SAP PRESS e-books

Print or e-book, Kindle or iPad, workplace or airplane: Choose where and how to read your SAP PRESS books! You can now get all our titles as e-books, too:

- By download and online access
- For all popular devices
- And, of course, DRM-free

Convinced? Then go to www.sap-press.com and get your e-book today.

Operational Data Provisioning with SAP BW/4HANA®

SAP PRESS is a joint initiative of SAP and Rheinwerk Publishing. The know-how offered by SAP specialists combined with the expertise of Rheinwerk Publishing offers the reader expert books in the field. SAP PRESS features first-hand information and expert advice, and provides useful skills for professional decision-making.

SAP PRESS offers a variety of books on technical and business-related topics for the SAP user. For further information, please visit our website: *www.sap-press.com*.

Thorsten Lüdtke, Marina Lüdtke
SAP BW/4HANA 2.0: The Comprehensive Guide
2021, 663 pages, hardcover and e-book
www.sap-press.com/4544

Anil Bavaraju
Data Modeling for SAP HANA 2.0
2019, 432 pages, hardcover and e-book
www.sap-press.com/4722

Colle, Dentzer, Hrastnik
Core Data Services for ABAP (2nd Edition)
2022, 648 pages, hardcover and e-book
www.sap-press.com/5294

Butsmann, Fleckenstein, Kundu
SAP S/4HANA Embedded Analytics: The Comprehensive Guide (2nd Edition)
2021, 432 pages, hardcover and e-book
www.sap-press.com/5226

Denis Reis
SAP Analysis for Microsoft Office—Practical Guide
2021, 569 pages, hardcover and e-book
www.sap-press.com/5155

Renjith Kumar Palaniswamy

Operational Data Provisioning with SAP BW/4HANA®

Rheinwerk
Publishing

Editor Rachel Gibson
Acquisitions Editor Hareem Shafi
Copyeditor Melinda Rankin
Cover Design Graham Geary
Photo Credit Shutterstock.com: 390014632/© PowerUp
Layout Design Vera Brauner
Production Hannah Lane
Typesetting III-satz, Germany
Printed and bound in the United States of America, on paper from sustainable sources

ISBN 978-1-4932-2406-7
© 2023 by Rheinwerk Publishing, Inc., Boston (MA)
1st edition 2023

Library of Congress Cataloging-in-Publication Control Number: 2023024529

Contents at a Glance

Dear Reader,

Did you pick up a "quarantine hobby" in 2020? Mine was collage.

I've never been much of an artist, so collage was the perfect way to play around with creativity without having to paint or draw. However, it does require an eye for design: taking many pieces and turning them into one bigger picture, and figuring out how clashing designs and contrasting colors can work together. Part of the puzzle of collaging is finding the right base materials to use. Hunting around the house for bits and pieces of ephemera that I can add to a collage is one of its perks. It feels like magic to take something that would have once been trash—an old receipt in an interesting color, a clothing tag with a fun design, or even a misplaced button—and turn it into a work of art.

Much like collage, data provisioning allows you to collect bits and pieces from many different sources, all of which contribute to the same bigger picture (in this case, that's your SAP system). As postcards, pamphlets, and tissue paper make up a collage, the data you're collecting—whether it's from SAP HANA calculation views, CDS views, or other SAP BW systems—will become the foundation of your system. With the help of expert author Renjith Kumar Palaniswamy, you'll learn how to use operational data provisioning to make data staging and extraction easier than ever.

What did you think about *Operational Data Provisioning with SAP BW/4HANA*? Your comments and suggestions are the most useful tools to help us make our books the best they can be. Please feel free to contact me and share any praise or criticism you may have.

Thank you for purchasing a book from SAP PRESS!

Rachel Gibson
Editor, SAP PRESS

rachelg@rheinwerk-publishing.com
www.sap-press.com
Rheinwerk Publishing · Boston, MA

Contents

5   Extracting Logistics Data   143

6   Extracting Master Data   283

7 Extracting Inventory Management Data 311

8 Extracting Financial Data 373

9 Extracting SAP ERP Human Capital Management Data

10 Generic Extraction from SAP S/4HANA

11 Extracting SAP BW 7.x Data into SAP BW/4HANA

12 Extracting Data Using CDS Views

13 Extraction Using Open ODS Views

Preface

Welcome to *Operational Data Provisioning with SAP BW/4HANA!* With the release of SAP BW/4HANA, data staging and extraction is now based on the operational data provisioning (ODP) framework, instead of the service application interface (SAPI)-based framework that was used in classical SAP Business Warehouse (SAP BW) 7.x systems. More migrations from SAP BW 7.x to SAP BW/4HANA have been happening in recent years. The common questions that arise during SAP BW/4HANA greenfield implementations (or migrations) are often related to the usage of ODP for data extraction requirements and how it impacts the daily data loads. The primary goal of this book is to address ODP-based extraction and explain how to use data staging in SAP BW/4HANA.

The book starts with the step-by-step process to create SAP BW/4HANA data models and helps you build a strong foundation in data modeling. Then, you'll see how to implement end-to-end SAP BW/4HANA data staging from an SAP S/4HANA system using the ODP framework. Since ODP is used across many different applications and enterprise resource planning (ERP) systems, we'll cover all aspects of ODP in the initial chapters. In later chapters, we'll focus on individual SAP S/4HANA application-based data extraction—for example, the extraction of sales data will be different from that of finance-based data.

This book will cover the data staging process in detail, using SAP-standard extractors across multiple applications such as sales, inventory management, purchasing, and finance. We'll cover the steps to create custom extractors and walk through how to consume them in SAP BW/4HANA. We'll show how to create core data services (CDS) views that support analytics and how to consume them in SAP BW/4HANA. (Nowadays, more customers are using CDS-based extraction, and there are many standard CDS views delivered by SAP.) We'll also walk through steps to create SAP HANA calculation views for SAP BW/4HANA modeling. This book also covers SAP HANA smart data access and SAP HANA smart data integration at a high level, helping you understand when to use these options for efficient data modeling. The data staging options discussed will enable you to architect SAP BW/4HANA systems using a mixed modeling approach for better performance and real-time reporting.

Objective of the Book

For customers with an SAP BW system landscape, there may be installations of SAP BW with different versions, and there may be new migrations to SAP BW/4HANA 2.0. This book helps explain the architecture of SAP BW/4HANA and the ODP framework. It provides you with an understanding of the step-by-step process of data staging and extraction in SAP BW/4HANA from multiple applications in SAP S/4HANA. This book also helps you learn and implement mixed modeling in SAP BW/4HANA 2.0.

The core aim of this book is to enable readers to create more efficient mixed data modeling by combining SAP HANA-based objects and SAP BW/4HANA-based objects in all their projects. This optimization of performance and enablement of real-time analytical reporting are the primary goals.

Target Audience

The target audience of this book is as follows:

- Consultants and users with experience in SAP BW 7.X versions or SAP BW/4HANA 1.0.
- Business intelligence (BI) developers, analytics architects, and team leads who want to implement data staging using mixed modeling for new SAP BW/4HANA 2.0 implementation or migration projects.
- IT managers and project managers who are planning to implement SAP BW/4HANA 2.0 in their landscape or upgrade their previous system to SAP BW/4HANA 2.0.

Additionally, any SAP consultant who wants to learn about SAP BW/4HANA 2.0 without prior experience can use this book to obtain detailed information about the product and its offerings.

Structure of the Book

This book is divided into 15 chapters, as follows:

- **Chapter 1** deals with the history and the roadmap of SAP BW/4HANA 2.0. We focus on the features that differentiate SAP BW/4HANA 2.0 from its previous versions. The design principles of SAP BW/4HANA are also discussed in detail. The major change in SAP BW/4HANA extraction deals with data staging, so we cover the fundamentals of the ODP layer in this chapter.
- **Chapter 2** covers data modeling in SAP BW/4HANA 2.0. You'll learn about all the important SAP BW objects used in data modeling. We'll use flat file-based extraction and create end-to-end data modeling in SAP BW/4HANA 2.0, starting from extraction to reporting. The data flow will be covered step by step, providing more details at the backend level when an object is created or activated.
- **Chapter 3** walks through the steps for creating a source system. When you want to extract data from any sender system into SAP BW/4HANA 2.0, it should have connectivity to that system. You can consider SAP BW as the receiver and all other sys-

tems that send data as sender systems. The systems that send data to the SAP BW system are called *source systems* in a broader context but are referred to as *DataSources* in an SAP BW/4HANA context. The source system must be created in SAP BW/4HANA. Creating the source system involves multiple activities and requires assistance from the Basis team, as it involves providing essential authorization and creating background users.

- **Chapter 4** provides details on standard SAP extractors across different functional areas in SAP S/4HANA. You'll learn about different extractor types and will understand the differences between each type.

- **Chapter 5** covers logistics-based extractors such as sales and distribution, purchasing, and quality management. We'll discuss the fundamentals of logistics extraction and review different update methods, like queue delta and direct delta. You'll learn how to implement logistics extraction in SAP BW/4HANA. We'll cover the required steps in SAP S/4HANA followed by the SAP BW/4HANA-based steps. Additionally, we'll explain how to extract initial data as well as the process of delta extraction. We'll cover other logistics extractions such as purchasing and quality management. Finally, you'll learn how to validate the data in Transaction ODQMON after the extraction is executed.

- **Chapter 6** discusses extracting master data from various functional areas. You'll learn about the different types of master data-based extractors and understand the differences between each type.

- **Chapter 7** provides details on SAP BW/4HANA extractors for materials management-inventory management areas. You'll start by learning about the basic functional terms used in materials management and inventory management. Then, we'll review noncumulative key figures and their importance. We'll explore multiple extractors available for inventory management extraction. This chapter will guide you through the flat file-based approach to load inventory management data and help you understand how the backend table behaves during extraction. You'll also learn how to implement the SAP-delivered inventory management optimization (IMO)-based data flow in SAP BW/4HANA 2.0.

- **Chapter 8** covers finance application-based extractors and explains how to extract data using SAP-delivered extractors. It covers the end-to-end extraction process from SAP S/4HANA source systems. In SAP S/4HANA, the financial management modules deal with the core finance data, such as accounts receivable, accounts payable, and the general ledger. You will learn about the Universal Journal table ACDOCA and how to extract data from this table using the standard SAP extractors. Understanding the functional basis of table ACDOCA, which is discussed in the first few sections, will help you better grasp the SAP BW extraction process.

- **Chapter 9** covers human resources (HR)-based extractors and explains how to extract data using SAP-delivered extractors. It covers the end-to-end extraction process from SAP S/4HANA source systems. In SAP S/4HANA, the human capital management modules deal with the management of core HR data, such as personal administration, payroll, and personal time management. Understanding the functional basis discussed in the first sections will enhance your understanding of the SAP BW extraction process.

- **Chapter 10** provides step-by-step details on creating custom extractors. These customer-generated extractors need to be created end-to-end in an SAP S/4HANA source system. The SAP BW/4HANA data modeling objects need to be created based on these custom extractors. Custom extractors are used when the standard SAP-delivered extractors cannot fulfill the business requirements.

- **Chapter 11** provides options to extract data from an SAP BW system into SAP BW/4HANA 2.0. When customers migrate from SAP BW 7.x to SAP BW/4HANA using shell conversion, where the data is not migrated, they need a way to bring in the data from the old system. In such cases, loading data from the old InfoProviders becomes necessary.

- **Chapter 12** describes the steps to create CDS views in an SAP S/4HANA system. You'll learn about basic annotations as well as analytics annotations, which enable CDS views to be consumed in SAP BW/4HANA. This chapter explains the data provisioning options from SAP HANA to SAP BW/4HANA 2.0 using CDS views in a step-by-step process. These methods help you transition from traditional SAP extractor-based data extraction to the new CDS-based extraction, enabling a more optimized extraction.

- **Chapter 13** describes the virtual data provisioning options from SAP HANA to SAP BW/4HANA 2.0.You will learn how to consume tables from SAP HANA to SAP BW without altering the data in SAP BW. Effective data modeling can be achieved with more virtualization options for data extraction.

- **Chapter 14** describes the steps to create SAP HANA calculation views in SAP S/4HANA and discusses the virtual data provisioning options from SAP HANA to SAP BW/4HANA 2.0. Effective data modeling can be achieved using the virtualization option for the data extraction.

- **Chapter 15** walks through multiple data provisioning options from an SAP HANA or non-SAP HANA system to SAP BW/4HANA. These data provisioning methods will help you define and architect the analytics strategy for the complex landscapes during SAP BW/4HANA implementations.

We recommend reading this book sequentially from Chapter 1 onwards, but if you have previous knowledge of ODP and/or SAP BW/4HANA, then you can go directly to the chapter that you wish to read.

Acknowledgments

Many thanks to the SAP PRESS team, especially the acquisitions editor, Hareem Shafi, who helped with the chapter organization and book structure creation. She was very cooperative in addressing any queries related to the book length and organization. I would also like to express my gratitude to the development editor, Rachel Gibson, who has been extremely helpful throughout the entire process of writing this book. Her input and suggestions for appropriate edits have been invaluable. Thanks to Melinda Rankin, the copyeditor, for her assistance in the final stage of edits. She diligently checked for grammatical errors and ensured the accuracy of product names and versions. Special thanks to the cover designer, Graham Geary, for designing the beautiful cover of this book. I would like to extend my heartfelt appreciation to all the members of the SAP PRESS team who contributed to the preparation of this book, from the initial draft phase to the printing phase. Their outstanding teamwork has been remarkable. Thanks to the SAP Americas Center of Expertise (CoE) leadership team, namely Thomas Walter (Global Head Premium Hub, SAP CoE), Balaji Rao Gaddam (VP and Head, SAP CoE North America), and Suhan Hegde (Director, CoE Analytics, SAP Americas), for their constant encouragement in publishing the quality book to SAP community. Thanks to my colleagues and friends in the SAP CoE North America Analytics team for all their support. Thanks to all the SAP BW/4HANA development team colleagues, SAP Product Support team colleagues, and SAP Community network members. Finally, many thanks to my parents Palaniswamy and Sarojini, my wife Mathumathi, my children Diya and Ram, my brother Manivannan, and all my family members and friends for their extended support while writing this book.

We hope you enjoy reading the book. Happy learning!

Chapter 1
Introduction

In this chapter, we look at the history of SAP BW/4HANA and how it has evolved. We'll focus on the features that make SAP BW/4HANA different from its successors and discuss its design principles in detail. The major change to SAP BW/4HANA extraction is in data staging, and we'll cover the fundamentals of operational data provisioning in this chapter.

In this chapter, you'll learn about the history and timeline of SAP BW/4HANA 2.0, then learn about its core design principles. The SAP BW objects associated with each design principle are explained in detail. We'll also cover Layered Scalable Architecture++ (LSA++) and offer insights for installing SAP HANA Studio and Eclipse. Finally, we'll give you an introduction to operational data provisioning (ODP) and learn about its architecture. You'll learn how ODP is used in real-time delta monitoring and how to use the different views in the ODP framework.

1.1 History of SAP BW/4HANA

In this section, we'll discuss the evolution of SAP BW/4HANA. The first release of SAP BW was 1.2A in 1998. The next major release was SAP BW 3.5 in 2004. In that same year, SAP NetWeaver was released, and SAP made a lot of changes to SAP BW by introducing many new objects. These changes were released as SAP BW 7.0. This release was the basis for all further major developments. From 2005 to 2011, releases started from 7.0 and went through 7.31. In 2010, there was an initial prerelease of the SAP HANA platform, followed by support for SAP HANA for SAP NetWeaver Business Warehouse, announced in the last quarter of 2011. From 2012 on, there was continuous evolution of SAP BW and SAP HANA. An illustration of the major evolution points is provided in Figure 1.1.

Since 2016, there have been many changes to SAP BW/4HANA, with changes and new innovations introduced in multiple support packages. Figure 1.2 shows the major SAP BW/4HANA releases.

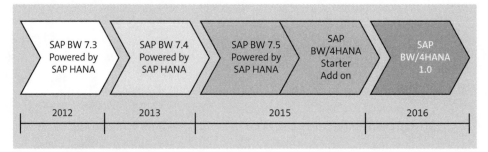

Figure 1.1 Evolution of SAP BW/4HANA

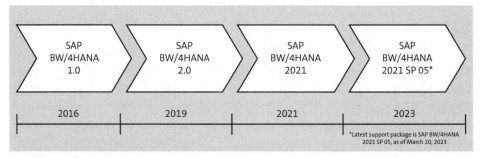

Figure 1.2 SAP BW/4HANA Releases

1.2   SAP BW/4HANA Overview and Design Principles

When you compare SAP BW/4HANA with the SAP BW 7.X versions, it's a completely new product that includes some features from the legacy application plus lots of new features and functionalities. It was developed using new design principles and aimed at utilizing the full power of SAP HANA.

When SAP BW/4HANA was introduced, these were its fundamental design principles:

- **Simplicity**
  SAP BW/4HANA aims to be simple to use and reduce complexity. The core focus is on reducing the end-to-end development time and running at a lower cost. This results in a reduction of many objects from the previous version; we'll cover that in the next section. In the classical SAP BW versions, there were close to 10 objects, but with the simplified design principles this number was reduced to four. The details of the objects are shown in Figure 1.3.

  In addition, SAP BW/4HANA has removed other legacy SAP BW functionality. For example, data modeling in SAP GUI is no longer supported: you need to use SAP BW modeling tools for data modeling, and SAP BW BEx query designer is not supported.

- **Openness**
  You bring data from different sources into SAP BW/4HANA and consume data from the SAP BW system, so you need to manage all kinds of data, and integration of data

with all systems has been made easier. The integration between SAP BW/4HANA and SAP HANA allows for the direct consumption of SAP BW/4HANA data via the generated SQL views. This enables exposing SAP BW/4HANA models as native SAP HANA views, and these automatically generated views can be consumed in SAP HANA to build new SAP HANA models or can be consumed by visualization tools. Refer to Figure 1.4 to see how SAP BW/4HANA objects are exposed to the SAP HANA layer.

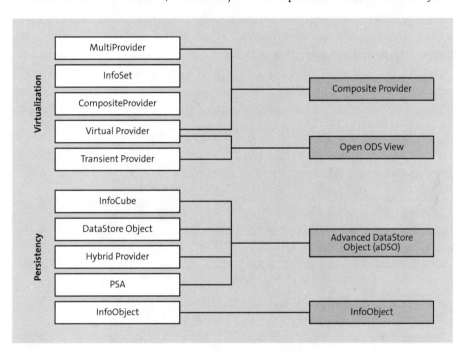

Figure 1.3 Simplified Data Model

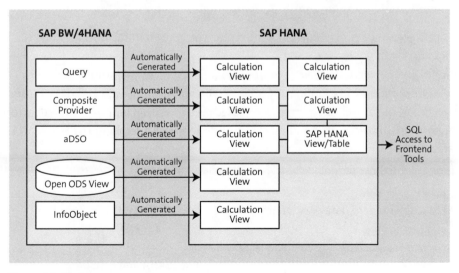

Figure 1.4 Openness

■ **Modern interface**
This principle ensures that users have simple access to data through easy-to-use tools with the Eclipse UI. Modern interfaces are available for business users, developers, and administrators.

■ **High performance**
SAP BW/4HANA is designed to use the full potential of SAP HANA to leverage large amounts of data in real time. There are designs to push the OLAP functionality and complex computations down to the SAP HANA database. The SAP BW/4HANA objects are designed to enable this pushdown. SAP HANA–specific libraries can be utilized that run in the SAP HANA platform. There are many ways to do a code pushdown, such as executing the data transfer process (DTP) in SAP HANA and creating SAP HANA transformations with ABAP Managed Database Procedures (AMDPs) to push the complex ABAP logic down (refer to Figure 1.5).

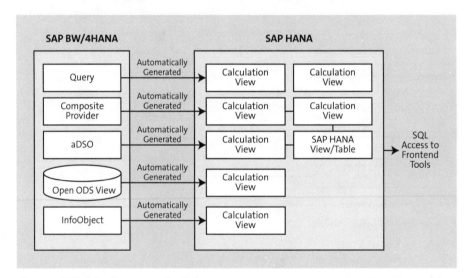

Figure 1.5 High Performance: Push Down

With the new objects, there have been many other changes, like from LSA to LSA++. LSA++ introduces an operational layer by enabling reporting on advanced DataStore objects (aDSOs), as well as a virtual layer based on SAP HANA composite providers to support virtual data marts, and queries can be accessed directly in the SAP HANA database.

These are the three new objects:

– **aDSO**
Used for standard data persistency

– **Open ODS view**
Defines the reusable SAP BW data warehouse semantics on field-based structures

- **Composite provider**
  Defines virtual data marts on persistence objects (aDSOs/InfoObjects) and/or open ODS views and SAP HANA calculation views or a combination of both

LSA++ has the following layers:

- **Operational DataStore layer**
  This is an entry layer that offers services such as queries and reports. The services offered are as follows:
  - Pare down and extend the data acquisition later services
  - Immediate query and reporting options
  - Early and simple integration of data in a data warehouse using LSA++ for simplified data warehousing

- **EDW propagation**
  This data propagation layer provides semantic and value standardization for data from different sources in a highly harmonized form. In the propagation layer, a standard principle applies: extract once, deploy many. The data propagation layer serves as a persistent architected data mart and is the basis for the virtual data mart layer. The data is saved and consolidated in standard aDSOs and in InfoObjects. Note that all the major data warehousing services are implemented in the LSA++ propagation layer.

- **Corporate memory**
  This layer contains the complete history of the loaded data from the source systems. This is filled separately in the architected data marts. This can be used as a source for the reconstruction without accessing the source system again.

- **Architect data mart**
  This layer serves as a query access layer if a query cannot be built in the propagation or open ODS layer; this is used when there is additional business logic involved. Most of the business requirements can be built with the propagation later and virtual data mart layer. A persistent architected data mart layer is built only if those layers aren't options. These architected data marts are defined based on aDSOs and InfoObjects. There are separate templates for the aDSOs for the data mart layer, like Reporting on Union of Active Table and Inbound Queue, which will make an aDSO behave like an InfoCube.

- **Virtual data mart**
  This layer combines data from a persistence provider (aDSO or InfoObject) with virtual providers (union/joins). Here the layer doesn't represent a strict limit, which means you can combine the objects from the open ODS layer with objects from the propagation layer or architected data mart layer. See Figure 1.6 for more details.

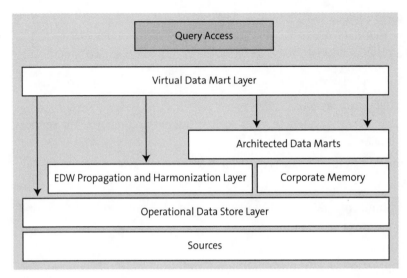

Figure 1.6 LSA++

If you want to set up SAP BW/4HANA, the options shown in Figure 1.7 are available.

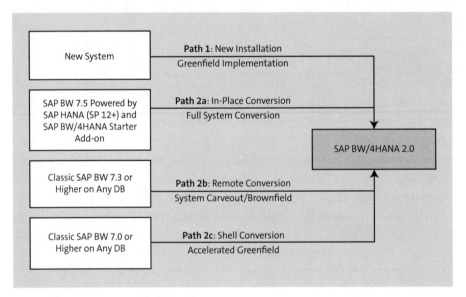

Figure 1.7 Path to SAP BW/4HANA 2.0

1.3   Eclipse and SAP HANA Studio

To work in SAP BW/4HANA, you need to have either the latest version of SAP HANA Studio or the latest version of Eclipse. In the following sections, we'll walk through the steps to install SAP HANA Studio and other SAP BW modeling tools. We'll also describe how to connect them to your SAP BW/4HANA system.

1.3.1 Installing SAP HANA Studio

To install SAP HANA Studio, follow these steps:

1. Go to *https://launchpad.support.sap.com/#/softwarecenter*.

2. Search for "SAP HANA Studio".

3. Click the **SAP HANA STUDIO 2** link.

4. Download the latest revision of SAP HANA Studio 2.

5. The file will be a SAR file type, and the file name will start with *I*, as shown in Figure 1.8.

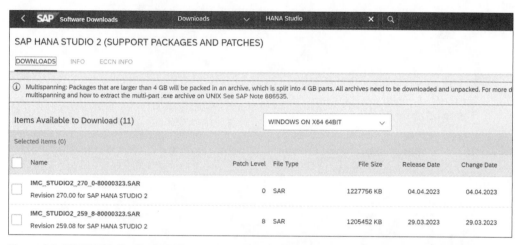

Figure 1.8 SAP HANA Studio SAR File

6. Click the first SAR file and it will start downloading. Save that SAR to a folder in your C drive.

7. Download the CAR file from the software corner. This is an EXE file (search for "SAP-CAR"; see Figure 1.9).

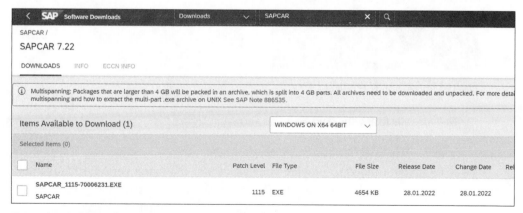

Figure 1.9 SAPCAR File

8. Now save the SAPCAR file in the same location in your local workstation, as shown in Figure 1.10.

Name	Date modified	Type	Size
IMC_STUDIO2_270_0-80000323.SAR	4/26/2023 5:27 PM	SAR File	1,227,756 KB
SAPCAR_1115-70006231.EXE	4/26/2023 5:28 PM	Application	4,655 KB

> Windows (C:) >   HANA Studio New

Figure 1.10 Files

9. Rename the downloaded SAPCAR****.EXE file to SAPCAR.EXE (see Figure 1.11).

Name	Date modified	Type	Size
IMC_STUDIO2_270_0-80000323.SAR	4/26/2023 5:27 PM	SAR File	1,227,756 KB
SAPCAR.EXE	4/26/2023 5:28 PM	Application	4,655 KB

Figure 1.11 After Rename

10. Now open the command prompt in Windows and type CMD. It will take you to the screen shown in Figure 1.12.

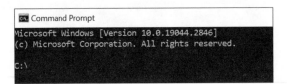

```
Microsoft Windows [Version 10.0.19044.2846]
(c) Microsoft Corporation. All rights reserved.

C:\
```

Figure 1.12 Command Prompt

11. Now use the CD command to go into a specific directory by typing "CD<Folder name>". For example, CD Desktop will go to your **Desktop** folder. In this case, go to the directory where your file is located (see Figure 1.13).

```
C:\            >cd HANA STUDIO NEW

C:\            \HANA Studio New>_
```

Figure 1.13 Command Prompt

12. Now use the following command, as shown in Figure 1.14:

```
sapcar -xvf <I*.sar>
```

Note that you need to provide your exact SAR file name here. In the example shown, you would therefore enter this command:

```
sapcar -xvf IMC_STUDIO2_270_0-80000323.SAR
```

```
C:              \HANA Studio New>sapcar -xvf IMC_STUDIO2_270_0-80000323.SAR
```

Figure 1.14 Syntax

13. Once you press [Enter], the file will be extracted, as shown in Figure 1.15.

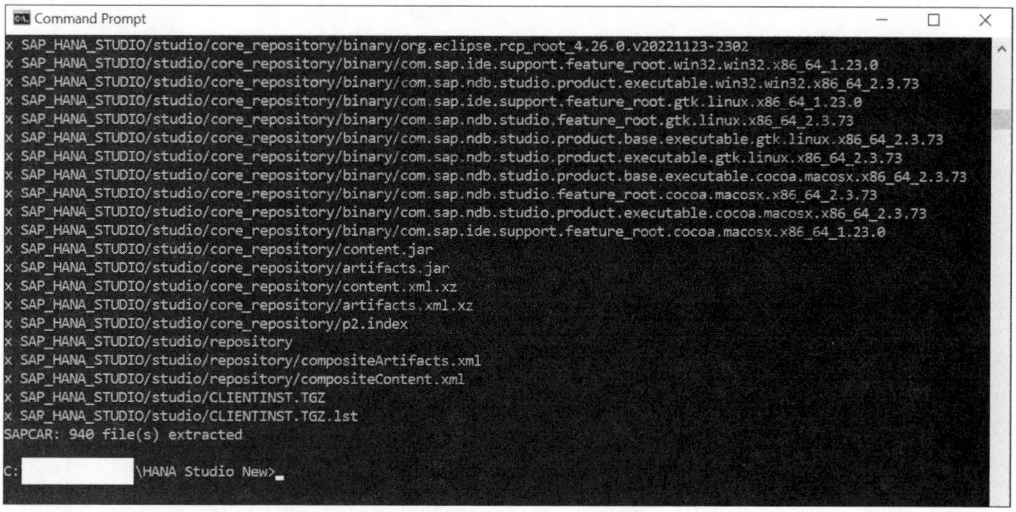

```
Command Prompt                                                                          —  □  ×
x SAP_HANA_STUDIO/studio/core_repository/binary/org.eclipse.rcp_root_4.26.0.v20221123-2302
x SAP_HANA_STUDIO/studio/core_repository/binary/com.sap.ide.support.feature_root.win32.win32.x86_64_1.23.0
x SAP_HANA_STUDIO/studio/core_repository/binary/com.sap.ndb.studio.product.executable.win32.win32.x86_64_2.3.73
x SAP_HANA_STUDIO/studio/core_repository/binary/com.sap.ide.support.feature_root.gtk.linux.x86_64_1.23.0
x SAP_HANA_STUDIO/studio/core_repository/binary/com.sap.ndb.studio.feature_root.gtk.linux.x86_64_2.3.73
x SAP_HANA_STUDIO/studio/core_repository/binary/com.sap.ndb.studio.product.base.executable.gtk.linux.x86_64_2.3.73
x SAP_HANA_STUDIO/studio/core_repository/binary/com.sap.ndb.studio.product.executable.gtk.linux.x86_64_2.3.73
x SAP_HANA_STUDIO/studio/core_repository/binary/com.sap.ndb.studio.product.base.executable.cocoa.macosx.x86_64_2.3.73
x SAP_HANA_STUDIO/studio/core_repository/binary/com.sap.ndb.studio.feature_root.cocoa.macosx.x86_64_2.3.73
x SAP_HANA_STUDIO/studio/core_repository/binary/com.sap.ndb.studio.product.executable.cocoa.macosx.x86_64_2.3.73
x SAP_HANA_STUDIO/studio/core_repository/binary/com.sap.ide.support.feature_root.cocoa.macosx.x86_64_1.23.0
x SAP_HANA_STUDIO/studio/core_repository/content.jar
x SAP_HANA_STUDIO/studio/core_repository/artifacts.jar
x SAP_HANA_STUDIO/studio/core_repository/content.xml.xz
x SAP_HANA_STUDIO/studio/core_repository/artifacts.xml.xz
x SAP_HANA_STUDIO/studio/core_repository/p2.index
x SAP_HANA_STUDIO/studio/repository
x SAP_HANA_STUDIO/studio/repository/compositeArtifacts.xml
x SAP_HANA_STUDIO/studio/repository/compositeContent.xml
x SAP_HANA_STUDIO/studio/CLIENTINST.TGZ
x SAP_HANA_STUDIO/studio/CLIENTINST.TGZ.lst
SAPCAR: 940 file(s) extracted

C:              \HANA Studio New>
```

Figure 1.15 Extracted File

14. When you open the folder where you've stored the files, it will look as shown in Figure 1.16.

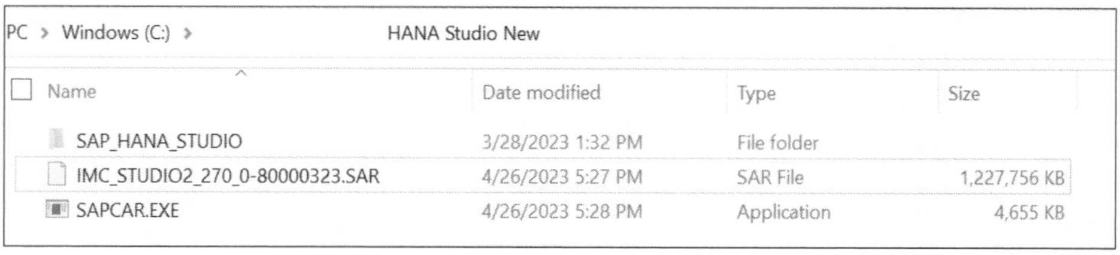

Name	Date modified	Type	Size
SAP_HANA_STUDIO	3/28/2023 1:32 PM	File folder	
IMC_STUDIO2_270_0-80000323.SAR	4/26/2023 5:27 PM	SAR File	1,227,756 KB
SAPCAR.EXE	4/26/2023 5:28 PM	Application	4,655 KB

PC > Windows (C:) >   HANA Studio New

Figure 1.16 SAP HANA Studio Folder

15. Double-click the **SAP_HANA_Studio** folder to see its contents, as shown in Figure 1.17.

16. Double-click **hdbsetup.exe**. If you do not have SAP HANA Studio installed already, you can install a new instance of it. Otherwise, you can choose to update your existing version, as shown in Figure 1.18.

17. Click **Next** and follow the wizard, as shown in Figure 1.19.

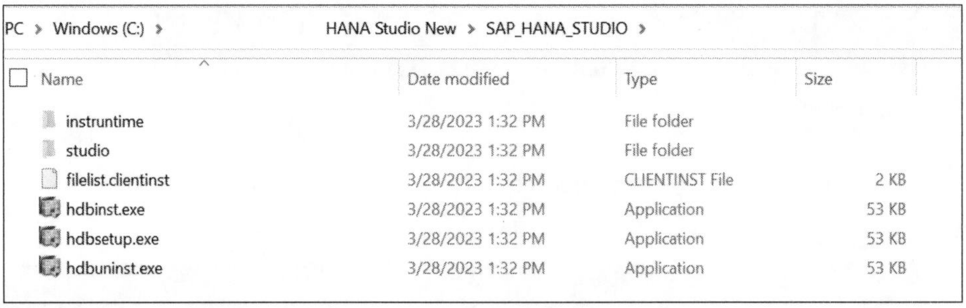

Name	Date modified	Type	Size
instruntime	3/28/2023 1:32 PM	File folder	
studio	3/28/2023 1:32 PM	File folder	
filelist.clientinst	3/28/2023 1:32 PM	CLIENTINST File	2 KB
hdbinst.exe	3/28/2023 1:32 PM	Application	53 KB
hdbsetup.exe	3/28/2023 1:32 PM	Application	53 KB
hdbuninst.exe	3/28/2023 1:32 PM	Application	53 KB

PC > Windows (C:) >   HANA Studio New > SAP_HANA_STUDIO >

Figure 1.17 SAP HANA Studio

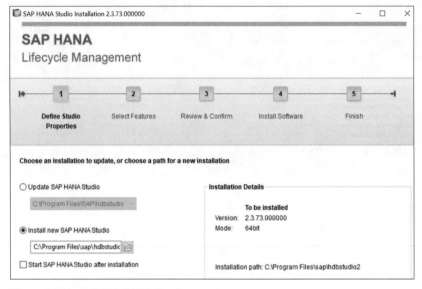

Figure 1.18 Install SAP HANA Studio

Figure 1.19 Installation Wizard

18. You will see the options shown in Figure 1.20. Click **Next** and complete the setup. If there are any errors, right-click **hdbsetup.exe** and select **Run as Administrator** from the context menu. Similarly, you can install Eclipse if you want to use it. Once the installation is done, open SAP HANA Studio or Eclipse.

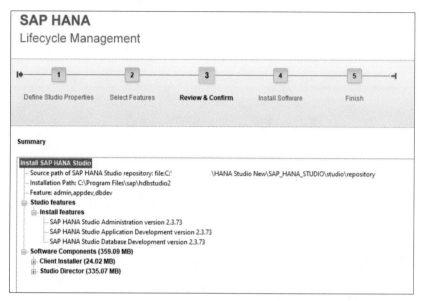

Figure 1.20 Review and Confirm Option

1.3.2 Installing SAP BW/4HANA Modeling Tools

To install SAP BW/4HANA modeling tools and ABAP development tools, follow these steps:

1. First, go to the following URL: *https://tools.hana.ondemand.com/#bw*. Here, you can find the latest URL for the SAP BW/4HANA modeling tools in step 3 under **Procedure**, as shown in Figure 1.21. (In this example, the URL is *https://tools.hana.ondemand. com/2023-03*.

2. Once you open SAP HANA Studio, follow the path **Help • Install New Software...**, as shown in Figure 1.22.

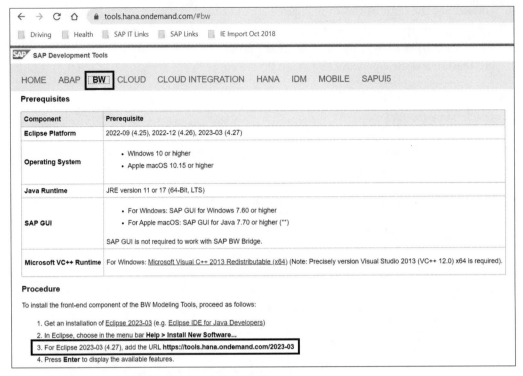

Figure 1.21 SAP BW/4HANA Modelling Tools

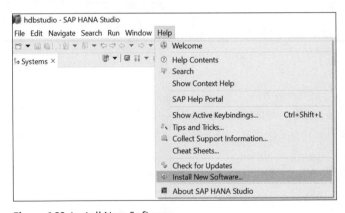

Figure 1.22 Install New Software

3. Now enter the URL from the first step (*https://tools.hana.ondemand.com2023-03*), as shown in Figure 1.23.

4. If you select **Modeling Tools for SAP BW/4HANA and SAP BW powered by SAP HANA**, you'll see the options shown in Figure 1.24.

5. Click **Finish** to complete the installation.

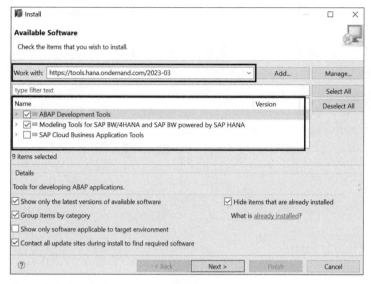

Figure 1.23 BW-MT

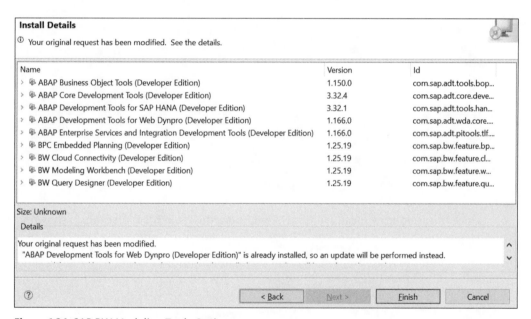

Figure 1.24 SAP BW Modeling Tools Options

1.3.3   Adding an SAP BW/4HANA System

Once you have installed SAP HANA Studio and Eclipse, follow these steps, as shown in Figure 1.25:

❶ Open the SAP BW/4HANA modeling tools perspective in Eclipse or SAP HANA Studio.

❷ Choose the **BW Project** option to create a new project.

❸ You will see a list of systems that are maintained in your SAP GUI. Choose the SAP BW/4HANA system.

❹ Provide the details of the SAP BW/4HANA system, such as **System ID**, **Application Server**, and **Instance Number** (you can get this information from the SAP GUI or Basis team). Then choose **Next**.

❺ You will be asked to provide the logon data, like the **Client**, **User**, and **Password** for the system. Choose **Finish** and the system will be added.

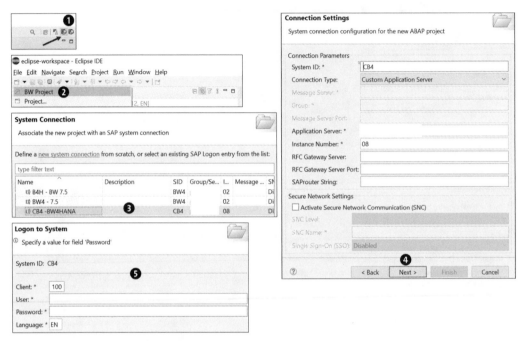

Figure 1.25 Adding SAP BW/4HANA System in Eclipse

Once this is done, you can see the system under the **Project Explorer** tab, as shown in Figure 1.26.

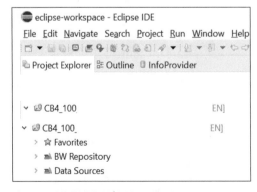

Figure 1.26 SAP BW/4HANA System

1.4 Overview of Operational Data Provisioning

Before we get into operational data provisioning (ODP), let's talk about the Service Application Interface (SAPI). This is the interface that was used in classical SAP BW systems from the beginning. The interface primarily used the RFC, and the delta is managed by the delta queue, which can be seen in Transaction RSA7. But if you've worked on RSA7, you might have felt that it had limited functionality, apart from the delta handling and management. Meanwhile, SAP BW systems were able to connect to multiple systems like DB Connect and other non-SAP systems, so there was a requirement for new approaches to provision the data from various sources that can be connected to SAP BW with minimal effort, and the approach was expected to have very good performance with traditional delta-handling capabilities, like SAPI. With the RSA7-based SAPI, the issue of missing deltas was quite complex, as the delta queue cannot have the current delta for next extraction *and* the previously loaded delta that will be used to reload if the delta was unsuccessful. ODP was introduced to solve this issue. The concept of ODP was available in SAP BW for a long time, but since classical SAP BW systems supported both SAPI and ODP, users could choose either framework. With SAP BW/4HANA, however, ODP is the default framework to connect to other systems for data provisioning.

ODP provides a technical infrastructure that a user can use to support two application scenarios: operational analytics and data extraction and replication. *Operational analytics* helps perform reporting and analysis based on the application data model without replicating data in the data warehouse. But because we're interested mostly in the data warehouse, we'll focus more on the next part.

Data extraction and replication combines multiple systems, providers, and senders.

In this section, you'll learn about ODP features and architecture and understand how to expose SAP extractors to the ODP framework. The data extraction and acquisition process in ODP is discussed in detail.

1.4.1 ODP Features and Architecture

The following are some of the features available with ODP:

- ODP enables an *extract once, deploy many* architecture for sources. This means that the data changes to a queue can be requested by more than one subscriber.
- The ODP framework has a unified configuration and provides a monitoring framework for all the provider and subscriber types.
- Unlike RSA7, you have configurable data retention period in ODP, and you have the option to store data in the operational delta queue (ODQ) for a specified time even after it's been read by applications. The default retention period is 24 hours.

- The ODQ offers highly efficient compression, which enables data compression rates of up to 90%.
- Parallelization options are available when there is high volume.
- ODP offers unified technology for data provisioning and consumption in SAP BW/4HANA.
- ODP acts as a hub for all data flowing into SAP BW/4HANA from multiple external sources.
- The ODQ unifies configuration and monitoring for all provider and subscriber types.

With this information in mind, let's now review the architecture of ODP, as illustrated in Figure 1.27.

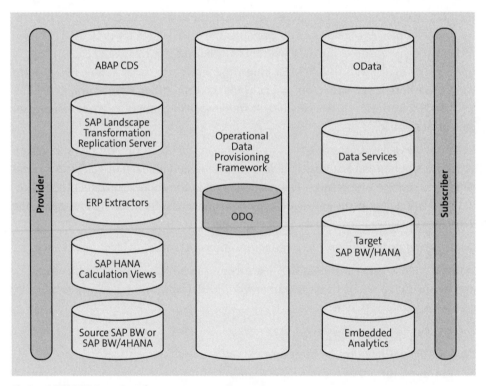

Figure 1.27 ODP Framework

In the ODP framework, there can be multiple subscribers or consumers that get data from providers. The following are the possible subscribers:

- **SAP BW**
  Beginning with release 7.30 SP 8 or 7.31 SP 5, SAP BW consumes data exposed via ODP from other systems. Both RFC and HTTP/SOAP communication channels are supported. Starting with SAP NetWeaver 7.40 SP 5, the context for DataSources and extractors also are available for SAP BW consumption.

- **OData**
  OData providers provide REST-based OData services. The SAP BW InfoProviders can be exposed via OData in ODP for lightweight consumption of data in SAP business systems. This interface requires SAP Gateway.

- **SAP Data Services**
  SAP Data Services release 4.2 SP 1 can extract data from ODP, transform and standardize them, and then load them to different target systems. It uses the RFC-based implementation of the consumer interface to connect to SAP NetWeaver systems.

- **SAP NetWeaver embedded analytics**
  If an ODP context offers operational data providers for embedded analytics, it's possible to define and execute an SAP BW query directly on the operational data provider. It isn't necessary to replicate the data into SAP BW. The SAP BW query is defined and executed locally on top of a transient InfoProvider, which is implicitly derived from ODP. The list of available ODP-based transient InfoProviders and their details can be displayed in SAP GUI with Transaction RSRTS_ODP_DIS.

There are multiple providers that can send data to the subscribers in the ODP framework, as follows:

- **ODP SAP Landscape Transformation Replication Server queue**
  Using the ODP infrastructure and the trigger-based replication of SAP Landscape Transformation Replication Server, data can be transferred in real time from an ABAP system to one or more data warehouse systems. SAP Landscape Transformation Replication Server acts as a provider for the ODP infrastructure. It can make tables from SAP sources available as delta queues. This provider implementation is available starting with Data Migration Server (DMIS) 2011 SP 5 and SAP NetWeaver 7.30 SP 8.

- **ODP ABAP CDS views**
  Core data services (CDS) views enhance SQL to allow defining and consuming semantically rich data models natively in the SAP HANA database. The key concept for expressing semantics of CDS models is annotations, which are attached to elements of a model (e.g., entities or views). By applying annotations with analytical semantics, CDS views can be annotated such that the resulting metadata would allow for generating transient ODP providers. This technology is core for SAP S/4HANA Analytics and has been added to the ODP framework staring with SAP BW 7.5.

- **ODP SAP HANA information views**
  This context makes analytic views, calculation views, and associated attribute views defined in an SAP HANA system release of 1.0 SP 4 and up available as (transient) ODP providers in a connected SAP NetWeaver 7.30 SP 5+ system. Attribute views and analytic views are now obsolete and only calculation views are currently available.

ODP SAP HANA information views allow replicating the view data into another data warehouse system or performing SAP BW queries directly on SAP HANA views. Such queries can be defined on top of transient SAP BW InfoProviders, which are provided for the transient ODP providers and can be identified by the prefix "2H" in their names.

Consumers access these ODP providers via the RFC implementation of the ODP consumer interface. This implementation opens the possibility to shift business logic from ABAP-based SAP BW warehousing and query layers to the SAP HANA database. Examples include calculations of key figures, restricted key figures, currency conversions, and joins and unions, which can be defined in SAP HANA views. The results of such calculations can then also be accessed via ODP.

- **ODP SAP BW**
  This exposes most data as ODP providers for replication purposes. Starting with release 7.40 SP 5, the following object types are supported: DSO, InfoCube, semantically partitioned object (SPO), hybrid provider, MultiProvider, InfoSets, and queries released as InfoProviders and InfoObjects for master data, texts, and hierarchies. The ODP providers are accessible via the RFC implementation of the ODP consumer interface.

- **ODP SAP extractors**
  This context exposes SAP BW DataSources as ODP providers. An SAP BW DataSource defines an extraction structure that is filled by an extractor implementing the logic to retrieve the relevant data from the ABAP system. There are application-specific extractors, each of which is hard-coded. In addition, there are generic extractors for tables, views, and application areas such as logistics, profitability analysis, special purpose ledger, and human resources. Without additional configuration, the ODP framework supports DataSources that have been released by the application owner since SAP NetWeaver 7.0 SPS 23. Most released DataSources are part of SAP Business Suite. Consumers access these ODPs via the RFC implementation of the ODP consumer interface.

We'll be extracting data from an SAP ERP or SAP S/4HANA system for the examples ahead. This is a widely used scenario, so it will be helpful to cover it here.

1.4.2   Introduction to ODP SAP Extractors

With the ODP framework, SAP BW DataSources are exposed to ODP. An SAP BW DataSource defines an extraction structure that is filled by an extractor implementing the logic to retrieve the relevant data from the ABAP system. Without additional configuration, the ODP framework supports DataSources that have been released by the application owner since SAP NetWeaver 7.0 SPS 23 (see Figure 1.28).

You can connect an SAP system, such as an SAP Business Suite or SAP ERP system, as an ODP provider. The objects that represent the interface of the SAP system with the ODP framework are DataSources (SAP extractors) activated from the SAP BusinessObjects Business Intelligence (SAP BusinessObjects BI) content or generated individually by users. Communication is performed using the standard RFC you use when you connect to the source system traditionally.

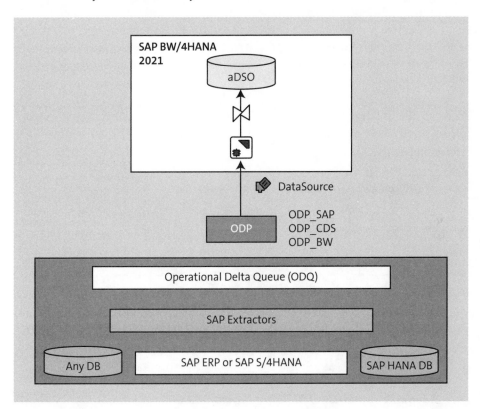

Figure 1.28 SAP Extractors

Starting from SAP BW/4HANA, data provisioning using ODP based on SAP extractors is a mandatory replacement for the previous usage of DataSources from SAP source systems using the SAP Service API and transactional RFC (tRFC) outbound delta queue (Transaction RSA7) standards. Therefore, the classical delta queue is replaced in the ODP framework. As an alternative, there are ODP delta queues available with many more services than before (Transaction ODQMON).

Now let's discuss the prerequisites for using the ODP framework:

1. To enable the use of ODP data replication in your system, you must first implement the Support Packages described in the following SAP Notes:
   – SAP Note 1521883 (ODP Replication API 1.0) for SAP_BASIS < 730
   – SAP Note 1931427 (ODP Replication API 2.0) for SAP Basis >= 730
2. Most of the delivered SAP extractors are already released for ODP replication. You can release the corresponding DataSources by implementing the steps in SAP Note

2232584 and executing the BS_ANLY_DS_RELEASE_ODP program, as shown in Figure 1.29.

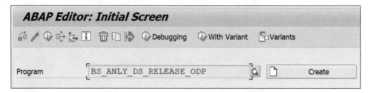

Figure 1.29 Release of SAP Extractors to ODP

3. You can use this report in your SAP ERP or SAP S/4HANA system. It will execute directly and won't offer any selection prompts. The results of the extraction are shown in Figure 1.30.

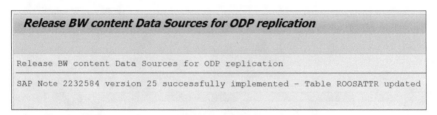

Figure 1.30 Report Result

4. Now you can view table ROOSATTR (DataSource Attributes) to see the status. Filter table ROOSATTR provide the field OLTPSOURCE with 2LIS_11* and execute. The results shown in Figure 1.31.

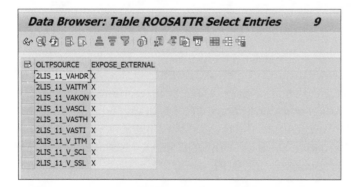

Figure 1.31 Table ROOSATTR Showing SAP-Delivered DataSources

5. You can see that DataSources released and thus available for ODP extraction are listed in table ROOSATTR with an active flag in the **EXPOSE_EXTERNAL** column.

> **SAP-Delivered ODP-Enabled Extractors**
>
> During SAP BW/4HANA implementation, a general requirement is to get the list of all SAP-standard extractors that are enabled and released for ODP in an Excel list, as in the attachment to SAP Note 2232584 (*ODP_Enabled_FullList_SAP_Note2235284.xls*).

6. If you want to expose user-generated SAP DataSources to ODP, then you need to first implement the steps described in SAP Note 2350464 (Creation of Generic Data-Source in RSO2—Automatic Release for ODP).

7. If the data store still isn't released, you can use the RODPS_OS_EXPOSE program in Transaction SE38 to release user-defined extractors directly in the relevant source system, as shown in Figure 1.32.

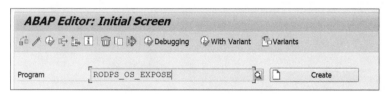

Figure 1.32 ODP Expose Report

8. The selection will be as shown in Figure 1.33.

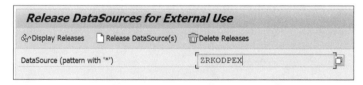

Figure 1.33 DataSource Selection

9. After exposing the ODP provider, you will see an entry like the one shown in Figure 1.34. The ZRKODPEX DataSource will show an **X** in the **EXPOSE_EXTERNAL** field.

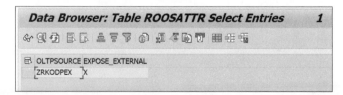

Figure 1.34 After Exposing

1.4.3   Data Extraction Essentials

In SAP BW/4HANA, you'll generally replicate the DataSource and activate it using the **Activate** icon. Once you active the DataSource, you'll see the DataSource maintenance screen with tabs like **Overview**, **Extraction**, and **Fields**. On the **Extraction** tab, you'll see the extractor-specific properties (Figure 1.35).

SAP BW/4HANA only uses DTP, so you'll see the properties like those shown in Figure 1.36 that are inherited from the DataSource.

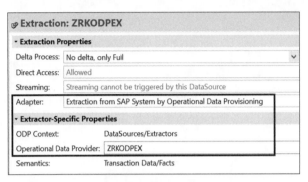

Figure 1.35 Extraction Properties

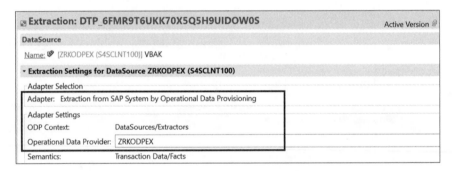

Figure 1.36 DTP Properties

1.4.4 Data Acquisition Process in ODP

When you try to extract data from the SAP source system, the ODP framework uses multiple calls to complete the extraction. There are three important calls: open, fetch, and close.

Figure 1.37 provides an overview of the architecture. The process steps for each type of call are as follows:

- **Open**
  - The subscriber agent (DTP for SAP BW, trigger job for DataSource) sends a request for data.
  - The extractor in the source system starts the extraction job and sends an acknowledgment to the agent.
  - The extraction job (asynchronously) writes data to the ODQ as it extracts.

- **Fetch**
  - The agent waits for the data from the ODQ. (The agent will wait up to two hours for data from the extractor. If the extractor doesn't return any data within this time, failure is assumed.)
  - Data is sent from the delta queue to the subscriber.
- **Close**
  - The subscriber receives a "no more data" indicator from the ODQ.
  - Once the subscriber finishes updating its target successfully, it sends confirmation to the ODQ. (For SAP BusinessObjects-based DataSources, there is an implicit close.)

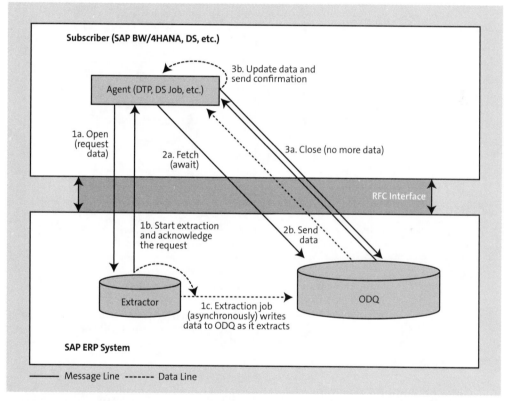

Figure 1.37 Data Acquisition Process

In the source system, the delta records are written in two ways, as shown in Figure 1.38: push (type D) and pull (type E). Most of the SAP extractors use one of these two options.

The following are the steps for each delta process:

- **Push (type D)**
  - Open call: Locates the request.
  - First fetch: "Cuts" the data packages and picks up the first package.

- Further fetches: Pick up further data packages; this can be done in parallel from the queue.

- **Pull (type E)**
  - Open call: Starts an asynchronous extraction job that calls the extractor.
  - First fetch: Has to wait until the extraction job writes something in the queue, then cuts the data packages and picks the first package.
  - Further fetches: Picks up further data packages; in this case, the degree of parallel pickup is limited to the availability packages (buffering) in the delta queue. In the worst-case scenario (when the extractor isn't writing faster than the subscriber is consuming; that is, there's no buffering), it would be serial.

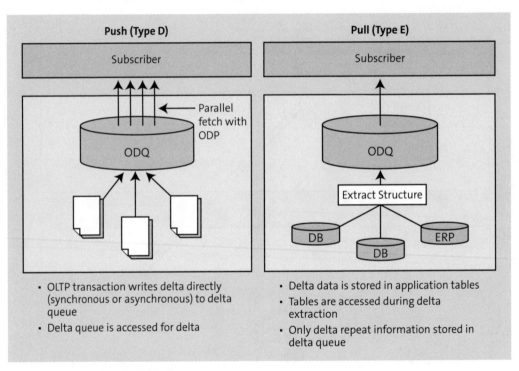

Figure 1.38 Push and Pull

A summary of all types of ODP is shown in Figure 1.39.

Essential Tables in ODP

There are a few important tables in ODP management that you should know based on the kind of data load:

- Table ODQDATA_C contains compressed init request data.
- Table ODQDATA_F contains compressed full request data.
- Table ODQDATA contains compressed delta request data.

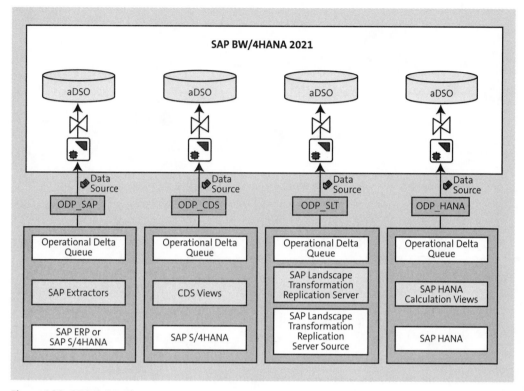

Figure 1.39 ODP Extraction

1.4.5 Monitoring

The Delta Queue Monitor (Transaction ODQMON) is the first entry point for analysis of delta issues. It allows you to monitor delta queues in various views, such as the following:

- Queue view
- Subscription view
- Requests view
- Units view

Note that for pull extractors only, there is an extraction job. Push extractors write directly to the queue. The naming conventions used for extraction job logs are as follows:

- Delta extraction jobs: *ODQR*D*
- Initial extraction jobs: *ODQR*C*
- Full extraction jobs: *ODQR*F*

The Transaction ODQMON initial screen is shown in Figure 1.40.

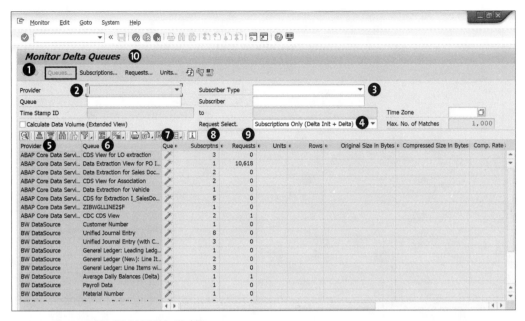

Figure 1.40 ODQMON Initial Screen

Once you open Transaction ODQMON screen, as shown in Figure 1.40, the default view will be the queue view. Here you'll see the following information:

❶ The **Queues** view is selected by default. It shows an overview of all ODP-enabled delta queues and information about the number of subscriptions, number of new requests, and more.

❷ The **Provider** can be selected here.

❸ The **Subscriber Type** can be selected.

❹ Under **Request Select.** (request type), you can filter the results (**Full**, **Init**, **Delta**).

❺ The **Provider** will be displayed.

❻ The technical name or description of the **Queue** is shown.

❼ The **Queue status** (active or inactive) is indicated.

❽ The total number of **Subscriptions** for the queue is listed here.

❾ The total number of **Requests** based on the subscription for the queue is listed here.

❿ This icon will toggle between the technical name and description.

Once you double-click the **Queues** view, it will take you to the **Subscriptions** view (see Figure 1.41), which will give an overview of all subscribers connected to a delta queue. Detailed information on each subscriber (subscriber, subscription number of transferred requests) is shown here.

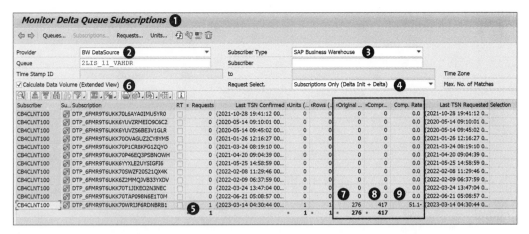

Figure 1.41 Subscriptions View

You can see the following options in Figure 1.41:

❶ The **Subscriptions** button is greyed out, indicating you're in the subscriptions view.

❷ **Provider** is set to **BW DataSource** and the **Queue** is the technical name of the Data-Source. (You also have the option to select **ABAP Core Data Services**, **HANA Information Views**, **ODP Introspektion**, or **SAP NetWeaver Business Warehouse** as the **Provider**.)

❸ The type of **Subscriber** is shown; here it's **SAP Business Warehouse**, as we're extracting data to SAP BW/4HANA.

❹ Under **Request Select.**, there are filter options for the type of **Request** (init or delta). The default value is **Subscriptions Only (Delta Init + Delta)**.

❺ The total number of requests and the associated subscriptions along with the associated DTP are listed here.

❻ If you select the **Calculate Data Volume (Extended View)** checkbox, then you can see the compression rates (by bytes and percentage).

❼ This is the original size of the records processed in bytes.

❽ This is the compressed size in bytes.

❾ This is the compression percentage.

There is also a **Trash** icon in this view, which will let you delete a subscription if required.

If you want to see more details, double-click on a subscription and it will take you to the next view, an overview of all picked up requests. Detailed information is shown for each request (subscriber subscription, full/delta request, date of request, related background job). This view shows the delta queue content depending on the subscribers (see Figure 1.42).

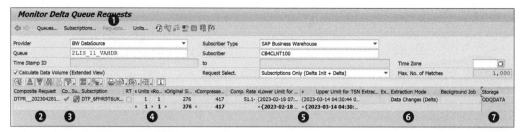

Figure 1.42 Requests View

As shown in Figure 1.42, you have the following options:

❶ The greyed-out **Requests** button indicates that you're in the requests view.

❷ The **Composite Request** column shows the DTP request number from SAP BW/4HANA.

❸ Here you can see the composite request status and the DTP associated with it.

❹ Here you can see the units and rows information for the request.

❺ In this area, you can see the lower and upper transaction sequence number (TSN) for the request.

❻ The extraction mode is shown here—in this case, delta extraction.

❼ The storage will show you the table associated with it. Here it's table ODQDATA as the mode is delta.

Let's go over some important details in this view. We'll create a new initialization for a new DSO, so we'll see the requests view as shown in Figure 1.43.

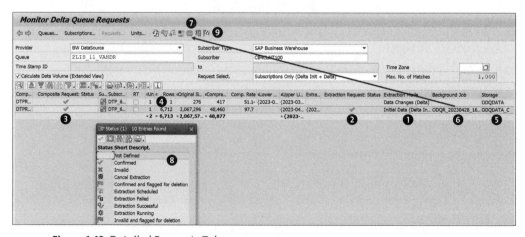

Figure 1.43 Detailed Requests Tab

The following details are shown in Figure 1.43:

❶ You can see that this is an initialization request.

❷ The **Extraction Request: Status** is green.

❸ The **Composite Request: Status** is green.

❹ You can see the total number of rows extracted and that the compression ratio is 97.7%.

❺ Since this is an init request, the table is ODQDATA_C.

❻ This request has created a **Background Job** for the extraction request. if you click the **Job** icon that the arrows points to, you can see the logs.

❼ If the extraction job has failed, you can use this icon to repeat the job.

❽ If the request has failed, it can be closed with this **Close Request** button.

Extraction Request Status versus Composite Request Status

What's the difference between the **Extraction Request: Status** flag and the **Composite Request: Status** flag?

The **Extraction Request: Status** flag shows the status of the extraction (job). Here, data is written from the application to the ODQ. (The status field is not used for a push delta without an extraction job.)

The **Composite Request: Status** flag shows the status from the subscriber perspective (if the request has been picked up or not). The final status is set by the subscriber during loading.

If you want to see the background job, you can click the row and the **Job** icon, and you will see the popup with the job overview. Once you select an ODQR job name, you'll see the job log, as shown in Figure 1.44.

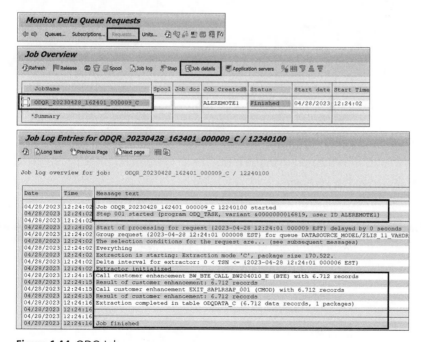

Figure 1.44 ODQ Job

Figure 1.45 shows the status change process in Transaction ODQMON.

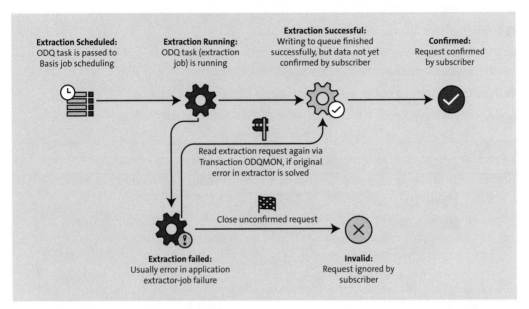

Figure 1.45 Status Change Process

A sample failed request is shown in Figure 1.46.

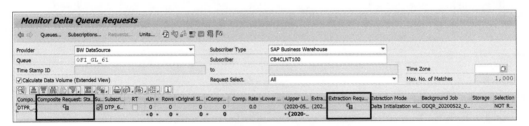

Figure 1.46 Failed Request

Now select the **Units** view (see Figure 1.47), where you can see the following:

❶ **Units** is greyed out, showing you're in the units view.

❷ The **Time Stamp ID** of the extraction is shown here.

❸ The **Subscriber** logical system ID is shown.

❹ The total number of **Rows** that are extracted is shown here.

❺ The **Unit Number** is shown if you double-click either **Unique Time Stamp ID** or **Rows** (for example, if there are 100 units in the **Rows** column, then you'll see 100 records' details in this section.)

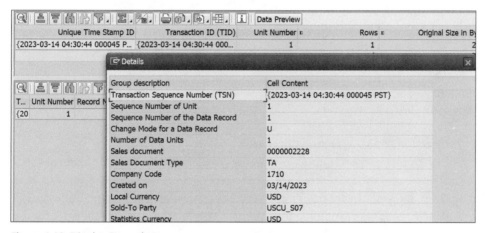

Figure 1.47 Units View

Choosing the **Display** icon  will show the complete details of the records (see Figure 1.48)

Figure 1.48 Display Record

Now, let's walk through some other options that are available in ODP:

- **ODQ Cleanup**

  In Transaction ODQMON, selecting the **Goto · Reorganize Delta Queues** menu item lets you clean up the old ODQ queues. Once you select this item, you will see the details of the retention period. The default value is 24 hours (see Figure 1.49).

  These are the details of the parameters:

  - **Recovery** is used to clean up the requests from tables ODQREQQUE, ODQTSNLOG, ODQ-DATA, ODQDATA_C, and ODQDATA_F.

  - **Data with Low Relevance** is used to close unconfirmed full requests.

  - **Data with Average Relevance** is used to delete task manager responses for ODQ (table ODQRESP).

  When a delta queue is activated, the reorganization run (program ODQ_CLEANUP) is scheduled automatically if there is no periodic scheduling yet. The periods specified can be modified either by manually scheduling them before the first delta request or by subsequently changing the automatically scheduled job.

Figure 1.49 ODQ Cleanup

- **Transaction RSA3 (Extraction Checker)**
  The extractor checker (Transaction RSA3) was widely used in the SAPI world to check the contents of the SAP extractors. You can test Transaction RSA3 for full and delta updates and you can set the parameters to increase the result count. But with SAP S/4HANA, you can't use this transaction for all scenarios. It does still work for the extractor, however, and throughout this book we will use this transaction as we are more concerned about the record count for reconciliation purposes. Check the Data-Source that you created based on table VBAK to see how many records are in it. To do so, use Transaction RSA3 in SAP S/4HANA. The result is shown in Figure 1.50.

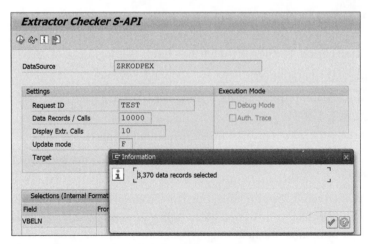

Figure 1.50 Transaction RSA3: Extractor Checker

- **Report RODPS_REPL_TEST**

  With SAP S/4HANA, you have an ABAP report that serves as a test tool for extraction. You can open Transaction SE38 and execute this report with certain selections, like the ODP context and the ODP name (which is the DataSource name), and you can choose the settings for the execution. Note that executing this report will create an entry for the DataSource in Transaction ODQMON, but it will be a test directory only (see Figure 1.51).

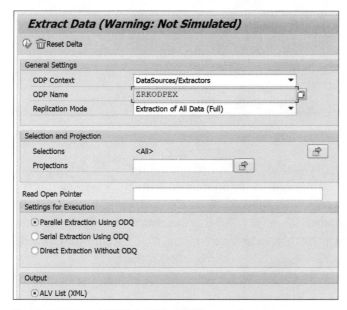

Figure 1.51 Report RODPS_REPL_TEST

The results are shown in Figure 1.52.

Extract Data with/from {2023-04-29 06:28:17 000023 PST}

VBELN	ERDAT	ERZET	ERNAM	ANGDT	BNDDT	AUDAT	VBTYP	TR	AUART	AU...
0060000003	10/24/2017	11:51:07	S4H_SD			10/24/2017	K	0	RK	102
0000000050	10/17/2017	11:39:01	S4H_SD			10/17/2017	C	0	TA	
0000001972	11/01/2019	11:20:01	S4H_SD			11/01/2019	C	0	TA	
0000002198	05/27/2020	14:49:07	I044912			05/27/2020	C	0	TA	
0040000001	10/16/2017	12:33:29	S4H_SD			10/16/2017	G	4	VC01	
0020000114	03/20/2019	04:00:28	S4H_PAI	03/20/2019	03/24/2019	03/20/2019	B	2	AG	

Figure 1.52 Result

In Transaction ODQMON, you can view this data, as shown in Figure 1.53.

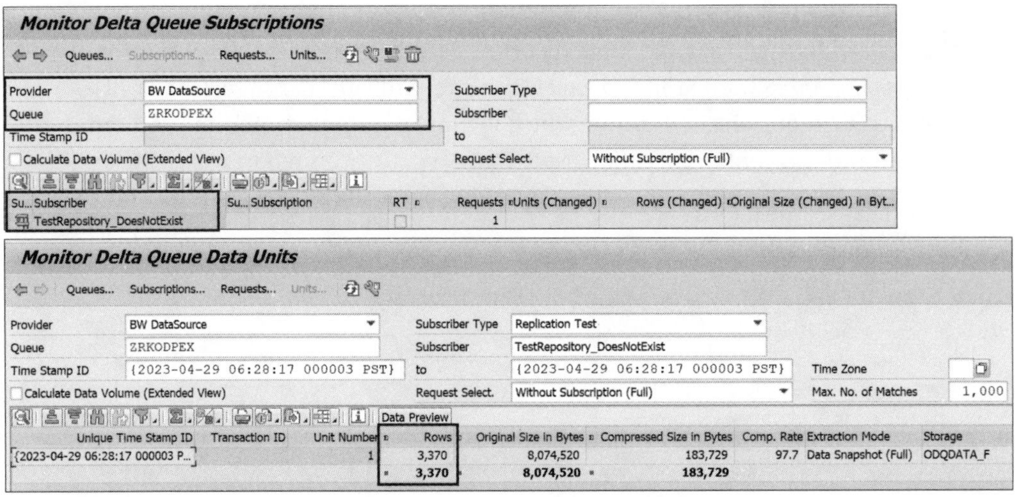

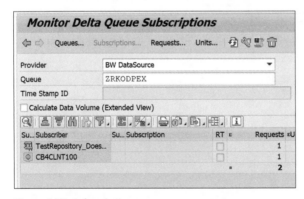

Figure 1.53 Transaction ODQMON

You can see that the provider is an SAP BW DataSource, and the Queue field contains the name of the DataSource. Note that the **Subscriber** field shows **TestRepository_DoesNotExist**; this is the result of the report. When you get into the units view, you can see that the total number of rows is 3,370. This matches the info in Transaction RSA3. We encourage you to use this report for your simulation purposes, but for testing we'll be using Transaction RSA3 widely throughout this book.

After you extract the data, you'll see one more subscription, as shown in Figure 1.54.

Figure 1.54 Subscription

1.5   Summary

In this chapter, you learned about the history of SAP BW/4HANA, followed by an overview of the product and its design principles. Then you learned about Eclipse and SAP HANA Studio, and we discussed how to install SAP HANA Studio and the SAP BW modeling tools. The last section of this chapter focused on an overview of operational data provisioning, in which we covered the detailed features and architecture of ODP. You also learned about ODP-based SAP extractors and data extraction essentials. Finally, we discussed the data acquisition process in ODP and ODP-based monitoring using the operational delta queue.

In the next chapter, we'll focus on creating an SAP BW/4HANA data model using a flat file, and we'll discuss the SAP BW/4HANA objects. We'll create an end-to-end data load and examine the SAP BW/4HANA objects that will be used in the data staging and modeling scenarios.

Chapter 2
Data Modeling in SAP BW/4HANA

This chapter will cover data modeling in SAP BW/4HANA. You'll learn about the all-important SAP BW objects used in data modeling, and we'll use flat file–based extraction to create end-to-end data modeling in SAP BW/4HANA from extraction to reporting. Once you complete this chapter, you'll have enough information to create data models in SAP BW/HANA.

This chapter covers the fundamentals of data modeling in SAP BW/4HANA. We'll walk step by step through the process to create objects and load data using a flat file. We'll start with data modeling in SAP BW/4HANA and cover details such as InfoAreas, InfoObjects, and DTP. Then, you'll learn about the advanced properties of InfoObjects. In Section 2.10, you'll learn about the creation of advanced data store objects (aDSOs). Finally, you'll learn about the creation of SAP HANA composite providers and walk through creating an SAP BW query.

2.1 Creating InfoAreas

InfoAreas are used to group a user's development objects. In SAP BW/4HANA installations, you'll see SAP-delivered InfoAreas such as SAP and its associated application areas: sales and distribution, materials management, and so on. To create an InfoArea, follow these steps:

1. Log into the SAP BW/4HANA system in the SAP BW modeling tools perspective. Right-click **BW Repository** and select **New** · **InfoArea** from the context menu. Provide the **Name** of the InfoArea and a **Description** as shown in Figure 2.1.

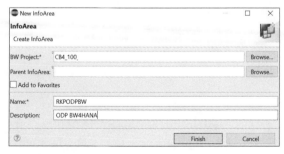

Figure 2.1 InfoArea Creation

2. Select **Finish**; your screen should look as shown in Figure 2.2.

Figure 2.2 InfoArea

3. You can add the InfoArea to your favorites via the context menu as shown in Figure 2.3.

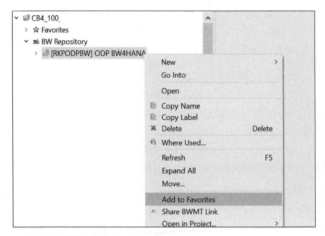

Figure 2.3 Add to Favorites

4. The InfoArea will now be added to your **Favorites** folder, as shown in Figure 2.4.

Figure 2.4 Favorites

Now that you've created an InfoArea, you can create other SAP BW/4HANA objects.

2.2   Creating Source Systems

In SAP BW/4HANA, you need to create source systems for SAP S/4HANA or other systems to extract data from them. SAP BW/4HANA supports only ODP source systems. There are a lot of steps to create a SAP source system that connects to SAP S/4HANA and other contexts, as we'll discuss in Chapter 3 on how to create an ODP source system for multiple contexts. For now, for understanding data modeling, you'll create a simple flat file source system in SAP BW/4HANA that will connect to a local workstation and fetch CSV or TXT files into SAP BW/4HANA. Follow these steps:

1. In the SAP BW/4HANA modeling tools, switch to the **Project Explorer** tab (making sure that you log onto the right SAP BW/4HANA system).

2. You can see the **Data Sources** folder here, shown in Figure 2.5.

Figure 2.5 Data Sources Folder

3. Right click the folder and choose **New** · **Source System**. Provide the **Name** and **Description** of your source system, as shown in Figure 2.6.

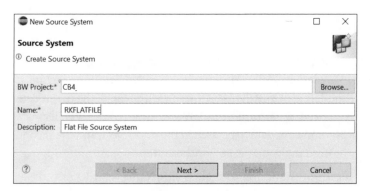

Figure 2.6 Flat File Source System

4. Select **Next**, then select **File** and click **Finish** (see Figure 2.7).

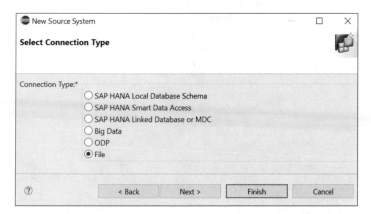

Figure 2.7 File Source System

5. You can activate the source system using the **Activate** icon 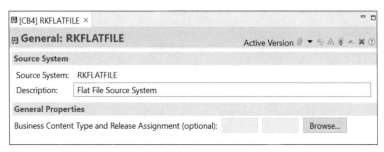 in the SAP BW modeling tools. Once it's activated, you will see the **Active Version** text, as shown in Figure 2.8.

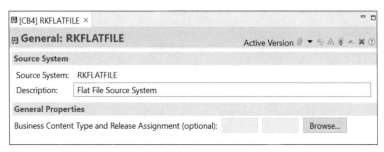

Figure 2.8 Flat File Source System

You can add this source system to your favorites if desired.

2.3   Creating Flat File Sources

You'll load the data from the flat file on your local workstation, so that will be the source of the SAP BW/4HANA data modeling. This process is called *flat file extraction*. It requires end-to-end data modeling in SAP BW/4HANA, so we'll cover all the major data modeling activities that you need to perform in SAP BW/4HANA. To start, you'll create two flat files: the first one is for master data to be used in the InfoObject, and the second is for transaction data to be used in the aDSO. Follow these steps:

1. Open Excel on your local workstation and create a simple file with 10 records, as shown in Figure 2.9. First save it as an XLS file, then save it as a CSV file.

	A	B	C	D	E
1	Customer Number	Customer Name	Customer State	Customer City	Customer Location
2	C001	Customer 1	NY	New York	Time Square
3	C002	Customer 2	PA	Philadelphia	West Chester
4	C003	Customer 3	NY	New York	Wall street
5	C004	Customer 4	PA	Philadelphia	Newtown Square
6	C005	Customer 5	NY	New York	Hudson Valley
7	C006	Customer 6	MA	Boston	Harward Square
8	C007	Customer 7	CA	SanFransisco	Solano
9	C008	Customer 8	MA	Boston	New England
10	C009	Customer 9	CA	SanFransisco	Santa Clara
11	C010	Customer 10	PA	Philadelphia	Malvern

Figure 2.9 Customer Master DataSource

2. Create a new Excel file. Make sure that the primary key in the first file is available in this second file. In our case, the primary key is **Customer Number**, so we used the same customer numbers in both files, as shown in Figure 2.10. Save your new Excel

file in both XLS and CSV formats, as you did for the first file. You should have four files in total.

	A	B	C
1	Customer Number	Customer Country	Sales Amount
2	C001	USA	100
3	C002	USA	200
4	C003	USA	300
5	C004	USA	400
6	C005	USA	500
7	C006	USA	600
8	C007	USA	700
9	C008	USA	800
10	C009	USA	900
11	C010	USA	1000

Figure 2.10 Customer Sales: Transaction Data

2.4   Creating a DataSource

A DataSource is a core object that contains the extraction logic of any extractors in any source system. There are many DataSources that you can extract from SAP S/4HANA, the SAP HANA database, flat files, and DB Connect. Chapter 5 through Chapter 9 deals with the SAP-delivered DataSources, but in this chapter you'll create a DataSource yourself based on a flat file. To do so, follow these steps:

1. Create an application component. Open the SAP BW modeling tools and log on to the SAP BW/4HANA system. In the **DataSource** folder , find the relevant source system, right-click on it, and select **New · Application Component**, as shown in Figure 2.11.

Figure 2.11 Application Component

2. Fill in the mandatory **Name** and **Description** fields for the application component, as shown in Figure 2.12. Once complete, choose **Finish** to complete the creation of the application component.

3. Find the source system you created via the **DataSources · File** menu option, or choose the source system from your favorites. Right-click the source system and select **New · DataSource**, as shown in Figure 2.13.

4. A wizard will open with the screen shown in Figure 2.14. Click **Next**.

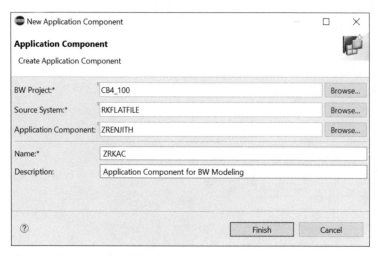

Figure 2.12 Name of Application Component

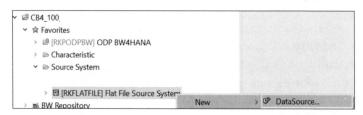

Figure 2.13 Source System

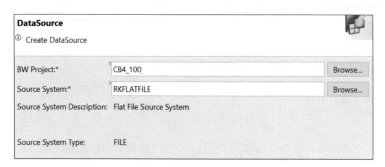

Figure 2.14 Wizard

5. You will see the screen shown in Figure 2.15, where you can select a template or source object. You can choose any of the options here based on your object, but for now, select **None**.

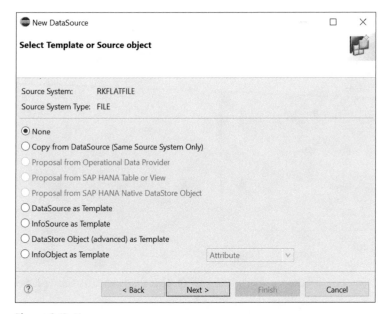

Figure 2.15 None

6. Click **Next** and complete the **Application Component**, **Name**, **Description**, and **Data-Source Type** fields, as shown in Figure 2.16.

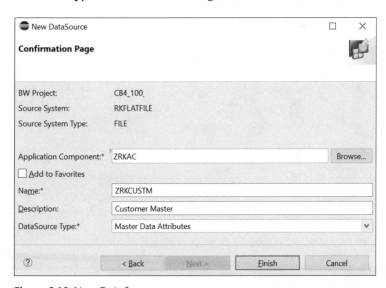

Figure 2.16 New DataSource

7. Once you select **Finish**, you'll see the screen shown in Figure 2.17. This is the **Overview** tab for DataSource maintenance.

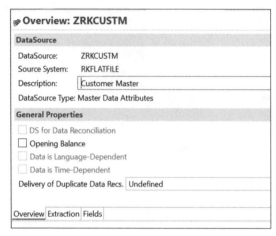

Figure 2.17 Overview Tab

8. Select the **Extraction** tab, as shown in Figure 2.18 ❶. The fields in this tab will be blank initially.

9. Provide the file path of your CSV file and enter "1" in the **Ignore Header Rows** field to ignore the first row, which is the header row. Enter a comma character (",") as the **Data Separator** and a semicolon (";") as the **Escape Sign** ❷.

10. Select **Derive Fields from File** ❸. This will show a popup window. Choose **Next** and the system will provide the proposal. Click **Finish** as shown in Figure 2.19.

11. Click the next tab, which is **Fields** (see Figure 2.20).

12. Activate the DataSource using the ⚙ icon.

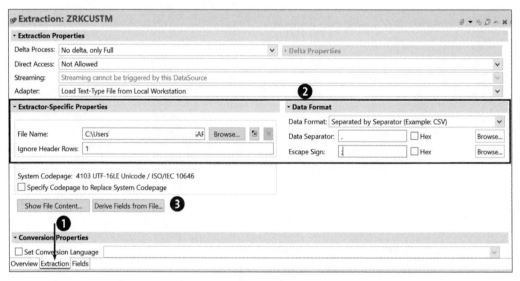

Figure 2.18 Values

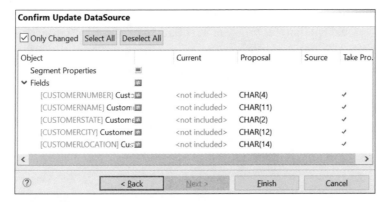

Figure 2.19 Proposal

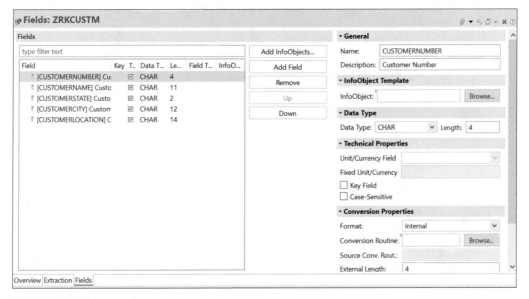

Figure 2.20 Fields

13. Once the DataSource is activated, you can see it in the backend table (RSDS) with **A** version (meaning the object is active), as shown in Figure 2.21.

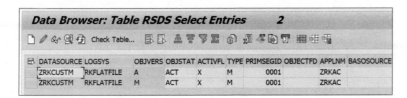

Figure 2.21 Backend Table

14. Next, create and activate one more DataSource, following the same process outlined in the previous steps, except that this time you'll set **DataSource Type** to **Transactional Data** (see Figure 2.22).

Figure 2.22 Customer Sales DataSource

15. You'll see the three fields for transaction data, as shown in Figure 2.23.

Figure 2.23 DataType for Transaction Data

16. You can see that both DataSources are displaying only the A version, as shown in Figure 2.24 in table RSDS.

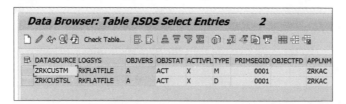

Figure 2.24 DataSource List

2.5   Creating InfoObjects

Business evaluation objects are known in SAP BW as *InfoObjects*. InfoObjects are the smallest units in SAP BW. They are used to depict information in a structured form required for creating InfoProviders. InfoObjects are divided into characteristics, key figures, units, time characteristics, and technical characteristics. InfoObjects with attributes or texts can also be InfoProviders in their own right.

Characteristics are sorting keys, such as company code, product, customer group, fiscal year, period, or region. *Key figures* provide the values that are reported on in a query. Key figures can include quantity, amount, or number of items.

Beginning with SAP BW 7.5, modeling in the Data Warehousing Workbench (SAP GUI) has been replaced by Eclipse-based modeling tools. Eclipse modeling tools provide a unified modeling environment for configuration, management, and maintenance of SAP BW and SAP HANA metadata objects.

If you need to create an InfoObject, then you need to use the SAP BW/4HANA modeling tools in Eclipse. Right-click your InfoArea and select **New · InfoObject** from the context menu. Then you'll create the InfoObject type characteristics that will be used in the master data InfoObject. In this case, in the DataSource for master data, we have the following fields: **Customer Number**, **Customer Name**, **Customer State**, **Customer City**, and **Customer Location**.

Of these, **Customer Number** is the primary key and we will create that as the master data InfoObject. The InfoObject will use the other fields as attributes, as illustrated in Figure 2.25.

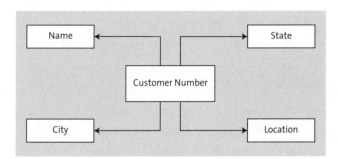

Figure 2.25 Master Data Attributes

The process is to create the attribute InfoObjects first before you use them in the master data InfoObject. Let's create the first InfoObject, customer name. From the data modelling context menu, select **New · InfoObject** to create a new InfoObject (see Figure 2.26). You know that its length is 11 characters, per the DataSource (see Figure 2.27).

Select the **CHAR—Character String** for **Data Type** and **11** as the **Length**. Because we have an uppercase and lowercase combination, you can select the **Case Sensitive** option as shown in Figure 2.27. You can see that **ZRKCUNAME** is the technical name.

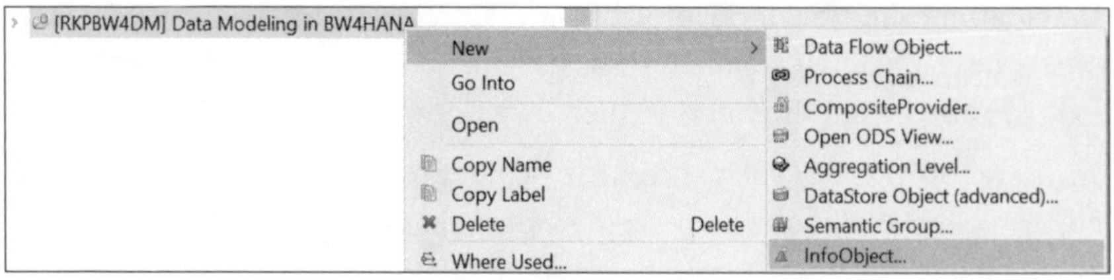

Figure 2.26 InfoObject Creation

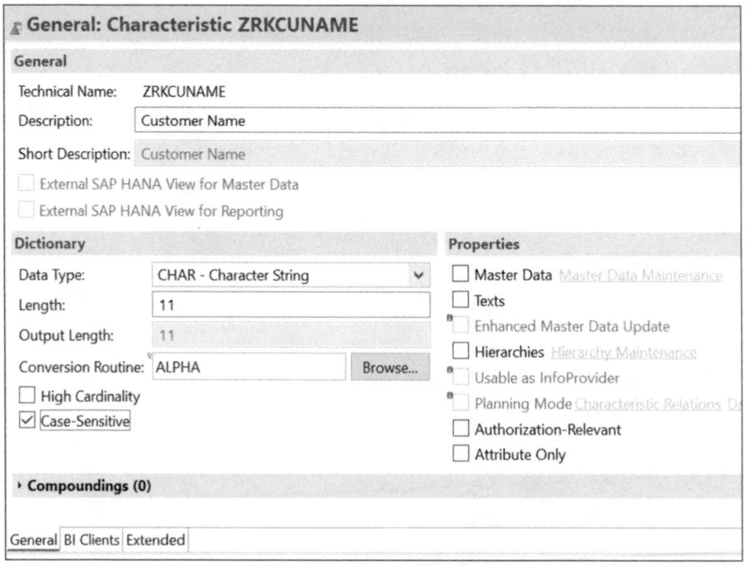

Figure 2.27 Customer Name

Activate this InfoObject using the icon and it will be stored in table RSDIOBJ as the **A** version. Similarly, create three other InfoObjects (see Figure 2.28):

- Customer state, which is type CHAR2, meaning the length of character is 2

InfoObject	V	Typ	Stat	Field Name	Short Description	BW-MT InfoObject: InfoArea
ZRKCUCITY	A	CHA	ACT	/BIC/ZRKCUCITY	Customer City	RKPBW4DM
ZRKCULOC	A	CHA	ACT	/BIC/ZRKCULOC	Customer Location	RKPBW4DM
ZRKCUNAME	A	CHA	ACT	/BIC/ZRKCUNAME	Customer Name	RKPBW4DM
ZRKCUST	A	CHA	ACT	/BIC/ZRKCUST	Customer State	RKPBW4DM

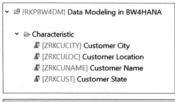

Figure 2.28 InfoObject Attributes

- Customer city, which is type CHAR12
- Customer location, which is type CHAR14

Their fields are **ZRKCUST, ZRKCUCITY**, and **ZRKCULOC**, respectively.

Next, create the master data InfoObject as shown in Figure 2.29, then choose **Finish** to complete the InfoObject creation.

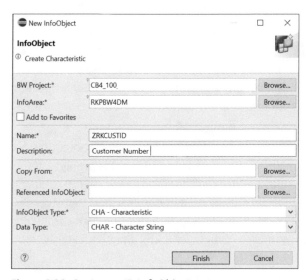

Figure 2.29 Customer ID InfoObject

When you return to the landing screen, you will see the **General**, **BI Clients**, and **Extended** tabs in the **General** screen (see Figure 2.30). There are many checkboxes on this screen that will alter the properties of the InfoObjects. We'll explore those next.

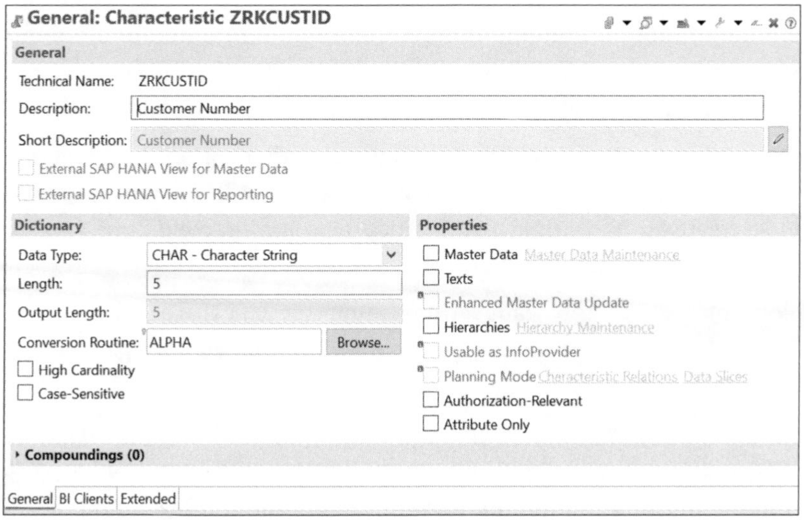

Figure 2.30 InfoObject Maintenance Screen

In the **Dictionary** section, there will be an option to select the **Data Type** and its associated **Length.** The following types are available:

- **CHAR**, a character field that can be filled with alphanumeric characters
- **NUMC**, a data type with which only numbers can be entered
- **DATS**, which has a length set to eight characters and the format YYYYMMDD
- **TIMS**, which has a length set to six characters and the format is HHMMSS

The **High Cardinality** property allows you to create more than 2,000,000,000 characteristic attributes for a characteristic. Because a characteristic with high cardinality has several restrictions, you should only set this property if you really expect several characteristic attributes. A characteristic with high cardinality has no persistent SID values and no SID table. It therefore cannot be used in hierarchies or as a navigational attribute.

Only use the **High Cardinality** option if you expect that the SID limit of 2,000,000,000 will not be sufficient. Otherwise, create the characteristic without this property. If the **High Cardinality** property is set, the characteristic will not have persistent SID values or an SID table, as noted previously, so it can only be used in InfoProviders that store the key value and not the SID value of the contained characteristics. The **High Cardinality** property is only supported for CHAR and NUMC data types with a length greater than or equal to 10.

The **Case Sensitive** option allows the system to differentiate between uppercase and lowercase letters when values are entered. If it isn't set, the system converts all letters into uppercase letters. No conversion occurs during the load process or during transformation. This means that values with lowercase letters cannot be posted to an InfoObject that doesn't allow lowercase letters. Once you specify the data type of an InfoObject, you'll see many checkboxes on the right side, which we'll walk through next.

The **Attribute Only** option specifies that the characteristic can be used only as a display attribute for another characteristic, not as a navigation attribute.

If you flag a characteristic as **Authorization-Relevant**, the authorization check will run whenever the query is worked on. Set the **Authorization-Relevant** flag for a characteristic if you want to create authorizations that restrict the selection conditions for this characteristic to single characteristic values.

Now let's explore some of the important settings in master data that will be used in real-time scenarios. These settings will impact the InfoObject-based table generation. Let's walk through them one by one.

Selecting the **Master Data**, **Text**, and **Hierarchies** checkboxes enables an InfoObject to have master data, which means that you will see an additional table in the InfoObject maintenance area for the **Master Data/Texts** and **Attributes** tabs (see Figure 2.31).

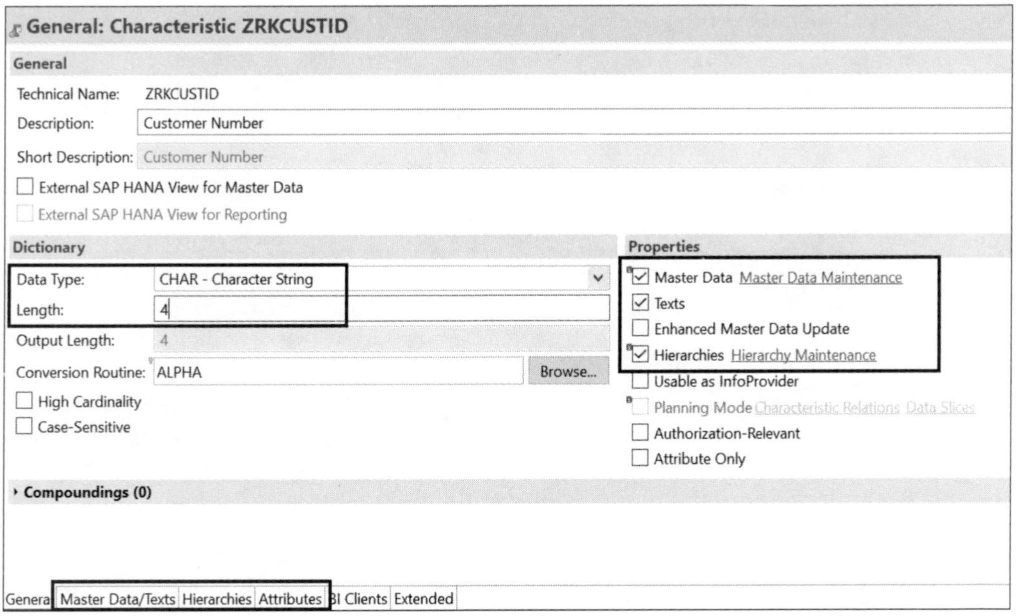

Figure 2.31 Master Data: Text, Attributes, and Hierarchies

When you go to the **Master Data/Texts** tab, you'll see two sections: the top half is for **Master Data/Text** and the bottom half is for **Hierarchies**. In the **Master Data/Text** section, you can see these details (see Figure 2.32):

- **Texts**
  If the characteristic contains texts, you must select at least one text. The **Short Text** (20 characters) option is set by default, but you can also choose **Medium Text** (40 characters) or **Long Text** (60 characters). If you choose the **Long Text Is Extra Long** option, the long text is of type SSTRING and can have up to 1,333 characters.

- **Language-Dependent**
  You can specify whether the texts in the text table are language-dependent. If you specify language-dependent, the language is a key field in the text table. Otherwise, there is no language field in the text table.

- **Time-Dependent**
  You can specify whether the texts are time-dependent. If so, the date is included in the key for the text table.

As shown in Figure 2.33, if you select the **Attributes** tab ❶, you can add additional InfoObjects, by using the **Add** button ❷. Select the InfoObject you wish to add ❸, then press OK ❹.

Master Data/Texts: Characteristic ZRKCUSTID

Read Access		Texts	
Access Type: Generic Access	✎ Details...	☑ Short Text	☐ Language-Dependent
		☐ Medium Text	☐ Time-Dependent
		☐ Long Text	
		☐ Long Text is Extra Long	

Configure Authorization

☐ Master Data Maintenance with Authorization Check

Hierarchies: Characteristic ZRKCUSTID

Hierarchy Type		Remote Hierarchy Properties	
Hierarchy Type: Standard	⌄	Remote Hierarchy Class: No values maintained	✎ Details...
☐ Version-Dependent			
☐ Time-Dependent			

Time-Dependent Properties	Miscellaneous
○ Entire Hierarchy is Time-Dependent	☐ Intervals Permitted in Hierarchy
○ Time-Dependent Hierarchy Structure	☐ Reverse +/- Sign for Nodes
☐ Use Temporal Hierarchy Join	

▸ **External Characteristics in Hierarchies (0)**

Figure 2.32 Master Data/Texts and Hierarchies

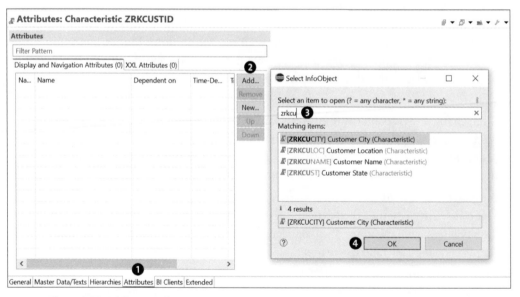

Figure 2.33 Adding Attributes

Now you can see the final status, as shown in Figure 2.34. This can be derived by adding all the attribute InfoObjects.

You can see that for the **ZRKCUCITY** navigation attribute, the checkbox for **Navigation** is enabled, and in **Navigation Attribute Properties**, the **Navigation Attribute Name** is shown as **ZRKCUSTID_ZRKCUCITY**, which denotes that this is based on the customer ID. You'll see how this will be connected in the tables after data loading.

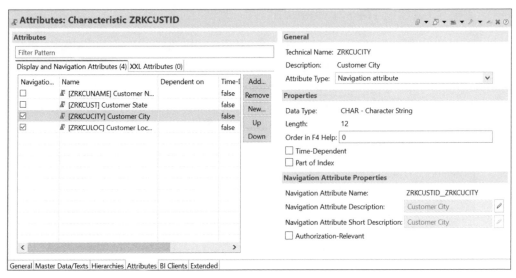

Figure 2.34 Display and Navigation Attributes

Now you need to activate the InfoObject. Open Transaction SE16 and search for the name of your InfoObject. You'll see a list of all tables that are generated; in this example, the InfoObject is ZRKCUSTID. If you need to find the tables generated, open Transaction SE16 and enter the InfoObject with * as the prefix and suffix. (For example, search for "*ZRKCUSTID*" and then search for "*ZRKCUSTID*"). Then press F4 in Transaction SE16 (see Figure 2.35).

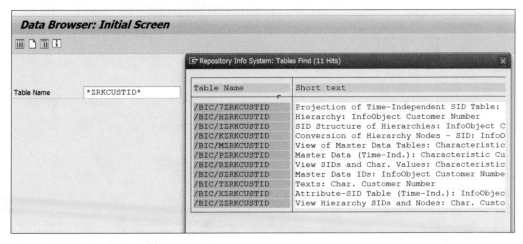

Figure 2.35 Master Data Tables

2.6   Creating Transformations

There are two options to create transformations: from the InfoObject or with the data-flow available in SAP BW/4HANA. For this section, we'll focus on the InfoObject-based flow. Follow these steps to create a transformation:

1. In the master data InfoObject you created earlier, right-click the InfoObject and choose • **New** • **Transformation** (see Figure 2.36).

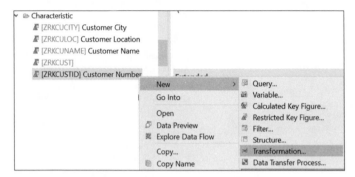

Figure 2.36 Create Transformation

2. You'll see the **New Transformation** window (see Figure 2.37). Here you create the transformation from the InfoObject. The **Target** section will have the **Object Type** set to **InfoObject—Attribute**, and the **Object Name** (ZRKCUSTID) is filled in by default. In the **Source** section, set **Object Type** as **DataSource** and set **Object Name** to **ZRK-CUSTM**. You'll see the associated source system, which is **RKFLATFILE**.

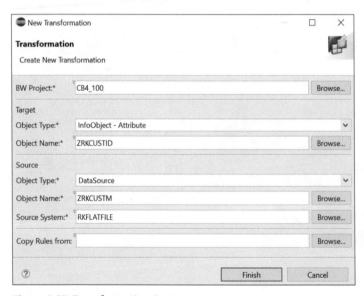

Figure 2.37 Transformation Source

3. Once you click **Finish** (Figure 2.37), you'll see the transformation maintenance area, including the **General** tab, shown in Figure 2.38. Here you'll see details such as the technical name and description of the transformation, as well as the **Target** (InfoObject **ZRKCUSTID**) and **Source** (DataSource **ZRKCUSTM**). You'll also see the details for the **Runtime Properties** and **Global Routines**, where you can create the **Start Routine**, **End Routine**, and **Expert Routines** that will help cleanse and harmonize your data.

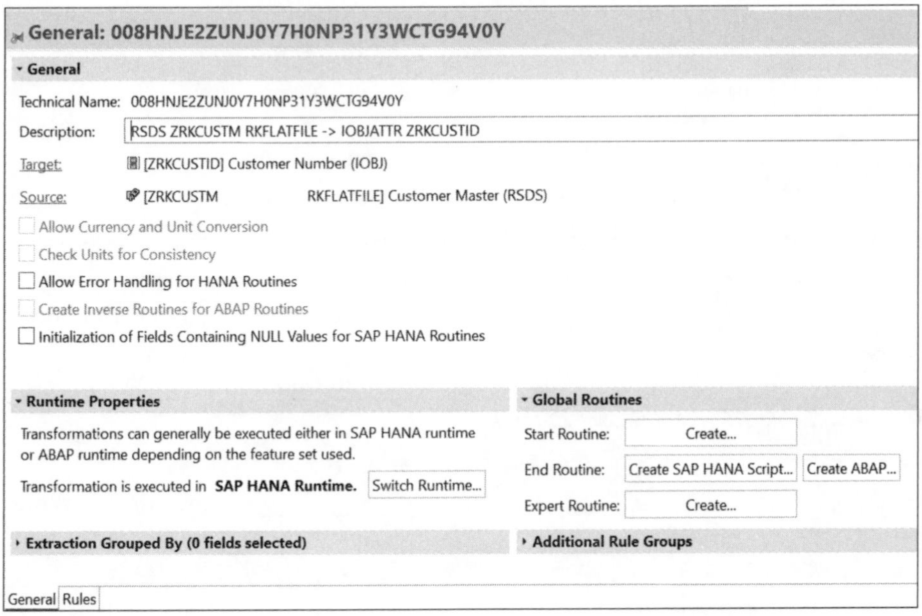

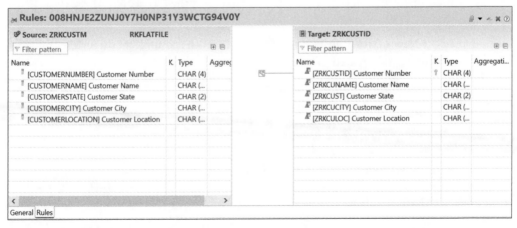

Figure 2.38 General Tab

4. Next, choose the **Rules** tab (see Figure 2.39), where you can see or define the mapping between the source and the target.

Figure 2.39 Rules Tab

5. Map the source to the target by dragging fields from the left side (**Source: ZRK-CUSTM**) to the right side (**Target: ZRKCUSTID**), as shown in Figure 2.40.

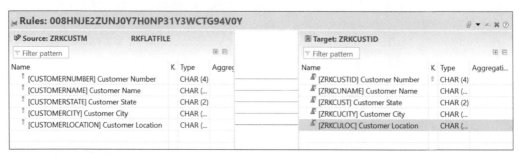

Figure 2.40 Mapping

Once the transformation is activated using the 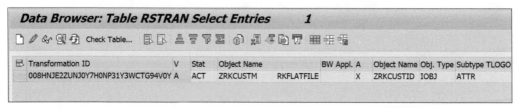 icon, you can see that table RSTRAN is filled as shown in Figure 2.41. The transformation ID will be the primary key of this table. The **Stat** column refers to the status; if it's **ACT**, that means the transformation is active.

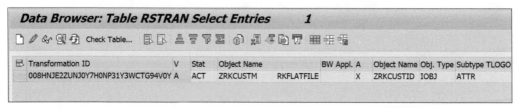

Figure 2.41 Table RSTRAN

2.7   Creating a Data Transfer Process

Once a transformation is created, you need to create the DTP. Follow these steps to do so:

1. Choose **New • Data Transfer Process (DTP)** from the context menu for the transformation you just created (see Figure 2.42).

Figure 2.42 DTP Creation

2. A popup for the target and source appears. Set the source as the DataSource (**ZRK-CUSTM**) and set the target (**ZRKCUSTID**), then click the **Next** button in the wizard (see Figure 2.43).

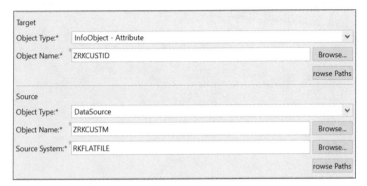

Figure 2.43 Target and Source

3. Choose **Finish** and you will see the DTP maintenance screen, shown in Figure 2.44. You can see multiple tabs here to review the DTP maintenance and execution. The default tab is **General**.

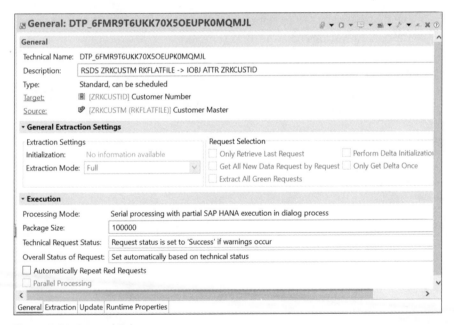

Figure 2.44 General Tab

4. Go to the **Extraction** tab to see the properties of the DataSource (see Figure 2.45). Because the DTP is based on the DataSource, the extraction setting will have the same values as you provided for the DataSource.

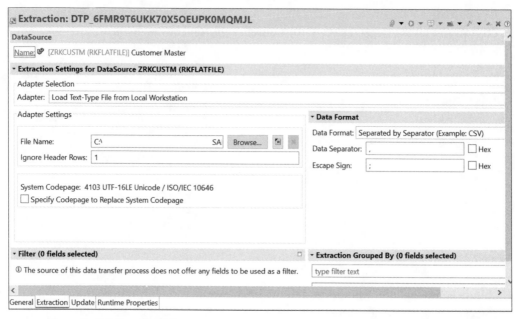

Figure 2.45 Extraction Tab

5. Go to the **Update** tab (see Figure 2.46) for the update settings details. There is no need to change the default settings here for this example.

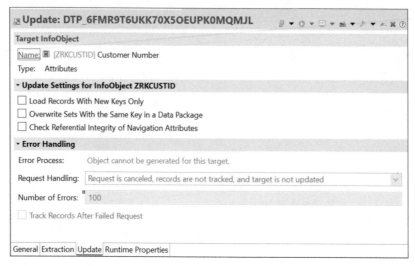

Figure 2.46 Update Tab

6. Now activate and execute the DTP as shown in Figure 2.47. You'll see the DTP settings, including the target InfoObject ❶. You can execute the DTP with the **Start**

execution of data transfer process 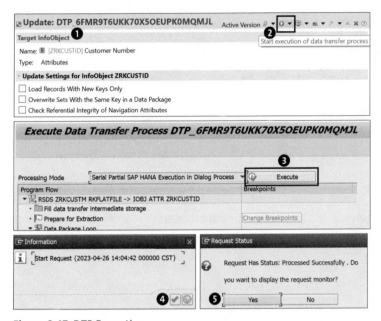 ▼ icon ❷. Execution of DTP can be started with the **Execute** button ❸. Choose the green checkmark in the **Information** popup to start the DTP request ❹. If the DTP request has completed successfully, you'll see a success message ❺.

Figure 2.47 DTP Execution

7. You can see the status as shown in Figure 2.48. If the request is green, then the DTP extraction has completed successfully. You can see the request ID and the start date and time of the request.

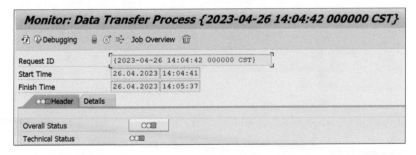

Figure 2.48 DTP Monitor

8. On the screen shown in Figure 2.48, if you choose the target 🎯 icon you'll go to the request maintenance section of the InfoObject (see Figure 2.49). Right-click the **Activation Request** and choose **Display Active Data (Time-Independent)**.

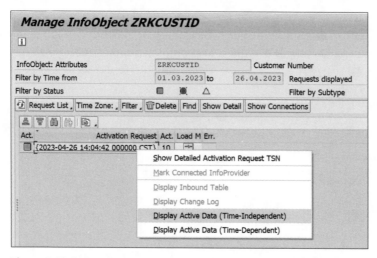

Figure 2.49 Request

9. Here the data is shown as in Figure 2.50. The data that you see is for the master data for the P table. It stores the values of the time-independent attributes for the InfoObject.

Data Browser: Table /BIC/PZRKCUSTID Select Entries   11

Customer Number	V	Change flag (I inserted / D deleted)	Customer Name	Customer State	Customer City	Customer Location
C001	A		Customer 1	NY	New York	Time Square
C002	A		Customer 2	PA	Philadelphia	West Chester
C003	A		Customer 3	NY	New York	Wall street
C004	A		Customer 4	PA	Philadelphia	Newtown Square
C005	A		Customer 5	NY	New York	Hudson Valley
C006	A		Customer 6	MA	Boston	Harward Square
C007	A		Customer 7	CA	SanFransisco	Solano
C008	A		Customer 8	MA	Boston	New England
C009	A		Customer 9	CA	SanFransisco	Santa Clara
C010	A		Customer 10	PA	Philadelphia	Malvern

Figure 2.50 Time-Independent Data

Let's examine the tables that were filled in during the data loading process, starting with the SID table. The SID table is created as shown in Figure 2.51. Refer to the **SID** field that has a number that starts at **2**, as that is the default value that the **SID** starts at when you load any master data InfoObject.

Data Browser: Table /BIC/SZRKCUSTID Select Entries   11

Customer Number	SID	Flag: Value in check tables	Value in Provider/Attribute (only releva	(obsolete)
	0	X	X	
C001	2	X	X	
C002	3	X	X	
C003	4	X	X	
C004	5	X	X	
C005	6	X	X	
C006	7	X	X	
C007	8	X	X	
C008	9	X	X	
C009	10	X	X	
C010	11	X	X	

Figure 2.51 SID Table

You can also see that the SID tables for the navigation attributes are also created once the data loading is completed. Figure 2.52 shows the SID tables for customer city ❶, customer location ❷, and customer name ❸. Note that the SID table for the ZRKCUNAME InfoObject (customer name) was not created, as that is a general InfoObject. The SID table will be created only when the master data is enabled.

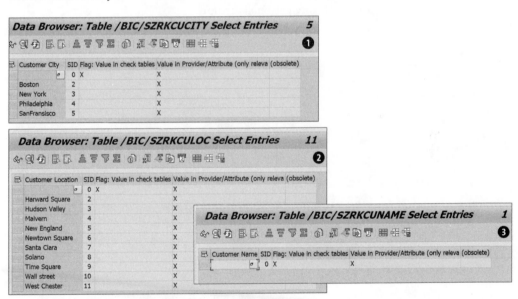

Figure 2.52 SID Tables

Now you can see the M table, which is the master data view (Figure 2.53). The M table will have the "/BIC/M" followed by the InfoObject name. In our case, the InfoObject name is ZRKCUSTID, so the M table is table /BIC/MZRKCUSTID. The prefix of the table will be "/BIO" if the InfoObject is SAP-delivered. You can see this table in Transaction SE16. Click on **/BIC/MZRKCUSTID** and use the **Execute** icon to execute the table.

Data Browser: Table /BIC/MZRKCUSTID Select Entries   11

Customer Number	V	Customer Name	Customer State	Customer City	Customer Location
	A				
C001	A	Customer 1	NY	New York	Time Square
C002	A	Customer 2	PA	Philadelphia	West Chester
C003	A	Customer 3	NY	New York	Wall street
C004	A	Customer 4	PA	Philadelphia	Newtown Square
C005	A	Customer 5	NY	New York	Hudson Valley
C006	A	Customer 6	MA	Boston	Harward Square
C007	A	Customer 7	CA	SanFransisco	Solano
C008	A	Customer 8	MA	Boston	New England
C009	A	Customer 9	CA	SanFransisco	Santa Clara
C010	A	Customer 10	PA	Philadelphia	Malvern

Figure 2.53 Master Data View

Now let's see how the navigation attributes are connected. Figure 2.54 shows how SIDs are stored in the X table (table /BIC/X ZRKCUSTID):

❶ Master data view

❷ Table for navigational attribute

❸ SID table for customer city navigational attribute

❹ SID table for customer location navigational attribute

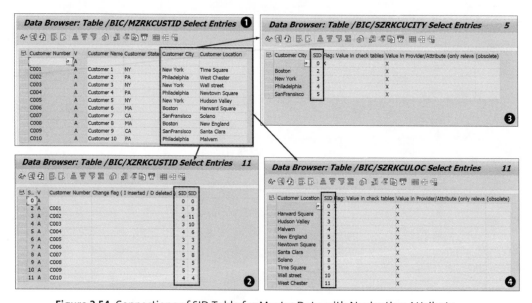

Figure 2.54 Connections of SID Table for Master Data with Navigation Attribute

If you can correlate the four tables shown in Figure 2.54, you'll know how the values from the master data view table correlate to the navigation attribute table for the master data InfoObject. It stores the SIDs of the city and location from both SID tables so that the data is made consistent.

For example, consider Customer C003. The Customer City is New York and the Customer Location is Wall Street. In the SID table for Customer City, the SID for New York is 3. In the SID table for Customer Location, the SID for Wall Street is 10. So how is this information getting stored?

In table /BIC/XZZRKCUSTID table, check row **C003** in the last two columns; for City and Location it has **3** and **10**, the SIDs, and you know these numbers mean NY and Wall Street as per SID mapping. You can do the same test for other rows by connecting the tables. This will give a very solid foundation to understand how master data tables connect with each other to provide accurate results.

2.8   Creating Key Figures

Now let's create the other InfoObjects to load the transaction data. Based on the customer sales DataSource, you have two characteristics (customer number and customer country) and one key figure (sales amount). You already have an InfoObject for the customer number, so you only need to create the InfoObject characteristic for the customer country and the sales amount key figure. Follow these steps to do so:

1.   Right-click the InfoArea and choose **New • Create Key Figure**. Then fill out the InfoObject screen as shown in Figure 2.55 and click **Finish**. (Refer back to Section 2.1 for more details on creating InfoObjects.)

Figure 2.55 Key Figure Options

2. On the key figure maintenance screen shown in Figure 2.56, you'll see the following options:

   - **Aggregation**
     Here you specify the function (**MAX/MIN/SUM**) that determines how the key figure is aggregated by default for the same key. For **Exception Aggregation**, you define when you need the key figure to be aggregated in SAP Business Explorer using the reference characteristic for it:

     • **Minimum (MIN)**
       The minimum value of all the values in this column is displayed in the results row.

     • **Maximum (MAX)**
       The maximum value of all the values in this column is displayed in the results row.

     • **Total (SUMMATION)**
       The total of all the values in this column is displayed in the results row.

   - **Standard Aggregation**
     These are aggregation functions such as summation average. For example, **Monthly Sales: Normal Summation** will give the total sales.

   - **Exception Aggregation**
     Use this when a normal summation would not yield correct results. The aggregation is done with reference to an external characteristic (mostly time). For example, **Yearly Population: Normal Summation** will not give the correct results, but you can use an exception aggregation for the last value and year as reference.

   - **High Precision**
     If you choose **High Precision**, the OLAP processor calculates internally with packed numbers that have 31 decimal places. This results in greater accuracy and fewer rounding differences. Normally, the OLAP processor calculates with floating point numbers.

   - **Noncumulative**
     If you set the **Noncumulative** flag, the key figure becomes a noncumulative key figure.

   - **Attribute Only**
     With this setting, the key figure that is created can only be used as an attribute for another characteristic. It cannot be used as a key figure in the InfoCube.

3. Activate the key figure using the 🔘 icon. You can see the list of all InfoObjects that were created under the **Characteristic** and **Key Figure** folders (Figure 2.57).

General: Key Figure ZRKCUSLS

General	
Technical Name:	ZRKCUSLS
Description:	Customer Sales
Short Description:	Customer Sales

Dictionary

		Properties
Key Figure Type:	Integer ▾	☐ High Precision
Data Type:	INT4 - 4-Byte Integer, -2.147.483.648 to +2.147.483.647 ▾	☐ Stock Coverage
		☐ Non-Cumulative
		☐ Attribute Only

Aggregation

		BI Clients	
Aggregation:	Summation ▾	Display:	Not Defined
Exception Aggregation:	▾ ✎	Description:	Use short description
Referenced Characteristic:	Browse...	Decimal Places:	Not Defined

Currency/Unit

		Read Access Logging	
○ Fixed Currency:	Browse...	Business Area:	
○ Currency InfoObject:	Browse...	Log Domain:	

General

Figure 2.56 Key Figure Maintenance Screen

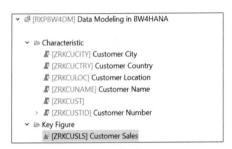

Figure 2.57 InfoObjects List

2.9   InfoObjects Advanced Properties

In this section, you'll learn how to use an InfoObject as an InfoProvider. You'll also learn about the enhanced master data update and how to enable external views so that an SAP BW object is consumed in the SAP HANA layer.

2.9.1   Usable as InfoProvider

When you choose the **Usable as InfoProvider** option on the **InfoObject Maintenance** screen on the **Master Data** tab, you can indicate that an InfoObject of type characteristic is an InfoProvider if it has attributes, as shown in Figure 2.58. The data is then loaded into the master data tables using the transformation rules.

You can also define SAP BW queries for the master data of the characteristic. There will be no additional table generated because of this property.

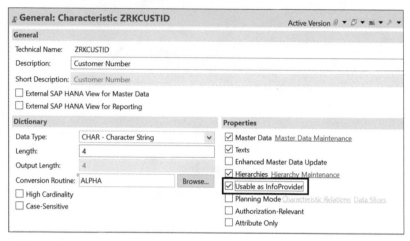

Figure 2.58 Usable as InfoProvider

2.9.2   Enhanced Master Data Update

Let's create a copy of the master data InfoObject you created earlier (see Figure 2.59). To create the copy, right-click the InfoArea and choose **New · InfoObject**. In the popup window, provide the name and description of the InfoObject. You'll see a **Copy From** option, via which you need to provide the name of the InfoObject that you wish to copy.

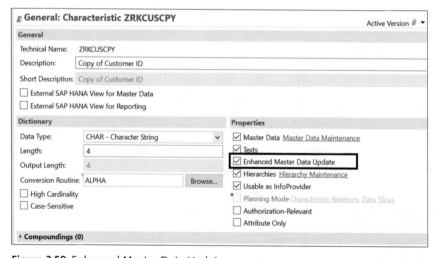

Figure 2.59 Enhanced Master Data Update

After you've created the InfoObject copy, activate it using the 🔳 icon. You'll see that four additional tables are generated, as shown in Figure 2.60.

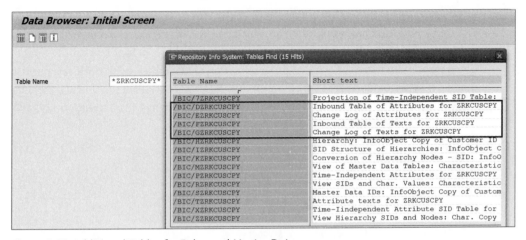

Figure 2.60 Additional Tables for Enhanced Master Data

For characteristics with attributes and/or texts, you can select the **Enhanced Master Data Update** checkbox. This enables parallel loading of data. For this process, the attribute receives additional tables. It then has a structure like a (advanced) DataStore object with an inbound table and a change log. The enhanced master data update is an advantage if you want to load a large quantity of data or load data from multiple DataSources simultaneously. You can also load deltas from one InfoObject into another InfoObject.

The data is initially loaded in parallel into the inbound table. When activated, the change log and the attribute and text tables of the InfoObject are updated. The activation can be processed in parallel in the ABAP runtime or in the SAP HANA runtime for SAP HANA 2.0 patch 03 (see Figure 2.61).

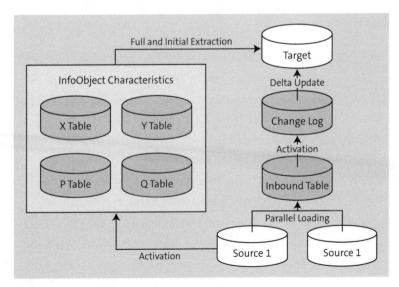

Figure 2.61 Enhanced Master Data: Load Process

As you can see, the activation creates the standard master data tables, like P, Q, X, and Y. The initial and full data is fetched from this table, but when there is enhanced master data the additional inbound and change log tables get the data for delta for the target. If you want to increase the parallel processing during the data load to optimize performance, that can be done from Transaction RSDMD_SETTINGS. There you click the **Edit** button to the right of **Process Settings** and establish settings for **Activation** and **SID Generation** (see Figure 2.62).

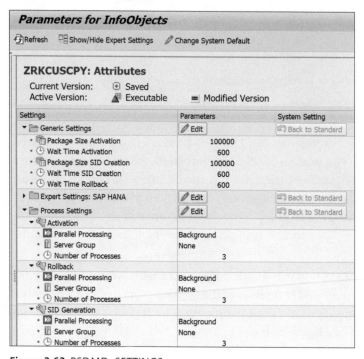

Figure 2.62 RSDMD_SETTINGS

The following is a list of all backend tables that are created upon activation of a master data InfoObject:

- /BI*/S<INFOOBJECTNAME> stores the SID values for the characteristic key values found in the P, Q, or T table.

- /BI*/M<INFOOBJECTNAME> is a database view defined as the union of time-dependent and time-independent master data attributes.

- /BI*/P<INFOOBJECTNAME> stores values of time-independent attributes.

- /BI*/Q<INFOOBJECTNAME> stores values of time-dependent attributes.

- /BI*/X<INFOOBJECTNAME> stores the SID values for time-independent navigation attributes. It exists if the characteristic has at least one time-independent navigation attribute.

- /BI*/Y<INFOOBJECTNAME>stores the SID values for time-dependent navigation attributes. It exists if the characteristic has at least one time-dependent navigation attribute.

- /BI*/T<INFOOBJECTNAME> stores time-independent and time-dependent texts.

2.9.3   Enable External View

If you choose the **External SAP HANA View for Reporting** option in the InfoObject, then it will create the external views in the SAP HANA database, and these views can then be consumed by SAP HANA applications. To enable automatic generation of external views, select the two checkboxes shown in Figure 2.63: **External SAP HANA View for Master Data** and **External SAP HANA View for Reporting**. Figure 2.63 shows these checkboxes both before activation ❶ and after activation ❷.

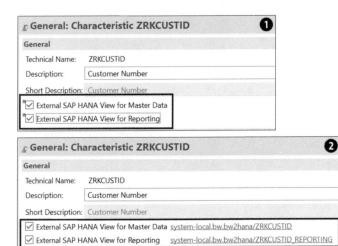

Figure 2.63 External SAP HANA View

You can see the generated external SAP HANA view once you get into the SAP HANA system in the admin console view (see Figure 2.64). Follow this path: **System ID of HANA DB · Content Folder · System Local Package · BW · bw2hana · Calculation Views**.

Your user needs the authorization to display the SAP HANA calculation views and perform a data preview; in most organizations, this authorization is granted by the Basis or security team. Once you have the authorization to display the data from SAP HANA calculation views, you can right-click an SAP HANA calculation view, choose **Data Preview**, and view the results (see Figure 2.65). Make sure that in the **Properties** tab, you have **Classical Analytic Privileges** set to avoid any authorization issues. Also set the **Client** to **Cross-Client** in the **View Properties** tab in Figure 2.65.

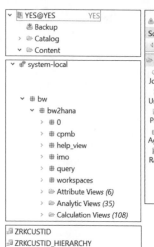
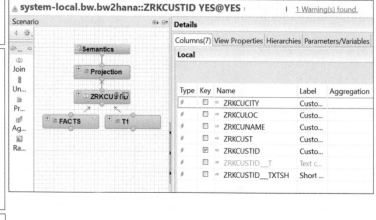

Figure 2.64 Generated SAP HANA Views

ZRKCUCITY	ZRKCULOC	ZRKCUNAME	ZRKCUST	ZRKCUSTID
New York	Time Square	Customer 1	NY	C001
Philadelphia	West Chester	Customer 2	PA	C002
New York	Wall street	Customer 3	NY	C003
Philadelphia	Newtown Squ...	Customer 4	PA	C004
New York	Hudson Valley	Customer 5	NY	C005
Boston	Harward Square	Customer 6	MA	C006
SanFransisco	Solano	Customer 7	CA	C007
Boston	New England	Customer 8	MA	C008
SanFransisco	Santa Clara	Customer 9	CA	C009
Philadelphia	Malvern	Customer 10	PA	C010

▽ Filter pattern ⏚ **11 rows retrieved - 359 ms**

Figure 2.65 Data Preview of SAP HANA View

In your SAP BW/4HANA system, make sure you enabled the view generation in Transaction RS2HANA_VIEW as shown in Figure 2.66. Provide the path in the **SAP HANA Package** field; you can maintain the path that's shown, **system-local.bw.bw2hana**. Then choose the checkboxes **Limit replication** and **Assign View Privileges** in the **Authorizations** area. **Assignment Type** should be set to "D". Provide your **DB Connection Name**.

Settings for external SAP HANA view for BW objects

General view settings

SAP HANA Package	system-local.bw.bw2hana
HDI Support Mode	Deployment into Repository Version 1
☑ Enforce SQL engine execution	
☐ Text for time characteristics	
☐ Multi-Tenant Enabled	
☐ Optimized column view	
☐ Add measures w/o decimal shift	

Authorizations

Assignment Type	D
DB Connection Name	YES
☑ Limit replication	
☑ Assign View Privileges	
SAP HANA Role	SAP_BW_MODEL_GENERATION

Figure 2.66 SAP HANA View Generation Settings

2.10   Creating Advanced Data Store Objects

Now that you have all the InfoObjects, you can start creating aDSOs to load the transaction data. To start, you need to create a new aDSO (see Figure 2.67). Right-click the InfoArea and choose **New · DataStore Object (advanced)**.

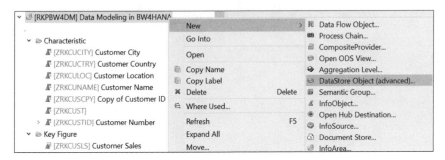

Figure 2.67 aDSO Creation

Provide the **Name** of the aDSO, choose the **DataSource**, and press **Finish** (see Figure 2.68).

You'll see the initial aDSO screen, as shown in Figure 2.69 ❶. Select **Standard DataStore Object**, and choose the **Write Change Log** checkbox ❷.

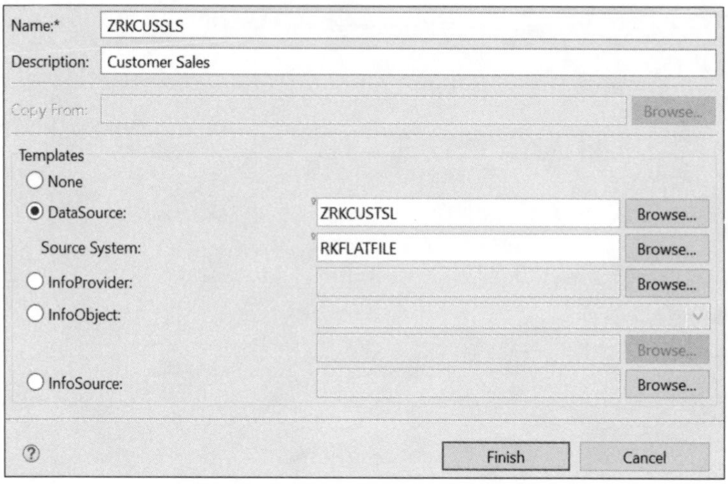

Figure 2.68 aDSO Name

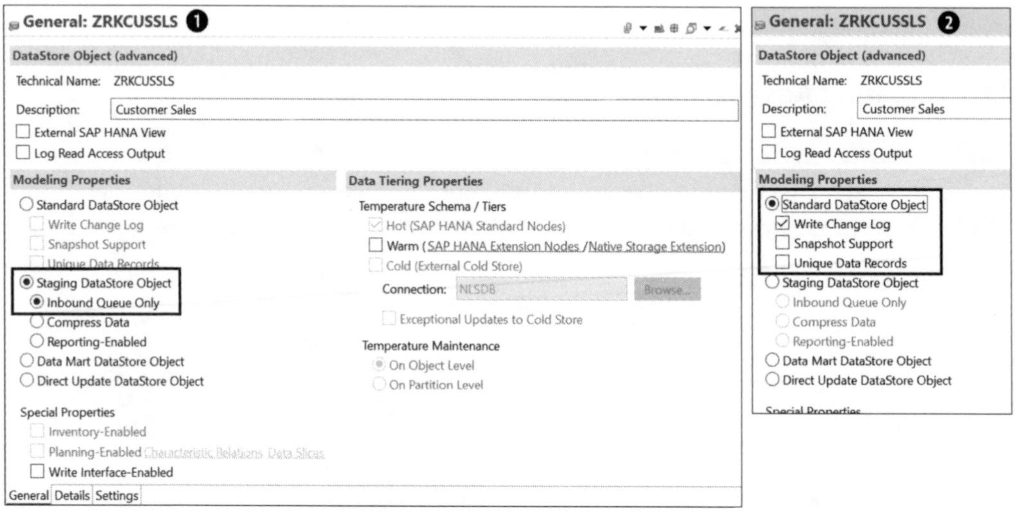

Figure 2.69 aDSO Initial Screen

When the **Write Change Log** box is checked, data is also written to the change log table once the activation process starts. If an aDSO is required to feed to other data targets, then a change log table is usually used to create delta updates to the target. The activation process involves comparing inbound data with the active table. Based on that, it creates deltas and stores them in the change log table. Once the target is ready to receive the delta data, the change log delta records are pushed into the target.

When this aDSO of a standard type with a change log is activated, it will create three major aDSO tables: an inbound table, active table, and change log table. Three views also will be created, one each for extraction, reporting, and external access.

In the aDSO maintenance, open the **Details** tab to see the fields from the DataSource. Then follow these steps, as outlined in Figure 2.70:

❶ Choose the aDSO field.

❷ Click **Change Type**.

❸ Search for the InfoObject name and then select the matching InfoObject.

❹ Select **OK** once you've chosen the right InfoObject.

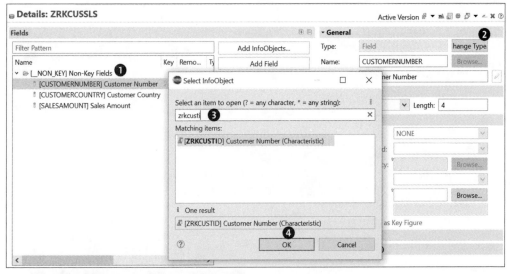

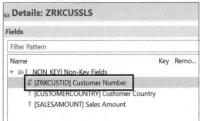

Figure 2.70 Change Type

Now you can manage the aDSO keys, as shown in Figure 2.71:

❶ Choose **Manage Keys**.

❷ Choose the InfoObject that will be used as the primary key (here, it's ZRKCUSTID; you can see it in bottom section of the screen titled **Keys**). Press **OK**.

❸ Now you can see the primary key icon.

Next, you'll activate the aDSO using the 🔧 icon. After activation, check the tables that are generated (see Figure 2.72).

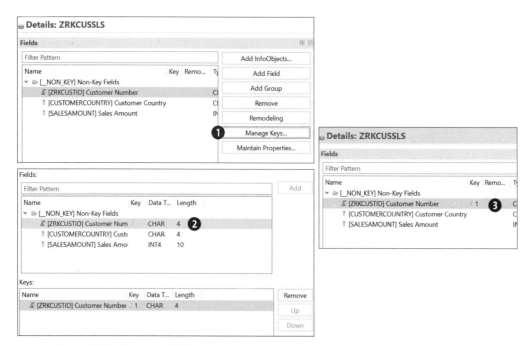

Figure 2.71 Manage aSDO Keys

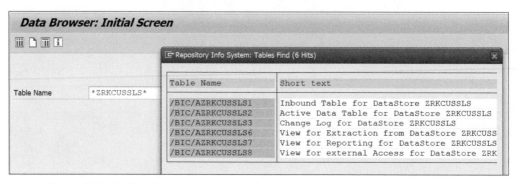

Figure 2.72 aDSO Tables

When an aDSO is generated in a customer namespace, its name will begin with */BIC*. If the aDSO is delivered by SAP, you'll see */BIO*. Here are the naming conventions for the major aDSO tables:

- **/BIC/A<ADSONAME>1 (inbound table)**
  This table is like the "new" table that loads data into the classic DSO. Data gets extracted via the InfoPackage/DTP and gets loaded into the inbound table.

- **/BIC/A<ADSONAME>2 (active data table)**
  An active table is where data resides for reporting purposes. In some instances (in SAP BW 7.4 and onwards), data from an active table can be combined with data from an inbound table for reporting.

- /BIC/A<ADSONAME>3 (change log table)

  If delta changes need to be pushed further to data targets, then the activation program pushes the delta data to the changelog table. If there are no data targets to feed, the changelog table can be left blank. This is slightly different from how the classic DSO functionality works.

Let's explore the aDSO types based on these three tables. The standard aDSO flow is shown in Figure 2.73.

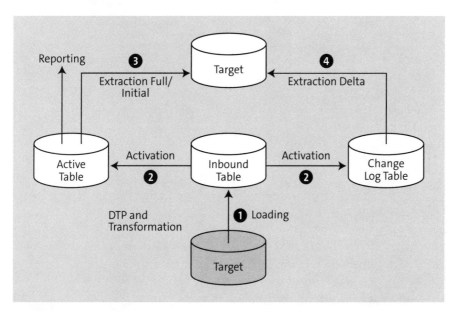

Figure 2.73 Standard aDSO

If you view the inbound table (Figure 2.74), you'll see a new field called **RECORDMODE**.

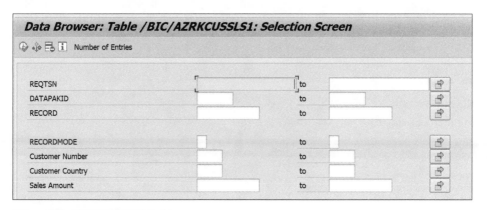

Figure 2.74 RECORDMODE Field

You can create the DTP and transformation for the sales DataSource (ZRKCUSTSL) to the aDSO that you created earlier (refer back to Figure 2.70). Create the missing mapping in the **Rules** tab as shown in Figure 2.75.

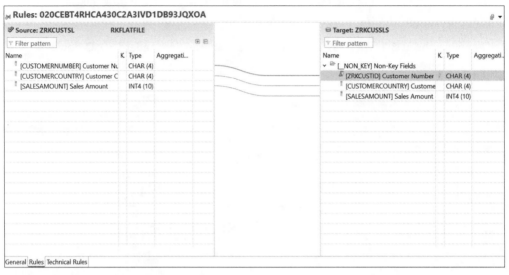

Figure 2.75 Mapping in Rules

If you now view the technical rules, you'll see ORECORDMODE. This field is required for aDSO delta management (see Figure 2.76).

Figure 2.76 ORECORDMODE

Now activate the transformation using the ⬛ icon. Create the DTP, activate it, and execute it. You can see this is successful as shown in Figure 2.77. (See Section 2.7 for more details.)

Figure 2.77 DTP Status

Click the **Administer Data Target** icon ⬚ and you'll see the **Load Request** time stamp there, as shown in Figure 2.78.

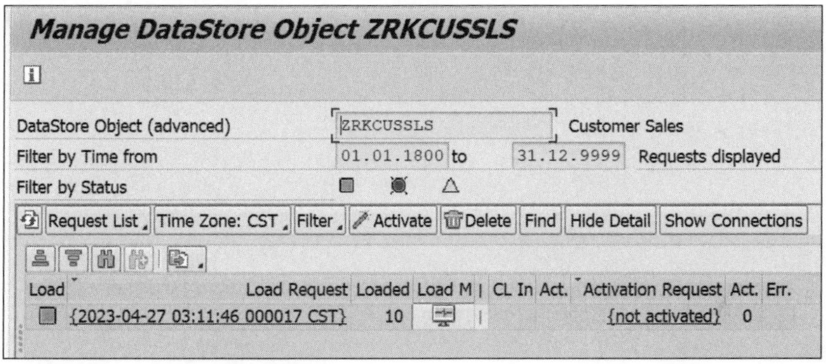

Figure 2.78 Load Request

Now let's check the backend tables. Figure 2.79 shows the inbound table ❶, change log table ❷, and active data table ❸ after the DTP execution and before the load request activation

From the aDSO, choose the **Manage DataStore Object (advanced)** option. In the **Manage DataStore Object** window (see Figure 2.80), the load request is shown. In this example, only the inbound table has data; the other two tables do not. Activate the inbound request via the context menu of the request, as shown in Figure 2.80.

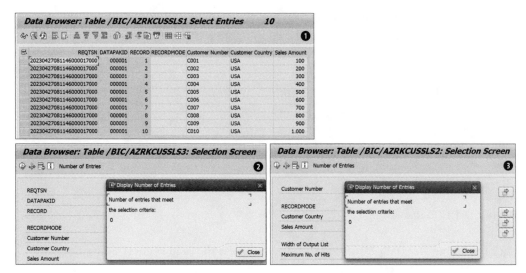

Figure 2.79 ADSO Tables: After DTP Load

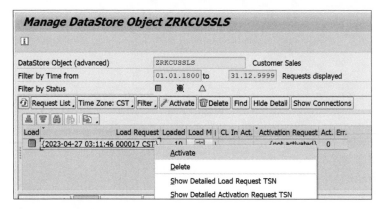

Figure 2.80 Activate DTP Request

Once the DTP request is activated, you'll see the screen shown in Figure 2.81.

Manage DataStore Object ZRKCUSSLS

DataStore Object (advanced)	ZRKCUSSLS	Customer Sales
Filter by Time from	01.01.1800 to 31.12.9999	Requests displayed	1
Filter by Status	■ ▓ △	

Request List | Time Zone: CST | Filter | Activate | Delete | Find | Hide Detail | Show Connections

Load	Load Request	Loaded	Load M	CL In Act.	Activation Request	Act. Records Err.
✓	{2023-04-27 03:11:46 000017 CST}	10			{2023-04-27 03:22:44 000007 CST}	10

Figure 2.81 DTP Activation

You can now see the transaction sequence number (TSN) with the time stamp–based value—for example, 2023-04-27—for both the load request and activation request.

Let's discuss the tables again. During the activation, the data from the inbound table will be moved to the change log table and active table, and once the request is activated the inbound table will be deleted. When the records are loaded for the first time, the value for ORECORDMODE will be N in the change log, which means it's a new record. Figure 2.82 shows the inbound table ❶, change log table ❷, and active data table ❸ after DTP execution and after the load request activation.

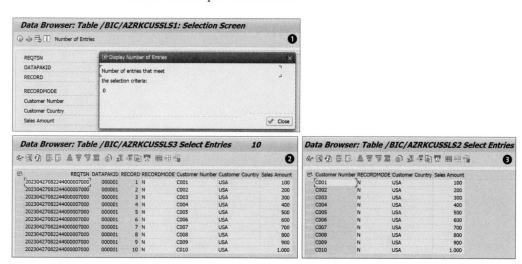

Figure 2.82 ADSO Tables after Activation

Delta Handling in aDSO

The new and changed records are extracted frequently in SAP BW/4HANA, such as when there is any change in the previously extracted value, like when the quantity of a sales amount changes. Based on the primary key settings and key figure aggregation, when the previous stored record is loaded, the ORECORDMDOE field in the aDSO will check the change log table before inserting into the active table. If the record exists, then it will act accordingly. We'll explore this further after testing the SAP HANA composite provider.

With the data in the active table, it's time to create the SAP HANA composite provider.

2.11   Creating an SAP HANA Composite Provider

To create an SAP HANA composite provider, follow these steps:

1. Right-click the InfoArea choose **New** · **Composite Provider**, as shown in Figure 2.83.

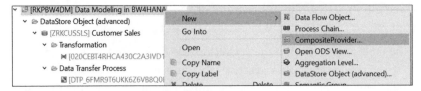

Figure 2.83 SAP HANA Composite Provider

2. The popup shown in Figure 2.84 will open. Provide the name of the SAP HANA composite provider and choose the source.

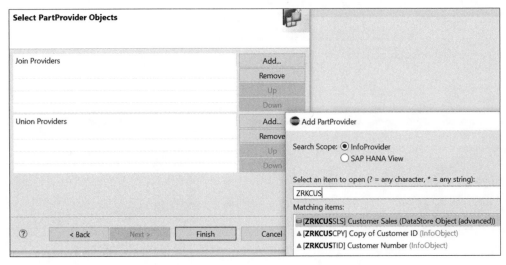

Figure 2.84 Choose SAP HANA Composite Provider and Source

3. Once you click **Finish**, the system will take you to the screen shown in Figure 2.85. Here, first choose the **Scenario** tab ❶. Then choose the aDSO and select **Create Assignments** ❷. Now you'll see the mappings from **Source** to **Target** ❸.

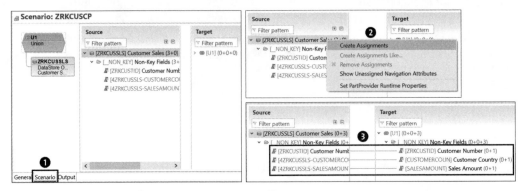

Figure 2.85 SAP HANA Composite Provider Maintenance

4. You might have noticed that the mappings for the customer city and customer location aren't shown here. To make those available, right-click the aDSO name in the **Source** window and select the **Show Unassigned Navigation Attributes** option, as shown in Figure 2.86.

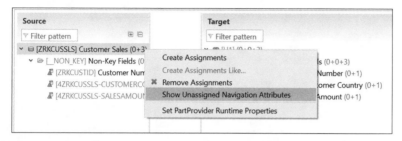

Figure 2.86 Navigation Attributes in SAP HANA Composite Provider

5. Now you can see the mappings as shown in Figure 2.87. Here, choose the navigational attributes fields in the sender ❶. Then right-click the fields and choose **Create Assignments** ❷. Finally, do the same for the other navigational fields and you can see the mappings from source to target ❸.

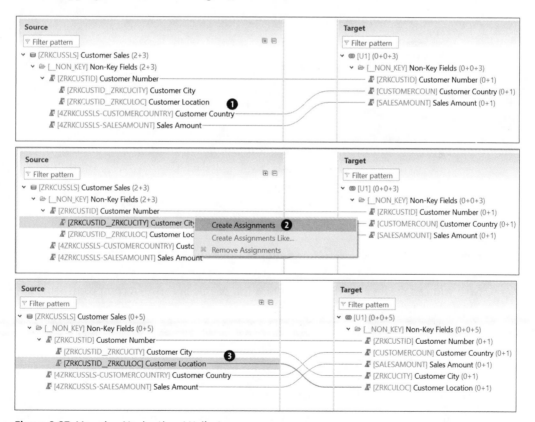

Figure 2.87 Mapping Navigation Attributes

6. Once all the mappings are completed, check the **Output** tab and make sure that all fields are available (see Figure 2.88).

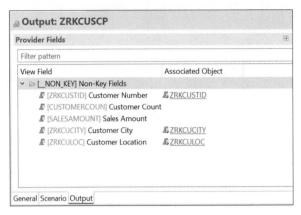

Figure 2.88 Output Tab

7. Active the SAP HANA composite provider with the 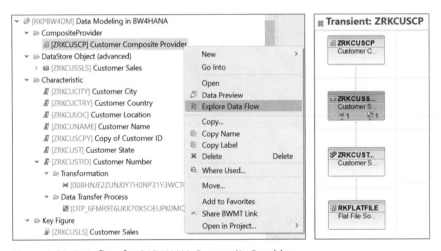 icon. It will create an **A** version entry in table RSOHCPR, as shown in Figure 2.89.

Figure 2.89 Dataflow for SAP HANA Composite Provider

Now you can create an SAP BW query on top of this SAP HANA composite provider, which we'll discuss in the next section.

2.12   Creating an SAP BW Query

To create the SAP BW query, follow these steps:

1. Right-click the SAP HANA composite provider and choose **New** · **Query** (see Figure 2.90).

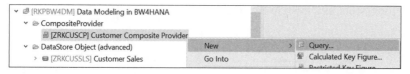

Figure 2.90 Create New Query

2. Enter a name for the query in the wizard. Once you press ⌷Enter⌷, you'll see the **Query Maintenance** window (see Figure 2.91).

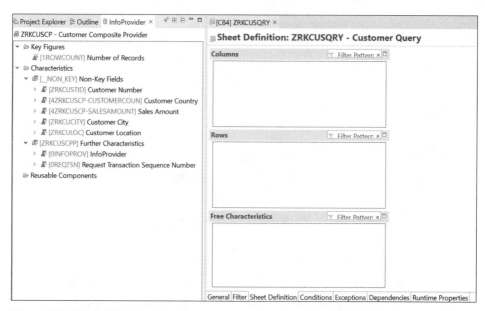

Figure 2.91 Sheet Definition

3. Double-click the InfoObject master data item in the **Rows** window and choose the fields that are the attributes (see Figure 2.92)—for example, **Customer Name**, **Customer State**, **Customer City**, or **Customer Location**.

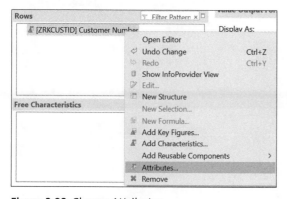

Figure 2.92 Choose Attributes

4. You can see the results, as shown in Figure 2.93.

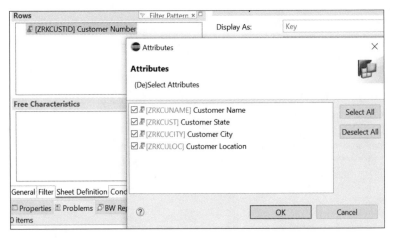

Figure 2.93 Attributes

5. Choose the other objects as shown in Figure 2.94:

   - Choose the InfoProvider view in Query Designer ❶.
   - Click a characteristic—for example, **Customer Country** ❷.
   - Bring the characteristic to the **Rows** window by dragging it from the InfoProvider View ❸.
   - Now drag the **Sales Amount** object to the **Rows** window ❹.
   - You can now see the **Sales Amount** key figure is in the **Rows** window ❺.
   - In the **Result Output Format** area, you can choose the **Never** option if you don't want to sum up similar values ❻.

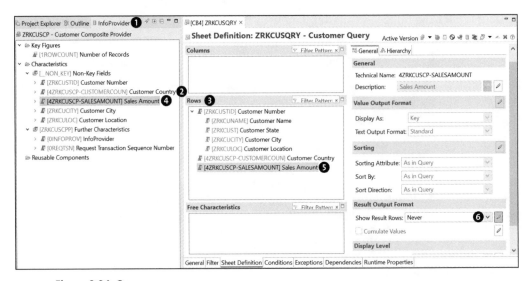

Figure 2.94 Query

6. Make sure that you set **Show Result Rows** to **Never** for all InfoObjects, like **Customer Number**, **Customer Country**, and **Sales Amount**.

7. Now save the query and do a data preview using the 🗗 icon (see Figure 2.95).

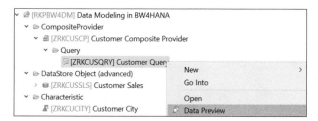

Figure 2.95 Query Data Preview

8. You can see the results as shown in Figure 2.96.

Customer Number	Customer Name	Customer State	Customer City	Customer Location	Customer Country	Sales Amount
C001	Customer 1	NY	New York	Time Square	USA	100
C002	Customer 2	PA	Philadelphia	West Chester	USA	200
C003	Customer 3	NY	New York	Wall street	USA	300
C004	Customer 4	PA	Philadelphia	Newtown Square	USA	400
C005	Customer 5	NY	New York	Hudson Valley	USA	500
C006	Customer 6	MA	Boston	Harward Square	USA	600
C007	Customer 7	CA	SanFransisco	Solano	USA	700
C008	Customer 8	MA	Boston	New England	USA	800
C009	Customer 9	CA	SanFransisco	Santa Clara	USA	900
C010	Customer 10	PA	Philadelphia	Malvern	USA	1000

[CB4] ZRKCUSQRY - Customer Query

Columns · Data Grid

Rows:
- Customer Number
- Customer Country
- Sales Amount

Figure 2.96 Data Preview

With this, you have completed the data extraction.

2.13 Summary

In this chapter, you learned about the design principles of SAP BW/4HANA, and you're now aware of the new objects used for data modeling. We covered data staging using flat files and the differences between master data and transaction data. We focused on creating the master data InfoObjects and analyzed the different tables that are created during the activation and data loading processes. Data staging for the transaction data aDSO has been completed, and we have tested an SAP HANA composite provider based on the aDSO. You also now know how to create an SAP BW query based on the SAP HANA composite provider. With this chapter completed, you should have a solid foundation for data modeling in SAP BW/4HANA.

Chapter 3

Creating an Operational Data Provisioning Source System

To extract data from any system into SAP BW/4HANA, you need connectivity to that system. SAP BW will be a receiver and all other systems that send data are sender systems. Sender systems are also called source systems in a broader context, or DataSources in an SAP BW/4HANA context. The source system must be created in SAP BW/4HANA, which involves multiple activities and requires some assistance from the Basis team for some essential authorizations and creation of background users.

With SAP BW/4HANA, the default source system connectivity takes place through the operational data provisioning (ODP) framework. This chapter explains how to create an ODP source system in SAP BW/4HANA for multiple sources, like SAP systems, SAP HANA systems, and local database connectivity. You'll learn about the steps in the creation of the ODP source system and about the importance of the source system and its impact on the data staging.

You'll start learning the steps to create the logical system in Section 3.1, then you'll learn about the users that need to be created in the sender and receiver systems, along with the required authorizations that help with data extraction. You'll learn how to create and test Remote Function Call (RFC) destinations between the sender and received systems. With all these prerequisites in place, in Section 3.2 you'll learn how to create an ODP SAP source system in SAP BW/4HANA, which will enable you to extract data from SAP S/4HANA or an SAP ERP system using SAP-delivered business content DataSources. Once the source system is created, you'll learn how to check the backend tables related to the source system and do the validation in the same sections.

3.1 Introduction to Source Systems

This section covers the details of the SAP BW/4HANA source system. Here you'll learn about the technical architecture of the source system.

3.1.1   Logical System

When data is distributed between different systems within a network, the systems must be identifiable—and that's where the logical system comes into play. In simple terms, a logical system is an application system in which applications work together on a common data basis. In SAP terms, the logical system is also called a client. When we say that a logical system is used to uniquely identify a system on a network, that means that no two systems in a network should have the same logical system. Each system in an SAP network will have a system ID of three characters, plus three digits for client number. For example, you can have an SAP BW production system name of BPD with a client of 200. When you create a logical system, you need to follow the standard naming conventions that SAP recommends. A logical system name will be <System ID>CLNT<Client Number>; based on this, the logical system in our example will be named BWDCLNT200.

When you log onto the SAP system, you need to provide the **Client**, as shown in Figure 3.1.

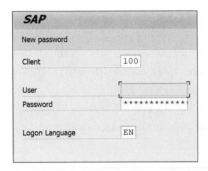

Figure 3.1 SAP Logon Screen with Client

Once you log onto the system, you can see the system ID set as **CB4** and the Client set as **100** as shown in Figure 3.2. (The **CB4** system ID is just used for the purposes of our example.) In this way, you can get the system ID and client details for any SAP system.

Based on the system ID and client, if you need to create a logical system for this example, it will be named CB4CLNT100.

Let's walk through how to create a logical system. Enter Transaction SALE, and navigate to **Basic Settings • Logical Systems** as shown in Figure 3.3. There you will find the **Define Logical System** option.

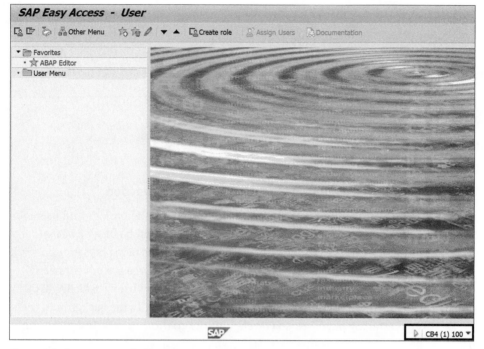

Figure 3.2 System ID and Client

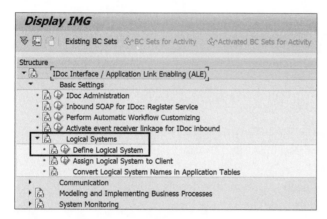

Figure 3.3 Define Logical System

Once you select **Define Logical System**, you can see the option for creating a logical system. If you click **New Entries**, you can provide the **Log.System** number and **Name** as shown in Figure 3.4.

Change View "Logical Systems": Overview

New Entries 🗋 🖺 ↺ 🖺 🖺 🖺 🗟

Logical Systems

Log.System	Name
CB4CLNT000	CB4CLNT000
CB4CLNT100	CB4 Client 100
CB4SDA	S4E HANA Calc
CB4VIEW	CB4 HANA Views

Figure 3.4 Define Logical System

3.1.2 Creating Background Users for SAP BW/4HANA Extraction

Once you've created the logical system, you need to create the background users for SAP BW/4HANA extraction. For the extraction, the users must be of type *background* because most of the SAP BW/4HANA data extraction happens using background work process. Two background users need to be created for the source system connectivity: one user in the sender system named ALEREMOTE and another user in SAP BW/4HANA named BWREMOTE. These two names are often used to identify the background users for SAP BW data staging purposes, so you should stick to these names. The background users can be created using Transaction SU01, which will open the screen shown in Figure 3.5. You can enter "BWREMOTE" in the **User** field and click the **Create** 🗋 icon at the far left.

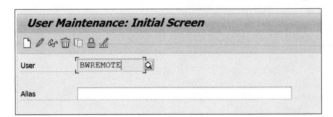

User Maintenance: Initial Screen

🗋 ✎ ⚸ 🗑 🗐 🔒 🖋

User   BWREMOTE   🔍

Alias

Figure 3.5 BWREMOTE Background User in SAP BW/4HANA

After you choose **Create**, you'll need to provide the details shown in Figure 3.6. Select **Service** for the **User Type** as and provide the SAP BW logon password in the **New Password** field. Finally, save using the **Save** icon 🖫 on the same screen.

You now should be able to log onto the SAP BW/4HANA system using this BWREMOTE user and password. Open the **Profile** tab and add the S_BI_WX_RFC profile, as shown in Figure 3.7. This profile will help in the SAP BW/4HANA extraction process.

Once you've created the background user in SAP BW/4HANA, you need to create the background user named ALEREMOTE in SAP S/4HANA. Use Transaction SU01 to create the user, setting **User Type** to **System**, as shown in Figure 3.8.

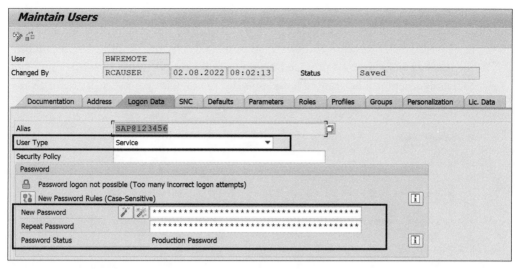

Figure 3.6 Create BWREMOTE User

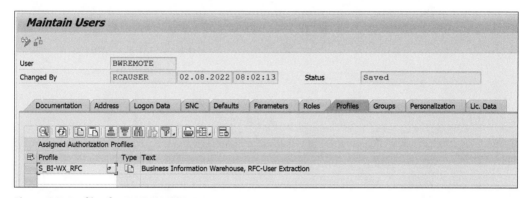

Figure 3.7 Profiles for BWREMOTE User

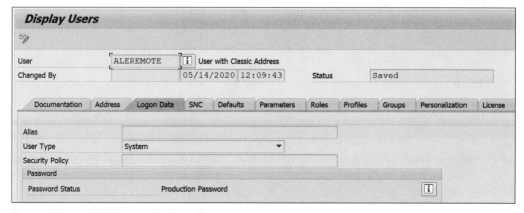

Figure 3.8 ALEREMOTE User in SAP S/4HANA

The background user in SAP S/4HANA should have profiles assigned to enable data extraction from SAP S/4HANA to SAP BW/4HANA. The essential profile required is S_BI-WX_RFC, which takes care of the extraction-related activities. Another important profile is called SAP_ALL. If it's provided, then you will have all access with this user—but that assignment can be granted based on a discussion with your security team. In any case, make sure your user has the S_BI-WX_RFC profile assigned, as shown in Figure 3.9.

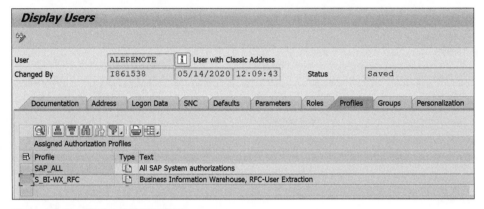

Figure 3.9 Profile for ALREMOTE User

Note

The RFC user on SAP BW/4HANA, receiving data from an OLTP (SAP S/4HANA or SAP ERP) system, should have the S_BI-WHM_RFC profile, while the RFC user on SAP S/4HANA or SAP ERP receiving requests from the SAP BW/4HANA system should have the S_BI-WX_RFC profile. A human administrator on both systems should have the S_RS_ALL profile. You can find detailed information about this in SAP Note 1478123 (FAQ: SAPI Source System).

When you create a source system, the system should be allowed to make changes. To make these settings, you need to work with your Basis team. Open Transaction SCC4 in both the SAP S/4HANA and SAP BW/4HANA systems and click the client number that you need to work with; you'll see the screen shown in Figure 3.10. There, you need to maintain **Changes to Repository and Cross-Client Customizing Allowed**. The Basis team will not make this setting in a production system, but you can make this change and then, once the source system is created, ask them to revert to the old settings. Make sure you select the right **Client** and verify the **Logical System**. Then choose the **Automatic Recording of Changes** radio button and enable **Changes to Repository and Cross-Client Customizing Allowed**. This activity must be done in both SAP S/4HANA and SAP BW/4HANA.

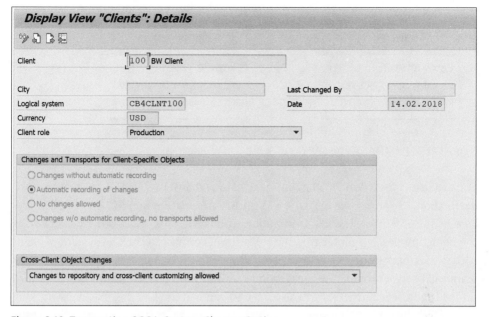

Figure 3.10 Transaction SCC4: System Change Options

3.1.3   RFC Destination

Once you've created the background users in SAP S/4HANA and SAP BW/4HANA, the next step is to create an RFC destination. In most organizations, a Basis team will take care of creating these users and RFC destinations. But as an SAP BW consultant, you should be aware of these concepts to know how the systems are communicating to fetch the data. SAP systems across a network communicate through RFC to send requests and receive data, and you define RFC destinations in your systems to manage the communication process and parameter handling. With an RFC destination, you can log on from one system into the remote system. Certain settings in both the sender and receiver systems must be maintained to enable this feature. As a best practice, an RFC destination can have same name as the logical system; for example, if you need the system CB4 to connect with S4S, which has the logical system name S4SCLNT100, then the RFC destination should also be named S4SCLNT100. This will help you identify the system easily. Consider the scenario shown in Figure 3.11, where the system communicates with the RFC destination.

SAP BW/4HANA communicates with SAP S/4HANA using RFC destination S4SCL-NT100, which is equivalent to the logical system name of SAP S/4HANA; similarly, SAP S/4HANA communicates with SAP BW/4HANA using RFC destination CB4CLNT100.

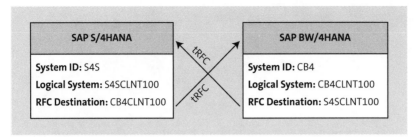

Figure 3.11 SAP S/4HANA and SAP BW/4HANA Communication

You can use Transaction SM59 in SAP S/4HANA and SAP BW/4HANA to create an RFC destination. As you can see in Figure 3.12, the RFC destination for SAP BW/4HANA is created in SAP S/4HANA. The **RFC Destination** with name CB4CLNT100 is created, and as the name implies, it denotes that the system will connect to the CB4 system of client 100. It uses background **User** BWREMOTE to connect to SAP BW/4HANA. The Basis team will need to provide the background user BWREMOTE's user name and password on the **Logon & Security** tab. You also need to confirm the RFC destination is working successfully by clicking the **Remote Logon** button and executing the **Connection Test**.

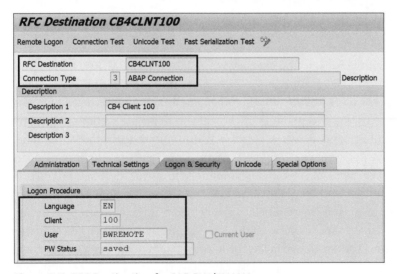

Figure 3.12 RFC Destination for SAP BW/4HANA

Similarly, you can create an RFC destination for SAP S/4HANA in the SAP BW/4HANA system. As you can see in Figure 3.13, the RFC destination S4SCLNT100 denotes that it's going to connect to the S4S system of client 100, and it uses the ALEREMOTE user to log onto the system.

It's always best practice to create the RFC destination with the name of the logical system that you are going to connect to. If you try to create the ODP source system without creating an RFC destination, it will generate the RFC destination based on the source system name that you provided by default when creating the ODP source system, but then later you will need to assign the username and password in the RFC destination as it will initially be blank. For example, if you try to create the ODP source system with the name S4STEST, then an RFC destination name with S4STEST will be generated with blank logon data in which you need to provide the remote logon details. This is why we suggest that you create the RFC before creating the ODP source system.

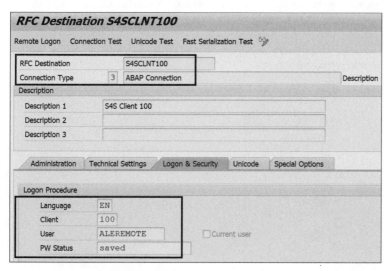

Figure 3.13 RFC Destination for SAP S/4HANA

3.2   Creating an ODP Source System

In this section, you'll learn how to create an ODP SAP source system in SAP BW/4HANA. If you need to extract data from a system like SAP S/4HANA or SAP ERP, then you need to have source system connectivity of type ODP SAP. This will enable you to extract data from the sender system into SAP BW/4HANA. You need to fulfill the prerequisites described in the previous section before starting this ODP system creation.

3.2.1   SAP BW/4HANA and ODP Source System Types

When you want to extract data from SAP S/4HANA, you need to do so in Eclipse via the SAP BW modeling tools perspective. Open the SAP BW/4HANA system and you'll see a folder called **Data Sources**. In the SAP BW/4HANA system, this folder will contain all the ODP connectivity-based information, so in a SAP BW/4HANA context, you can think of the **Data Source** folder as the source system. As shown in Figure 3.14, you can find multiple options for creating an ODP source system under **DataSources**:

❶ **[ODP_BW]** refers to the ODP source system of type BW.

❷ **[ODP_SAP]** refers to ODP extraction from ERP systems like SAP S/4HANA.

❸ **[ODP_HANA]** refers to ODP extraction from SAP HANA calculation views.

❹ **[ODP_SLT]** refers to extraction of data from SAP Landscape Transformation Replication Server queues.

❺ **[ODP_CDS]** enables you to extract data from the CDS views defined in the sender system.

❻ **[ODP]ODP—Other Contexts** can have many combinations of the other categories.

❼ **[FILE]** is used to connect to the local files like MS-Excel based data uploads.

❽ **[HANA_LOCAL]** is based on SAP HANA and is used to connect to the local SAP HANA database schema and extract data.

❾ **[HANA_SDA]** is based on SAP HANA and is used to extract data from other databases.

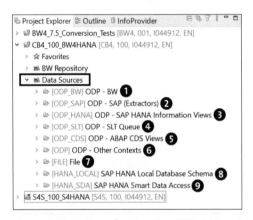

Figure 3.14 Options for Creating ODP Source System

You can see the same options if you log onto Transaction RSA1 in your SAP BW/4HANA system. They are visible in the **Source Systems** folder, as shown in Figure 3.15.

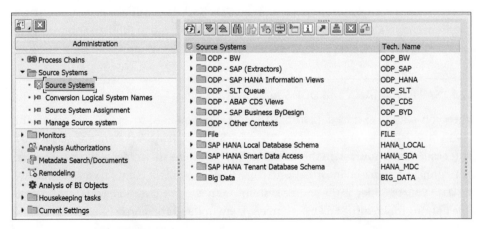

Figure 3.15 Transaction RSA1 and Source System

As you have seen, the SAP BW modeling tools will be in sync with the background Transaction RSA1 shown in Figure 3.15. Let's see how we can use each of these ODP system types and how to create an ODP source system.

3.2.2   Creating an ODP Source System for SAP S/4HANA and SAP ERP

If you need to extract data from SAP S/4HANA or SAP ERP, then you need to create an ODP_SAP-based source system. To do so, follow these steps:

1. Make sure that you have RFC destinations created for the sender and receiver. Now open the SAP BW modeling tools and select the SAP BW modeling perspective, then log onto the SAP BW/4HANA system. From the context menu of **[ODP_SAP]** under the **Data Sources** folder, select **New · Source System...** as shown in Figure 3.16.

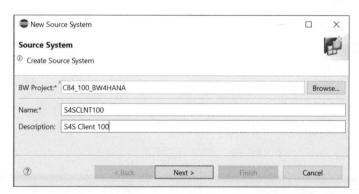

Figure 3.16 Creating ODP_SAP Source System

2. You'll see the screen shown in Figure 3.17. Provide the ODP source system **Name** and its **Description**, then select **Next**.

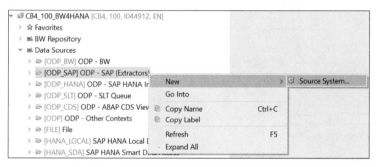

Figure 3.17 Name and Description

3. Set the **Connection Type** to **ODP**, as shown in Figure 3.18.

4. Next, you'll choose the type of system and RFC, as shown in Figure 3.19.

5. After you click **Next**, you'll see the details on the **Confirmation Page**, as shown in Figure 3.20.

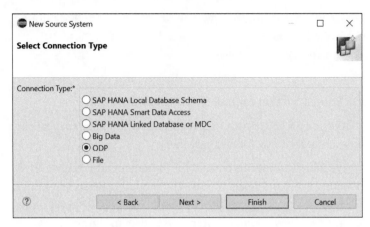

Figure 3.18 Connection Type

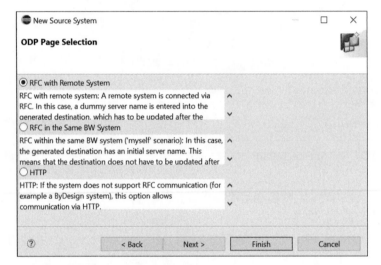

Figure 3.19 RFC Selection for Source System

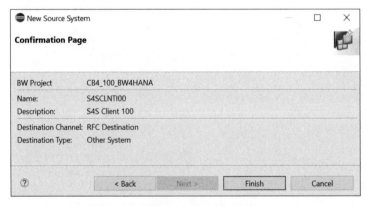

Figure 3.20 Confirmation Page

6. Click **Finish**. The ODP_SAP source system will be created, as shown in Figure 3.21.

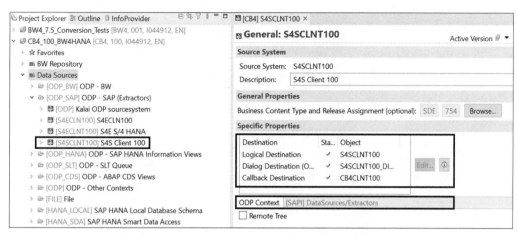

Figure 3.21 ODO_SAP Source System for S4S System

As you can see in Figure 3.21, S4SCLNT100 is the source system name of type ODP_SAP. You can also see multiple options in the **Specific Properties** section. Let's start with **Logical Destination** in which the value in the **Object** column is S4SCLNT100. This field is used to connect to the remote SAP S/4HANA system or SAP ERP system. You'll see the RFC destination of the source system in this object as a value.

Next, we have **Dialog Destination** in which the value in the **Object** column is S4SCLNT100_DIALOG. This is used to connect to a remote system with a dialog user, and it's optional. The **Callback Destination** has the value CB4CLNT100 in the **Object** column. It's used to connect from the remote system to SAP BW/4HANA system. The **Status** column has green checkmarks for all destinations, which means that they're all working fine and there is no issue with this ODP connectivity. You can see that **ODP Context** is maintained as **[SAPI] DataSources/Extractors**, which means it pulls data from the SAPI extractors. There is a **Remote Tree** checkbox here. The upload tree menu in the source system maintenance toolbar is associated with the status of the remote tree in the source system.

For example, the ODP SAP upload tree functionality brings up the hierarchy defined in the source system application component, as shown in Figure 3.22. This means you can specify some sources that can deliver a hierarchical grouping of source objects (trees) whether the grouping should be copied to the DataSource tree for the specific source system. If you do not copy the tree from the source or the source cannot deliver a hierarchical grouping, the generic application component hierarchy defined for the non-replicated source systems is used as the grouping for the source tree. But if the **Remote Tree** checkbox is selected, you can update the hierarchical grouping from the source by pressing **Upload Tree** (an icon) in the editor toolbar, as shown in Figure 3.22.

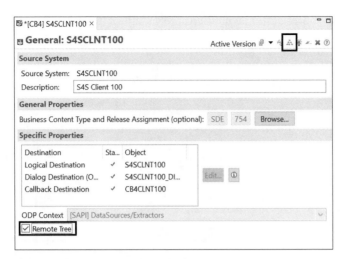

Figure 3.22 Remote Tree in ODP_SAP

In terms of **ODP Context**, as shown in Figure 3.23, it's set to **[SAPI]**. Other options are available, and you can select them based on the ODP source system that you create. In our scenario, it's **[SAPI] DataSources/Extractor** because we're connecting to an SAP system with ODP_SAP.

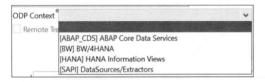

Figure 3.23 ODP Context

If you want to check if the ODP connection is fine, you can do that from Transaction RSA1. Right-click the source system (**S4SCLNT100**) and choose **Check**, as shown in Figure 3.24.

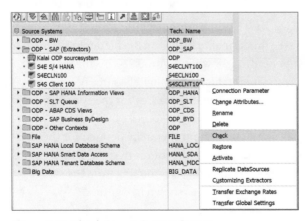

Figure 3.24 Check Source System Status

You'll then see the result of the consistency check. It will show a status message, as shown in Figure 3.25. This will ensure that your ODP SAP connectivity is working fine.

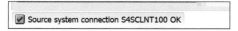

Figure 3.25 Consistency Check Status

3.2.3   Creating ODP Source in SAP BW Context

You will need the data from your SAP BW/4HANA system for an ODP source system. There might be also scenarios where you will need to connect to other SAP BW systems, so you can create an ODP source with an SAP BW context. Follow these steps:

1. When you try to create the source system as shown in Figure 3.26, from the **Data-Sources** folder in the SAP BW modeling tools, you need to provide the name of the ODP SAP BW source system, as shown in Figure 3.27. You need to provide the name per the naming conventions; here we're using **CB4** in the example. Choose **Next**.

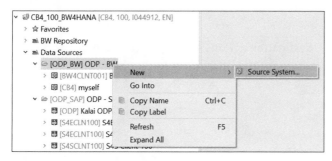

Figure 3.26 SAP BW ODP Context

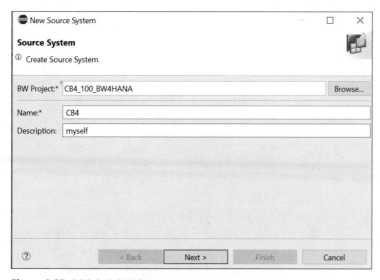

Figure 3.27 ODP SAP BW Source System Name

2. Now you will see the screen shown in Figure 3.28. Set the **Connection Type** as **ODP** and choose **Next**.

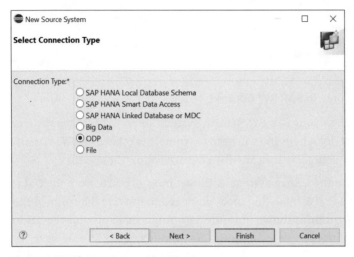

Figure 3.28 Choose Connection Type

3. You should now see the RFC destination options shown in Figure 3.29. Choose **RFC in the Same BW System**, which means CB4 will connect to CB4 using CB4's own RFC destination. Click **Finish**.

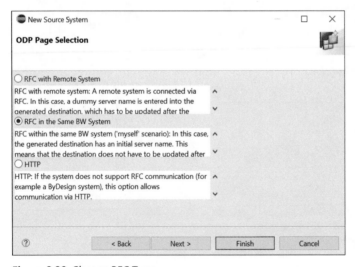

Figure 3.29 Choose RFC Type

4. You'll now need to choose the RFC in same SAP BW system, and you'll see that a source system of type ODP_BW is created. In Figure 3.30, you can see the source system is QB4 and callback destination is CB4CLNT100, which is the same as the SAP BW/4HANA system. You'll also see that the ODP context is SAP BW/4HANA.

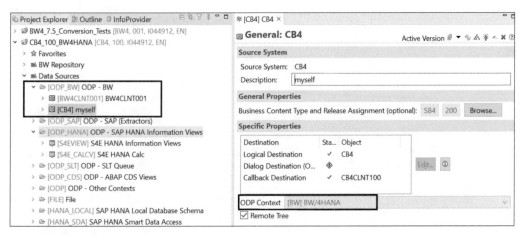

Figure 3.30 Validate Source System

5. As you can see in Figure 3.30, the callback destination is CB4CLNT100, which is for the same SAP BW/4HANA system. This will check for the logical system name of the SAP BW system and use the RFC destination based on same name. If you open Transaction SM59 in SAP BW/4HANA, you can see **RFC Destination** set to CB4CNT100, as shown in Figure 3.31, and that BWREMOTE is the background user that will connect to the SAP BW/4HANA system. You know from Section 3.1.2 that this user has all the required profiles.

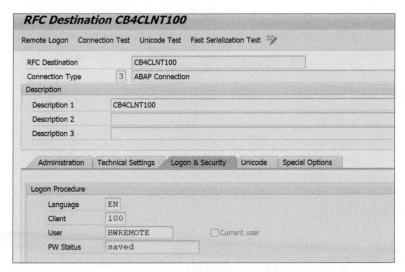

Figure 3.31 RFC Destination for ODP SAP BW Callback

6. If you need to check from SAP GUI, you can open Transaction RSA1 and check the **Source Systems** folder. There you can see that **CB4** is in the **ODP—BW** folder and the description is shown as **myself**. The icon that describes this source system will be

used in a DataMart scenario to transfer data between the same systems, as shown in Figure 3.32.

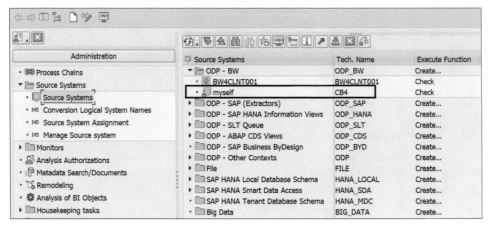

Figure 3.32 Transaction RSA1 Checks

3.2.4   Creating an ODP Source System in an SAP HANA Context

When you have an SAP HANA–based system, there will a requirement to fetch data from the SAP HANA database into your SAP BW/4HANA system. Follow these steps to do so:

1. Log into Eclipse, open the SAP BW modeling tools, and select the SAP BW/4HANA system. Right-click the **Data Sources** folder to create the ODP source based on an SAP HANA context by following the path **New · Source System**, as shown in Figure 3.33.

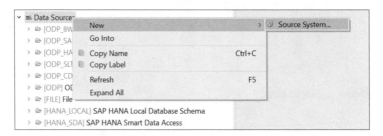

Figure 3.33 ODP Source: SAP HANA Context

2. Provide the source system **Name**, making sure that you have an RFC destination created with the same name and that it's working properly. As you can see in Figure 3.34, S4SVIEW will be the source system name in this example.

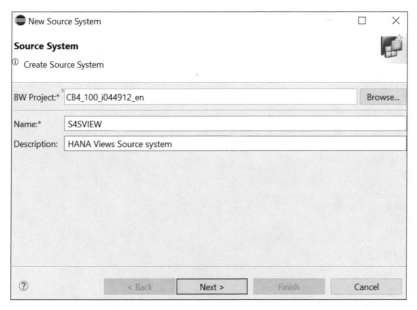

Figure 3.34 SAP HANA Source System Name

3. Once you choose **Next**, the system will prompt for the connection type. Choose **ODP** as shown in Figure 3.35.

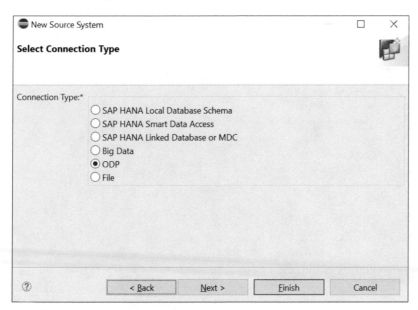

Figure 3.35 Select Connection Type

4. Click **Next** again, then choose **RFC with Remote System**, as shown in Figure 3.36. You've already created this RFC and tested it.

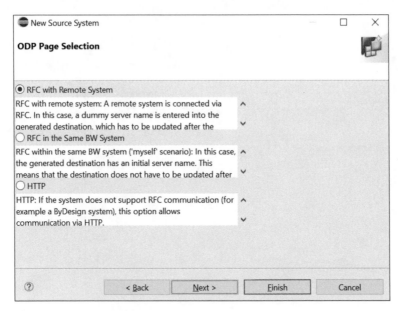

Figure 3.36 RFC Type

5. Click **Next** to see a confirmation of all the details filled in so far, as shown in Figure 3.37.

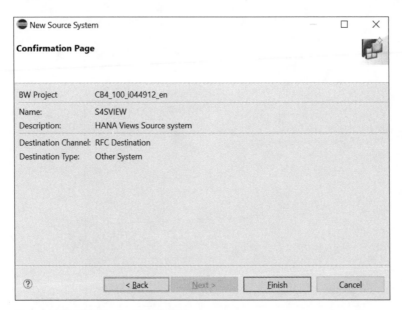

Figure 3.37 ODP Context Validation

6. When you click **Finish**, the ODP_HANA source system is created, as shown in Figure 3.38. You might need to activate the source system if it's inactive via the icon.

Figure 3.38 ODP_HANA Source System

7. You can see the **ODP_HANA** source system folder in the **Data Sources** folder, as shown in Figure 3.39.

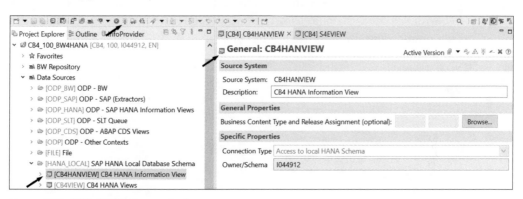

Figure 3.39 ODP_HANA Source System

3.2.5   Creating an ODP Source System in a CDS View Context

You'll need the data from your sender system when you have CDS views. For that, you need to create an RFC destination that connects to the source system that has CDS views, and then you need to use the same name for the source system.

Create a source system named S4SCDS using these steps:

1. Follow the same steps as shown earlier in Figure 3.33: log onto the SAP BW/4HANA system in the SAP BW modeling tools perspective, right-click the **Data Sources** folder, and choose **New · Source System**.

2. Next, give the **Name** of the system, as shown in Figure 3.40.

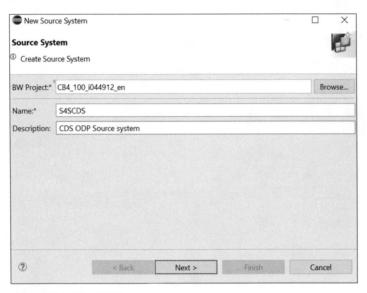

Figure 3.40 ODP CDS Source

3. Choose **ODP** for the **Connection Type** (refer back to Figure 3.35) and click **Next**. Select **RFC with Remote System** (as shown previously in Figure 3.36) and you will see the **Confirmation Page**, as shown in Figure 3.41.

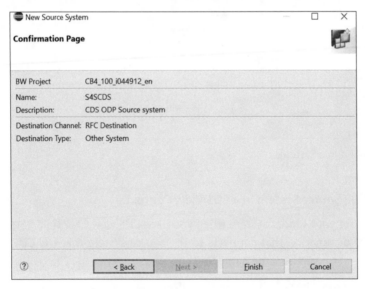

Figure 3.41 Confirmation for ODP CDS

4. Once you press **Finish**, the ODP CDS system is created. Set the **ODP Context** as **ABAP Core Data Services**, as shown in Figure 3.42, and then activate using the ⚙ icon.

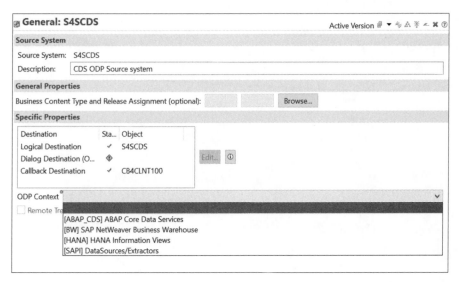

Figure 3.42 ODP Context

5. The source system is now created under the **CDS_ODP** folder, and the **ODP Context** shown on the right-hand side is **ABAP_CDS** for the source system, as shown in Figure 3.43.

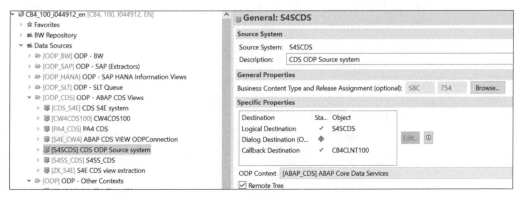

Figure 3.43 ODP_CDS Source System

3.2.6 Access Local SAP HANA Database Schema

If you need to access the data stored in the local SAP BW schema of the SAP HANA database, then you can use the **HANA_LOCAL** option under the **Data Sources** folder of the SAP BW/4HANA system. You need to log onto Eclipse and choose the SAP BW modeling tools perspective, then log onto the SAP BW/4HANA system, right-click the **Data Sources** folder, and select **New • Source System**.

Once you've provided the source system **Name** and selected **Next**, as shown in Figure 3.44, you'll see the option to choose the **Connection Type**, as shown in Figure 3.45.

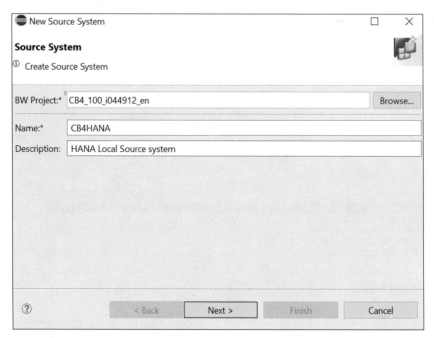

Figure 3.44 SAP HANA Source System

Select **Next** to get to the schema screen shown in Figure 3.46. In this case, we're selecting a specific SAP BW schema for access.

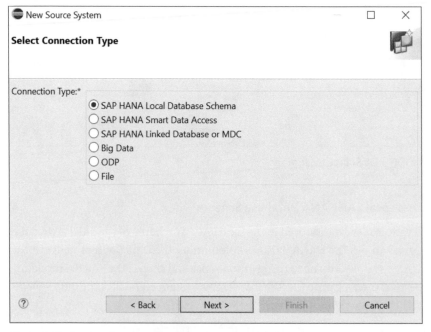

Figure 3.45 Connection Type: SAP HANA Local Database Schema

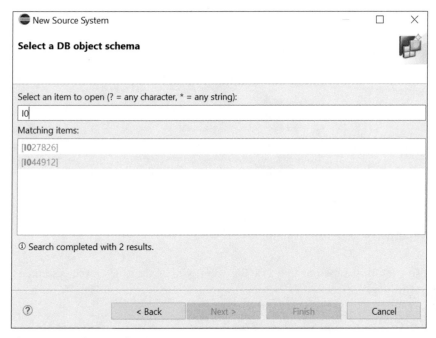

Figure 3.46 Schema Selection

After you select the schema and choose next, you can continue to the **Confirmation Page** shown in Figure 3.47.

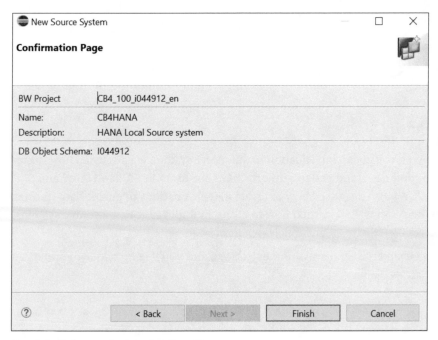

Figure 3.47 Source System Confirmation

When you choose **Finish**, the source system will be created under the **HANA_LOCAL** folder. If it's not active, then you need to activate it using the 🔲 icon. You'll see that **Owner/Schema** will refer to the schema that you selected, as shown in Figure 3.48.

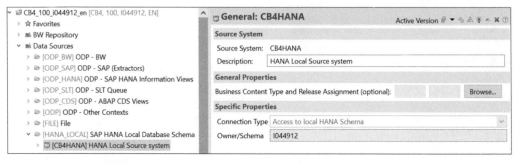

Figure 3.48 HANA_LOCAL source system

You can also use other schemas like **SYS_BIC** when you create the source system, as shown in Figure 3.49.

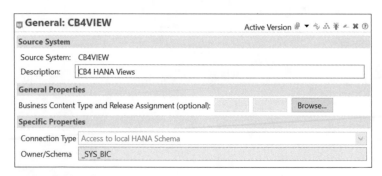

Figure 3.49 HANA_LOCAL for _SYS_BIC Schema

3.3   Summary

In this chapter, you got an introduction to the source system. We discussed how to create background users and assign authorizations for users in SAP S/4HANA and SAP BW/4HANA. We also discussed how to create RFC destinations to enable data transfer between the systems. You learned how to create multiple ODP-based source systems, like ODP_SAP, ODP_CDS, ODP_BW, and SAP HANA local systems.

In the next chapter, we'll discuss SAP extractors, and you'll learn about the multiple types that are available.

Chapter 4
Working with SAP Extractors

This chapter discusses standard SAP extractors in different functional areas in logistics. You'll learn about the extractor types and the differences between them.

When you want to extract data from any SAP ERP system into SAP BW/4HANA, you need *extractors* or DataSources that fetch and send data between the two systems. In this chapter, you'll be introduced to the extractors in each functional area in Section 4.1.

There are many extractors that are delivered across multiple functional areas, and each functional area has its own logic to send historical and delta records to SAP BW/4HANA using DataSources. You'll learn about the types of SAP-delivered extractors in Section 4.2. You'll explore the logistics Extractors in Section 4.2.1, where we'll focus on logistics applications like sales and distribution, materials management, purchasing, plant maintenance, and so on. Then we'll talk about the finance extractors in Section 4.2.2, with extractors for areas like accounts receivable, accounts payable, and the general ledger. Finally, we'll look at human resources extractors in Section 4.2.3.

Section 4.3 looks at generic extractors, and then you'll learn about installing SAP BusinessObjects Business Intelligence (SAP BusinessObjects BI) content in Section 4.4. Once you complete the chapter, you'll have a strong foundation for learning about data loading from SAP S/4HANA in later chapters.

4.1   Introduction to SAP Extractors

This section covers types of SAP ERP systems and their associated SAP BusinessObjects BI content and discusses the availability of SAP extractors and DataSources.

> **SAP ERP System and Extractors**
>
> SAP BW/4HANA can be connected to SAP ERP and SAP S/4HANA. There have been major functional-level changes between these two systems, and new tables have replaced some old tables in SAP S/4HANA. The important SAP S/4HANA versions start from SAP S/4HANA 1610, which was released in May 2016, and the latest version is SAP S/4HANA 2022. Most of the SAP business content extractors that worked with SAP ERP are still used in SAP BW/4HANA. A few DataSources are depreciated with SAP

133

> S/4HANA. For some DataSources, alternatives have been provided in SAP S/4HANA. We'll focus on the most common application areas here and their associated extractors, where most SAP BW reporting is used.

To extract data from SAP ERP, many DataSources have been developed by SAP across multiple application components. These DataSources can be accessed using specific transactions in SAP S/4HANA or SAP ERP systems. For SAP BW systems, these Data-Sources have been updated and shipped using the BI_CONT add-on, which can be installed in SAP BW 7.X systems; for example, SAP BusinessObjects BI content 7.57 is the add-on for 7.5. It includes SAP HANA–optimized business content. When SAP BW/4HANA is used, you'll see two new components: BW4CONT and BW4CONTB. BW4-CONTB contains objects like InfoAreas, application components, InfoObjects, and so on. BW4CONT has dataflows, aDSOs, CompositeProviders, InfoSources, and transformations. You can see the BW4CONT component in Figure 4.1.

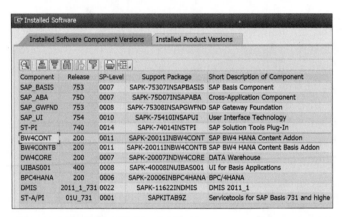

Figure 4.1 BW4CONT and BW4CONTB

Types of SAP extractors include the following:

- **Application-specific**
  - Business content extractors—widely used
  - Customer-generated extractors—not used much with SAP S/4HANA
- **Cross-application**
  - Generic extractors
  - Custom CDS views

4.2   SAP-Delivered Business Content Extractors

For application-specific business content extractors, SAP delivers the business content completely, which means the DataSource is already developed by SAP. During the implementation, it's enough to activate the DataSource and consume the data from the source system. SAP-delivered extractors include logistics extractors, finance extractors, and HR extractors. Let's look at these extractors in detail in the following sections.

4.2.1   Logistics Extractors

SAP has delivered many DataSources to extract data from logistics-based applications, including the following functional applications:

- Sales and distribution
- Purchasing
- Materials management
- Shop floor control
- Quality management
- Plant maintenance
- Invoice verification

The DataSources can be accessed from Transaction LBWE in SAP S/4HANA (the Logistics Cockpit), which has information about all logistics DataSources. Each logistics application is identified with a unique two-digit number, as you can see in Figure 4.2.

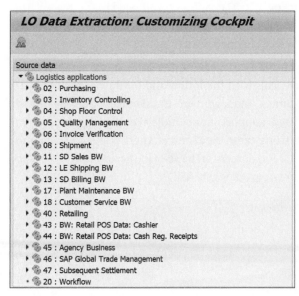

Figure 4.2 LO Cockpit

When you expand any application component number, you can see the details of the extractors that are delivered by SAP under **Extract Structures**, as shown in Figure 4.3.

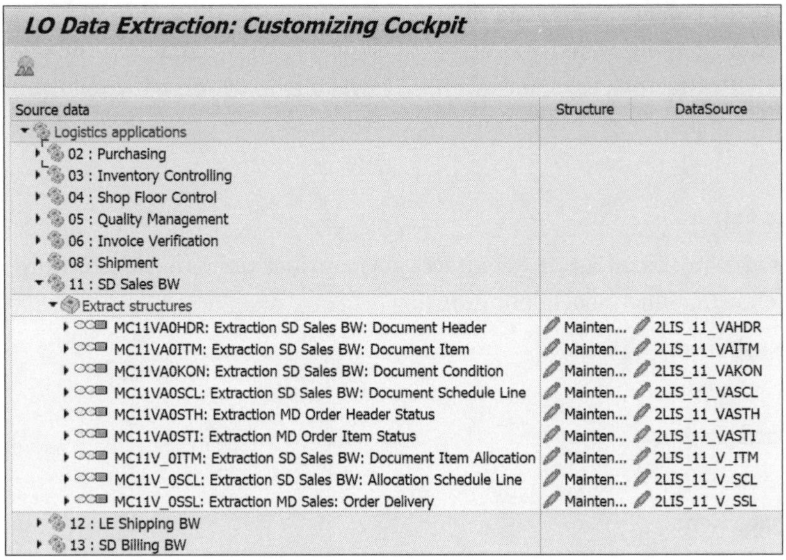

Figure 4.3 Extractors in LO Cockpit

Application component 11, SD Sales BW, which is used to extract sales and distribution data, has many DataSources, as listed in Figure 4.3. Chapter 5 will discuss how to use these DataSources and extract data to SAP BW/4HANA.

When extracting the data from the logistics DataSources, you need to fill in the setup table, which is a temporary table for loading the historical data, and then use the logistics-based delta logic to get the new and changed records.

When handling scenarios like inventory management, the data should not be cumulated in SAP BW because inventory deals with the inflow and outflow of materials. To handle such scenarios, use materials management DataSources that deal with extraction of inventory data. They support noncumulative key figures in SAP BW/4HANA. When extracting data using these DataSources, there is an additional process that needs to be followed. The DataSources can be seen in the application component for inventory management, as shown in Figure 4.4.

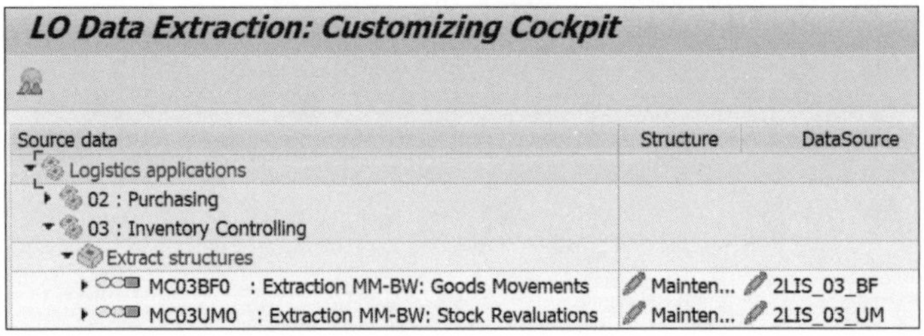

Figure 4.4 Inventory Management Extractors

4.2.2 Finance Extractors

There are many SAP standard-delivered DataSources that extract data from finance application components. The common finance applications used most commonly until SAP BW 7.5 include the following:

- Accounts receivables
- Accounts payable
- New general ledger

With SAP S/4HANA, there has been a major change in finance applications and how data is stored in the tables; many old finance tables have been replaced by table ACO-DOCA. With SAP S/4HANA, new DataSources based on table ACDOCA have been delivered to replace old finance DataSources. You can see the OFI_ACDOCA_10 and OFI_ACDOCA_20 DataSources in Figure 4.5.

```
Installation of DataSource from Business Content

🗗 🗐 🗐 🗐   Set Section  🔍 🗗 Content Delta    Activate DataSources   Version Comparison   Display Log

              ──────OFI_ACDOCA_10      🔳 Unified Journal Entry
              ──────OFI_ACDOCA_20      🔳 Unified Journal Entry (with Currency type)
              ──────OFI_GL_1           🔳 General ledger: Transaction figures
              ──────OFI_GL_10          🔳 General Ledger: Leading Ledger Balances
              ──────OFI_GL_11          🔳 General Ledger: Balances of Leading Ledger via Line Items
              ──────OFI_GL_12          🔳 General Ledger: Balances of Leading Ledger via Delta Queue
              ──────OFI_GL_14          🔳 General Ledger (New): Line Items Leading Ledger
```

Figure 4.5 Table ACDOCA and Finance DataSources

Unlike logistics DataSources, there is no need for a setup table to do a historical data load here. Finance extractors use timestamps for fetching new and changed records in delta extraction. You'll learn more about this logic in Chapter 5.

4.2.3 HR Extractors

You may need to extract data from HR or SAP ERP Human Capital Management–based applications for SAP BW reporting, and SAP has delivered DataSources for these scenarios. Note that SAP SuccessFactors is also used for many HR-based activities, and SAP BW/4HANA can also extract from that application. An example of the personnel administration application is shown in Figure 4.6.

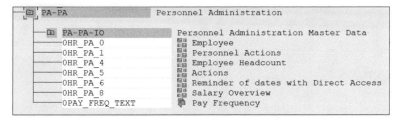

```
─🗀 PA-PA                      Personnel Administration
  └🗀
    ──🗀 PA-PA-IO              Personnel Administration Master Data
      ──────0HR_PA_0          🔳 Employee
      ──────0HR_PA_1          🔳 Personnel Actions
      ──────0HR_PA_4          🔳 Employee Headcount
      ──────0HR_PA_5          🔳 Actions
      ──────0HR_PA_6          🔳 Reminder of dates with Direct Access
      ──────0HR_PA_8          🔳 Salary Overview
      ──────0PAY_FREQ_TEXT    🔳 Pay Frequency
```

Figure 4.6 HR Personnel Administration DataSources

You can also see the DataSources for payroll and time management in Figure 4.7.

PT		Time Management
PT-IO		Time Management Master Data
0HR_PT_1		Times from personal work schedule
0HR_PT_2		Actual personnel times
0HR_PT_3		Quota movements

Figure 4.7 HR Time Management DataSources

SAP HANA-Optimized Business Content

When you install the latest SAP BusinessObjects BI content add-on, you'll get SAP HANA–optimized business content objects. There are many in-memory objects, like aDSOs and SAP HANA composite providers. These objects support new data models that follow recommendations based on Layered Scalable Architecture++ (LSA++).

DataSource Enhancement

In any SAP-delivered extractor, there is an option to enhance the standard extractor. If you have a business requirement that can be achieved by enhancing a standard extractor, like adding a few fields, that's possible with DataSource enhancement. You need to enhance the DataSource fields and, if required, write the enhancement logic to extract the data for the enhanced fields. If the business requirement is so complex that an enhancement won't be enough, then the only option is to create a custom Data-Source based on the business requirement by creating your own extractor, as we'll discuss in the next section.

4.3 Generic Extractors

When the SAP-delivered business content-based extractors can't meet your business requirements, then you can create generic extractors or user-developed extractors. The end-to-end process of creating an extractor and enabling the delta process should be done by the extractor developer who is implementing the solution. SAP has provided multiple methods to create custom DataSources, including the following:

- Generic DataSource based on views
- Generic DataSource based on InfoSets
- Generic DataSource based on function modules
- SAP BW BAdI providers
- Custom CDS views
- Custom SAP HANA calculation views

When you want to create a generic DataSource in SAP S/4HANA, you can use Transaction RSO2. It will have various options to create the DataSource, as shown in Figure 4.8.

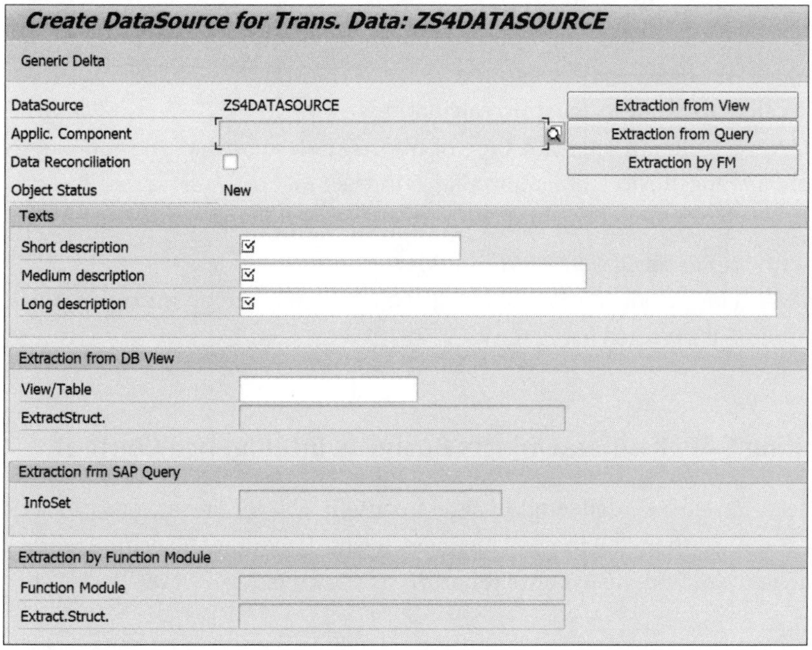

Create DataSource for Trans. Data: ZS4DATASOURCE

Generic Delta

DataSource	ZS4DATASOURCE		Extraction from View
Applic. Component			Extraction from Query
Data Reconciliation	☐		Extraction by FM
Object Status	New		

Texts

Short description	☑
Medium description	☑
Long description	☑

Extraction from DB View

| View/Table | |
| ExtractStruct. | |

Extraction frm SAP Query

| InfoSet | |

Extraction by Function Module

| Function Module | |
| Extract.Struct. | |

Figure 4.8 Generic DataSource Creation: Transaction RSO2

Transaction RSO2 will work only in the SAP S/4HANA or SAP ERP source system. In SAP BW/4HANA, you can only display the DataSource; the **Create** option will be disabled, as shown in Figure 4.9.

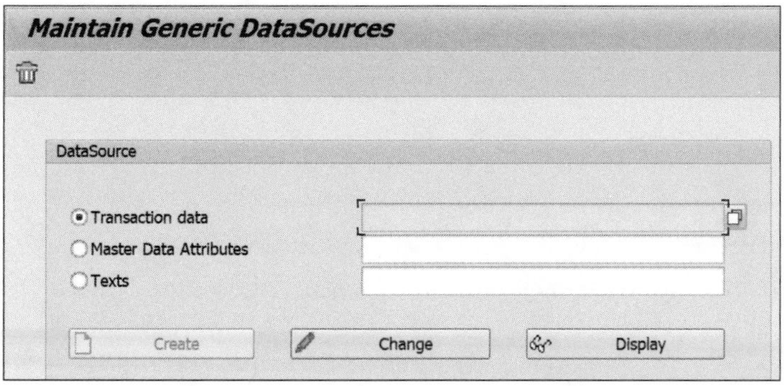

Maintain Generic DataSources

DataSource

⦿ Transaction data

○ Master Data Attributes

○ Texts

| Create | | Change | | Display |

Figure 4.9 Transaction RSO2: SAP BW/4HANA

Because Transaction RSO2 is not available in SAP BW/4HANA, the alternate option is to create the generic DataSource within the SAP BW/4HANA system, using the following options:

- **ABAP CDS views (using custom logic)**
  ABAP CDS views help you create complex and semantically rich data models. Using CDS views, you can create views based on table fields according to application-specific needs for your business. These CDS views are a kind of virtual data model that allows direct access to the tables.

- **SAP HANA calculation views (custom calculations)**
  An SAP HANA calculation view is a type of information view that you can use to define more advanced slices of data available in the SAP HANA database. You can create joins and projections on tables that reside in the database.

- **BAdI InfoProvider as an ODP SAP BW provider**
  A BAdI InfoProvider is an InfoProvider that you can enhance by means of ABAP implementation. It's created using the RSO_BADI_PROVIDER BAdI.

4.4   Installing SAP BusinessObjects Business Intelligence Content

When you need to use SAP-delivered business content objects or dataflows in SAP BW/4HANA, you need to install the SAP BusinessObjects BI content. Execute Transaction RSA1, and you can find the **BI Content** button, as shown in Figure 4.10.

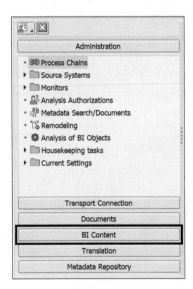

Figure 4.10 BI Content Option

Once you choose **BI Content**, you will have the option to install required objects, as shown in Figure 4.11:

❶ Choose **Object Types**.

❷ Choose the object type that you need to install and click **Choose Objects**. The system will show a popup with a list of available objects based on the type.

❸ Select the SAP BusinessObjects BI content object that you want to install (you can use the **Search** icon to find an object).

❹ Choose **Transfer Selections**, which will collect all the related objects upward and downward for installation. For example, if you choose an aDSO, then the downwards objects in the dataflow for the aDSO are InfoObjects, DataSources, and transformations. The upwards objects are SAP HANA composite providers and the associated queries. All these objects will be collected for the installation.

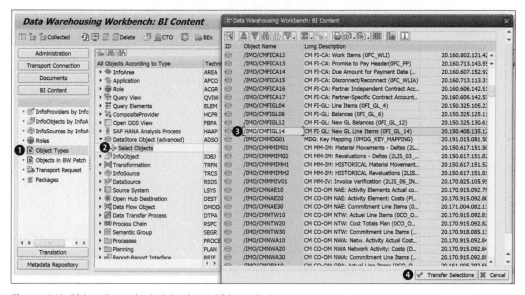

Figure 4.11 Object Types in SAP BusinessObjects BI Contents

When installing, you will have option to group objects as shown in Figure 4.12, with the following options:

- **Only Necessary Objects** will collect the important objects for the required SAP BW object that needs to be installed.

- **Data Flow Before** will collect all the objects that connect to the current object; for example, for an aDSO, you'll get the InfoObject, transformations, and so on.

- **Data Flow Afterwards** will collect all objects above the current installation object. For example, the aDSO will get all objects that have queries and other reporting elements.

- **Data Flow Before and After** will collect all data flow–based objects like InfoObjects, transformations, aDSOs, queries, and so on.

Once you've decided on a grouping option, you can install the object with the **Install** option, as shown in Figure 4.13.

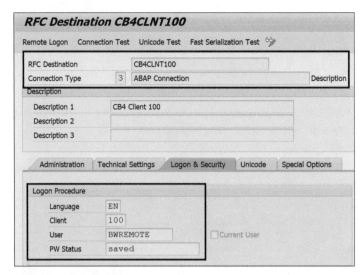

Figure 4.12 Grouping

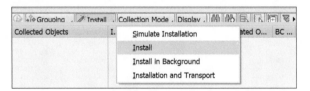

Figure 4.13 Install SAP BusinessObjects BI Content Object

4.5   Summary

In this chapter, you learned the basics of SAP extractors. We looked at the different types of extractors across different functional areas. We walked you through the standard-delivered extractors in the LO cockpit and explained how the application numbers are used in logistics extractors. We also walked through the different categories of extractors in finance applications. Finally, we looked at the extractors used in HR applications. You also learned about generic extractors and the steps to install the BI content objects in an SAP BW/4HANA system. These basics will be used as the foundation for data staging from the next chapter on.

In the next chapter, we'll focus on extracting data from SAP logistics applications to SAP BW/4HANA. This will be one of the most important chapters in the book. We'll detail the steps thoroughly so that the data staging can be understood from end to end.

Chapter 5
Extracting Logistics Data

This chapter provides details about logistics application–based extractors for areas like sales and distribution, purchasing, and quality management. It explains how to extract data from these extractors and covers end-to-end extraction from the SAP S/4HANA source system.

Most SAP BW/4HANA reporting is based on the data from ERP systems such as SAP S/4HANA or SAP ERP, and almost all ERP systems have logistics (LO) applications at their core. This chapter provides the details of logistics application–based extractors for areas like sales and distribution and purchasing. We'll discuss how to extract data from systems like SAP ERP and SAP S/4HANA using these extractors. End-to-end data extraction from the SAP S/4HANA source system is also covered in this chapter.

In this chapter, we'll begin with a logistics extraction overview in Section 5.1 and will discuss the architecture of logistics extractors at a table level. Before sending data into SAP BW, you need to fill in setup tables in SAP S/4HANA, which is discussed in Section 5.2. You then test the data extraction, followed by replicating the DataSource into SAP BW/4HANA using an ODP SAP framework as a source system. Finally, you extract the data from SAP S/4HANA using an SAP BW dataflow, as explained in Section 5.3. You will learn about the Transaction ODQMON and how to use it to check the extraction in Section 5.4. You finally you complete the extraction process with data validation between SAP BW/4HANA and SAP S/4HANA, which is explained in Section 5.5. Then we will discuss the steps to extract logistics data from other applications in Section 5.6. Understanding the steps in this chapter will give you a strong foundation to start your SAP BW/4HANA implementation project.

5.1 Logistics Extraction with the ODP Framework

This section covers the architecture of the logistics extraction framework, such as extraction methods and delta update modes, with detailed insights and table-level information.

5.1.1   Logistics Extraction Overview

SAP BW/4HANA is a packaged data warehouse based on SAP HANA. It's an on-premise data warehouse layer of SAP Business Technology Platform and it helps enterprises to do more analytical reporting. Meanwhile, SAP S/4HANA is an enterprise resource planning (ERP) business suite based on SAP HANA's in-memory database. It's more focused on day-to-day transactional processing and helps to save operational day-to-day transactional data. To get better insights about a company, you need the operational and transactional data from SAP S/4HANA to be extracted into SAP BW/4HANA for the purposes of analytical reporting to help in decision-making. The data stored in ERP systems like SAP S/4HANA will have more transactional information for day-to-day reporting, but for analytical reports you need summarized information about specific activities, such as sales or purchasing. But how do you transfer the transactional data to a system that help you generate analytical reports?

To achieve this, many fields in the transactional table need not be transferred to SAP BW/4HANA for analytical reporting. *Extractors* have been designed to solve this problem; they are separate structures that have the fields that need to be sent to SAP BW/4HANA. Logistics extraction deals with the process of extracting essential data from applications like sales and distribution, materials management, purchasing, and quality management into SAP BW/4HANA for analytical reporting purposes. SAP has delivered standard objects to support these objects, and these are called *business content extractors*.

5.1.2   Architecture

This section covers the design and architecture of logistics extractors in SAP S/4HANA. Extractors are core SAP-based objects that help to extract data from the sender SAP S/4HANA or SAP ERP system into an SAP BW/4HANA system.

The extract structures are a fundamental part of the extraction concept. These are SAP ERP ABAP Data Dictionary (DDIC) structures that contain relevant fields, whose data contents are transferred from the transaction data table level data through the DataSource to SAP BW when you activate the relevant extraction process.

Most of the extract structures for applications—like 11, which deals with sales; 12, which deals with shipping; and 13, which deals with billing—and many more applications in the logistics cockpit that deals with other functional components are structured in such a way so that most of the fields within the structure are filled directly from the field contents of the logistics information systems (LIS) communication structures. Some additional fields are determined in the extraction module. Every LIS communication structure is used to fill an extract structure of the specific datasource. When you're adding extra fields whose field names are identical in several LIS communication structures intended for use in an extractor, it's possible to assign the LIS communication structures from which the data contents are transferred uniquely.

However, this doesn't mean that you can include a field with the same named extract structure.

This extract structure concept allows you to include other fields without modification—as well as user-defined fields, which were included using append technology in the corresponding include of the LIS communication structure—in the extract structures. They are then automatically filled with the values from the corresponding LIS communication structure. Figure 5.1 describes the complete architecture of logistics extractors.

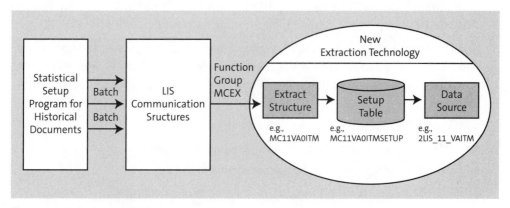

Figure 5.1 Overview of LO Extractors

An *SAP BW DataSource* is a structure created in a source system like SAP ERP or SAP S/4HANA and replicated to SAP BW/4HANA. Maintaining a DataSource in a source system means making changes related to the DataSource. This could be adding/deleting fields or checking the flags in the DataSource like the hide and selection flags. Also, if the DataSource is provided in the logistics cockpit, changes can be made there too depending on how the extraction of data is made for that DataSource. Extraction could be flat file extraction of multiple flat structures (hierarchies). There are two major types of DataSource:

- DataSource for transaction data
- DataSource for master data, which includes:
  - DataSource for attribute
  - DataSource for texts
  - DataSource for hierarchies

If you need to use SAP-delivered extractors, then you need to install the business intelligence (BI) content add-on in your SAP S/4HANA system. *BI Cont* and *BI Content Ext* are preconfigured sets of roles and related information models like DataSources, InfoObjects, InfoSources, in-memory optimized aDSOs, transformations, queries, and much more. In most organizations, the installation of BI content is carried out by the Basis team. If you need to test this extraction, install the latest BI content add-on in SAP BW/4HANA.

Let's start with an SAP-delivered BI content-based DataSource for LO extraction, a part of the business content that uses the following naming convention: *2LIS_ <Application_Component>_<Event>_<Suffix>*.

2LIS is common for all Logistics based DataSources. It's followed by the application component number, a two-digit number that provides information related to a functional application; for example, when you see 11 in any DataSource, that specifies that the DataSource belongs to sales-related applications and extracts the data from sales tables. When you see 12 as the application component, then the DataSource fetches data related to shipping. If you see application component 13, it will deal with billing.

In a DataSource name, the event code gives a high-level overview of the transaction name that provides the data for the application. For example, event VA means creating, changing, and displaying orders. The following events are used in sales-based DataSources:

- Event VA means creating, changing, or deleting orders.
- Event VB means creating, changing, or deleting quotations.
- Event VC means creating, changing, or deleting deliveries.
- Event VD means creating, changing, or deleting billing documents.

In any logistics DataSource, there will be a suffix that informs you what level of data is extracted from the sender system into SAP BW/4HANA. For standard SAP-delivered DataSources, you'll commonly see the following suffixes for logistics DataSources:

- HDR represents header data.
- ITM represents item data.
- SCL represents schedule line data.
- KON represents conditions data.

SAP BW/4HANA DataSource Naming Conventions

Consider the SAP-standard DataSource for sales, 2LIS_11_VAHDR. 2LIS is a common prefix for all standard logistics extractors. When you see 11, you should know that the DataSource extracts data from application component 11, which means sales. Then you see the two-character event code is VA, so you know that it deals with extraction of sales order creation/changes. Finally, the three-character suffix HDR tells you that the header data is extracted using this DataSource.

Each DataSource has a component called an *extraction structure*. The general naming syntax for an extraction structure is *Extraction structure MC<Application><Event/ group of events>0<Suffix>*, where MC is derived from the associated communication structures and <Suffix> is optional.

As an example, for events and groups in an SAP BW DataSource, the extraction structure for the `2LIS_11_VAITM` DataSource is `MC11VA0ITM`. Similarly, if you consider other applications, the extraction structure for the purchasing-based `2LIS_02_HDR` DataSource is `MC02M_OHDR`, where M* indicates the group for the events. (You can see the events for sales as an example of this later in Section 5.1.3, Figure 5.20.) Similarly for purchasing, you can see the following events in the logistics cockpit:

- MA denotes actions related to purchase orders.
- MD represents the delivery schedule.
- ME represents the contract.
- MF represents a request.

The *setup table* is widely used for extracting data in LO extraction. The reason to use a setup table is that the logistics applications in SAP do not want to allow access to direct application tables, so the setup table is an intermediate table between the application and SAP BW. This table will be filled in based on steps carried out in SAP S/4HANA. When requesting data from SAP S/4HANA for the first time, it will fetch this setup table, which generally uses the following naming convention: <Extraction structure>SETUP.

Setup Table Naming Conventions

The naming convention for the setup table is the extraction structure followed by the word SETUP. For example, the setup table for `2LIS_11_VAITM` will start with the extraction structure name, `MC11VA0ITM`, followed by SETUP—so the name will be `MC11-VAOHDRSETUP`.

In the SAP BW context, *extractors* enable the upload of business data from source systems into the data warehouse. They're programs that can be used to retrieve data from the source system and transfer it to an SAP BW system. When fetching the data in the sender system, extractors use the extract structure to find the related fields in the transfer structure to send the relevant the data to the SAP BW system.

For most of the logistics DataSources, the extractor named `MCEX_BW_LO_API` contains the ABAP code that helps extract data from SAP S/4HANA into SAP BW/4HANA. If you need to see the code of this function module, you can check Transaction SE37.

All the information related to the DataSource is maintained in table `ROOSOURCE`. Enter your DataSource name to see all relevant details about it, as shown in Figure 5.2.

If the **REALTIME** field is set to X, which means that this is a real-time source. The **Real-Time Enabled** indicator determines whether a DataSource can supply real-time data. In SAP BW/4HANA, the *streaming process chain* concept lets you fetch near-real-time data.

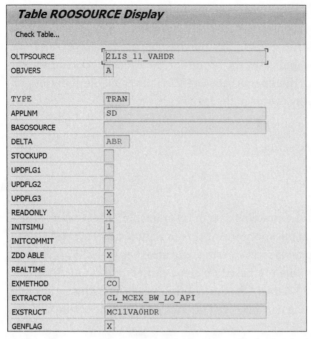

Figure 5.2 Table ROOSOURCE in SAP ERP and SAP S/4HANA

Every DataSource can use any of the following extraction methods:

- V: DDIC name of the transparent table or the databank view used for generic extraction.

- F1: Name of the function module for the extraction (template in the function group RSAX, FB RSAX_BIW_GET_DATA).

- F2: Name of the function module for the extraction (template in the function groups RSAX, FB RSAX_BIW_GET_DATA_SIMPLE).

- D: DDIC name of the name from which texts are to be extracted.

- Q: Functional area of the ABAP query (<4.6) or InfoSet of the InfoSet Query (>4.6).

- A: For reasons of consistency, the DDIC name of the append structure.

If you need more information about the DataSource, open Transaction RSA2. This transaction, for the DataSource repository, will give you all information about the DataSource. As you can see in Figure 5.3, all the details related to the 2LIS_11_VAHDR DataSource is available in multiple tabs. You can get information about the **Extractor**, **ODP Extractor**, and **Extract Structure.**

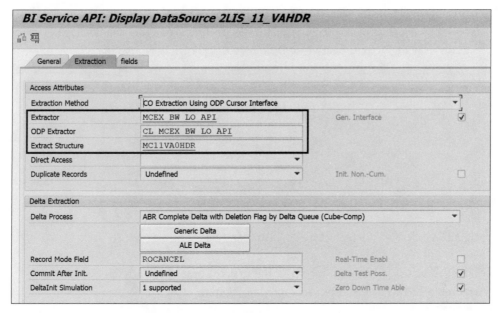

Figure 5.3 Transaction RSA2 for DataSource Information

The interaction of the LIS communication structures with the extract structures is controlled,
among other things, by the extract structure administration table, table TMCEXCFS, in
which information about the fields that you have selected or fields that are not available for selection is contained for all LIS communication structures. Table TMCEXCFS (LO
Data Extraction: Field Status of Communication Structures) provides the extract structure name in the **ESTRU** input field (MC11VA0HDR in Figure 5.4).

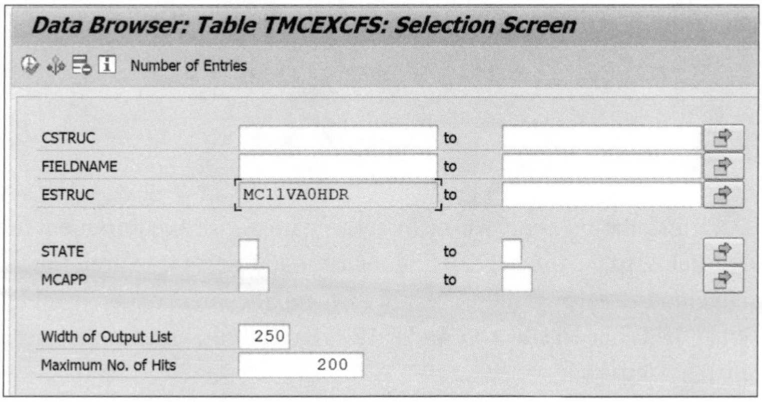

Figure 5.4 Extractor Administration Table

You can provide the extract structure name that was derived from Transaction RSA2 or table ROOSOURCE as shown in Figure 5.4. It will show the **STATE** for each field, with possible entries being **Active**, **Inactive**, or **Disallowed**, as shown in Figure 5.5.

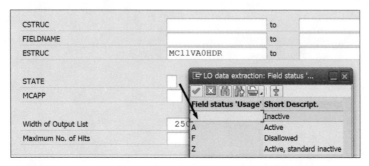

Figure 5.5 Selections for Extractor Administration Table

The filed status is given as output in the first column of table TMCEXCFS, as shown in Figure 5.6. **CSTRU** here stands for *communication structure*.

CSTRUC	FIELDNAME	ESTRUC	STATE	MCAPP
MCVBAK	ANGDT	MC11VA0HDR	A	11
MCVBAK	AUART	MC11VA0HDR	A	11
MCVBAK	AUGRU	MC11VA0HDR	A	11
MCVBAK	BNDDT	MC11VA0HDR	A	11
MCVBAK	BUKRS	MC11VA0HDR	A	11
MCVBAK	ERDAT	MC11VA0HDR	A	11
MCVBAK	FAKSK	MC11VA0HDR	A	11
MCVBAK	HWAER	MC11VA0HDR	A	11
MCVBAK	KUNNR	MC11VA0HDR	A	11
MCVBAK	KURST	MC11VA0HDR	A	11
MCVBAK	KVGR1	MC11VA0HDR	A	11
MCVBAK	KVGR2	MC11VA0HDR	A	11
MCVBAK	KVGR3	MC11VA0HDR	A	11
MCVBAK	KVGR4	MC11VA0HDR	A	11
MCVBAK	KVGR5	MC11VA0HDR	A	11
MCVBAK	LIFSK	MC11VA0HDR	A	11

Figure 5.6 Table TMCEXFS Output

In any SAP BW/4HANA installation, there will be many scenarios with a requirement to have custom-created fields, to customize existing fields or add fields that aren't provided by an SAP-delivered extractor. If there are any such enhancements, then in table TMCEXCFZ, all additional fields like **FIELDNAME** and **ESTRU** that the customer has chosen are recorded as shown in Figure 5.7.

If you need to check the extract structures that are assigned to a DataSource, you can use table TMCEXACT as shown in Figure 5.8. In addition, table TMCEXACT shows the activation status for the extractions. The DataSource is generated based on these tables (e.g., according to the enhancement of an extract structure).

Dictionary: Display Table

⇦ ⇨ | ⁹⁷ ⁹⁵ 🗂 | 𝔞⁶ ✎ ⇥ | 🚠 ≞ ▢ 🛈 | 🎚 ⅲ   Technical Settings   Append Structure...

| Transparent Table | TMCEXCFZ | 🗂 Active |
| Short Description | LO Data Extraction: Field Status Comm. Structures (Customer) | |

| Attributes | Delivery and Maintenance | Fields | Input Help/Check | Currency/Quantity Fields | Indexes |

✂ 🗐 🗂 🗄 🗃   ⬇ 🗐 🗐 ⬆   🔍 Search   Built-In Type

Field	Key	Initi...	Data element	Data Type	Length	Decimal...	Coordinate	Short Description
CSTRUC	✓	✓	SQTAB	CHAR	30	0	0	Source table
FIELDNAME	✓	✓	FIELDNAME	CHAR	30	0	0	Field Name
ESTRUC	✓	✓	TABNAME	CHAR	30	0	0	Table Name

Figure 5.7 Table for Customer-Defined Field Information

Dictionary: Display Table

⇦ ⇨ | ⁹⁷ ⁹⁵ 🗂 | 𝔞⁶ ✎ ⇥ | 🚠 ≞ ▢ 🛈 | 🎚 ⅲ   Technical Settings   Append Structure...

| Transparent Table | TMCEXACT | 🗂 Active |
| Short Description | LO Data Extraction: Activate Data Sources/Update | |

| Attributes | Delivery and Maintenance | Fields | Input Help/Check | Currency/Quantity Fields | Indexes |

✂ 🗐 🗂 🗄 🗃   ⬇ 🗐 🗐 ⬆   🔍 Search   Built-In Type

Field	Key	Initi...	Data element	Data Type	Length	Decimal...	Coordinate	Short Description
CLIENT	✓	✓	MANDT	CLNT	3	0	0	Client
ESTRUC	✓	✓	STFNA	CHAR	30	0	0	Field name in the generated DDIC structure
ISOURCE	☐	✓	ROOSOURCER	CHAR	30	0	0	DataSource (OSOA/OSOD)
ISGEN	☐	☐	ROGENAPPL	CHAR	1	0	0	Flag: InfoSource was generated
UPDACT	☐	☐	KBTCHX	CHAR	1	0	0	Indicator: Extraction structure updated
ADDHEADER	☐	☐	ADDHEADER	CHAR	1	0	0	Additional header entry
MCAPP	☐	☐	MCAPP	CHAR	2	0	0	Number of application

Figure 5.8 DataSource Assignment and Generation

When you choose to display the table contents using the ⅲ button, you'll see the details of **ESTRCU**, which is the extract structure, and its assignment to the DataSource, which is shown under **ISOURCE** in Figure 5.9.

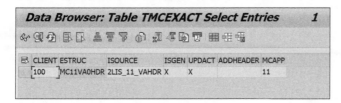

Data Browser: Table TMCEXACT Select Entries   **1**

⇖ ⚙ 🗗 | 🗐 🗐 | ≞ ⤒ ⤓ | 🗐 🗐 ⬆ 🗐 🗑 | 🎛 🎚 🎛

CLIENT	ESTRUC	ISOURCE	ISGEN	UPDACT	ADDHEADER	MCAPP
100	MC11VA0HDR	2LIS_11_VAHDR	X	X		11

Figure 5.9 Sample Result from Table TMECXACT

5.1.3 Update Method

When implementing SAP BW/4HANA for the first time, you need to consider using a full upload or delta upload. In a *full upload*, the historical data from SAP S/4HANA can be fetched and stored in SAP BW/4HANA persistence objects like aDSOs. Once all historical records are fetched, the next step is to prepare SAP S/4HANA to constantly send the new and changed records to SAP BW/4HANA. This process of capturing new and changed records in SAP S/4HANA and sending them to SAP BW/4HANA is called a *delta update*. LO DataSources support multiple modes to capture and send these new and changed records. This can be seen in the logistics cockpit (Transaction LBWE). For the standard-delivered DataSources, you can see three different update methods:

- **Direct delta**
  When the direct delta update mode is selected in the logistics cockpit, each and every document posting in SAP ERP or SAP S/4HANA for the specific application will trigger the delta. For example, if you create a sales order, then the delta postings are directly written into the delta queue—Transaction RSA7 for SAP ERP or Transaction ODQMON when the DataSource is exposed via ODP. This extraction mode will have an impact on the extraction performance when there are too many document postings as each and every document needs a specific work process to update the delta queue. But in a large customer landscape, there will be more ERP-based document postings per hour, and the new documents get added to the delta queue each time, so this will consume more work process.

- **Queued delta**
  When queue delta update mode is selected in the logistics cockpit, the new and changed records for the specific application are collected intermittently in a queue called the extraction queue. These records can be seen using Transaction LBWQ in SAP ERP or SAP S/4HANA. Once the queue reaches a certain threshold, like 10,000 documents, then a collection run background job that was scheduled by the cockpit will be triggered, and it will send the data from extraction queue (Transaction LBWQ) to the delta queue (Transaction RSA7 or ODQMON). This mode is widely used as its performance is more optimal. That's because the extraction job doesn't use a work process for each and every changed document; it sends the documents at certain threshold numbers.

- **Nonserialized V3 update**
  With SAP S/4HANA, we do not recommend using the nonserialized V3 update method. But in SAP ERP, when this mode is selected, the new and changed documents are sent to the update tables before the documents are moved to the delta queue in Transaction RSA7. The extraction data of the application being viewed is written to the update queue with a V3 update module and is kept there until the data is read with an update collection run and processed.

Let's start with the *nonserialized V3 update mode*. With this update mode, the extraction data of the application in question continues to be written to the update tables using a V3 update module and is retained there until the data is read and processed by a collective update run.

You need to note that in this mode, the delta records may not arrive in the same order in SAP BW as they were generated in the OLTP system. This can cause problems in SAP BW when using old ODS objects in classical SAP BW systems. The nonserialized V3 update method doesn't ensure the serialization of the document update to the aDSO objects and is not recommended if serialization is desired.

The question that many customers ask is about the usage of the delta modes. Due to the design of the data targets in SAP BW and for the application in question, it's irrelevant whether the extraction data is transferred to SAP BW in the sequence in which the data was generated. The dataflow is shown in Figure 5.10. Although this diagram is based on classical SAP BW objects, the flow is still applicable to SAP BW/4HANA as these operations are primarily carried out in the source system.

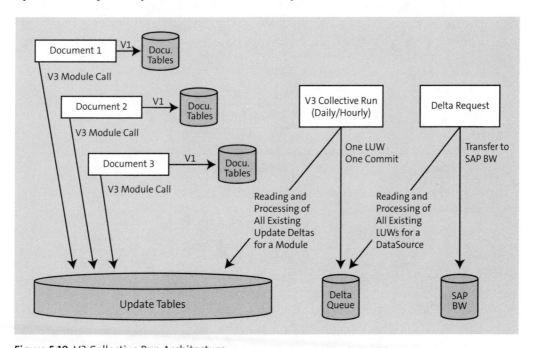

Figure 5.10 V3 Collective Run Architecture

Nonserialized V3 Update Mode in ODP

The nonserialized V3 update mode is not suitable for ODP-based extraction. SAP BW/4HANA supports only ODP-based extraction, so it's not recommended to use this option in your implementations.

In Figure 5.11, the document flow from the sender (SAP S/4HANA) to SAP BW is explained in detail. When a document posting like a sales order happens in SAP S/4HANA, it updates the core database application tables, which is called a V1 update. When the setup table is filled in for the application, it will fill the associated setup tables and will have documents to be transferred to SAP BW. As we discussed at the beginning of this section, this is called a *full upload* or an *initial upload*. This is a very important step when SAP BW is implemented for the first time, and while filling the setup table, customers should ensure that there is business downtime, which means there should be a document-free posting period. The reason for downtime is that when the setup table is being filled, it will refer to the standard application tables, and if document postings happened during this time, then the setup table will miss some documents. The data in the setup table is extracted to SAP BW into an aDSO using a DataSource. Once the setup table fill is completed, then downtime can be released for document postings. SAP BW will store the initial data load in the aDSO from the sender SAP BW system.

If V3 jobs are scheduled through the logistics cockpit framework, then they're sent to change document header tables like table VBDATA. As V3 jobs are scheduled, the V3 collective run will pick data from the change header table for the delta management tables.

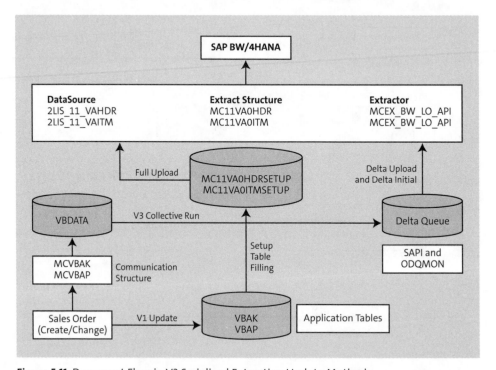

Figure 5.11 Document Flow in V3 Serialized Extraction Update Method

With a *queued delta* process, the extraction data from the concerned application is collected in an extraction queue as shown in Figure 5.12, then the data is transferred to the delta queue, in a similar manner as the V3 update, with an update collection run. The delta queue can be viewed using Transaction ODQMON with the ODP framework, and in systems other than SAP BW/4HANA it can be seen in Transaction RSA7.

With this update mode, the extraction data for the affected application is compiled in an extraction queue (instead of in the update data) and can be transferred to the SAP BW delta queues by an update collective run, as previously executed during the V3 update. Up to 10,000 delta extractions of documents to a logical unit of work (LUW) in the SAP BW delta queues are cumulated in this way per DataSource, depending on the application.

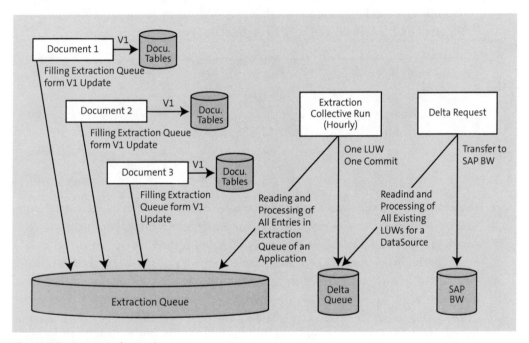

Figure 5.12 Queue Delta Logic

There are many advantages of using a queued delta, and most companies with large SAP BW landscapes follow this approach in their complex SAP BW landscapes. A few of the benefits of a queued delta are listed here:

- By writing in the extraction queue within the V1 update process, the serialization of documents is ensured by using the enqueue concept for the applications.

- By collecting data in the extraction queue that is processed regularly (preferably hourly, as recommended), this process is especially recommended for customers with a high occurrence of documents.

- The collective run uses the same reports as before: RMBWV3<Appl.-No.>. Here, <Appl.-No.> should be replaced with a 2-digit application component number. For example, if you need to run the report to clear the extraction queue for a sales application with application number 11 in Transaction LBWE, the report name will be RMBWV311.

- By collecting new document data during the delta init request, the downtime in the initialization process can be reduced for the reconstruction run (filling of the setup tables). V1 is immeasurably more burdened than V3.

- Collective runs perform better than the serialized V3. The critical aspect of multiple languages in particular does not apply here.

- Event handling is not possible. In contrast to the V3 collective run, a definite end for the collective run is measurable, and a subsequent process can be scheduled. After the collective run for an application has ended, an event (&MCEX_11) is automatically triggered that, if defined, can be used at the start of the subsequent job.

Queue Delta Collective Run

If you use this method, it is also necessary to schedule a job (LIS_BW_VB_APPLICA-TION_XX, where XX can be the application component number) to regularly transfer the data to the BW delta queues (update collective run). However, you should note that reports delivered using the logistics extract structures customizing cockpit are used during this scheduling.

The data flow from the sender system to a target SAP BW system is explained in Figure 5.12. For example, the sales document postings trigger a V1 update, which saves the record in application tables like VBAK/VBAP. If the delta queue is selected as the update mode for the DataSource in the logistics cockpit, there's no change in the full update, but with the new delta posting, both the new and the changed documents will be stored in the extraction queue (Transaction LBWQ). This is a very important change in the delta handling with the delta queue method. The queue gets incremented when there is a new or change document posting, and it will a have certain threshold for a maximum number of records. Once the max records threshold is reached or if the periodic extraction job (LIS_BW_VB_APPLICATION_11) scheduled for the sales application is executed, then data from Transaction LBWQ (Extraction Queue) is cleared and moved to the delta queue. SAP BW fetches data only from the delta queue Transaction ODQMON of SAP S/4HANA or Transaction RSA7 of systems other than SAP S/4HANA. Figure 5.13 gives detailed insights into the delta queue-based flow.

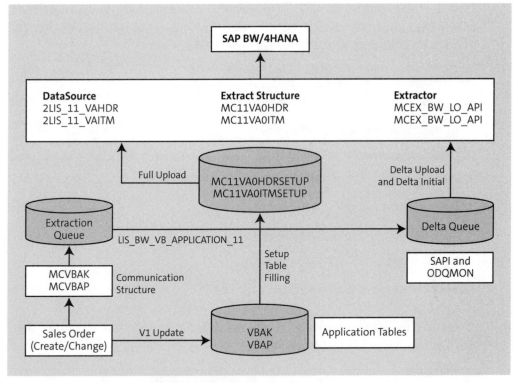

Figure 5.13 Document Flow in Delta Queue Update Method

Delta Queue Considerations

In the following cases, the extraction queues should never contain any data. They should be emptied using collective run reports before these activities:

- Importing a support package
- Performing SAP ERP and SAP S/4HANA upgrades
- Importing plug-in Support Packages
- Executing a plug-in upgrade

When more than 10,000 document changes (creating, changing, or deleting a document) are performed each day for the application in question, it's a good idea to consider the delta queue approach as it can help to use work processes more optimally.

Many reports are used in the maintenance of the delta queue mode. The delta for the logistics extractor is generally moved depending on the setup of job control in Transaction LBWE. If there is a requirement to manually move the delta, you can run the programs depending on application components.

Use the programs listed in Table 5.1 to move the deltas manually. Go to Transaction SE38 in SAP ERP and run the relevant program to move data from Transaction LBWQ to Transaction ODQMON, which is based on the ODP framework.

Application	Program
02 Purchasing	RMBWV302
03 Inventory Controlling	RMBWV303
04 Shop Floor Control	RMBWV304
08 Shipment	RMBWV308
11 SD Sales BW	RMBWV311
12 LE Shipping BW	RMBWV312
13 SD Billing BW	RMBWV313

Table 5.1 Queue Delta: ABAP Reports for Collective Run

If you need to find more reports like this, search for "RMBWV3*" in Transaction SE38. You'll get the list shown in Figure 5.14.

Program Name	Report title
RMBWV302	BW - V3 Update: PP Application
RMBWV303	BW - Application 03 Update (Inventory Management)
RMBWV304	BW - V3 Update: PP Application
RMBWV305	BW-V3 Posting, Application QM
RMBWV306	BW-V3 Posting Application 06
RMBWV308	BW V3 Posting Application LE-TRA
RMBWV311	
RMBWV312	
RMBWV313	
RMBWV317	BW V3 Updating, Application 17: Plant Maintenance
RMBWV318	BW-V3 Update Application 18: Customer Service
RMBWV340	BW - V3 Update: PP Application
RMBWV343	BW - V3 Update: PP Application
RMBWV344	BW - V3 Update: PP Application
RMBWV345	Update Request Analysis and Processing Tool
RMBWV346	Program RMBWV346
RMBWV347	Program RMBWV347

Figure 5.14 Reports Used in Delta Queue Scenario

In a *direct delta*, the extracted data is transferred directly to the delta queue with the document posting. Thus, the sequence of the transfer of documents agrees with the chronological order of data creation.

With the *direct delta update mode*, extraction data is transferred directly to the SAP BW delta queues every time a document is posted. In this way, each document posted with delta extraction is converted to exactly one LUW in the related SAP BW delta queues. If you're using this method, then there's no need to schedule a job at regular intervals to transfer the data to the SAP BW delta queues.

There's a performance factor implication with this updated mode: the number of LUWs per DataSource increases significantly in the SAP BW delta queues because the deltas of many documents are not summarized into one LUW in the SAP BW delta queues.

Direct Delta Mode Usage

If you're using this update mode, note that you cannot post any documents during delta initialization in an application from the start of the recompilation run in the OLTP until all delta init requests have been successfully updated in SAP BW. Otherwise, data from documents posted in the meantime is irretrievably lost. Due to performance implications, avoid this mode as much as possible.

There is a certain restriction for using a direct delta—for example, when a maximum of 10,000 document changes (creating, changing, or deleting documents) are accrued between two delta extractions for the application in question. A (considerably) larger number of LUWs in the SAP BW delta queue can result in terminations during extraction, so in this scenario it's best practice to consider the alternate update method options.

When SAP S/4HANA doesn't have too many documents posting between delta intervals, then definitely there's an advantage in using the direct delta update mode. Here are some scenarios where you can consider choosing the direct delta update mode:

- By writing in the delta queue within the V1 update process, the serialization of documents is ensured by using the enqueue concept for applications.

- For customers with a low occurrence of documents, the process is recommended if downtime is possible in the initialization process during the reconstruction and the delta init request.

- V1 is more heavily burdened by this process than V3 or the delta queue. But for customers with less document occurrence or postings, this is certainly not critical as it will not impact the performance of the SAP S/4HANA system.

- Extraction is independent of the V2 update.

- Additional monitoring of update data or extraction queue does not apply.

The data flow in direct delta update mode is explained in Figure 5.15. As you know, the document postings in SAP S/4HANA update the backend tables related to the application. The major change in direct delta is in the way the new and changed records are sent to the delta queue and the frequency with which they're sent. In direct delta, as soon as the V1 update is completed, the record is immediately sent to the delta queue. Here each LUW is used to send the record to the delta queue. Once the record is available in the delta queue, SAP BW/4HANA process chains will fetch the data from the delta queue at the regular interval. Figure 5.16 shows the status of dataflow.

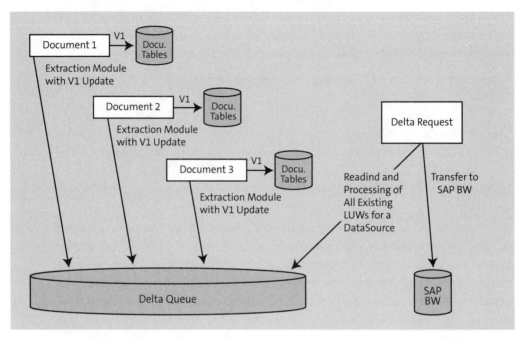

Figure 5.15 Direct Delta Architecture

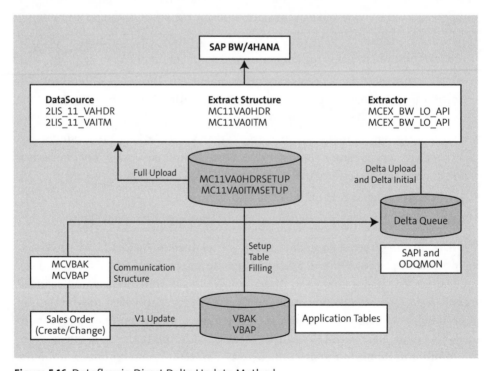

Figure 5.16 Dataflow in Direct Delta Update Method

We have seen three update methods so far, and these are stored in the new Customizing table TMCEXUPD (LO Data Extraction: Update Control of Applications), shown in Figure 5.17. The **MCAPP** field denotes the application, and the **UPDATE MODE** field indicates the update mode.

Figure 5.17 Table for Update Control

As shown in Figure 5.18, when you view table TMCEXUPD in Transaction SE16, it lists all the application components that are extracted by LO extractors, such as 02 for purchasing, 03 for inventory, 11 for sales, 12 for shipping, and 13 for billing. You can see that in the **MCAPP** field. When the DataSource is enabled for delta, then the update mode associated with the application is listed in the **UPDATE_MODE** field.

Data Browser: Table TMCEXUPD Select Entries   17

CLIENT	MCAPP	UPDATE_MODE	UPD_HEAD_COUNT	MULTI_PROCESS	MAX_TASKS	SERVER_GROUP	BACKUP_RUNS	BACKUP_DAYS
100	02	B	000000		0		0	0
100	03	B	000000		0		0	0
100	04	B	000000		0		0	0
100	05	B	000000		0		0	0
100	06	A	000000		0		0	0
100	08	B	000000		0		0	0
100	11	A	000000		0		0	0
100	12	B	000000		0		0	0
100	13	B	000000		0		0	0
100	17	B	000000		0		0	0
100	18	B	000000		0		0	0
100	40	B	000000		0		0	0
100	43	B	000000		0		0	0
100	44	B	000000		0		0	0
100	45	B	000000		0		0	0
100	46	B	000000		0		0	0
100	47	B	000000		0		0	0

Figure 5.18 Sample Result of Update Control Table in SAP S/4HANA

Let's discuss the sales and distribution DataSource to understand the complete logic. In the SAP-delivered LO DataSource, you need to open Transaction LBWE (LO Data Extraction: Customizing Cockpit), shown in Figure 5.19. This transaction is called the logistics cockpit generally.

LO Data Extraction: Customizing Cockpit

Source data	Structure	DataSource	Update	Update Mode
▸ 08 : Shipment			Job Control	Queued Delta
▾ 11 : SD Sales BW			Job Control	Direct Delta
▾ Extract structures				
▸ MC11VA0HDR: Extraction SD Sales BW: Document Header	Mainten...	2LIS_11_VAHDR	Active	
▸ MC11VA0ITM: Extraction SD Sales BW: Document Item	Mainten...	2LIS_11_VAITM	Active	
▸ MC11VA0KON: Extraction SD Sales BW: Document Condition	Mainten...	2LIS_11_VAKON	Active	
▸ MC11VA0SCL: Extraction SD Sales BW: Document Schedule Line	Mainten...	2LIS_11_VASCL	Active	
▸ MC11VA0STH: Extraction MD Order Header Status	Mainten...	2LIS_11_VASTH	Active	
▸ MC11VA0STI: Extraction MD Order Item Status	Mainten...	2LIS_11_VASTI	Active	
▸ MC11V_0ITM: Extraction SD Sales BW: Document Item Allocation	Mainten...	2LIS_11_V_ITM	Active	
▸ MC11V_0SCL: Extraction SD Sales BW: Allocation Schedule Line	Mainten...	2LIS_11_V_SCL	Active	
▸ MC11V_0SSL: Extraction MD Sales: Order Delivery	Mainten...	2LIS_11_V_SSL	Active	
▾ 12 : LE Shipping BW			Job Control	Queued Delta
▾ Extract structures				
▸ MC12VC0HDR: Extraction LE Shipping BW: Document Header	Mainten...	2LIS_12_VCHDR	Active	
▸ MC12VC0ITM: Extraction LE Shipping BW: Document Item	Mainten...	2LIS_12_VCITM	Active	
▸ MC12VC0SCL: Extraction LE Shipping BW: Schedule Line Deliver	Mainten...	2LIS_12_VCSCL	Active	
▾ 13 : SD Billing BW			Job Control	Queued Delta
▾ Extract structures				
▸ MC13VD0HDR: Extraction SD Billing Document BW: Document Hea	Mainten...	2LIS_13_VDHDR	Active	
▸ MC13VD0ITM: Extraction SD Billing Document BW: Document Iten	Mainten...	2LIS_13_VDITM	Active	
▸ MC13VD0KON: Extraction SD Billing Documents BW: Document Cc	Mainten...	2LIS_13_VDKON	Active	
▸ 17 : Plant Maintenance BW			Job Control	Queued Delta
▸ 18 : Customer Service BW			Job Control	Queued Delta

Figure 5.19 Overview of SD DataSource in the Logistics Cockpit

Let's discuss events based on the logistics cockpit. The delta in SAP S/4HANA is triggered based on the event fields shown in Transaction LBWE as per Figure 5.19.The DataSource shows the events in SAP S/4HANA in which you can transfer data to SAP BW. You can find the event under each extract structure.

Consider that transactions such as VA01, VA02, and so on are frequently used the by end user in sSales and distribution applications. Transaction VA01 is used to create a sales order and Transaction VA02 is used to change an existing sales order. These transactions create or change the entries in backend application tables like VBAK/VBAP, but how does SAP S/4HANA know these changes need to be sent to SAP BW? When an event related to a DataSource is used, it triggers the delta related to the DataSource. You can see the events for application 11, sales, in Figure 5.20.

When you make any change in a VA-based event like VA02, then these changes are captured as a delta, and it will be sent to the SAP BW system. Similarly, you can see the events related to shipping DataSources in Figure 5.21.

▼ 🔘 Extract structures			
▼ ⌕▣ MC11VA0HDR: Extraction SD Sales BW: Document Header	✏ Mainten...	✏ 2LIS_11_VAHDR	✏ Active
▼ ☆ Events			
• VA : Sales order: sched.agreement			
• VB : Quotation: contract			
▼ ⌕▣ MC11VA0ITM: Extraction SD Sales BW: Document Item	✏ Mainten...	✏ 2LIS_11_VAITM	✏ Active
▼ ☆ Events			
• VA : Sales order: sched.agreement			
• VB : Quotation: contract			
▶ ⌕▣ MC11VA0KON: Extraction SD Sales BW: Document Condition	✏ Mainten...	✏ 2LIS_11_VAKON	✏ Active
▶ ⌕▣ MC11VA0SCL: Extraction SD Sales BW: Document Schedule Line	✏ Mainten...	✏ 2LIS_11_VASCL	✏ Active

Figure 5.20 Events Related to Sales Header

▼ 🔘 12 : LE Shipping BW		Job Control	✏ Queued Delta
▼ 🔘 Extract structures			
▼ ⌕▣ MC12VC0HDR: Extraction LE Shipping BW: Document Header	✏ Mainten...	✏ 2LIS_12_VCHDR	✏ Active
▼ ☆ Events			
• VC : Delivery			
▼ ⌕▣ MC12VC0ITM: Extraction LE Shipping BW: Document Item	✏ Mainten...	✏ 2LIS_12_VCITM	✏ Active
▼ ☆ Events			
• VC : Delivery			
▼ ⌕▣ MC12VC0SCL: Extraction LE Shipping BW: Schedule Line Deliver	✏ Mainten...	✏ 2LIS_12_VCSCL	✏ Active
▼ ☆ Events			
• VC : Delivery			
▼ 🔘 13 : SD Billing BW		Job Control	✏ Queued Delta
▼ 🔘 Extract structures			
▼ ⌕▣ MC13VD0HDR: Extraction SD Billing Document BW: Document Hea	✏ Mainten...	✏ 2LIS_13_VDHDR	✏ Active
▼ ☆ Events			
• VD : Billing document			
▼ ⌕▣ MC13VD0ITM: Extraction SD Billing Document BW: Document Iter	✏ Mainten...	✏ 2LIS_13_VDITM	✏ Active
▼ ☆ Events			
• VD : Billing document			
▶ ⌕▣ MC13VD0KON: Extraction SD Billing Documents BW: Document Co	✏ Mainten...	✏ 2LIS_13_VDKON	✏ Active

Figure 5.21 Events Related to Shipping

So far, you've seen information related to a DataSource. When doing an implementation or in a support project, you'll need all details relevant to the DataSource. To see the features of the DataSource and the options it has, you can check table ROOSOURCE, shown in Figure 5.22. The **DELTA** field indicates the delta method that a DataSource uses.

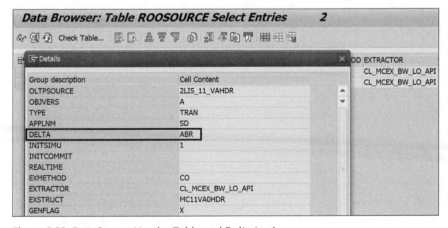

Figure 5.22 DataSource Header Table and Delta Logic

As you can see in Figure 5.23, various types of delta modes are supported by SAP BW DataSources, and the details can be seen in Table RODELTAM. Check the **DELTA** and **TXTLG** fields for their descriptions.

Data Browser: Table RODELTAM Select Entries   20

DELTA	ONLYFULL	UPDM_NIM	UPDM_BIM	UPDM_AIM	UPDM_ADD	UPDM_DEL	UPDM_RIM	DREQSER	DELTATYPE	TXTLG
								1		Delta Only by Full Upload (ODS or InfoPackage Selection)
A			X					2	A	ALE Update Pointer (Master Data)
ABR	X	X	X			X		2	D	Complete Delta with Deletion Flag by Delta Queue (Cube-Comp)
ABR1	X	X	X			X		1	D	Like Method 'ABR' But Serialization Only by Requests
ADD				X				1	E	Additive Extraction by Extractor (e.g. LIS Info Structures)
ADDD				X				1	D	Like 'ADD' But by Delta Queue (Cube-Compatible)
AIE			X					2	E	After-Images by Extractor (FI-GL/AP/AR)
AIED			X			X		2	E	After-Images with Deletion Flag by Extractor (FI-GL/AP/AR)
AIM			X					2	D	After-Images by Delta Queue (e.g. FI-AP/AR)
AIMD			X			X		2	D	After-Images with Deletion Flag by Delta Queue (e.g. BtB)
CUBE				X				0	E	InfoCube Extraction
D								2	D	Unspecific Delta by Delta Queue (Not ODS-Compatible)
E								2	E	Unspecific Delta by Extractor (Not ODS-Compatible)
FIL0			X					2	F	Delta by File Import with After-Images
FIL1				X				2	F	Delta by File Import with Delta Images
NEWD	X							0	D	Only New Records (Inserts) by Delta Queue (Cube-Compatible)
NEWE	X							0	E	Only New Records (Inserts) by Extractor (Cube-Compatible)
O		X	X	X				0	E	
ODS	X	X	X			X		1	E	ODS Extraction
X								2	X	Delta Unspecified (Do Not Use!)

Figure 5.23 Table RODELTAM for DataSource Delta Information

5.1.4   DataSource Activation

When you're working for the first time in SAP S/4HANA, make sure you have the latest valid business content add-on installed in your system. When you're doing a greenfield or fresh SAP BW/4HANA implementation in an SAP S/4HANA source system, you need to execute Transaction RSA9 one time in the system to the transfer application component hierarchy to Transaction RSA5. When you open Transaction RSA5 (Installation of DataSource from Business Content), it will display the SAP ERP application components and associated DataSources, as shown in Figure 5.24. For example, the sales and distribution application can be expanded by clicking the folder icon ⊞ to the left of **SD**. Then you'll see a list of all the related sales and distribution DataSources.

To activate an SAP DataSource, follow this process, as shown in Figure 5.25:

❶ Choose a DataSource name.

❷ Activate the DataSource from this list by selecting the **Activate DataSource** button.

❸ Check if the DataSource is enabled for ODP by checking the correct checkmark icon 📝 to the left.

You can choose any DataSource—for example, 2LIS_11_VAHDR, listed under the **SD-IO** application component. Once you select the DataSource, click **Activate DataSource** to activate the DataSource in the source system. You might see a popup for a transport request. In that case, provide a valid transport request for activation.

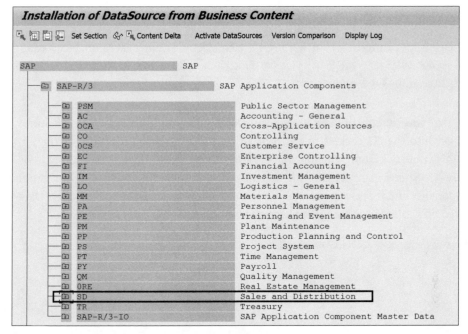

Figure 5.24 Transaction RSA5: List of All DataSources

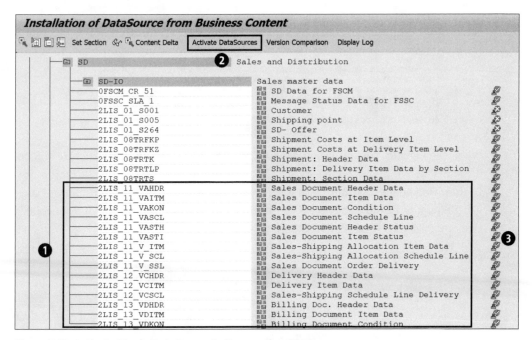

Figure 5.25 Activate Single DataSource in Transaction RSA5

> **DataSource Activation**
>
> Once the DataSource is activated from Transaction RSA5 as shown in Figure 5.25, it can be seen in table ROOSOURCE as A version, which means it's active. Refer back to Figure 5.22 to view the table contents.

Now that you've seen all the details about DataSources and their associated features, let's get into the LO cockpit to perform all DataSource-related activities in the SAP S/4HANA source system. The logistics cockpit can be accessed via Transaction LBWE. Figure 5.26 shows the details of the logistics cockpit, including the list of application components and their related DataSources. For example, sales and distribution Data-Source 2LIS_11_VAHDR is part of application component 11 (SD Sales BW).

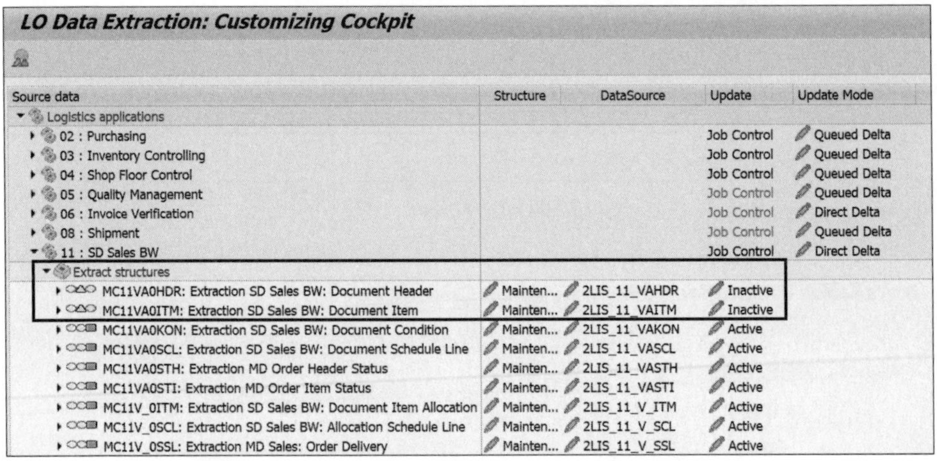

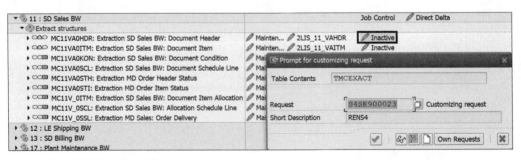

Figure 5.26 Logistics Cockpit: Application Component and DataSource

When the logistics cockpit is launched for the first time, the extract structure will be listed as **Inactive**, as shown in Figure 5.27. Click **Inactive** and you will see the **Prompt for Customizing Request** popup. Once you provide the request and press enter, it will trigger the popup message shown in Figure 5.28. This sets the V3 update that does collective processing for each change document to active.

Figure 5.27 Activate DataSource

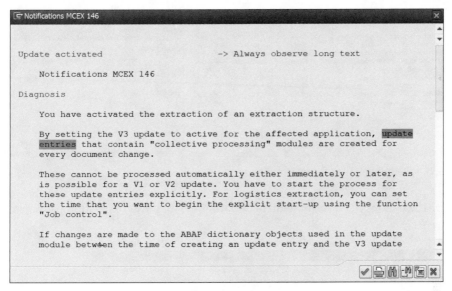

Figure 5.28 Activate LO: Prompt for V3 Update Confirmation

Once you choose the checkmark icon ✅, as shown in Figure 5.28, the DataSource will be activated and it can start extracting the data from the sender system. You can see that DataSource 2LIS_11_VAHDR is changed to **Active**, visible below **Job Control** in Figure 5.29.

	Job Control	Direct Delta
▼ 🔮 11 : SD Sales BW		
▼ 🔮 Extract structures		
▼ ∞ MC11VA0HDR: Extraction SD Sales BW: Document Header	🖉 Mainten... 🖉 2LIS_11_VAHDR	🖉 Active
▼ ⭐ Events		
• VA : Sales order: sched.agreement		
• VB : Quotation: contract		
▶ ∞ MC11VA0ITM: Extraction SD Sales BW: Document Item	🖉 Mainten... 🖉 2LIS_11_VAITM	🖉 Inactive

Figure 5.29 Activate the Logistics-Sales and Distribution HDR DataSource

Now let's activate the other DataSource for the item too (see Figure 5.27). The result is shown in Figure 5.30, where DataSource 2LIS_11_VAITM is **Active** now.

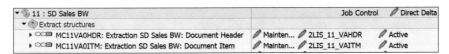

	Job Control	Direct Delta
▼ 🔮 11 : SD Sales BW		
▼ 🔮 Extract structures		
▶ ∞ MC11VA0HDR: Extraction SD Sales BW: Document Header	🖉 Mainten... 🖉 2LIS_11_VAHDR	🖉 Active
▶ ∞ MC11VA0ITM: Extraction SD Sales BW: Document Item	🖉 Mainten... 🖉 2LIS_11_VAITM	🖉 Active

Figure 5.30 Activate Logistics Item DataSource

Once the DataSource is activated, you need to schedule the job for periodic update processing. To do this, choose **Job Control** as shown in Figure 5.31 and the click **Start Date**. This will open a popup, as shown in Figure 5.32.

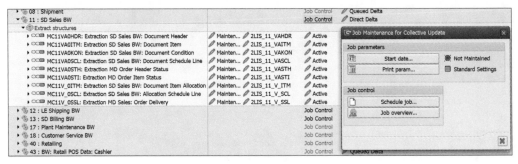

Figure 5.31 Scheduling V3 Job for LO DataSource

You have the option to choose **Immediate** or **Date/Time** for the job execution, as shown in Figure 5.32.

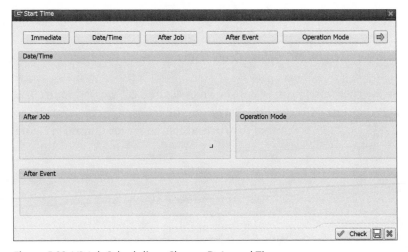

Figure 5.32 V3 Job Scheduling: Choose Date and Time

Based on the entry from Figure 5.32, once the data and time are selected, you can see that the **Start Date** is maintained and the **Job Parameters** are green, as shown in Figure 5.33. This step will complete the V3 job scheduling process for the DataSource.

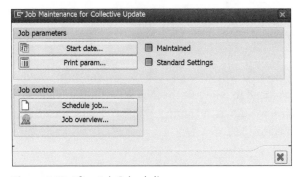

Figure 5.33 After Job Scheduling

5.2 Logistics Data Extraction in SAP S/4HANA

This section covers the steps to expose an SAP DataSource to the ODP framework and extract data into SAP BW/4HANA using business content DataSources. We'll also start to fill the setup table in SAP S/4HANA and you'll learn how to see the results in Service Application Interface (SAPI)- and ODP-based transactions.

5.2.1 Exposing Logistics DataSource to Operational Data Provisioning

SAP BW DataSources are delivered by the business content addon. When you need to use these DataSources in SAP BW/4HANA, you need to make sure that they're exposed to ODP. Follow these steps to check if the DataSource is enabled for ODP:

1. **Perform an ODP check in Transaction RSA5.**

   The DataSources that are exposed to ODP can be seen in the logistics cockpit via Transaction RSA5. When you see the green arrow icon for any DataSource, that it means it's exposed to ODP. Open Transaction RSA5 in SAP S/4HANA to view the screen shown in Figure 5.34.

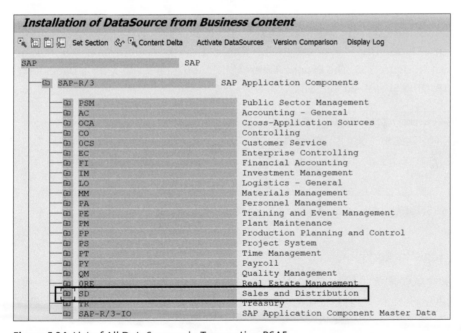

Figure 5.34 List of All DataSources in Transaction RSA5

If the icon has a checkmark as shown in Figure 5.35, then the DataSource is enabled for ODP. Choose the folder icon.

Installation of DataSource from Business Content

🔲 🔲 🔲 🔲   Set Section   🔗 🔲 Content Delta   Activate DataSources   Version Comparison   Display Log

🗂 SD-IO	Sales master data
─── 0FSCM_CR_51	SD Data for FSCM
─── 0FSSC_SLA_1	Message Status Data for FSSC
─── 2LIS_01_S001	Customer
─── 2LIS_01_S005	Shipping point
─── 2LIS_01_S264	SD- Offer
─── 2LIS_08TRFKP	Shipment Costs at Item Level
─── 2LIS_08TRFKZ	Shipment Costs at Delivery Item Level
─── 2LIS_08TRTK	Shipment: Header Data
─── 2LIS_08TRTLP	Shipment: Delivery Item Data by Section
─── 2LIS_08TRTS	Shipment: Section Data
─── 2LIS_11_VAHDR	Sales Document Header Data
─── 2LIS_11_VAITM	Sales Document Item Data
─── 2LIS_11_VAKON	Sales Document Condition
─── 2LIS_11_VASCL	Sales Document Schedule Line
─── 2LIS_11_VASTH	Sales Document Header Status
─── 2LIS_11_VASTI	Sales Document Item Status
─── 2LIS_11_V_ITM	Sales-Shipping Allocation Item Data
─── 2LIS_11_V_SCL	Sales-Shipping Allocation Schedule Line
─── 2LIS_11_V_SSL	Sales Document Order Delivery
─── 2LIS_12_VCHDR	Delivery Header Data
─── 2LIS_12_VCITM	Delivery Item Data
─── 2LIS_12_VCSCL	Sales-Shipping Schedule Line Delivery
─── 2LIS_13_VDHDR	Billing Doc. Header Data
─── 2LIS_13_VDITM	Billing Document Item Data
─── 2LIS_13_VDKON	Billing Document Condition

Figure 5.35 Checkmark to Indicate DataSource Is Exposed to ODP

2. **Check table ROOSATTR in SAP S/4HANA.**

When a DataSource is exposed to SAP HANA, it can be seen in table ROOSATTR, as shown in Figure 5.36. The **Expose_External** field must be set to X for a DataSource (**OLTPSOURCE**) enabled for ODP.

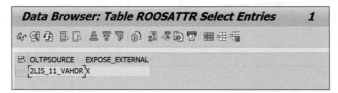

Figure 5.36 Table to Check DataSource Exposed to ODP

5.2.2   Logistics Cockpit

The logistics cockpit in SAP S/4HANA contains all SAP BW DataSources based on logistics applications. The cockpit can be accessed via Transaction LBWE as shown in Figure 5.37. You'll see the following options:

❶ Application component list

❷ V3 job schedule

❸ Update mode (V3/queue/direct) for delta handling

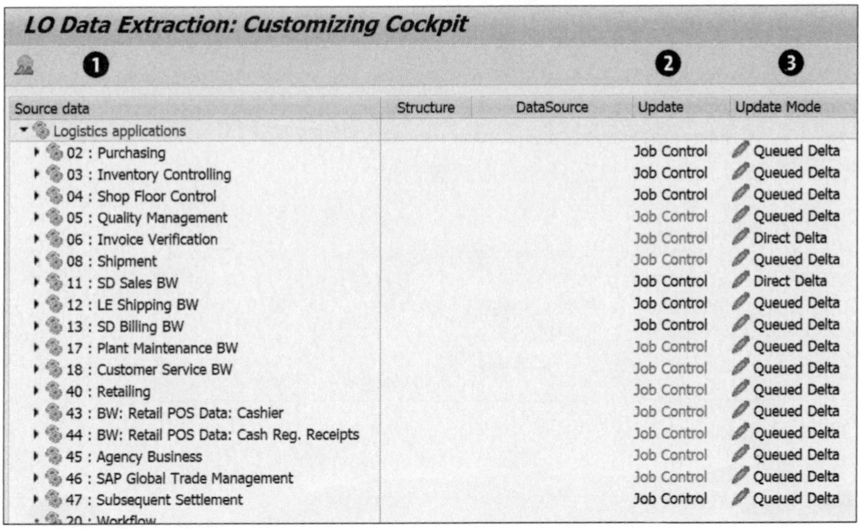

Figure 5.37 Logistics Cockpit

5.2.3   Filling the Setup Table and Testing the Extraction

Logistics DataSources have setup tables that need to be filled before extracting the data into SAP BW/4HANA. The following setup table name has a naming convention based on the extraction structure name: *Restructuring table (setup table) <Extraction structure>SETUP*.

Setup Table: Naming Convention

As an example of the setup table naming convention, consider the 2LIS_11_VAHDR DataSource. The setup table name is based on the extraction structure: MC11VA0HDR followed by SETUP. The associated restructuring setup table will be MC11VA0HDRSETUP.

Here are a few more examples:

- 2LIS_11_VAHDR would be MC11VA0HDRSETUP.
- 2LIS_11_VAITM would be MC11VA0ITMSETUP.
- 2LIS_11_VAITM would be MC11V_0ITMSETUP.

As shown in Figure 5.38, the extraction structure (**Structure**) is based on the DataSource. The setup table, as shown in Figure 5.39, will have SETUP as a suffix added to the extraction structure.

The setup table for DataSource has SETUP added to the end of the extraction structure. With this naming process, you can see the associated setup table, as shown in Figure 5.39. For example, for DataSource 2LIS_11_VAHDR, the extraction structure is MC110VAHDR, so the setup table name will be MC11VA0HDRSETUP.

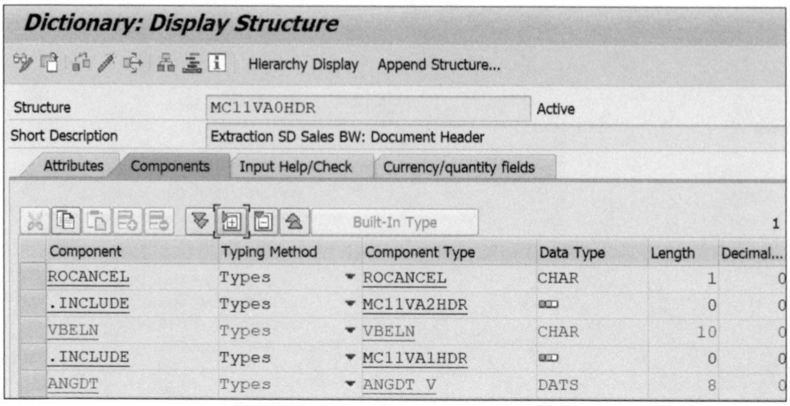

Figure 5.38 Extraction Structure

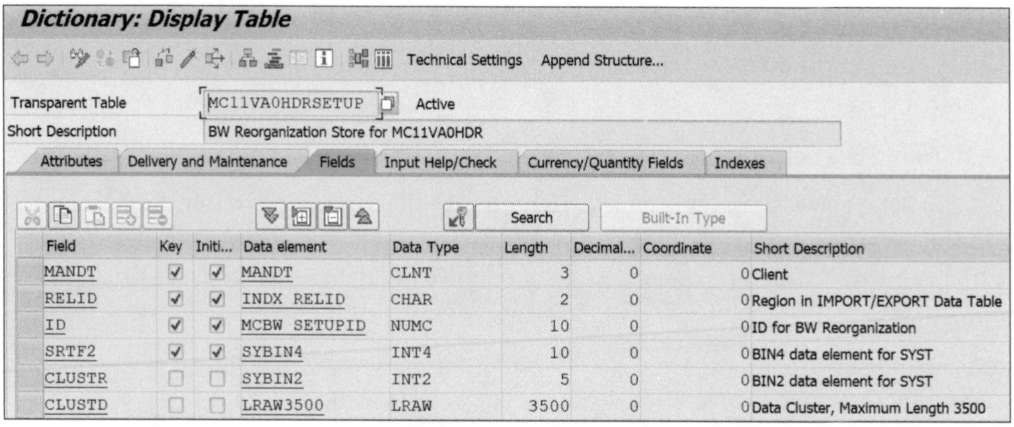

Figure 5.39 Setup Table for LO DataSource

You can always check the contents of the setup table in Transaction SE11 or SE16. From the screen shown in Figure 5.39, click the **Table Contents** icon [icon] or press [Ctrl] + [Shift] + [F10] to view the contents of the setup table and check the total number of entries.

Clearing the Setup Table

It's best practice to clear the contents of the setup table before filling the setup table; otherwise, it will cause duplicate records to be sent to SAP BW/4HANA. To clear the setup table, use Transaction LBWG and provide the application component number and execute. It will delete all entries of the setup table. For example, if you need to clear all the sales-based setup table content, then you can open Transaction LBWG, provide 11, and execute. That will drop all contents of all setup tables for all Data-Sources under application component 11.

Now that we've covered the details of the setup table, it's time to fill the setup table in SAP S/4HANA. We'll start this activity from the transaction level. Once you're aware of this process, you can use reports to fill the setup table directly for specific application components. Follow these steps in order:

1. Open Transaction SBIW. This will show the **Display IMG** screen (Figure 5.40 ❶).
2. Expand **Settings for Application-Specific DataSources (PI)** ❷.
3. Expand **Logistics** ❸.
4. Expand **Initialization** ❹.
5. Expand **Filling in the Setup Table** ❺.
6. Expand **Application-Specific Setup of Statistical Data** ❻.

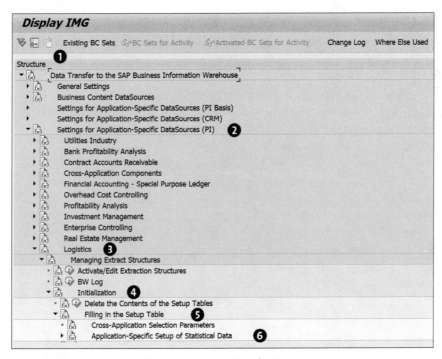

Figure 5.40 IMG Path to Fill Setup Table in SAP S/4HANA

7. Once you expand **Application-Specific Setup of Statistical data**, as shown in Figure 5.41 ❶, you can see the options for filling the setup table for multiple applications ❷: inventory, sales, deliveries, billing, and so on.
8. The screen shown in Figure 5.42 opens. Fill out the following important fields: **Name of Run** ❶; and the **Termination Date** and **Termination Time** ❷, which should always be in the future. Click the **Execute** icon 🕹 ❸ or press F8 to fill the setup table.

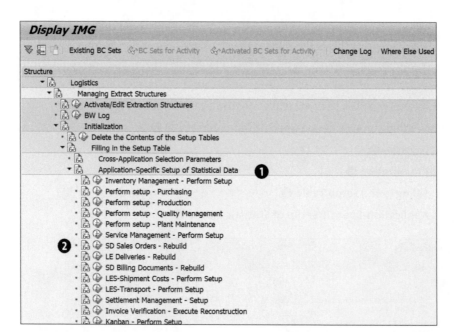

Figure 5.41 IMG Path to Fill Setup Table for SD Sales Order

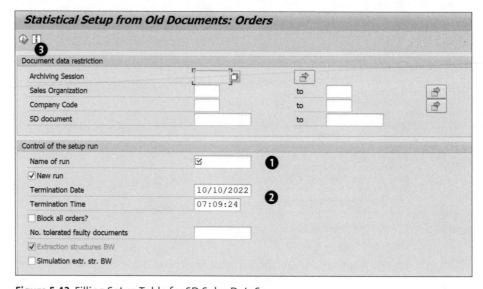

Figure 5.42 Filling Setup Table for SD Sales DataSources

Setup Table Filling: Performance Optimization

When extracting large volumes of data in SAP BW/4HANA, the selections available under **Document Data Restriction** (Figure 5.43) can be used to parallelize the setup table filling. This helps to reduce the downtime in SAP S/4HANA, which will be a core requirement for any business. For example, you can create multiple setup table executions for different company codes like 1000, 2000, and 3000 in parallel, or create multiple setup table executions for different sales organizations.

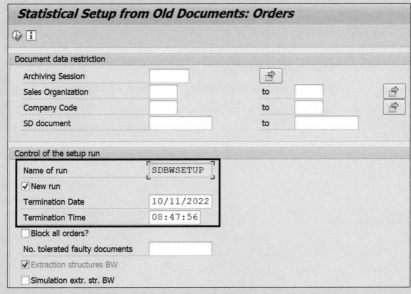

Figure 5.43 Filling Setup Table for SD DataSource: Input Parameters

9. Once the **Execute** option is selected, you'll get the popup message shown in Figure 5.44. It will take some time to fill the setup table and make sure that SAP S/4HANA doesn't have any document postings during that period if it's an implementation project.

Figure 5.44 Start to Fill Setup Table

Reports for Setup Table Filling

You can come to the same screen by using the standard report delivered by SAP. For filling the setup table for a sales application, execute Transaction OLI7BW. This will take you to the same screen as shown in Figure 5.43. Similarly, you can use Transaction OLI8BW for filling the setup table for shipping applications and Transaction OLI9BW for filling the setup table for billing applications.

10. Now the setup table can be viewed using Transaction RSA3 (Extraction Checker—S-API). This is widely used in the Service API methodology that was common in SAP BW and can be used to check the extractors for simulating the records that will be sent to the SAP BW system. This still works in SAP S/4HANA, but there you can use the ODP framework to check the simulated record count. To check the setup table contents, execute Transaction RSA3 to see the screen shown in Figure 5.45, then follow these steps:

❶ Provide the SAP BW **DataSource** name.

❷ There will be default numbers entered in the **Data Records / Calls** and **Display Extr. Calls** fields. The system shows 100 data records with 10 display calls, with 99 records per data package, so it can list a maximum of 990 records for a data package.

❸ The **Update Mode F** implies that this is a full upload.

❹ Execute with the button to view the contents of the setup table.

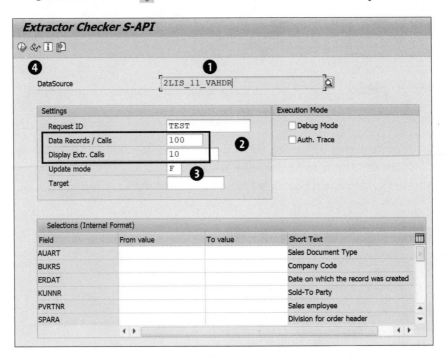

Figure 5.45 Steps to Check Contents of Setup Table for DataSource

11. The popup shown in Figure 5.46 is the total number of records selected based on the info shown in Figure 5.45.

Figure 5.46 Total Records Selected Based on Provided Input Parameters

12. Once you choose the **Enter** button , you can see the options shown in Figure 5.47 at the bottom of the Transaction RSA3 screen. There will be options to see the results in **ALV Grid** format or **List** format; when you select an option, the results will be shown accordingly.

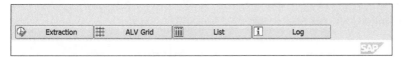

Figure 5.47 Transaction RSA3 Results

13. Choose the **List** button to see the results shown in Figure 5.48.

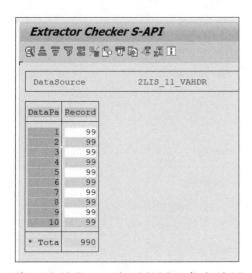

Figure 5.48 Transaction RSA3 Results in List Format

14. Because you already set **Data Records / Call** to 100 and **Display Extr. Calls** to 10 (refer back to Figure 5.45), the list shows 99 records in 10 data packages, which makes it count to 990. When you click a data package, such as **1** in Figure 5.48, you'll see 99 records displayed, as shown in Figure 5.49. The left and right arrow icons ◀ ▶ shown in Figure 5.49 let you navigate to the fields to the left and right.

Extractor Checker S-API

| DataSource | 2LIS_11_VAHDR |
| Struktur | MC11VAOHDR |

Valid From	Orders(ANZAU	Sale	Ord	Valid To(B	CoCo	On(ERDAT)	Bi	Local	Sold-To(KU	ExRa	Cus	Cus	Cus	Cus	Cus	De	FY	Employee	C	Di	Curre	SD Doc.(V
	1	OR			1710	10/06/2017		USD	17100003								K4			00	USD	2
	1	OR			1710	10/06/2017		USD	17100001								K4			00	USD	3
	1	OR			1710	10/08/2017		USD	USCU_L10								K4			00	USD	4
	1	OR			1710	10/08/2017		USD	USCU_L10								K4			00	USD	22
	1	OR			1710	10/08/2017		USD	USCU_S07								K4			00	USD	23
	1	OR			1710	10/08/2017		USD	USCU_S03								K4			00	USD	24
	1	OR			1710	10/06/2017		USD	USCU_S15								K4			00	USD	25
	1	OR			1710	10/08/2017		USD	USCU_L04								K4			00	USD	26
	1	OR			1710	10/08/2017		USD	USCU_L02								K4			00	USD	27
	1	OR			1710	10/08/2017		USD	USCU_L09								K4			00	USD	28
	1	OR			1710	10/08/2017		USD	USCU_S05								K4			00	USD	29
	1	OR			1710	10/08/2017		USD	USCU_S17								K4			00	USD	30
	1	OR			1710	10/08/2017		USD	USCU_L03								K4			00	USD	31
	1	OR			1710	10/08/2017		USD	USCU_L08								K4			00	USD	32
	1	OR			1710	10/08/2017		USD	USCU_S10								K4			00	USD	33
	1	OR			1710	10/08/2017		USD	USCU_S06								K4			00	USD	34
	1	OR			1710	10/08/2017		USD	USCU_S09								K4			00	USD	35
	1	OR			1710	10/08/2017		USD	USCU_L01								K4			00	USD	36
	1	OR			1710	10/08/2017		USD	USCU_S15								K4			00	USD	37
	1	OR			1710	10/08/2017		USD	USCU_L04								K4			00	USD	38
	1	OR			1710	10/08/2017		USD	USCU_L10								K4			00	USD	39

Figure 5.49 Transaction RSA3 Results in List Format for Data Package 1

15. Refer back to Figure 5.47. When you choose the **ALV Grid** option, you'll see the results in the format shown in Figure 5.50 for DataSource 2LIS_11_VAHDR. The **Data Package (Number of Recs)** field has drilldown options; here it's showing **1 (99)**, which means it's showing the first data package and 99 records.

Result of Extraction of DataSource 2LIS_11_VAHDR

Data Package (Number of Recs): 1 (99)

Cancel	SD Doc.	Valid From	SaTy	OrdRs	Valid To	CoCode	Created on	BB	LCurr	Sold-To	ERTy	Grp1	Grp2	Grp3	Grp4	Grp5	DIBI	Employee	Curr.	Doc.Cat.	Req.Div.Dt	SOff.	SGrp	SOrg.	DChl	Curr.DI	DocCa	Orders	FV
	2	OR			1710		10/06/2017		USD	17100003									USD	C	10/06/2017			1710	10	USD	00	1	K4
	3	OR			1710		10/06/2017		USD	17100001									USD	C	10/06/2017			1710	10	USD	00	1	K4
	4	OR			1710		10/08/2017		USD	USCU_L10									USD	C	10/08/2017			1710	10	USD	00	1	K4
	22	OR			1710		10/08/2017		USD	USCU_L10									USD	C	10/09/2017			1710	10	USD	00	1	K4
	23	OR			1710		10/08/2017		USD	USCU_S07									USD	C	10/09/2017			1710	10	USD	00	1	K4
	24	OR			1710		10/08/2017		USD	USCU_S03									USD	C	10/09/2017			1710	10	USD	00	1	K4
	25	OR			1710		10/08/2017		USD	USCU_S15									USD	C	10/09/2017			1710	10	USD	00	1	K4
	26	OR			1710		10/08/2017		USD	USCU_L04									USD	C	10/09/2017			1710	10	USD	00	1	K4
	27	OR			1710		10/08/2017		USD	USCU_L02									USD	C	10/09/2017			1710	10	USD	00	1	K4
	28	OR			1710		10/08/2017		USD	USCU_L09									USD	C	10/09/2017			1710	10	USD	00	1	K4
	29	OR			1710		10/08/2017		USD	USCU_S05									USD	C	10/09/2017			1710	10	USD	00	1	K4
	30	OR			1710		10/08/2017		USD	USCU_S17									USD	C	10/09/2017			1710	10	USD	00	1	K4
	31	OR			1710		10/08/2017		USD	USCU_L03									USD	C	10/09/2017			1710	10	USD	00	1	K4
	32	OR			1710		10/08/2017		USD	USCU_L08									USD	C	10/09/2017			1710	10	USD	00	1	K4
	33	OR			1710		10/08/2017		USD	USCU_S10									USD	C	10/09/2017			1710	10	USD	00	1	K4
	34	OR			1710		10/08/2017		USD	USCU_S06									USD	C	10/09/2017			1710	10	USD	00	1	K4
	35	OR			1710		10/08/2017		USD	USCU_S09									USD	C	10/09/2017			1710	10	USD	00	1	K4
	36	OR			1710		10/08/2017		USD	USCU_L01									USD	C	10/09/2017			1710	10	USD	00	1	K4
	37	OR			1710		10/08/2017		USD	USCU_S15									USD	C	10/09/2017			1710	10	USD	00	1	K4
	38	OR			1710		10/08/2017		USD	USCU_L04									USD	C	10/09/2017			1710	10	USD	00	1	K4
	39	OR			1710		10/08/2017		USD	USCU_L10									USD	C	10/09/2017			1710	10	USD	00	1	K4

Figure 5.50 Transaction RSA3 Results: ALV Grid format

16. If you need to see other data packages, choose them from the dropdown, which will show the package listing as shown in Figure 5.51.

17. As you can see in Figure 5.51, there are 99 records in 10 data packages and hence 990 records do not comprise the complete set of records in the setup table. In a real-time SAP BW/4HANA implementation, you'll see a huge volume of data in SAP S/4HANA tables, and in those scenarios, you need to check the setup table for the DataSources directly in Transaction SE16 with the naming convention that was

shown earlier in Figure 5.39. Now you can check the setup table for 2LIS_11_VAHDR, which is MC11VA0HDRSETUP. Open Transaction SE16 and provide this table name. Once you see the screen shown in Figure 5.52, choose the **Number of Entries** button to see the total entries in the table. The **Display Number of Entries** popup window shows the total count of records that a setup for a specific DataSource has; in this case, there are 6,712 entries in the setup table.

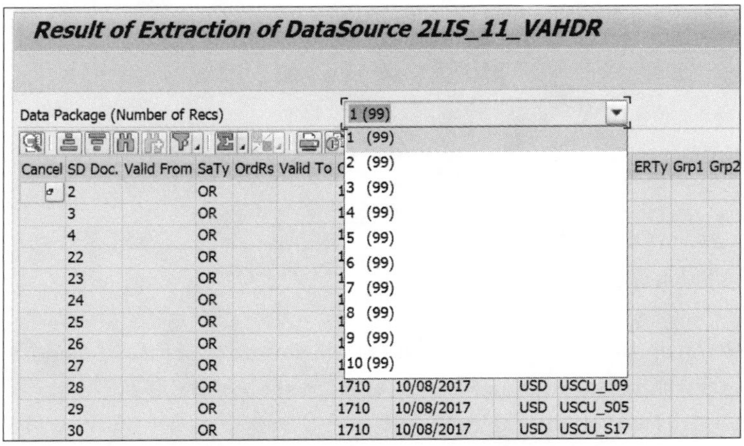

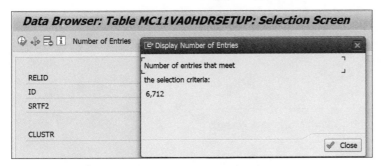

Figure 5.51 Transaction RSA3 Results: ALV Grid and Package Selection

Figure 5.52 Check Complete Contents of Setup Table

18. Now you might have a question: Figure 5.52 shows 6,712 records, so why does Transaction RSA3 only display 90 records? The reason for this behavior is that **Data Records / Call** was set to 100 and **Display Ext Call** was set to 10, so it can display a maximum of 99 records in 10 packages for a total of 990 records. Remember that Transaction RSA3 is only used for simulation purposes. If you need to see all the records in Transaction RSA3, use the options shown in Figure 5.53. You can see that **Data Records / Calls** is increased to 10,000, which means that one data package will have 9,999 records with up to 10 **Display Extr. Calls**, so this option will display up to 99,990 records. In this case, there are only 6,712 records in the setup table, so the

first data package will contain the full number of records. Once this data is entered, click the **Execute** icon to move to the next screen.

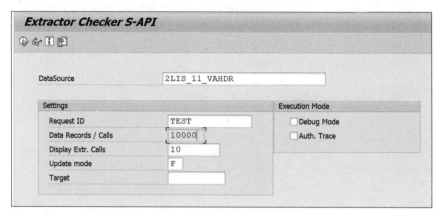

Figure 5.53 RSA3 Simulation with More Records

19. You can now see the option to display the results in ALV grid or list format; choose **List** to see the screen shown in Figure 5.54. Here, you can see that **DataPa** (data package 1) has 6,712 records without any split.

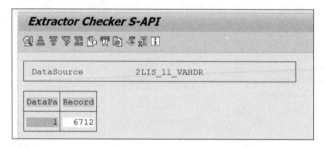

Figure 5.54 Transaction RSA3 with More Data Records

5.2.4   Testing Setup Table Extraction Replication Using ODP Framework

Until now you have seen how to fill the setup table and check it using Transaction RSA3, which is based on the Service API (S-API). But in SAP BW/4HANA, the ODP framework is supported for the extraction. Although you can use Transaction RSA3 for checking the contents of the setup table, when you're using SAP BW/4HANA, it's also good to use the new reports that are designed for the ODP-based framework. Let's look at that option now. Once you've filled the setup table, to test the total records that are fetched, you can open Transaction SE38 and try to execute report RODPS_REPL_TEST, as shown in Figure 5.55.

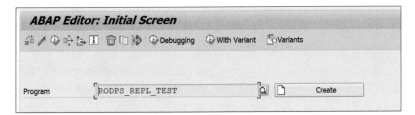

Figure 5.55 Setup Simulation for ODP-Based DataSource

After you enter "RODPS_REPL_TEST" into the **Program** field as shown in Figure 5.55, click the **Execute** icon ⊕ or press [F8] to see the input fields for the report. You'll see the screen shown in Figure 5.56 after execution. Here, you'll need to fill the input fields as follows:

❶ Because you're using the standard SAP extractors, you can choose **DataSource/ Extractors**.

❷ In the **ODP Name** field, provide the name of the SAP DataSource that you want to simulate the results of.

❸ In **Max Number of Displayed Rows**, you can set the maximum value to expect.

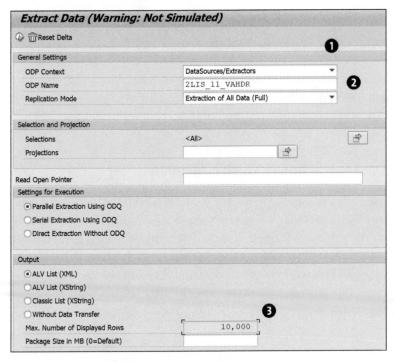

Figure 5.56 Report RODPD_REPL_TEST Parameters

You can leave the other fields as set. For example, replication mode can be set to **Extraction of All Data (Full)**, which means it will get data from the setup table. You can leave the **Parallel Extraction Using ODQ** button as is.

Once you execute, you'll see the results as shown in Figure 5.57. This will display all the records from the setup table, and you can use the output to validate the data required for SAP BW extraction. During the SAP BW/4HANA implementation, this can help SAP BW consultants test the data before extracting it to SAP BW/4HANA.

Extract Data with/from {2022-11-04 16:15:14 000065 PST}								
RCVBELN	ANGDT	AUART AU...	BNDDT	BUKRS	ERDAT	FA...	HWAER	KUNNR
0000000002		TA		1710	10/06/2017		USD	0017100003
0000000003		TA		1710	10/06/2017		USD	0017100001
0000000004		TA		1710	10/08/2017		USD	USCU_L10
0000000022		TA		1710	10/08/2017		USD	USCU_L10
0000000023		TA		1710	10/08/2017		USD	USCU_S07
0000000024		TA		1710	10/08/2017		USD	USCU_S03
0000000025		TA		1710	10/08/2017		USD	USCU_S15
0000000026		TA		1710	10/08/2017		USD	USCU_L04
0000000027		TA		1710	10/08/2017		USD	USCU_L02
0000000028		TA		1710	10/08/2017		USD	USCU_L09
0000000029		TA		1710	10/08/2017		USD	USCU_S05
0000000030		TA		1710	10/08/2017		USD	USCU_S17
0000000031		TA		1710	10/08/2017		USD	USCU_L03
0000000032		TA		1710	10/08/2017		USD	USCU_L08

Figure 5.57 Report RODPS_REPL_TEST: Results of Execution

Now you know how to fill a setup table for a LO extractor and check the setup table contents in Transaction RSA3 and report RODPS_REPL_TEST. This will give you a strong foundation when you work on any SAP BW project.

5.3   Logistics Data Extraction in SAP BW/4HANA

In this section, you'll learn how to replicate an ODP-based DataSource to SAP BW/4HANA and create an aDSO that will get data based on the ODP DataSource. This will be followed by creating a transformation and a data transfer process (DTP) to load data into the aDSO, then checking the data in the aDSO and in Transaction ODQMON in the SAP S/4HANA system. This will help you understand the complete end-to-end SAP BW/4HANA data extraction process in LO extraction. The same steps will apply to most LO DataSources.

5.3.1   Replicating ODP DataSources in SAP BW/4HANA

To this point, you've seen the steps in the SAP S/4HANA source system. In this section, we'll walk through the steps to be done in SAP BW/4HANA system to extract data from the sender ERP system:

1. Before replicating the ODP DataSource, you need to make sure that the SAP BW/4HANA system has an ODP source system, as discussed in Chapter 3. In the SAP BW/4HANA modeling tools, you need to check for the SAP S/4HANA source system. Right-click the desired source system from the **ODP_SAP** folder, as shown in Figure 5.58.

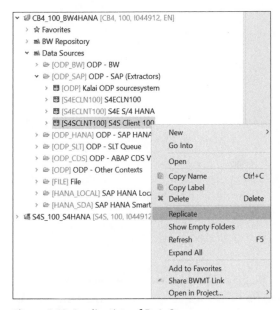

Figure 5.58 Replication of DataSource

2. You'll see the popup shown in Figure 5.59.

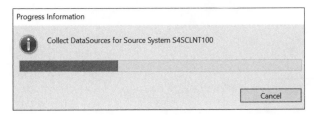

Figure 5.59 Collection of DataSource

3. The system will collect all eligible DataSources and list them as shown in Figure 5.60:

   - **Select Displayed DataSource ❶**: If this is selected, then all DataSources shown will be selected and the checkbox will be enabled.
   - **Deselect Displayed DataSources ❷**: This will remove the checkbox for all DataSources listed.
   - **DataSource ❸**: This section represents the DataSources that can be replicated from the sender system. You have the option to select and deselect DataSources here.

183

– **Filter Pattern ❹**: This is used to select only specific DataSources for replication. This will save the time needed to replace and activate extraneous DataSources.

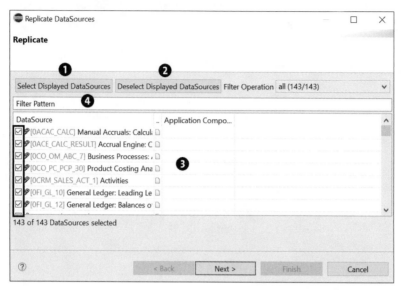

Figure 5.60 Replication Options

4. In this scenario, first choose **Deselect Displayed DataSources**. The checkboxes will be disabled for all the DataSources listed (in this example, 143). Next, enter "2LIS_11" as the filter pattern. You can see the details of 2LIS_11_VAHDR and other DataSources that follow that pattern, as shown in Figure 5.61. Note that the **Next** option is disabled now.

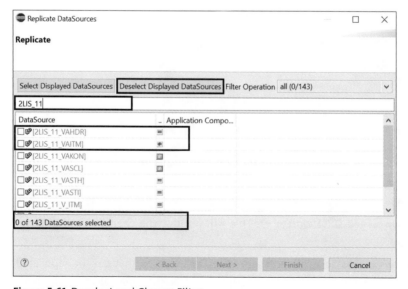

Figure 5.61 Deselect and Choose Filter

5. In Figure 5.61, you see that 0 of 143 DataSources were selected. This means that we didn't select any DataSources for replication. You can also see that checkbox for the 2LIS_11_VAHDR DataSource is also disabled. You need to enable the checkboxes for **2LIS_11_VAHDR** and **2LIS_11_VAITM**, as shown in Figure 5.62. Once you do this, the **Next** option will be enabled and you will see **2 of 143 DataSources Selected**.

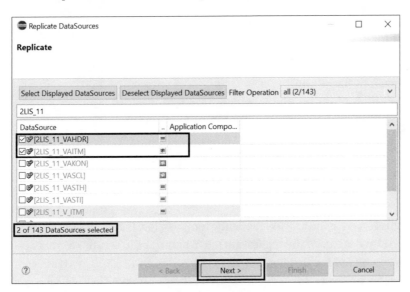

Figure 5.62 Select DataSources for Replication

6. Choose **Next**, and you will see the popup shown in Figure 5.63. If you're doing the replication for the first time, you'll see that the **Activate New DataSources** checkbox will be selected and enabled; any time after that, you'll see the **Activate Updated DataSources** option. This will make sure that all changes in the sender DataSource will be updated in the target SAP BW/4HANA system. For example, if you added a field in a DataSource in the sender system, then when you try to replicate the Data-Source, it will update the DataSource structure in SAP BW/4HANA.

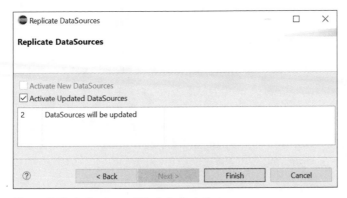

Figure 5.63 Activate and Update DataSource

Replication: Best Practice

It's best practice to replicate the DataSource in SAP BW/4HANA when there is any change to the structure in SAP ERP or SAP S/4HANA. Many times, you modify a Data-Source with added fields or updated enhancement logic. If you don't replicate the DataSource after those steps, then SAP BW/4HANA will not have that information updated.

7. Click **Finish** to complete the replication process. Replication will start in the background, as shown in Figure 5.64.

Figure 5.64 Popup for Replication

8. You can see this screen in the SAP BW modeling tools as a tab. If you click **Refresh**, you can see the final status of the replication job. You can see in Figure 5.65 that saving has been completed for DataSources 2LIS_11_VAHDR and 2LIS_11_VAITM. Note that the DataSource shows its associated source system name; in this case, it's S4SCLNT100. This tells you that a DataSource is always tied to its source system.

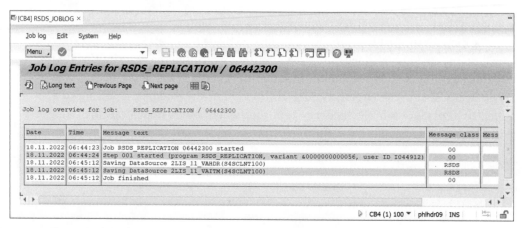

Figure 5.65 Replication Job Overview

9. You need to check if the DataSource is available in the source system folder. Expand the source system folder as shown in Figure 5.66 and use the scroll bar to drill down and see if the DataSource is replicated.

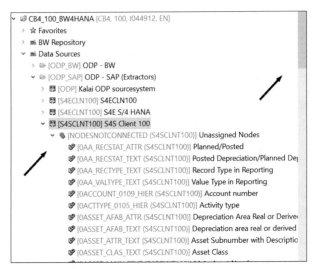

Figure 5.66 Checking Replication

10. You can find both the DataSources, and if you double-click **2LIS_11_VAHDR**, you can see the details of the DataSource and its status; here it's shown as **Active** in Figure 5.67. But if it's not active, then you need to manually activate the DataSource by using the **Activate** icon in the SAP BW modeling tools, as shown in Figure 5.67.

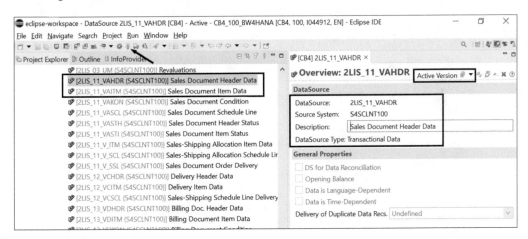

Figure 5.67 DataSource Status

11. Because the DataSource is activated, it will be updated in the SAP BW/4HANA back-end tables. The table-level validation can help you in SAP BW implementation and support projects. If you need to check that a specific DataSource is active at the table level, you can see that in table RSDS, as shown in Figure 5.68:

❶ Choose the arrow icon to provide more than one selection.

❷ Provide the list of all DataSource names that you need to check—in this case, 2LIS_11_VAHDR and 2LIS_11_VAITM.

❸ Once the DataSource list is provided, choose the **Execute** icon. This will take you to the next screen, as shown in Figure 5.69.

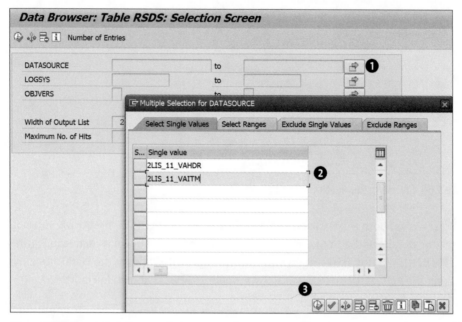

Figure 5.68 Check DataSource Status

12. In the screen shown in Figure 5.69, you need to provide the name of the SAP S/4HANA source system so that you will only see results for that specific source system.

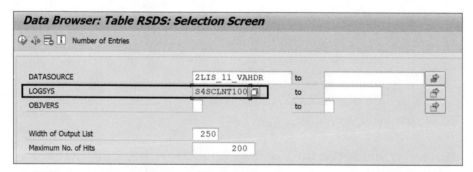

Figure 5.69 Selection Screen

13. The results are shown in Figure 5.70, where you can see that the DataSource name is 2LIS_11_VAHDR, it has its associated source system as S4SCLNT100, and you can see **OBJVERS** as **A**. You will always see three statuses for a DataSource: **D** stands for

delivered, **M** stands for modified, and **A** stands for active. If you need to use a
DataSource for extraction of data, then **OBJVERS** needs to show **A** and **OBJSTAT**
needs to show **ACT**.

Data Browser: Table RSDS Select Entries   6

DATASOURCE	LOGSYS	OBJVERS	OBJSTAT	ACTIVFL	TYPE	PRIMSEGID	OBJECTFD	APPLNM	BASOSOURCE	DELTA	STOCKUPD
2LIS_11_VAHDR	S4SCLNT100	A	ACT	X	D	0001				ABR	
2LIS_11_VAHDR	S4SCLNT100	D	INA		D	0001				ABR	
2LIS_11_VAHDR	S4SCLNT100	M	ACT	X	D	0001				ABR	
2LIS_11_VAITM	S4SCLNT100	A	ACT	X	D	0001				ABR	
2LIS_11_VAITM	S4SCLNT100	D	ACT		D	0001				ABR	
2LIS_11_VAITM	S4SCLNT100	M	ACT	X	D	0001				ABR	

Figure 5.70 DataSource Status

SAP-Delivered DataSource Activation Report

In some scenarios, you might need to activate a DataSource using SAP-delivered
reports. There might be some instances where the replication of a DataSource will not
activate the DataSource as expected, in which case using SAP-delivered report RSDS_
DATASOURCE_ACTIVATE_ALL will help you. This report will be very handy in implementation and support projects.

14. The process of replicating a DataSource is common for all extraction scenarios. The
DataSource must be active before it's used for extraction. Use Transaction SE38 to
execute report RSDS_DATASOURCE_ACTIVATE_ALL, as shown in Figure 5.71.

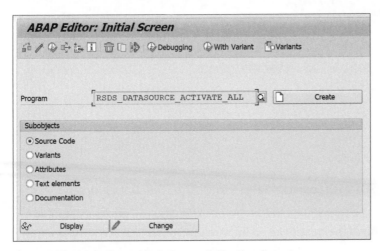

Figure 5.71 SAP-Delivered DataSource Activation Report

15. Provide the name of the **DataSource** and the **Source System** to start activation, as
shown in Figure 5.72.

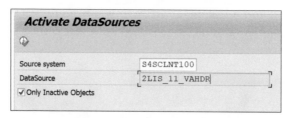

Figure 5.72 Selections for DataSource Activation

16. Note that the report will work on inactive objects if the **Only Inactive Objects** check-box is selected. If the object is already active, then you can uncheck it, as we've done here because the DataSource is already active. In a real-world scenario, you'll often use this report for inactive DataSources. Once you click **Execute** or press ⌐F8⌐, the DataSource will be activated. You can see the results in Figure 5.73.

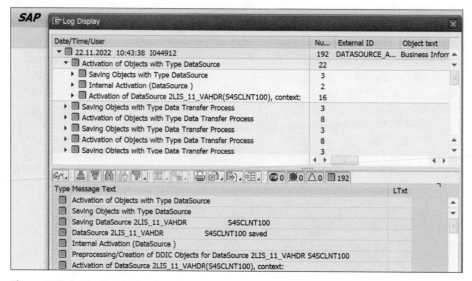

Figure 5.73 Activation Log

Now you have successfully replicated the DataSource from the source system and activated it.

5.3.2 Creating aDSOs with Logistics Sales and Distribution DataSources

Once you've activated a DataSource in SAP BW/4HANA, you can create a dataflow for extraction. This involves the creation of an InfoArea and other SAP BW/4HANA objects for data persistency.

Creating an InfoArea

Let's start by creating an InfoArea for the example project, using these steps:

1. Create an InfoArea as shown in Figure 5.74. (Refer back to Chapter 2 for more information on creating InfoAreas.)

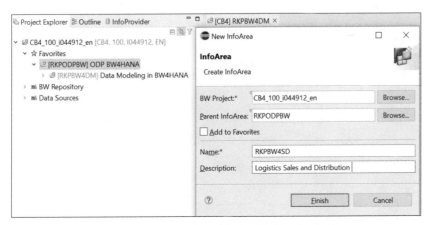

Figure 5.74 Info Area for Logistics Sales and Distribution Extraction

2. After you finish creating the InfoArea, you can see the **RKPBWSD** subfolder, as shown in Figure 5.75.

Figure 5.75 Info Area after Creation

Creating Logistics Sales and Distribution Header aDSO

Once the InfoArea is created, the next step is to create the aDSO based on the two Data-Sources that you activated. To create an aDSO, follow these steps:

1. Creating a logistics-sales and distribution header aDSO. Right-click on **Logistics Sales and Distribution** from the **Project Explorer**, then select **New • DataStore Object (advanced)**, as shown in Figure 5.76.

2. You can create an aDSO based on the 2LIS_11_VAHDR SD header DataSource. You learned how to create an aDSO in Chapter 2. Now enter the following information, as shown in Figure 5.77:

   ❶ Provide the aDSO **Name (ZSDHDR)** and **Description**.

   ❷ Choose the **DataSource** that will be used as a reference for the aDSO creation along with the source system. You can use the **Browse** option to choose the **Data-Source** and **Source System**.

   ❸ Complete the process by clicking **Finish**.

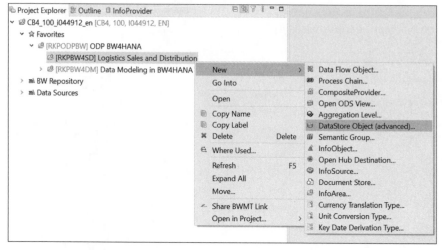

Figure 5.76 aDSO Creation

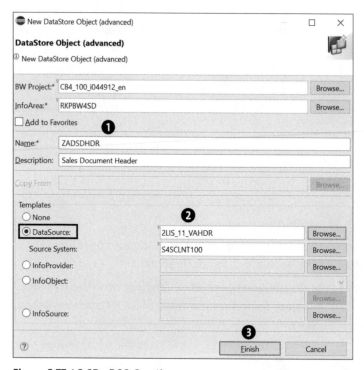

Figure 5.77 LO SD aDSO Creation

3. You'll see the aDSO maintenance screen. Choose the options as shown in Figure 5.78. Choose the **Standard DataStore Object** radio button and the **Write Change Log** checkbox, which can be seen in the **General** tab.

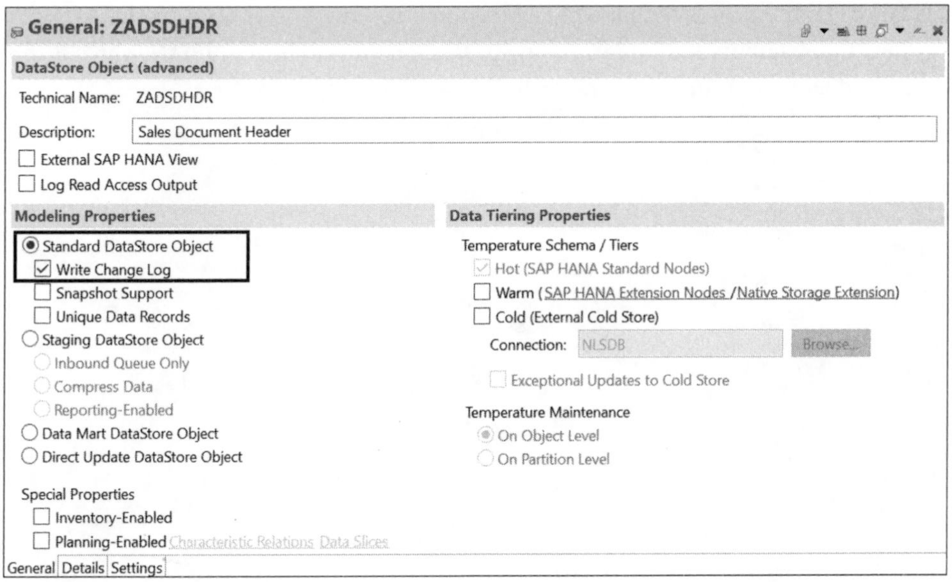

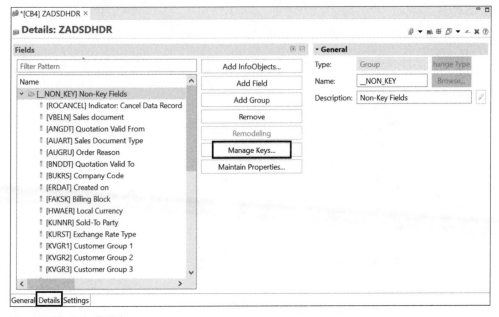

Figure 5.78 aDSO Maintenance

4. Once the **General** tab details are populated, choose the **Details** tab at the bottom to see the screen shown in Figure 5.79. On this tab, you can choose the primary key for the aDSO. This key will enable the aDSO to do aggregations such as overwriting when there are duplicate records.

Figure 5.79 Details Tab

5. You need to make sure that when you choose the key, you choose a *primary key* (a field that has a unique value). In the SD DataSource, that field is **VBELN**, which is the sales document number, as shown in Figure 5.80.

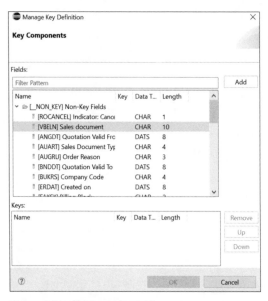

Figure 5.80 Choose Key Fields

6. Once you double-click the key, you can see it in the **Keys** window, as shown in Figure 5.81.

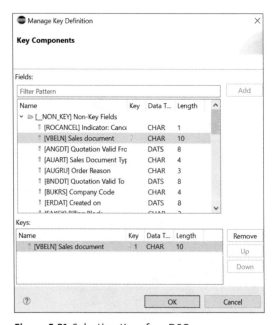

Figure 5.81 Selecting Keys for aDSO

7.   Choose **OK** to complete the process. This will take you to the screen shown in Figure 5.82. You can leave the **Settings** tab as it is for now. You'll see that the icon for the aDSO is not active.

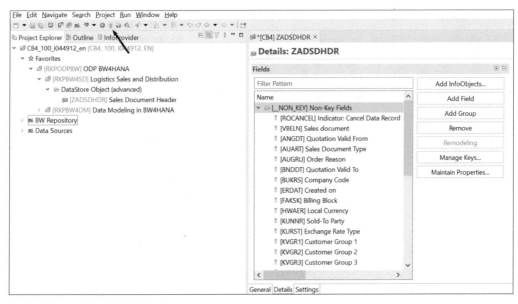

Figure 5.82 Activating aDSOs

8.   Once the aDSO is activated using the 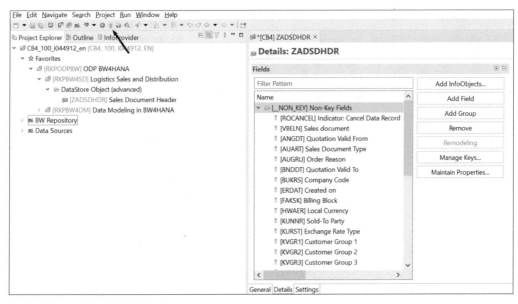 icon in the SAP BW modeling tools, you'll see that the aDSO will look as shown in Figure 5.83.

Figure 5.83 aDSO after Activation

9.   Follow the same steps you used earlier to create the second aDSO for the SD item. You can name the new ADSO ZASDITM. Here ITM means item. Choose the DataSource as 2LIS_11_VAITM from S4SCLNT100, as shown in Figure 5.84.

10. Once you choose **Finish**, follow the same steps as for in general table based on Figure 5.84, then choose the **Details** tab, but in this aDSO, you need to have two key fields: sales document header (**VBELN**) and sales document item number (**POSNR**). Every sales document will have a line item, which helps to identify duplicates during the extraction process (see Figure 5.85).

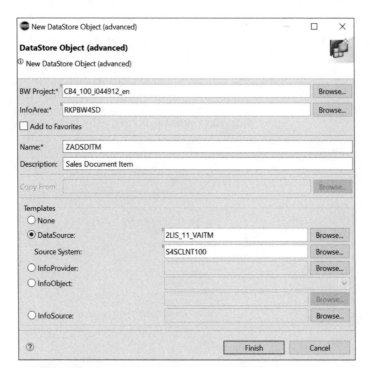

Figure 5.84 LO SD Item aDSO

Figure 5.85 LO SD Item aDSO

11. Now you can activate the aDSO, and the status will be as shown in Figure 5.86.

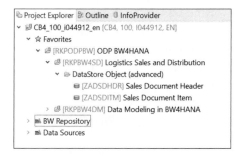

Figure 5.86 aDSO List

You now know how to create an aDSO based on the DataSource. Do you know why we created two aDSOs, one for the header and one for the item? The reason is that we join the contents of these two aDSOs with an SAP HANA composite provider using the appropriate primary key for our reporting requirements.

Creating Transformations

Next you can create your SAP BW/4HANA-based transformations for the aDSOs you have created. To do this, you can follow these steps:

1. Return to the aDSO for the logistics-sales and distribution header (ZADSDHDR). From the context menu, choose **New • Transformation**, as shown in Figure 5.87.

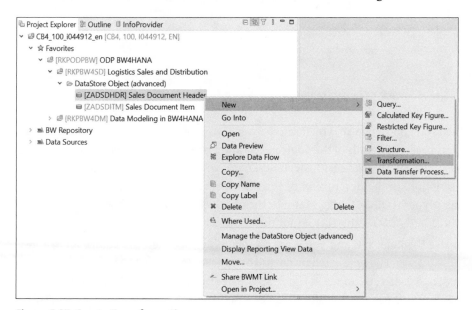

Figure 5.87 Create Transformation

2. On the next screen, you can see that the **Target** fields are populated automatically because you're creating a transformation from a target object that is an aDSO. Next

you need to choose the source object type for the transformation and the object name, which will create the mappings between the source and the target aDSO. Provide the object name as DataSource. For this demo, we choose the associated name **2LIS_11_VAHDR** which is the DataSource for the logistics-sales and distribution header. Make sure you choose the DataSource from the right ODP sender source system. In our case we are getting data from the **S4SCLNT100** system, which is SAP S/4HANA, and thus you can see the logical system name along with the DataSource in Figure 5.88.

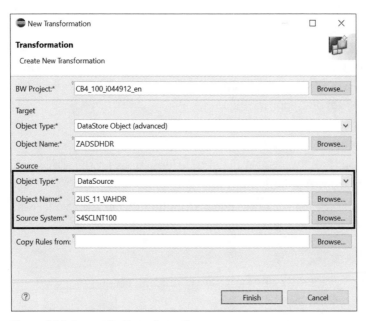

Figure 5.88 Source for Transformation

3. Once you choose **Finish**, you'll see the transformation maintenance screen, where you can see the details of the **Source** and **Target** objects in the **General** tab, as shown in Figure 5.89. You can see the technical name of the transformation along with the description. In the description of the transformation, you'll see the transportable object type (TLOGO). In this example, the TLOGO is **RSDS**, which stands for the Data-Source, and **ADSO** is the TLOGO for the aDSO.

4. Choose the **Rules** tab and you'll see the mappings between the **Source** and **Target**. These rules will be populated by default as you created the aDSO based on the same DataSource. As you can see in Figure 5.90, **Sales Document (VBELN)** from DataSource **2LIS_11_VAHDR** is mapped to sales document (**VBELN**) in the target aDSO (**ZADS-DHDR**) to the **VBELN** field. These mappings are very important as they enable the dataflow from the source fields to the target fields.

Figure 5.89 Transformation Creation: General Tab

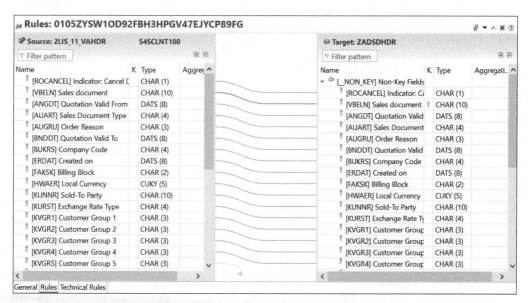

Figure 5.90 Transformation Rules Tab

5. Choose the **Technical Rules** tab in transformation maintenance. This has mappings to the target ORECORDMODE field. There is no need to change anything here. The screen should look as shown in Figure 5.91.

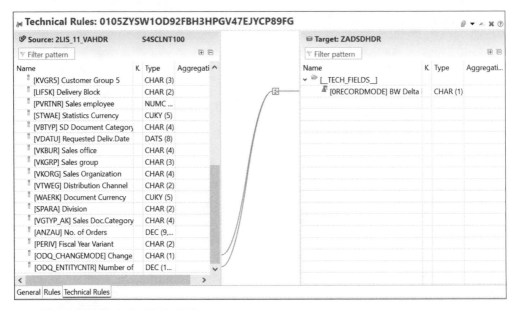

Figure 5.91 Technical Rules Tab

6. Once you have validated the **General**, **Rules**, and **Technical Rules** tabs of the transformation, you can activate the transformation using the **Activate** icon ![icon] in Eclipse. Once the transformation is activated, you can see the details as shown in Figure 5.92.

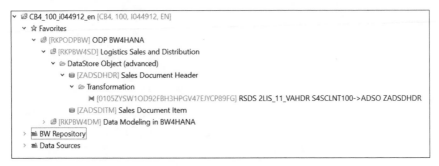

Figure 5.92 Transformation: Logistics Header aDSO

7. Repeat the same steps to create a new transformation for an aDSO for the LO SD item ZADSITM. For this aDSO, the source will be the sales document item DataSource, which is **2LIS_11_VAITM**, based on S4SCLNT10. The item DataSource will have an additional key field of the item number along with the header number. The mappings in Figure 5.93 show how the sales document (**VBELN**) along with item (**POSNR**) fields from DataSource 2LIS_11_VAITM are mapped to the target ZADSDITM aDSO.

8. Once you activate the transformation using the ![icon] icon, you can see the final status as shown in Figure 5.94.

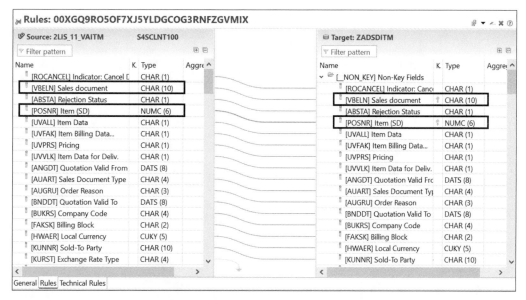

Figure 5.93 Transformation Rules: Sales Item aDSO

Figure 5.94 Transformation after Activation

Creating DTPs

Once you have created the transformation for the DataSource and aDSO, you can create the DTP for the same. Follow these steps:

1. First, expand the logistics header aDSO folder and find the **Transformation** folder. Choose **New · Data Transfer Process...** from the context menu, as shown in Figure 5.95.

2. You'll see the popup shown in Figure 5.96, which provides the source and target details for the DTP. The source is DataSource 2LIS_11_VAHDR and the target is aDSO ZADSDHDR.

3. Once you choose **Next**, you'll see the confirmation screen, which will give the source and target objects as shown in Figure 5.97. Click **Finish**.

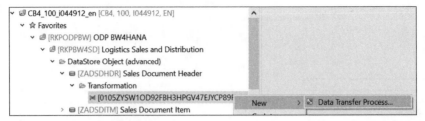

Figure 5.95 Create DTP for LO Header

Figure 5.96 LO Header DTP Source and Target

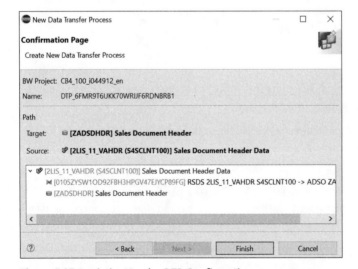

Figure 5.97 Logistics Header DTP Confirmation

4. The DTP maintenance screen will now be available. It shows the source and target object names, and it has multiple tabs. **General** will be the first tab shown. It contains the extraction mode and package size settings, which you can see in Figure 5.98.

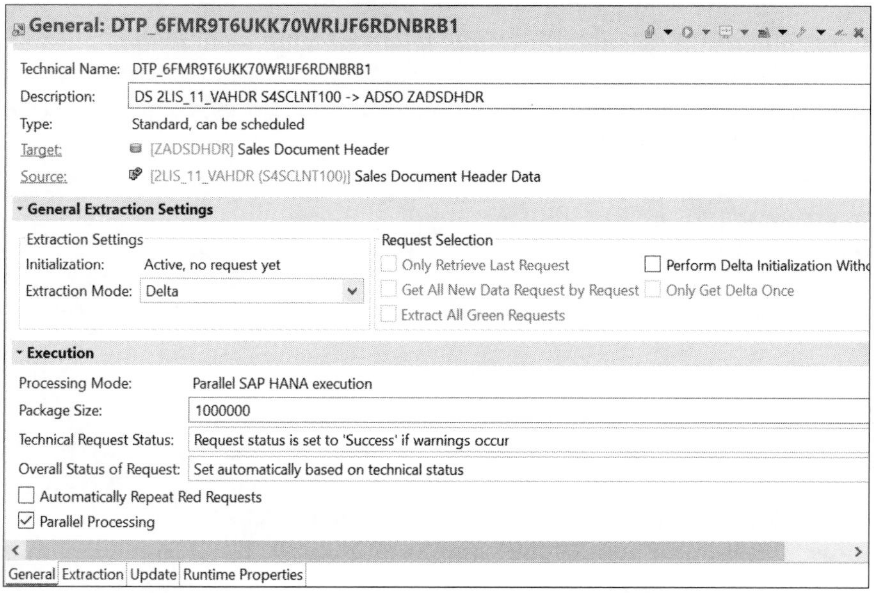

General: DTP_6FMR9T6UKK70WRIJF6RDNBRB1	
Technical Name:	DTP_6FMR9T6UKK70WRIJF6RDNBRB1
Description:	DS 2LIS_11_VAHDR S4SCLNT100 -> ADSO ZADSDHDR
Type:	Standard, can be scheduled
Target:	[ZADSDHDR] Sales Document Header
Source:	[2LIS_11_VAHDR (S4SCLNT100)] Sales Document Header Data

▾ General Extraction Settings

Extraction Settings

| Initialization: | Active, no request yet |
| Extraction Mode: | Delta |

Request Selection

☐ Only Retrieve Last Request   ☐ Perform Delta Initialization With...
☐ Get All New Data Request by Request   ☐ Only Get Delta Once
☐ Extract All Green Requests

▾ Execution

Processing Mode:	Parallel SAP HANA execution
Package Size:	1000000
Technical Request Status:	Request status is set to 'Success' if warnings occur
Overall Status of Request:	Set automatically based on technical status
☐ Automatically Repeat Red Requests	
☑ Parallel Processing	

General | Extraction | Update | Runtime Properties

Figure 5.98 Logistics Header DTP Maintenance

DTP Extraction Mode

You can see that the extraction mode is delta in the DTP, which is the default setting. But when you execute the DTP for the first time, it will function like a full update in that it will fetch all historical records and update the timestamp for the next delta extraction.

---

5. Click the next tab, **Extraction**. It shows that **Adapter** is set to **Extraction from SAP System by Operational Data Provisioning**, and **ODP Context** is of type **DataSources/ Extractors**. There is also an option to filter the data extraction based on certain fields that are available. You can choose these to restrict the data, as shown in Figure 5.99.

6. Next, we'll walk through the other two tabs, **Update** and **Runtime Properties**. In the **Update** tab, you have a **Trigger Database Merge** option and an **Error Handling** requests option. You can leave the default settings as they are, as shown in Figure 5.100. In **Runtime Properties**, you can define the number of parallel processes and choose background servers for optimal performance when there is a large volume of data, as shown in Figure 5.101.

In the **Runtime Properties** tab, you'll see the **Number of Parallel Process** for background processing. Setting this number to its maximum value will enable more parallelization, as shown in Figure 5.101.

7. Once all settings are maintained, you can activate the DTP using the ⚙ icon, and it will be visible in the data flow under the **DataStore Object (Advanced)** folder, as shown in Figure 5.102. The folder contains the ZADSDHDR aDSO, which has the Data-Source 2LIS_11_VAHDR transformation that gets data from table RSDS, and a DTP is created based on this transformation.

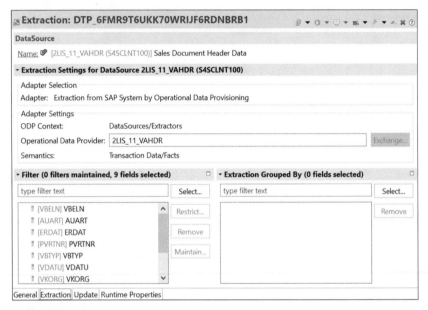

Figure 5.99 DTP: Extraction Tab for LO Header

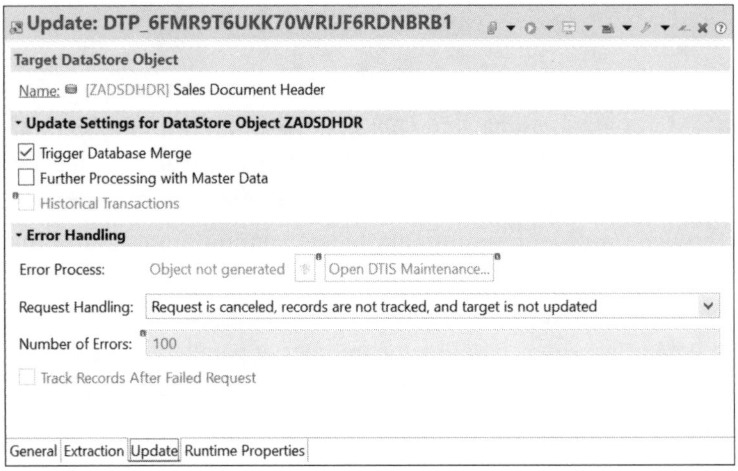

Figure 5.100 Update Tab

Figure 5.101 Runtime Properties Tab

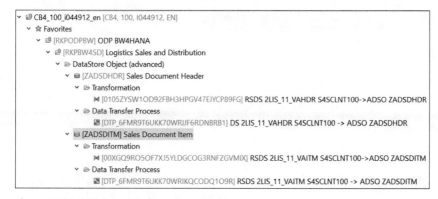

Figure 5.102 LO Header Data Flow

8. Follow the same steps that you did for creating the DTP for the ZADSDHDR sales document header aDSO to create the DTP for the ZADSDITM sales document item aDSO. Figure 5.103 shows the flow after the DTP is created.

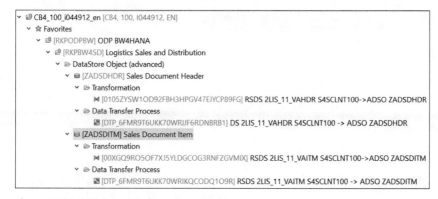

Figure 5.103 DTP For LO Sales Document Item

5.3.3   Data Extraction from SAP S/4HANA to SAP BW/4HANA: Full Upload

Once you've created DTPs for both the aDSOs, ZADSDHDR for the header and ZADSDITM for the item, you can execute the DTP to load data from SAP S/4HANA to SAP BW/4HANA for both DTPs. The first execution of the DTP will bring in all the records from the setup table that you filled in a *full upload*. But before that, you can see the total contents of the setup table in SAP S/4HANA for the two different DataSources. To do so, use Transaction RSA3 for the DataSource **2LIS_11_VAHDR,** which is for the sales header, and the result will show that 6,712 records are extracted (see Figure 5.104).

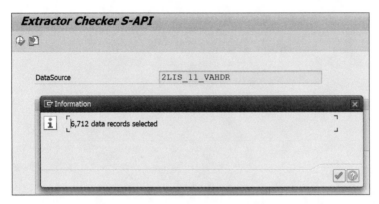

Figure 5.104 Simulation for 2LIS_11_VAHDR

Execute Transaction RSA3 in SAP S/4HANA system to see the total records for 2LIS_11_VAITM. You can see that 6,780 records will be extracted (see Figure 5.105).

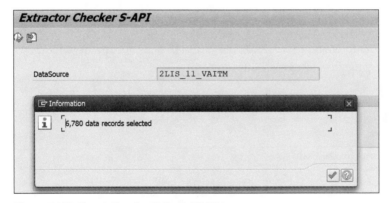

Figure 5.105 Simulation for 2LIS_11_VAITM

With the total records in SAP S/4HANA, if you now execute the DTP for the first time using the ⬤ ▼ icon, it will extract all these records into SAP BW/4HANA. Execute the DTP for the sales document header aDSO as shown in Figure 5.106.

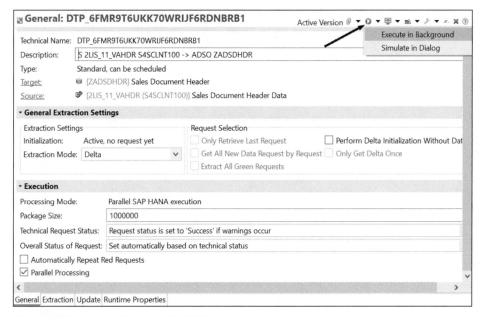

Figure 5.106 Execute Sales Header DTP

Once you execute the DTP, it pops up a message with a **Execute and Open Monitor** option, which you should select. This will take you to SAP BW/4HANA web cockpit. Provide your user name and password if you're using it for the first time, as shown in Figure 5.107.

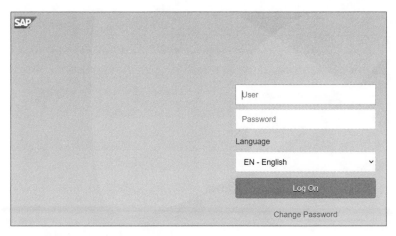

Figure 5.107 SAP BW/4HANA Web cockpit

Once you log into the web cockpit, you can see the status of the extraction, as shown in Figure 5.108.

You can see that 6,712 data records are selected, which matches the results of Transaction RSA3, shown earlier in Figure 5.104. These records will be in the inbound table of the aDSO. Now you need to activate this request to move it and change the log table and active table. For that, you need to click **Manage Request**, shown in Figure 5.108.

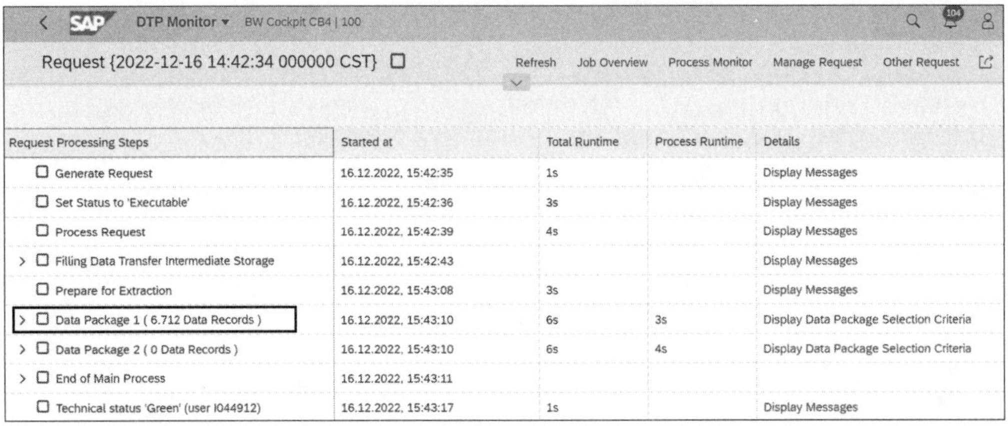

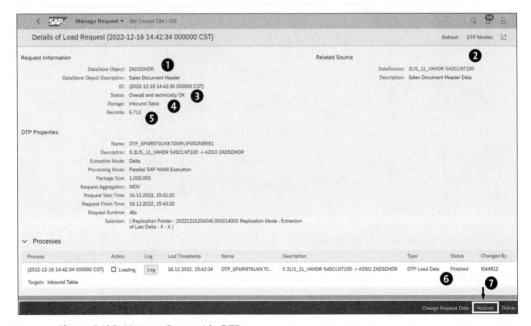

Figure 5.108 DTP Status

This will take you to the screen shown in Figure 5.109, which shows the following options:

❶ aDSO name

❷ Source name; here, DataSource 2LIS_11_VAHDR

Figure 5.109 Manage Request in DTP

❸ Overall status of DTP extraction

❹ aDSO table details, with data records now in the inbound table

❺ Total records extracted

❻ Final status of DTP extraction

❼ **Activate** button to enable you to activate the aDSO request and move data from the inbound table to the active and change log tables

Let's first check the contents of the inbound table. To do so, click **Inbound Table**, and you will see the options shown in Figure 5.110.

Request Information

DataStore Object:	ZADSDHDR
DataStore Object Description:	Sales Document Header
ID:	{2022-12-16 14:42:34 000000 CST}
Status:	Overall and tech
Storage:	Inbound Table
Records:	6,712

Definition

Contents

Figure 5.110 Inbound Table Contents

Select **Contents** to see the contents of the inbound table, as shown in Figure 5.111.

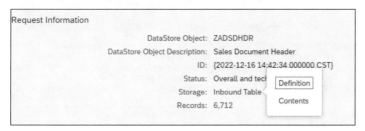

Display Inbound Table of ZADSDHDR

Table Size: 6,712
Matching Filter: 6,712

REQTSN:	DATAPAKID:	RECORD:	Max Rows:
=2022121620423400000000 ⊗			200

Adapt Filters Go

Details

REQTSN	DATAPAKID	RECORD	RECORDMODE	VBELN	ROCAN...	ANGDT	AUART	AUGRU	BNDDT	BUKRS	ERDAT	FAKS
{2022-12-16 14:42:34 000000 CST}	1	1		0000000002			TA			1710	06.10.2017	
{2022-12-16 14:42:34 000000 CST}	1	2		0000000003			TA			1710	06.10.2017	
{2022-12-16 14:42:34 000000 CST}	1	3		0000000004			TA			1710	08.10.2017	
{2022-12-16 14:42:34 000000 CST}	1	4		0000000022			TA			1710	08.10.2017	
{2022-12-16 14:42:34 000000 CST}	1	5		0000000023			TA			1710	08.10.2017	
{2022-12-16 14:42:34 000000 CST}	1	6		0000000024			TA			1710	08.10.2017	
{2022-12-16 14:42:34 000000 CST}	1	7		0000000025			TA			1710	08.10.2017	
{2022-12-16 14:42:34 000000 CST}	1	8		0000000026			TA			1710	08.10.2017	
{2022-12-16 14:42:34 000000 CST}	1	9		0000000027			TA			1710	08.10.2017	
{2022-12-16 14:42:34 000000 CST}	1	10		0000000028			TA			1710	08.10.2017	
{2022-12-16 14:42:34 000000 CST}	1	11		0000000029			TA			1710	08.10.2017	

Display In Internal Format Manage

Figure 5.111 Inbound Table Contents

You can also see the same contents in the backend. To do so, log onto the SAP BW/4HANA GUI, open Transaction SE16, and search for the aDSO tables. To find the tables related to the aDSOs, you can enter "*<aDSOName>*" as shown in Figure 5.112. In our example, we'll enter "*ADSDHDR*", which is the header aDSO name.

Select the inbound table that ends with 1, and when you see the contents of the table, you can view the same records (as shown in Figure 5.113 and Figure 5.114) that you saw in the SAP BW/4HANA web cockpit.

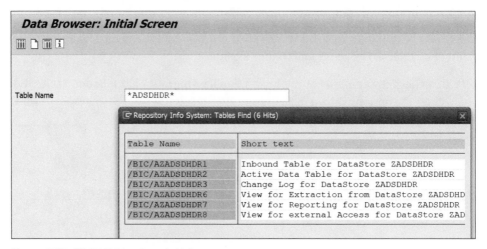

Figure 5.112 ADSO Tables Search Help

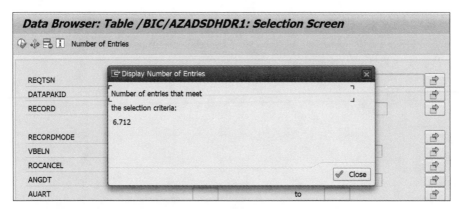

Figure 5.113 Inbound Table Entries

	REQTSN	DATAPAKID	RECORD	RECORDMODE	VBELN	ROCANCEL	ANGDT	AUART	AUGRU	BNDDT	BUKRS	ERDAT	FAKSK	HWAER	KUNNR
	20221216204234000000000	000001	1		0000000002			TA			1710	06.10.2017		USD	0017100003
	20221216204234000000000	000001	2		0000000003			TA			1710	06.10.2017		USD	0017100001
	20221216204234000000000	000001	3		0000000004			TA			1710	08.10.2017		USD	USCU_L10
	20221216204234000000000	000001	4		0000000022			TA			1710	08.10.2017		USD	USCU_L10
	20221216204234000000000	000001	5		0000000023			TA			1710	08.10.2017		USD	USCU_S07
	20221216204234000000000	000001	6		0000000024			TA			1710	08.10.2017		USD	USCU_S03
	20221216204234000000000	000001	7		0000000025			TA			1710	08.10.2017		USD	USCU_S15
	20221216204234000000000	000001	8		0000000026			TA			1710	08.10.2017		USD	USCU_L04
	20221216204234000000000	000001	9		0000000027			TA			1710	08.10.2017		USD	USCU_L02
	20221216204234000000000	000001	10		0000000028			TA			1710	08.10.2017		USD	USCU_L09
	20221216204234000000000	000001	11		0000000029			TA			1710	08.10.2017		USD	USCU_S05

Figure 5.114 Inbound Table Contents

Note that the active table and change log table will be empty at this time. Check the active table for the aDSO (see Figure 5.115) that ends with 2; you can get this result in the list when you search for "*<aDSONAME>*" in Transaction SE16 as you saw earlier in Figure 5.112.

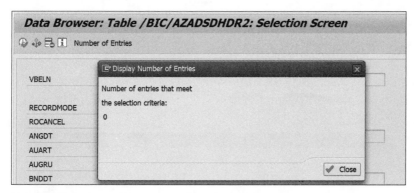

Figure 5.115 Active Table Entries: Before Activation

After you've checked the entries in active table, the next step is to check the change log table. You can find the change log table by viewing the aDSO table that ends with 3. For the change log table, choose the number of entries and you'll see the results shown in Figure 5.116.

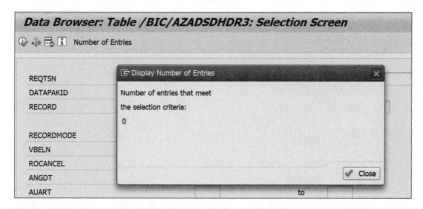

Figure 5.116 Change Log Table Entries: Before Activation

If you choose the ⟨ icon, you'll go back to the manage request screen, which you saw earlier in Figure 5.109. Click the **Activate** option on this screen, and it will take you to the screen shown in Figure 5.117. Click **Activate** again.

Figure 5.117 Activation of Request

When you click **Refresh**, you can see the request count increase in the **Processes** section. The details are as shown in Figure 5.118:

❶ The first execution of DTP created entries in the inbound table.

❷ The activation of the inbound request moved the data from the inbound table to the active and change log tables.

Figure 5.118 aDSO Request: After Activation

❸ After the data was moved to the active and change log tables, the entries in the inbound table were deleted.

❹ If you click the link to the right of **Activation Request**, shown in Figure 5.118, it will take you to the screen shown in Figure 5.119.

Figure 5.119 Activation Request Contents

If you select the **Active Data Table** and choose **Contents**, you will see the records there, as shown in Figure 5.120.

VBELN	RECORDMODE	ROCANCEL	ANGDT	AUART	AUGRU	BNDDT	BUKRS	ERDAT	FAKSK	HWAER	KUNNR
0000000002	N			TA			1710	06.10.2017		USD	0017100003
0000000003	N			TA			1710	06.10.2017		USD	0017100001
0000000004	N			TA			1710	08.10.2017		USD	USCU_L10
0000000022	N			TA			1710	08.10.2017		USD	USCU_L10
0000000023	N			TA			1710	08.10.2017		USD	USCU_S07
0000000024	N			TA			1710	08.10.2017		USD	USCU_S03
0000000025	N			TA			1710	08.10.2017		USD	USCU_S15
0000000026	N			TA			1710	08.10.2017		USD	USCU_L04
0000000027	N			TA			1710	08.10.2017		USD	USCU_L02

Figure 5.120 Active Table Records

The records will be decreased here when there is any aggregation. Now you can see the contents of all tables again by choosing the inbound table that ends with 1 and checking the number of entries. The number of entries in the inbound table is now zero, as shown in Figure 5.121.

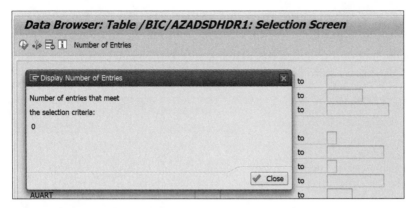

Figure 5.121 Inbound Table: After Activation

Check the active table: it might have reduced entries due to aggregation (see Figure 5.122).

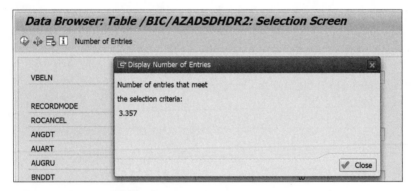

Figure 5.122 Active Table: After Activation

Also check the change log table after activation (see Figure 5.123).

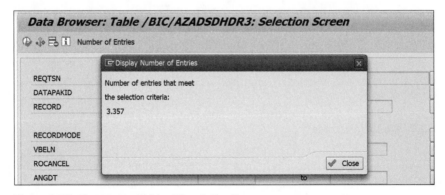

Figure 5.123 Change Log Table: After Activation

In the change log, you can see a field called **RECORDMODE**, which is in the fourth column of the change log table. It helps to maintain the delta consistency, as shown in Figure 5.124.

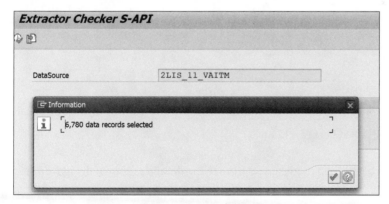

Data Browser: Table /BIC/AZADSDHDR3 Select Entries   200

REQTSN	DATAPAKID	RECORD	RECORDMODE	VBELN	ROCANCEL	ANGDT	AUART	AUGRU	BNDDT	BUKRS	ERDAT	FAKSK	HWAER	KUNNR
20221216212706000007000	000001	1	N	0000000002			TA			1710	06.10.2017		USD	0017100003
20221216212706000007000	000001	2	N	0000000003			TA			1710	06.10.2017		USD	0017100001
20221216212706000007000	000001	3	N	0000000004			TA			1710	08.10.2017		USD	USCU_L10
20221216212706000007000	000001	4	N	0000000022			TA			1710	08.10.2017		USD	USCU_L10
20221216212706000007000	000001	5	N	0000000023			TA			1710	08.10.2017		USD	USCU_S07
20221216212706000007000	000001	6	N	0000000024			TA			1710	08.10.2017		USD	USCU_S03
20221216212706000007000	000001	7	N	0000000025			TA			1710	08.10.2017		USD	USCU_S15
20221216212706000007000	000001	8	N	0000000026			TA			1710	08.10.2017		USD	USCU_L04
20221216212706000007000	000001	9	N	0000000027			TA			1710	08.10.2017		USD	USCU_L02
20221216212706000007000	000001	10	N	0000000028			TA			1710	08.10.2017		USD	USCU_L09
20221216212706000007000	000001	11	N	0000000029			TA			1710	08.10.2017		USD	USCU_S05
20221216212706000007000	000001	12	N	0000000030			TA			1710	08.10.2017		USD	USCU_S17
20221216212706000007000	000001	13	N	0000000031			TA			1710	08.10.2017		USD	USCU_L03
20221216212706000007000	000001	14	N	0000000032			TA			1710	08.10.2017		USD	USCU_L08

Figure 5.124 Change Log Table: Record Mode

As you saw in the previous section, the value of **RECORDMODE** will be based on the value of primary key. Here the value **N** in the **RECORDMODE** field indicates that for this aDSO, this is a new record.

Next, we'll discuss data loading for the sales document item. You'll follow the same steps to load the data for the sales document item aDSO that you did for loading the sales document header aDSO. View the Transaction RSA3 results before you start, as shown in Figure 5.125.

Extractor Checker S-API

DataSource   2LIS_11_VAITM

Information

ℹ   6,780 data records selected

Figure 5.125 DataSource 2LIS_11_VAITM in RSA3

Now you can load the DTP. You can see that it loaded the same number of records, as shown in Figure 5.126.

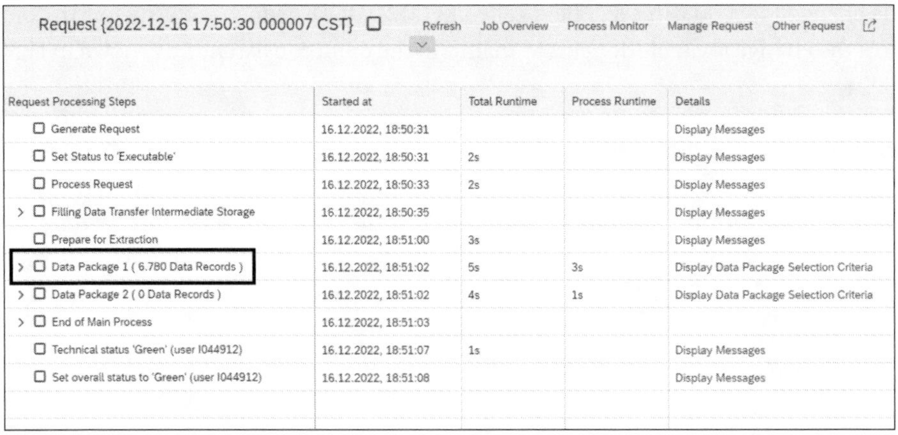

Figure 5.126 DTP Load status

When you select **Manage Request**, you can see the details, as shown in Figure 5.127.

Figure 5.127 Inbound Table Checks for Item

After the activation of the load request, you can see the details as shown in Figure 5.128.

Now you know how to load the DTP and activate the request in an aDSO. In the next section, we'll see how this was handled in the ODP in SAP S/4HANA.

Figure 5.128 After Activation

5.4 Transaction ODQMON: Logistics Full Upload

When the DTP is executed, it creates a request for extraction and is sent to the source system—S4SCLNT100 in our case. You can use Transaction ODQMON to monitor the status of the extraction during the runtime. With the DTP job completed, let's check the transaction in SAP S/4HANA to understand the extraction process. Now, log into SAP S/4HANA and execute Transaction ODQMON.

Figure 5.129 shows the details of the transaction:

❶ In the **Provider** field, choose **BW DataSource** as you're using the SAP-delivered Data-Source for extraction.

❷ The subscriber is SAP BW/4HANA, so you need to choose **SAP Business Warehouse** for the **Subscriber Type**.

❸ Choose the **Subscriber**; in our case, it's the system ID of SAP BW/4HANA, which is **CB4CLNT100**.

❹ In **Request Select**, choose **Subscriptions Only (Delta Init + Delta)**. There is also an option to choose **All** from the dropdown.

❺ In the **Queue** area, you can see the queue description. If you need to see the technical name, then you need to press the wrench icon ❾.

❻ In **Queue: Status**, you can see if the queue is active or inactive.

❼ You can see the total subscriptions in the **Subscrptns** column.

❽ The total request count can be derived from the **Requests** column.

❾ When you click the wrench icon, the queue descriptions ❺ will change to technical names. Most often, SAP BW consultants prefer to use technical names instead of descriptions.

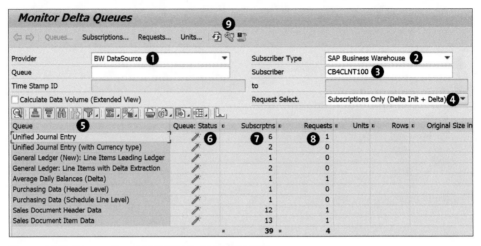

Figure 5.129 Transaction ODQMON in SAP S/4HANA

Click the wrench icon ❾ and you'll see the queue technical names, which include the DataSource names 2LIS_11_VAHDR and 2LIS_11_VAITM, as shown in Figure 5.130.

Monitor Delta Queues

Provider	BW DataSource	▾		Subscriber Type	SAP Business Warehouse	▾	
Queue				Subscriber	CB4CLNT100		
Time Stamp ID				to			
☐ Calculate Data Volume (Extended View)				Request Select.	Subscriptions Only (Delta Init + Delta)	▾	

Queue	Queue: Status	Subscrptns	Requests	Units	Rows	Original Size in Bytes	Compressed Size
0FI_ACDOCA_10	🖊	6	1				
0FI_ACDOCA_20	🖊	2	0				
0FI_GL_14	🖊	1	0				
0FI_GL_4	🖊	2	0				
0FI_GL_61	🖊	1	1				
2LIS_02_HDR	🖊	1	0				
2LIS_02_SCL	🖊	1	0				
2LIS_11_VAHDR	🖊	12	1				
2LIS_11_VAITM	🖊	13	1				
	▪	39 ▪	4				

Figure 5.130 Transaction ODQMON with Technical Names

Double-click **2LIS_11_VAHDR**, which has 12 subscriptions and one request. That will take you to the **Subscriptions** details screen shown in Figure 5.131, with the **Subscription** time stamp and the **Last TSN Confirmed** date and the **Created On** date. Note that the subscription is created by an SAP BW background user for the source system: **ALEREMOTE1**.

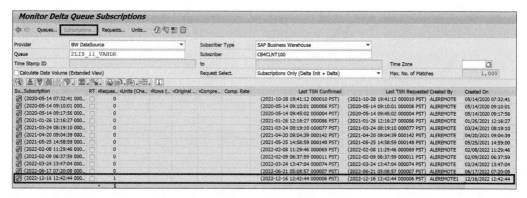

Figure 5.131 Transaction ODQMON: Subscriptions

You can click the **Subscription** row to see more details, as shown in Figure 5.132.

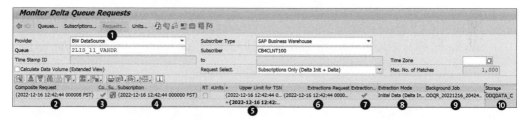

Figure 5.132 Transaction ODQMON: Request Details

Note that in Transaction ODQMON the composite request time is based on PST, but in SAP BW/4HANA it was CST, so there will be a difference of two hours between the two time zones (i.e., CST is two hours ahead of PST). If you see the time in the SAP BW/4HANA system, it will be **{2022-12-16 14:42:34 000000 CST}**, as shown earlier in the **ID** field in Figure 5.110. But it's **{2022-12-16 12:42:44 000008 PST}** in Transaction ODQMON in Figure 5.132.

Now let's walk through the details of the **Requests** screen:

❶ The **Requests** button is greyed out, indicating you are in the requests area.

❷ The **Composite Request** column number is filled with the PST time stamp.

❸ The **Composite Request Status** column has a green checkmark.

❹ The **Subscription** column is filled with the time stamp.

❺ The **Upper Limit for TSN** column is selected based on the subscription time stamp.

❻ The request that is generated from SAP BW/4HANA is filled in the **Extractions Request** column.

❼ The final status of the extraction request is shown as successful.

❽ The **Extraction Mode** is **Initial Data** because it's the first load.

⑨ The SAP BW/4HANA extraction request will trigger a job for ODP extraction, and that job name will start with ODQR*.

⑩ The table where the data is stored, table ODQDATA_C, will be used for this initial load.

If you need to recheck the time stamp, you can have a quick look in the DTP extraction monitor in the web cockpit. The **ID** field shows the timestamp (Figure 5.133).

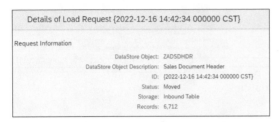

Details of Load Request {2022-12-16 14:42:34 000000 CST}

Request Information

DataStore Object:	ZADSDHDR
DataStore Object Description:	Sales Document Header
ID:	{2022-12-16 14:42:34 000000 CST}
Status:	Moved
Storage:	Inbound Table
Records:	6,712

Figure 5.133 Request ID in SAP BW/4HANA

As shown in Figure 5.132, in Transaction ODQMON, from the queue view, you can go to the units view. There, click the **Composite Request** number and it will take you to the units section, as shown in Figure 5.134.

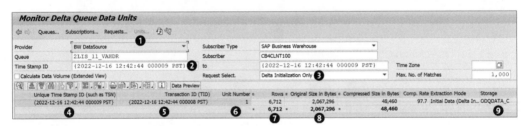

Figure 5.134 Transaction ODQMON: Units

You can see the following details on this screen:

① **Units** is greyed out, which means you're in the units section.

② Timestamp ID is generated based on the extraction time.

③ Because the DTP is executed for the first time, this is a delta initialization, which sets the time.

④ The TSN is based on the extraction time.

⑤ The transaction ID is again based on the time.

⑥ The unit number increased based on extraction.

⑦ The rows count (6,712) gives you the total number of data records. You can validate this in the SAP BW/4HANA aDSO.

⑧ The original size will be compressed in ODP. In this case, the rate is 97.7.

⑨ The storage is in table ODQDATA_C.

5.5   Delta Extraction based on ODP in Logistics Extraction

You've seen how to extract the full upload in SAP BW/4HANA. But consider that if an organization is already using SAP S/4HANA for ERP automation, it will have active document postings when the SAP BW/4HANA implementation is going on. So, the implementation steps involve extracting all the historical data from SAP S/4HANA to a certain time, and that's done with a full upload, which initializes the time stamp of extraction. Once the DTP is executed the first time, it will be like a full upload with delta initialization. It will bring the records from the setup table, and the same execution time stamp is set in the ERP system, which will try to look for any new and changed records for associated tables related to the DataSource that is initialized. These records will be stored in the delta queue. With ODP, you can view these records in Transaction ODMON. And when you execute the DTP from SAP BW/4HANA again, these delta records are extracted; this process is called *delta extraction*.

In this section, we'll explain the basic settings to enable the delta in LO extraction. We'll also discuss the update mode settings. Then we'll post the documents in SAP S/4HANA that will enable the delta postings to be extracted to SAP BW/4HANA. You'll learn how to extract the delta in LO extraction, and finally we'll check Transaction ODQMON to see the status of the delta extraction and check multiple views for data reconciliation.

5.5.1   Settings for Logistics Delta Extraction in SAP S/4HANA

As you learned in Section 5.1.3, there are many types of update modes in Transaction LBWE. To check the status of an update mode, you can open the transaction again, as shown in Figure 5.135.

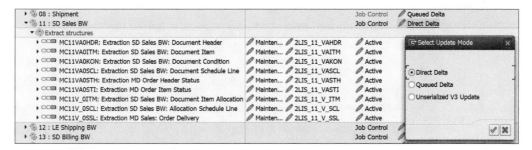

Figure 5.135 Update Modes in LO

All the LO DataSources have these update modes: **Direct Delta**, **Queued Delta**, and **Unserialized V3 Update**. You can choose the type of mode that you need. Let's look first at queue delta mode, which is used widely across all organizations. It's shown in Figure 5.136.

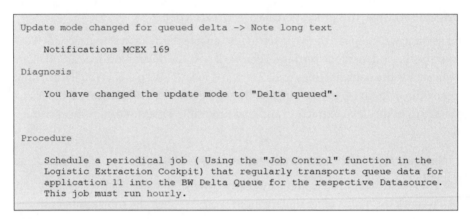

Figure 5.136 Update Mode Selection

When the **Queued Delta** update mode is selected, you'll see the popup shown in Figure 5.137, which specifies the steps that you need to do. Choose the enter icon ✔, then provide the transport request if prompted by a popup.

```
Update mode changed for queued delta -> Note long text

    Notifications MCEX 169

Diagnosis

    You have changed the update mode to "Delta queued".


Procedure

    Schedule a periodical job ( Using the "Job Control" function in the
    Logistic Extraction Cockpit) that regularly transports queue data for
    application 11 into the BW Delta Queue for the respective Datasource.
    This job must run hourly.
```

Figure 5.137 Queue Delta Popup

Once you've selected all options in the previous popups, you'll see that the final update mode is selected as **Queued Delta**, as shown in Figure 5.138.

▼ 🔲 11 : SD Sales BW		Job Control	🖉 Queued Delta
▼ 🔲 Extract structures			
▶ ⌀⌀▣ MC11VA0HDR: Extraction SD Sales BW: Document Header	🖉 Mainten...	🖉 2LIS_11_VAHDR	🖉 Active
▶ ⌀⌀▣ MC11VA0ITM: Extraction SD Sales BW: Document Item	🖉 Mainten...	🖉 2LIS_11_VAITM	🖉 Active
▶ ⌀⌀▣ MC11VA0KON: Extraction SD Sales BW: Document Condition	🖉 Mainten...	🖉 2LIS_11_VAKON	🖉 Active
▶ ⌀⌀▣ MC11VA0SCL: Extraction SD Sales BW: Document Schedule Line	🖉 Mainten...	🖉 2LIS_11_VASCL	🖉 Active
▶ ⌀⌀▣ MC11VA0STH: Extraction MD Order Header Status	🖉 Mainten...	🖉 2LIS_11_VASTH	🖉 Active
▶ ⌀⌀▣ MC11VA0STI: Extraction MD Order Item Status	🖉 Mainten...	🖉 2LIS_11_VASTI	🖉 Active
▶ ⌀⌀▣ MC11V_0ITM: Extraction SD Sales BW: Document Item Allocation	🖉 Mainten...	🖉 2LIS_11_V_ITM	🖉 Active
▶ ⌀⌀▣ MC11V_0SCL: Extraction SD Sales BW: Allocation Schedule Line	🖉 Mainten...	🖉 2LIS_11_V_SCL	🖉 Active
▶ ⌀⌀▣ MC11V_0SSL: Extraction MD Sales: Order Delivery	🖉 Mainten...	🖉 2LIS_11_V_SSL	🖉 Active

Figure 5.138 Update Mode Confirmation

Click **Job Control** and you'll see the new popup shown in Figure 5.139.

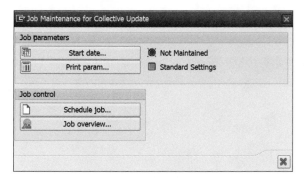

Figure 5.139 Job Control Maintenance

From the screen shown in Figure 5.139, you can choose these standard settings, as shown in Figure 5.140:

❶ Choose **immediate** or **Date/Time**.

❷ Choose the **Periodic Job** checkbox if you need to schedule a job at a specific interval.

❸ Choose the **Periodic Values** checkbox to see the **Periodic Values** popup.

❹ You can choose **Hourly**, **Daily**, or **Weekly**. In most scenarios, you can choose **Hourly**, then click the ✅ icon for the term check and then choose the ✅ icon again.

Figure 5.140 Setting Hourly Jobs

223

You can see the statuses under **Job Parameters** for **Start Date** and **Print Parameters** are green, as shown in Figure 5.141.

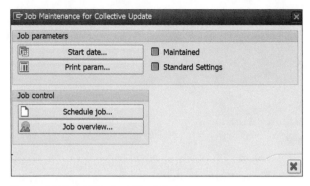

Figure 5.141 Job Control Final Status

If you click the **Job Overview** button, you can see the statuses of scheduled, released, and finished jobs, as shown in Figure 5.142.

Job name	Scheduled	Released	Ready	Active	Finished	Canceled
LIS-BW-VB_APPLICATION_11_100		X				
LIS-BW-VB_APPLICATION_11_100					X	
LIS-BW-VB_APPLICATION_11_100					X	
LIS-BW-VB_APPLICATION_11_100					X	
LIS-BW-VB_APPLICATION_11_100					X	
LIS-BW-VB_APPLICATION_11_100					X	
LIS-BW-VB_APPLICATION_11_100					X	
LIS-BW-VB_APPLICATION_11_100					X	

Job Overview: Alphabetic — Job log, Release, Refresh, Spool, Step

Figure 5.142 Job Overview

5.5.2   Post a Delta in SAP S/4HANA

In any organization, there will be document postings happening every day, so after the full upload is completed and initialized, the new and changed documents are captured as delta. In this section, we'll post a new sales order in the SAP S/4HANA system, and that will trigger a delta. To create a sales order, you can use Transaction VA01; in general, this activity will be done by the application team or end users in the application regularly.

To test the delta extraction, first create a new sales order with Transaction VA01 as shown in Figure 5.143. Provide the details as required, as shown in Figure 5.144.

Figure 5.143 Sales Order Creation

Create Standard Order: Overview

Standard Order		Net Value	700.00	USD
Sold-To Party	USCU S07	
Ship-To Party	USCU S07	
Cust. Reference	4500045060	Cust. Ref. Date	

| Sales | Item Overview | Item detail | Ordering party | Procurement | Shipping | Configuration | Reason for rejection |

Complete Div.	☐	Total Weight	10	G
Delivery Block	▼	Volume	0.000	
Billing Block	▼	Pricing Date	02/18/2023	
Pyt Terms	NT30	Net Due in 30 Days	
Inco. Version		
Incoterms	CFR	
Inco. Location1	Cost & Freight	

All Items

Item	Material	Req. Segment	Order Quantity	Un	S	Item Description
10	MZ-TG-Y120		10	PC	✓	Y120 Bike

Figure 5.144 Sales Order Creation

Press **Save** and you'll see the popup shown in Figure 5.145, which tells you the sales order is saved. This implies that the order is saved in the database table.

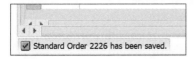

Figure 5.145 Created Sales Order

This popup means the V1 update is finished and sales order 2226 is created in the standard tables in the database. You can refer to that by checking table VBAK. First, check if the sales order is there in Transaction VA03.

You can use Transaction VA03 to see this sales order; the screen will look as shown in Figure 5.146.

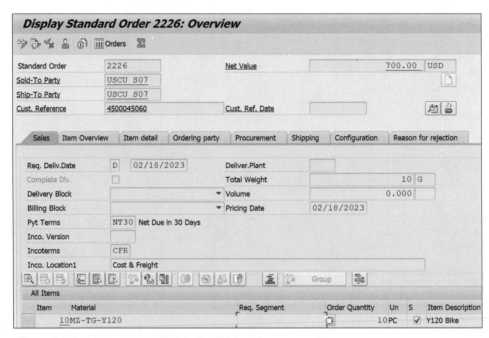

Figure 5.146 Transaction VA03: Display Sales order

Use table VBAK to see this sales order. We'll use the field description to match Transaction VA03. The field is displayed as shown in Figure 5.147.

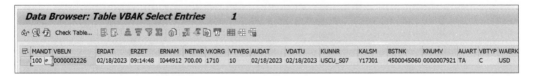

Figure 5.147 Table VBAK Fields for Sales Order

If you need to see the technical names or the descriptions of the fields, select **Setting · User Parameters** from the menu bar, as shown in Figure 5.148.

Now choose **Field Name** (by default, the SAP table will have **Field Label** selected), as shown in Figure 5.149.

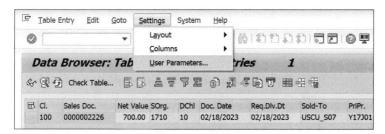

Figure 5.148 User Parameters for Table

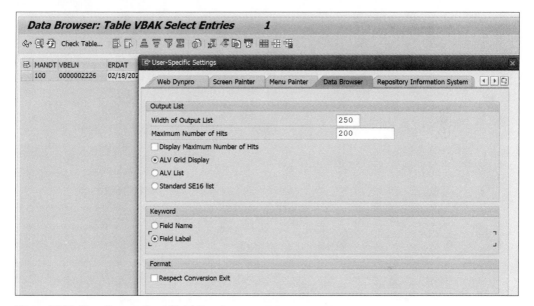

Figure 5.149 User Parameters: Field Name

Once you press `Enter`, you'll see the details shown in Figure 5.150. You can see fields such as **Sales Doc.**, **Net Value**, sales organization (**SOrg**), and others, like document date (**Doc. Date**). Sold-To has the value **USCU_S07**, which is the customer.

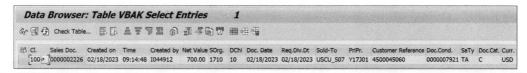

Figure 5.150 Table VBAK with Field Names

Because the delta is of type queued delta, you can see if there is any change in Transaction ODQMON in SAP S/4HANA, as shown in Figure 5.151. When you open Transaction ODQMON and enter "2LIS_11_VAHDR" in the **Queue** field, you'll see the details shown in Figure 5.151.

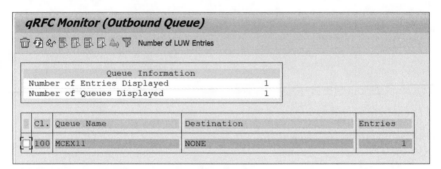

Figure 5.151 Transaction ODQMON: Subscriptions

In SAP S/4HANA, let's check Transaction LBWQ, which is the extraction queue. You can see that **MCEX11** is the queue name for application 11, as shown in Figure 5.152. Notice that the **Entries** column has the value 1, which means there is a change in the document, and that can be sent to the delta queue with the extraction job that you have scheduled (shown earlier in Figure 5.142).

qRFC Monitor (Outbound Queue)

🗑 🔁 ⬚ ⬚ ⬚ ⬚ ⬚ ⬚ ⬚ Number of LUW Entries

```
                    Queue Information
    Number of Entries Displayed            1
    Number of Queues Displayed             1
```

Cl.	Queue Name	Destination	Entries
100	MCEX11	NONE	1

Figure 5.152 Transaction LBWQ: Extraction Queue

In Figure 5.152, double-click the **MCEX11** row to view the data, as shown in Figure 5.153.

qRFC Monitor (Outbound Queue)

🗑 🔁 ⬚ ✏ 🔒 🔓 🔓 Immediately 🔓 Without activation

Cl.	Queue Name	Destination	Entries	Status	Date 1	Time 1	Next	Next	Wait for queue
100	MCEX11	NONE	1	NOSEND	02/18/2023	09:43:12	02/18/2023	09:43:12	

Figure 5.153 Extraction/Outbound Queue Data

Create one more record, as shown in Figure 5.154. You need to use the Transaction VA01 for this; follow the same steps that were shown earlier in Figure 5.143 to Figure 5.145.

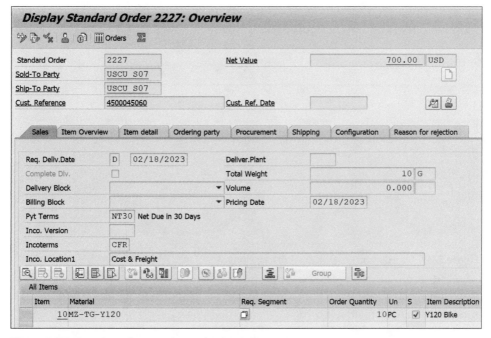

Figure 5.154 Creation of New Sales Order Record

After the creation of the sales order, you'll see the confirmation message shown in Figure 5.155.

Figure 5.155 Second Record

Now in SAP S/4HANA, open Transaction SE16 and check table VBAK, as shown in Figure 5.156. Provide the selection for the **Sales Doc.** field as the sales document number that you created. For this example, enter "2226" and "2227" in the field and then press ⊕. This will take you to the data browser for table VBAK, showing the two records that you created.

Figure 5.156 Delta Records

Check Transaction ODQMON again. Enter "2LIS_11_VAHDR" in the **Queue** field and you can see the subscriber with the target SAP BW/4HANA system, along with the details of

229

the subscription and request. Select a row and double-click it. You'll then be in the subscriptions view, as shown in Figure 5.157.

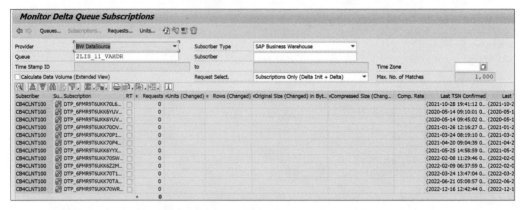

Figure 5.157 Transaction ODQMON: Subscriptions

Now log onto SAP BW/4HANA and execute the DTP as shown in Figure 5.158. In the DTP monitor, you need to do following:

❶ Expand the aDSO for the SD header DataSource **2LIS_11_VAHDR**.

❷ Double-click the DTP for the SD header DataSource.

❸ Check the **Source** and **Target** for the DTP.

❹ The default **Extraction Mode** will be **Delta**.

❺ Execute the DTP. You'll see an option to open the monitor; choose **Yes**.

Figure 5.158 DTP for LO SD Header

You'll be asked to log into the SAP BW web cockpit. Once you've provided the logon credentials, the data load status can be seen as shown in Figure 5.159. Make sure you check the following options:

❶ Check the total records that are loaded; in this case, it's two records.

❷ To view the status of the request, click **Manage Request**.

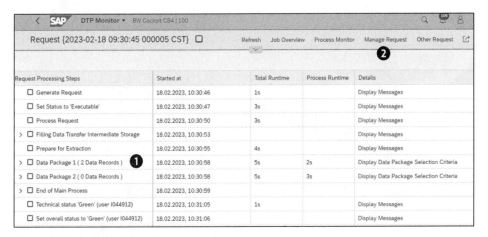

Figure 5.159 Data Load Monitor

Once you choose **Manage Requests**, you'll see the screen shown in Figure 5.160.

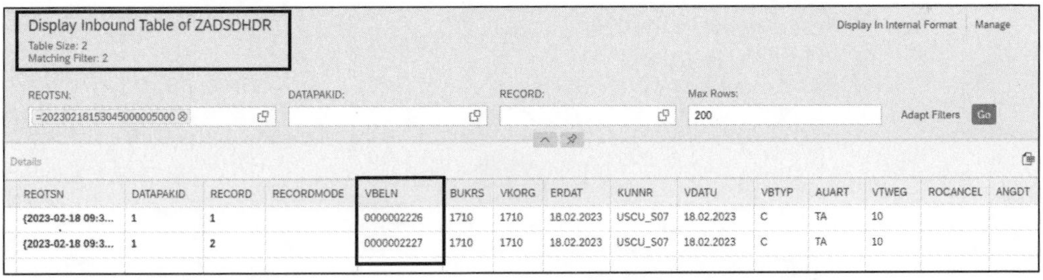

Figure 5.160 Manage Requests

You can see that **Storage** is **Inbound Table** and the number of records is **2**. If you need to see the contents of the aDSO, you can click the **Inbound Table · Contents**, as shown in Figure 5.161.

Request Information

DataStore Object: ZADSDHDR
DataStore Object Description: Sales Document Header
ID: {2023-02-18 09:30:45.000005 CST}
Status: Overall and tec
Storage: Inbound Table
Records: 2

Definition

Contents

Figure 5.161 Inbound Table Contents

You'll then see the records that were created, as shown in Figure 5.162.

To check the request status, follow the steps shown in Figure 5.163: right-click **[ZADS-DHDR]** and select **Manage the DataStore Object (Advanced)**.

Now you'll see the screen shown in Figure 5.164. You'll notice the request at the top has **2** records and **Storage** is **Inbound Table**.

Figure 5.162 Inbound Table Contents

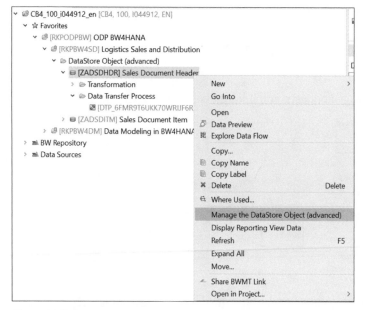

Figure 5.163 Manage aDSO

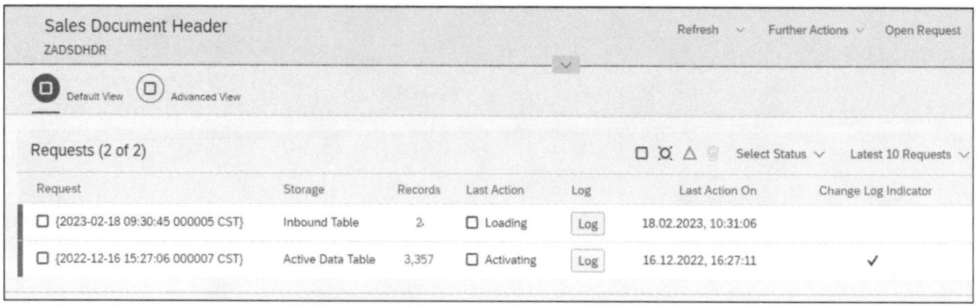

Figure 5.164 Manage aDSO: View Records

If you want to see the status of an aDSO in an SAP GUI format, you can use Transaction RSMNG in SAP BW/4HANA to access the screen shown in Figure 5.165. In the **DataStore Object (Advanced)** selection field, enter "ZASDHDR" as the aDSO name and execute using the icon.

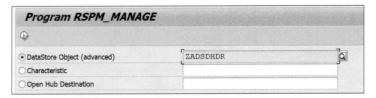

Figure 5.165 Transaction RSMNG

You'll then see the same status in GUI format, as shown in Figure 5.166.

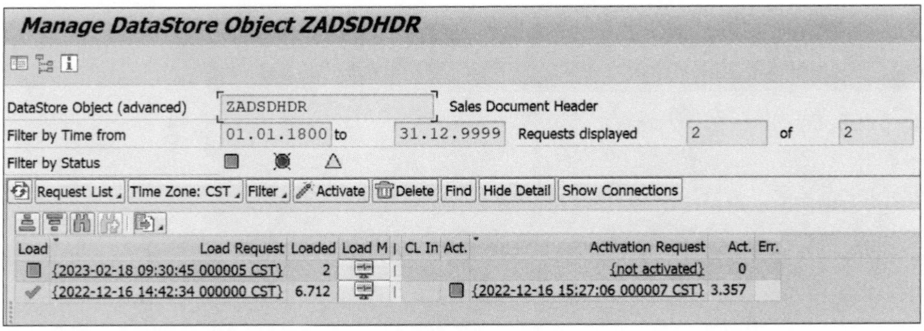

Figure 5.166 Transaction RSMNG: View Status in GUI Format

The load request and activation request options are available for the full upload, but for the delta upload you'll see only the load request. To see the activation request, you need to activate the load request. You can use the web cockpit to do this. Enter the web cockpit and click **Activate**, as shown in Figure 5.167.

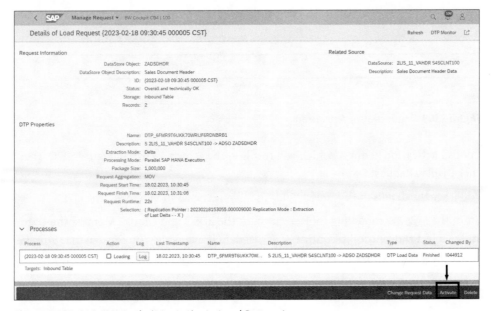

Figure 5.167 SAP BW Cockpit to Activate Load Request

Confirm the popup using the ![icon] icon and continue to see the **Activate Request by Request** option, as shown in Figure 5.168. (This setting is optional.) Click the **Activate** button.

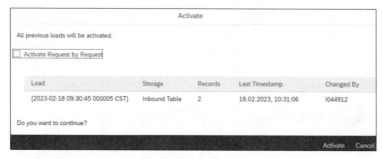

Figure 5.168 Continue to Activate

Now you can see that the request is activated (see Figure 5.169).

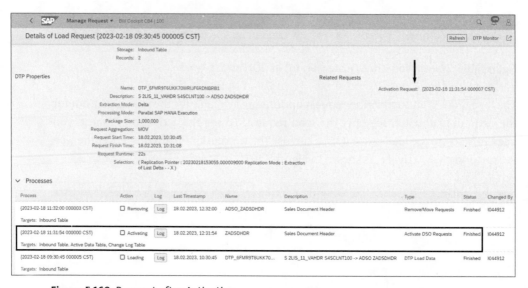

Figure 5.169 Request after Activation

Choose **Activation Request**, which will result in the screen shown in Figure 5.170. Then click **Display Request Data**.

You'll see the details of the added fields in table VBELN, as shown in Figure 5.171.

From the SAP BW modeling tools, right-click the aDSO and choose **Manage the Datastore Object (Advanced)** to confirm if active data is available. You can see that **Storage** will be now show **Active Data Table** with **Records** set to **2**, as shown in Figure 5.172.

Figure 5.170 Activate Table Display Request Data

Figure 5.171 Data in Active Table of aDSO

Figure 5.172 Manage ADSO to See Data

The same can be verified from Transaction RSMNG for the aDSO. You can see that the delta load has a **Load Request** and **Activation Request** with two total records, as shown in Figure 5.173.

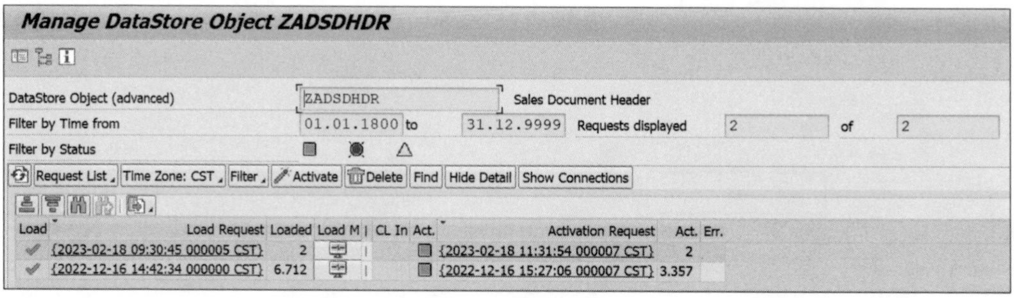

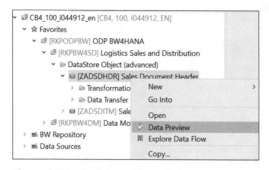

Figure 5.173 Transaction RSMNG for Delta Load Test

Now do a data preview of the aDSO, as shown in Figure 5.174. In the SAP BW modeling tools, right-click the aDSO and choose **Data Preview**.

Figure 5.174 aDSO Data Preview

Move all the **Free Characteristics** entries to **Rows** to see the data, as shown in Figure 5.175. You can move the free characteristics by dragging the fields from the **Free Characteristics** window to the **Rows** window.

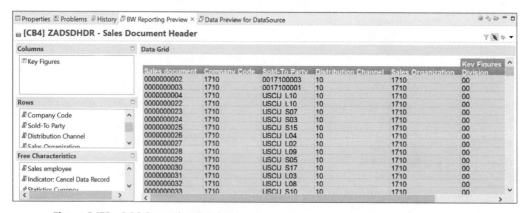

Figure 5.175 aDSO Reporting Preview

Choose the **Filter** icon ( ) to open a popup for filtering. Here, double-click **Sales Document** to open another popup, **Edit Filter**. In the **Values** input field in the popup, add the filter values for the sales order; for example start with "2227" and you'll see the sales document. You can double-click that value and it will be moved to the **Filter Definition** section. Similarly, add the next sales document that you created, as shown in Figure 5.176. You've now set two sales document as filters in the aDSO reporting preview.

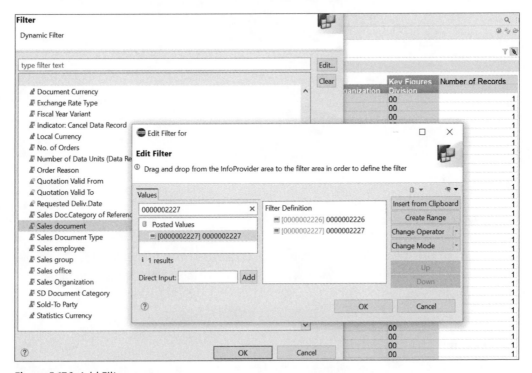

Figure 5.176 Add Filter

You can see these data records for **Sales Document**, which are set for filtering as shown in Figure 5.177.

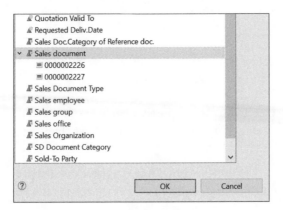

Figure 5.177 Confirm filter Records

Once you choose **OK**, you'll see the two records from the aDSO, as shown in Figure 5.178.

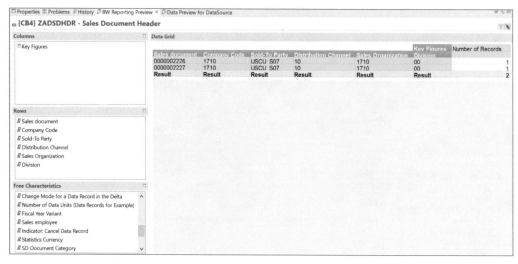

Figure 5.178 Filtered Delta Records

You can also search for the aDSO active table like this from Transaction SE16. The table name that ends with 2 (/BIC/AZADSDHDR2) is an active table. Choose that table as shown in Figure 5.179.

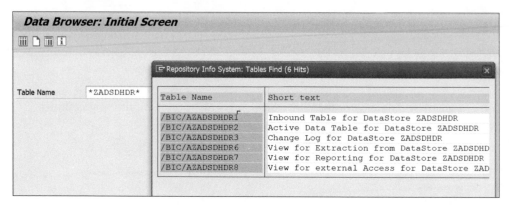

Figure 5.179 List of aDSO Tables

In the Transaction SE16 **Data Browser** screen, you can see the **Number of Entries** button. Use it to check the number of entries as shown in Figure 5.180. You can see that there are 3,359 records.

Now filter only for delta records. This can be done by providing the values of the two sales documents in the **VBELN** input field. Choose and you will see the results shown in Figure 5.181.

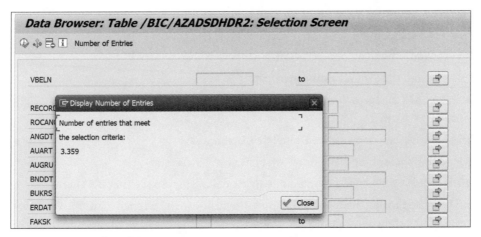

Figure 5.180 Number of Entries

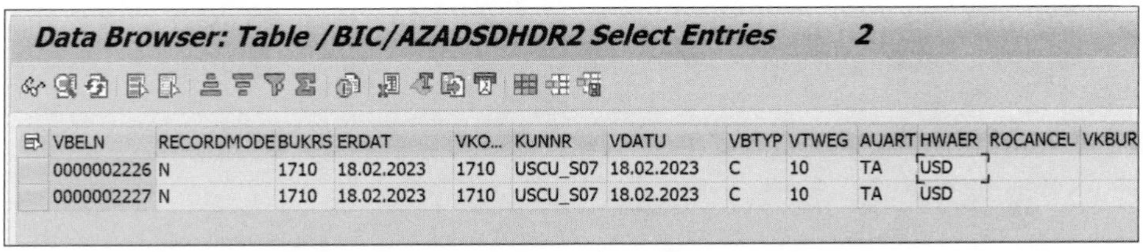

Data Browser: Table /BIC/AZADSDHDR2 Select Entries   2

VBELN	RECORDMODE	BUKRS	ERDAT	VKO...	KUNNR	VDATU	VBTYP	VTWEG	AUART	HWAER	ROCANCEL	VKBUR
0000002226	N	1710	18.02.2023	1710	USCU_S07	18.02.2023	C	10	TA	USD		
0000002227	N	1710	18.02.2023	1710	USCU_S07	18.02.2023	C	10	TA	USD		

Figure 5.181 Validating Delta Records in aDSO Active Table

You can now confirm that delta records are available in the aDSO active table for SAP BW reporting. Next, we'll check to see what happened in Transaction ODQMON.

5.5.3 Transaction ODQMON Checks for Delta Extraction

Open Transaction ODQMON in SAP S/4HANA to see what happened after the delta extraction. First, see if the extraction queue has data. You can see that after delta extraction, there will not be any data, as shown in Figure 5.182.

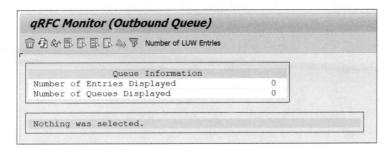

Figure 5.182 Extraction Queue

Now in SAP BW/4HANA, go back to Transaction ODQMON and provide the details as shown in Figure 5.183:

❶ By default, when you open ODQMON, **Queues** will be selected.

❷ Choose **BW DataSource** as the provider.

❸ Choose **SAP Business Warehouse** as the subscriber type because you're sending data to SAP BW/4HANA.

❹ The request selection can be **Delta Init + Delta**.

❺ Find the label for the DataSource that has been extracted.

❻ The request will be incremented due to the delta; you can see that it's **1** here.

❼ If you need to see the technical names, then choose the wrench icon 🔧. You'll see the results shown in Figure 5.183, where the queue names have changed to the technical description values instead of the technical names. For example, you'll see **Sales Document Header** instead of **2LIS_11_VAHDR**. If you need to see the technical names again, click the same icon 🔧 once more and it will toggle between names and descriptions of the queues or DataSources.

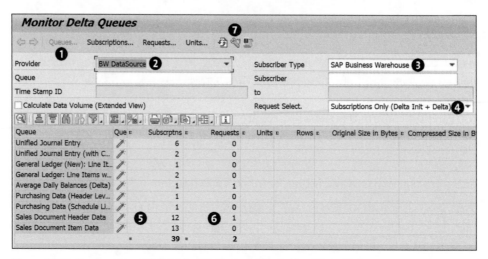

Figure 5.183 Transaction ODQMON with Technical Details of DataSources

Then follow these steps, as shown in Figure 5.184:

❶ You are now in **Subscriptions**.

❷ The subscription is based on the DTP on the time stamp listed.

❸ There is a new **Request**.

❹ The **Last TSN Confirmed** shows a time stamp.

❺ The **Last TSN Requested** is shown.

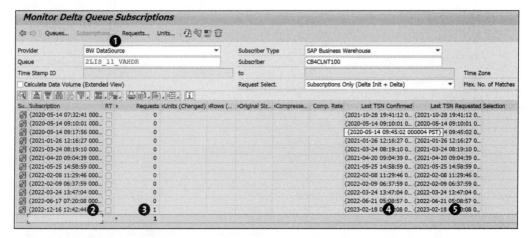

Figure 5.184 Subscriptions in Transaction ODQMON

Once you double-click the subscription ❷, it will take you to the request section, with the details shown in Figure 5.185:

❶ This shows that you are in **Requests**.

❷ The composite request is the DTP subscription that finished for the delta.

❸ The green checkmark indicates that the last composite request was successful.

❹ You'll see the last successful DTP subscription that created the full load and initialized the delta.

❺ The lower TSN is the first load from the DTP that did the initialization. That time was used to capture the delta records.

❻ The upper limit for the TSN is the current delta-based time, so any records after this time will be extracted in the next delta.

❼ The extraction mode is delta, which means that it captured the new and changed records.

❽ The table used to handle this delta mode is ODQDATA.

Figure 5.185 Transaction ODQMON: Requests

When you double-click the composite request row ❷, you'll be taken to the units section shown in Figure 5.186, which includes the following components:

241

❶ **Units** section

❷ Unique TSN

❸ Transaction ID

❹ Total rows

❺ Extraction mode delta

❻ Storage table

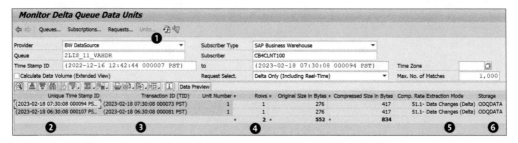

Figure 5.186 Units

You can double-click each row to see the record values, as shown in Figure 5.187.

Figure 5.187 Row 1

You can see that **VBELN** is **2227**, and if you double-click the next row, you can see the next value for **VBELN**, **2226**, as shown in Figure 5.188.

Figure 5.188 Row 2

To view all fields in a table format, click the **Display** icon, which is shown above the
ODQ_T column (see Figure 5.189).

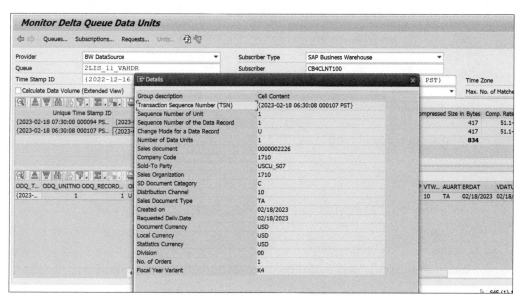

Figure 5.189 View Single Record in Column Format

To see the records in table ODQDATA, copy the transaction ID and enter a selection in table
ODQDATA as shown in Figure 5.190.

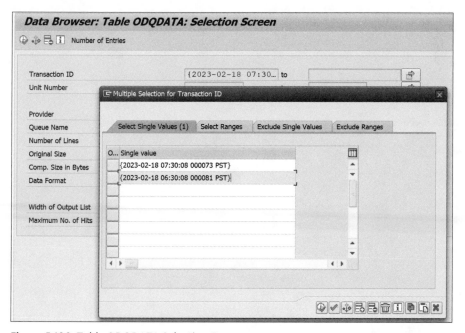

Figure 5.190 Table ODQDATA Selection Screen

You can see the results as shown in Figure 5.191.

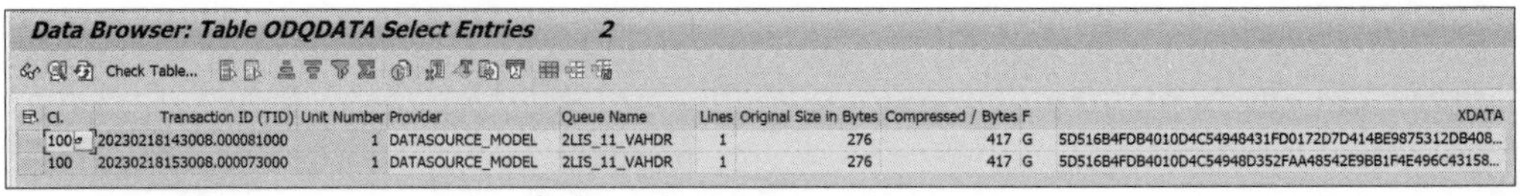

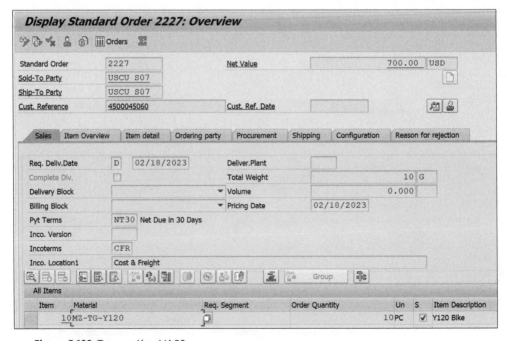

Figure 5.191 Table ODQDATA Results

The data cannot be interpreted as its in XDATA format, but you know how to view the table. You can do so using Transaction ODQMON, which will show all the details stored in this table. It's best practice to use Transaction ODQMON to view the status of the extraction.

5.5.4 Loading the Logistics Sales Document Item aDSO Using ODP

In this section, you'll learn how to load the sales document item data from SAP S/4HANA to SAP BW/4HANA. First we'll view the data in application tables like VBAP that store line-item-level data and then use a DTP to load the data from 2LIS_11_VAITM. Finally we'll execute the DTP and check Transaction ODQMON for the logistics line item extraction.

Transaction VA03 has certain values and material numbers along with the quantity, as shown in Figure 5.192.

Figure 5.192 Transaction VA03

This information is stored in table VBAP as shown in Figure 5.193. It has the item number for the material and its equivalent material name, along with the net value and quantity.

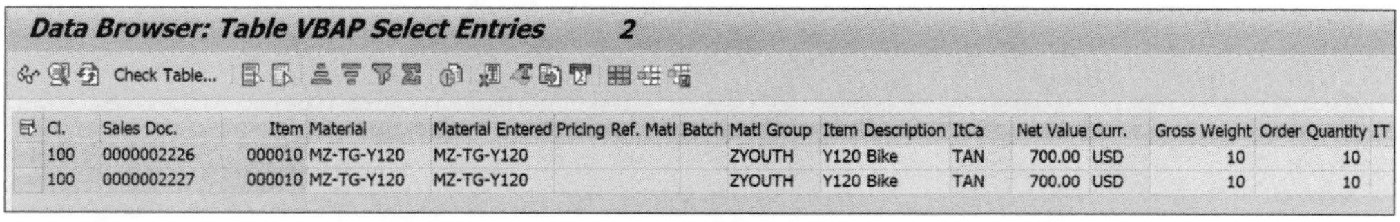

Data Browser: Table VBAP Select Entries	2											

Cl.	Sales Doc.	Item Material	Material Entered	Pricing Ref. Matl	Batch	Matl Group	Item Description	ItCa	Net Value Curr.		Gross Weight	Order Quantity IT
100	0000002226	000010 MZ-TG-Y120	MZ-TG-Y120			ZYOUTH	Y120 Bike	TAN	700.00	USD	10	10
100	0000002227	000010 MZ-TG-Y120	MZ-TG-Y120			ZYOUTH	Y120 Bike	TAN	700.00	USD	10	10

Figure 5.193 Table VBAP for Sales Document Data

If you need to extract the item-level data, then you need to use a different DataSource. In logistics and sales and distribution, we have 2LIS_11_VAITM for this purpose. Because the delta is posted and the table already has data, it's enough to execute the DTP for the sales document DataSource. Before executing the DTP, check Transaction ODQMON in the sender system as shown in Figure 5.194. You need to check for the 2LIS_11_VAITM queue.

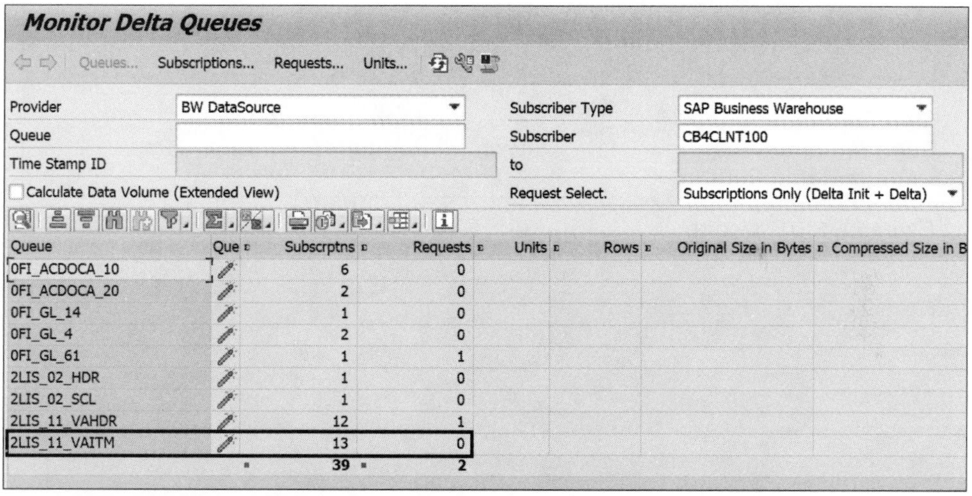

Figure 5.194 Transaction ODQMON for SD Item DataSource

Now execute the DTP using ▶ ▼ for the aDSO that fetches data from the 2LIS_11_VAITM DataSource, as shown in Figure 5.195.

As you can see in Figure 5.195, the **Source** of the DTP is **2LIS_11_VAITM** and **Target** is the **ZADSDITM** aDSO for the sales document item. Execute the DTP as showed earlier in Figure 5.103 and check the contents in the inbound table, as shown in Figure 5.196.

Now click **Manage Request** and it will open the screen that has information about the load request. Click the **Inbound Table** to check it and it will open a popup window. Choose **Display Contents**, where you can see two delta records are created, as shown in Figure 5.197.

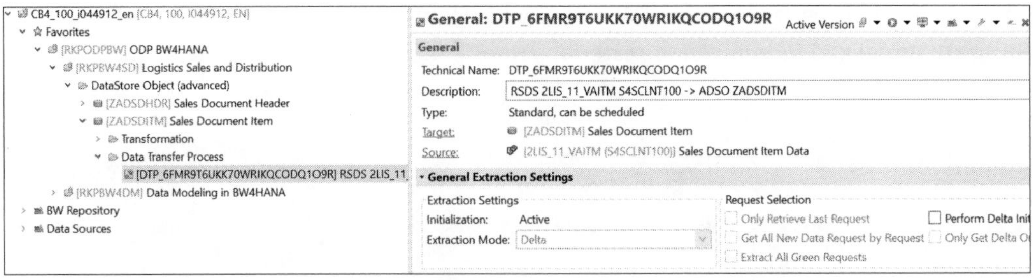

Figure 5.195 DTP for Logistics Item Data Extraction

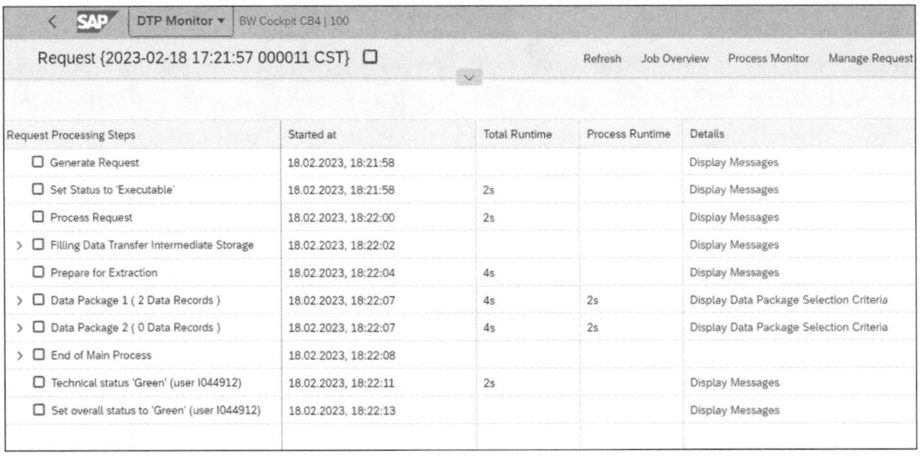

Figure 5.196 DTP Monitor

Figure 5.197 Inbound Table for Sales Document Item

Activate the load request by selecting the **Activate** button and check the data (see Figure 5.198).

Figure 5.198 After aDSO Activation

From the SAP BW modeling tools, check the aDSO data preview, as shown in Figure 5.199. To do so, right-click the aDSO and select **Manage DataStore Object (Advanced)**.

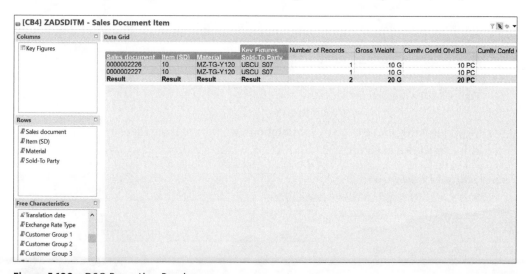

Figure 5.199 aDSO Reporting Preview

Check the aDSO active table (see Figure 5.200), where you can see the two records that were posted.

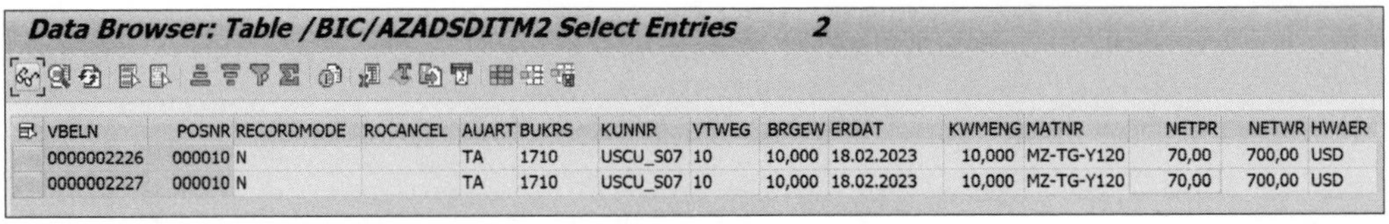

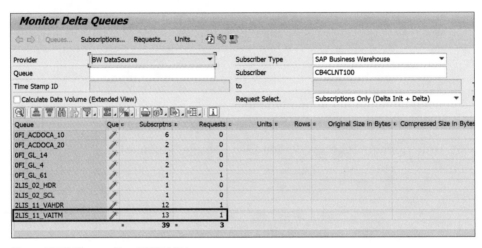

Figure 5.200 aDSO Active Table for Sales Item

5.5.5   Transaction ODQMON for Logistics Sales Item

Now you can check Transaction ODQMON in the SAP S/4HANA system. It will give you the details of the queue as shown in Figure 5.201. Choose the **2LIS_11_VAITM** Data-Source, where you can see the new request.

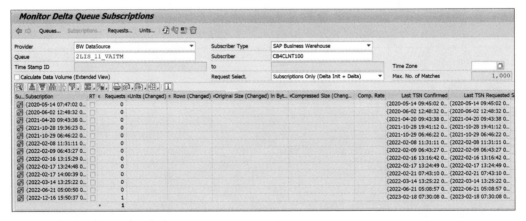

Figure 5.201 Transaction ODQMON

Now select the queue to go to **Subscriptions**, where you'll see there are many subscriptions, as shown in Figure 5.202.

Figure 5.202 Subscriptions

Choose the last row, where you see **Requests** set to **1**. This will take you to the request details. You can see the **Composite Request** has a green checkmark, which means it's successful (see Figure 5.203).

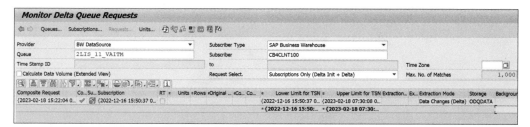

Figure 5.203 Requests Section

Click the composite request, which will open the **Units** section. As shown in Figure 5.204, it has multiple rows.

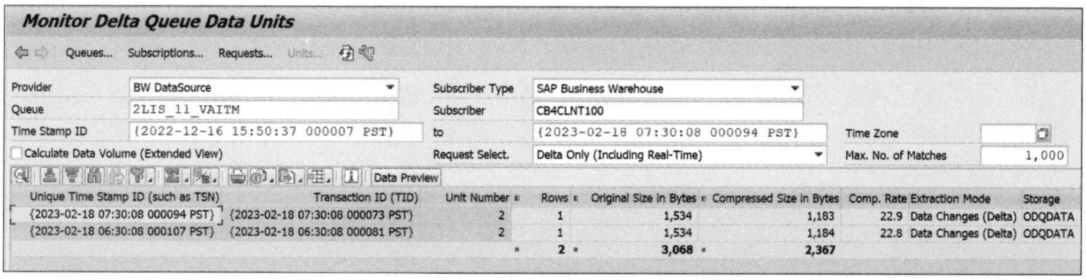

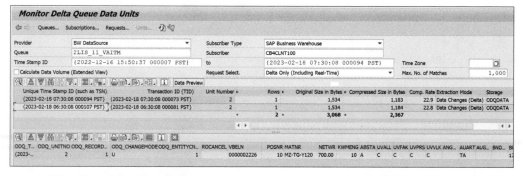

Figure 5.204 Units Section

Choose each row to view the records available in the same screen, as shown in Figure 5.205.

Figure 5.205 Check Rows from Bottom

To see the records in each row, first check the row, double-click on that row, and you'll see the screen shown in Figure 5.206, where row 1 is selected. Similarly you can double-click row 2 to see the contents of that row.

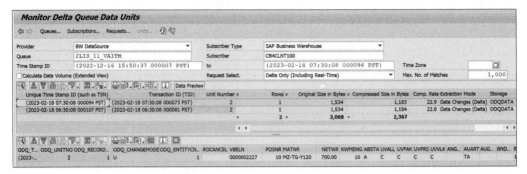

Figure 5.206 View Delta Records in Units

Now you've seen how to load the delta to SAP BW/4HANA and validate it in Transaction ODQMON. To reorganize the delta queue, follow menu path **Goto • Reorganize Delta Queue** (see Figure 5.207).

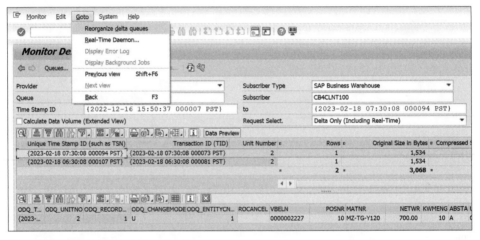

Figure 5.207 Delta Queue: Reorganize

Note that the delta queue is by default valid for 24 hours. You can see that from this menu and that the **Recovery** period is 24 hours (see Figure 5.208).

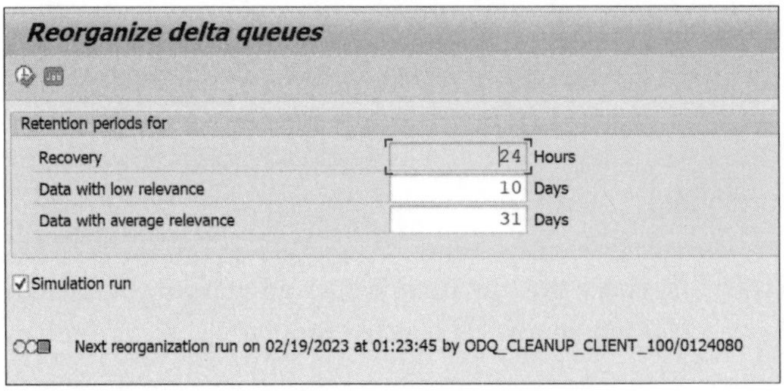

Figure 5.208 Delta Queue: Reorganization Details

With this, you've completed the data flow for LO extraction, covering the sales and distribution application module.

5.6   Extracting Logistics DataSources from Other Applications

This section provides the details of logistics extractors across different functional areas based on the logistics cockpit. In the previous section, we focused only on sales-based LO extraction, but here you'll learn about other logistics-based extractor types and understand the differences between them. Once you complete this section, you'll know the key differences of logistics extractors in various SAP functional applications and how to use them in SAP BW/4HANA data staging.

In SAP S/4HANA, there are many application modules that deal with management of procurement and checks for quality management, production planning, and finally plant maintenance. To start, we'll focus on the basics of each functional module and learn the important terms used in the module in the SAP BW reporting perspective. The functional basis that we will build first will help you to understand the SAP BW extraction process better.

We'll start with the organization structure used in purchasing and the steps to fill the setup table for purchasing. We'll also discuss data staging of purchasing data. Finally, we'll discuss the plant maintenance component.

5.6.1   Introduction to Logistics-Based Functional Modules

In an ERP system, there will be many functional areas that deal with sales, purchasing, production, finance, and so on. In Chapter 4, we discussed how to use LO-based sales data and extract the data into SAP BW/4HANA. In a greenfield implementation, you need to extract the data from all other functional modules, so as an SAP BW architect, you'll need to understand the basics of SAP ERP– or SAP S/4HANA–based dataflows and how tables are connected in the system. You know how to load the data into SAP BW/4HANA, so we'll focus on the kinds of DataSources that SAP provides for each extractor and how to use them.

In Transaction LBWE, shown in Figure 5.209, you can see several application components identified with two-digit numbers. For example, you can see **02** for **Purchasing** and **03** for **Inventory Controlling**. From earlier sections, you know how to work with application component 11, which is for sales, 12 for shipping, and 13 for billing. In any SAP BW/4HANA greenfield implementation, more focus will be given to extract data that is listed from the functional areas of the application components in the logistics cockpit, so this is must-know information for SAP BW consultants.

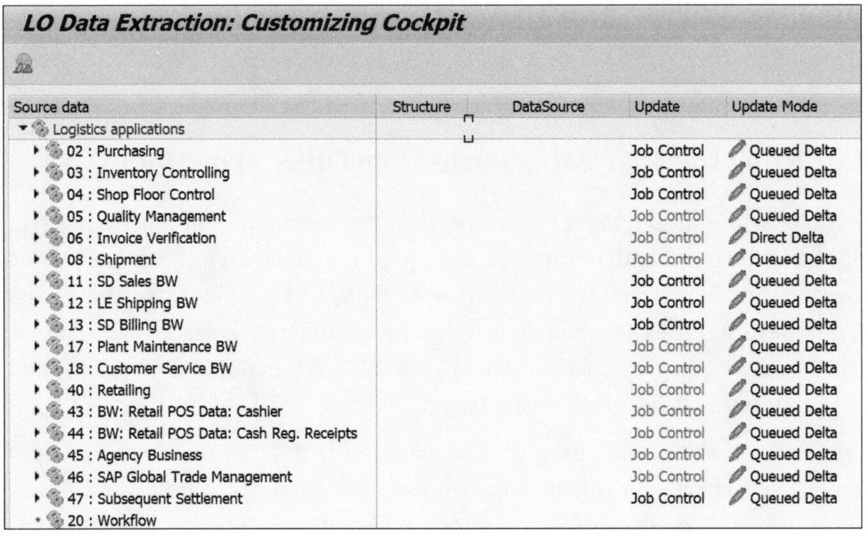

Source data	Structure	DataSource	Update	Update Mode
Logistics applications				
02 : Purchasing			Job Control	Queued Delta
03 : Inventory Controlling			Job Control	Queued Delta
04 : Shop Floor Control			Job Control	Queued Delta
05 : Quality Management			Job Control	Queued Delta
06 : Invoice Verification			Job Control	Direct Delta
08 : Shipment			Job Control	Queued Delta
11 : SD Sales BW			Job Control	Queued Delta
12 : LE Shipping BW			Job Control	Queued Delta
13 : SD Billing BW			Job Control	Queued Delta
17 : Plant Maintenance BW			Job Control	Queued Delta
18 : Customer Service BW			Job Control	Queued Delta
40 : Retailing			Job Control	Queued Delta
43 : BW: Retail POS Data: Cashier			Job Control	Queued Delta
44 : BW: Retail POS Data: Cash Reg. Receipts			Job Control	Queued Delta
45 : Agency Business			Job Control	Queued Delta
46 : SAP Global Trade Management			Job Control	Queued Delta
47 : Subsequent Settlement			Job Control	Queued Delta
20 : Workflow				

Figure 5.209 Logistics Cockpit

Now let's check some of the important functional areas in the logistics cockpit and see how to fill the setup table and understand the logic behind each DataSource in the next sections.

5.6.2 Extraction of Purchasing Data into SAP BW/4HANA

In any organization, purchasing is an important element, and it's a part of materials management (MM). The major tasks of purchasing includes procuring materials or services from vendors, determining the best possible sources for your procurement needs, monitoring the delivery of payments, and checking that the goods arrived in the organization. In general, you need to understand the procurement cycle at a very high level; this will be common across SAP ERP and SAP S/4HANA.

As you can see in Figure 5.210, when an organization needs to produce a product, it needs raw materials. The purchase requirement is sent to purchasing team, which tries to find the right source and vendor to buy the raw materials. Once the vendor is finalized, the team raises a purchase order (PO) that will have multiple components and conditions and delivery schedules. Once the PO is finalized, the organization needs to get the goods via a goods receipt process, which increases the available inventory. The organization also needs to make a payment to the vendor for the purchased goods based on the invoice receipt process, which finally impacts the payment processing and adjusts the accounts in the FI area. When you work on the extraction of purchasing data, these are general terms that you'll come across, so clarity into this flow will help you to choose the best extractors for your data modeling needs.

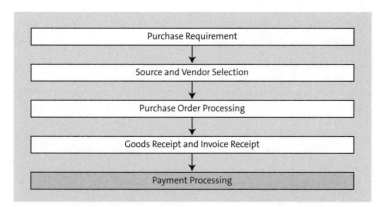

Figure 5.210 Purchasing Dataflow

In the following sections, you'll learn about the extraction of purchasing data into SAP BW/4HANA, filling the setup table, and loading the data for the purchasing-based application into SAP BW/4HANA. Then finally you'll use an SAP HANA composite provider to check the purchasing data preview.

Introduction to Purchasing Extractors

Let's look at the extractors used in this context, as shown in Figure 5.211. In SAP S/4HANA, you can use Transaction LBWE and select application component 02 to view the list of all purchasing DataSources.

LO Data Extraction: Customizing Cockpit

Source data	Structure	DataSource	Update	Update Mode
Logistics applications				
02 : Purchasing			Job Control	Queued Delta
Extract structures				
MC02M_0ACC: Extraction Purchasing (Account)	Mainten...	2LIS_02_ACC	Inactive	
MC02M_0CGR: Produced Activity: Delivery of Confirmations	Mainten...	2LIS_02_CGR	Inactive	
MC02M_0HDR: Extraction Purchasing (Header)	Mainten...	2LIS_02_HDR	Active	
MC02M_0ITM: Extraction Purchasing (Item)	Mainten...	2LIS_02_ITM	Active	
MC02M_0SCL: Extraction Purchasing (Schedule Line)	Mainten...	2LIS_02_SCL	Active	
MC02M_0SCN: Produced Activity: Confirmation of Schedule Line	Mainten...	2LIS_02_SCN	Active	
MC02M_0SGR: Produced Activity: Delivery of Schedule Lines	Mainten...	2LIS_02_SGR	Inactive	

Figure 5.211 Logistics-Materials Management Purchasing Extractors

You can see the list of all DataSources for category 02, purchasing components. The first DataSource **2LIS_02_ACC** is in a red status and the **Job Control** is inactive; these scenarios are very common in greenfield implementations.

To understand the behavior for this status, open table ROOSOURCE. As shown in Figure 5.212, the **OLTP Source Version** is **D**, which means that DataSource 2LIS_02_ACC is in the delivered state. This is the reason it appears red in Transaction LBWE: it needs to be activated.

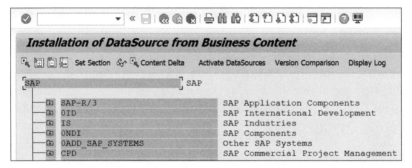

Figure 5.212 Table ROOSOURCE

To activate the DataSource, open Transaction RSA5 in SAP S/4HANA as shown in Figure 5.213.

Figure 5.213 Transaction RSA5

If you need to expand all nodes, this can be done by placing your cursor on **SAP** and clicking the icon button on the application toolbar, as shown in Figure 5.214. This will open all subfolders under **SAP**, and then you can use the **Find** icon from the toolbar under **Menu**. This will open up the **Find** window popup, in which you can provide the DataSource name—for example, "2LIS_02_ACC"—in the **Find** input. Then click the **Enter** icon or press Enter to search for the DataSource.

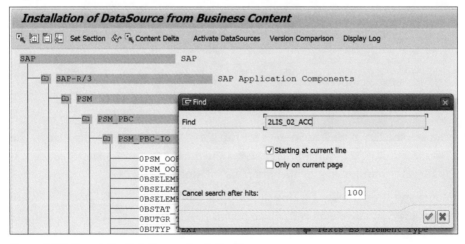

Figure 5.214 Search for DataSource for Activation

Activate the DataSource using the **Activate DataSource** button, and you will see it in table ROOSOURCE, as shown in Figure 5.215.

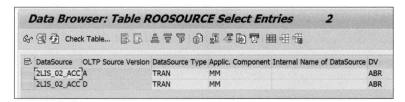

DataSource	OLTP Source Version	DataSource Type	Applic. Component	Internal Name of DataSource	DV
2LIS_02_ACC	A	TRAN	MM		ABR
2LIS_02_ACC	D	TRAN	MM		ABR

Figure 5.215 After Activation

After the activation of DataSource 2LIS_02_ACC, you'll see that the list of extract structures will not be in red, as shown in Figure 5.216.

LO Data Extraction: Customizing Cockpit

Source data	Structure	DataSource	Update	Update Mode
▼ Logistics applications				
▼ 02 : Purchasing			Job Control	Queued Delta
▼ Extract structures				
MC02M_0ACC: Extraction Purchasing (Account)	Mainten...	2LIS_02_ACC	Inactive	
MC02M_0CGR: Produced Activity: Delivery of Confirmations	Mainten...	2LIS_02_CGR	Inactive	
MC02M_0HDR: Extraction Purchasing (Header)	Mainten...	2LIS_02_HDR	Active	
MC02M_0ITM: Extraction Purchasing (Item)	Mainten...	2LIS_02_ITM	Active	
MC02M_0SCL: Extraction Purchasing (Schedule Line)	Mainten...	2LIS_02_SCL	Active	
MC02M_0SCN: Produced Activity: Confirmation of Schedule Line	Mainten...	2LIS_02_SCN	Active	
MC02M_0SGR: Produced Activity: Delivery of Schedule Lines	Mainten...	2LIS_02_SGR	Inactive	

Figure 5.216 After Activation

To active the job control, click the **Inactive** option listed under the **Update** column for the specific DataSource. A few popups will open, and finally the DataSource will be activated; this was discussed in detail in Chapter 4. You can see that DataSource 2LIS_02_ACC is now active, as shown in Figure 5.217.

Source data	Structure	DataSource	Update	Update Mode
▼ Logistics applications				
▼ 02 : Purchasing			Job Control	Queued Delta
▼ Extract structures				
MC02M_0ACC: Extraction Purchasing (Account)	Mainten...	2LIS_02_ACC	Active	
MC02M_0CGR: Produced Activity: Delivery of Confirmations	Mainten...	2LIS_02_CGR	Inactive	
MC02M_0HDR: Extraction Purchasing (Header)	Mainten...	2LIS_02_HDR	Active	
MC02M_0ITM: Extraction Purchasing (Item)	Mainten...	2LIS_02_ITM	Active	
MC02M_0SCL: Extraction Purchasing (Schedule Line)	Mainten...	2LIS_02_SCL	Active	
MC02M_0SCN: Produced Activity: Confirmation of Schedule Line	Mainten...	2LIS_02_SCN	Active	
MC02M_0SGR: Produced Activity: Delivery of Schedule Lines	Mainten...	2LIS_02_SGR	Inactive	

Figure 5.217 Job Control Active

As you can see in Figure 5.217, the list of all DataSources that are used to extract purchasing data is available. These are under application component 02. The most frequently used DataSources are as follows:

- 2LIS_02_HDR, purchasing header

- 2LIS_02_ITM, purchasing item

- 2LIS_02_SCL, purchasing schedule line

2LIS_02_HDR extracts all the header-level data related to a purchasing document. If you need to know the tables involved, you can choose **Maintenance**. It will take you through a few popups, and finally you'll see the screen shown in Figure 5.218.

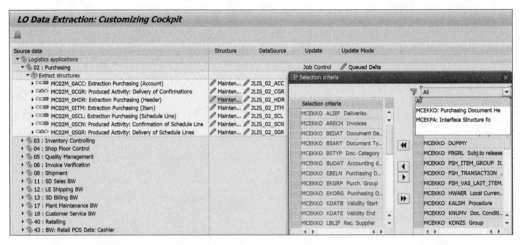

Figure 5.218 DataSource Structure Maintenance and Source Tables

MCEKKO and **MCEKPA** are shown in the dropdown. All the fields are based on the communication structure. You can see the communication structure from Transaction SE11: choose the **Datatype** radio button and give the structure name, as shown in Figure 5.219.

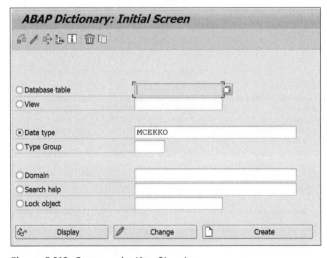

Figure 5.219 Communication Structure

Select **Display**, and you can see the structure fields for **MCEKKO**, as shown in Figure 5.220.

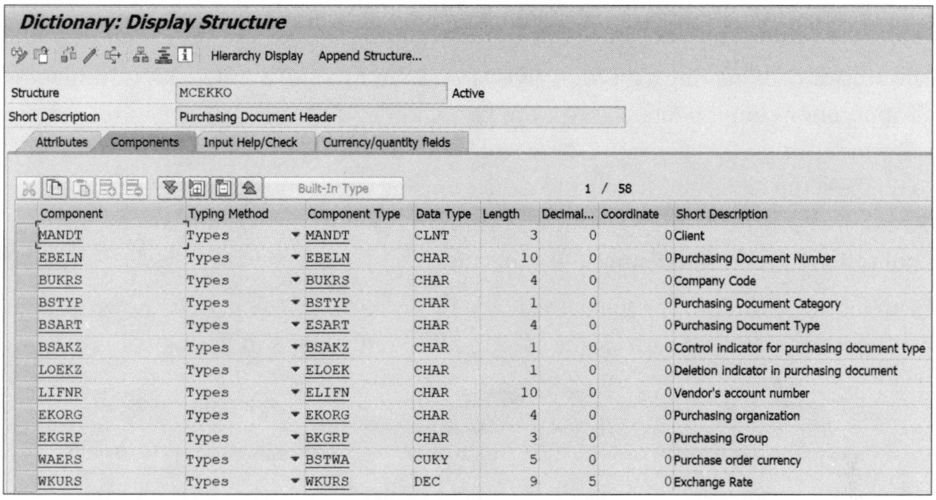

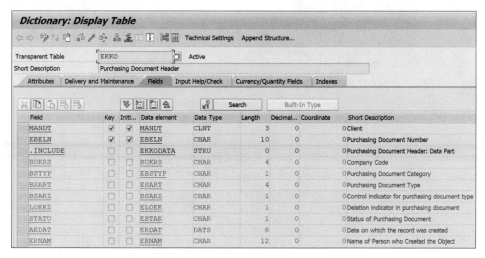

Figure 5.220 Communication Structure for Purchase Header

The communication structure has all the fields required for the DataSource. This process of checking communication structures is common for all LO DataSources with all application components.

If you look at the fields, you can see that **EBELN** is the purchase document number. You can get the base for this structure from the structure name; in our case, the table for **MCEKKO** is EKKO and the table for **MCEKPA** is EKPA. Let's look at the contents of table EKKO, which is the base for the communication structure. You'll find that **EBELN** is the primary key, which means it can be connect to other tables (see Figure 5.221).

Figure 5.221 Table EKKO

When you extract data from DataSource 2LIS_02_HDR, most of the records are fetched from the same tables EKKO and EKPA.

Filling the Setup Table for Purchasing DataSources

The process of extracting data from an LO DataSource to SAP BW/4HANA is similar for all application components, so once you know how to do it for one DataSource, it's the same for all other DataSources. Like LO sales extraction, there is a separate transaction to fill the setup table, but there's also a Customizing transaction that will have all these details in one place. In SAP S/4HANA, in Transaction SBIW, use menu path **Settings for Application-Specific DataSource (PI) · Logistics**.

From logistics, you can see the path shown in Figure 5.222. The path is shown here to highlight that the same path can be used to fill all setup tables in the logistics cockpit.

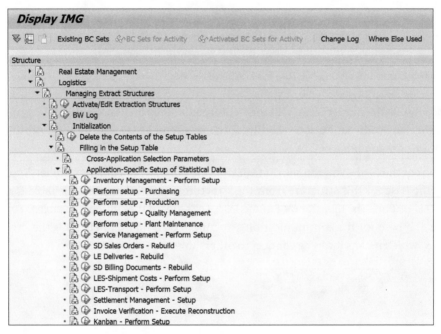

Figure 5.222 Purchasing Setup Table Filling

Once you execute the **Perform Setup—Purchasing** activity, you can see the transaction to fill the setup table, as shown in Figure 5.223. Note that the same screen can be accessed via Transaction OLI3BW. You'll see a similar screen as you saw for the SD sales setup table filling. Provide the **Name of Run** and **Termination Time** (which must be in the future) to start filling the setup table.

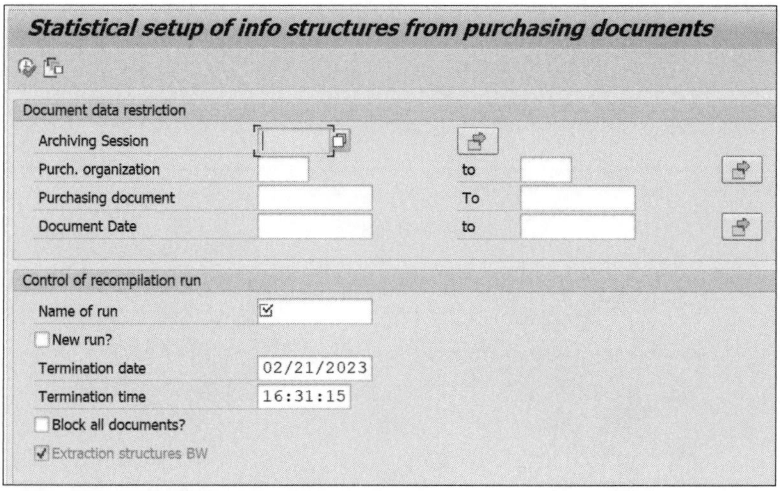

Figure 5.223 Setup Purchasing DataSources

After executing the setup table, you can see the records in Transaction RSA3. This step will populate the setup table for all DataSources listed under application component 02. A sample DataSource is shown in Figure 5.224.

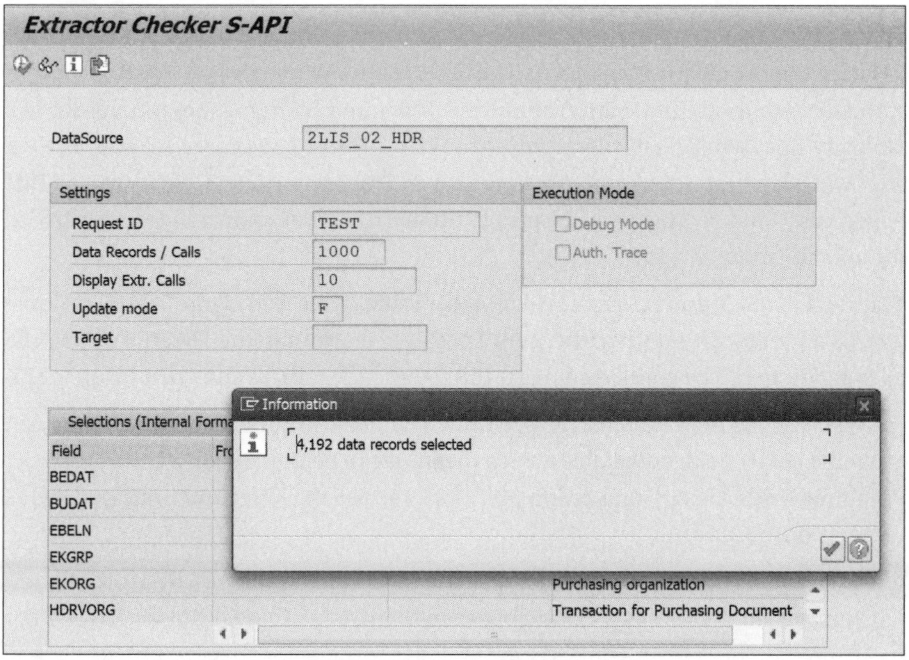

Figure 5.224 Transaction RSA3 for DataSource 2LIS_02_HDR

Replication Test

You can use report RODPS_REPL_TEST in Transaction SE38 instead of Transaction RSA3, as shown in Figure 5.225.

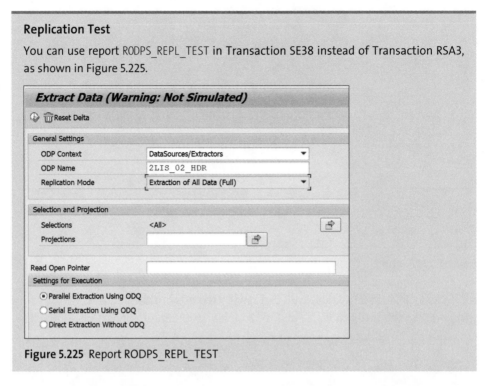

Figure 5.225 Report RODPS_REPL_TEST

Let's check the results for DataSource 2LIS_02_ITM also. With this DataSource, you can extract the item-level information about the purchase order. In general, an order will have many line items, so it's common for 2LIS_02_ITM to have more records as each header will have more item records. Note that in Transaction RSA3, we increased **Display Records / Calls** to 1,000 and **Display Extr.Calls** to 100, as shown in Figure 5.226, to accommodate more records.

In Transaction RSA3, you can now see the other DataSource (see Figure 5.226). In Transaction LBWE, you can see that the item DataSource also has the **EBELN** field, so the header and item can be connected to get the required details, as shown in Figure 5.227.

As you can see, the item DataSource gets data from tables EKKO, EKPA, and EKPO. You can see that the **EBELN** field is available, which means it can be used to join the tables to get the required fields. Using Transaction SQVI, you can see the join conditions quickly, as shown in Figure 5.228.

Tables EKKO and EKPO are joined with key field **EBELN**, which is the purchase order number. If you need to find the association between them, you can use Transaction SQVI or you can directly check from Transaction SE11 and see the fields that can be used for the join. When modeling the aDSO in SAP BW/4HANA, you need to use the same field or associated InfoObject when you try to join at the SAP HANA composite provider level.

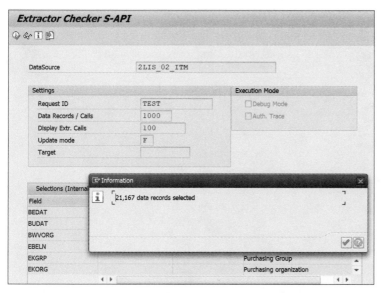

Figure 5.226 Transaction RSA3 for DataSource 2LIS_02_ITM

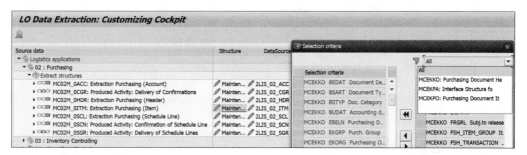

Figure 5.227 Item DataSource 2LIS_02_ITM

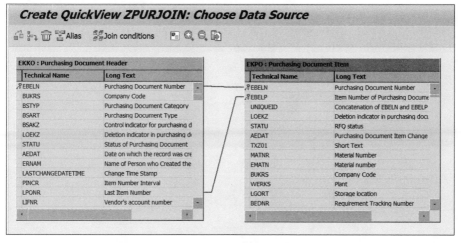

Figure 5.228 Transaction SQVI for Checking Table Joins

Loading Purchasing Data in SAP BW/4HANA

Once the setup table is completed, make sure the DataSource is replicated in SAP BW/4HANA, then create an aDSO based on the DataSource, as shown in Figure 5.229.

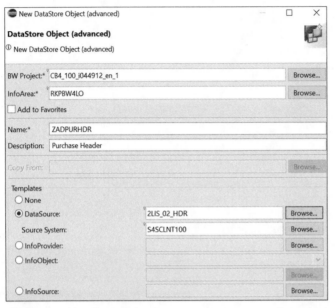

Figure 5.229 aDSO For Purchase Header

In the **Details** tab of the aDSO, choose **Manage Keys**. Now you need to define **EBELN** as a key field, as shown in Figure 5.230.

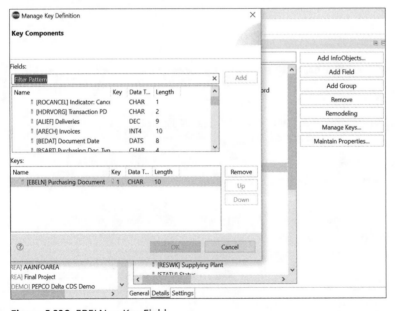

Figure 5.230 EBELN as Key Field

After you activate the aDSO using the 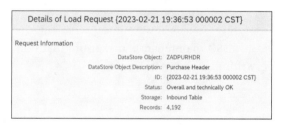 icon, create the transformation and DTP for DataSource 2LIS_02_HDR as shown in Figure 5.231.

```
✓ 🖳 CB4_100_i044912_en_1 [CB4, 100, I044912, EN]
   ✓ ☆ Favorites
      ✓ 🖳 [RKPODPBW] ODP BW4HANA
         ✓ 🖳 [RKPBW4LO] Logistics General Extraction
            ✓ 🖿 DataStore Object (advanced)
               ✓ ▣ [ZADPURHDR] Purchase Header
                  ✓ 🖿 Transformation
                     ⋈ [00JHN59WFJ7MI6QS70EXXMIHQCE6275B] RSDS 2LIS_02_HDR S4SCLNT100->ADSO ZADPURHDR
                  ✓ 🖿 Data Transfer Process
                     ⧉ [DTP_6FMR9T6UKK6Z6OAPE7ZOOKMUR] RSDS 2LIS_02_HDR S4SCLNT100 -> ADSO ZADPURHDR
            > 🖳 [RKPBW4SD] Logistics Sales and Distribution
            > 🖳 [RKPBW4DM] Data Modeling in BW4HANA
      > 🖹 BW Repository
      > 🖹 Data Sources
```

Figure 5.231 DTP and Transformation

Execute the DTP and check that the inbound table matches via Transaction RSA3, as shown in Figure 5.232. It has 4,192 records.

```
Details of Load Request {2023-02-21 19:36:53 000002 CST}

Request Information
                  DataStore Object:  ZADPURHDR
      DataStore Object Description:  Purchase Header
                               ID:  {2023-02-21 19:36:53 000002 CST}
                           Status:  Overall and technically OK
                          Storage:  Inbound Table
                          Records:  4,192
```

Figure 5.232 aDSO Inbound Table

Once the activation is completed, the records will move from the inbound table to the active table, and the total records will be reduced or increased based on the transformation rules, which help to cleanse and enhance the data from sender to the target. Now do the same for 2LIS_02_ITM and create the DTP and transformation; start with the aDSO, as shown in Figure 5.233.

```
ⓘ New DataStore Object (advanced)

BW Project:*   CB4_100_i044912_en_1                              [ Browse... ]
InfoArea:*     RKPBW4LO                                          [ Browse... ]
☐ Add to Favorites

Name:*         ZADPURITM
Description:   Purchase Item
Copy From:     [                                        ]        [ Browse... ]

Templates
○ None
◉ DataSource:                    2LIS_02_ITM                     [ Browse... ]
   Source System:                S4SCLNT100                      [ Browse... ]
```

Figure 5.233 Purchase Item

When assigning keys to the aDSO, check the source table keys. An aDSO has an over-write property, and if the keys aren't defined properly it will overwrite with the last value—so check the key fields of the source table in SAP S/4HANA. In table EKPO, you can see that fields **EBELN** and **EBELP** are key, as shown in Figure 5.234.

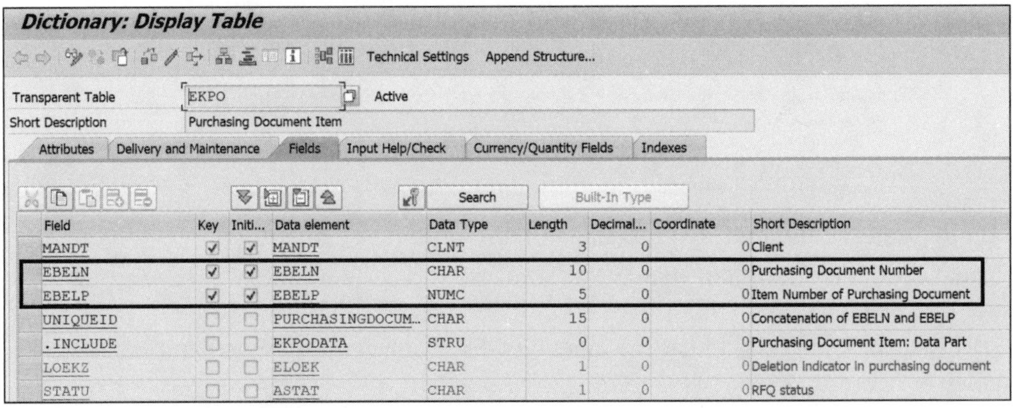

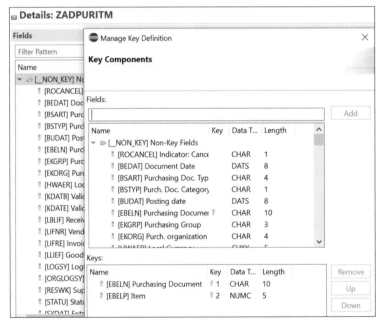

Figure 5.234 Key Fields in Source Table

Now in the SAP BW modeling tools, in the aDSO maintenance, make sure that both fields are selected as keys to prevent overwriting, as shown in Figure 5.235.

Figure 5.235 Manage Keys for aDSO

Now activate the aDSO and create the DTP and transformation. The dataflow is shown in Figure 5.236, where you can see details such as DTP, transformation, and DataSource.

```
∨  🗗 [RKPODPBW] ODP BW4HANA
    ∨  🗗 [RKPBW4LO] Logistics General Extraction
        >  🗁 CompositeProvider
        ∨  🗁 DataStore Object (advanced)
            >  🖿 [ZADPURHDR] Purchase Header
            ∨  🖿 [ZADPURITM] Purchase Item
                ∨  🗁 Transformation
                    ▶ [06L6NOM9XAFS1SPPBYGLT69W4L1STJD1] RSDS 2LIS_02_ITM S4SCLNT100->ADSO ZADPURITM
                ∨  🗁 Data Transfer Process
                    🗋 [DTP_6FMR9T6UKK6Z6OAQQ9XMB6DRK] RSDS 2LIS_02_ITM S4SCLNT100 -> ADSO ZADPURITM
        >  🗗 [RKPBW4SD] Logistics Sales and Distribution
        >  🗗 [RKPBW4DM] Data Modeling in BW4HANA
    >  📕 BW Repository
    >  📕 Data Sources
```

Figure 5.236 DTP and Transformation for LO Purchasing Item

Next execute the DTP using ⏵ ▼ and view the inbound table. The records count is shown in Figure 5.237.

Details of Load Request {2023-02-22 05:54:17 000006 CST}	
Request Information	
DataStore Object:	ZADPURITM
DataStore Object Description:	Purchase Item
ID:	{2023-02-22 05:54:17 000006 CST}
Status:	Overall and technically OK
Storage:	Inbound Table
Records:	21,167

Figure 5.237 Inbound Table for Purchase Item

Then activate the aDSO using⟳, which will populate the activation request. To test the keys' behavior, check table EKPO for any PO document with several line items. When you click a column and choose the Σ icon for the **NETPR** and **NETWR** columns, you'll see the PO document shown in Figure 5.238.

EBELN	EBELP	MATNR	MATKL	MENGE	NETPR	NETWR
4500000098	00001	MZ-RM-R200-01	ZFRAME	12.000	701.37	8,416.44
4500000098	00002	MZ-RM-R200-02	ZHANDLE	12.000	20.63	247.56
4500000098	00003	MZ-RM-R200-03	ZSEAT	12.000	20.63	247.56
4500000098	00004	MZ-RM-R200-04	ZWHEEL	24.000	61.89	1,485.36
4500000098	00005	MZ-RM-R200-05	ZFORK	12.000	165.03	1,980.36
4500000098	00006	MZ-RM-R200-06	ZBRAKES	12.000	103.14	1,237.68
4500000098	00007	MZ-RM-R200-07	ZGEARS	12.000	288.80	3,465.60
4500000098	00008	MZ-RM-R200-08	ZPEDAL	12.000	185.66	2,227.92
4500000098	00009	MZ-RM-R200-09	ZTRAIN	12.000	453.83	5,445.96
					▪ 2,000.98	▪ 24,754.44

Data Browser: Table EKPO Select Entries   9

Figure 5.238 EKPO Sample for PO Document: SAP S/4HANA

Now open the aDSO table for the purchasing item and check for the same PO document in the aDSO active table that ends with 2. You'll see that the results match with the results shown in Figure 5.238. This is possible due to the addition of **EBELN** and **EBELP** as keys; otherwise the aDSO could have overwritten all keys and you could have seen only the last record in the active table. Instead, as expected, you'll see the same nine records in the active table of the aDSO, as shown in in Figure 5.239.

Data Browser: Table /BIC/AZADPURITM2 Select Entries						9		
RECORDMO...	EBELN	EBELP	MATNR	MATKL	MENGE ☰	NETPR ☰	NETWR	LIFNR
N	4500000098	00001	MZ-RM-R200-01	ZFRAME	12	701,37	8.416,44	USSU-VSF02
N	4500000098	00002	MZ-RM-R200-02	ZHANDLE	12	20,63	247,56	USSU-VSF02
N	4500000098	00003	MZ-RM-R200-03	ZSEAT	12	20,63	247,56	USSU-VSF02
N	4500000098	00004	MZ-RM-R200-04	ZWHEEL	24	61,89	1.485,36	USSU-VSF02
N	4500000098	00005	MZ-RM-R200-05	ZFORK	12	165,03	1.980,36	USSU-VSF02
N	4500000098	00006	MZ-RM-R200-06	ZBRAKES	12	103,14	1.237,68	USSU-VSF02
N	4500000098	00007	MZ-RM-R200-07	ZGEARS	12	288,80	3.465,60	USSU-VSF02
N	4500000098	00008	MZ-RM-R200-08	ZPEDAL	12	185,66	2.227,92	USSU-VSF02
N	4500000098	00009	MZ-RM-R200-09	ZTRAIN	12	453,83	5.445,96	USSU-VSF02
						▪ 2.000,98	▪ 24.754,44	

Figure 5.239 aDSO Active Table with PO as Selection: SAP BW/4HANA

Check the Purchasing Data Preview with an SAP HANA Composite Provider

The last step in the data modeling will be the creation of an SAP HANA composite provider by joining the relevant tables. The SAP HANA composite provider can be used as a base for the SAP BW/4HANA reporting. To do this, first create an SAP HANA composite provider as shown in Figure 5.240. Right-click the InfoAres and select **New · HANA Composite Provider**.

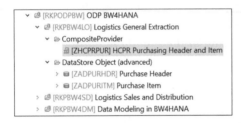

Figure 5.240 SAP HANA Composite Provider for Purchasing

Figure 5.241 shows the join conditions for the SAP HANA composite provider:

❶ The SAP HANA composite provider is based on an **Inner Join**.

❷ The ADSO for the purchasing head is part of the join.

❸ The ADSO for the purchasing item is part of the join.

❹ The join condition is based on the following equation: *Header ADSO – EBELN = Item ADSO – EBELN*. Here, EBELN is the field that is used to connect both the ADSO.

❺ Select the fields that you need for output, which will be displayed in the final report.

Figure 5.241 SAP HANA Composite Provider Modeling

You can see the results in Figure 5.242.

Source data	Structure	DataSource	Update	Update Mode
▾ ⬡ Logistics applications				
▾ ⬡ 02 : Purchasing			Job Control	⬦ Queued Delta
▾ ⬡ Extract structures				
▸ ⬤⬜ MC02M_0ACC: Extraction Purchasing (Account)	⬦ Mainten...	⬦ 2LIS_02_ACC	⬦ Active	
▸ ⬤⬜ MC02M_0CGR: Produced Activity: Delivery of Confirmations	⬦ Mainten...	⬦ 2LIS_02_CGR	⬦ Inactive	
▸ ⬤⬜ MC02M_0HDR: Extraction Purchasing (Header)	⬦ Mainten...	⬦ 2LIS_02_HDR	⬦ Active	
▸ ⬤⬜ MC02M_0ITM: Extraction Purchasing (Item)	⬦ Mainten...	⬦ 2LIS_02_ITM	⬦ Active	
▸ ⬤⬜ MC02M_0SCL: Extraction Purchasing (Schedule Line)	⬦ Mainten...	⬦ 2LIS_02_SCL	⬦ Active	
▸ ⬤⬜ MC02M_0SCN: Produced Activity: Confirmation of Schedule Line	⬦ Mainten...	⬦ 2LIS_02_SCN	⬦ Active	
▸ ⬤⬜ MC02M_0SGR: Produced Activity: Delivery of Schedule Lines	⬦ Mainten...	⬦ 2LIS_02_SGR	⬦ Inactive	

Figure 5.242 SAP HANA Composite Provider Results after Join: Data Preview

Now you know how to model SAP BW/4HANA with standard purchasing DataSources, so let's recap all the business content DataSources in purchasing. As shown in Figure 5.242, in any greenfield or support projects, you'll deal with these DataSources:

- 2LIS_02_ACC has information about purchasing data at the account level. Some of the useful tables include EKKO, EKPO, and EKKN, where the account assignments are stored.
- 2LIS_02_CGR is for produced activity: delivery of confirmation.
- 2LIS_02_HDR is for purchase header.
- 2LIS_02_ITM is for purchase item.
- 2LIS_02_SCL is for purchase schedule lines that get data from tables EKKO, EKPO, EKET.
- 2LIS_02_SCN is for confirmation of schedule lines.
- 2LIS_02_SGR is for delivery of schedule lines.

5.6.3   Other Logistics-Based Applications and DataSources

In this section, we'll cover other commonly used logistics extraction-based applications. We'll try to cover the applications based on Transaction LBWE.

Shop Floor

The production planning (PP) application in SAP ERP helps in forecasting of demand and provides essential data that helps organizations plan manufacturing capacity and activity against consumer demand. Accurate production planning is a base requirement for effective supply chains. Production planning is fully integrated with sales, materials management, purchasing, and quality management (QM). You can think of it this way: The sales module gets a sales order for thousands of units of a product and checks the inventory to view available supply. If there isn't enough inventory, then the product needs to be produced at the plant. To produce product, the company needs materials, and purchasing handles procurement of materials. When getting the procured raw materials, they must be tested for quality via quality management. If the material passes the quality checks, it's sent to production for final production of the product, which then is sent to inventory for sales availability. This is the high-level integration among these areas, which is more than sufficient for SAP BW/4HANA extraction.

In this section, you'll learn about other LO-based DataSources: shop floor extraction, QM extraction, and invoice verification.

Overview

There are few terms that you need to remember from the production planning perspective. When creating a material master, you'll have options to add entries like sales data, purchase data, material planning data, production planning data, and quality management data, plus accounting and costing, so the material master is like the central master data of an organization for any material. In the production planning perspective, those data are stored in tables related to specific applications. For example, using Transaction MM01, you can create a material master. It will ask you to choose the views, so let's choose a few views related to production planning which is materials requirement planning (MRP; see Figure 5.243).

There are a few terms that need to be understood when extracting data from production planning:

- A *bill of material* (BOM) is a list of components together with the quantity required to produce the product. This is used in material requirements planning and product costing.
- A *work center* is a machine or a group of machines with which the production operations are performed. This is also used in task list operations called *routings*.

- A *routing* is the sequence of the operations performed at the work center. It specifies the machine, labor, time, and so on for the execution of specific operations.

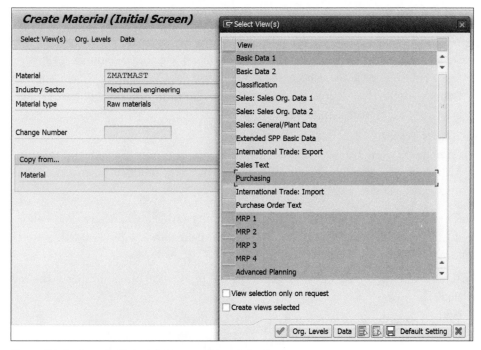

Figure 5.243 Sample Material Master: Views Selection

In SAP S/4HANA 1909, in the logistics cockpit, you can see the extractors for shop floor control in production planning (see Figure 5.244).

LO Data Extraction: Customizing Cockpit

Source data	Structure	DataSource	Update	Update Mode
▼ 🌐 Logistics applications				
▸ 🌐 02 : Purchasing			Job Control	🖉 Queued Delta
▸ 🌐 03 : Inventory Controlling			Job Control	🖉 Queued Delta
▼ 🌐 04 : Shop Floor Control			Job Control	🖉 Queued Delta
▼ 🌐 Extract structures				
▸ ◯◯▥ MC04PE0ARB: Extraction PP-BW: Reporting Points of REM	🖉 Maintenance	🖉 2LIS_04_PEARBPL	🖉 Active	
▸ ◯◯▥ MC04PE0COM: Extraction PP-BW: Repetitive Manufacturing Compo	🖉 Maintenance	🖉 2LIS_04_PECOMP	🖉 Active	
▸ ◯◯▥ MC04PE0MAT: Extraction PP-BW: Repetitive Manufacturing Mater	🖉 Maintenance	🖉 2LIS_04_PEMATNR	🖉 Active	
▸ ◯◯▥ MC04PK0KAN: Extraction PP-BW: Kanban	🖉 Maintenance	🖉 2LIS_04_PKKANBAN	🖉 Active	
▸ ◯◯▥ MC04P_0ARB: Extraction PP-BW: Work Center View from PP/PP-PI	🖉 Maintenance	🖉 2LIS_04_P_ARBPL	🖉 Active	
▸ ◯◯▥ MC04P_0COM: Extraction PP-BW: Component View from PP/PP-PI	🖉 Maintenance	🖉 2LIS_04_P_COMP	🖉 Active	
▸ ◯◯▥ MC04P_0MAT: Extraction PP-BW: Material View from PP/PP-PI	🖉 Maintenance	🖉 2LIS_04_P_MATNR	🖉 Active	

Figure 5.244 Logistics Cockpit: Production Planning

Note that a few DataSources are depreciated in SAP BW/4HANA, so you need to make sure that you're using the right DataSource for the flow or using in-memory-optimized business intelligence (BI) content. These DataSources are used:

- **2LIS_04_P_MATNR**

  Material view from production planning-process industries. This DataSource is used to extract data from the production order header into SAP BW.

- **2LIS_04_P_ARBPL_20**

  Work center view from production planning-process industries. You won't see this DataSource in Transaction LBWE, but it's normal. Usage of DataSource 2LIS_04_P_ARBPL is also allowed, and both DataSources use same structure, MC04P_0ARB. The DataSource has transaction data from the manufacturing process about order operations as well as work center–based information.

- **2LIS_04_P_COMP**

  Component view from production planning-process industries. This DataSource helps to find the details of material consumption for the production process and has information about material components.

When you work on the logistics-production planning extracts, you need to know about frequently used tables. The important tables that help with SAP BW extraction are as follows:

- Table AFKO, Order Header Data PP Orders (AUFNR, production order number, is the key field)
- Table AFPO, Order Item (AUFNR and POSNR are key fields)

The join conditions in SAP BW/4HANA for an SAP HANA composite provider will be based on the **AUFNR** field.

Extraction of Production Planning Data

To extract data using production planning DataSources, you need to follow the same process as for extracting data from the logsitics DataSources:

1. Delete the setup table using Transaction LBWG for component 04.
2. Activate the required DataSource in Transaction RSA5.
3. Activate the DataSource and job control in Transaction LBWE.
4. Fill the setup table in SAP ERP or SAP S/4HANA.
5. Replicate the DataSource in SAP BW/4HANA.
6. Create the SAP BW/4HANA models or install the in-memory flows from the business content.
7. Use the DTP to execute the full load, which fetches data from the setup table, and then initialize the delta.
8. Execute the DTP again to fetch the subsequent delta.

Filling the Setup Table for Production Planning DataSources

You can follow this path in Transaction SBIW to fill the setup table (see Figure 5.245):
Settings for Application-Specific DataSource (PI) · Logistics · Initialization · Filling the Setup table · Application-Specific Setup of Statistical Data ·Perform Setup- Production.

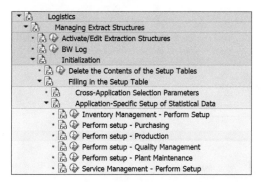

Figure 5.245 Transaction SBIW Path for Filling Production Setup Table

You can also use Transaction OLI4BW to fill the setup table for application 04. The screen is shown in Figure 5.246.

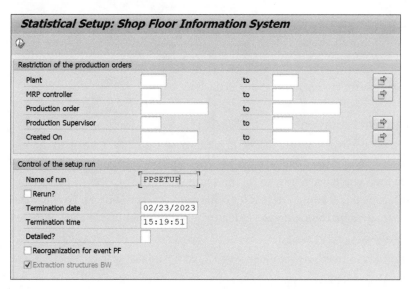

Figure 5.246 Setup Table for Production Planning

The next steps are the same as those you would follow to use a standard SAP-delivered IMO objects dataflow, as shown in Figure 5.247, where you have the SAP delivered Data-Source that is used for the SAP BW extraction. Upon extraction, it sends the data to the aDSO in the corporate memory layer. When you execute the DTP, this ADSO will be populated. Next, we have the EDW core layer, which has the InfoSource that gets data from the corporate memory layer ADSOs; then the aDS, which is based on the Info-Source; and finally, we have the virtual layer, where the SAP HANA composite provider is available for reporting purposes. The SAP HANA composite provider will join the ADSO based on the EDW layer.

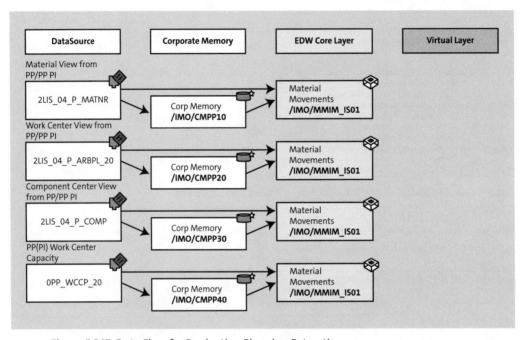

Figure 5.247 Data Flow for Production Planning Extraction

Quality Management Extraction

In this section, we'll cover the details of logsitics-based quality management extraction. You'll learn about the quality management DataSources available in Transaction LBWE, and then you'll learn how to fill the setup table. The process to extract the data from this setup table is similar to that for other logistics DataSources. To check the list of quality management DataSources, see Figure 5.248. Some important DataSources are 2LIS_05_QE1 and 2LIS_05_QE2.

The most useful DataSources are as follows:

- 2LIS_05_QE1, inspection result general data
- 2LIS_05_QE2, inspection result quantitative data
- 2LIS_05_QUVDN, inspection lot / usage decision
- 2LIS_05_QONOTIF, quality notification
- 2LIS_05_QOITEM, quality notification item
- 2LIS_05_QOCAUSE, quality notification causes
- 2LIS_05_QOACTY, quality notification activities
- 2LIS_05_QOTASK, quality notification tasks

LO Data Extraction: Customizing Cockpit

Source data	Structure	DataSource	Update	Update Mode
▼ Logistics applications				
▶ 02 : Purchasing			Job Control	Queued Delta
▶ 03 : Inventory Controlling			Job Control	Queued Delta
▶ 04 : Shop Floor Control			Job Control	Queued Delta
▼ 05 : Quality Management			Job Control	Queued Delta
▼ Extract structures				
▶ MC05Q00ACT: Extraction QM-BW: Notification Activity	Maintenance	2LIS_05_Q0ACTY	Active	
▶ MC05Q00CSE: Extraction QM-BW: Notification Cause	Maintenance	2LIS_05_Q0CAUSE	Active	
▶ MC05Q00ITM: QM-BW Extraction: Notification Item	Maintenance	2LIS_05_Q0ITEM	Active	
▶ MC05Q00NTF: QM-BW Extraction: Notification	Maintenance	2LIS_05_Q0NOTIF	Active	
▶ MC05Q00TSK: QM-BW Extraction: Notification Task	Maintenance	2LIS_05_Q0TASK	Active	
▶ MC05Q1_0IN: QM-BW Extraction: Inspection Characteristic Resu	Maintenance	2LIS_05_QE1	Active	
▶ MC05Q2_0IN: QM-BW Extraction: Inspection Char. Results (Quan	Maintenance	2LIS_05_QE2	Active	
▶ MC05QV0UDN: QM-BW Extraction: Usage Decision for Inspection	Maintenance	2LIS_05_QVUDN	Active	

Figure 5.248 QM DataSources in Transaction LBWE

Most of the data comes from the following tables:

- QAMV, Characteristics Specification for Inspection Processing
- QAMR, Characteristics Result during Inspection Processing
- QASR, Sample Results for Inspection Characteristics
- QAPP, Inspection Point

To fill the setup tables for quality management, use Transaction SBIW. Follow this path, as shown in Figure 5.249: **Settings for Application-Specific DataSource (PI) · Logistics · Initialization · Filling the Setup Table · Application-Specific Setup of Statistical Data · Perform Setup—Quality Management**.

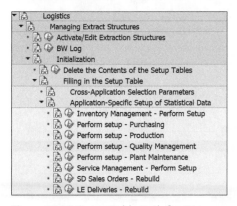

Figure 5.249 Setup Table Path for QM

You can also use Transaction OLIQBW if you prefer; the results are shown in Figure 5.250. You'll see here that the setup table can be filled based on notifications and inspections.

Set Up BW Structures for Quality Management

Reconstruct				
☐ Notifications (Event Q0)				
Notification		to		
☐ Inspection Lot (Event QV)				
☐ Inspection Results (Event QE)				
Inspection Lot	0	to	0	

Control Reconstruction Run	
Name of Run	QMTEST
Termination date	02/24/2023
Termination Time	00:00:00
☐ Block all documents	

Figure 5.250 QM Setup Table

Figure 5.251 shows the dataflow for quality management. Where you have the Data-Source that sends the data to the aDSO in the corporate memory layer and then we have the EDW core layer which has InfoSource that gets data from the corporate memory, then we have the aDSO based on the InfoSource and finally we have the virtual layer where the SAP HANA composite provider is available for reporting purposes.

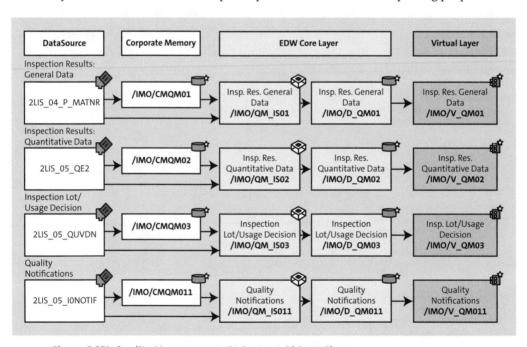

Figure 5.251 Quality Management: BI Content Objects Flow

Invoice Verification

The invoice verification application helps to extract invoice data from SAP ERP. It's used to analyze the invoice verification process. The DataSource helps to analyze invoices at an aggregated or at detailed level. There is one DataSource for this application component, under application component 06, as shown in Figure 5.252.

LO Data Extraction: Customizing Cockpit				
Source data	Structure	DataSource	Update	Update Mode
▼ 🕸 Logistics applications				
▶ 🕸 02 : Purchasing			Job Control	🖉 Queued Delta
▶ 🕸 03 : Inventory Controlling			Job Control	🖉 Queued Delta
▶ 🕸 04 : Shop Floor Control			Job Control	🖉 Queued Delta
▶ 🕸 05 : Quality Management			Job Control	🖉 Queued Delta
▼ 🕸 06 : Invoice Verification			Job Control	🖉 Direct Delta
▼ 🕲 Extract structures				
▶ ⚙ MC06M_0ITM: Extraction Structure BW	🖉 Mainten...	🖉 2LIS_06_INV	🖉 Active	

Figure 5.252 Invoice Verification

The tables used to fetch the data for this DataSource are RBKP (Invoice Header) and RSEG (Invoice Item). The path in Transaction SBIW is **Settings for Application-Specific Data-Source (PI) · Logistics**, as shown in Figure 5.253.

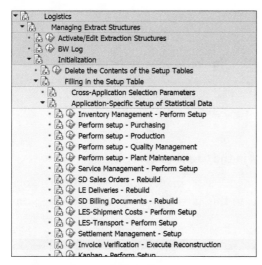

Figure 5.253 Setup Table Filling

You can also use Transaction OLI6BW to access the screen to fill the setup table for the invoice verification application–based DataSource, as shown in Figure 5.254.

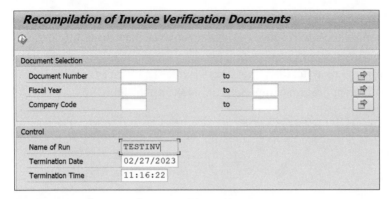

Figure 5.254 Screen to Fill Setup Table

Figure 5.255 shows the dataflow for the invoice verification. Where you have the Data-Source that sends the data to the aDSO in the corporate memory layer and then we have the EDW core layer which has InfoSource that gets data from the corporate memory, then we have the aDSO based on the InfoSource and finally we have the virtual layer where the SAP HANA composite provider is available for reporting purposes.

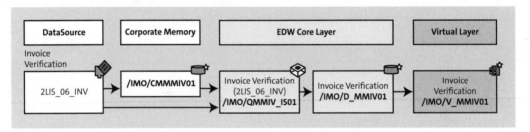

Figure 5.255 Invoice Verification: SAP BusinessObjects BI Content Flow

5.6.4   Asset Management Components in the Logistics Cockpit

There are two application components related to asset management–based extraction: plant maintenance and customer service. In this section, we'll discuss both applications and their DataSources.

Plant Maintenance Extraction

In this extraction, you can get the details of asset management across the company. Assets can be based on plants or services for the materials, as shown in Figure 5.256.

In the maintenance structure, you'll see that most of the plant maintenance Data-Sources get data from tables such as QMEL (Quality Notification), QMFE (Notification Item), and QMMA (Notification Activity).

Source data	Structure	DataSource	Update	Update Mode
▸ ⬡ 11 : SD Sales BW			Job Control	✎ Queued Delta
▸ ⬡ 12 : LE Shipping BW			Job Control	✎ Queued Delta
▸ ⬡ 13 : SD Billing BW			Job Control	✎ Queued Delta
▾ ⬡ 17 : Plant Maintenance BW			Job Control	✎ Queued Delta
▾ ⊚ Extract structures				
▸ ⊂⊃ MC17I00ACT: PM-BW Extraction: Notification Activity	✎ Mainten...	✎ 2LIS_17_I0ACTY	✎ Active	
▸ ⊂⊃ MC17I00CSE: PM-BW Extraction: Notification Cause	✎ Mainten...	✎ 2LIS_17_I0CAUSE	✎ Active	
▸ ⊂⊃ MC17I00ITM: PM-BW Extraction: Notification Item	✎ Mainten...	✎ 2LIS_17_I0ITEM	✎ Active	
▸ ⊂⊃ MC17I00NTF: PM-BW Extraction: Notification	✎ Mainten...	✎ 2LIS_17_I0NOTIF	✎ Active	
▸ ⊂⊃ MC17I00TSK: PM-BW Extraction: Notification Task	✎ Mainten...	✎ 2LIS_17_I0TASK	✎ Active	
▸ ⊂⊃ MC17I30HDR: PM-BW Extraction: Order	✎ Mainten...	✎ 2LIS_17_I3HDR	✎ Active	
▸ ⊂⊃ MC17I30OPR: Extraction PM-BW: Order Process	✎ Mainten...	✎ 2LIS_17_I3OPER	✎ Active	

LO Data Extraction: Customizing Cockpit

Figure 5.256 Transaction LBWE for Plant Maintenance

To fill the setup table, in Transaction SBIW follow menu path **Settings for Application-Specific DataSource (PI) · Logistics · Initialization · Filling the Setup Table · Application-Specific Setup of Statistical Data · Perform Setup Plant Maintenance**, as shown in Figure 5.257.

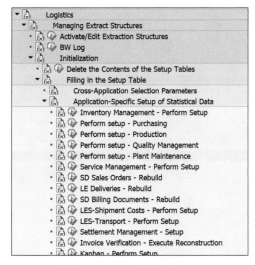

Figure 5.257 Transaction SBIW Path for PM Setup Table Filling

If you click **Perform Setup—Plant Maintenance**, it will take you to the screen shown in Figure 5.258. You can also use Transaction OLIIBW to call this screen.

Figure 5.259 shows the dataflow for the plant maintenance extraction. Where you have the DataSource that sends the data to the aDSO in the corporate memory layer and then we have the EDW core layer which has InfoSource that gets data from the corporate memory, then we have the aDSO based on the InfoSource and finally we have the virtual layer where the SAP HANA composite provider is available for reporting purposes.

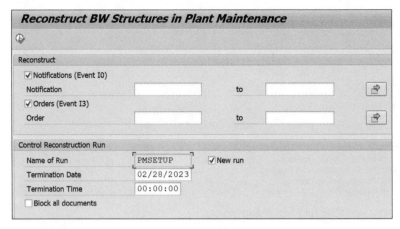

Figure 5.258 Plant Maintenance Setup Table

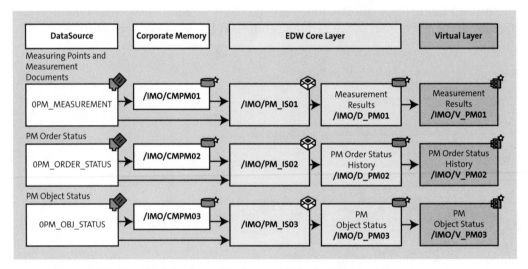

Figure 5.259 Plant Maintenance: SAP BusinessObjects BI Content Flow

Customer Service

The customer service process is similar to plant maintenance. You'll notice the similarity in the DataSources, as shown in Figure 5.260.

The path to fill the setup table from Transaction SBIW is as shown in Figure 5.261: **Settings for Application-Specific DataSource (PI)** · **Logistics** · **Initialization** · **Filling the Setup Table** · **Application-Specific Setup of Statistical Data** · **Service Management—Perform Setup**.

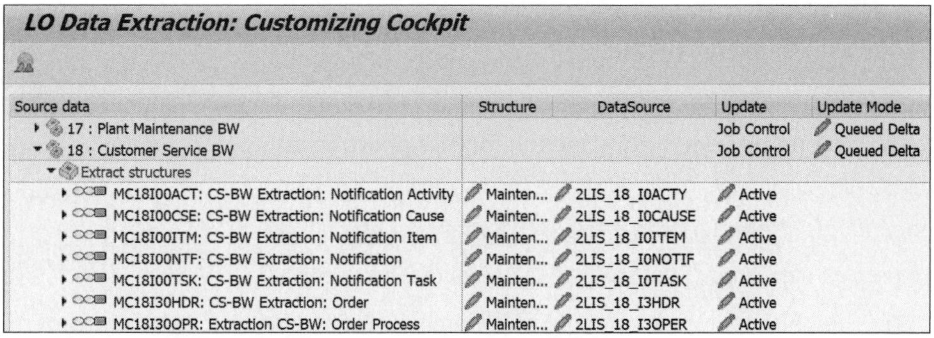

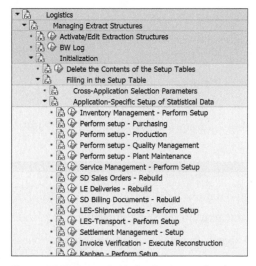

Figure 5.260 Transaction LBWE for Customer Service

Figure 5.261 Setup Path for Customer Service

Transaction OLISBW can be used to reach to the same screen, as shown in Figure 5.262.

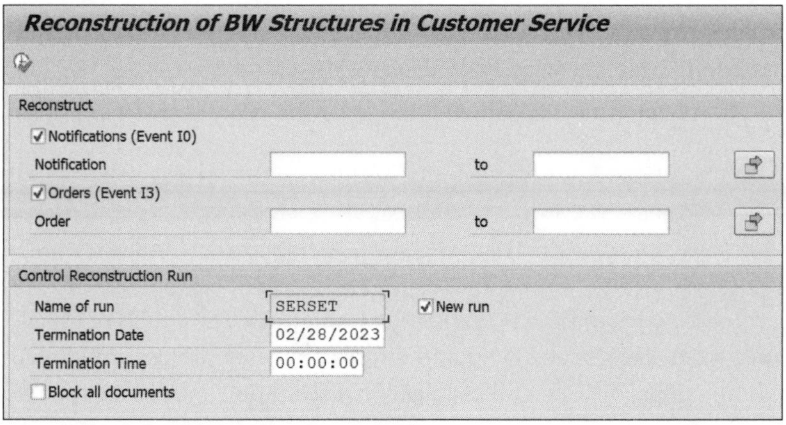

Figure 5.262 Setup for Customer Service

Once you fill the setup table as shown in Figure 5.262 using Transaction OLISBW, it will be available for the full upload.

5.6.5   Setting Up Logistics Extraction for All Applications

We've now walked through all the details for filling setup tables for all application components. Let's summarize the details in a couple of lists.

To prepare data staging for SAP S/4HANA, follow these steps:

1. Transfer the application component hierarchy using Transaction RSA9 (one time).
2. Delete the setup table from all LO application components based on number from Transaction LBWE.
3. Install the SAP BW DataSource with Transaction RSA5.
4. Activate the DataSource in the logistics cockpit in Transaction LBWE.
5. Select the update mode in Transaction LBWE.
6. Make sure the Transaction LBWE job control is green.
7. Fill the setup table based on Transaction SBIW.
8. Check the contents of the setup table using Transaction RSA3 or report RODPS_REPL_ TEST.

To implement the dataflow and fetch data in SAP BW/4HANA, follow these steps:

1. Install the SAP BusinessObjects BI content dataflow.
2. Replicate the SAP-delivered DataSource and activate the DataSource.
3. Connect the dataflow based on the /IMO objects as per the data flow for the application.
4. If the /IMO flow is not used, create the Dataflow using an aDSO.
5. Create the transformation and DTP.
6. Execute the DTP. The first load will be init with data load. It will create the subscription in Transaction ODQMON.
7. Once the delta is initialized, the next DTP will be the delta load.
8. Add the delta DTP to the process chain and schedule the process chain at regular intervals.

5.7   Summary

In this chapter, you learned about the LO extraction framework. The details of the different extraction modes like queued delta and direct delta were discussed in detail, along with a basic functional overview of the sales and distribution application module and the tables and transactions used in the applications. We discussed the steps to active DataSources in SAP S/4HANA and fill the setup tables for applications in sales. You learned how to use the logistics cockpit for SAP BW/4HANA extraction. Now you can do the LO extraction and check the data in Transaction ODQMON for reconciliation purposes.

With the completion of the end-to-end extraction based on the logistics extraction views, you're ready to build the SAP BW/4HANA model to extract data from the SAP S/4HANA system using the SAP-delivered extractors. Understanding this logic will be mandatory as large SAP BW/4HANA implementation projects will have the reporting requirements based on data from SAP S/4HANA systems. LO extraction plays a key role in fetching data from the SAP S/4HANA and SAP ERP systems.

We also covered a basic functional overview of purchasing and other important logistics applications, and the tables and transactions used in the applications were discussed in detail. You're aware now of the functional flows that trigger the data in each application. We discussed the steps to active DataSources and fill the setup tables for each application. With the completion of the dataflow based on the logistics extraction views now you are ready to build the SAP BW/4HANA model to extract the data from SAP S/4HANA system using the SAP-delivered extractors. We discussed all the major extractors available in the logistics cockpit. Understanding this logic will be mandatory in large SAP BW/4HANA implementation projects as the business requirements for SAP BW analytical reports will be based on data from the SAP S/4HANA system.

In the next chapter, we'll focus on extracting the master data from SAP S/4HANA using the SAP-delivered standard extractors.

Chapter 6
Extracting Master Data

This chapter explains extracting master data from different functional areas. You'll learn about the master extractor types and understand the differences of each type. This chapter also covers the standard SAP-delivered master data frequently used in logistics applications and shows you how to load the data from SAP S/4HANA to SAP BW/4HANA 2.0. Once you complete this chapter, you'll be able to identify the relevant master data InfoObjects for data modeling and use them for the SAP BW/4HANA data staging requirements for analytical reporting scenarios.

When a document is posted in an online transactional processing (OLTP) system, it's stored in backed application tables. The data stored is categorized as master data or transactional data. You can see that the data dictionary in SAP also distinguishes between the tables that store master data and transactional data. In general, *master data* is the core data used for any business transaction. In any OLTP system, when a transaction document like a sales order or purchase order is posted, then it needs the associated master data to complete the document creation. These master data are preconfigured or maintained when the ERP system is implemented. It can be said that *transactional data* is created based on the existing master data. Consider, for example, a sales order for a thousand units of a product. It needs the product master data that is stored already.

In this chapter, we'll start by explaining master data from an SAP BW perspective in Section 6.1. We'll also discuss various mater data that can be extracted from SAP S/4HANA in Section 6.2 and see how that can be used in the SAP BW/4HANA data modeling and reporting. You'll learn why master data extraction is essential for accurate reporting. In Section 6.3, you'll learn how to install master data in SAP BW and how to load data from master data tables using extractors by using the SAP-delivered business content to extract master data for all application-based SAP BW/4HANA data staging or extractions.

6.1 Introduction to Master Data in SAP S/4HANA

You have already learned how to post transactional data in the SAP S/4HANA system. There are many transaction codes that help you achieve this. Once transactional data is posted, it creates a transaction document number, like a sales order number, for example. Let's review the screen where you create a sales order using Transaction VA01. We'll display a sales order and get a functional understanding of what master data is and how it's used in OLTP.

Figure 6.1 shows the following details:

❶ **Sold-to Party** and **Ship-to Party** are standard master data elements in sales and distribution, and the values shown here are the master data values stored in master data tables.

❷ The **Material** name listed here will be part of the material master table.

❸ Once you provide the **Order Quantity**, then based on the master data from the material table, other calculations are performed.

❹ The **Total Weight** is calculated by order quantity × gross weight. Here, the order quantity is 10, and the weight per material is 1, meaning the total weight is 10.

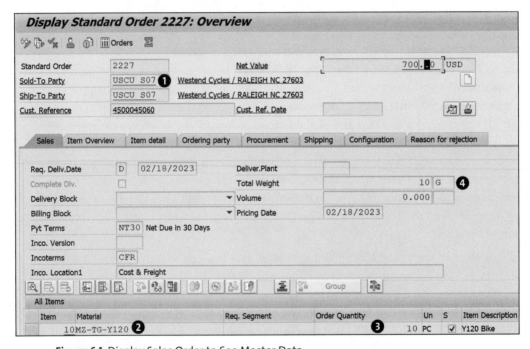

Figure 6.1 Display Sales Order to See Master Data

In SAP S/4HANA, you create the customer master using Transaction BP, where BP stands for business partner. In this transaction, provide the sold-to party in the **BusinessPartner** field, as shown in Figure 6.2.

Once you press ⌈Enter⌋, you'll see the details of the business partner, as shown in Figure 6.3, including **Partner**, **Description**, and **Name.**

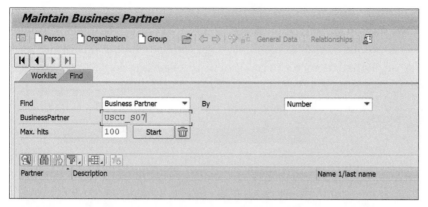

Figure 6.2 Finding Business Partner Details

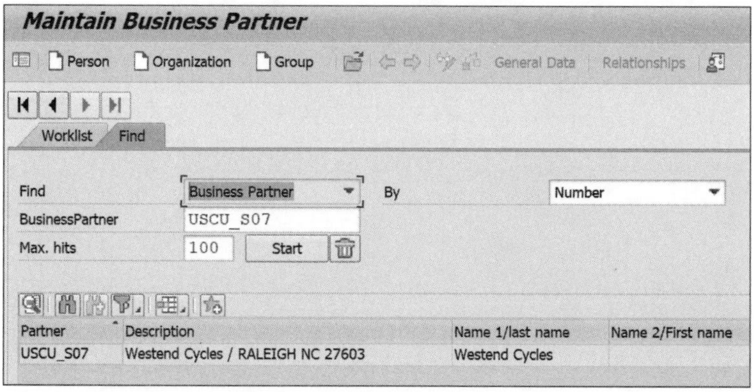

Figure 6.3 Partner ID and Description

Once the business partner is created, it gets stored in the backend master data table. Table KNA1 is the master table for customers. If you need to find the details of a customer, you can provide the customer ID in the **Customer** field in table KNA1 to see the details, as shown in Figure 6.4.

Cl.	Customer	Cty	Name 1	Name 2 City	PostalCode Rg	SearchTerm Street Telephone 1 Fax Number One-time Address	Name 1	Name 2 City	Title
100	USCU_S07	US	Westend Cycles	RALEIGH 27603	NC	CBK15	0000023660 WESTEND CYCLES	RALEIGH	Company

Figure 6.4 Table KNA1: General Data in Customer Master

Now you know how the sold-to party got details such as name and address once you provided the sold-to party number in the sales order creation. The sold-to-party details are already stored in the database tables and are used when creating the transactional data.

Now let's see where the master data for the material in the sales order creation is stored. To view that, open Transaction MM03. This transaction can be used to examine a material with various views, like basic data, sales data, purchasing, quality management, and so on. In this example, choose all views by selecting select all the views button as shown in Figure 6.5.

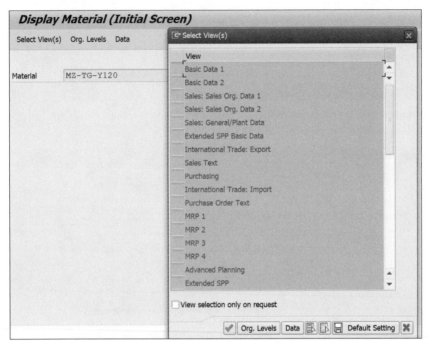

Figure 6.5 Transaction MM03 for Material Display

Once you choose the **Enter** icon ✔, you can see the complete master data of the material from all view perspectives. Each view is in its own tab, and you can select each tab to see the different views of the material. Figure 6.6 shows the following details:

❶ This is the material name that you see in sales order creation.

❷ This is the material description seen on the sales order screen.

❸ This is the weight of the material; here, it's **1**. This was part of the calculation of total weight shown in Figure 6.1

❹ The weight unit is G here, which is called in the sales order.

❺ You can see different tabs to see the views for the material.

Now if you display table MARA in Transaction SE16 and execute it using the ⊕ icon, you'll see that it holds all the master data for a specific material. Let's check table MARA for a few fields that we are interested in. For example, we'll now look at all material numbers available in the SAP S/4HANA system and get the material-related information from table MARA, as shown in Figure 6.7.

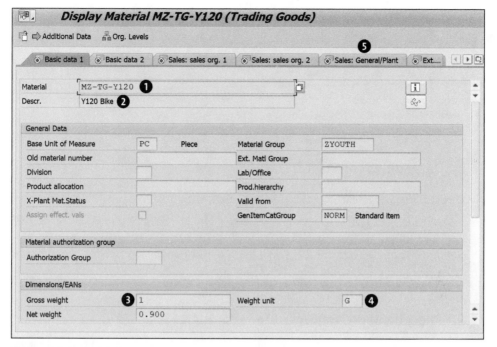

Figure 6.6 Material View

Data Browser: Table MARA Select Entries 200

Check Table...

Material	Maint. status	MTyp	I	Matl Group	BUn	OUn	Gross weight	Net weight	WUn	Volume	Width	Height	Unit of Dimension
000000000000000011	KDP	FERT	M		ST					0.000			
000000000000002101	K	FERT	M		ST					0.000			
CM-FL-V01	KCLVDBGA	KMAT	M	L004	ST		3	2	KG	0.000			
CM-MLFL-KM-VXX	KCLVDBGA	KMAT	M	L004	ST		1,000	1,000	KG	0.000			
CM-WPR-SYSTEM	KC	KMAT	M		EA					0.000			
EWMS4-01	KLEVDB	HAWA	M	L001	ST		18	18	KG	8.000	20	20	CM
EWMS4-02	KLEVDB	HAWA	M	L001	ST		4	4	KG	3.000	10	30	CM
EWMS4-10	KLEVDB	HAWA	M	L001	ST		225	225	KG	144.000	120	30	CM
EWMS4-11	KLEVDB	HAWA	M	L001	ST		150	150	KG	135.000	30	90	CM
EWMS4-20	KCLEVDB	HAWA	M	L001	ST		150	150	KG	135.000	30	90	CM
EWMS4-40	KLEVDB	HAWA	M	L001	ST		1	1	KG	5.000	20	16	CM
EWMS4-41	KLEVDB	HAWA	M	L001	ST		1	1	KG	3.000	18	14	CM
EWMS4-42	KLEVDB	HAWA	M	L001	ST		150	150	KG	135.000	30	90	CM
EWMS4-50	KLVDABG	FERT	M	L004	ST		55	55	KG	144.000	40	30	CM
EWMS4-502	KLEVDBG	ROH	M	L002	ST		1	1	KG	13.000	0	0	CM

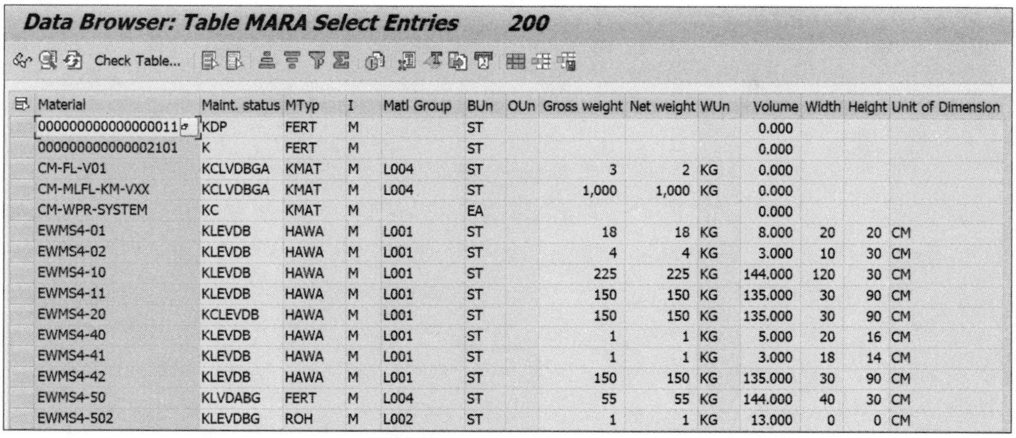

Figure 6.7 Material Master

In Transaction SE16 for table MARA, you can select a material such as MZ-TZ-Y120 and click . Then, as shown in Figure 6.8, you'll see the details of material MZ-TZ-Y120, which was used for the sales order creation.

With this screen, now you know how the master data is used in SAP S/4HANA to create the transactional data.

Data Browser: Table MARA Select Entries   1

Material	Maint. status	MTyp	I	Matl Group	BUn	OUn	Gross weight	Net weight	WUn	Volume	Width	Height	Unit of Dimension
MZ-TG-Y120	KDELBVQ	HAWA	M	ZYOUTH	ST		1	0.900	G	0.000			

Figure 6.8 Display Material with Selection for Sales Order

6.2   DataSource for Master Data

In this section, you'll learn how to check the master DataSource in SAP S/4HANA and how to check the status of the DataSource in backend tables in Section 6.2.1. You'll learn about the different types of master data that are available, such as attributes, texts, and hierarchies. Then in Section 6.2.2, you'll learn about the DataSource for the material master.

6.2.1   Check the Master DataSource in SAP S/4HANA

With a strong understating of master data, now let's look at all the important master DataSources used in SAP BW/4HANA extraction. Without the master data, the reporting in SAP BW will be incomplete, so during the implementation you should make sure that you extract the relevant master data before extraction of transactional data. If you want to load master data for LO-based extraction, then most of them are found in Transaction RSA5 in the path **SAP · SAP-R/3 · LO · LO-IO**, as shown in Figure 6.9.

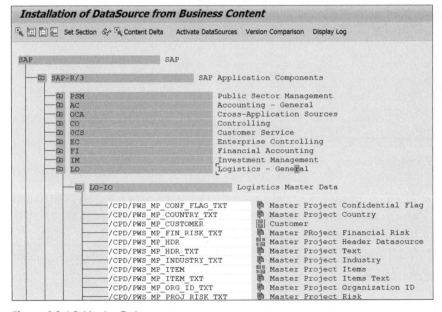

Figure 6.9 LO Master Data

Next, we'll search for the master DataSource for customer. Click the **Search** icon 🔍 and search for "OCUSTOMER", as shown in Figure 6.10.

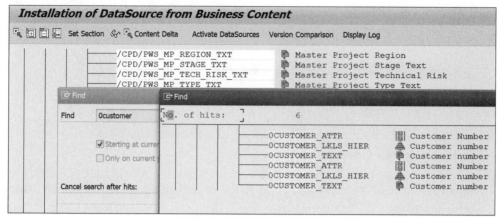

Figure 6.10 Finding Relevant Master Data Using Search Icon

Once you've found the relevant master data, such as **OCUSTOMER_ATTR**, you can choose that row. There is an option to activate the master DataSource from here, but first check if the DataSource is active. You can check this in table ROOSOURCE. Search for the table with the InfoObject name; for example, here we'll search for "OCUSTOMER*", which will return results for all the DataSources that start with OCUSTOMER, as shown in Figure 6.11.

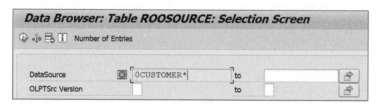

Figure 6.11 Selections for DataSource

Once you execute the table with filtering for DataSources that begin with **OCUSTOMER***
and click the ⊕ icon, the results will be shown as in Figure 6.12.

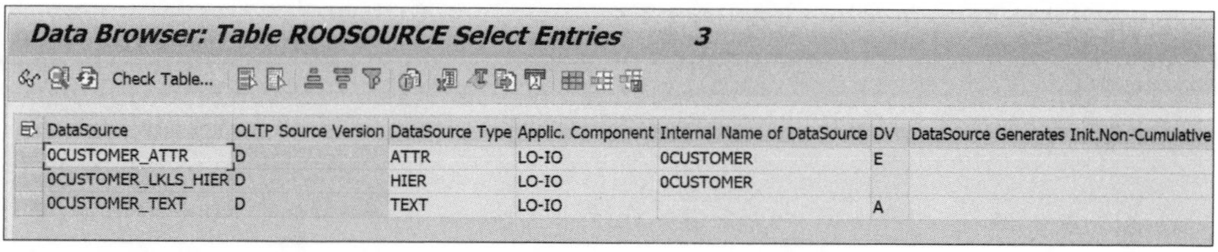

DataSource	OLTP Source Version	DataSource Type	Applic. Component	Internal Name of DataSource	DV	DataSource Generates Init.Non-Cumulative
Data Browser: Table ROOSOURCE Select Entries 3						
OCUSTOMER_ATTR	D	ATTR	LO-IO	OCUSTOMER	E	
OCUSTOMER_LKLS_HIER	D	HIER	LO-IO	OCUSTOMER		
OCUSTOMER_TEXT	D	TEXT	LO-IO		A	

Figure 6.12 OCUSTOMER DataSources

If the **OLTP Source Version** column shows **D**, that means the DataSource is the delivered version. To use this DataSource for extraction, it needs to be an active version. To activate the DataSource, go to Transaction RSA5, as shown in Figure 6.13. Choose a specific DataSource like **OCUSTOMER_ATTR** or **OCUSTOMER_TEXT** and select the **Activate Data-Sources** button as shown in Figure 6.13.

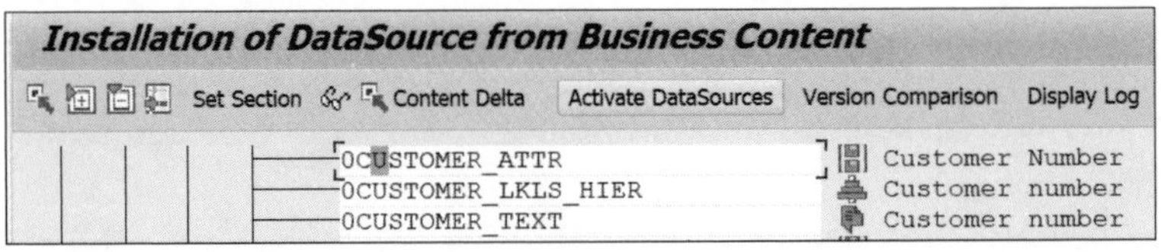

Figure 6.13 Activate Customer DataSource

Now activate OCUSTOMER_TEXT (shown in Figure 6.12), then open Transaction SE16 and open table ROOSOURCE. Do a refresh using the ⟳ icon of the table ROOSOURCE output. You can see that an A version will be generated, as shown in Figure 6.14.

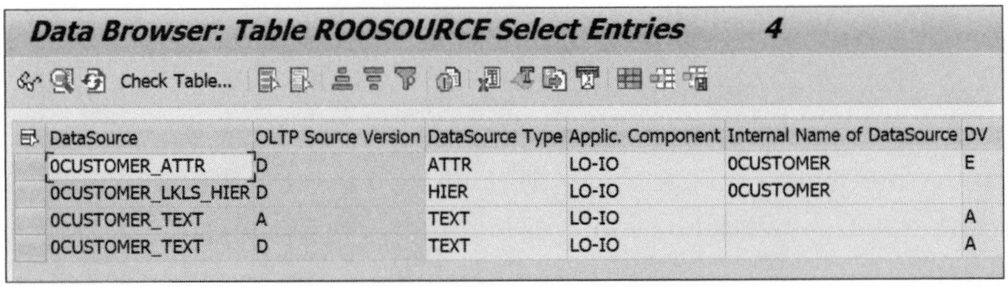

Data Browser: Table ROOSOURCE Select Entries   4

DataSource	OLTP Source Version	DataSource Type	Applic. Component	Internal Name of DataSource	DV
OCUSTOMER_ATTR	D	ATTR	LO-IO	OCUSTOMER	E
OCUSTOMER_LKLS_HIER	D	HIER	LO-IO	OCUSTOMER	
OCUSTOMER_TEXT	A	TEXT	LO-IO		A
OCUSTOMER_TEXT	D	TEXT	LO-IO		A

Figure 6.14 Active Version for Text Table

Now activate the other two DataSources (OCUSTOMER_ATTR and OCUSTOMER_LKLS_HIER) in the same way from Transaction RSA5 and check table ROOSOURCE again, as shown in Figure 6.15.

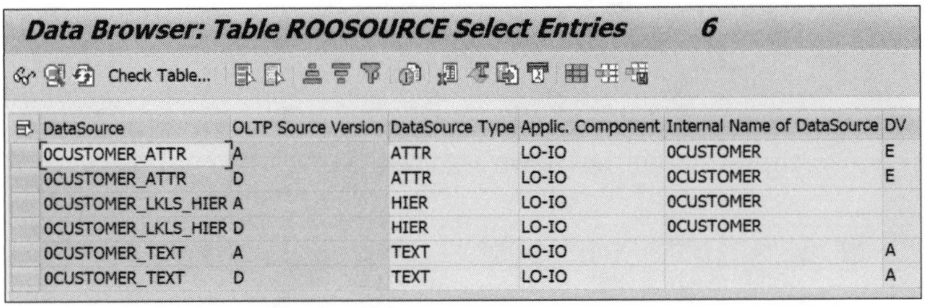

Data Browser: Table ROOSOURCE Select Entries   6

DataSource	OLTP Source Version	DataSource Type	Applic. Component	Internal Name of DataSource	DV
OCUSTOMER_ATTR	A	ATTR	LO-IO	OCUSTOMER	E
OCUSTOMER_ATTR	D	ATTR	LO-IO	OCUSTOMER	E
OCUSTOMER_LKLS_HIER	A	HIER	LO-IO	OCUSTOMER	
OCUSTOMER_LKLS_HIER	D	HIER	LO-IO	OCUSTOMER	
OCUSTOMER_TEXT	A	TEXT	LO-IO		A
OCUSTOMER_TEXT	D	TEXT	LO-IO		A

Figure 6.15 DataSources with A Version

In general, for an SAP BW extraction, there will be three master data sources:

- DataSource for master data to extract attributes
- DataSource for master data to extract texts
- DataSource for master data to extract hierarchies

This is why you see three DataSources for 0CUSTOMER. Once you've activated a Data-Source in Transaction RSA5, the data can be viewed in report RSA3, as shown in Figure 6.16, or in ABAP report RODPS_REPL_TEST.

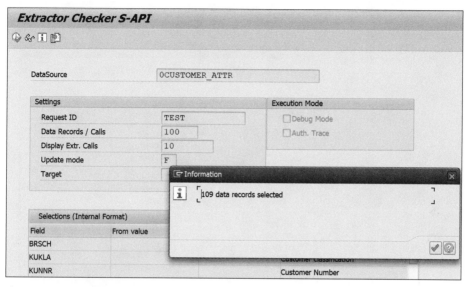

Figure 6.16 Simulation

From Transaction RSA3, once the popup of 109 records selected is shown, you can choose the **ALV Grid** option ▦ to view the records, as shown in Figure 6.17.

Result of Extraction of DataSource 0CUSTOMER_ATTR

Data Package (Number of Recs)   1 (100)

Customer	Address	Title	OrBlk	Street	City	Created on	Group	Cty
1000010	24637			3475 Deer Creek	Palo Alto	11/09/2018	CUST	US
1000049	24746			Hauptstr. 10	Walldorf	02/18/2019	CUST	DE
1000110	25590	Company		Sector 12	NAVI MUMBAI	10/10/2021	CUST	IN
1000111	25592	Company		1	NAVI MUMBAI	10/10/2021	CUST	IN
3000000	24728				Frankfurt	02/14/2019	DEBI	DE
10100002	23744	Company		Platnerstraße 45	Chemnitz	10/17/2017	CUST	DE
10100003	23768	Company		Römerstraße 1230	Budenheim	10/17/2017	CUST	DE
10100004	23770	Company		Lahnbergweg 23	Wetzlar	10/17/2017	CUST	DE
10100005	23780	Company		Heinrichstraße 1020	Steinhagen	10/17/2017	CUST	DE

Figure 6.17 Result of Simulation

You can group the fields that you need by choosing the layout option ▦. Now you can filter using the **Filter** icon ▼. for the field KUNNR (which is used for storing sold-to party information), which is customer **USCU_S07**, as shown in Figure 6.18.

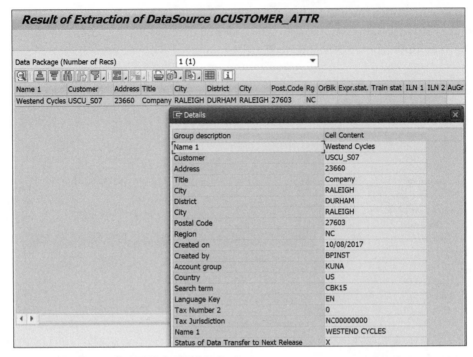

Figure 6.18 Transaction RSA3 for Sold-to Party

When you extract the OCUSTOMER_ATTR DataSource, it will bring in the fields that are displayed to the SAP BW/4HANA master data InfoObject that can be used in SAP BW reporting. If you need to see the extractor and the extract structure, you can use Transaction RSA2, which will display the details shown in Figure 6.19. You can see that the **Extractor** is MDEX_CUSTOMER_MD, which is an ABAP-based function module, and the **Extract Structure** is BIW_KNA1_S, which will have all the fields for the extraction.

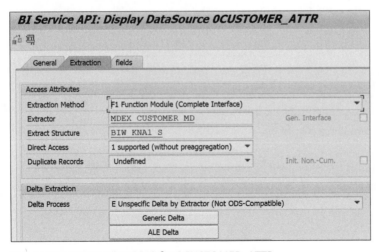

Figure 6.19 Transaction RSA2 for OCUSTOMER_ATTR

If you double-click in the **Extractor** field, there will be a standard SAP code that is used to fetch the data during the SAP BW extraction process. You can see that tables like KNA1, which we discussed earlier in Section 6.1, were used in the selection. This explains the logic of extraction of attributes and the source for the data, as shown in Figure 6.20.

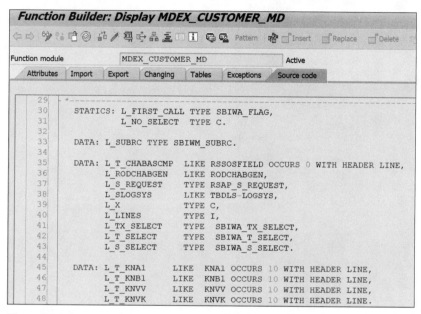

Figure 6.20 Extractor for 0CUSTOMER_ATTR

It can be important to know all the fields and their properties that are handled by a DataSource. Table ROOSFIELD is used for that purpose. Open the table and either execute it without a selection or provide the field if necessary. When you see the **Relevance** for an extractor set to **Y**, that means the field is sent to SAP BW for extraction. If it's set to **N**, then that field will not be sent to SAP BW for extraction. This table will be used to analyze the reason for missing data in any of transactional data and master data extraction, as shown in Figure 6.21.

Now if you choose the extract structure from the screen that was shown in Figure 6.19, you'll see the fields that will be extracted. You'll see the list of all fields in the **Component** column, as shown in Figure 6.22.

You can use the same simulation options to execute Transaction RSA3 and check the 0CUSTOMER_TEXT DataSource, as shown in Figure 6.23.

DataSource	OLTP Source Version	Field Name	Properties of a DataSource Field	Ref. field	Field Inverted if Canceled
0CUSTOMER_ATTR	A	KUNNR	X		
0CUSTOMER_ATTR	D	KUNNR	X		

Group description	Cell Content
DataSource	0CUSTOMER_ATTR
OLTP Source Version	A
Field Name	KUNNR
Properties of a DataSource Field	X
Ref. field	
Field Inverted if Canceled	
F4 Type for a DataSource Field	
Extractor for Input Help	
Relevance for Standard Extractor(s)	Y
DataSource Key Field	
Selection Options	0

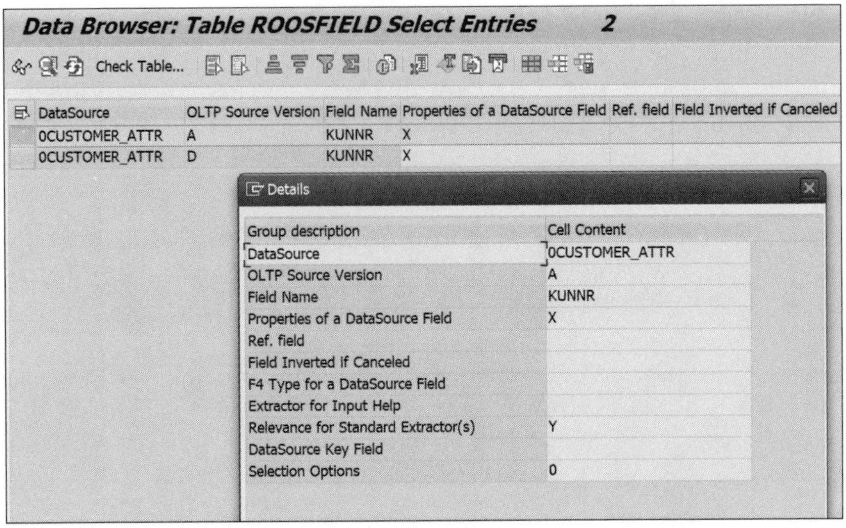

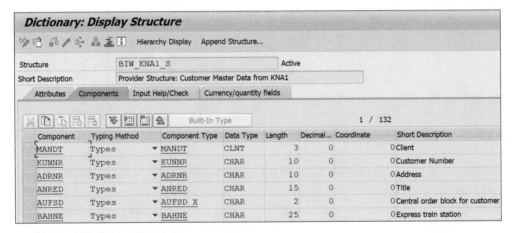

Figure 6.21 Table ROOSFIELD for Selection

Component	Typing Method	Component Type	Data Type	Length	Decimal...	Coordinate	Short Description
MANDT	Types	MANDT	CLNT	3	0	0	Client
KUNNR	Types	KUNNR	CHAR	10	0	0	Customer Number
ADRNR	Types	ADRNR	CHAR	10	0	0	Address
ANRED	Types	ANRED	CHAR	15	0	0	Title
AUFSD	Types	AUFSD_X	CHAR	2	0	0	Central order block for customer
BAHNE	Types	BAHNE	CHAR	25	0	0	Express train station

Figure 6.22 Extract Structure

Customer	Name 1
USCU_S07	Westend Cycles

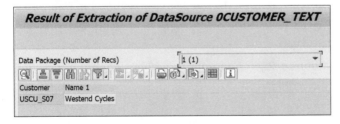

Figure 6.23 Transaction RSA3: 0CUSTOMER_TEXT

6.2.2   DataSource for Material Master

Once you log onto the SAP S/4HANA system, in Transaction RSA5 you can see Data-Sources like OMATERIAL, as shown Figure 6.24, for extracting the material master.

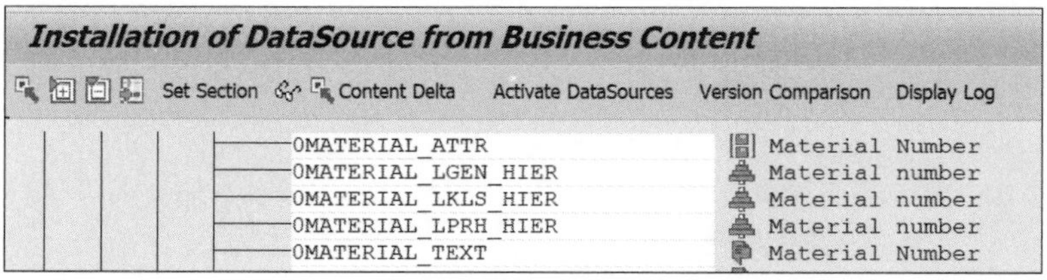

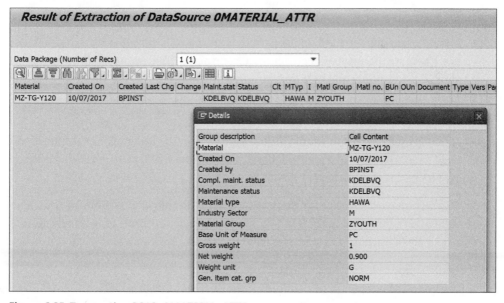

Figure 6.24 DataSource for Material Master Extraction

There are different types of master data like ATTR, TEXT, and HIER for the DataSources for material masters, like OMATERIAL_ATTR, OMATERIAL_TEXT, and OMATERIAL_LGEN_HIER. The steps to extract data from the SAP S/4HANA system the same as for other logistics-based extractions: you need to activate the DataSource first and test the data for the DataSource, like OMATERIAL_ATTR, with Transaction RSA3.

Let's look at the data for OMATERIAL_ATTR, which was used in the sample sales order creation. The results for attribute data are shown in Figure 6.25, based on the execution of Transaction RSA3.

Figure 6.25 Transaction RSA3: OMATERIA_ATTR

Once you display the data from Transaction RSA3 for the material MZ-TG-Y120, you can see that the **Gross Weight** is **1** and **Weight Unit** is **G**, as captured by this extractor. With this, you can see how an SAP transaction is connected to backend tables and how the

SAP BW DataSources get those data. Knowing about this extraction logic is essential for effective data extraction.

Now let's see the text data for a material based on OMATERIAL_TEXT, as shown in Figure 6.26.

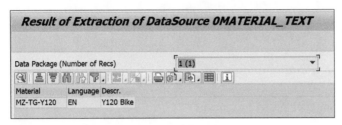

Figure 6.26 Transaction RSA3: OMATERIAL_TEXT

You can see that the material description is based on this DataSource, so if you need your SAP BW reports to have the material description in the results, then this Data-Source must be connected to the OMATERIAL InfoObject.

6.3   Standard Logistics InfoObjects with Master Data

There are various SAP-delivered business content InfoObjects of type master data. In general, master InfoObjects are divided into the following categories:

- Attributes are the separate InfoObjects that are logically subordinate to characteristics. There are many types of attributes, like display attributes, navigation attributes, and time-dependent and time-independent attributes.

- Text type master data holds descriptions of fields. The data is stored in a text table as small, medium, or large descriptions.

- Hierarchy data serves to enable drilldown based on the nodes. For example, if you need to see the sales of a material based on a region, that can be determined based on a hierarchy structure.

In this section, you'll learn how to install master data InfoObjects from the business content and then how to replicate the master data from SAP S/4HANA. Finally, in Section 6.3.3 you'll learn how to load data from the master DataSource to SAP BW/4HANA.

6.3.1   Install Master Data InfoObjects from Business Content

Before loading master data into SAP BW/4HANA, you need to install the standard business content for master data; for example, OCUSTOMER is the InfoObject for extracting the customer master data, so you need to install this from SAP BW/4HANA with Transaction RSA1. You can do so following these steps, as shown in Figure 6.27:

❶ Choose **BI Content** from Transaction RSA1.

❷ Choose the object type **InfoObject** and click **Select Objects**. This will take you to the next popup, where you can search using the **Find** icon 🔍 for "0CUSTOMER". You'll see the InfoObject in the results.

❸ Choose **0CUSTOMER** from the list.

❹ Choose **Transfer Selections**.

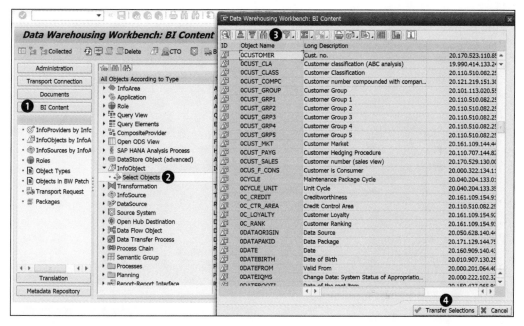

Figure 6.27 Steps for Business Content Installation

Now make groupings per your requirements. Here, we'll choose **Only Necessary Objects** for the example, as shown in Figure 6.28.

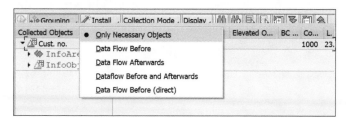

Figure 6.28 Grouping

Next choose the **Install** option. That will install the InfoObject in the SAP BW/4HANA system.

After the installation is completed, you'll see the logs for successful completion. You can choose the option to install in the background (see Figure 6.29). If instead you install via the dialog, you need to confirm various popups and assign the transport package and workbench request as per your requirements. This step will try to collect many InfoObject attributes and activate them because the master data InfoObject for OCUSTOMER relies on many other InfoObjects as attributes for its structure. During activation, you can see info in the status bar, shown in Figure 6.30, that will keep changing. It will show **Checking InfoObject** followed by an InfoObject name. Once all the InfoObjects are checked, it will begin the activation process.

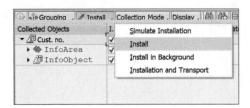

Figure 6.29 Install OCUSTOMER

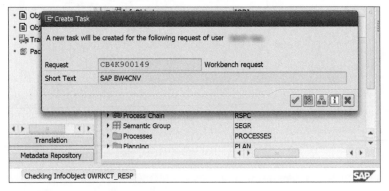

Figure 6.30 Status Bar Updates

You can see messages in the status bar indicating the processing status, as shown in Figure 6.31, where it shows **Creation of DDIC Objects for InfoObject**, which means the tables are created for the InfoObject.

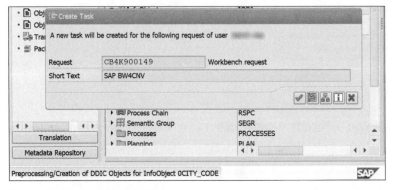

Figure 6.31 Creation of DDIC Objects

Once the creation is completed, you'll see the activation process happening, as shown in Figure 6.32.

Figure 6.32 Activation Process

When this is completed, the logs are shown (see Figure 6.33). The activation status is green for all logs.

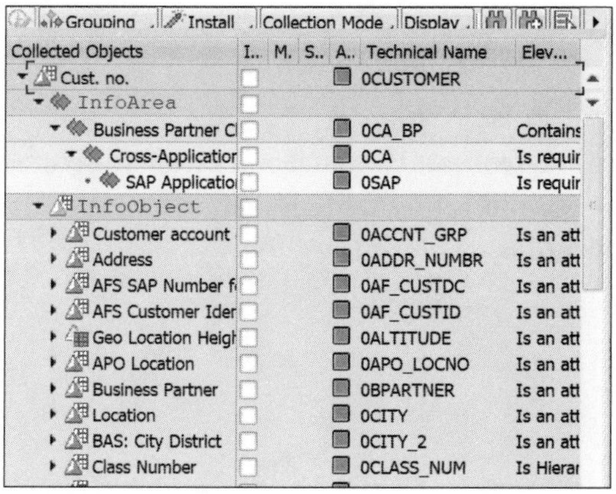

Collected Objects	I..	M.	S..	A..	Technical Name	Elev...
Cust. no.	☐			☐	0CUSTOMER	
InfoArea	☐					
Business Partner C	☐			☐	0CA_BP	Contains
Cross-Application	☐			☐	0CA	Is requir
SAP Applicatio	☐			☐	0SAP	Is requir
InfoObject	☐					
Customer account	☐			☐	0ACCNT_GRP	Is an att
Address	☐			☐	0ADDR_NUMBR	Is an att
AFS SAP Number f	☐			☐	0AF_CUSTDC	Is an att
AFS Customer Ider	☐			☐	0AF_CUSTID	Is an att
Geo Location Heigh	☐			☐	0ALTITUDE	Is an att
APO Location	☐			☐	0APO_LOCNO	Is an att
Business Partner	☐			☐	0BPARTNER	Is an att
Location	☐			☐	0CITY	Is an att
BAS: City District	☐			☐	0CITY_2	Is an att
Class Number	☐			☐	0CLASS_NUM	Is Hierar

Figure 6.33 Logs

You can refer to table RSDIOBJ to see the status of the InfoObjects, as shown in Figure 6.34.

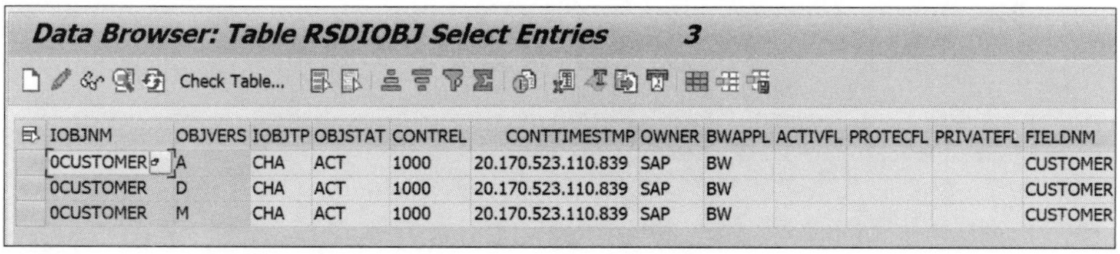

Data Browser: Table RSDIOBJ Select Entries   3

IOBJNM	OBJVERS	IOBJTP	OBJSTAT	CONTREL	CONTTIMESTMP	OWNER	BWAPPL	ACTIVFL	PROTECFL	PRIVATEFL	FIELDNM
0CUSTOMER	A	CHA	ACT	1000	20.170.523.110.839	SAP	BW				CUSTOMER
0CUSTOMER	D	CHA	ACT	1000	20.170.523.110.839	SAP	BW				CUSTOMER
0CUSTOMER	M	CHA	ACT	1000	20.170.523.110.839	SAP	BW				CUSTOMER

Figure 6.34 InfoObject Status

With this, you can confirm that the InfoObject is activated. Perform the same steps for the standard InfoObject OMATERIAL in Transaction RSA1 with the **BI Content** option, and activate the InfoObject. You'll see that the **A** versions will be created for the InfoObjects, as shown in Figure 6.35.

IOBJNM	OBJVERS	IOBJ...	OBJSTAT	CONTREL	CONTTIMESTMP	OWNER	BWAPPL	ACTIVFL	PROTECFL	PRIVATEFL	FIELDNM
0CUSTOMER	A	CHA	ACT	1000	20.170.523.110.839	SAP	BW				CUSTOMER
0CUSTOMER	D	CHA	ACT	1000	20.170.523.110.839	SAP	BW				CUSTOMER
0CUSTOMER	M	CHA	ACT	1000	20.170.523.110.839	SAP	BW				CUSTOMER
0MATERIAL	A	CHA	ACT	1000	20.170.519.131.406	SAP	BW	X			MATERIAL
0MATERIAL	D	CHA	ACT	1000	20.170.519.131.406	SAP	BW	X			MATERIAL
0MATERIAL	M	CHA	ACT	1000	20.170.519.131.406	SAP	BW	X			MATERIAL

Data Browser: Table RSDIOBJ Select Entries   6

Check Table...

Figure 6.35 0MATERIAL Status

6.3.2   InfoObjects and Master Data–Based Sources

Before starting the extraction, make sure you replicate the DataSource from the corresponding SAP S/4HANA system. Right-click the source system and select **Replicate** from the context menu, as shown in Figure 6.36.

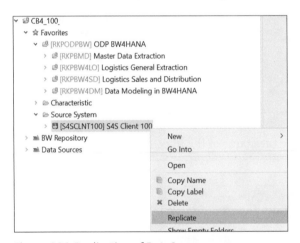

Figure 6.36 Replication of DataSource

On the next screen, first deselect all the listed DataSources; this will help you choose only the required objects for replication. Filter for "OCUS" and choose the resulting three DataSources. Click **Select Displayed DataSources**. You'll see that 3 of 185 are selected, as shown in Figure 6.37.

Choose **Select Displayed DataSources** and search for "OMAT" to see DataSources that start with OMAT. Choose these DataSources by selecting the option **Select Displayed DataSources**. Six DataSources will be selected, as shown in Figure 6.38.

Now you'll see **6 of 185 DataSources Selected**. These will be created or updated as shown in Figure 6.39.

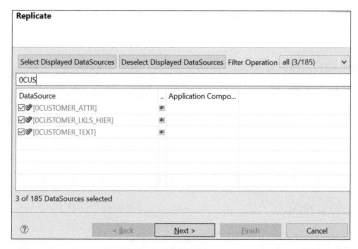

Figure 6.37 Replication for 0CUSTOMER

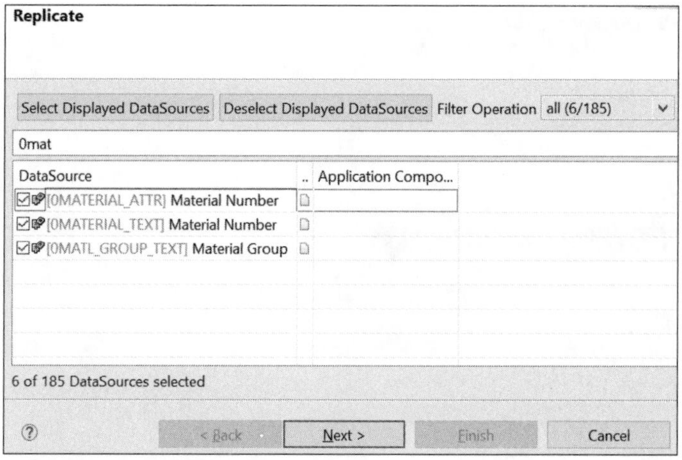

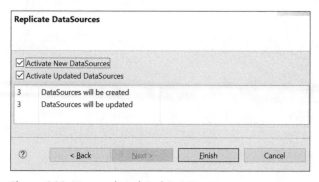

Figure 6.38 0MATERIAL Selection

Figure 6.39 New and Updated DataSources

Choose **Finish** to complete the process. It will create a job that starts with **RSDS_REPLICATION**, and it can be seen in Transaction SM37, as shown in Figure 6.40.

Job Log Entries for RSDS_REPLICATION / 22525600
Long text
Previous Page
Next page
Job log overview for job: RSDS_REPLICATION / 22525600
Date
Time
Message text
27.02.2023 22:52:57 Job RSDS_REPLICATION 22525600 started
27.02.2023 22:52:57 Step 001 started (program RSDS_REPLICATION, variant &0000000000058, user ID

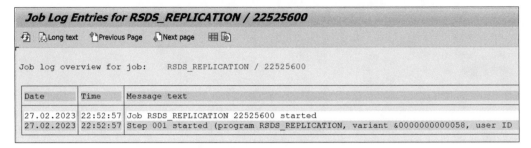

Figure 6.40 DataSource replication tab

To understand the behavior, check table RSDS before this job finishes. You can see that there are no entries for one of the DataSources, as shown in Figure 6.41.

Data Browser: Table RSDS: Selection Screen
Number of Entries
DATASOURCE
0CUSTOMER*
to
LOGSYS
S4SCLNT100
to
OBJVERS
A
to
Display Number of Entries
Number of entries that meet
the selection criteria:
0
Close

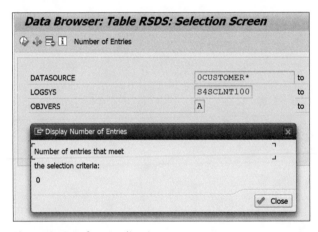

Figure 6.41 Before Replication

Once the replication of the DataSource has started, you can see the status of the replication job, as shown in Figure 6.42.

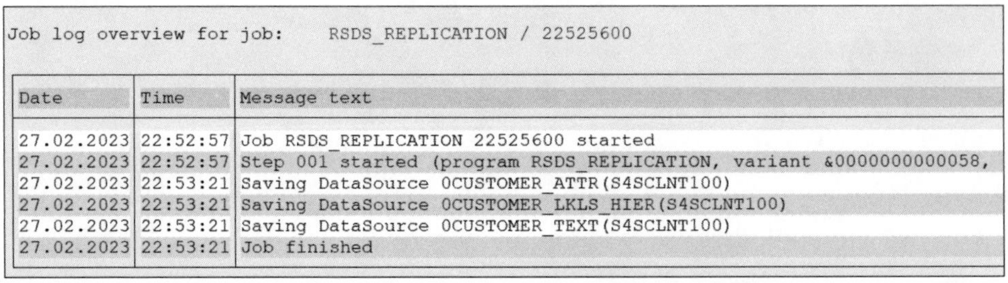

Job log overview for job: RSDS_REPLICATION / 22525600
Date
Time
Message text
27.02.2023 22:52:57 Job RSDS_REPLICATION 22525600 started
27.02.2023 22:52:57 Step 001 started (program RSDS_REPLICATION, variant &0000000000058,
27.02.2023 22:53:21 Saving DataSource 0CUSTOMER_ATTR(S4SCLNT100)
27.02.2023 22:53:21 Saving DataSource 0CUSTOMER_LKLS_HIER(S4SCLNT100)
27.02.2023 22:53:21 Saving DataSource 0CUSTOMER_TEXT(S4SCLNT100)
27.02.2023 22:53:21 Job finished

Figure 6.42 After Replication

6.3.3   Load the Data from the Master Data Source to the InfoObject

Now create the transformation from master data–based DataSources to InfoObjects. In this example, we'll create the transformation from DataSource 0CUSTOMER_ATTR to Info-Object 0CUSTOMER, as shown in Figure 6.43.

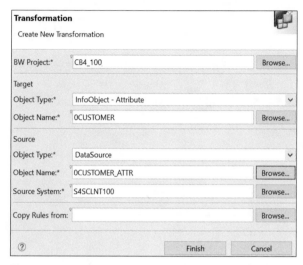

Figure 6.43 Transformation

Create a DTP based on the transformation created in the previous step. You can see the DTP settings as shown in Figure 6.44.

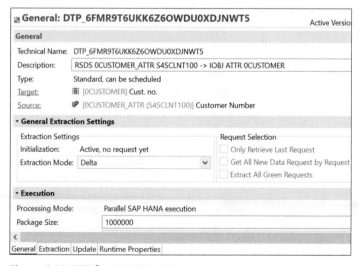

Figure 6.44 DTP for 0CUSTOMER

Activate the DTP using the ⬚ icon. Before executing, you need to check two things. First, check table ROOSGEN as shown in Figure 6.45. You'll see that there is no OCUSTOMER DataSource in this list.

Data Browser: Table ROOSGEN Select Entries   17

DataSource	Src. System	DWH System	Method	TransferStructure	IDocSegm.	Structure	Field	Message type
OFI_ACDOCA_10	S4HCLNT100	$ODQ_DUMMY	T				6FMR9T6UKK6YUVW9NJDZ3XA4U	
OFI_ACDOCA_20	S4HCLNT100	$ODQ_DUMMY	T				6FMR9T6UKK70T20LPWE5435VA	
OFI_GL_14	S4HCLNT100	$ODQ_DUMMY	T				6FMR9T6UKK6YUZ56JGSZ2WK0G	
OFI_GL_4	S4HCLNT100	$ODQ_DUMMY	T				6FMR9T6UKK70WEDW1RHNBFJDA	
OFI_GL_61	S4HCLNT100	$ODQ_DUMMY	T				6FMR9T6UKK6YUWNYMWB2OD51C	
OMATERIAL_ATTR	S4HCLNT100	$ODQ_DUMMY	T				6FMR9T6UKK6Z2E0BPBZTJ0FAX	RS0001
OPOC_BUSINESS_ACTIVITY	S4HCLNT100	$ODQ_DUMMY					12Y48MZQ449GSD5WAMI4EZ5X6	
OPOC_PRC_INSTANCE	S4HCLNT100	$ODQ_DUMMY					12Y48MZQ449GSD5WBCJ2954FU	
OPOC_PRC_KPI	S4HCLNT100	$ODQ_DUMMY					12Y48MZQ449GSD5W8RQY8HBXZ	
OPOC_PRC_STEP_INSTANCE	S4HCLNT100	$ODQ_DUMMY					12Y48MZQ449GSD5W876WD9SQE	
2LIS_02_HDR	S4HCLNT100	$ODQ_DUMMY	T				6FMR9T6UKK70L7D33DMPYLMRO	
2LIS_02_ITM	S4HCLNT100	$ODQ_DUMMY	T				6FMR9T6UKK6Z6OAQU8FEQEQCB	
2LIS_02_S011	S4HCLNT100	$ODQ_DUMMY					6FMR9T6UKK70SMIL33J41SJ34	
2LIS_02_SCL	S4HCLNT100	$ODQ_DUMMY	T				6FMR9T6UKK70L6YIPS3Q1PUI0	
2LIS_11_VAHDR	S4HCLNT100	$ODQ_DUMMY	T				6FMR9T6UKK6YUVZN3TI7S9XC1	
2LIS_11_VAITM	S4HCLNT100	$ODQ_DUMMY	T				6FMR9T6UKK6YUVZNSTLT7PMTL	
2LIS_13_VDITM	S4HCLNT100	$ODQ_DUMMY					6FMR9T6UKK6YYTP3QEZCNZIN5	

Figure 6.45 Table ROOSGEN

The second thing is to log onto SAP S/4HANA and check Transaction ODQMON in the sender system. You'll see that OCUSTOMER is not in the list, as shown in Figure 6.46.

Monitor Delta Queues

Queues...   Subscriptions...   Requests...   Units...

Provider	BW DataSource	Subscriber Type	SAP Business Warehouse
Queue		Subscriber	
Time Stamp ID		to	
☐ Calculate Data Volume (Extended View)		Request Select.	Subscriptions Only (Delta Init + Delta)

Queue	Que	Subscrptns	Requests	Units	Rows	Original Size in Bytes	Compressed Size in B
OFI_ACDOCA_10		6	0				
OFI_ACDOCA_20		2	0				
OFI_GL_14		1	0				
OFI_GL_4		2	0				
OFI_GL_61		1	1				
2LIS_02_HDR		2	0				
2LIS_02_ITM		1	0				
2LIS_02_SCL		1	0				
2LIS_11_VAHDR		12	0				
2LIS_11_VAITM		13	0				
		41	1				

Figure 6.46 Transaction ODQMON

Now execute the DTP using the ⬚ icon and see the contents of the inbound table, as shown in Figure 6.47.

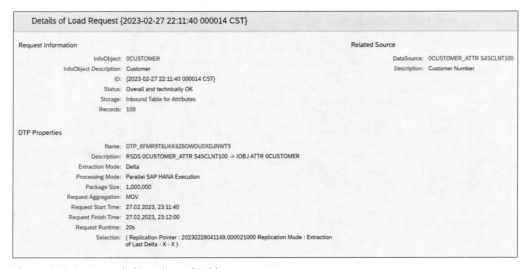

Figure 6.47 Data Loaded in Inbound Table

By this time, the data in SAP S/4HANA may have been populated. Let's first activate the data in SAP BW/4HANA from the manage request screen by selecting the **Activate** button. You can see the status of the activation in Figure 6.48.

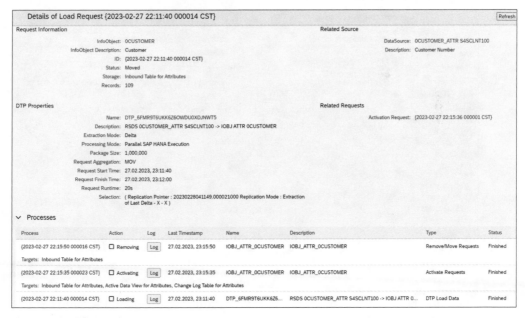

Figure 6.48 After Activation

Now let's look at table ROOSGEN again, you can see that OCUSTOMER_ATTR is now available with the message type set to RS0006, as shown in Figure 6.49.

Data Browser: Table ROOSGEN Select Entries   18

DataSource	Src. System	DWH System	Method	TransferStructure	IDocSegm.	Structure	Field	Message type
0CUSTOMER_ATTR	S4HCLNT100	$ODQ_DUMMY	T				6FMR9T6UKK6Z6OWDYRCPQE7WB	RS0006
0FI_ACDOCA_10	S4HCLNT100	$ODQ_DUMMY	T				6FMR9T6UKK6YUVW9NJDZ3XA4U	
0FI_ACDOCA_20	S4HCLNT100	$ODQ_DUMMY	T				6FMR9T6UKK70T20LPWE5435VA	
0FI_GL_14	S4HCLNT100	$ODQ_DUMMY	T				6FMR9T6UKK6YUZ56JGSZ2WK0G	
0FI_GL_4	S4HCLNT100	$ODQ_DUMMY	T				6FMR9T6UKK70WEDW1RHNBFJDA	
0FI_GL_61	S4HCLNT100	$ODQ_DUMMY	T				6FMR9T6UKK6YUWNYMWB2OD51C	
0MATERIAL_ATTR	S4HCLNT100	$ODQ_DUMMY	T				6FMR9T6UKK6Z2E0BPBZTJ0FAX	RS0001
0POC_BUSINESS_ACTIVITY	S4HCLNT100	$ODQ_DUMMY					12Y48MZQ449GSD5WAMI4EZ5X6	
0POC_PRC_INSTANCE	S4HCLNT100	$ODQ_DUMMY					12Y48MZQ449GSD5WBCJ2954FU	
0POC_PRC_KPI	S4HCLNT100	$ODQ_DUMMY					12Y48MZQ449GSD5W8RQY8HBXZ	
0POC_PRC_STEP_INSTANCE	S4HCLNT100	$ODQ_DUMMY					12Y48MZQ449GSD5W876WD9SQE	
2LIS_02_HDR	S4HCLNT100	$ODQ_DUMMY	T				6FMR9T6UKK70L7D33DMPYLMRO	
2LIS_02_ITM	S4HCLNT100	$ODQ_DUMMY	T				6FMR9T6UKK6Z6OAQU8FEQEQCB	
2LIS_02_S011	S4HCLNT100	$ODQ_DUMMY					6FMR9T6UKK70SMIL33J41SJ34	
2LIS_02_SCL	S4HCLNT100	$ODQ_DUMMY	T				6FMR9T6UKK70L6YIPS3Q1PUI0	
2LIS_11_VAHDR	S4HCLNT100	$ODQ_DUMMY	T				6FMR9T6UKK6YUVZN3TI7S9XC1	
2LIS_11_VAITM	S4HCLNT100	$ODQ_DUMMY	T				6FMR9T6UKK6YUVZNSTLT7PMTL	
2LIS_13_VDITM	S4HCLNT100	$ODQ_DUMMY					6FMR9T6UKK6YYTP3QEZCNZIN5	

Figure 6.49 Table ROOSGEN: 0CUSTOMER_ATTR

Check Transaction ODQMON in the sender system again and you'll be able to see the queue for 0CUSTOMER_ATTR now, as shown in Figure 6.50.

Monitor Delta Queues

Provider	BW DataSource	Subscriber Type	SAP Business Warehouse
Queue		Subscriber	
Time Stamp ID		to	
☐ Calculate Data Volume (Extended View)		Request Select.	Subscriptions Only (Delta Init + Delta)

Queue	Que	Subscrptns	Requests	Units	Rows	Original Size in Bytes	Compressed Size in Byte
0CUSTOMER_ATTR		1	1				
0FI_ACDOCA_10		6	0				
0FI_ACDOCA_20		2	0				
0FI_GL_14		1	0				
0FI_GL_4		2	0				
0FI_GL_61		1	1				
2LIS_02_HDR		2	0				
2LIS_02_ITM		1	0				
2LIS_02_SCL		1	0				
2LIS_11_VAHDR		12	0				
2LIS_11_VAITM		13	0				
		42	2				

Figure 6.50 ODQMON Queues

Once you double-click a row in the **Queues** column, you'll land in the subscriptions area. You'll see the details shown in Figure 6.51. The subscriber is the SAP BW system, and you can see the subscription details.

Once you choose the row, you'll see the request view, as shown in Figure 6.52. You can see that **Extraction Mode** is set to **Initial Data**, as shown in Figure 6.52.

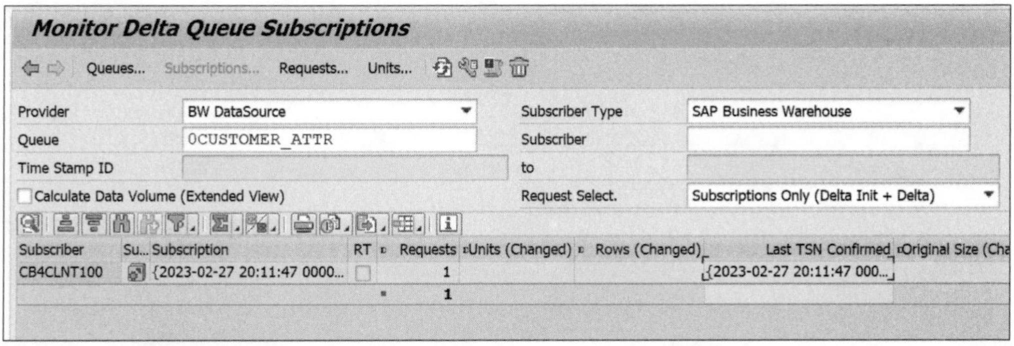

Figure 6.51 Transaction ODQMON: Subscriptions

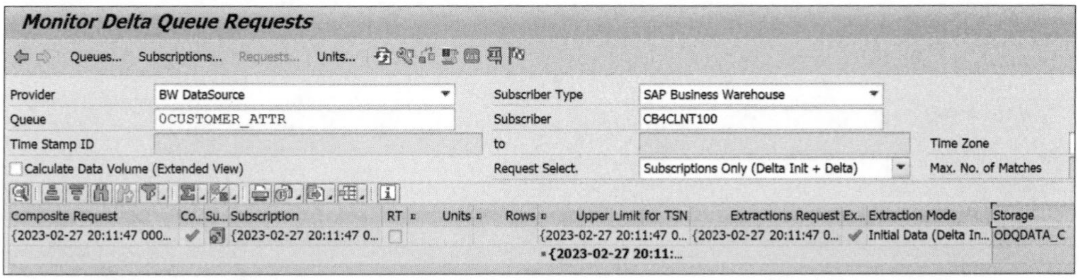

Figure 6.52 Transaction ODQMON: Requests

From the request, you can navigate to the **Units** view tab, where you can get the details of the number of rows extracted in the **Rows** column. You can see that 109 rows are there with a compression rate (**Comp. Rate**) of 96.4, as shown in Figure 6.53.

Figure 6.53 Transaction ODQMON: Units

You can see the data in the rows double-clicking a row. You'll see the list of all records in the **Units** tab, as shown in Figure 6.54.

You can search for the sold-to party (**KUNNR**) from the **Find** icon. You'll see that USCU_ S07 is part of the list that was extracted, as shown in Figure 6.55.

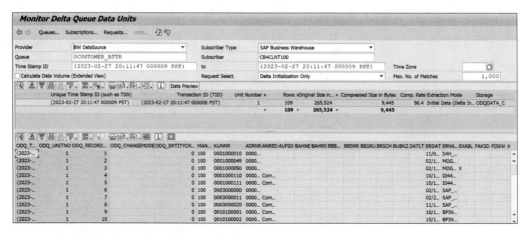

Figure 6.54 Units Tab: Check Records

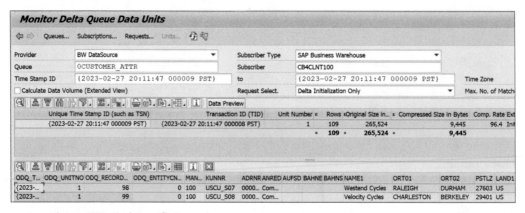

Figure 6.55 Find Specific Records

For data validation, you should check for the same record in the master data (0CUSTOMER) with the data preview option and set a filter option from the aDSO data preview. The result is shown in Figure 6.56.

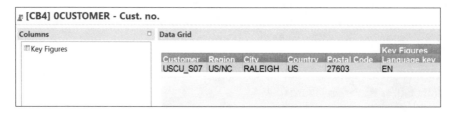

Figure 6.56 Master Data: Data Preview

You can also see the backend table for master data to check the availability of the customer data, as shown in Figure 6.57.

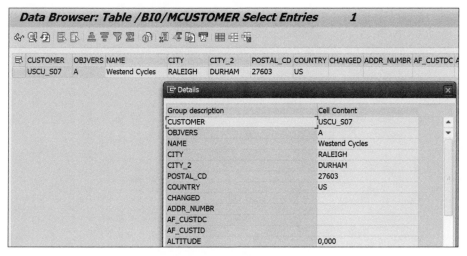

Figure 6.57 Master Data: View Table Checks

6.4   Summary

With the completion of this chapter, you've learned the basics of master data in SAP. You've seen the different types of master data and walked through a sample material master. You learned about the installation of master data InfoObjects from the business content, and you learned how to load that master data–based InfoObject. These master data will be used along with the transactional data for SAP BW reporting.

In the next chapter, we'll focus on extracting data from inventory management, which is part of materials management, to SAP BW/4HANA. This will be one of the most important chapters in the book as the logic will be different with the introduction of noncumulative key figures. We'll try to make the steps more detailed so that the data staging can be understood from end to end.

Chapter 7

Extracting Inventory Management Data

This chapter provides details of SAP BW/4HANA extractors across different functional areas. You'll learn about the extractor types and understand the differences of each type. We begin with an introduction to inventory management and review the basic functional terms used in this context. We then cover the inventory management extraction logic based on the SAP-delivered extractors as well as detailed insights into non-cumulative key figures. Finally, we'll implement a materials management-inventory management extraction into BW/4HANA 2.0, show how the system updated multiple backend tables, and install the standard SAP delivered Inventory data flow for SAP BW extraction.

In SAP S/4HANA, inventory management deals with the management of material stocks in terms of value, quantity, and movement. There is always an inbound and outbound movement of stocks in any industry, so efficient inventory maintenance is critical for any industry's profitability. To start, we'll focus on the very basics of inventory management and learn about important terms used in this area to understand the SAP BW reporting perspective. If you can understand the functional basis that we'll discuss in the first sections, it will help you understand the SAP BW extraction process better.

In this chapter, we'll start with the organization structure used in material management and the key definitions of the material handling process. Then you'll learn about the DataSources in SAP S/4HANA that extract data from the inventory management–based tables. Because the materials management SAP BW extraction is unique and complex among the logistics DataSources as the stocks cannot be cumulated, we'll see how SA PBW/4HANA inventory management uses the concept of a noncumulative key figure–based approach to extract the data from inventory and present analytical reports on top of those materials. We'll then focus on how to install the dataflow for SAP HANA–optimized inventory management in SAP BW/4HANA and activate those flows to extract full and delta loads from SAP S/4HANA.

7.1   Introduction to Inventory Management in SAP BW/4HANA

From an ERP system perspective, the business process that involves tracking materials, which can be raw or finished goods, is *inventory management*. The whole process involves multiple stages, such as ordering materials, storing materials, and using those materials. In most manufacturing industries, inventory management is a key application module and has an impact on profitability. Understanding the functional flow of inventory management will help in SAP BW/4HANA data modeling. Inventory management is part of materials management, so let's first look at the materials management organization structure at a very high level. Understanding this flow will be useful when you do the extraction of inventory management data from SAP S/4HANA.

As shown in Figure 7.1, any industry that uses material management in SAP S/4HANA will have these flows:

- The *client* is the highest unit in the SAP system. It's self-contained and has separate master data along with the associated tables. Data stored at the client level can be accessed by all company codes. A client can have many company codes.

- The *company code* is the central organization unit of external accounting for which complete self-contained bookkeeping can be maintained. The data stored in one company cannot be accessed from other company codes.

- A *plant* is an organization within logistics. It helps the enterprise in production, procurement, and materials planning. A company code can have many plants for different manufacturing requirements.

- The *storage location* is used to store the inventory of raw materials. It's where the stocks are physically stored.

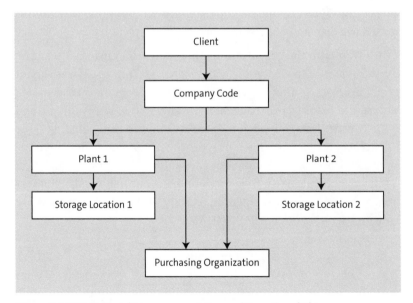

Figure 7.1 SAP Material Management General Functional Flow

- A *purchase organization* is an area within logistics that helps with purchasing requirements.

Now you know about the organizational structure for material management. Purchasing and inventory management are key subareas of material management. In this chapter, we'll focus on how to extract the inventory management data from the SAP S/4HANA system. Although inventory management is part of logistics, the extraction of data into SAP BW is very complex as it deals with stocks, materials, and quantities. Let's look at some additional definitions before we get into SAP BW.

Materials management helps to oversee the flow of materials and products in a warehouse. The optimal maintenance of inventory helps with profitability. The SAP process starts with managing receipts of supplies to prevent overstocking, with a focus on the movement of inventories and their counts. To understand the data extraction, you need to understand these concepts at a very high level.

A *goods receipt* is the physical inbound movement of goods into an inventory or warehouse. It's a goods movement that posts goods that are received from an external vendor or are in plant production. All types of goods receipts will result in the increase of stock in the data warehouse.

A *goods issue* is the physical outbound movement of goods from an inventory or warehouse. It's a goods movement that posts goods that are sent from a warehouse to customers or vendors, or even sent to plant for production purposes. All types of goods issues will result in a decrease of stock in the data warehouse.

An *internal movement* happens when a material is transferred from one storage location to another. It's a kind of plant-to-plant movement; for example, a material can be taken from inventory and sent for quality inspection, and if it's successful, then it's sent to production (see Figure 7.2).

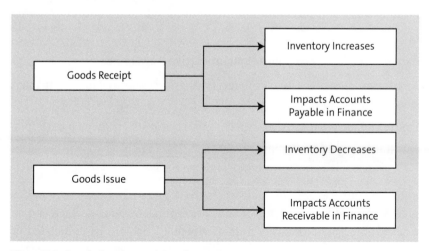

Figure 7.2 Goods Receipt and Goods Issue

A *material movement* is the movement of materials or finished goods from one plant/ storage location to another for any purpose. It can be for production or even final distribution. SAP has a three-digit code that helps you find the reason for a material movement, called a *movement type*. These codes indicate the purpose of the material movement. Some standard movement types are as follows:

- Movement type 101 with movement indicator B is used for goods receipt from a purchase order.

- Movement type 101 with movement indicator F is used for goods issue for a production order.

- Movement type 201 is used for goods issues concerning cost center.

- Movement type 311 is used for stock transfer from one storage location to another.

- Movement type 601 is for goods issues for outbound delivery.

Valuated stocks are those that post values in the company's accounts. These stock types define the state, usage, and usability of material. Types of valuated stocks include the following:

- *Unrestricted stock* can be used readily.

- *Quality inspection stock* is retained for quality inspection.

- *Blocked stock* is stock that has been rejected due to quality issues.

7.2   Inventory Management Extraction Logic

In this section, we'll walk through the steps in SAP S/4HANA to extract MM-IM data into SAP BW/4HANA. We'll start with the DataSources and discuss a few MM-IM-based terms to understand the data load efficiently. Then we'll follow up with filling setup tables for the inventory DataSources.

7.2.1   Fundamentals of Inventory and Noncumulative Key Figures

With a basic understanding of the inventory terms, you now know that inventory management deals with the following:

- Stock quantity and stock values of any specific material available in the plant

- Movements (incoming and outgoing) of materials from one place to another (storage location, plant), called goods receipts and goods issues

Because the stock quantity in any company will increase and decrease on a day-to-day basis, the quantity cannot be cumulated or added over time. In general, when you do an SAP BW extraction, you extract the numerical values that can be cumulated or added, called *cumulative values*, and they are cumulated using the key characteristics and time. For example, consider sales revenue: when you extract these data, you just sum up the revenue per day based on the customer number. But with inventory management, we deal with the materials and their quantities based on the inbound and outbound move concerning a specific time; for example, you can have a goods receipt (inflow) of 50 on the first day that increases the inventory stock quantity, and a goods issue (outflow) of 30 the next day that decreases the inventory quantity, so these values are measured with reference to a specific period of time. This makes them not able to be cumulated over time—and if they are, it creates the wrong data. There is a special way to handle these kinds of noncumulative values in SAP BW/4HANA, and that makes the inventory extractors and the extraction process unique and complex in the logistics extraction area.

For example, consider that on April 1 the stock quantity of a material is 50. On April 2, 10 units are sent out (outflow), which makes the stock quantity 40. To get the current stock balance as of April 2, you can't add or cumulate the stock of April 1 and 2; that will add up 50 + 40 for a total of 90, and you know that's wrong as there are only 90 units in the inventory. The actual total stock for that material by end of April 2 is only 40 units. These values are *noncumulative*, which means that you cannot cumulate or sum up the values in general. So you need to have a time reference when you deal with this kind of noncumulative value; for example, you need to ask what the stock quantity of the material is as of April 2 or April 1.

There are two other important concepts in inventory data loading:

- **Validity period**
  The validity period defines the time frame when the key figure with a quantity and value is valid. You can see the contents of this in the validity table. The validity table defines the range of the characteristic values for which the noncumulative key figure is valid.

  Let us say your class SAP BW-based InfoCube has OCALDAY as a time characteristic. It has data from 01/01/2022 to 12/31/2022. If you run a query and check the stock balance per day per plant, it will calculate balances for each plant and show them starting from 01/01/2022 onward.

  However, if you had a plant that only became operational on 06/01/2022, you wouldn't want to see a zero-stock balance for it starting from 01/01/2022 (or say when calculating the average, take as if stock existed from 01/01/2022) but from the date the plant existed—that is, 06/01/2022.

  In this case, if your validity table had only OCALDAY, your report would show 0 stock for each day from 01/01/2022 to 06/01/2022 for this new plant, which isn't preferable—but if you defined it at the plant level, then you would see the report starting at 06/01/2022, while it will start from 01/01/2022 for other plants.

- **Reference pointer**

  The reference pointer is used in the time reference for noncumulative key figures. The reference point table contains the reference points for noncumulative key figures. The reference characteristics are always the most granular time characteristics used in the aDSO; for example, if OCALDAY is the most granular InfoObject in the aDSO, then that is the reference characteristic, and reference pointers are stored in the reference table.

Essentials Terms in Materials Management-Inventory Management Extraction In SAP BW/4HANA

In the classical SAP BW 7.X system, inventory cubes are modeled using a concept called *marker update*, which will update the reference points. There were many series of steps involved in that process, but with the innovations in SAP BW/4HANA, the logic of the marker update is pushed down to the data staging DTPs with special fields. So if you're from the classical SAP BW world, you need to understand that there is a change in the handling of inventory data in SAP BW/4HANA. These are some of the related key terms that we will use throughout this chapter:

- *Inflow* will increase the stock quantity for material in the plant.
- *Outflow* will decrease the stock quantity for material in the plant.
- The *current stock balance* is calculated using the inflows and outflows for a material in a specific plant based on the day.

In SAP BW/4HANA, the stocks are modeled as *noncumulative key figures* as they cannot be cumulated over time. These key figures are summarized (over time) by using the exception aggregation (last value, first value, minimum, maximum, average). In general, a noncumulative key figure is modeled in SAP BW/4HANA using the corresponding field for the noncumulative value change or the corresponding fields for inflows or outflows. You can determine the current noncumulative value or the noncumulative value at a particular point in time. To do this, you use the current, end noncumulative, and noncumulative changes and/or the inflows and outflows. In our inventory scenarios, we'll use the noncumulative key figures with corresponding fields for inflows or outflows.

With this approach, there will be two additional cumulative key figures as InfoObjects for noncumulative key figures: one for inflow and the other for outflow.

When you install the OTOTALSTCK key figure from the business content, you can see the key figure in SAP BW/4HANA, as shown in Figure 7.3.

Figure 7.3 0TOTALSTCK Key Figure

You can see the following details for the key figure in the **General** tab:

❶ The noncumulative key figure name (**Technical Name, 0TOTALSTCK**).

❷ The **Data Type** of the key figure, **QUAN** (quantity).

❸ The **Aggregation**, **Summation**; and the **Exception Aggregation**, **Last Value**. The reference characteristics for the aggregation are mostly the most granular InfoObject, 0CALDAY.

❹ The currency unit is based on the 0BASE_UOM InfoObject.

❺ In the properties, **Noncumulative** is selected, marking this key figure as a noncumulative key figure.

If you choose the **Noncumulative** tab next to **General**, you can see the other two key figures that are involved (see Figure 7.4). The key figures are **0RECTOTSTCK** for received stock and **0ISTOTSTOCK** for issues.

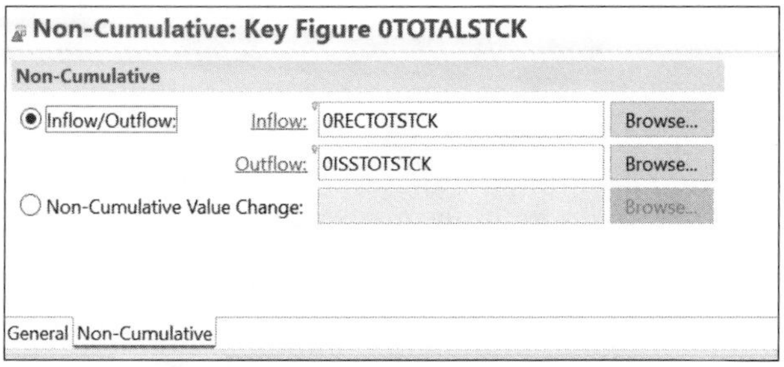

Non-Cumulative: Key Figure 0TOTALSTCK

Non-Cumulative

- ⦿ Inflow/Outflow:
  - Inflow: 0RECTOTSTCK — Browse...
  - Outflow: 0ISSTOTSTCK — Browse...
- ◯ Non-Cumulative Value Change: — Browse...

General | Non-Cumulative

Figure 7.4 Noncumulative Key Figures

Figure 7.5 shows other key figure details for the inflow ❶ and outflow ❷, such as the **Description**, **Key Figure Type**, **Aggregation** details, and **Currency/Unit** details.

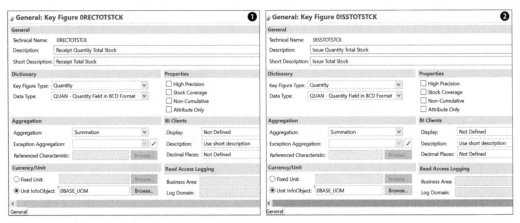

Figure 7.5 Inflow and Outflow Key Figure Properties

So when you add the OTOTALSTCK key figure in an aDSO, then it will add the following key figures too: OISSTOTSTCK, ORECTOTSTCK, and OBASE_UOM.

7.2.2   Understanding the Inventory Management Extraction Logic in SAP BW/4HANA

Let's use a simple flat file-based data load to understand the logic of materials management-inventory management extraction. Follow these steps:

1. Create a few flat files for data loading. Here we've created an Excel file and stored it in CSV format for the data load. Figure 7.6 shows the first flat file for the initial balance.

	A	B	C	D	E
1	CALDAY	MATERIAL	PLANT	STOCK_QUANTITY	UNIT
2	20230403	MAT001	P100	100	EA
3	20230403	MAT002	P100	200	EA
4	20230403	MAT003	P100	300	EA
5	20230403	MAT004	P200	400	EA
6	20230403	MAT005	P200	500	EA

Figure 7.6 Table: Initial Balance

2. You need to create a flat file source system under **DataSource · File · New · Source system** and give your source system name in the **Source System** field. In this example, name the source system **ZRKFILE** and once it's created, activate it using the icon if required (see Figure 7.7).

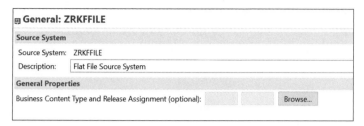

Figure 7.7 Flat File Source System

3. Use the flat file framework to upload this to a DataSource. Create a new DataSource as shown in Figure 7.8; see Chapter 2, Section 2.4 for a refresher on uploading flat files to SAP BW/4HANA.

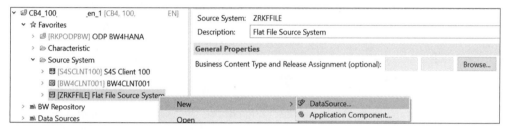

Figure 7.8 DataSource Creation

4. Follow the wizard, which will prompt you to provide the name of the DataSource and its description. Name the DataSource "ZRKINVOPBAL". You'll see the details provided in Figure 7.9.

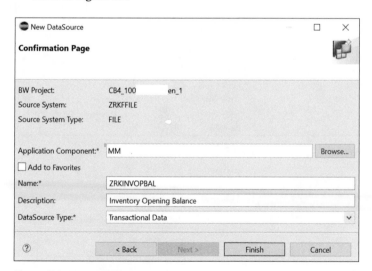

Figure 7.9 New DataSource

5. After choosing the **Finish** button, you'll see the DataSource has been created in SAP BW/4HANA. Open the DataSource and choose the **Opening Balance** option for the DataSource, as shown in Figure 7.10.

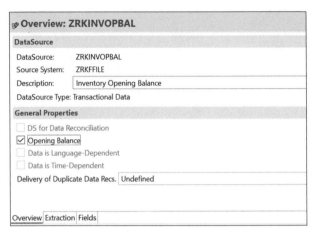

Figure 7.10 Overview Tab: Opening Balance

6. In the DataSource maintenance screen, choose the **Extraction** tab and provide the details as shown in Figure 7.11. Click the **Browse** button to the right of **File Name** and select the CSV file. Set **Data Seperator** to " , " and **Escape Sign** to " ; " (including the spaces in both cases). If you have any header row in the source flat file, add the value 1 in **Ignore Header Rows**.

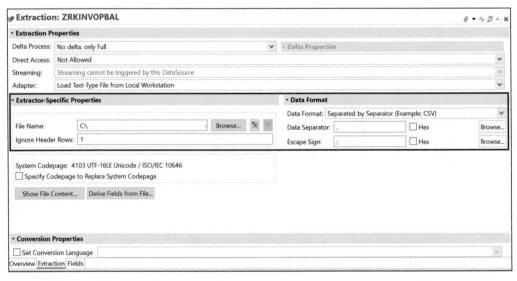

Figure 7.11 Extraction Tab

7. Click **Derive Fields from File** and you'll see the popup shown in Figure 7.12.

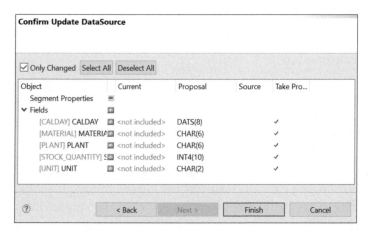

Figure 7.12 Derive Field from File

8. Select **Finish** and you'll see the list of all field names, such as **CALDAY**, **MATERIAL**, **PLANT**, **STOCK_QUANTITY**, and **UNIT**, in the **Fields** tab (see Figure 7.13).

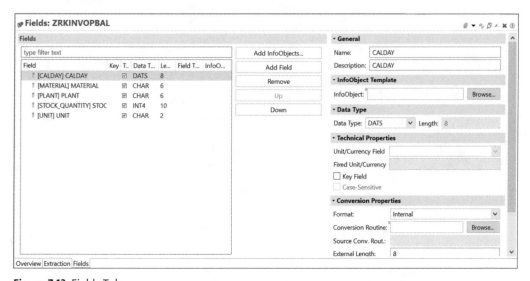

Figure 7.13 Fields Tab

9. In the **Fields** tab of the DataSource, review and update all fields as necessary. For example, select **MATERIAL** and adjust the data type to **CHAR** (**Length 40**) and then **PLANT** to **CHAR** (**Length 4**) and make the **STOCK QUANTITY** data type **QUAN** (**Length 17**) and **UNIT** data type **UNIT** (**Length 3**; see Figure 7.14). This can be done by selecting each field and updating the length field manually.

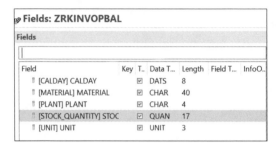

Figure 7.14 Adjusted Datatype

10. Activate the DataSource using the ⬛ icon. The next step is to create the aDSO based on this DataSource (see Figure 7.15). To create the aDSO, you'll provide the DataSource name (`ZRKINVOPBAL`) as the template. You can see that the DataSource is based on the **ZRKFILE** flat file.

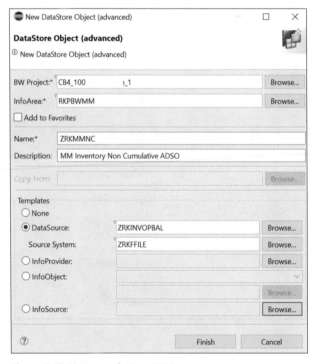

Figure 7.15 Noncumulative aDSO

11. Now choose **Finish** and you'll see the screen shown in Figure 7.16. You'll see the **General** tab of the aDSO. Choose the **Data Mart DataStore Object** option and make sure that **Special Properties** has the **Inventory Enabled** checkbox selected.

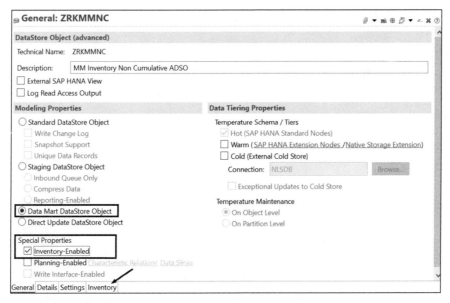

Figure 7.16 aDSO General Tab

12. Select the **Details** tab of the aDSO. For all the fields, assign the **Type** and choose **Change Type to Its Equivalent InfoObject** (see Figure 7.17).

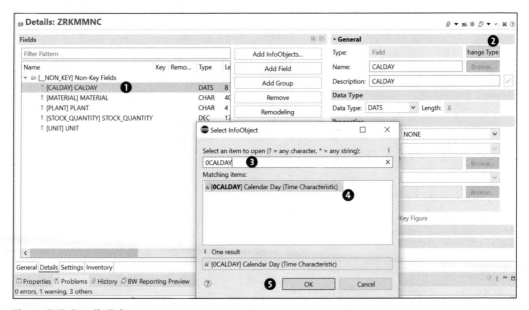

Figure 7.17 Details Tab

Here are the details shown in Figure 7.17:

❶ Select the fields by double-clicking them.

❷ Select the **Change Type** button.

❸ In this window, you need to search for the standard InfoObject, so type "0CAL-DAY".

❹ In the matching items, you can see the **0CALDAY** result; choose it.

❺ Select the **OK** button to change the type for the field.

13. You can see that the **CALDAY** field with the ▯ icon is now changed to an InfoObject with the 🔏 icon, as shown in Figure 7.18.

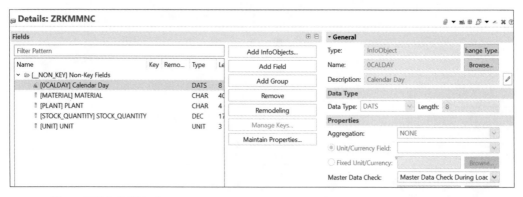

Figure 7.18 InfoObject

14. Now change other fields like **Material** to **0MATERIAL** and **Plant** to **0PLANT** and **Totalstck** to **0TOTALSTCK**. When you replace **STOCK_QUANTITY** with **0TOTALSTCK**, additional key figures will be added, as shown in Figure 7.19.

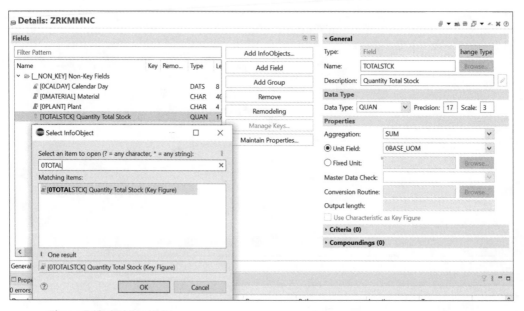

Figure 7.19 0TOTALSTCK

324

15. Now if you press **OK**, you'll see the screen shown in Figure 7.20. These are the new fields that will be added. You can see **0TOTALSTCK** for **Quantity** stock and **0ISSTOT-STCK** for **Issue Quantity**, and **0RECTOTSTCK**, which is the **Receipt Quantity** stock, and **0BASE_UOM** for **Base Unit of Measure**.

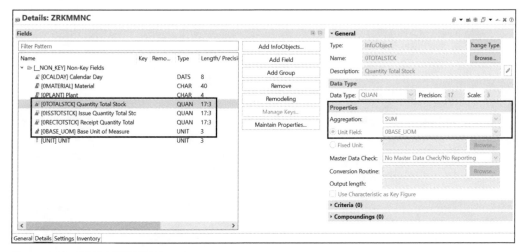

Figure 7.20 0TOTALSTCK Field

16. Because you already have 0BASE_UOM, you don't need the UNIT field; it can be removed in the aDSO. There are no mappings required for this field from the sender to the target so you can leave it unmapped. The status is shown in Figure 7.21.

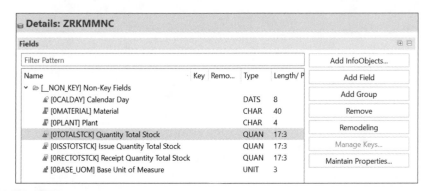

Figure 7.21 aDSO Status

17. When you choose the **Inventory** tab, you can see the reference characteristics for **0CALDAY**, as shown in Figure 7.22.

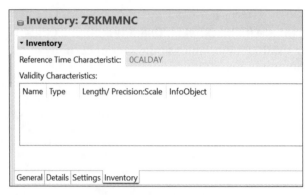

Figure 7.22 Inventory Reference Characteristics

18. Once you create and activate the aDSO, you can see that the inbound tables, active table, and change log tables are generated as shown in Figure 7.23.

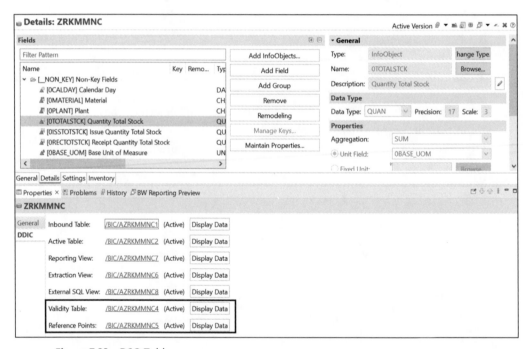

Figure 7.23 aDSO Tables

19. Create the transformation from the DataSource (ZRKFFILE) to the aDSO (ZRKMMNC). You can see the default mapping as shown in Figure 7.24.

20. Create an additional mapping manually from **STOCK_QUANITY** to **0RECTOTSTOCK** and it will also map, then activate the transformation using the ⚙ icon (Figure 7.25). Create a DTP (Figure 7.26).

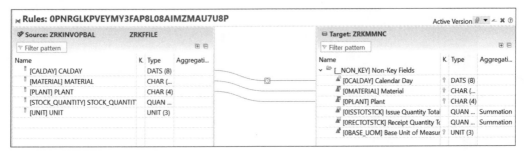

Figure 7.24 Transformation Default Mapping

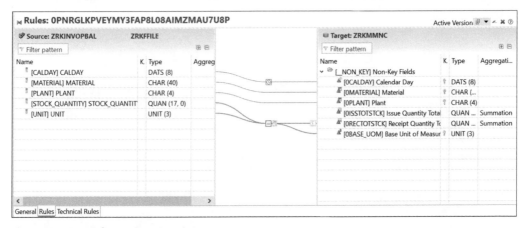

Figure 7.25 Transformation Mapping

You can see that the **Extraction Mode** is **Initial Noncumulative for Noncumulative Values** (Figure 7.26).

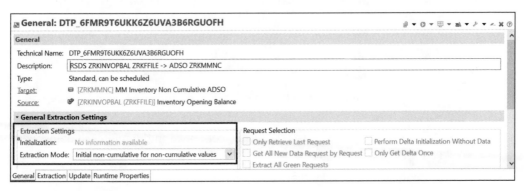

Figure 7.26 DTP Mode

21. Now activate the DTP using the ⬛ icon and execute the DTP using the ⬤ ▼ icon. The status is shown in Figure 7.27.

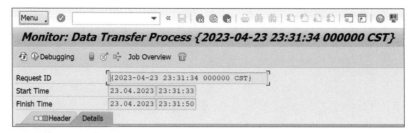

Figure 7.27 DTP Status

22. Click the ⊙ icon shown in Figure 7.27. You can see the activation request as shown in Figure 7.28.

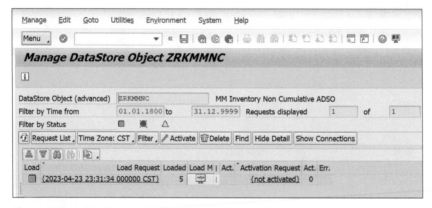

Figure 7.28 Activation Request

23. Figure 7.29 shows the contents of the inbound table. Note that **RECORDTP** is **1** and **RECTOTSTCK** has the value from the CSV file. While writing the initial stock balances into the inbound table, SAP BW/4HANA filled the technical field for the record type (RECORDTP) with the value 1 because noncumulative DataStore objects use the RECORDTP field to differentiate among the following:

   – The reference points with RECORDTP = 1

   – The records that are not yet (semantically) contained in the reference points with RECORDTP = 0

   – Records that are already (semantically) contained in the reference points with RECORDTP = 2

   Because the data is only in the inbound table and not yet moved to the reference table, you'll see **RECORDTP** as 1 in the inbound table.

24. The inbound table that ends with 1 will have an entry, and the validity table that ends with 4 will be filled with the request TSN, which will have a timestamp value. Figure 7.30 shows the validity table ❶, reference point table ❷, and extraction view

table ❸. The extraction view that ends with 6 (the extraction view table) has data with RECORDTP set to 1.

Data Browser: Table /BIC/AZRKMMNC1 Select Entries   **5**

REQTSN	DATAPAKID	RECORD	RECORDMODE	RECORDTP	CALDAY	MATERIAL	PLANT	ISSTOTSTCK	RECTOTSTCK	BASE_UOM
20230424043134000000000	000001	1		1	03.04.2023	MAT001	P100	0	100	EA
20230424043134000000000	000001	2		1	03.04.2023	MAT002	P100	0	200	EA
20230424043134000000000	000001	3		1	03.04.2023	MAT003	P100	0	300	EA
20230424043134000000000	000001	4		1	03.04.2023	MAT004	P200	0	400	EA
20230424043134000000000	000001	5		1	03.04.2023	MAT005	P200	0	500	EA

Figure 7.29 Inbound Table

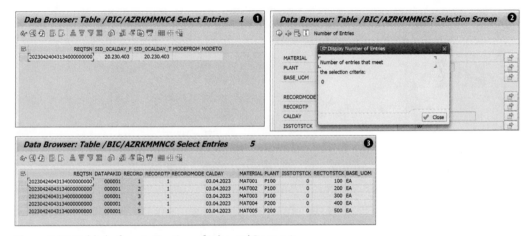

Data Browser: Table /BIC/AZRKMMNC4 Select Entries   **1** ❶

REQTSN	SID_0CALDAY_F	SID_0CALDAY_T	MODEFROM	MODETO
20230424043134000000000	20.230.403	20.230.403		

Data Browser: Table /BIC/AZRKMMNC5: Selection Screen ❷

MATERIAL
PLANT
BASE_UOM

RECORDMODE
RECORDTP
CALDAY
ISSTOTSTCK

Display Number of Entries

Number of entries that meet
the selection criteria:
0

✔ Close

Data Browser: Table /BIC/AZRKMMNC6 Select Entries   **5** ❸

REQTSN	DATAPAKID	RECORD	RECORDTP	RECORDMODE	CALDAY	MATERIAL	PLANT	ISSTOTSTCK	RECTOTSTCK	BASE_UOM
20230424043134000000000	000001	1	1		03.04.2023	MAT001	P100	0	100	EA
20230424043134000000000	000001	2	1		03.04.2023	MAT002	P100	0	200	EA
20230424043134000000000	000001	3	1		03.04.2023	MAT003	P100	0	300	EA
20230424043134000000000	000001	4	1		03.04.2023	MAT004	P200	0	400	EA
20230424043134000000000	000001	5	1		03.04.2023	MAT005	P200	0	500	EA

Figure 7.30 Table before Activation of Inbound Request

25. Activate the aDSO using the 🔳 icon. This will populate the reference point table as shown in Figure 7.31. During activation, the following things happen:

   – Entries in the inbound table will get deleted.
   – The validity table ❶ request TSN will be set to 0.
   – The reference point table ❷ will be updated; you can see that RECORDTP in this table is 1.
   – The extraction view table will reset the request TSN.

Data Browser: Table /BIC/AZRKMMNC4 Select Entries   **1** ❶

REQTSN	SID_0CALDAY_F	SID_0CALDAY_T	MODEFROM	MODETO
00000000000000000000000	20.230.403	20.230.403		

Data Browser: Table /BIC/AZRKMMNC5 Select Entries   **5** ❷

MATERIAL	PLANT	BASE_UOM	RECORDMODE	RECORDTP	CALDAY	ISSTOTSTCK	RECTOTSTCK
MAT001	P100	EA		1	03.04.2023	0	100
MAT002	P100	EA		1	03.04.2023	0	200
MAT003	P100	EA		1	03.04.2023	0	300
MAT004	P200	EA		1	03.04.2023	0	400
MAT005	P200	EA		1	03.04.2023	0	500

Figure 7.31 After ADSO Activation of Inbound Request

You can see that in the aDSO, **RECORDTP** is set to **1**, which means it contains the initialization records with the initial stock balance. This reference point will be updated when there is a request with a new delta movement and that inbound request is activated. You can think of reference points as an equation: *reference points = initialization, plus or minus the delta movement value.* So you need always to ensure that all reference points are updated for the correct query result. Note that the reference table doesn't have a request identifier field such as REQTSN because it stores the reference points aggregated over time on the granularity defined by a characteristic selected by the user; in this case, OCALDAY.

You can also open the extraction view table to see the contents of the view, and you'll note that the request TSN will be set to 0, as shown in Figure 7.32.

Data Browser: Table /BIC/AZRKMMNC6 Select Entries   5

REQTSN	DATAPAKID	RECORD	RECORDTP	RECORDMODE	CALDAY	MATERIAL	PLANT	ISSTOTSTCK	RECTOTSTCK	BASE_UOM
00000000000000000000000	000000	0	1		03.04.2023	MAT001	P100	0	100	EA
00000000000000000000000	000000	0	1		03.04.2023	MAT002	P100	0	200	EA
00000000000000000000000	000000	0	1		03.04.2023	MAT003	P100	0	300	EA
00000000000000000000000	000000	0	1		03.04.2023	MAT004	P200	0	400	EA
00000000000000000000000	000000	0	1		03.04.2023	MAT005	P200	0	500	EA

Figure 7.32 Extraction view

26. Now you need to extract the delta movements, so create the XLS and CSV files as shown in Figure 7.33. For the initial test purposes, create the Excel file exactly like the one shown.

	A	B	C	D	E	F
1	CALDAY	MATERIAL	PLANT	RECEIVED	ISSUED	UNIT
2	20230405	MAT001	P100	0	50	EA
3	20230406	MAT001	P100	100	0	EA
4	20230407	MAT002	P100	100	0	EA
5	20230408	MAT002	P100	0	30	EA
6	20230409	MAT003	P100	0	250	EA
7	20230410	MAT003	P100	100	50	EA
8	20230411	MAT004	P200	150	0	EA
9	20230412	MAT005	P200	0	50	EA

Figure 7.33 Delta Movements

27. Now create a DataSource based on this flat file and activate the DataSource using the ![icon] icon. Make sure that you do not select the checkbox for the **Opening Balance** checkbox (Figure 7.34). (See Chapter 2, Section 2.4 for more information about how to create the DataSource.)

28. Figure 7.35 shows the fields for you to review. Note that the **RECEIVED** and **ISSUED** fields have the type **QUAN** (quantity) and the **UNIT** field is mapped to **UNIT**.

Figure 7.34 Delta Movements DataSource

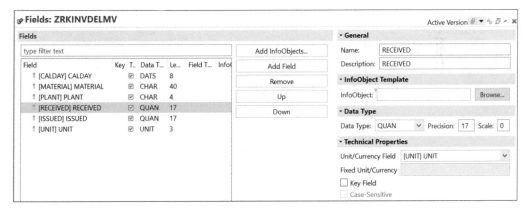

Figure 7.35 DataSource Fields

29. Now create the transformation from the previous aDSO to this DataSource and activate the aDSO using the ⬚ icon (see Figure 7.36). (See Chapter 2, Section 2.4 for how to create the DataSource and Section 2.10 for how to create an aDSO.)

Figure 7.36 Transformation

30. Do the mapping manually as shown in Figure 7.37. You need to drag the fields from sender to receiver, making sure you connect the **RECEIVED** field from the DataSource to **RECEIPT** in the target aDSO, **ZRKMMNC**, and the **ISSUED** field in the DataSource to

the **ISSUE** quantity in the target, and then **UNIT** will be connected in both. Figure 7.37 shows the transformations both before mapping ❶ and after mapping ❷.

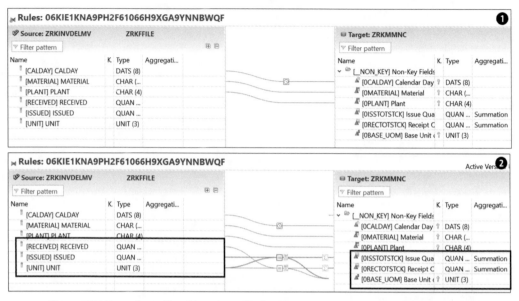

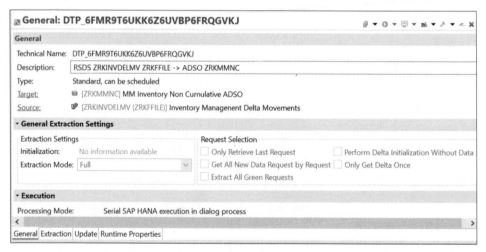

Figure 7.37 Transformation Mapping of Delta Movements

31. Create the DTP based on the transformation as shown in Figure 7.38.

Figure 7.38 DTP Properties

32. You can see that the DTP is full. Activate the DTP using 🔲 and execute it using the ⏵ ▼ icon. You can see the details in Figure 7.39.

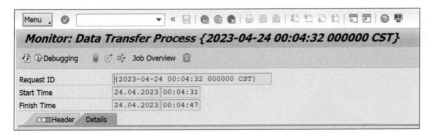

Figure 7.39 DTP Request

33. Once the DTP is completed, the load request is added to the aDSO as shown in Figure 7.40.

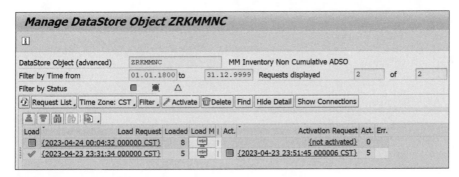

Figure 7.40 ADSO Administration

34. Now let's check the tables, starting with the inbound table that ends with 1. Note that RECORDTP is set to 0 (see Figure 7.41).

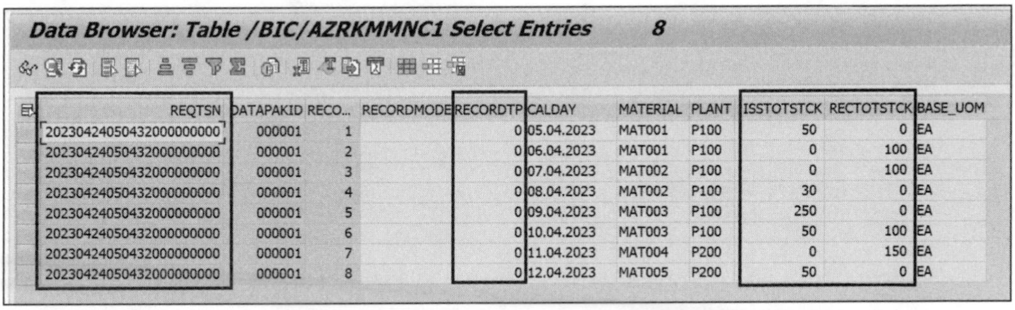

REQTSN	DATAPAKID	RECO...	RECORDMODE	RECORDTP	CALDAY	MATERIAL	PLANT	ISSTOTSTCK	RECTOTSTCK	BASE_UOM
20230424050432000000000	000001	1		0	05.04.2023	MAT001	P100	50	0	EA
20230424050432000000000	000001	2		0	06.04.2023	MAT001	P100	0	100	EA
20230424050432000000000	000001	3		0	07.04.2023	MAT002	P100	0	100	EA
20230424050432000000000	000001	4		0	08.04.2023	MAT002	P100	30	0	EA
20230424050432000000000	000001	5		0	09.04.2023	MAT003	P100	250	0	EA
20230424050432000000000	000001	6		0	10.04.2023	MAT003	P100	50	100	EA
20230424050432000000000	000001	7		0	11.04.2023	MAT004	P200	0	150	EA
20230424050432000000000	000001	8		0	12.04.2023	MAT005	P200	50	0	EA

Figure 7.41 Inbound Table: Delta Movements

35. From Transaction SE16, check the validity table that ends with 4. You can see the new request and its timestamp (see Figure 7.42).

36. From Transaction SE16, check the reference point table. There won't be any change as the aDSO inbound request isn't yet activated (see Figure 7.43).

Data Browser: Table /BIC/AZRKMMNC4 Select Entries   2

REQTSN	SID_0CALDAY_F	SID_0CALDAY_T	MODEFROM	MODETO
00000000000000000000000	20.230.403	20.230.403		
20230424050432000000000	20.230.405	20.230.412		

Figure 7.42 Validity Table: Delta Movements

Data Browser: Table /BIC/AZRKMMNC5 Select Entries   5

MATERIAL	PLANT	BASE_UOM	RECORDMODE	RECORDTP	CALDAY	ISSTOTSTCK	RECTOTSTCK
MAT001	P100	EA		1	03.04.2023	0	100
MAT002	P100	EA		1	03.04.2023	0	200
MAT003	P100	EA		1	03.04.2023	0	300
MAT004	P200	EA		1	03.04.2023	0	400
MAT005	P200	EA		1	03.04.2023	0	500

Figure 7.43 Reference Point Table: Before Activation

37. In Transaction SE16, also check the extraction view table that ends with 6. It will have the expected data (see Figure 7.44).

Data Browser: Table /BIC/AZRKMMNC6 Select Entries   13

REQTSN	DATAPAKID	RECORD	RECORDTP	RECORDMODE	CALDAY	MATERIAL	PLANT	ISSTOTSTCK	RECTOTSTCK	BASE_UOM
00000000000000000000000	000000	0	1		03.04.2023	MAT001	P100	0	100	EA
00000000000000000000000	000000	0	1		03.04.2023	MAT002	P100	0	200	EA
00000000000000000000000	000000	0	1		03.04.2023	MAT003	P100	0	300	EA
00000000000000000000000	000000	0	1		03.04.2023	MAT004	P200	0	400	EA
00000000000000000000000	000000	0	1		03.04.2023	MAT005	P200	0	500	EA
20230424050432000000000	000001	1	0		05.04.2023	MAT001	P100	50	0	EA
20230424050432000000000	000001	2	0		06.04.2023	MAT001	P100	0	100	EA
20230424050432000000000	000001	3	0		07.04.2023	MAT002	P100	0	100	EA
20230424050432000000000	000001	4	0		08.04.2023	MAT002	P100	30	0	EA
20230424050432000000000	000001	5	0		09.04.2023	MAT003	P100	250	0	EA
20230424050432000000000	000001	6	0		10.04.2023	MAT003	P100	50	100	EA
20230424050432000000000	000001	7	0		11.04.2023	MAT004	P200	0	150	EA
20230424050432000000000	000001	8	0		12.04.2023	MAT005	P200	50	0	EA

Figure 7.44 Extraction View Table: Before Activation of Inbound Request

38. Activate the inbound request of the aDSO using the **Activate** button. You can see the activation request as shown in Figure 7.45.

39. The inbound table that ends with 1 will be empty, so first check the validity table that ends with 4. As shown in Figure 7.46, it shows one request.

40. Check the active data table that ends with 2, as shown in Figure 7.47. It shows the new result: RECORDTP will be 2.

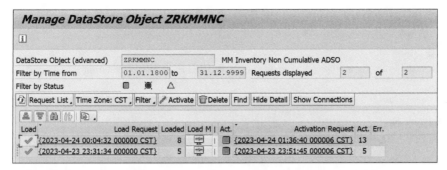

Figure 7.45 Activation of Inbound Request

Data Browser: Table /BIC/AZRKMMNC4 Select Entries   1

	REQTSN	SID_0CALDAY_F	SID_0CALDAY_T	MODEFROM	MODETO
00000000000000000000000		20.230.403	20.230.412		

Figure 7.46 Validity Table: After Activation

Data Browser: Table /BIC/AZRKMMNC2 Select Entries   8

MATERIAL	PLANT	BASE_UOM	RECORDMODE	RECORDTP	CALDAY	ISSTOTSTCK	RECTOTSTCK
MAT001	P100	EA	N	2	05.04.2023	50	0
MAT001	P100	EA	N	2	06.04.2023	0	100
MAT002	P100	EA	N	2	07.04.2023	0	100
MAT002	P100	EA	N	2	08.04.2023	30	0
MAT003	P100	EA	N	2	09.04.2023	250	0
MAT003	P100	EA	N	2	10.04.2023	50	100
MAT004	P200	EA	N	2	11.04.2023	0	150
MAT005	P200	EA	N	2	12.04.2023	50	0

Figure 7.47 Active Table: After Activation

41. Check the reference point table from Transaction SE16. You'll see the updated reference points with RECORDTP = 1 (see Figure 7.48).

Data Browser: Table /BIC/AZRKMMNC5 Select Entries   5

MATERIAL	PLANT	BASE_UOM	RECORDMODE	RECORDTP	CALDAY	ISSTOTSTCK	RECTOTSTCK
MAT001	P100	EA		1	03.04.2023	0	150
MAT002	P100	EA		1	03.04.2023	0	270
MAT003	P100	EA		1	03.04.2023	0	100
MAT004	P200	EA		1	03.04.2023	0	550
MAT005	P200	EA		1	03.04.2023	0	450

Figure 7.48 Reference Point Table

42. To calculate if this is correct, let's summarize it all. Figure 7.49 shows the initial balance ❶, the delta movements ❷, and the reference point table ❸.

	A	B	C	D	E
1	CALDAY	MATERIAL	PLANT	STOCK_QUANTITY	UNIT
2	20230403	MAT001	P100	100	EA
3	20230403	MAT002	P100	200	EA
4	20230403	MAT003	P100	300	EA
5	20230403	MAT004	P200	400	EA
6	20230403	MAT005	P200	500	EA
7					
❶					

	A	B	C	D	E	F
1	CALDAY	MATERIAL	PLANT	RECEIVED	ISSUED	UNIT
2	20230405	MAT001	P100	0	50	EA
3	20230406	MAT001	P100	100	0	EA
4	20230407	MAT002	P100	100	0	EA
5	20230408	MAT002	P100	0	30	EA
6	20230409	MAT003	P100	0	250	EA
7	20230410	MAT003	P100	100	50	EA
8	20230411	MAT004	P200	150	0	EA
❷	20230412	MAT005	P200	0	50	EA

Data Browser: Table /BIC/AZRKMMNC5 Select Entries   5

MATERIAL	PLANT	BASE_UOM	RECORDMODE	RECORDTP	CALDAY	ISSTOTSTCK	RECTOTSTCK
MAT001	P100	EA		1	03.04.2023	0	150
MAT002	P100	EA		1	03.04.2023	0	270
MAT003	P100	EA		1	03.04.2023	0	100
MAT004	P200	EA		1	03.04.2023	0	550
MAT005	P200	EA		1	03.04.2023	0	450

❸

Figure 7.49 Summary

You can use the following formula to check this logic:

RECTOTSTCK = (Initial Balance OR Reference Points) + Received Stock – Issued Stock

Some examples of how to use this formula are as follows:

- MAT001 = 100 + 100 – 50 = 150
- MAT002 = 200 + 100 – 30 = 270
- MAT003 = 300 + 100 - 250 -50 = 100
- MAT004 = 400 + 150 – 0 = 550
- MAT005 = 500 + 0 -50 = 450

With this logic, the SAP BW/4HANA system ensures that all activated delta movements are contained in the reference points. Updating the reference points semantically allows for time-based archiving of older delta movements. In addition, switching the record type from '0' to '2' keeps the content of the object coherent with the semantics of record types in DataStore objects. Just to recall:

- Record type 0 means that a record is not yet contained in the reference point.
- Record type 2 means that a record is already contained in the reference point.

By activating the request with delta movements, reference points were updated, so the record type switched from 0 to 2.

43. Next, we'll begin updating historical movements. Create DataSource ZRKINVHSIM based on the flat file shown in Figure 7.50 and activate the DataSource. Then create the transformation from the same DataSource, using similar mapping as that used in the delta movements (see Figure 7.51).

	A	B	C	D	E	F
1	CALDAY	MATERIAL	PLANT	RECEIVED	ISSUED	UNIT
2	20220305	MAT001	P100	50	0	EA
3	20220306	MAT001	P100	0	70	EA
4	20220307	MAT002	P100	60	0	EA
5	20220308	MAT002	P100	0	50	EA
6	20220309	MAT003	P100	0	70	EA
7	20220310	MAT003	P100	30	30	EA
8	20220311	MAT004	P200	90	0	EA
9	20220312	MAT005	P200	0	40	EA

Figure 7.50 Historical Movements

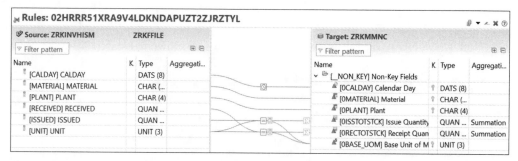

Figure 7.51 Rules

44. Create the DTP. In the **Update** tab, enable the checkbox for **Historical Transactions** (see Figure 7.52).

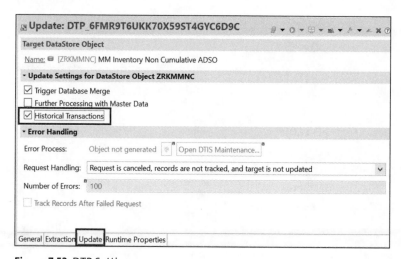

Figure 7.52 DTP Settings

45. Now execute the DTP using the ⬚ icon, and you can see the inbound table (see Figure 7.53).

Data Browser: Table /BIC/AZRKMMNC1 Select Entries   8

REQTSN	DATAPAKID	RECORD	RECORDMODE	RECORDTP	CALDAY	MATERIAL	PLANT	ISSTOTSTCK	RECTOTSTCK	BASE_UOM
20230424080310000000000	000001	1		2	05.03.2022	MAT001	P100	0	50	EA
20230424080310000000000	000001	2		2	06.03.2022	MAT001	P100	70	0	EA
20230424080310000000000	000001	3		2	07.03.2022	MAT002	P100	0	60	EA
20230424080310000000000	000001	4		2	08.03.2022	MAT002	P100	50	0	EA
20230424080310000000000	000001	5		2	09.03.2022	MAT003	P100	70	0	EA
20230424080310000000000	000001	6		2	10.03.2022	MAT003	P100	30	30	EA
20230424080310000000000	000001	7		2	11.03.2022	MAT004	P200	0	90	EA
20230424080310000000000	000001	8		2	12.03.2022	MAT005	P200	40	0	EA

Figure 7.53 Inbound Table

46. Now you can see the entry in the validity table, as shown in Figure 7.54.

Data Browser: Table /BIC/AZRKMMNC4 Select Entries   2

REQTSN	SID_0CALDAY_F	SID_0CALDAY_T	MODEFROM	MODETO
00000000000000000000000	20.230.403	20.230.412		
20230424080310000000000	20.220.305	20.220.312		

Figure 7.54 Validity Table

47. There will be no change in the reference point table as it's not activated; check the extraction view that ends with 6 (see Figure 7.55).

Data Browser: Table /BIC/AZRKMMNC6 Select Entries   21

REQTSN	DATAPAKID	RECORD	RECORDTP	RECORDMODE	CALDAY	MATERIAL	PLANT	ISSTOTSTCK	RECTOTSTCK	BASE_UOM
00000000000000000000000	000000	0	2		05.04.2023	MAT001	P100	50	0	EA
00000000000000000000000	000000	0	2		06.04.2023	MAT001	P100	0	100	EA
00000000000000000000000	000000	0	2		07.04.2023	MAT002	P100	0	100	EA
00000000000000000000000	000000	0	2		08.04.2023	MAT002	P100	30	0	EA
00000000000000000000000	000000	0	2		09.04.2023	MAT003	P100	250	0	EA
00000000000000000000000	000000	0	2		10.04.2023	MAT003	P100	50	100	EA
00000000000000000000000	000000	0	2		11.04.2023	MAT004	P200	0	150	EA
00000000000000000000000	000000	0	2		12.04.2023	MAT005	P200	50	0	EA
00000000000000000000000	000000	0	1		03.04.2023	MAT001	P100	0	150	EA
00000000000000000000000	000000	0	1		03.04.2023	MAT002	P100	0	270	EA
00000000000000000000000	000000	0	1		03.04.2023	MAT003	P100	0	100	EA
00000000000000000000000	000000	0	1		03.04.2023	MAT004	P200	0	550	EA
00000000000000000000000	000000	0	1		03.04.2023	MAT005	P200	0	450	EA
20230424080310000000000	000001	1	2		05.03.2022	MAT001	P100	0	50	EA
20230424080310000000000	000001	2	2		06.03.2022	MAT001	P100	70	0	EA
20230424080310000000000	000001	3	2		07.03.2022	MAT002	P100	0	60	EA
20230424080310000000000	000001	4	2		08.03.2022	MAT002	P100	50	0	EA
20230424080310000000000	000001	5	2		09.03.2022	MAT003	P100	70	0	EA
20230424080310000000000	000001	6	2		10.03.2022	MAT003	P100	30	30	EA
20230424080310000000000	000001	7	2		11.03.2022	MAT004	P200	0	90	EA
20230424080310000000000	000001	8	2		12.03.2022	MAT005	P200	40	0	EA

Figure 7.55 View

48. From Transaction SE16, check the active table that ends with 2. You can see the records as shown in Figure 7.56.

Data Browser: Table /BIC/AZRKMMNC2 Select Entries   8

MATERIAL	PLANT	BASE_UOM	RECORDMODE	RECORDTP	CALDAY	ISSTOTSTCK	RECTOTSTCK
MAT001	P100	EA	N	2	05.04.2023	50	0
MAT001	P100	EA	N	2	06.04.2023	0	100
MAT002	P100	EA	N	2	07.04.2023	0	100
MAT002	P100	EA	N	2	08.04.2023	30	0
MAT003	P100	EA	N	2	09.04.2023	250	0
MAT003	P100	EA	N	2	10.04.2023	50	100
MAT004	P200	EA	N	2	11.04.2023	0	150
MAT005	P200	EA	N	2	12.04.2023	50	0

Figure 7.56 Active Table

49. Now activate the request in the aDSO using the **Activate** button. There's no change in the reference pointer value; you can see it has five fields (see Figure 7.57). However, the active table has this entry, as shown in Figure 7.58.

Data Browser: Table /BIC/AZRKMMNC5 Select Entries   5

MATERIAL	PLANT	BASE_UOM	RECORDMODE	RECORDTP	CALDAY	ISSTOTSTCK	RECTOTSTCK
MAT001	P100	EA		1	03.04.2023	0	150
MAT002	P100	EA		1	03.04.2023	0	270
MAT003	P100	EA		1	03.04.2023	0	100
MAT004	P200	EA		1	03.04.2023	0	550
MAT005	P200	EA		1	03.04.2023	0	450

Figure 7.57 Reference Pointer

You can see that **ISSTOTSTCK** and **RECTOTSTCK** have the values shown in Figure 7.58.

Data Browser: Table /BIC/AZRKMMNC2 Select Entries   16

MATERIAL	PLANT	BASE_UOM	RECORDMODE	RECORDTP	CALDAY	ISSTOTSTCK	RECTOTSTCK
MAT001	P100	EA	N	2	05.04.2023	50	0
MAT001	P100	EA	N	2	06.04.2023	0	100
MAT001	P100	EA	N	2	05.03.2022	0	50
MAT001	P100	EA	N	2	06.03.2022	70	0
MAT002	P100	EA	N	2	07.04.2023	0	100
MAT002	P100	EA	N	2	08.04.2023	30	0
MAT002	P100	EA	N	2	07.03.2022	0	60
MAT002	P100	EA	N	2	08.03.2022	50	0
MAT003	P100	EA	N	2	09.04.2023	250	0
MAT003	P100	EA	N	2	10.04.2023	50	100
MAT003	P100	EA	N	2	09.03.2022	70	0
MAT003	P100	EA	N	2	10.03.2022	30	30
MAT004	P200	EA	N	2	11.04.2023	0	150
MAT004	P200	EA	N	2	11.03.2022	0	90
MAT005	P200	EA	N	2	12.04.2023	50	0
MAT005	P200	EA	N	2	12.03.2022	40	0

Figure 7.58 Active Table

The extraction view that ends with 6 will have this info based on the flat file data as a summary (see Figure 7.59).

Data Browser: Table /BIC/AZRKMMNC6 Select Entries   21

REQTSN	DATAPAKID	RECORD	RECORDTP	RECORDMODE	CALDAY	MATERIAL	PLANT	ISSTOTSTCK	RECTOTSTCK	BASE_UOM
00000000000000000000	000000	0	2		05.04.2023	MAT001	P100	50	0	EA
00000000000000000000	000000	0	2		06.04.2023	MAT001	P100	0	100	EA
00000000000000000000	000000	0	2		07.04.2023	MAT002	P100	0	100	EA
00000000000000000000	000000	0	2		08.04.2023	MAT002	P100	30	0	EA
00000000000000000000	000000	0	2		09.04.2023	MAT003	P100	250	0	EA
00000000000000000000	000000	0	2		10.04.2023	MAT003	P100	50	100	EA
00000000000000000000	000000	0	2		11.04.2023	MAT004	P200	0	150	EA
00000000000000000000	000000	0	2		12.04.2023	MAT005	P200	50	0	EA
00000000000000000000	000000	0	2		05.03.2022	MAT001	P100	0	50	EA
00000000000000000000	000000	0	2		06.03.2022	MAT001	P100	70	0	EA
00000000000000000000	000000	0	2		07.03.2022	MAT002	P100	0	60	EA
00000000000000000000	000000	0	2		08.03.2022	MAT002	P100	50	0	EA
00000000000000000000	000000	0	2		09.03.2022	MAT003	P100	70	0	EA
00000000000000000000	000000	0	2		10.03.2022	MAT003	P100	30	30	EA
00000000000000000000	000000	0	2		11.03.2022	MAT004	P200	0	90	EA
00000000000000000000	000000	0	2		12.03.2022	MAT005	P200	40	0	EA
00000000000000000000	000000	0	1		03.04.2023	MAT001	P100	0	150	EA
00000000000000000000	000000	0	1		03.04.2023	MAT002	P100	0	270	EA
00000000000000000000	000000	0	1		03.04.2023	MAT003	P100	0	100	EA
00000000000000000000	000000	0	1		03.04.2023	MAT004	P200	0	550	EA
00000000000000000000	000000	0	1		03.04.2023	MAT005	P200	0	450	EA

Figure 7.59 View

50. From Transaction SE16, open the validity table that ends with 5. It's been updated with the data from the historical Excel flat file, as shown in Figure 7.60.

Data Browser: Table /BIC/AZRKMMNC4 Select Entries   1

REQTSN	SID_0CALDAY_F	SID_0CALDAY_T	MODEFROM	MODETO
00000000000000000000	20.220.305	20.230.412		

Figure 7.60 Validity Table

51. Now that you understand the logic of materials management-inventory management extraction in SAP BW/4HANA, the next step is to create an SAP HANA composite provider for the materials management flow (see Figure 7.61). (Refer to Chapter 2, Section 2.11 for how to create the SAP HANA composite provider.)

52. Create a query on top of this aDSO by using **New · Query** to open the query maintenance. Choose the **Sheet Definition** tab (see Figure 7.62). (See Chapter 2, Section 2.12 for how to create a query.)

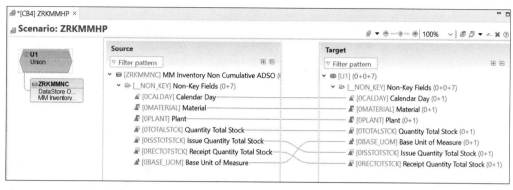

Figure 7.61 SAP HANA Composite Provider

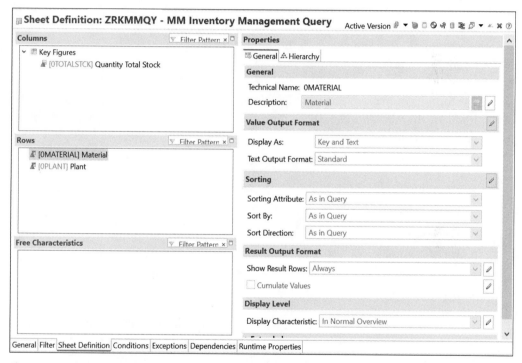

Figure 7.62 Sheet Definition

53. Do a data preview using the icon; it will refer to the formula that was used (see Figure 7.63).

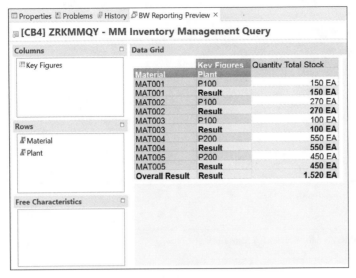

Figure 7.63 Data Preview

The formula from used took data the reference point table. When you include OCALDAY, it will use the most granular data, but now we're seeing the most recent noncumulative data. Here's the formula:

RECTOTSTCK = (Initial Balance OR Reference Points) + Received Stock – Issued Stock

Some examples of this formula in practice are as follows:

- *MAT001 = 100 + 100 – 50 = 150*
- *MAT002 = 200 + 100 – 30 = 270*
- *MAT003 = 300 + 100 - 250 -50 = 100*
- *MAT004 = 400 + 150 – 0 = 550*
- *MAT005 = 500 + 0 -50 = 450*

Once you completely understand the logic, you'll be able to understand and implement the materials management extraction logic based on the SAP-delivered extractors, as we'll discuss in the next section.

7.3   Implementing Inventory Management Extraction Using Logistics Cockpit DataSources

With the knowledge of the inventory flow in hand, we'll explain how to implement the SAP-delivered inventory dataflow and extract data from the standard materials management table in SAP S/4HANA. This section will cover an introduction to business content extractors for the inventory dataflow and the standard DataSources available for the materials management-inventory management extraction. Then you'll learn how to install the standard in-memory objects in SAP BW/4HANA for enabling the MM-IM extraction. Finally you'll fill the setup table for the standard extractors and use SAP-delivered in-memory objects to implement the materials management-inventory management extraction.

7.3.1 Business Content Extractors and Inventory Dataflow

In SAP ERP or SAP S/4HANA, there are three ODP-based standard business content extractors that cover stock balances, historical movements, and revaluations, including deltas as well. Inventory data load in SAP BW/4HANA can be implemented using these three DataSources. You need to know that due to noncumulative behavior in inventory, this extraction is slightly different from other logistics extractions, and this is a little complex if not understood in detail. Let's explore the extraction using standard business content extractors, starting with the SAP ERP or SAP S/4HANA perspective:

- **2LIS_03_BX**

  This DataSource is used to extract the opening stock balance that is stored in the ERP system tables like MARD and others. It extracts the stock balance on a detailed level (material, plant, storage location). The value that you fetch using this DataSource is the status of the inventory. Consider an example: The stock quantity on April 24 is 40. If you're filling the setup table for 2LIS_03_BX on April 24, then only the opening stock or the current stock will be loaded in the 2LIS_03_BX DataSource. This is the current stock value at the time of data load. So the SAP BW/4HANA system will update this as the initial stock. So what will happen to the other stock that was from after April 24? We have a separate extractor to load the delta material movements and the historical data from before that date.

- **2LIS_03_BF**

  This DataSource is used to extract the material movements into the SAP BW/4HANA system. This DataSource can extract historic and delta transactions, so it will load all the historical stock values of all the materials except the current stock value.

- **2LIS_03_UM**

  This DataSource is used to extract the data from evaluated revaluations in financial accounting (table BESG). In simple terms, it holds the value of the stock. This data is useful to update the valuated stock changes for the calculated stock balance in SAP BW/4HANA. As this DataSource is related to stock value, this information is less useful here; we're interested only in the quantity, so and it isn't used as widely as the other two extractors. But when you create the dataflow, it's good to create this flow also.

Next you need to understand the inventory flow in SAP BW/4HANA. All the objects in the dataflow discussed ahead will be available in the BI content and can be installed from Transaction RSA1, via the **BI Content** option. There are many objects in multiple

LSA++ layers, such as DataSources, corporate memory, enterprise data warehouse (EDW) core layer, and finally virtual layer (see Figure 7.64).

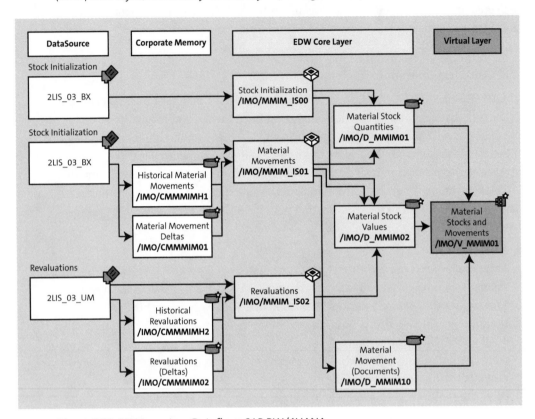

Figure 7.64 MM Inventory Dataflow: SAP BW/4HANA

The following business content is provided with SAP BW/4HANA content (software component BW4CONT):

- **Composite provider**
  - /IMO/V_MMIM01 – Material Stocks & Movements
- **Integrated warehouse layer (adDSOs)**
  - /IMO/D_MMIM01 – MM-IM: Material Stock – Quantities
  - /IMO/D_MMIM02 – MM-IM: Material Stock – Values
  - /IMO/D_MMIM10 – MM-IM: Material Movements
- **InfoSources**
  - /IMO/MMIM_IS00 – MM-IM: Stock Initialization (2LIS_03_BX)
  - /IMO/MMIM_IS01 – MM-IM: Material Movements (2LIS_03_BF)
  - /IMO/MMIM_IS02 – MM-IM: Revaluations (2LIS_03_UM)

- **Staging/corporate memory layer (aDSOs)**

  Note that SAP recommends loading the data through these DSOs:

  - /IMO/CMMMIMH1 – MM-IM: Historical Material Movements
  - /IMO/CMMMIMO1 – MM-IM: Material Movements Delta
  - /IMO/CMMMIMH2 – MM-IM: Historical Revaluations
  - /IMO/CMMMIMO2 – MM-IM: Revaluations – Delta

7.3.2   Installing IMO Objects in SAP BW/4HANA

Before implementing the materials management-inventory management extraction, make sure that you have installed all the latest SAP Notes related to SAP BW/4HANA transformations. You can get the updated transformation notes in SAP Note 2603241 (overview and summary of most important SAP Notes in the context of SAP BW transformation with SAP HANA and ABAP execution).

This SAP Note will have an XML attachment; download that XML file. Then run report Z_SAP_BW_NOTE_ANALYZER (available in the SAP Note). First use Transaction SE38 to create the ABAP report and then execute the report and use the **Load XML File** option (see Figure 7.65) to upload the XML file that you got from the note. Execute the report, and if you see any SAP Notes with a status of yellow or red, then you need to install all the SAP Notes in the same sequence from the output list.

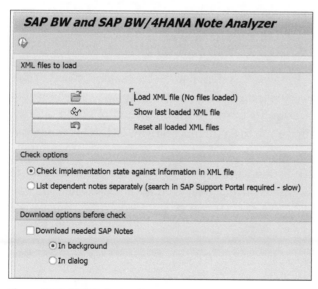

Figure 7.65 SAP Note Analyzer

Once all SAP Notes are completed, you can start installing the IMO objects. Follow these steps:

1. In SAP BW/4HANA, open Transaction RSA1 and select menu path **Administration** · **Source Systems** · **Source System Assignment**. Provide a two-digit ID for your sender SAP S/4HANA source system name. Figure 7.66 shows the status of the source system ID for logical system **S4SCLNT100** as blank initially ❶ and then with a value of **02** ❷.

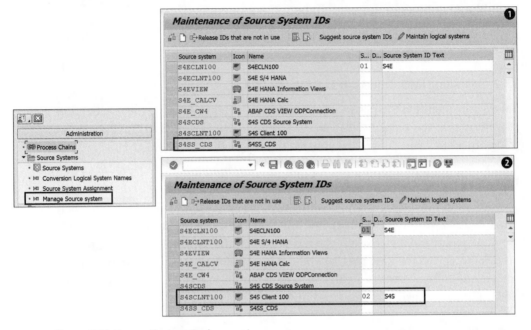

Figure 7.66 Source System Assignment

2. In SAP BW/4HANA, open Transaction RSA1 and select your source system in the right-hand folder. Right-click the source system name—for example, **S4SCLNT100**. From the context menu, choose the **Transfer Global Settings** option. This will ensure the currencies and units of measure are transferred from the source system, and it's a one-time activity. We encourage you to do this once SAP BW/4HANA is connected to any source system.

3. In SAP BW/4HANA, open Transaction RSA1 (see Figure 7.67). Choose **BI Content** ❶ and then in source system assignment, using the ▣ icon ❷, choose the relevant SAP S/4HANA source system (in this case, **S4SCLNT100** ❸) and press Enter or click the ✔ icon.

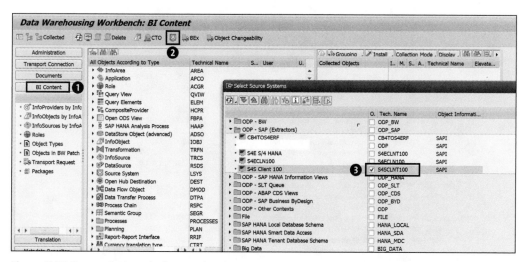

Figure 7.67 Source System Assignment

4. Choose **Select Objects** from the **Data Flow Object** section and search (see Figure 7.68).

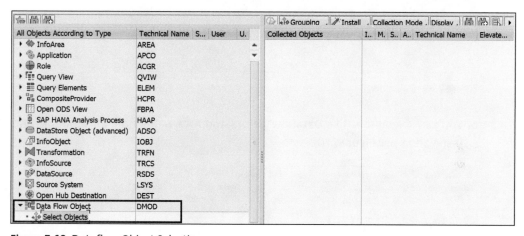

Figure 7.68 Dataflow Object Selection

5. Once you've found the dataflow object (**/IMO/DF_MMIM_01**), choose it and click **Transfer Selections** (see Figure 7.69).

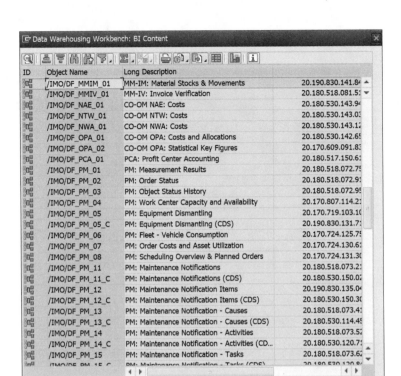

Figure 7.69 Dataflow

6. You can see options like **Dataflow Before and Afterwards** now for grouping and installation (see Figure 7.70).

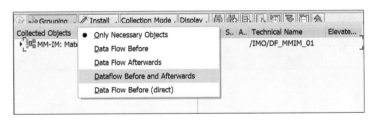

Figure 7.70 Grouping

7. Once you select **Dataflow Before and Afterwards**, you'll see the objects being collected after a few seconds. You'll see the screen shown in Figure 7.71. Expand the objects as shown.

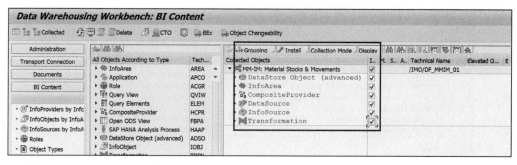

Figure 7.71 Objects

8. When you expand all the objects shown in Figure 7.71, you can see all the objects and choose the **Install** option (see Figure 7.72).

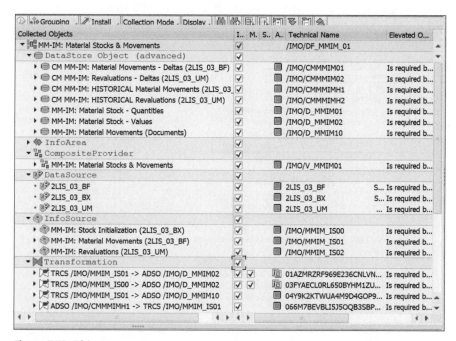

Figure 7.72 Objects

9. Choose **Install** (see Figure 7.73), then there will be a popup. Choose **Transfer All without Dialog** to install all the objects. Otherwise, choose **Install in the Background**. When you transfer in dialog, it will run the foreground and it takes time, but using the background will create a background job. In both cases, make sure the job is completed. Because this involves many objects for the first time, it will take a lot of time (multiple hours) to activate.

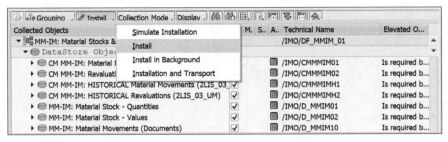

Figure 7.73 Install

10. If you open Eclipse and open the SAP BW repository, you'll see the InfoArea as shown in Figure 7.74. You'll see folders for the /IMO objects in materials management-inventory management, plus the SAP BW/4HANA objects that are installed, like aDSOs, SAP HANA composite providers, InfoSources, and so on.

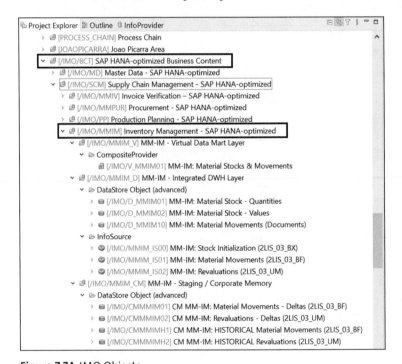

Figure 7.74 IMO Objects

11. If you expand the aDSO, you'll see the associated transformations (see Figure 7.75). If a transformation isn't active, you can activate it manually using the **Activate** ⚙ icon. (This process was covered in detail in Chapter 2.)

Now you've ensured that the right content is installed for the materials management extraction. Let's now move to SAP S/4HANA to fill the setup table.

```
˅ ⊌ [/IMO/MMIM] Inventory Management - SAP HANA-optimized
   ˅ ⊌ [/IMO/MMIM_V] MM-IM - Virtual Data Mart Layer
      ˅ ⊳ CompositeProvider
            ⊞ [/IMO/V_MMIM01] MM-IM: Material Stocks & Movements
   ˅ ⊌ [/IMO/MMIM_D] MM-IM - Integrated DWH Layer
      ˅ ⊳ DataStore Object (advanced)
         ˅ ⊟ [/IMO/D_MMIM01] MM-IM: Material Stock - Quantities
            ˅ ⊳ Transformation
                  ⋈ [0R4QN2QWJSLIZGGOQQT17GKNIG85MLEI] TRCS /IMO/MMIM_IS01->ADSO /IMO/D_MMIM01
                  ⋈ [0SGC5239X28U1ERT3UQEWLFQRPAP6ATI] TRCS /IMO/MMIM_IS00->ADSO /IMO/D_MMIM01
            › ⊳ Data Transfer Process
         ˅ ⊟ [/IMO/D_MMIM02] MM-IM: Material Stock - Values
            ˅ ⊳ Transformation
                  ⋈ [01AZMRZRF969E236CNLVN7N4HAHGS974] TRCS /IMO/MMIM_IS01->ADSO /IMO/D_MMIM02
                  ⋈ [03FYAECL0RL650BYHM1ZUYEE7YTNNCX9] TRCS /IMO/MMIM_IS00->ADSO /IMO/D_MMIM02
                  ⋈ [0MJYY95E3PYGHZ9LFTY8777XWJCZC1JG] TRCS /IMO/MMIM_IS02->ADSO /IMO/D_MMIM02
         ˅ ⊟ [/IMO/D_MMIM10] MM-IM: Material Movements (Documents)
            ˅ ⊳ Transformation
                  ⋈ [04Y9K2KTWUA4M9D4GOP9YI2FF9PU2QTJ] TRCS /IMO/MMIM_IS01->ADSO /IMO/D_MMIM10
      › ⊳ InfoSource
```

Figure 7.75 Corporate Memory

7.3.3   Filling the Setup Table for Inventory Data Loading

Follow these steps in SAP S/4HANA for filling the setup table for inventory data loading:

1. Use Transaction LBWG and enter "03" in the input field to delete the contents of the setup tables related to application component 03. This will avoid additional records when loading data.

2. From Transaction RSA5, activate DataSources 2LIS_03_BX, 2LIS_03_BF, and 2LIS_03_UM by choosing the rows for these DataSources and selecting the **Activate** button (see Figure 7.76).

```
Installation of DataSource from Business Content
🔍 📇 📄 📝  Set Section  🔍⌄ 🔍  Content Delta    Activate DataSources    Version Comparison    Display Log

        ───────2LIS_02_SGR        🔳🔳 Produced Activity: Delivery of Schedule Lines
        ───────2LIS_02_SRV        🔳🔳 Purchasing Data (External Services)
        ───────2LIS_03_BF         🔳🔳 Goods Movements From Inventory Management
        ───────2LIS_03_BX         🔳🔳 Stock Initialization for Inventory Management
        ───────2LIS_03_S091       🔳🔳 WM: Quantity flows
        ───────2LIS_03_S194       🔳🔳 MRP: Business Info Warehouse
        ───────2LIS_03_S195       🔳🔳 Material movements: storage location
        ───────2LIS_03_S196       🔳🔳 Goods movement: Plant
        ───────2LIS_03_S197       🔳🔳 Periodic storage location stock
        ───────2LIS_03_S198       🔳🔳 Periodic plant stock
        ───────2LIS_03_UM         🔳🔳 Revaluations
        ───────2LIS_06_INV        🔳🔳 Extraction of Invoice Verification Data into BW
```

Figure 7.76 Activate DataSources

3. Now open the logistics cockpit using Transaction LBWE, activate the two extractors, and make the mode queued delta. You won't see the extractor for 2LIS_03_BX here. As shown in Figure 7.77, the **Update** is **Active** for both extractors.

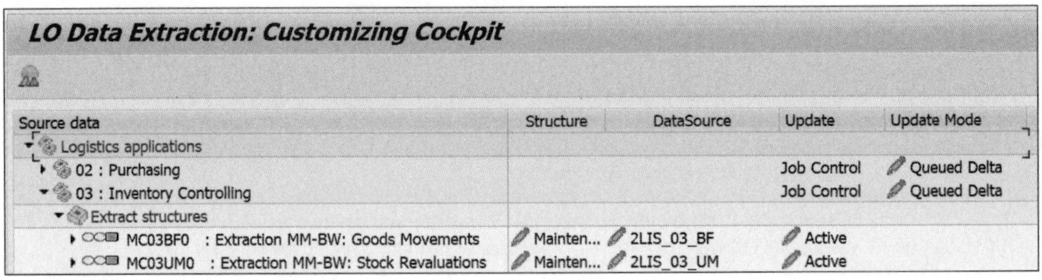

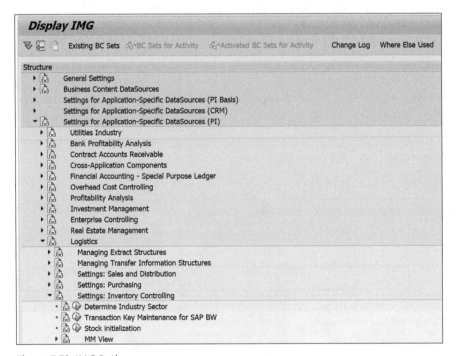

Figure 7.77 Logistics Cockpit

You're done with the basic steps to fill the setup table, but you need to make a few settings in the SAP ERP and SAP S/4HANA systems before filling setup table. To do so, follow these steps:

1. Open Transaction SBIW and follow the path shown in Figure 7.78: **Settings for Application-Specific DataSource (PI)** · **Logistics** · **Settings: Inventory Controlling** · **Determine Industry Sector**.

Figure 7.78 IMG Path

2. Once you select **Determine Industry Sector**, choose **Standard (Core)** before filling in the setup table. If the sector is different, you need to choose accordingly. For this example, choose **Standard (Core)** as shown in Figure 7.79.

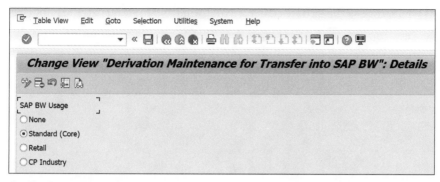

Figure 7.79 Settings

3. Execute Transaction BF11, then select the **BW** checkbox (see Figure 7.80).

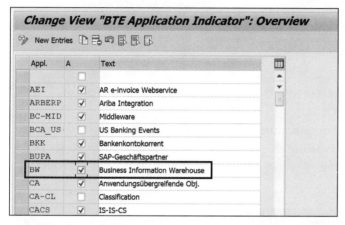

Figure 7.80 BF11 Transaction

One this is completed, fill the setup table, following these steps:

1. In SAP S/4HANA, open Transaction LBWE and delete the setup table for application component O3 by entering "03" and clicking the ![icon] icon (see Figure 7.81).

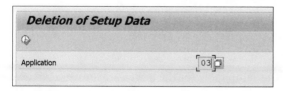

Figure 7.81 Delete Contents of Setup Table

2. Open Transaction MCNB to fill the 2LIS_03_BX DataSource, and change the **Time of Termination** to a future value. For example, if the time is 3 p.m. when you perform this step, set the value to, say, 6 p.m., or set the **Termination Date** to the next day. In

the ⌷F4⌷ help, choose the extract structure that will have the value **2LIS_03_BX** (see Figure 7.82).

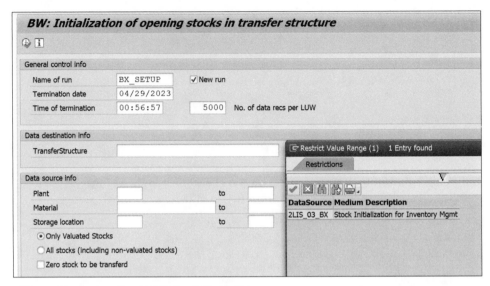

Figure 7.82 Transaction MCNB For 2LIS_03_BX

3. Once you've set the transfer structure as 2LIS_03_BX and set the termination time to a future date, execute this setup table filling process. It will show the popup in Figure 7.83. Once you choose the ✔ icon for the series of popups, the setup table will be filled.

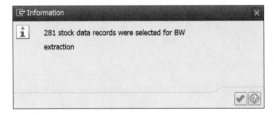

Figure 7.83 Setup Content

4. You can see the contents of the filled setup table in Transaction RSA3 (see Figure 7.84).

5. Use the Transaction OLI1BW to fill the setup table for the next DataSource, 2LIS_03_ BF, as shown in Figure 7.85. Make sure that you set the date or time to the future and click the ⊕ icon.

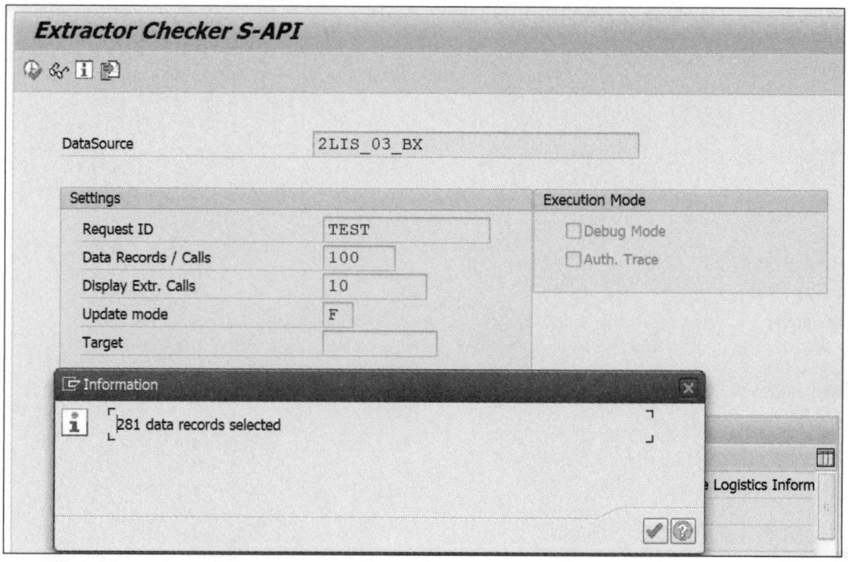

Figure 7.84 Simulation Run

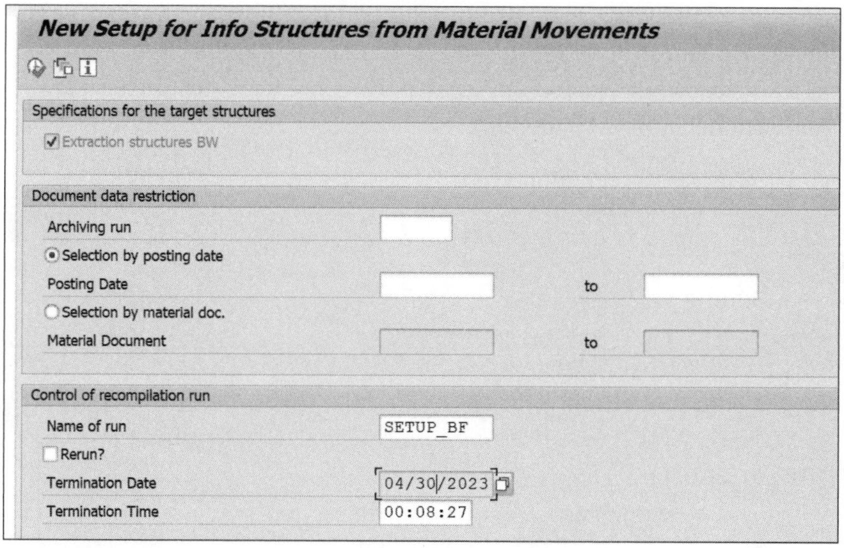

Figure 7.85 Transaction OLI1BW: 2LIS_03_BF

6. Once this is executed, you can see the setup table contents as shown in Figure 7.86. Use Transaction RSA3, provide the DataSource name "2LIS_03_BF", and click ⊕ to see the data.

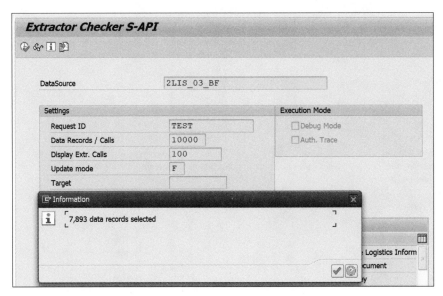

Figure 7.86 Setup Table Contents

7. You can also use report RODPS_REPL_TEST to validate this setup table content, but the execution of the report will create an entry in Transaction ODQMON with the subscriber as a test repository, so you can see that the contents match the results you saw in Transaction RSA3 (see Figure 7.87).

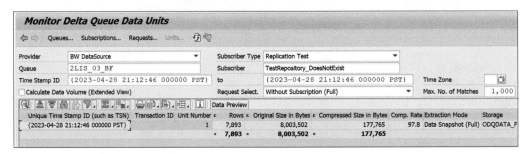

Figure 7.87 2LIS_03_BF Data

8. You can use Transaction OLIZBW to fill the setup table for 2LIS_03_UM. In this transaction, the **Company Code** field is mandatory, so you must provide the company code for which you're filling the setup table (see Figure 7.88).

9. Once this is completed, you can see the contents of the setup table as shown in Figure 7.89. Use Transaction RSA3 by entering the DataSource name, "2LIS_03_UM".

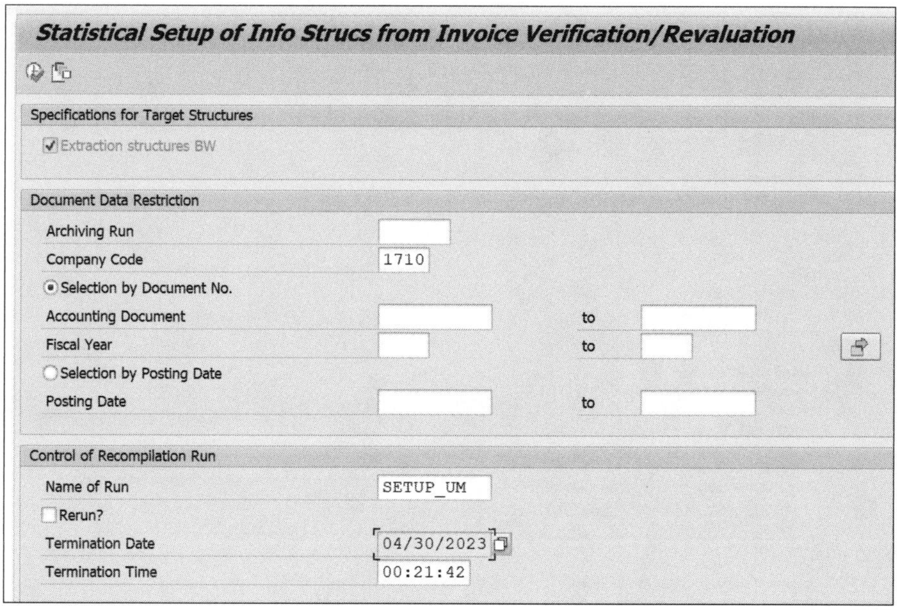

Figure 7.88 Transaction OLIZBW: 2LIS_03_UM

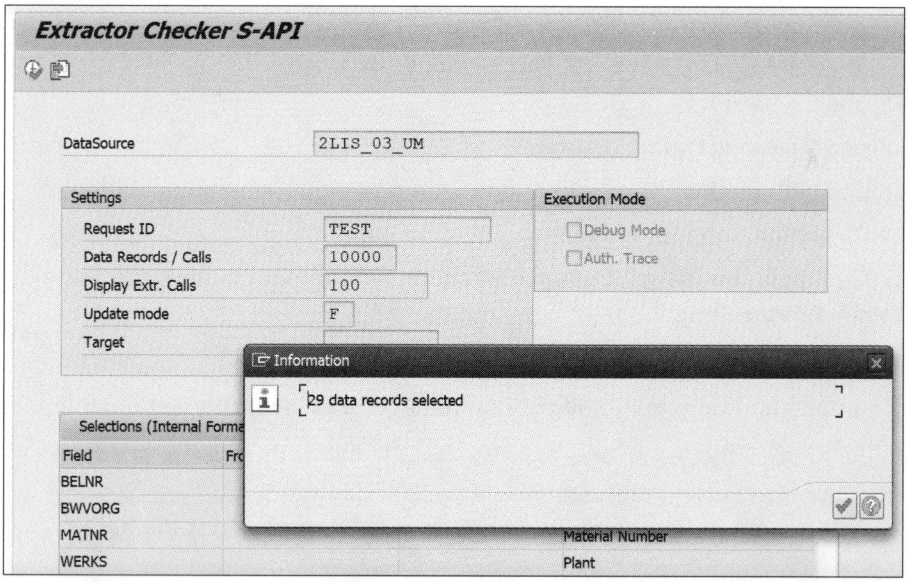

Figure 7.89 2LIS_03_UM: Setup Table Contents

Now you've filled the setup tables for all three DataSources. If you don't want to use the transactions to fill the setup tables, you can use the Transaction SBIW path to fill the setup tables. It will take you to the same transactions that we used earlier (see Figure 7.90).

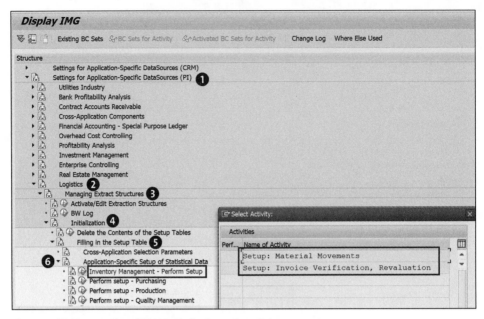

Figure 7.90 Transaction SBIW Path for Inventory Setup

Follow these steps, as shown in Figure 7.90:

❶ In Transaction SBIW, choose **Settings for Application-Specific DataSource (PI)**.

❷ Expand the **Logistics**.

❸ Expand **Managing Extract Structures**.

❹ Expand **Initialization**.

❺ Expand **Filling in the Setup Table**.

❻ Expand **Application-Specific Setup of Statistical Data** and choose **Inventory Management—Perform Setup**.

7.3.4   Implementing Logistics-Materials Management Inventory Data Loading

With the prerequisites completed in SAP S/4HANA, follow these steps to implement the logistics-materials management inventory data loading:

1. Replicate the 2LIS_03_BX, 2LIS_03_BF, and 2LIS_03_UM DataSources in SAP BW/4HANA and activate them.

2. Make sure that all the inventory flows are active, as shown earlier in Figure 7.76. If any objects are inactive, activate them using the ⚙ icon.

3. Start the data loading of 2LIS_03_BX. Implement this flow (see Figure 7.91), where you will create the full DTP from DataSource 2LIS_03_BX to the EDW core layer aDSO /IMO/D_DMMIM01. The DTP should have the **Extraction Mode** set to **Initial Noncumulative for Noncumulative Values**. Execute the DTP; this will be a one-time execution.

Similarly create the next DTP from 2LIS_03_BX with full DTP and **Extraction Mode** set to **Initial Noncumulative for Noncumulative Values** for one time.

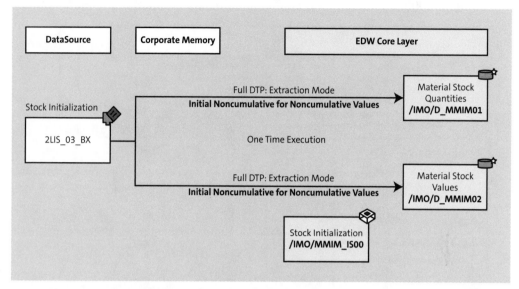

Figure 7.91 Implementing DataSource 2LIS_03_BX Data Flow

4. Open the /IMO/D_MMIM01 aDSO. Create the DTP based on the transformation there. You will have an InfoSource between the data flow, but the DTP can be created for the RSDS object. Figure 7.92 shows the following:

❶ The integrated data warehouse aDSO (/IMO/D_MMIM01) gets data through the two InfoSources.

❷ This is the transformation from the InfoSource (/IMO/MMIM_IS00) to the aDSO (/IMO/D_MMIM01).

❸ The InfoSource has the transformation from 2LIS_03_BX.

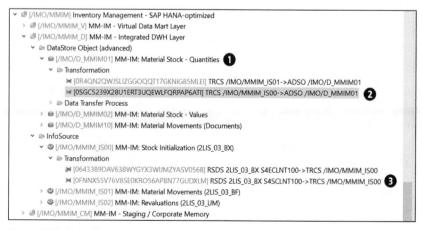

Figure 7.92 Dataflow

5. Right-click the aDSO (**/IMO/D_MMIM01**) and create the DTP for the two transformations (see Figure 7.93). Follow the path **New · Data Transfer Process** from both transformations.

Figure 7.93 Create DTP

6. For **Object Type** under **Source**, select **DataSource** (see Figure 7.94).

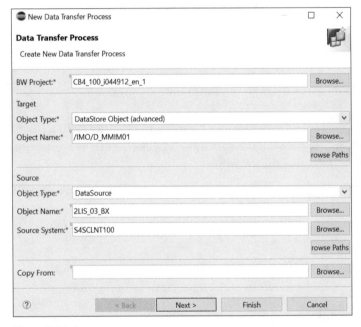

Figure 7.94 Source

7. When you choose **Next**, you can see that the InfoSource is also part of the flow (see Figure 7.95). Choose **Finish**.

8. In the DTP, you can see the sender or source as **DataSource RSDS**, which is **2LIS_03_BX**, and you will see that the **Extraction Mode** is **Initial Noncumulative for Noncumulative Values**. Execute this DTP only once using ▶ ▼ (see Figure 7.96).

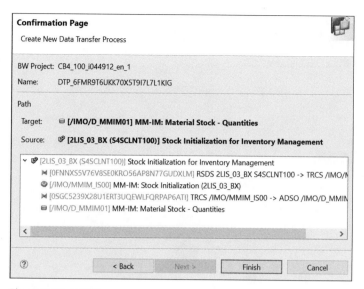

Figure 7.95 DTP Flow

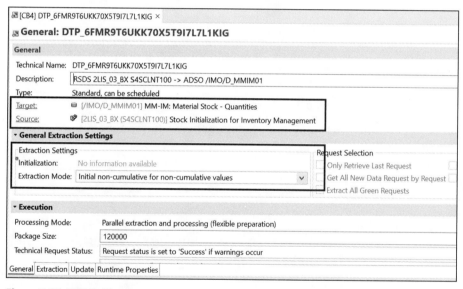

Figure 7.96 DTP Settings

9. Once you execute the DTP, you can see the extracted records (see Figure 7.97):

   ❶ Transaction RSA3 in SAP S/4HANA had 281 records, and the same number can be seen in the DTP request in SAP BW/4HANA.

   ❷ The transformation flow is from 2LIS_03_BX.

   ❸ 281 records are extracted based on this transformation flow.

   ❹ This transformation is from InfoSource /IMO/MMIM_IS00, as can be seen in the DTP flow.

❺ There are 279 records based on this flow.

❻ The final update happens here to the /IMO/D_MMIM01 aDSO.

❼ The final data for this aDSO is now 279.

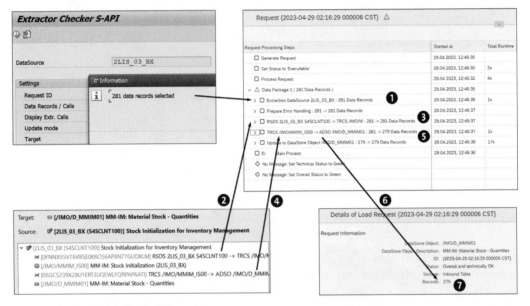

Figure 7.97 Extracted Records

Now you can check the tables using these steps:

1. Check the aDSO tables like /B1H/AD_MMIM011, /B1H/AD_MMIM012, and /B1H/AD_MMIM013 (see Figure 7.98).

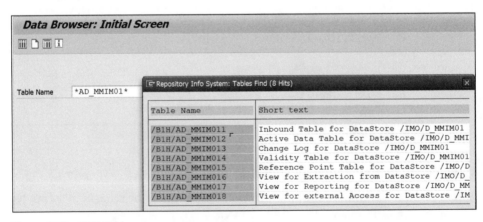

Figure 7.98 aDSO Tables

2. Once you choose the inbound table that ends with 1, you can see the inbound table will have an entry. Activate the aDSO using the 🔧 icon (see Figure 7.99).

Figure 7.99 aDSO Request Activation

3. As shown in Figure 7.100, you'll see the data in the validity table ❶ and reference point table ❷. You need to open the aDSO tables that end with 4 and 5—for example, /B1H/AD_MMIM014 for the validity table and /B1H/AD_MMIM05 for the reference table.

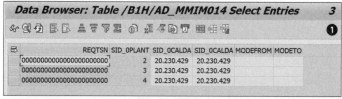

Figure 7.100 Table Contents

4. Create the DTP for /IMO/D_MMIM02 based on DataSource 2LIS_03_BX. This is a one-time action. Make sure you have the **Initial Noncumulative for Noncumulative Values** setting selected (see Figure 7.101).

Figure 7.101 DTP for /IMO/D_MMIM02

5. Execute the DTP using the ⊕ icon and you can see the results as shown in Figure 7.102.

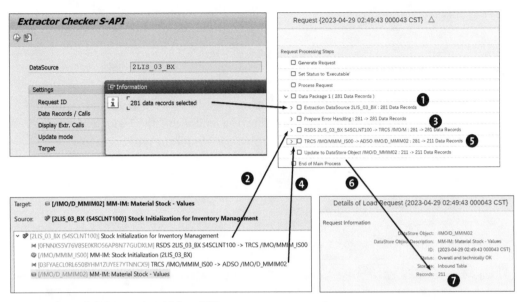

Figure 7.102 Inventory Values DTP

Here are the details:

❶ The initial extraction of DataSource 2LIS_03_BX in Transaction RSA3 is 281, and the same number can be seen in the DTP request in SAP BW/4HANA.

❷ This is the transformation from 2LIS_03_BX to InfoSource /IMO/MMIM_IS00 in the DTP flow.

❸ The result of the transformation is 281.

❹ The transformation from InfoSource /IMO/MMIM_IS00 to aDSO /IMO/D_MMIM02 in the DTP flow.

❺ The result of the transformation is 211 records.

❻ The update to the aDSO happens in this step.

❼ The aDSO inbound table is filled.

6. View the aDSO request, as shown in Figure 7.103. It can be seen from the Manage Request area.

7. Activate the request using the 🔳 icon to see the two tables shown in Figure 7.104: the validity table ❶ and the reference point table ❷.

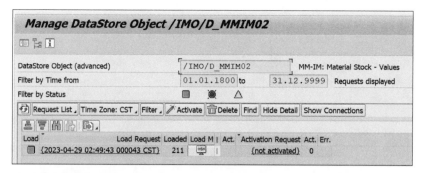

Figure 7.103 Inbound Table

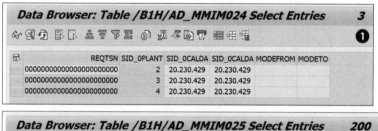

Figure 7.104 Tables

With this, you've completed the 2LIS_03_BX steps and loaded the initial balance for quantity and value. Now let's focus on the material movements using these steps:

1. To load the material movements 2LIS_03_BF, follow the flow in Figure 7.105. From the DataSource 2LIS_03_BF, you first execute the full DTP one time to the corporate memory aDSO /IMO/CMMMIMH1. Then load the data from /IMO/CMMMIMH1 to the EDW aDSOs /IMO/D_MMIM01, /IMO/D_MMIM02, and /IMO/D_MMIM10 using the settings highlighted in Figure 7.105. Once the full load is completed the next step is to initialize delta and load the delta. Execute the delta load from 2LIS_03_BF to /IMO/CMMMIMO1 and then execute the delta from /IMO/CMMMIMO1 to /IMO/D_MMIM01, /IMO/D_MMIM02, and / IMO/D_MMIM10.

2. Now create the full DTP (see Figure 7.106).

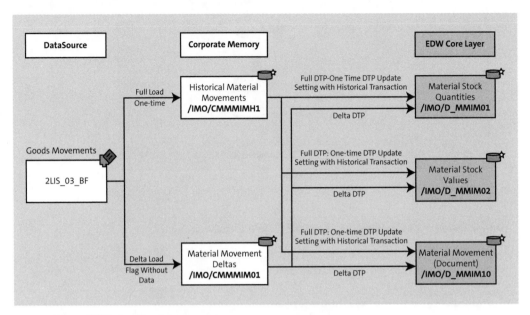

Figure 7.105 Loading Layer

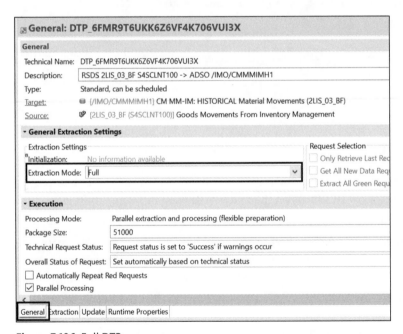

Figure 7.106 Full DTP

3. You'll see the popup shown in Figure 7.107, which will have the details of the target and the source. Enter "/IMO/CMMMIMH1" in **Target** and "2LIS_03_BF" in **Source**.

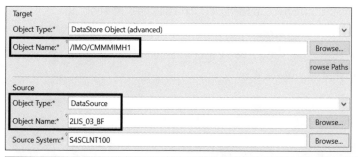

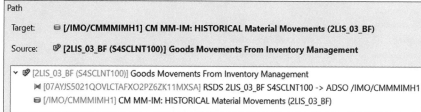

Figure 7.107 Full DTP

4. Execute the DTP using the ● ▼ icon. You can see the result in Figure 7.108.

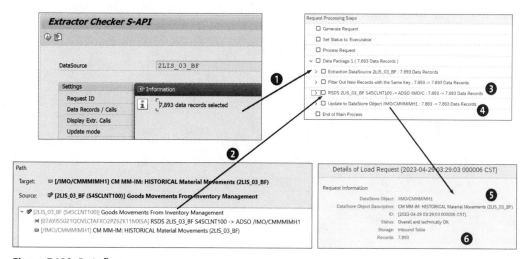

Figure 7.108 Dataflow

You can see these details:

● The Transaction RSA3 results match 2LIS_03_BF in SAP BW/4HANA: 7,893 records.

● The transformation is from 2LIS_03_BF to aDSO /IMO/CMMMIMH1 in the DTP flow.

● The result of the transformation is shown as 7,893 records.

● The update to the aDSO is happening here in SAP BW/4HANA; it updated 7,893 records.

❺ You can see the aDSO name here in the aDSO data as /IMO/CMMMIMH1.

❻ The inbound table has 7,893 records.

5. Because this aDSO is in staging status, you cannot activate it (see Figure 7.109). You can open aDSO /IMO/CMMMIMH1 to see it.

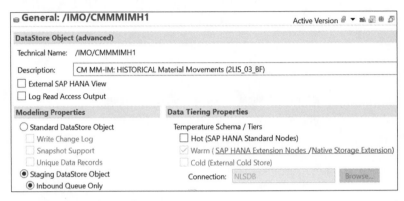

Figure 7.109 Staging Status

6. You can see that staging aDSO /IMO/CMMMIMH1 has an option for load request only, and not for the activation request (Figure 7.110).

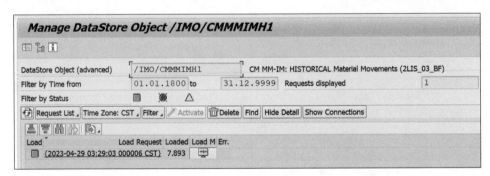

Figure 7.110 Staging aDSO

7. Now create the next DTP for the EDW layer for **/IMO/D_MMIM01** from **/IMO/CMMIMH1** using the option **Full One Time DTP** with the update settings set to **Historical Transactions**. This will have an InfoSource layer with a transformation in between. You can see the flow as shown in Figure 7.111.

Figure 7.111 Transformation for InfoSource and aDSO

The DTP settings will be as shown in Figure 7.112, with the checkbox for **Historical Transactions** enabled.

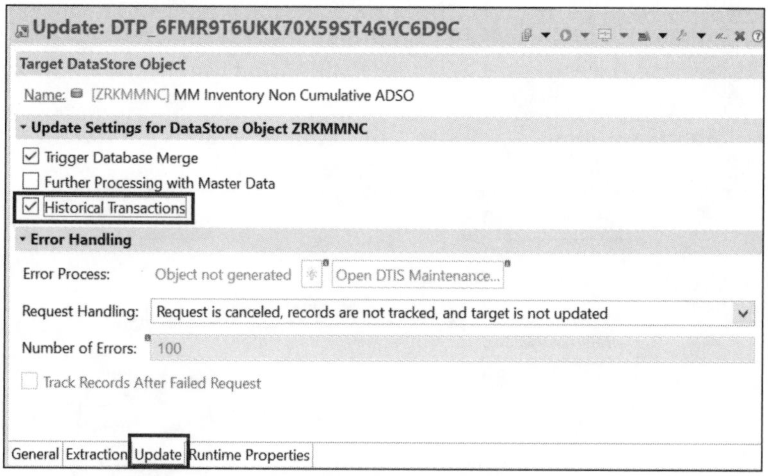

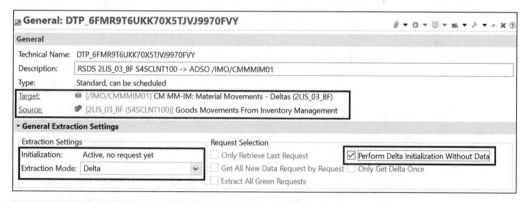

Figure 7.112 Historical Transactions

8. Complete all the flows shown earlier in Figure 7.105 for the historical load, which focuses on the /IMO/CMMMIMH1 objects and then on /IMO/D_MMIMO1, /IMO/D_MMIMO2, and /IMO/D_MMIMO3.

9. Next, complete the delta DTP flow D (see Figure 7.113), which loads from 2LIS_03_BF to /IMO/CMMMIMO1 and to /IMO/D_MMIMO1, /IMO/D_MMIMO2, and /IMO/D_MMIMO3.

Figure 7.113 Delta DTP Flow

10. Once all the delta DTPs are completed, complete the delta DTP between the staging and DWH layers for all the three aDSOs: /IMO/D_MMIMO1 (Material Stock Quantities), /IMO/D_MMIMO2 (Material Stock Values), and /IMO/D_MMIM10 (Material Movements, Documents). These delta DTPs will be used in the process chains for the daily execution.

11. Now complete the flow for the revaluation. As per this flow (see Figure 7.114), you need to start with the DTP creation from 2LIS_03_UM, and there is a full DTP from 2LIS_03_UM to corporate memory aDSO /IMO.CMMMIMH2. Then do the full DTP with the **Historical Transactions** setting enabled to EDW aDSO /IMO/D_MMIMO2, then load the delta from 2LIS_03_UM to the staging aDSO (/IMO/MMMIMO2) and use the delta DTP to load to EDW core layer /IMO/D_MMIMO2.

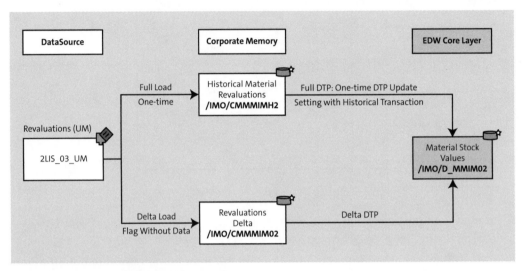

Figure 7.114 Material Revaluations

Once this flow is completed, this delta DTP can be included in the process chain. Then the regular execution of the process chain will bring in the delta movements and revaluations. This will complete the implementation of materials management-inventory management extraction in SAP BW/4HANA.

7.4   Summary

In this chapter you learned the fundamentals of the materials management inventory process in SAP. This functional knowledge will be the basis for materials management-inventory management data extraction. We discussed the steps to active the materials management-inventory management DataSources in SAP S/4HANA and fill the setup tables for applications in sales. You learned how the materials management-inventory management dataflow works in SAP BW/4HANA with noncumulative values and how the tables are filled and activated during the data load. You learned to make the configuration settings, which is unique for MM extraction, and now you know how to do the data staging of materials management-inventory management to SAP BW/4HANA.

With the completion of the end-to-end extraction based on the logistics extraction for materials management-inventory management, you're ready to build the SAP BW/4HANA model to extract the data from materials management-inventory management tables in the SAP S/4HANA system using the SAP-delivered extractors. Knowing this logic will be mandatory as large SAP BW/4HANA implementation projects will have reporting requirements based on the data from SAP S/4HANA systems. Materials management extraction plays a key role in fetching data from the inventory tables of SAP S/4HANA and SAP ERP systems.

In the next chapter, we'll focus on extraction of finance data from SAP ERP and SAP S/4HANA using the SAP-delivered standard extractors.

7

Chapter 8
Extracting Financial Data

This chapter covers finance application extractors. It explains how to extract data from these SAP-delivered extractors and the end-to-end extraction from the SAP S/4HANA source system. In SAP S/4HANA, financial management deals with the management of core finance data such as accounts receivable, accounts payable, and the general ledger. The functional basics that we'll discuss in the first sections will help you to understand the SAP BW extraction process better.

In any organization, financial accounting is very important. It deals with storing finance-based data and helps organizations to do transactional reporting based on financial data. Finance (FI) in SAP is integrated with areas like sales and distribution, materials management, purchasing, and more. There have been many changes in FI in SAP S/4HANA. From an SAP BW perspective, you use DataSources that support extraction from classical SAP ERP–based tables and the new tables based on SAP S/4HANA, so we'll offer a high-level overview of both perspectives here as SAP BW/4HANA reporting can get data from both these DataSources.

In this chapter, we'll start with an introduction to financial management. Then we'll discuss FI in SAP ERP systems in Section 8.1. The classical SAP standard extractors for FI-AR, FI-AP, and FI-GL are covered in Section 8.1.2. The changes in the new general ledger are discussed in Section 8.2. Then we'll check how to extract the FI asset account data from SAP S/4HANA in Section 8.3. The data from table ACDOCA is extracted using two standard DataSources, as we'll explain in Section 8.4. We'll also focus on how to install the dataflows for SAP HANA–optimized financial management in SAP BW/4HANA and activate those flows to extract full and delta loads from SAP S/4HANA.

8.1 Finance in SAP ERP Systems

In an SAP ERP system, the finance area is called FICO, for finance (FI) and controlling (CO). *Finance* has more subareas that deal with an organization's external financial requirements, like balance sheets, income statements, cash flow statements, and so on. It deals with accounts from customers and vendors. *Controlling* deals with an organization's internal requirements, like cost center–based reports and profit center-based reports. We'll begin this section by discussing the DataSources in these areas, and then we'll discuss open items in FI-AR and open items in FI-AP. You'll learn about the extraction of classical FI-based DataSources in Section 8.1.2 and you'll learn about the management of delta records and how to extract new and changed records in Section 8.1.3.

8.1.1   Finance in SAP

Finance has many subareas that help manage an organization's financial data. All these areas and their relationships to each other are shown in Figure 8.1.

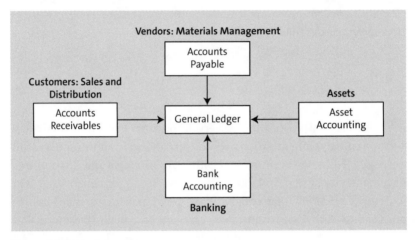

Figure 8.1 FI Modules

Let's walk through each module in more detail:

- *General ledger accounting (FI-GL)* has all the transactional-level details of the company: the accounts are used to prepare the financial statements, and the transactions that are recorded in other areas are reconciled in real time. The common ledger entries are customer transactions, vendor purchases, and transactions within the company. In simple terms, a *general ledger* is a set of numbered accounts a business uses to keep track of its financial transactions and prepare financial reports. Each account is a unique record summarizing a specific type of asset, liability, equity, revenue, or expense. A *chart of accounts* lists all the accounts in the general ledger. In general, a large business has thousands of accounts in a general ledger. In SAP, you can see the general ledger accounts in table SKA1. In the general ledger accounts' master table (chart of accounts), the SAKNR field will have the general ledger account number, which is 10 digits.

- *Accounts receivable (FI-AR)* is responsible for all the transactions based on customers. This area has the details of the customers' accounts. This is tightly integrated with sales and distribution, where the customer buys products and is responsible for paying the company—and so these accounts are accounts *receivable* to the company.

Postings made in AR are simultaneously recorded in the general ledger (receivables, customer down payments, etc.).

To help you better understand open items in FI-AR, we'll walk through an example and a few important terms. In sales and distribution, when a customer buys a product and a sale has been completed, it creates a billing document in table VBRK-VBLEN, and there will be an accounting document created in the line item tables BSID/BSAD. *Customer open items* means the billed or invoice amount is pending from the customer, yet to be received. Table BSID stores this information. *Customer closed items* means the amounts have been received from the customer; the payments are completed. Table BSAD stores this information.

- *Accounts payable* (FI-AP) is responsible for all the transactions based on vendors, so this area has the details of vendor accounts. This is tightly integrated into the MM-purchasing module, where the organization buys raw materials for production from different vendors and the company is responsible for paying the vendors once the materials are purchased; hence these accounts are accounts *payable* from the company. Postings made in AP are simultaneously recorded in the general ledger (payables, vendor down payments, etc.).

To help you better understand open items in FI-AP, we'll walk through an example and a few important terms. In material management purchasing, when an organization procures a material for production it creates a purchase order (PO). When a PO is created, an equivalent document in purchasing-based backend tables is also create. Then there will be an accounting document created in the line item tables BSIS/BSAD based on the purchase order. *Vendor open items* means the billed or invoice amount is pending to the vendor; it is yet to be paid. Table BSIS stores this information. *Vendor closed items* means the amounts have been paid to the vendor; the payment is completed. Table BSIK stores this information.

- *Asset accounting (FI-AA)* deals with the fixed assets of the company and stores all the details of the transactions based on fixed accounts (equipment, buildings, vehicles, and goodwill).

Some additional important terms to know that are used in most SAP BW extractions are credit and debit. Under the double-entry system, every business entry is recorded in two accounts: one account will receive a debit on the left side and the other account will receive a credit on right side of any double-entry bookkeeping.

In general, a *debit* is what comes in, or the receiver, or all the expenses and gains. A *credit* is what goes out, or the giver, or all the incomes and gains. To give a simple example, if you buy a phone for $1,000, then you've increased your physical assets (with the phone being a new asset). At the same time, another asset (your cash) has decreased. To summarize, the financial entry would look like this:

- Cell Phone Debit: $1,000
- Cash Credit: $1,000

Tables Used in Financial Management

In classical SAP ERP systems, general ledger transaction data is stored in table GLT0 and line items are stored in BSEG and BKPF. There are a few important FI DataSources in classical SAP BW extraction. These DataSources are still supported in SAP BW/4HANA.

The classical FI extractors are as follows:

- 0FI_AR_4—Customers: Line Items with Delta Extraction (takes data from tables BSID/BSAD)
- 0FI_AP_4—Vendors: Line Items with Delta Extraction (takes data from tables BSIK/BSAK)
- 0FI_GL_4—General Ledger: Line Items with Delta Extraction (takes data from tables BKPF/BSEG)

8.1.2 FI Classical DataSource Extraction from an SAP ERP System

The process to extract the data from the SAP ERP system is common for all FI areas, like AP, AR, and the general ledger. Follow these steps:

1. Activate the DataSource in Transaction RSA5. You can select the DataSource and choose the **Activate DataSource** button. In Figure 8.2, you can see the **0FI_AR_4** accounts receivable DataSource is selected, and it can be activated using **Activate DataSource** button.

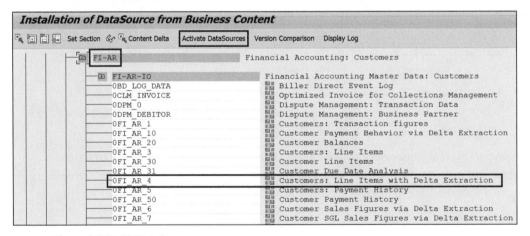

Figure 8.2 FI-AR DataSource

In Figure 8.3, you can see the **0FI_AP_6** accounts payable DataSource. In Figure 8.4, you can see the **0FI_GL_6** general ledger DataSource.

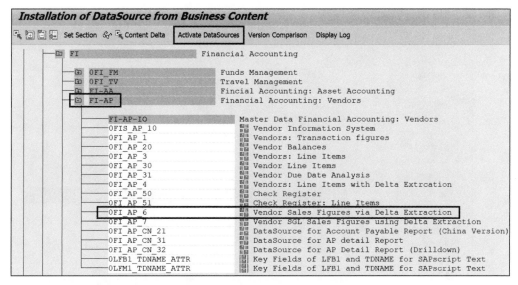

Figure 8.3 FI-AP DataSource

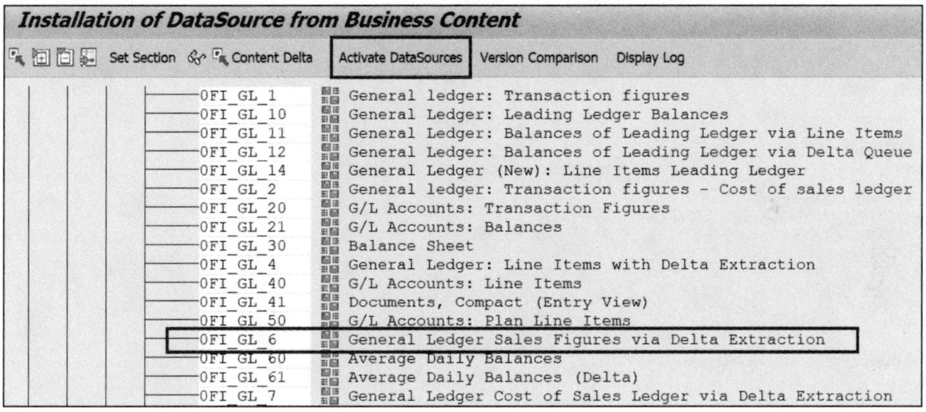

Figure 8.4 FI-GL DataSource

2. You can execute Transaction RSA3 or use the ABAP report RODPS_REPL_TEST in Transaction SE38 to see the total number of records for each extractor (see Figure 8.5).

3. Replicate the DataSource in SAP BW/HANA to activate it (see Figure 8.6). You can do the replication by right-clicking the relevant SAP S/4HANA source system under the **ODP_SAP** folder and choosing **Replicate**.

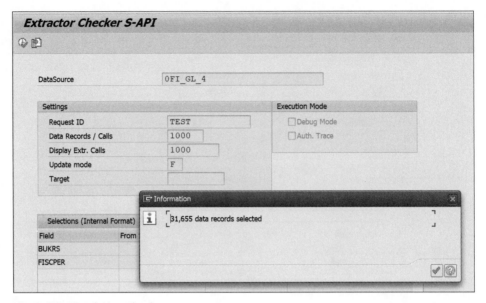

Figure 8.5 Simulation Checker

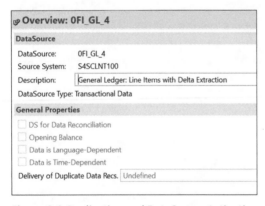

Figure 8.6 Replication and DataSource Activation

4. Create an aDSO and load the DTP (see Figure 8.7). You can create the aDSO based on the DataSource as the template and define the primary keys for the aDSO. Then create the transformation from the DataSource to the aDSO. Finally, from the transformation, you can create the DTP. (If you need a refresher on how to create an aDSO, refer to Chapter 1, Section 1.10.)

5. Execute the DTP using ◉ ▼ and see the contents of the inbound table of the aDSO (see Figure 8.8).

6. Log onto the SAP S/4HANA system and check Transaction ODQMON (see Figure 8.9). You can provide the DataSource name "0FI_GL_4" in the **Queue** field, and you'll see all the subscribers, as shown in Figure 8.9.

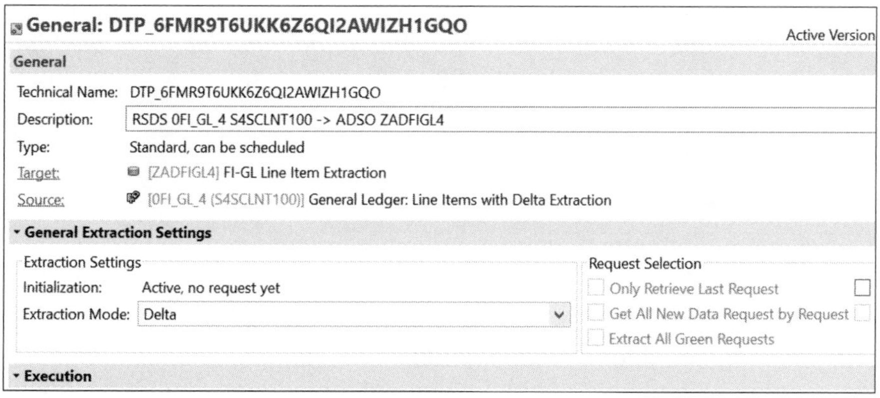

Figure 8.7 DTP

Figure 8.8 DTP Status

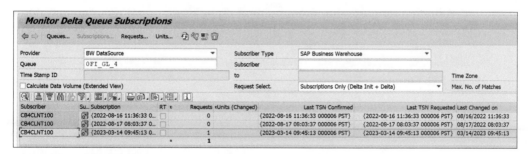

Figure 8.9 Subscriptions

From the **Subscriptions** tab, you can choose a row to get to the request view, and from the request view you can select a row to see the units view (see Figure 8.10).

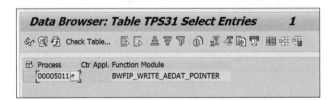

Figure 8.10 Total Records

8.1.3 Delta Management in Classical FI DataSources

Unlike LO DataSources with multiple update modes, the deltas in FI areas are handled by timestamp-based logic. The timestamp of the delta init is stored in the table as shown in Figure 8.11. You can see that **LAST_TS** is set to **X** in table BWOM2_TIMEST, which is the timestamp table for delta extraction (see Figure 8.11).

Data Browser: Table BWOM2_TIMEST Select Entries   3

MANDT	OLTPSOURCE	AEDAT	AETIM	UPDMODE	TS_LOW	TS_HIGH	LAST_TS	TZONE	DAYST
100	OFI_GL_4	08/16/2022	14:37:11	C	315,504,000,000	10,294,703,990,000		18,000-	X
100	OFI_GL_4	08/17/2022	11:04:04	C	315,504,000,000	10,294,703,990,000		18,000-	X
100	OFI_GL_4	03/14/2023	12:45:39	C	315,504,000,000	10,294,703,990,000	X	18,000-	X

Figure 8.11 Timestamp of Delta

Once the delta is initialized, table TPS31 (Process BTE) will have the **BWFIP_WRITEAEDAT_POINTER** entry in the Function Module column (see Figure 8.12).

Data Browser: Table TPS31 Select Entries   1

Process	Ctr	Appl.	Function Module
00005011			BWFIP_WRITE_AEDAT_POINTER

Figure 8.12 Table for BTE

This table will enable the recording of the changed documents in table BWFI_AEDAT. This table sets the last delta timestamp, and then the changed documents are stored in BWFI_AEDAT, so when a new document is posted it's written to BWFI_AEDAT with a timestamp like this: **20,210,112,180,445** (see Figure 8.13). Note that the timestamp value will vary based on the date and time when you executed the change.

There is a master table (BWOM_SETTINGS) that controls most FI DataSources and impacts the way they're executed, as shown in Figure 8.14, but this is an old extractor that isn't used much. We'll focus on the next DataSource category, safety intervals, instead.

Data Browser: Table BWFI_AEDAT Select Entries   200

Cl.	CoCd	DocumentNo	Year	Changed	Time	Time Stamp	Checkbox
100	1010	1900000000	2020	01/12/2021	13:04:45	20,210,112,180,445	
100	1010	1900000000	2021	01/12/2021	14:35:53	20,210,112,193,553	
100	1010	1900000001	2017	12/03/2020	07:58:23	20,201,203,125,823	
100	1010	2000000000	2021	01/12/2021	14:28:57	20,210,112,192,857	
100	1710	0100000000	2020	12/01/2020	08:28:23	20,201,201,132,823	

Figure 8.13 Table BWFI_AEDAT

Data Browser: Table BWOM_SETTINGS Select Entries

Cl.	DataSource	Field Name	Char
100		BWFIGLENQ	
100		BWFIGLLOG	
100		BWFILOWLIM	19910101
100		BWFINEXT	
100		BWFINOCHNG	
100		BWFINSAF	3600
100		BWFIORDBY	
100		BWFIOVERLA	
100		BWFISAFETY	1
100		BWFITIMBOR	020000
100		BW_CO_LOG	
100		CO_AREA_SL	
100		DELTIMEST	60

Figure 8.14 Table BWOM_SETTINGS

Tables for Delta Management in Classical FI Extraction

When you use OFI_*_6 or OFI_*_7, those extractors use BWFI_AEDA2 for the registration of the change log. When you use OFI_AP_8 or OFI_AP_9 and OFI_AP_10, those extractors use BWFI_AEDA3 for the registration of the change log.

The BWFINSAF field is used to define the **Safety Interval** for the delta extraction as 3,600, which is in seconds, so it's calculated as an hour (see Figure 8.15).

BWOM_SETTINGS Parameter

To update the parameter in Table BWOM_SETTINGS, you can use the **Create** button or use the function module in Transaction SE37 and execute function module BWOMU_PUT_ BWOM_SETTINGS. You can provide the DataSource name in **OLTPSOURCE** followed by the parameter name and parameter value.

You need to understand this table to know the delta logic used in FI: the timestamp-based delta. As shown in Figure 8.15, delta run 1 will have an upper limit and will set the lower limit timestamp. Then if the safety interval is set to 3,600 seconds (one hour), delta run 2 will extract all the records posted one hour before the start of the next extraction; that will be the lower limit. You can expect some duplicate records in this process as the time is overlapped, but these records are overwritten as the FI extraction uses the aDSO with an overwrite option. Delta run 2 will end by creating the new lower limit for the next extraction run, delta run 3, which uses the safety interval of one hour to extract the delta records.

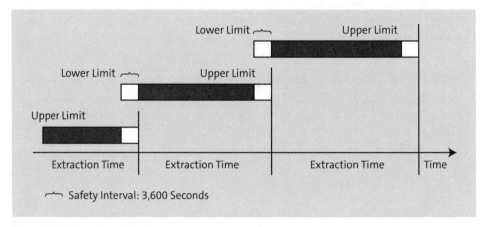

Figure 8.15 Timestamp Logic

The SAP-delivered DataSource will have different delta methods to handle how delta records are sent to the SAP BW system; for example, in FI the safety interval creates duplicate records that need to be handled by the overwrite option in the aDSO. So it has the delta method set as **After-Images with Deletion** (AIED). You can see the all the delta methods used by the SAP extractors in table RODELTAM in SAP S/4HANA (see Figure 8.16).

Data Browser: Table RODELTAM Select Entries   20

DELTA	ONLYFULL	UPDM_NIM	UPDM_BIM	UPDM_AIM	UPDM_ADD	UPDM_DEL	UPDM_RIM	DREQSER	DELTATYPE	TXTLG
	X								1	Delta Only by Full Upload (ODS or InfoPackage Selection)
A				X					2 A	ALE Update Pointer (Master Data)
ABR	X	X	X			X		2 D		Complete Delta with Deletion Flag by Delta Queue (Cube-Comp)
ABR1	X	X	X			X		1 D		Like Method 'ABR' But Serialization Only by Requests
ADD				X				1 E		Additive Extraction by Extractor (e.g. LIS Info Structures)
ADDD				X				1 D		Like 'ADD' But by Delta Queue (Cube-Compatible)
AIE			X					2 E		After-Images by Extractor (FI-GL/AP/AR)
AIED			X		X			2 E		After-Images with Deletion Flag by Extractor (FI-GL/AP/AR)
AIM			X					2 D		After-Images by Delta Queue (e.g. FI-AP/AR)
AIMD			X		X			2 D		After-Images with Deletion Flag by Delta Queue (e.g. BtB)
CUBE				X				0 E		InfoCube Extraction
D								2 D		Unspecific Delta by Delta Queue (Not ODS-Compatible)
E								2 E		Unspecific Delta by Extractor (Not ODS-Compatible)
FIL0			X					2 F		Delta by File Import with After-Images
FIL1				X				2 F		Delta by File Import with Delta Images
NEWD	X							0 D		Only New Records (Inserts) by Delta Queue (Cube-Compatible)
NEWE	X							0 E		Only New Records (Inserts) by Extractor (Cube-Compatible)
O		X	X	X				0 E		
ODS	X	X	X			X		1 E		ODS Extraction
X								2 X		Delta Unspecified (Do Not Use!)

Figure 8.16 Table RODELTAM

Now you can see the status of the delta method for the 0FI_AP_4 DataSource in table ROOSOURCE in Figure 8.17. Note the **AIE** indicator in the **Delta** column for after-images by extractor.

Data Browser: Table ROOSOURCE Select Entries 4

Check Table...

OLTPSOURCE	OBJVERS	TYPE	APPLNM	BASOSOURCE	DELTA	STOCKUPD	UPDFLG1	UPDFLG2	UPDFLG3	READONLY	INITSIMU	INITCOMMIT	ZDD_ABLE	REALTIME	EXMETHOD	EXTRACTOR
0FI_AP_4	D	TRAN	FI-AP		AIE					X	1				F1	BWFID_GET_FIAP_ITEM
0FI_AR_4	D	TRAN	FI-AR		AIE					X	1				F1	BWFID_GET_FIAR_ITEM
0FI_GL_4	A	TRAN	FI-GL		AIE					X	1				F1	BWFID_GET_FIGL_ITEM
0FI_GL_4	D	TRAN	FI-GL		AIE					X	1				F1	BWFID_GET_FIGL_ITEM

Figure 8.17 FI_*_4 Delta Logic

The AIE delta method needs an aDSO to handle the overwrite.

8.2 Finance Extraction with New General Ledger Based on SAP ERP System

To efficiently handle financial reporting, the new general ledger was introduced in FI, and additional tables have been created for this process. From an SAP BW perspective, it's enough to know the table names and the DataSources that are commonly used, including the following:

- FAGLFLEXA—General Ledger: Actual Line Items
- FAGLFLEXP—General Ledger: Planned Line Items
- FAGLFLEXT—General Ledger: Totals

Before diving into the extraction, let's first discuss leading and nonleading ledgers. In general, ledgers are used to record financial transactions in general accounting by account. In general accounting, there are several ledgers used in parallel. SAP has two types of ledgers:

- A *leading ledger* is the base ledger. You can define only one leading ledger, which starts with OL. It's a kind of parent ledger—for example, a ledger created for the base country. The leading ledger uses general ledger table FAGLFLEXT. A DataSource like 0FI_GL_4 extracts general ledger line items, and 0FI_GL_14 deals with the leading ledger line-item extraction.
- *Nonleading ledgers* are activated at the company code level: here you can create additional currencies, such as for ledgers created for countries outside the base country, and they follow the local accounting rules for the specific country. You use nonleading ledgers only in the SAP ERP system. To generate extractors or DataSources for nonleading ledgers, you can use Transaction FAGLBW03. To do so, you need to activate the FIN_GL_CI_1 SAP BW switch using Transaction SFW5 in your ECC system. For example, the extractor names for nonleading ledgers would be as follows:

– 3FI_GL_XX_SI where XX denotes the ledger name and SI is from the actual line items in table FAGLFLEXA

– 3FI_GL_XX_TT where XX denotes the ledger name and TT is from the totals in table AGLFLEXT

> **Note**
>
> Newly created nonleading ledger DataSources are not supported in SAP S/4HANA, but migrated nonleading ledgers can be used for DataSource assignment. There are separate DataSources to address this problem.

If you need to extract the new general ledger data based on the leading ledger, you can use two standard SAP-delivered DataSources: OFI_GL_10 and OFI_GL_14. We'll discuss these in the following sections.

8.2.1   Extraction Using OFI_GL_10

DataSource OFI_GL_10 is used to extract the totals record from the leading ledger in the new general ledger. The delta type is AIED. This provides the cumulative balance at the posting period level. For example, it can be used for balance sheet line items where cumulative data is reported, like fixed assets, current assets, and so on.

In SAP S/4HANA, use Transaction RSA2 to check the OFI_GL_10 properties, as shown in Figure 8.18. The **General** tab will have the **DataSource Type** as **Transaction Data** and the application component (**Appl.Component**) as **FI-GL**.

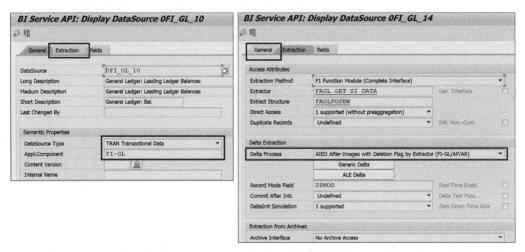

Figure 8.18 OFI_GL_10

The **Extraction** tab will have information about the **Extraction Method**, **Extractor**, and **Extract Structure**. You can see that the extractor has the suffix LE, for *leading ledger*. The delta process is AIED. First check the data in Transaction RSA3, and you can see the results shown in Figure 8.19.

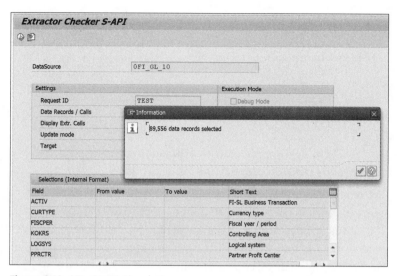

Figure 8.19 OFI_GL_10 Simulation

In SAP BW/4HANA, follow these steps to perform an extraction:

1. Replicate the OFI_GL_10 DataSource in the SAP ODP source system. You can also choose the exact application component for replication based on the **Appl.Component** value (refer back to Figure 8.18). You can see that application component is FI-GL. The replication of the DataSource will activate the DataSource in the SAP BW/4HANA system.

2. Once the DataSource is active, create an aDSO (ZADFIGL10) based on DataSource OFI_GL_10. You need to create the keys as this aDSO will overwrite based on the AIED delta. Refer to table FAGLFLEXT to understand the key fields; if the key fields aren't maintained properly, then the aDSO will overwrite the totals records. In most scenarios, SAP BW consultants will check with FI consultants based on the company's business processes and check with the reporting team for the key fields that will determine the data. In our example, we used most of the fields from the aDSO as key fields.

3. Create the transformation from DataSource OFI_GL_10 to aDSO ZADFIGL10 and create the DTP based on the transformation from the DataSource to the aDSO (see Figure 8.20).

```
✓ ⊕ [RKPBWFI] Financials Extraction
  ✓ ▷ DataStore Object (advanced)
    ✓ ▣ [ZADFIGL10] New GL ADSO - Totals Record- Leading Ledger
      ✓ ▷ Transformation
          ⋈ [05BS4JTM9AWH15LWXIBQF1JKVWRF5PO9] RSDS 0FI_GL_10 S4SCLNT100->ADSO ZADFIGL10
      ✓ ▷ Data Transfer Process
          ▣ [DTP_6FMR9T6UKK6Z6SQU9HYWYFGPZ] RSDS 0FI_GL_10 S4SCLNT100 -> ADSO ZADFIGL10
```

Figure 8.20 OFI_GL_10 Dataflow

4. You can also use extractors like OFI_GL_11 and OFI_GL_12 in your general ledger extraction (see Figure 8.21).

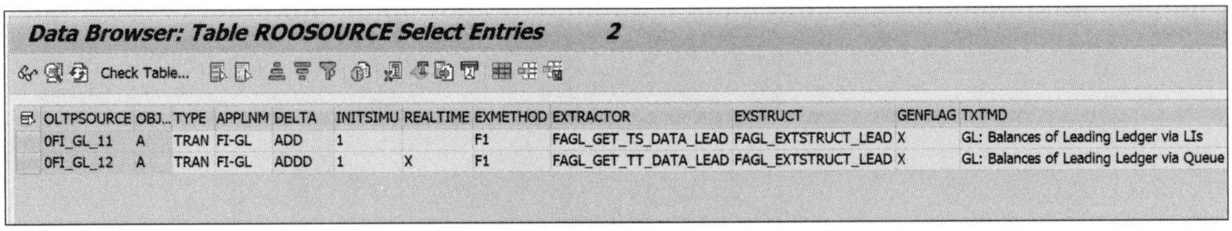

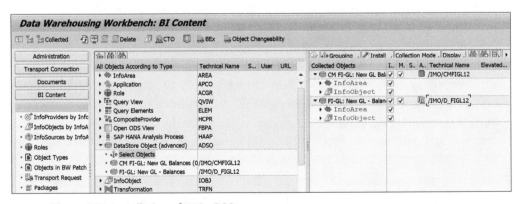

Figure 8.21 OFI_GL_11 and OFI_GL_12

You can see that the **Delta** field has the entries **ADD** (additive delta extraction via line-item extraction) and **ADDD** (delta extraction via delta queue).

5. You can use the new DataSources like OFI_GL_11 and OFI_GL_12 when you expect more performance in the data loads. There are a lot of steps to use OFI_GL_11, but in SAP BW/4HANA we suggest checking into the usage of OFI_GL_12. There is an IMO aDSO dataflow available for that. To install the IMO dataflow, you need to open Transaction RSA1 in SAP BW/4HANA, choose **BI Content**, and search for the aDSO— for example, search for "/IMO/CMFIGL12"—from the object types and install those in the system. You can get the details of the IMO objects from SAP Help documentation (see *https://help.sap.com/docs/BI_CONTENT_757/c644067f89c74ff38da2b9f765b e6cce/3b61c554ed0fb209e10000000a423f68.html*). You'll see the details of the object at the InfoSource level, staging level, corporate memory level, and integrated DWH layer level (see Figure 8.22).

Figure 8.22 Installation of IMO aDSO

6. After installation, you can see that aDSOs like /IMO/CMFIGL12 and /IMO/D_FIGL12 are active in the system (see Figure 8.23).

Data Browser: Table RSOADSO Select Entries   2

ADSONM	OBJVERS	CONTREL	CONTTIMESTMP	OWNER	BWAPPL	INFOAREA
/IMO/CMFIGL12	A	757	20.150.325.130.608	SAP		/IMO/FIGL_CM
/IMO/D_FIGL12	A	2000	20.190.429.145.213			/IMO/FIGL_D

Figure 8.23 IMO aDSOs

7. You can see the aDSO for the staging layer and the InfoSource, and an aDSO for the data mart layer, which is used for staging purposes in SAP BW/4HANA. You'll also see an SAP HANA composite provider in the virtual data mart layer, which will be used by SAP BW queries for reporting purposes. You need to replicate the DataSource and then connect the aDSO using the transformation and DTP, as shown in Figure 8.24.

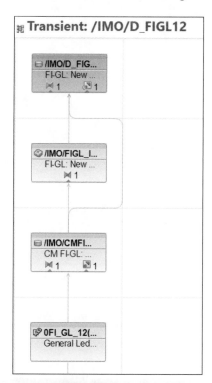

Figure 8.24 Dataflow

8.2.2   Extracting Using 0FI_GL_14

This is one of the important extractors used in general ledger extraction. This extractor is used when the new general ledger is enabled in any organization. It extracts the line items of the leading ledger. DataSource 0FI_GL_14 is used to extract line-item records from the leading ledger, based on the following tables:

- BKPF: Accounting Document Header
- BSEG: Accounting Document Segment
- FAGLFLEXA: General Ledger—Actual Line items

This DataSource provides detailed information about an account number at the day level, which is the posting date, and, for example, profit and loss line items. From a functional perspective, if you have a new general ledger in your SAP ERP system, you can use Transaction FBL3N to see the general ledger account line-item display. You can also use Transaction FAGLBO3.

You can see the details of the DataSource using Transaction RSA2, as shown in Figure 8.25, where you can see the **Extractor**, **Delta Process** set to **AIE**, and the **Extract Structure**.

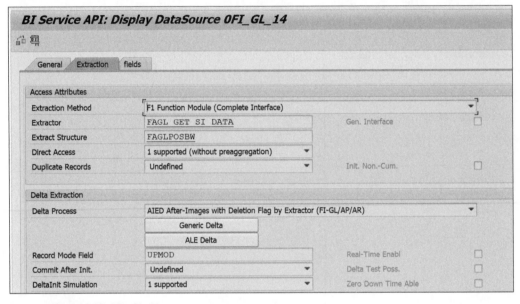

Figure 8.25 OFI_GL_14

The extraction process is similar to the steps that we discussed for DataSource OFI_GL_10 that was shown in Figure 8.20:

1. Replicate the OFI_GL_14 DataSource in SAP BW/4HANA.

2. Create an aDSO based on the DataSource and consume that in an SAP HANA composite provider.

3. There is an option to use IMO objects like /IMO/FIGL_IS14 for the InfoSource and /IMO/CMFIGL14 for corporate memory and /IMO/D_FIGL14 for the integrated data warehouse layer.

4. You can install SAP HANA composite provider /IMO/V_FIGL02 for the new general, which will by default get all the required aDSOs (see Figure 8.26).

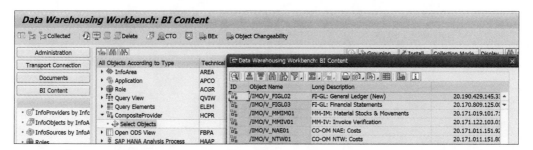

Figure 8.26 SAP HANA Composite Provider IMO

5. You can use the **Dataflow Before** option under the grouping area to bring in all the SAP BW objects used in the dataflow (see Figure 8.27).

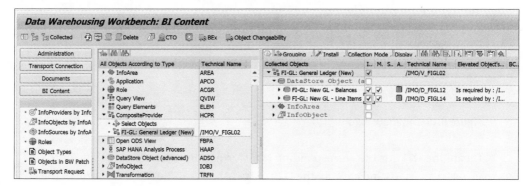

Figure 8.27 Install Dataflow

6. If you expand the aDSO, the IMO/D_FIGL12 and /IMO/D_FIGL14 objects will be visible, as shown in Figure 8.28.

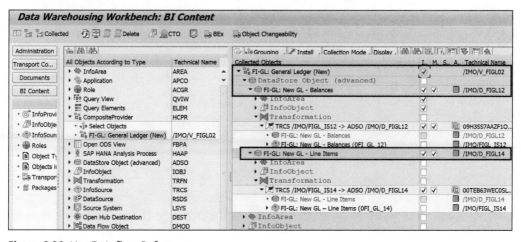

Figure 8.28 Use Dataflow Before

7. You can see the complete flow, which lists the RSDS and InfoSources for the two aDSOs (see Figure 8.29).

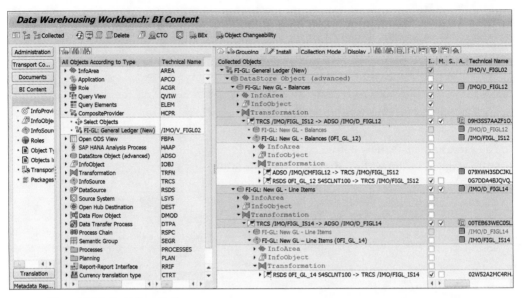

Figure 8.29 Dataflow Before

Create the DTP for the corresponding transformations that connect DataSource OFI_GL_14 to the aDSO and execute the DTP to load the data. The first execution of the DTP will bring in all records and then initialize the delta.

Delta management in OFI_GL_14 is done by first triggering the delta by posting a few financial documents. Replicate and execute the data extraction (see Figure 8.30).

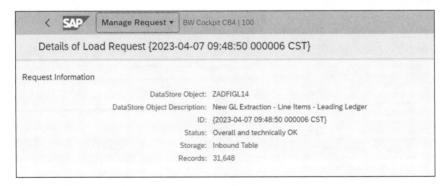

Figure 8.30 Data Load

Log onto SAP S/4HANA and open Transaction ODQMON. The status can be seen as shown in Figure 8.31.

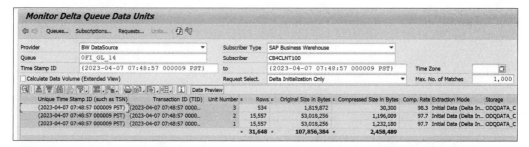

Figure 8.31 Transaction ODQMON

You can see the status of the DTP request in the web cockpit (see Figure 8.32). Note that **Storage** is set to **Inbound Table** and the **Records** count is **3,360**. You'll also see that **Extraction Mode** is **Delta**.

Details of Load Request {2023-04-07 10:33:06 000012 CST}

Request Information   Related Source

DataStore Object:	ZADFIGL14
DataStore Object Description:	New GL Extraction - Line Items - Leading Ledger
ID:	{2023-04-07 10:33:06 000012 CST}
Status:	Overall and technically OK
Storage:	Inbound Table
Records:	3,360

DTP Properties

Name:	DTP_6FMR9T6UKK6Z6T5N2MSMLZX5L
Description:	RSDS 0FI_GL_14 S4SCLNT100 -> ADSO ZADFIGL14
Extraction Mode:	Delta
Processing Mode:	Parallel SAP HANA Execution
Package Size:	1,000,000
Request Aggregation:	MOV
Request Start Time:	07.04.2023, 11:33:07
Request Finish Time:	07.04.2023, 11:33:27
Request Runtime:	20s
Selection:	(Replication Pointer : 20230407153312.000032000 Replication Mode : Extraction of Last Delta - - X)

Figure 8.32 Delta

You can see the delta in Transaction ODQMON in SAP S/4HANA (see Figure 8.33). Navigate from the queues area where the DataSource name is **0FI_GL_14** to the subscription view and from there to the request view, where you will find the composite request for the DTP. You can see the lower and upper timestamps based on the delta execution. Note that the first extraction is the initial data, which had only the upper timestamp, and the next extraction is the delta extraction with the previous upper timestamp as its new lower timestamp. It created a new upper limit (**2023-04-07 08:33:12...**) for the next delta extraction.

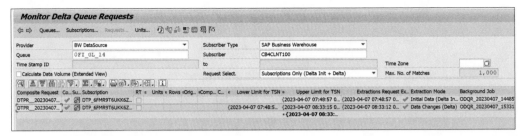

Figure 8.33 Transaction ODQMON: Request

The records match the last delta request you can see in the web cockpit (see Figure 8.34). Transaction ODQMON has 3,360 rows in the units view, and you can see the same records in the SAP BW DTP delta extraction.

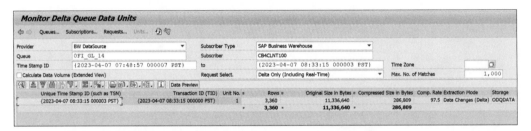

Figure 8.34 Transaction ODQMON: Unite

The delta for `OFI_GL_14` is updated in table `ROOSGENDLM`, where the `DELTID` field shows a YYYYMMDD timestamp (20230407153313) like the last delta (see Figure 8.35).

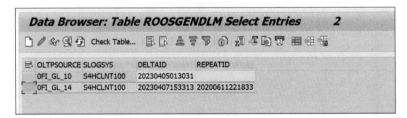

Figure 8.35 Last Delta

The delta for `OFI_GL_14` is based on table `FAGLFLEXA`, and the field is `TIMESTAMP`. When a document is created or changed it's reflected in this table. Based on the `DELTAID` field in table `ROOSGENDLM`, the delta is fetched, and you can see the `TIMESTAMP` field like this in table `FAGLFLEXA` (see Figure 8.36).

Data Browser: Table FAGLFLEXA Select Entries   200

Check Table...

RCLNT	RYEAR	DOCNR	RLDNR	RBUKRS	DOCLN	TIMESTAMP
100	2017	B000000001	0L	1710	000003	20,171,115,091,052
100	2017	B000000002	0L	1710	000003	20,171,115,095,708
100	2017	B000000003	0L	1710	000003	20,171,115,100,318
100	2017	B000000004	0L	1710	000003	20,171,116,130,349
100	2017	B000000005	0L	1710	000003	20,171,116,134,148
100	2017	B000000006	0L	1710	000003	20,171,116,135,712
100	2018	0100000000	0L	TA00	000001	20,210,303,231,144

Figure 8.36 Table FAGLFLEXA: Timestamp Field

8.3   Extracting Asset Accounting and Controlling Data from SAP ERP and SAP S/4HANA

In this section, you'll learn about extracting asset accounting and controlling data from SAP ERP and SAP S/4HANA. We'll start with an introduction to asset accounting and learn about the tables and the standard DataSources, then you'll learn about controlling application data extraction and about the various SAP-delivered DataSources in controlling applications.

8.3.1   Asset Accounting

The asset accounting (AA) area is used for managing fixed assets in an organization within an SAP system. In SAP ERP, the following tables are important for asset management:

- ANEK: Document Header Asset Posting
- ANEP: Asset Line items
- ANEA: Asset Line items for Proportional Values
- ANLC: Asset Value fields
- ANLP: Asset Periodic Values

The important DataSources that are used in asset accounting are as follows (if you use these DataSources for extraction scenarios, make sure you follow the below sequence when extracting from SAP BW/4HANA):

- OFI_GL_4: General ledger line items (if required)
- OASSET_ATTR_TEXT: Master data for asset subnumber
- OASSET_AFAB_ATTR: Depreciation area
- OFI_AA_11: FI-AA transactions with line-item details; data based on tables ANLC, ANEP, and ANEA
- OFI_AA_12: Posted depreciation; contains periodic values based on table ANLP (this is a very stable DataSource)

If you want to use the /IMO dataflow, then SAP delivers a composite provider (/IMO/V_FIAA01). If you install that with the dataflow before beginning the asset accounting process, you'll get all the required aDSOs for OFI_AA_11 and OFI_AA_12, as shown in Figure 8.37.

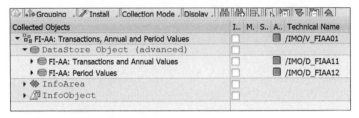

Figure 8.37 IMO Flow for FI-AA CompositeProvider

When you expand the aDSOs listed in Figure 8.37, you'll see the details of the corporate memory aDSO, as shown in Figure 8.38.

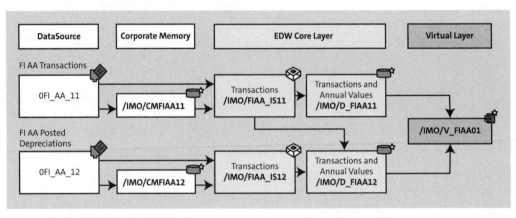

Figure 8.38 FI-AA IMO Dataflow

For SAP BW data loading, the process is like other FI-based data loads. The first step is to activate the DataSource in Transaction RSA5 in SAP S/4HANA, then log onto SAP BW/4HANA and replicate the relevant DataSource there and activate it. The next step is to create an aDSO based on the DataSource. Then create the transformation and DTP. Start the data load by executing the DTP using ▶ ▼, which will initialize the deltas in BWOM2_TIMEST. The LAST_TS flag will be set to X and the next delta will get the TS_HIGH values as the lower time of the new delta run.

8.3.2   Controlling Application–Based Extraction

FI deals with external reporting, while controlling (CO) applications help businesses analyze and deal with internal reporting. This includes managing and configuring the master data that covers cost and profit centers, and it deals with cost elements and functional areas. Its main advantage is planning: you can determine variances by comparing actual versus planned data to help your organization control the business flow. Because there are many applications in this area, we'll focus on the relevant information from an SAP BW perspective. Controlling DataSources can be categorized into the following groups:

- CO-OM: Overhead cost controlling—69+ DataSources in SAP S/4HANA
- CO-PA: Profitability analysis—14 DataSources
- CO-PC: Product cost controlling

CO-OM is further split into the following groups:

- 0CO_OM_CCA* for cost center–based costs and allocations, activities, and so on
- 0CO_OM_OPA* for order-based costs and allocations, activities, and so on
- 0CO_OM_NAE*, NTW*, and NWA* for network activity elements
- 0CO_OM_WBS* for work breakdown structures like budget or overall plan cost

---

Controlling DataSources

Some of the important DataSources are as follows:

- 0CO_OM_CCA_9—actual costs line items
- 0CO_OM_CCA_10—commitment line items
- 0CO_OM_CCA_30—statistical key figures
- 0CO_OM_CCA_40—actual line items
- 0CO_OM_OPA_40—actual line items
- 0CO_OM_OPA_1_D—plan totals
- 0CO_OM_WBS_6—actual line items
- 0CO_OM_WBS_7—commitment line items
- 0CO_PC_10—product cost analysis
- 0CO_PC_PCP_20—product cost estimates
- 0CO_PCP_30—product cost estimates itemization
- 0CO_OM_NAE_2—actual line items
- 0CO_OM_NTW_2—actual line items
- 0CO_OM_NWA_2—actual line items

Most of the DataSources in CO use tables like COEP (CO Objects Line Items), COSP, and COSS. Note that if you're using SAP S/4HANA, most of these are not required—but if you extract the data from SAP ERP, then you need to use these extractors.

8.4   Extracting Finance Data from SAP S/4HANA to SAP BW/4HANA

There have been a lot of changes in finance in SAP S/4HANA. As you have seen in previous sections, the classical version of FI used lots of tables for open items and closed items and a separate table for the general ledger. With the introduction of the new general ledger, there were tables for line items and totals records. You have seen the Data-Sources related to those tables. With SAP S/4HANA, there has been a major change in how FI is handled. A new table called ACDOCA is introduced in SAP S/4HANA. First, let's discuss this table before getting into SAP BW extraction.

8.4.1   Introduction to Table ACDOCA in SAP S/4HANA

Any SAP S/4HANA application consultant working in FI should know about table ACDOCA in detail, but from an SAP BW/4HANA consultant perspective, you just need to understand the high-level overview of ACDOCA and what kind of data you're extracting. Earlier versions of SAP used lots of totals tables, line-item tables, and index tables for efficient data retrieval, but in SAP S/4HANA aggregations or calculations can be performed on the fly from table ACDOCA. There's no need to store redundant information in multiple tables. With SAP S/4HANA, SAP has removed all the totals and index tables. The data in FI and CO are now collected in one table, ACDOCA. For this reason, it's called the *Universal Journal*. The simplified data model is shown in Figure 8.39.

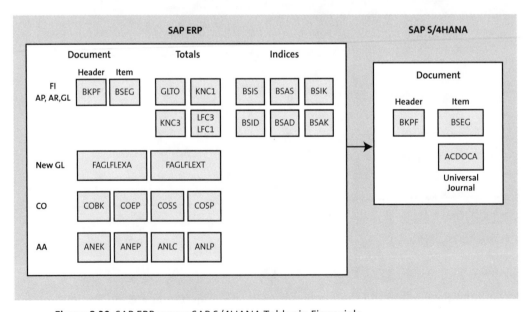

Figure 8.39 SAP ERP versus SAP S/4HANA Tables in Financials

In summary, the following tables were replaced by SAP HANA views with the same names:

- The line items, totals, and application index tables of general ledger accounting (GLTO, BSIS, BSAS, and FAGLFLEXA, FAGLFLEXT, FAGLBSIS, FAGLBSAS)

- The totals tables and application index tables of accounts receivable and accounts payable (KNC1, KNC3, LFC1, LFC3, BSID, BSIK, BSAD, BSAK)

- The line item and totals tables of controlling (COEP for certain value types, COSP, COSS)

- The material ledger tables for parallel valuations (MLIT, MLPP, MLPPF, MLCR, MLCD, CKMI1, BSIM)

- The asset accounting tables (ANEK, ANEP, ANEA, ANLP, ANLC)

Replacing these tables with views with the same names ensures the continuation of all read accesses to the tables mentioned.

With SAP Simple Finance, on-premise edition, you're provided with the universal data table ACDOCA, which contains all of the line item documents from FI, FI-AA, and CO. All postings of these applications are written to the new table after the installation and migration are complete.

Because ACDOCA is based on SAP S/4HANA, it utilizes the full potential of SAP HANA, like data compression and columnar storage options. For data reads, columnar storage is very effective. You can see that setting in Transaction SE11 under **ACDOCA · Technical Settings**, as shown in Figure 8.40. You can see that **Storage Type** is set to **Column Store**.

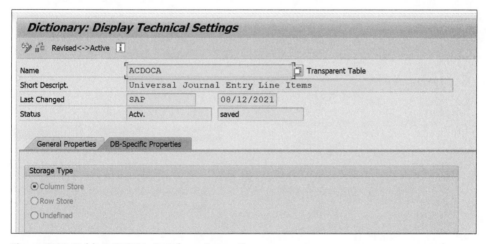

Figure 8.40 Table ACDOCA: Database Properties

Similarly, you can see that table ACDOCA uses lots of **Indexes** (see Figure 8.41). Refer to the column **Ind.** and you'll see five **ANL** indexes with the **DB Index Name ACDOCA~ANL**. Similarly, you'll see the **AWR, BEL, ONR**, and **POB** indexes, which are used to optimize the performance during the read from this table.

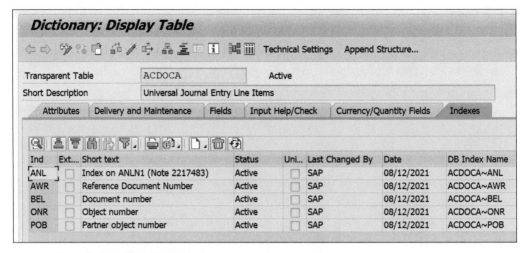

Figure 8.41 Table ACDOCA Indexes

When you open an index—for example, if you double-click **BEL**—you can see the complete details of the index, like field names. Here it uses **BELNR**, which is the accounting document number. If you select the **For Selected Database Systems** radio button, you can choose ⮕ to see a popup that tells you on what database the index is active. In this case, it shows **HDB**, for SAP HANA database (see Figure 8.42).

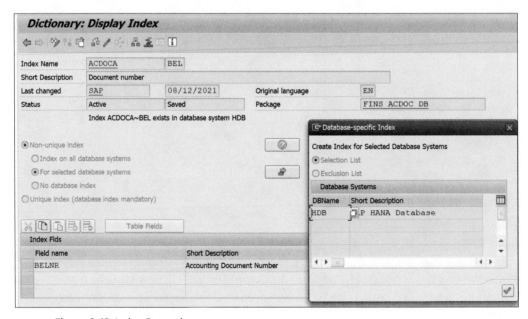

Figure 8.42 Index Example

8.4.2   DataSource for Table ACDOCA Extraction

To extract data from table ACDOCA, you have two standard extractors: OFI_ACDOCA_10 and OFI_ACDOCA_20.

OFI_ACDOCA_10

You can use the OFI_ACDOCA_10 DataSource for line items and aggregated balance reporting. This DataSource is delta-capable and can extract newly posted, cleared, reversed, and changed documents. This DataSource is also used for balance reporting on balance sheet accounts. Note that there are no standard BI content objects available for OFI_ACDOCA_10, so you can't install any dataflow in SAP BW/4HANA. If you plan to use OFI_ACDOCA_10, then you need to replicate the DataSource, then make sure that you have activated DataSource OFI_ACDOCA_10 (it should be in the A version in table RSDS) and create an aDSO based on the DataSource with the following key fields:

- OAC_LEDGER (RLDNR)
- OCOMP_CODE (RBUKRS)
- OFISCVARNT (PERIV)
- OFISCPER (FISCYEARPER)
- OAC_DOC_NR (BELNR)
- AC_DOC_LN (DOCLN)

You can then have a few data fields like these:

- OGL_ACCOUNT (RACCT)
- OSEGMENT (SEGMENT)
- OCOSTCENTER (RCNTR)
- ODEBCRED (DRCRK)
- ODOC_CURRKEY (RTCUR)
- ODEB_CRE_DC (TSL)
- OLOC_CURRKEY (RHCUR)
- ODEB_CRE_LC (HSL)
- OLOC_CURRC2 (RKCUR)
- ODEB_CRE_L2 (KSL)

You can add the fields to the aDSO based on your business requirements. Because FI can send the duplicate records, you need to make sure that in the SAP BW/4HANA transformation to the aDSO, all the key figures should have the aggregation set to **Overwrite** (see Figure 8.43).

Figure 8.43 aDSO Creation

Once the aDSO is created, in the **General** tab use the **Standard DSO Object** option and select the **Write Change Log** checkbox. Then select the **Details** tab and choose the relevant key fields that we discussed, and choose the data fields for the aDSO (see Figure 8.44).

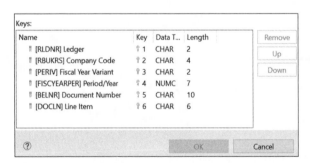

Figure 8.44 Key Fields

Activate the aSDO using the icon and create a transformation based on DataSource OFI_ACDOCA_10 (see Figure 8.45).

You can see the details of the transformation in Figure 8.46. **Target** is set to the aDSO name (ZACDOCA10) and **Source** to the DataSource, OFI_ACDOCA_10.

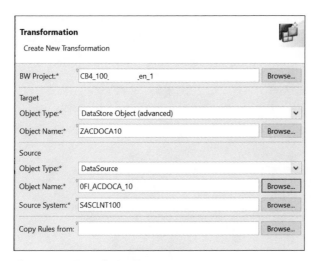

Figure 8.45 Transformation

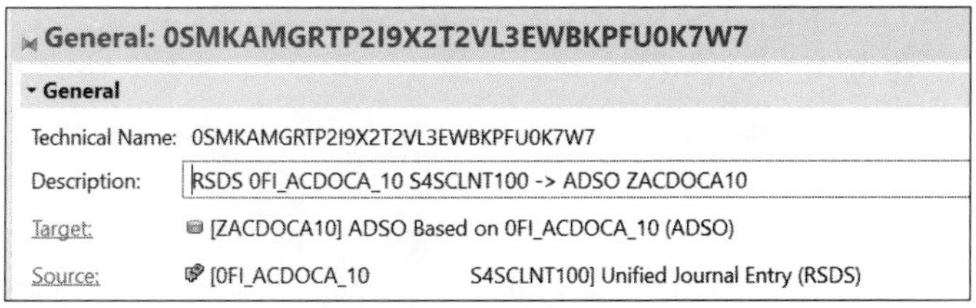

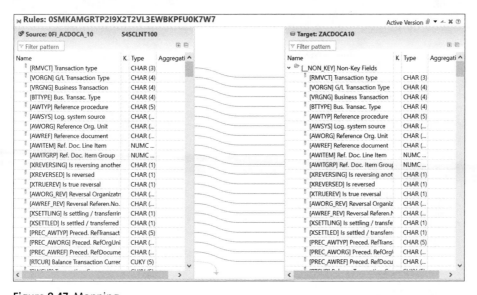

Figure 8.46 Transformation Details

Once the mapping is created, you can see the mappings between the source and the target as shown in Figure 8.47.

Figure 8.47 Mapping

Once the transformation is activated using the 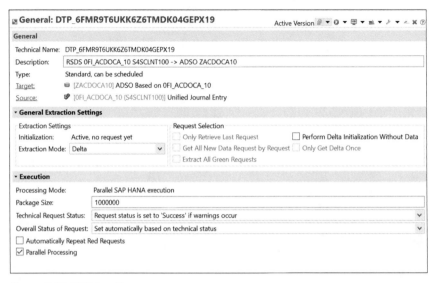 icon, the next step is to create the DTP as shown in Figure 8.48. The DTP is created based on the transformation that you created.

Figure 8.48 DTP Creation

You can see there are many fields in the **Extraction** tab under the **Filter** section. These fields for the filter are passed from the DataSource (OFI_ACDOCA_10) to the DTP that you are creating, as shown in Figure 8.49.

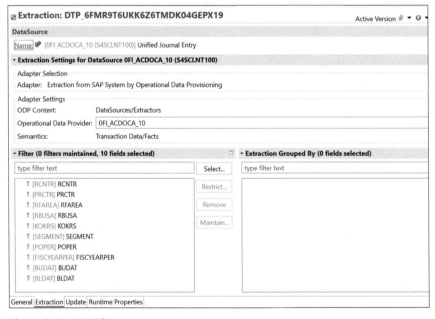

Figure 8.49 DTP Filters

Activate the DTP using the ![icon] icon. Before executing the DTP, open Transaction RSA3 in the SAP S/4HANA system. Enter the DataSource name, "0FI_ACDOCA_10", as the selection, and click ![icon] to see the data records that will be extracted. In Figure 8.50, you can see that 73,683 records will be extracted in the DTP.

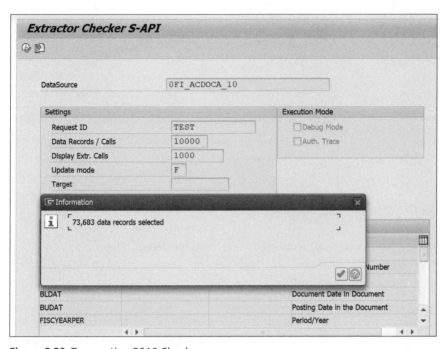

Figure 8.50 Transaction RSA3 Check

Now in SAP BW/4HANA, execute the DTP using ![icon] ▼ . This will execute the DTP and open the monitor in the web cockpit (see Figure 8.51).

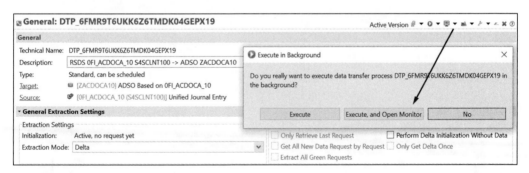

Figure 8.51 Execute and Monitor

You can see a **Delta Initialized without Data Transfer** checkbox. You can select that after the first full load is completed.

Now you can see the data in the SAP BW cockpit (see Figure 8.52). The extraction created **Data Package 1** and you can see a transformation from DataSource OFI_ACDOCA_10 to aDSO ZACDOC, with the record count as 73,683. The overall status is green.

Request {2023-04-10 23:11:55 000006 CST} ☐				Refresh Job Overview Process Monitor Manage Request
Request Processing Steps	Started at	Total Runtime	Process Runtime	Details
☐ Generate Request	11.04.2023, 00:11:56			Display Messages
☐ Set Status to 'Executable'	11.04.2023, 00:11:56	2s		Display Messages
☐ Process Request	11.04.2023, 00:11:58	2s		Display Messages
> ☐ Filling Data Transfer Intermediate Storage	11.04.2023, 00:12:00			Display Messages
☐ Prepare for Extraction	11.04.2023, 00:13:07	4s		Display Messages
⌄ ☐ Data Package 1 (73.683 Data Records)	11.04.2023, 00:13:09	8s	6s	Display Data Package Selection Criteria
☐ RSDS 0FI_ACDOCA_10 S4SCLNT100 -> ADSO ZACDOC : 73.683 -> 73.683 Data Records	11.04.2023, 00:13:11	6s		Display Messages More …
> ☐ Data Package 2 (0 Data Records)	11.04.2023, 00:13:09	4s	1s	Display Data Package Selection Criteria
> ☐ End of Main Process	11.04.2023, 00:13:11			
☐ Technical status 'Green' (user I044912)	11.04.2023, 00:13:18	1s		Display Messages
☐ Set overall status to 'Green' (user I044912)	11.04.2023, 00:13:19			Display Messages

Figure 8.52 DTP Monitor

Now look into the manage request area to see the table details (Figure 8.53). The load data has populated the inbound table, and you can see the count as 73,683, which matches the simulation check in Transaction RSA3.

Figure 8.53 Manage Request

Now you can activate the request using the **Activate** button, highlighted with an arrow in Figure 8.53, to move the data from the inbound table to the active table (see Figure 8.54).

Figure 8.54 Activation

When you click and choose the activation request number from the screen shown in Figure 8.54, you can see the details shown in Figure 8.55. Note that the **Storage** is **Active Data Table** and the **Records** count is **73,683**. In the **Processes** section, you can see the **Status** is **Finished**.

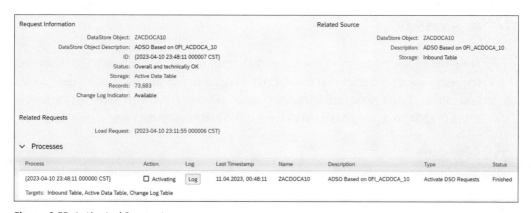

Figure 8.55 Activated Request

Open Transaction ODQMON in the sender SAP S/4HANA system (see Figure 8.56). You'll be in the default queue view. Provide the DataSource name, "0FI_ACDOCA_10", in the **Queue** field.

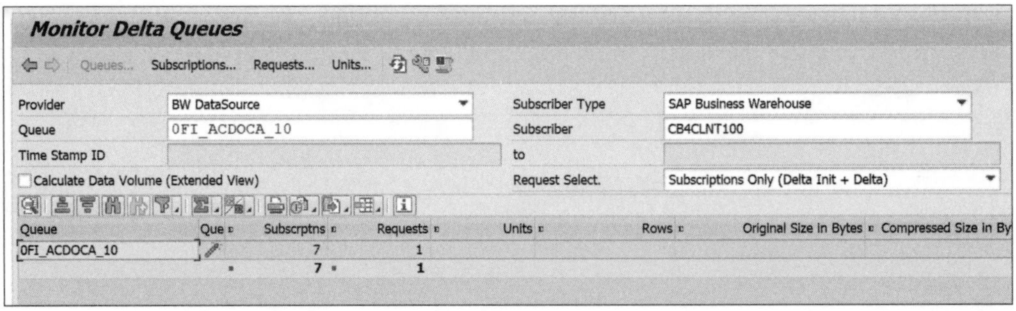

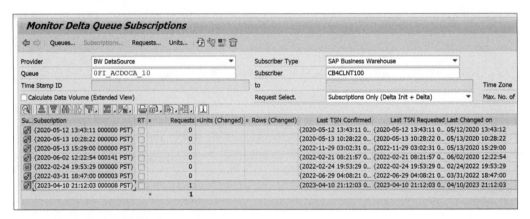

Figure 8.56 Transaction ODQMON: Queues

Once the OFI_ACDOCA_10 DataSource is available in the rows, double-click that row and you will be in the subscriptions view. You can see that the last row is the latest subscription (Figure 8.57). You'll see the latest subscription based on the date and the time that you executed the process.

Figure 8.57 Subscription

From the subscriptions view, double-click the row of your last subscription to see the requests view. You can see that the last DTP-based subscription is an init request, which you can see from the **Extraction Mode** field set to **Initial Data**. Also note that **Storage** is set to **ODQDATA_C**, which is used to store the initial request data (see Figure 8.58).

Figure 8.58 Init Request

From the request view, you can double-click the subscription row to go to the units view. In our example, we double clicked on the row in the subscription view to get to the units view (see Figure 8.59). In the units view, note that the **Rows** column shows **73,683**, the total number of records extracted by the DTP.

Monitor Delta Queue Data Units

Queues... Subscriptions... Requests... Units...

Provider	BW DataSource	Subscriber Type	SAP Business Warehouse		
Queue	0FI_ACDOCA_10	Subscriber	CB4CLNT100		
Time Stamp ID	{2023-04-10 21:12:03 000017 PST}	to	{2023-04-10 21:12:03 000017 PST}	Time Zone	
Calculate Data Volume (Extended View)		Request Select.	Delta Initialization Only	Max. No. of Matches	1,000

Data Preview

Unique Time Stamp ID (such as TSN)	Transaction ID (TID)	Unit No.	Rows	Original Size in B...	Compressed Size in Bytes	Comp. Rate	Extraction Mode	Storage
{2023-04-10 21:12:03 000017 PST}	{2023-04-10 21:12:03 000016 PST}	8	6,665	37,617,260	1,343,790	96.4	Initial Data (Delta In...	ODQDATA_C
{2023-04-10 21:12:03 000017 PST}	{2023-04-10 21:12:03 000016 PST}	7	9,574	54,035,656	1,916,321	96.5	Initial Data (Delta In...	ODQDATA_C
{2023-04-10 21:12:03 000017 PST}	{2023-04-10 21:12:03 000016 PST}	6	9,574	54,035,656	1,915,837	96.5	Initial Data (Delta In...	ODQDATA_C
{2023-04-10 21:12:03 000017 PST}	{2023-04-10 21:12:03 000016 PST}	5	9,574	54,035,656	1,925,216	96.4	Initial Data (Delta In...	ODQDATA_C
{2023-04-10 21:12:03 000017 PST}	{2023-04-10 21:12:03 000016 PST}	4	9,574	54,035,656	1,921,213	96.4	Initial Data (Delta In...	ODQDATA_C
{2023-04-10 21:12:03 000017 PST}	{2023-04-10 21:12:03 000016 PST}	3	9,574	54,035,656	1,917,472	96.5	Initial Data (Delta In...	ODQDATA_C
{2023-04-10 21:12:03 000017 PST}	{2023-04-10 21:12:03 000016 PST}	2	9,574	54,035,656	1,920,301	96.4	Initial Data (Delta In...	ODQDATA_C
{2023-04-10 21:12:03 000017 PST}	{2023-04-10 21:12:03 000016 PST}	1	9,574	54,035,656	1,921,649	96.4	Initial Data (Delta In...	ODQDATA_C
			73,683	**415,866,852**	**14,781,799**			

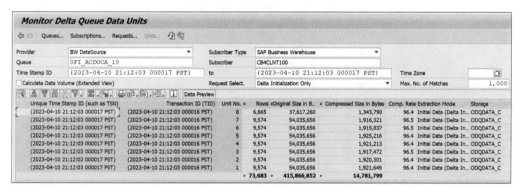

Figure 8.59 Units

If you want to see the storage table data, open Transaction SE11 and go to table ODQDATA_C (see Figure 8.60).

Data Browser: Table ODQDATA_C Select Entries 8

Check Table...

CLIENT	RID	UNITNO	MODELNAME	QUEUENAME	LINES	RAWSIZE	COMPSIZE	DATAFORMAT	XDATA
100	20230411041203.000017000	1	DATASOURCE_MODEL	0FI_ACDOCA_10	9,574	54,035,656	1,921,649	G	ECBD899F23C975E7F7A93EAA8F2167C891B85CAFEDF5ACAFB5770C...
100	20230411041203.000017000	2	DATASOURCE_MODEL	0FI_ACDOCA_10	9,574	54,035,656	1,920,301	G	ECBD8B9F23D955E7F9C9AACACAACEA76B7DDB8F1ECB0CBF6BE776...
100	20230411041203.000017000	3	DATASOURCE_MODEL	0FI_ACDOCA_10	9,574	54,035,656	1,917,472	G	ECBD899F2BC955EFF9A9DBB7AAEEBD76B717DC9879B3F5AC6F864...
100	20230411041203.000017000	4	DATASOURCE_MODEL	0FI_ACDOCA_10	9,574	54,035,656	1,921,213	G	ECBD899F234956E7F989CC8C8CC8ACBE68687A766677B6F63E6AA5...
100	20230411041203.000017000	5	DATASOURCE_MODEL	0FI_ACDOCA_10	9,574	54,035,656	1,925,216	G	ECBD899F234956E7F989CC8C88ACECEEAAEAEA2E7A76F6AADD1DF...
100	20230411041203.000017000	6	DATASOURCE_MODEL	0FI_ACDOCA_10	9,574	54,035,656	1,915,837	G	ECBD899F23C975E7F7A9EEAAAEEE1E9243511C71BDB6E5595F6B6B...
100	20230411041203.000017000	7	DATASOURCE_MODEL	0FI_ACDOCA_10	9,574	54,035,656	1,916,321	G	ECBD899F244956DFF9C9AACACCAA9A93611AB4D21E25EDAD56F89...
100	20230411041203.000017000	8	DATASOURCE_MODEL	0FI_ACDOCA_10	6,665	37,617,260	1,343,790	G	ECBD899F23D955EFF9C9AACACAAA6ABBDB3618BF796F967EB30F8...

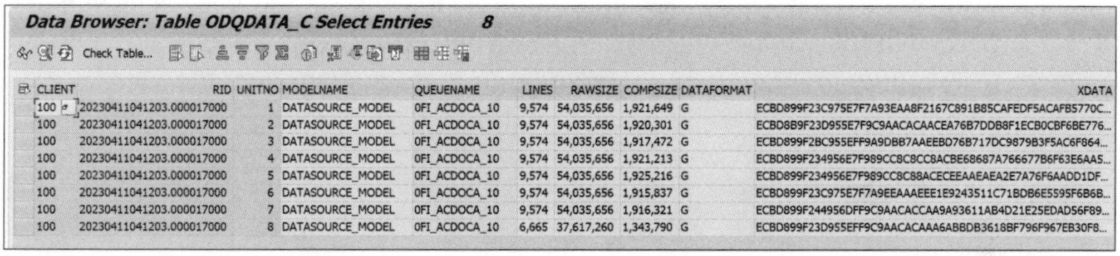

Figure 8.60 Table ODQDATA_C

Once you've extracted the DTP for the first time, the delta will be initialized. The next step is to load the new and changed documents, which you can do using these steps:

1. Make sure you have completed the execution of the DTP that did the delta initialization. When you start the DTP for the first time, the delta can be initialized for all the relevant periods/years that an organization wants to report. You can see the details in the FISCPERYEAR field (fiscal year). The selections that you provide in the DTP will be used as the base for the delta initialization.
2. When you try to do the initialization, it's best practice to have a posting-free period; if there are no postings in table ACDOCA during the delta init, there will be less chance of missing records.

   Once the delta is initialized, the newly posted and changed/reversed/cleared documents will be written to the delta queue and will be extracted in the next delta run.

Next, we'll discuss posting and extracting the delta. Let's change a FI document in SAP S/4HANA, which will trigger the delta for SAP BW/4HANA. Follow these steps:

In SAP S/4HANA, use Transaction FBO2 to change a FI document in SAP S/4HANA. The screen will have various selections, as shown in Figure 8.61. It will have the **Document Number**, **Company Code**, and **Fiscal Year** as selections; to change a document, you need to provide these fields.

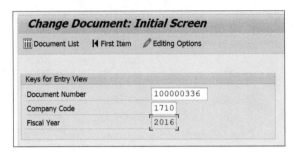

Figure 8.61 Transaction FBO2

3. Once you have provided the details as per Figure 8.61 and pressed Enter, you can see the line item details, as shown in Figure 8.62. You'll see there are three line items. Note that the **Data Entry View** area has header details such as **Document Number**, **Document Date**, and so on. In the line item details, you can see details such as company code, line item number, and the account number followed by the description. There are three line items in this example, as shown in Figure 8.62.

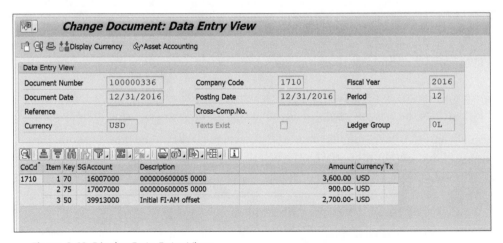

Figure 8.62 Display Data Entry View

4. To trigger the delta, change line item 1. Enter new text in the **Text** field, as shown in Figure 8.63. You can see that in the **Additional Details** section, in **Text**, we've added "Change 4 12".

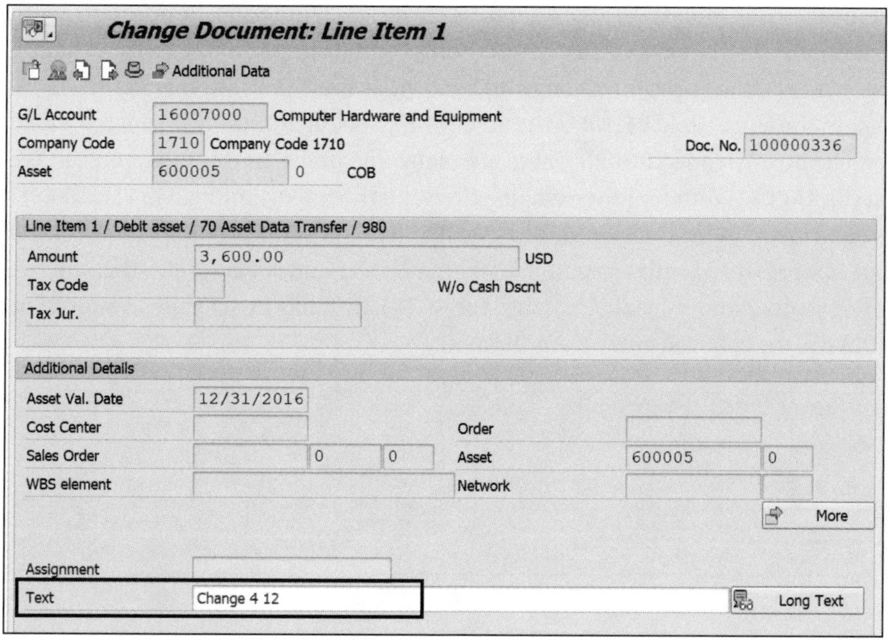

Change Document: Line Item 1

Additional Data

G/L Account	16007000 Computer Hardware and Equipment	
Company Code	1710 Company Code 1710	Doc. No. 100000336
Asset	600005 0 COB	

Line Item 1 / Debit asset / 70 Asset Data Transfer / 980

Amount	3,600.00	USD
Tax Code		W/o Cash Dscnt
Tax Jur.		

Additional Details

Asset Val. Date	12/31/2016		
Cost Center		Order	
Sales Order	0 0	Asset	600005 0
WBS element		Network	

More

Assignment	
Text	Change 4 12

Long Text

Figure 8.63 Change Text

Save the document after the change using the ▢ icon. You'll see a message that the FI document is saved. To check the changes at the table level, check table ACDOCA and provide the details such as company code (RBUKRS), year (GJAHR), and accounting document number (BELNR) based on values shown earlier in Figure 8.61. The details can be entered as selections for table ACDOCA as shown in Figure 8.64.

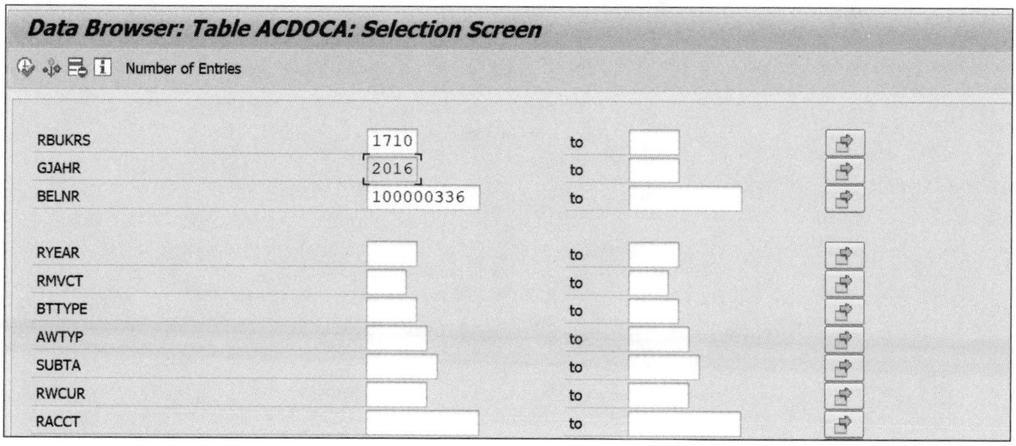

Data Browser: Table ACDOCA: Selection Screen

Number of Entries

RBUKRS	1710	to	
GJAHR	2016	to	
BELNR	100000336	to	
RYEAR		to	
RMVCT		to	
BTTYPE		to	
AWTYP		to	
SUBTA		to	
RWCUR		to	
RACCT		to	

Figure 8.64 Selections

409

5. Now execute the table to see the results, as shown in Figure 8.65. For line item 1 with the account number (**RACCT**) 16007000, **SGTXT** is reflected with the change that we have made. It has the value **Change 4 12** shown in the box. Note that **RLDNR** is **OL**, which is the ledger, and **BELNR** is the accounting document number, which is based on the company code **RBUKRS**. There are many line items. In this case, you can see that the **RACCT** is different for each line item and the important field in FI is **DRCRK**, the debit credit indicator. Here **S** is for **Debit** and **H** is for **Credit**. When you see H, the value is represented with a negative sign (-) as it's a credit. For example, this appears for line items 2 and 3. Finally, because the **SGTXT** field has the changed value, table ACDOCA has the changed entry from the delta.

Data Browser: Table ACDOCA Select Entries   3

	RCLNT	RLDNR	RBUKRS	GJAHR	BELNR	DOCLN	RYEAR	POPER	BUDAT	BUZEI	BSCHL	RACCT	TSL	DRCRK	RTCUR	SGTXT	BLDAT
	100	OL	1710	2016	0100000336	000001	2016	012	12/31/2016	001	70	0016007000	3,600.00	S	USD	Change 4 12	12/31/2016
	100	OL	1710	2016	0100000336	000002	2016	012	12/31/2016	002	75	0017007000	900.00-	H	USD		12/31/2016
	100	OL	1710	2016	0100000336	000003	2016	012	12/31/2016	003	50	0039913000	2,700.00-	H	USD		12/31/2016

Figure 8.65 Table ACDOCA

6. Now in SAP BW/4HANA, open the DTP and execute the delta DTP by executing the DTP with ▶ ▼. You'll see the delta request status as shown in Figure 8.66. Note that the **Extraction Mode** is **Delta** and note that **Records** has a value of **1**; it's the only value extracted as you've changed only one line item in SAP S/4HANA. That record is now extracted in the DTP delta execution.

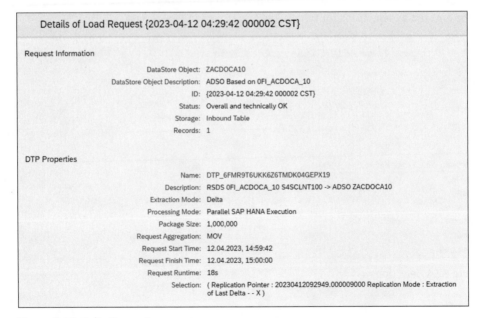

Details of Load Request {2023-04-12 04:29:42 000002 CST}

Request Information

DataStore Object: ZACDOCA10
DataStore Object Description: ADSO Based on 0FI_ACDOCA_10
ID: {2023-04-12 04:29:42 000002 CST}
Status: Overall and technically OK
Storage: Inbound Table
Records: 1

DTP Properties

Name: DTP_6FMR9T6UKK6Z6TMDK04GEPX19
Description: RSDS 0FI_ACDOCA_10 S4SCLNT100 -> ADSO ZACDOCA10
Extraction Mode: Delta
Processing Mode: Parallel SAP HANA Execution
Package Size: 1,000,000
Request Aggregation: MOV
Request Start Time: 12.04.2023, 14:59:42
Request Finish Time: 12.04.2023, 15:00:00
Request Runtime: 18s
Selection: (Replication Pointer : 20230412092949.000009000 Replication Mode : Extraction of Last Delta - - X)

Figure 8.66 Delta Request

7. When you click **Inbound Table**, you can see the exact record that you changed. Check the **SGTXT** column to see the value **Change 4 12** that you changed in SAP S/4HANA, as shown in Figure 8.67. This record is fetched using the delta DTP load.

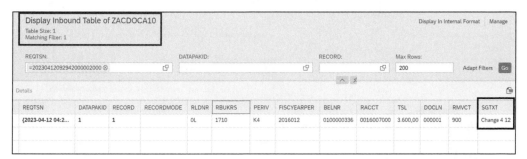

Figure 8.67 Inbound Table Content

8. To validate, log into SAP S/4HANA and open Transaction ODQMON. Check the **Queue** for **OFI_ACDOCA_10** to see the subscriptions. The last row is the subscription based on the **Last TSN Request** date. Choose the specific row shown in Figure 8.68, which has two requests.

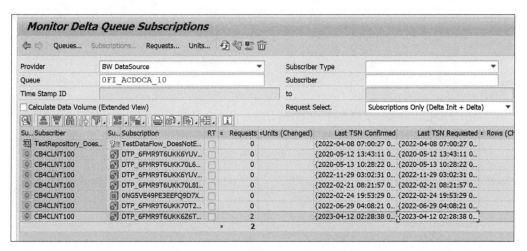

Figure 8.68 Transaction ODQMON

9. Once you choose the last request, you'll go to the **Request** view section shown in Figure 8.69. The **Upper Limit for TSN** has the delta execution timestamp; that is the delta request. You'll see that that **Extraction Mode** is **Data Changes (Delta)** and **Storage** is **ODQDATA**, which is the table for the delta extraction in ODP.

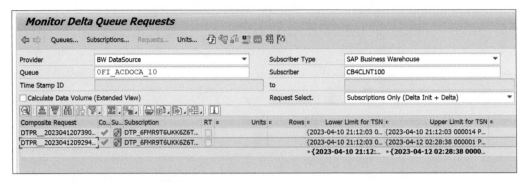

Figure 8.69 Requests with Timestamps

10. Once you double-click the second row shown in Figure 8.69, you'll go to the **Unit** section, where you can find the total records captured in the delta. Because you've changed only one record, the **Rows** column is set to **1**, as shown in Figure 8.70.

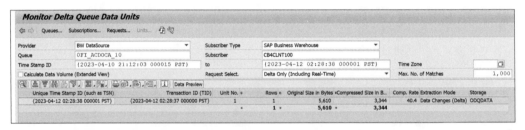

Figure 8.70 Units

11. If you double-click the main row listed, it will open a new row in the same units view. You can see the data of the delta record and will see that **Text** shows the value that you changed, **Change 4 12**, as shown in Figure 8.71.

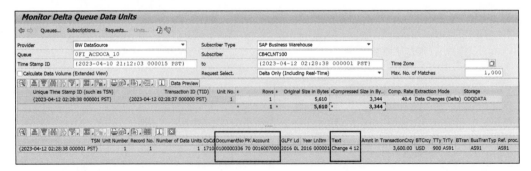

Figure 8.71 Data

12. You can also see that the change in the document number is captured in table BWFI_ AEDAT (see Figure 8.72). The timestamp is also updated in the **TIMEST** field along with the company code (**BUKRS**), accounting document number (**BELNR**), and fiscal year (**GJAHR**).

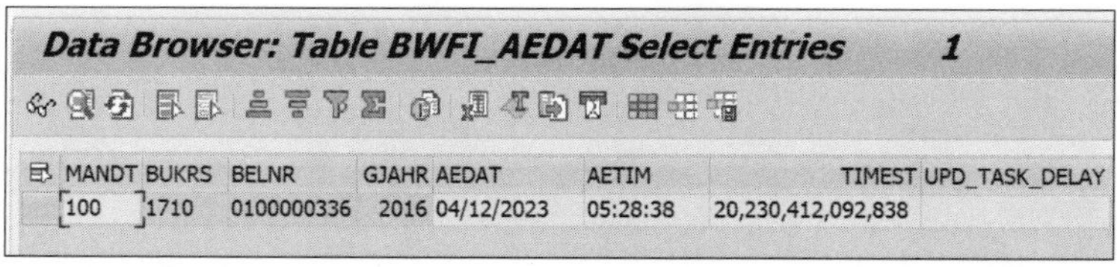

Figure 8.72 Timestamp Capture

Here in table BWFI_AEDAT, you can get the timestamp (**TIMEST**) for when you updated the document number. Because this timestamp was above the last delta extraction, this document was selected for the delta. You can use this table in Figure 8.72 for the analysis of delta records.

> **Note**
>
> Remember that the delta mode for OFI_ACDOCA_10 is AIMD, so the overwrite in aDSO will support this.

OFI_ACDOCA_20

OFI_ACDOCA_20 can be used for balances and/or financial statement reporting. When used in delta mode, it extracts only newly posted documents, including the line items created by the balance carry forward program (B* items with ACDOCA-BSTAT = 'C', which only exist in table ACDOCA).

Because OFI_ACDOCA_10 and OFI_ACDOCA_20 extract the same data from ACDOCA but in another form (OFI_ACDOCA_20 creates its record for each currency type), check whether you have to use OFI_ACDOCA_20 if you're using OFI_ACDOCA_10 already. Using OFI_ACDOCA_20 in addition to OFI_ACDOCA_10 creates a much higher volume in SAP BW and costs additional resources and performance (especially when running the balance carry forward program) on the SAP ERP side.

It's important to note that there are two new fields in this DataSource: **BALANCE** and **TURNOVER** (see Figure 8.73). **BALANCE** is a noncumulative key figure. Because the extraction of **BALANCE** can result in an extremely high data volume, especially if you use daily ledgers, please check whether you need the **BALANCE** key figure in your reporting. Often, a report on **BALANCE** for period 7 can be replaced by a report on **TURNOVER** for periods 0–7, for example.

The **OFI_ACDOCA_20** field in the standard extraction process doesn't fill the **BALANCE** cumulative key figure due to data volume and performance reasons. If you need the DataSource to fill that, then you can update table BWOM_SETTINGS with this new entry as shown in Figure 8.74. In the **OLTPSOURCE** field, enter "OFI_ACDOCA_20", and in the **PARAM NAME** field, enter "BWFIBALREQ". Enter "X" for **PARAMVALUE**.

Data Browser: Table ROOSFIELD Select Entries   2

&r 🔲 🔄 Check Table...   🔲 🔲 🔺 ▽ ▽ Σ 🔘 🔳 🔳 🔳 🔳 ⊞ ⊞ ⊞

🔲 OLTPSOURCE	OBJVERS	FIELD	SELECTION	UNIFIELDNM	STORNO	F4TYPE	F4EXTRAKT	NOTEXREL	KEYFLAG_DS	SELOPTS
OFI_ACDOCA_20	A	BALANCE		CURRUNIT				Y		0
OFI_ACDOCA_20	A	TURNOVER		CURRUNIT				Y		0

Figure 8.73 Table ROOSFIELD Sample

Table BWOM_SETTINGS Insert

Reset

MANDT	100
OLTPSOURCE	OFI_ACDOCA_20
PARAM NAME	BWFIBALREQ
PARAM VALUE	X

Figure 8.74 Table BWOM_SETTINGS for Balance Calculation

You can see the difference in Figure 8.75, which shows table BWOM_SETTING before ❶ and after ❷ the parameter. Once the parameter is added to table BWOM_SETTING, you'll see that the **Cuml.Bal** field has the data now.

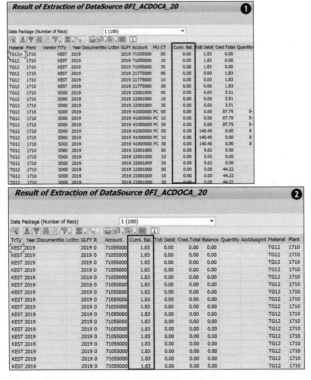

Figure 8.75 Parameter Impact on Results

The delta behavior is different for OFI_ACDOCA_20. As shown in Figure 8.76, the delta is **ADDD**, so this is an additive extractor and overwrite is not supported. Thus, you need to make sure all the data posted to table ACDOCA is extracted only once.

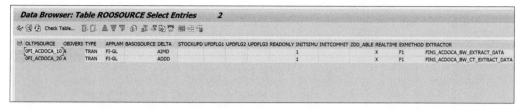

Figure 8.76 Delta for OFI_ACDOCA_20

To perform an extraction using the OFI_ACDOCA_20 DataSource, follow these steps:

1. Log onto the SAP BW/4HANA system. From the relevant source system, replicate the OFI_ACDOCA_20 DataSource in SAP BW/4HANA and then activate it.

2. Create an aDSO based on the OFI_ACDOCA_20 DataSource and then maintain the key fields for extracting the aggregated data (see Figure 8.77).

Keys:			
Name	Key	Data T...	Length
[RLDNR] Ledger	1	CHAR	2
[RBUKRS] Company Code	2	CHAR	4
[GJAHR] Fiscal Year	3	NUMC	4
[RACCT] Account Number	4	CHAR	10
[PRCTR] Profit Center	5	CHAR	10
[RCNTR] Cost Center	6	CHAR	10

Figure 8.77 Key Fields

You can also use key fields like RLDNR, RBUKRS, GJAHR, BELNR, and DOCLN if you're extracting detailed data.

3. Then you can create the transformation based on DataSource OFI_ACDOCA_20 and create the DTP based on the transformation with the full mode. Activate the DTP using the 🔹 icon (see Figure 8.78).

4. Now execute the DTP using ▶ ▼ in full update mode and test the records. The first execution will have the load request that will populate the inbound table. Activate the aDSO request, which will populate the active and change log tables (see Figure 8.79).

5. Log onto the SAP S/4HANA system and check Transaction ODQMON as shown in Figure 8.80.

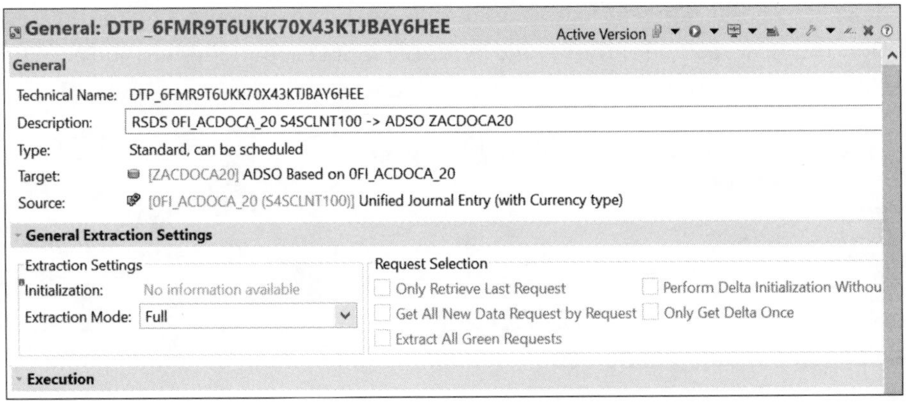

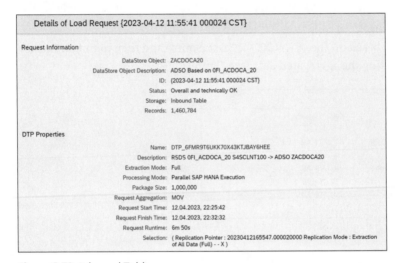

Figure 8.78 DTP Mode

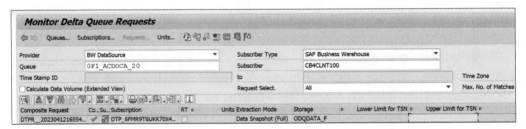

Figure 8.79 Inbound Table

Figure 8.80 Full Update

6. Staring from the queue view, provide the name of the DataSource, "OFI_ACDOCA_ 20". Go to the subscription view and then to the request view and finally to the units view. There you can see the total number of records in Transaction ODQMON: **1,460,784** (see Figure 8.81).

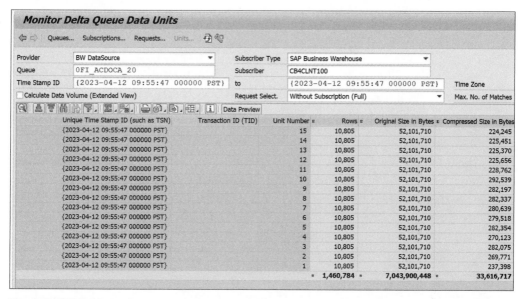

Figure 8.81 Total Records

7. Now come back to SAP BW/4HANA. Open the DTP and execute the init without data (see Figure 8.82). This will ensure that only the delta init is updated in the source system and no records are extracted. The reason to use this option is that you already extracted the records using full update mode; now you just need to initialize the delta.

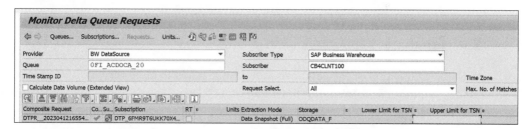

Figure 8.82 Init without Data

8. To see the status of the DTP execution, in SAP S/4HANA, open Transaction ODQMON and go to the requests view (see Figure 8.83). You'll see the details of the subscription and that **extraction Mode** is **Delta Initialization** and **Storage** is **ODQ-DATA_F**.

9. For the last step, run the delta DTP and go to Transaction ODQMON in SAP S/4HANA (Figure 8.84). You can see that in the request view, **Extraction Mode** is **Data Changes (Delta)** and **Storage** is **ODQDATA**.

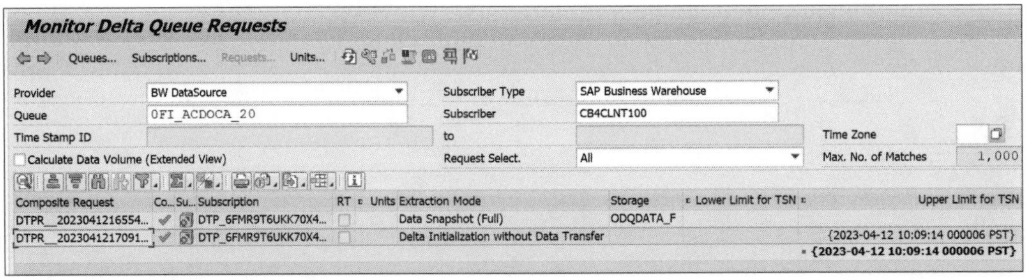

Figure 8.83 Delta Init

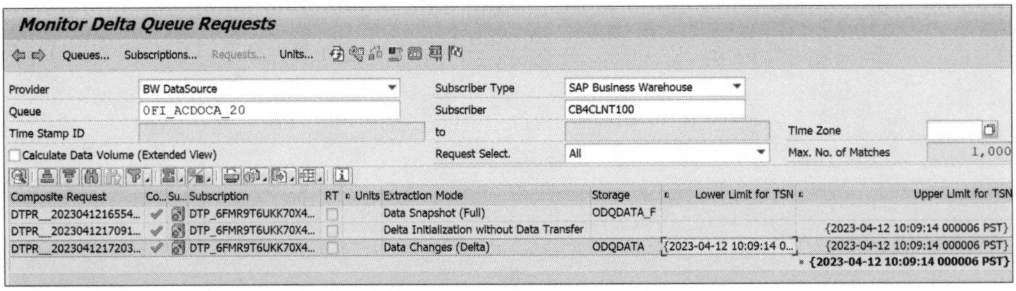

Figure 8.84 ODQ Delta

If you post a document now in SAP S/4HANA, it can be a new document or it can be a document change; because the delta is initialized for the DataSource, from the next DTP load, the new and changed documents will be fetched in the delta load.

8.5   Summary

With the completion of the dataflows, now you're ready to build the SAP BW/4HANA model to extract data from SAP S/4HANA or SAP ERP using SAP-delivered business content DataSources to extract the financial data. You've learned about the application-level details of finance and know the differences between the classical general ledger and new general ledger. You've also learned how to do effective data modeling on table ACODOCA. Knowing about a mix of classical and new extractors will help you design more efficient data models during an SAP BW/4HANA implementation.

In the next chapter, we'll focus on extracting data from SAP ERP Human Capital Management to SAP BW/4HANA.

Chapter 9

Extracting SAP ERP Human Capital Management Data

This chapter discusses extractors for SAP ERP Human Capital Management data. In S/4HANA, human capital deals with the management of core human resources (HR) data such as personnel administration, payroll, and personnel time management. If you can understand the functional basis that we'll discuss in first sections, it will help you to understand the SAP BW extraction process better.

In this chapter, we'll start with an introduction to SAP ERP Human Capital Management in Section 9.1. We'll go over basic terminology in the same section, including a discussion of InfoTypes. The SAP standard extractors for HR are covered in Section 9.2. HR-PA DataSources are discussed in Section 9.2.1. HR master data extraction is discussed in Section 9.2.2. HR-PY DataSources are discussed in Section 9.2.3. HR-PT DataSources are discussed in Section 9.2.4. Then we'll focus on SAP S/4HANA extraction. We'll also focus on how to install the dataflow for SAP HANA–optimized HR objects in SAP BW/4HANA and how to activate those flows to extract full and delta loads from SAP S/4HANA.

9.1 Introduction to Human Capital Management in SAP BW/4HANA

This section covers types of SAP ERP systems and their associated BI content, and it discusses the availability of SAP extractors and DataSources. From an SAP ERP system perspective, the business process that involves the management of human capital is called SAP ERP Human Capital Management. The whole human capital process involves other important areas for the management of personnel administration (PA), payroll management (PY), and personnel time management (PT).

HR data is stored in *InfoTypes*. These start with a two-letter prefix followed by five numerals. For example, **PA0001** is an InfoType containing information about an employee, such as personnel number, start date, end date, organization unit, and so on, as shown in Figure 9.1.

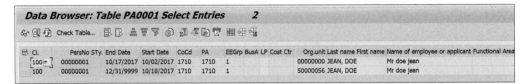

Figure 9.1 Infotype

SAP ERP Human Capital Management InfoTypes can be accessed with Transaction PA20. If you need to view employee details, they can be seen in Transaction PA20, which is used to display the HR master record, as shown in Figure 9.2.

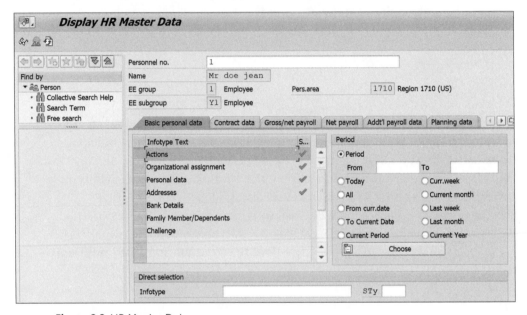

Figure 9.2 HR Master Data

With Transaction PA20, you can see details about an employee. The **Personnel No.** field, which assigns the employee number, is set to **1** in the example. When you press Enter, you can see details for that employee on multiple tabs, like **Basis Personal Data**, **Contract Data**, **Payroll**, and so on. In the **Basis Personal Data** tab, click the **Actions** view button, highlighted in the figure, then click the **Display** icon. You'll see the screen shown in Figure 9.3, which will have details of the actions, such as **Action Type**, set here to **Hiring**, and other information, such as **Employment Status**.

Similarly, if you choose to select another InfoType, it will show you the pertinent data. For example, select **Addresses** from the main screen of Transaction PA20 to see address details, as shown in Figure 9.4.

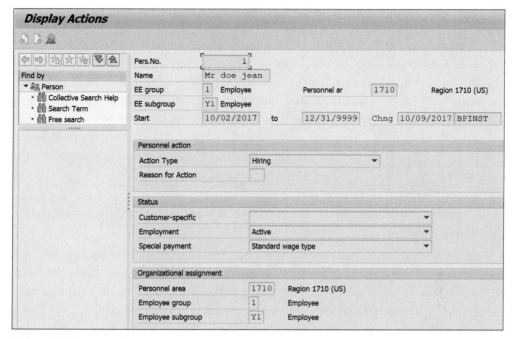

Figure 9.3 Display Actions

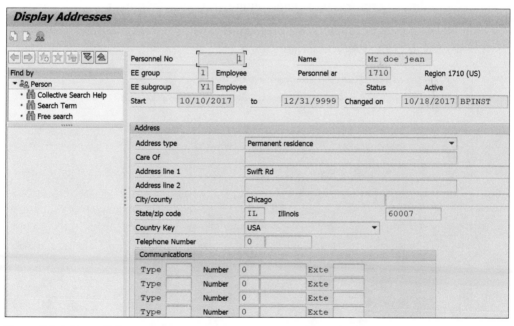

Figure 9.4 Address Data

9.2   Human Resources DataSources Overview

There are three major categories of HR DataSources that deal with applications related to SAP ERP Human Capital Management, such as payroll, which focuses on managing salaries and wages. Time extraction DataSources will track employee time, and there are also DataSources to fetch data related to employee personnel administration: employment date, type, and so on. These three categories are as follows:

- Payroll DataSources: 0HR_PY*
- Time extraction DataSources: 0HR_PT*
- Personnel administration DataSources: 0HR_PA*

You need to have the P_BAS_ALL and P_PLAN_ALL authorizations for the background user (e.g., ALEREMOTE) extracting the HR data.

In this section, you'll learn about the HR personnel administration DataSources that can be used to extract data to SAP BW/4HANA, then you'll learn about the various master data in HR-PA applications, followed by the DataSources in HR-PY for payroll. Finally, you'll learn about the DataSources related to HR-PT that extract time-related information for a specific employee.

9.2.1   Human Resources Personnel Administration DataSources

In Transaction RSA5, you can see the personnel administration DataSources in the path **SAP · SAP R/3 · PA · PA-PA** (see Figure 9.5).

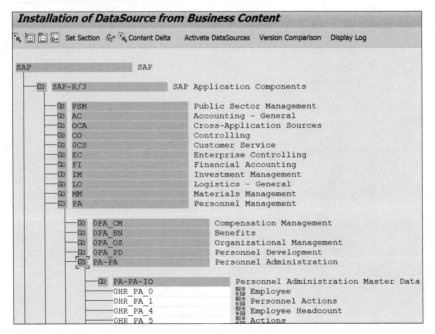

Figure 9.5 HR-PA Path

Some of the important DataSources supported in SAP S/4HANA are as follows:

- 0HR_PA_0: Employee
- 0HR_PA_1: Personnel Actions
- 0HR_PA_2: HR Structural Authorizations—Values
- 0HR_PA_3: HR Structural Authorizations—Hierarchies

To load an HR-PA DataSource, first check the simulation in Transaction RSA3 or execute report RODPS_REPL_TEST. Then log onto the SAP BW/4HANA system. Right-click the application component for the specific source to replicate the DataSource. Activate the DataSource and create an aDSO based on the created DataSource (see Figure 9.6).

Result of Extraction of DataSource 0HR_PA_1

Data Package (Number of Recs) 1 (28)

Calendar day	Pers.No.	Act.	ActR	S
10/02/2017	1	01		3
10/10/2017	2	01	01	3
09/06/2017	3	01	01	3
09/06/2017	4	01	01	3
01/01/2015	5	01	01	3
03/26/2018	6	01		3
03/26/2018	7	01		3
03/26/2018	8	01		3
03/26/2018	9	01		3
03/26/2018	10	01		3

Figure 9.6 0HR_PA_1

9.2.2   Master Data in Human Resources

There are many important master data DataSources in HR, including 0EMPLOYEE_ATTR. You can see the status of that DataSource in Transaction RSA3, as shown in Figure 9.7.

Result of Extraction of DataSource 0EMPLOYEE_ATTR

Data Package (Number of Recs) 1 (29)

Start Date	End Date	Pers.No.	RefPersNo.	CoCode	PA	Subarea	EEGrp	ESgrp	Org. Unit	Job	Position	CO area	MasterCCtr	PArea	CGrpg	Ty.	PSA	Grpg	PS group	Lv	UtilLvl	Ann.salary	Curr.	Empl. %	S	Entry Date
10/02/2017	10/17/2017	1		1 1710	1710	1710	1	Y1			99999999	A000		99	10						0.00		100.00	3	10/02/2017
10/18/2017	12/31/9999	1		1 1710	1710	1710	1	Y1	50000056		50000058	A000		99	10						0.00		100.00	3	10/02/2017
10/10/2017	12/31/9999	2		1 1710	1710	1710	1	Y1	50000000		50000001	A000		99	10						0.00		100.00	3	10/10/2017
09/06/2017	12/31/9999	3		3 1710	1710	1710	1	Y1			99999999	A000		99	10						0.00		0.00	3	09/06/2017
09/06/2017	12/31/9999	4		4 1710	1710	1710	1	Y1			99999999	A000		99	10						0.00		0.00	3	09/06/2017
01/01/2015	12/31/9999	5		5 DE01	DE01	0001	1	DU			99999999	DE01		99	01		3					0.00		0.00	3	01/01/2015
03/26/2018	12/31/9999	6		6 1710	1710	1710	1	Y1			99999999	A000	17101321	99	10						0.00		0.00	3	03/26/2018

Figure 9.7 0EMPLOYEE_ATTR

When you want to extract the data to SAP BW/4HANA, follow these steps:

1. Ensure that the user who extracts the data has authorization to extract the HR data; P_BAS_ALL will provide sufficient authorization. This must be provided by the Basis and security team.

2. Extract the relevant master data like OEMPLOYEE_ATTR and load the data to an Info-Object like OEMPLOYEE (see Figure 9.8). We discussed the extraction process in detail in Chapter 2.

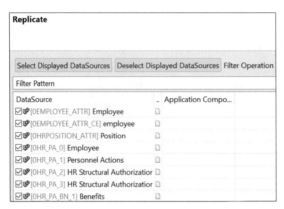

Figure 9.8 Replication in SAP BW/4HANA

3. In SAP BW/4HANA, from your specific SAP S/4HANA source system, replicate the required HR-PA DataSources as shown in Figure 9.8. This should activate the DataSource also; if it's not active, use the [icon] icon to activate the DataSource.

4. Once the DataSource is active, create the aDSO based on the HR DataSource and then create the transformation and DTP and load the data for the aDSO.

5. Use the master data InfoObject in the aDSO for reporting purposes.

9.2.3   Payroll Data Extraction

The important DataSources for payroll data extraction are as follows:

- **0HR_PY_1: Payroll Data**
  This DataSource uses table PA0003 (the HR master record), InfoType 003 (the payroll status), Table PA0000 (the HR master record with InfoTypes 000), Table T500L (the personnel country grouping), and Table PCL2 (HR Cluster 2), which is a cluster table that holds the amount values that are populated.

- **0HR_PY_CE_1: Payroll Data (CE) Enabled**
  This DataSource is used for the extraction of concurrent employment–based payroll data of all employees for a fixed period. This is provided in the context of concurrent employment (CE), which just means that an employee has more than one personnel assignment with one enterprise or several affiliated enterprises at the same time. For example, an IT company employee in one region may be sent to another location for a certain assignment for a limited period to deliver a special service.

- **OHR_PY_PP_1: Auditing Information for Posting Transfer**
  This DataSource is used for the transfer of information contained in the posting index to SAP BW. This DataSource supports delta uploads.

- **OHR_PY_PP_2: BIW Extraction for HR Posting Documents**
  This DataSource is used for the transfer of data contained in posting or reverse posting documents. This DataSource supports delta uploads.

9.2.4   Planned Time Data Extraction

The important DataSources for planned time data extraction are as follows:

- **OHR_PT_1 (planned time; data can be seen in PA20 at InfoType 0007)**
  This DataSource is used to extract the planned time and the labor data from the time management area. This DataSource supports delta uploads.

- **OHR_PT_2 (actual times and labor times; deals with the reporting times based on time types)**
  This DataSource is used to extract the actual time and labor data from time management; it supports delta uploads.

- **OHR_PT_3 (quota transaction; info on the days off that an employee is allowed to take each year)**
  This DataSource is used to extract the time quotas and employee data from time management. It DataSource can extract delta data.

The delta for PT is based on InfoType 439 and table PA0439. When you open table PA0439, the **Subtype** field reflects the DataSource delta initialization with a number. For example, subtype 0001 is for OHR_PT_1, subtype 0002 is for OHR_PT_2, and subtype 0003 is for OHR_PT_3. You can see the value 1001 in Figure 9.9.

MANDT	PERNR	SUBTY	OBJPS	SPRPS	ENDDA	BEGDA	SEQNR	AEDTM	UNAME
100	00000001	1001			12/31/9999	04/16/2023	000	04/16/2023	ALEREMOTE1
100	00000002	1001			12/31/9999	04/16/2023	000	04/16/2023	ALEREMOTE1
100	00000003	1001			12/31/9999	04/16/2023	000	04/16/2023	ALEREMOTE1
100	00000004	1001			12/31/9999	04/16/2023	000	04/16/2023	ALEREMOTE1
100	00000005	1001			12/31/9999	04/16/2023	000	04/16/2023	ALEREMOTE1
100	00000006	1001			12/31/9999	04/16/2023	000	04/16/2023	ALEREMOTE1

Figure 9.9 Table PA0439: SUBTY Field

When SAP ERP uses the Cross-Application Time Sheet (CATS), the personnel time entry is maintained using Transaction CAT2. Those data can be extracted by the SAP standard extractors. There are a few important extractors, like the following:

- OCA_TS_IS_1

  This DataSource contains data that was entered using CATS and that has been approved (status 30 and 50).

- OCA_TS_IS_2

  This DataSource is available for timesheet data that has not been approved but has been released for approval (status 20).

9.3   Summary

With the completion of the dataflow, you're ready to build the SAP BW/4HANA model to extract the data from HR system using the SAP-delivered business content DataSources to extract the HR data. You have learned the application-level details of SAP ERP Human Capital Management and now know the differences between HR-PA, HR-PY, and HR-PT. You have learned how to do effective data modeling based on HR DataSources. Knowing about a mix of classical and new extractors will help you design more efficient data models during the SAP BW/4HANA implementation.

In the next chapter, we'll focus on generic data extraction, which will enable you to build custom DataSources when standard DataSources can't satisfy your business requirements.

Chapter 10

Generic Extraction from SAP S/4HANA

This chapter provides the details to create custom extractors. These are the extractors that must be created from end to end in the SAP S/4HANA source system. The SAP BW/4HANA objects need to be created based on these custom extractors. These extractors will be used when the standard SAP-delivered extractors can't satisfy your business requirements.

Most application-based data can be extracted using the SAP-delivered standard DataSources, and you've seen most of them in the previous chapters. But if the standard DataSources don't suit your extraction requirements, you can create custom DataSources. These user-generated DataSources are called *generic DataSources*. There are multiple ways to create generic DataSources and consume them in SAP BW/4HANA.

In this chapter, we'll start with an introduction to generic DataSources in Section 10.1 and discuss their types. Next, we'll walk through the steps to create generic DataSources of different types starting in Section 10.1.2 and give an overview of essential transactions and tables used in this process. Finally, you'll learn how to consume these DataSources in SAP BW/4HANA in Section 10.2 and how to extract data for reporting purposes and check the ODQ for analysis and troubleshooting purposes.

10.1 Introduction to Generic DataSources

In any OLTP system, such as SAP ERP or SAP S/4HANA, there are many applications that help to run business processes, and these generate a lot of data that gets stored in many tables. As SAP uses standard tables to store the transactional data, the standard-delivered DataSources for many applications can access these tables for SAP BW data extraction purposes. There might be scenarios where the standard DataSources lack the fields that a business requires. In such scenarios, the first option is to see if the standard DataSource can be enhanced with the missing field and if you can write logic to populate that field. We'll describe that process in the next chapters. But if such enhancement isn't possible, then the only solution is to create a new DataSource that can meet your needs, and that's the focus of this chapter.

In this section, you'll learn about the business requirements to create a generic Data-Source and how to create the database view. You'll create a generic DataSource based on the database view and test the extraction.

10.1.1   Business Requirements

Assume that a company that uses SAP ERP or SAP S/4HANA needs to get the details of a sales order: the sales order number, order date, sales organization, net value, and the items purchased in that order, plus the material number and material group. This seems to connect multiple tables in sales, so let's create a custom DataSource.

The first step is to get the table-based connectivity for joins. In general, this information can be provided by the functional team that proposes the reporting requirement; many business blueprints will have tables and join conditions for the report. The tables that will be used for the current business requirement are VBAK (Sales Document: Header Data) and VBAP (Sales Document: Item data).

You also need to get the join conditions to fetch the data from these tables. For our scenario, VBAK can be joined with VBAP using the VBELN field (sales document number). This join provides the POSNR field (item number) to get the required fields from each table.

10.1.2   Create the Database View

The first step in generic DataSource creation is to create the database view that has the fields that can be used as the extract structure. If you're using SAP ERP, then you can use Transaction SE11 (Data Dictionary) for this purpose; the same transaction also can be used in SAP S/4HANA. Let's create the database view:

1. Open Transaction SE11 and choose the **Views** option. Provide the view name that you prefer. Because this is user-generated, use Y or Z as the prefix for your view name (see Figure 10.1).

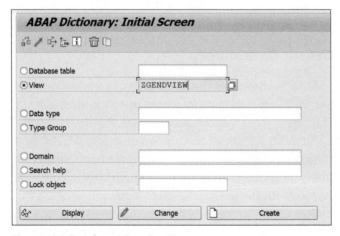

Figure 10.1 Database View Creation

2. Now choose **Create** to see the popup shown in Figure 10.2. Choose **Database View** and click the green checkmark.

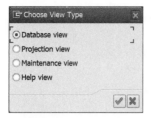

Figure 10.2 Database View

3. You'll see the screen shown in Figure 10.3, where you can provide the names of the output fields. The fields you enter here can be basically any field name that you prefer for the view output. The field name can be based on any existing table and its field. In this example, we'll use the fields for our view from table VBAK, such as VBELN and ERDAT.

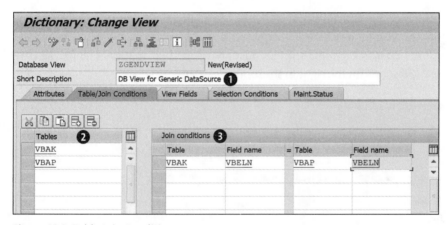

Figure 10.3 Table Join Conditions

You'll take the following steps on the screen shown in Figure 10.3:

❶ Provide a short description for the database view.

❷ Provide the list of tables that will be used for joins and field selection.

❸ Define the join conditions.

4. Once these conditions are provided, choose the **View Fields** tab, which will enable you to select the display fields for the view. Start with the first field, which is derived from table VBAK and based on field VBELN. Keep the **View Field** value as set. Now you can add any fields from the list of tables that you've selected. You can name your view field anything you'd like, but we maintained the same name here so that the logic will be clear. Choose the source table in the **Table** column and choose the source field in the **Field** column. After defining all view fields, press [Enter] and you'll see the screen shown in Figure 10.4.

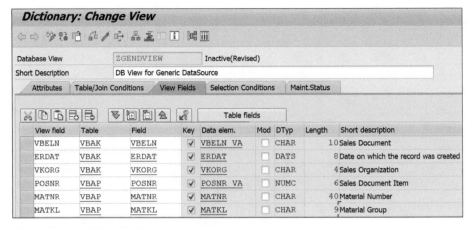

Figure 10.4 Add View Field

5. Now click the **Save** 🖫 icon and activate the view using the **Activate** icon 🔆. You can see that the **Database View** will now have the status **Active** next to the view name. Choose the **Display Contents** icon 🏛, just above the text that says Active 🏛. The icon is the last one on the right in the toolbar (see Figure 10.5).

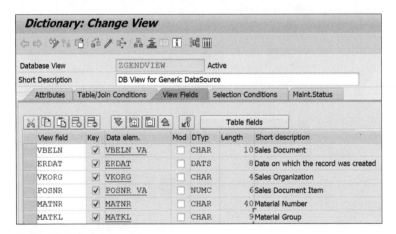

Figure 10.5 View Is Active

6. After choosing the **Display Content** icon, you can see the selection screen popup for the views, as shown in Figure 10.6. You can choose the **Number of Entries** button to see the total records available in the view.

7. If you need to see all the records, remove the limit of 200 in **Maximum No. of Hits** and choose the **Execute** icon 🕹 to see the view contents, as shown in Figure 10.7.

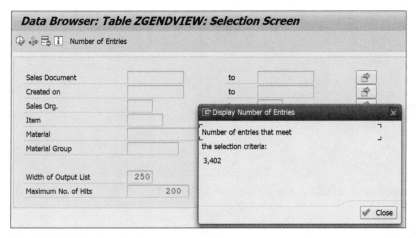

Figure 10.6 Selection Fields

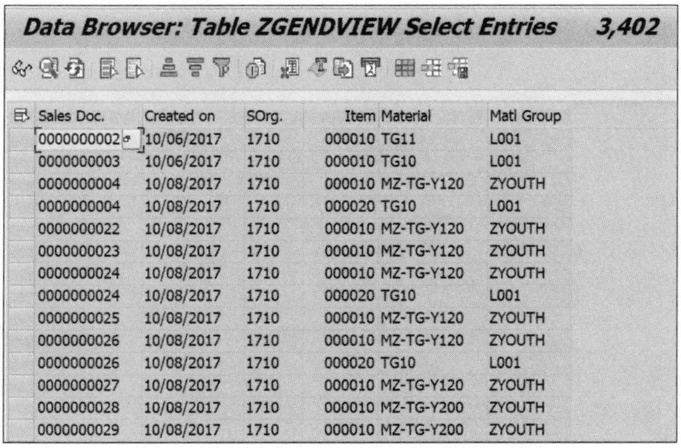

Figure 10.7 View Content Display

With this, you've created a database view that can be used for the creation of an SAP BW DataSource.

10.1.3 Create the Generic DataSource Based on the View

In the last section, you saw how to create a database view. Now let's create a generic DataSource based on that view. Follow these steps:

1. Open Transaction RSO2 in the source system; you'll see screen shown in Figure 10.8. This will allow you to create the DataSource. Choose the **Transaction Data** option and provide a view name that starts with Z.

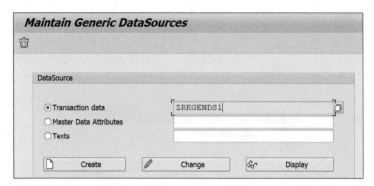

Figure 10.8 Create Generic DataSource of Type Transaction Data

2. Once you click **Create**, you'll see the screen shown in Figure 10.9. Enter the following information on this screen:

   ❶ Choose the application component (**Applic. Component**) where the DataSource can be listed; this can be used for replication also.

   ❷ You'll create this DataSource based on a view, so choose **Extraction from View** here.

   ❸ Provide the **Short**, **Medium**, and **Long Description**s for the DataSource.

   ❹ Because the DataSource is based on a view only, this option is enabled. Provide the database view name here.

   ❺ Press **Save**.

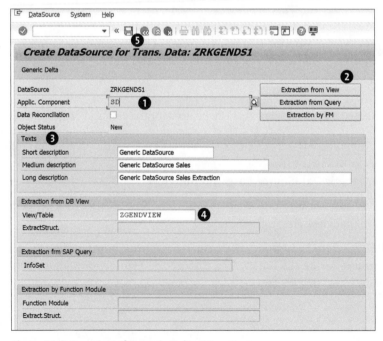

Figure 10.9 Creation of Generic Delta: View Type

3. Once you save, you'll see a popup for the package assignment and the transport request allocation. After confirming everything, you'll see the screen shown in Figure 10.10. Here, select the checkbox for in the **Selection** column for **VBELN** (**Sales Document**); this will be reflected in the DTP from SAP BW/4HANA.

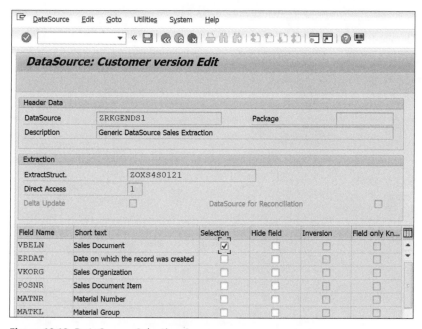

Figure 10.10 DataSource Selection Screen

4. Choose **Save** and you'll see the message shown in Figure 10.11 in the status bar. This will confirm that the **DataSource has been saved successfully**.

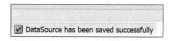

Figure 10.11 DataSource Status

10.1.4   Checking DataSource Metadata

Once the DataSource is created, you can see the metadata from tables and transactions. Let's start with the standard table, which stores the header information of the DataSource.

1. Open table ROOSOURCE and provide the DataSource name in the **DataSource** field, as shown in Figure 10.12. Click the **Execute** icon.

2. You'll see the details shown in Figure 10.13. You can see that **DataSource Extraction Method** is set to **V**, for *view*, and **DataSource Extractor** is set to **ZGENDVIEW**, the view that you created earlier in Transaction SE11.

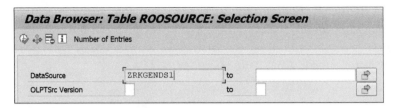

Figure 10.12 DataSource Selection

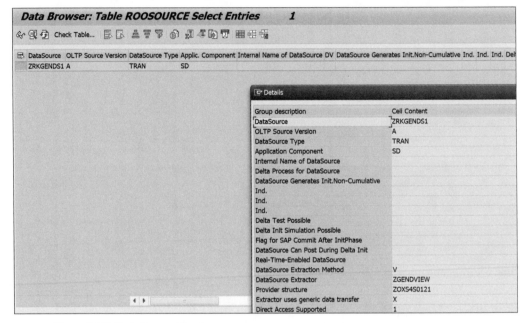

Figure 10.13 DataSource Header

3. Open table ROOSFIELD and examine the fields and their properties based on the table (see Figure 10.14). You can see that **VBELN** shows **X** in the **Properties of a DataSource Field** column per its selection enabled in table ROOSFIELD, which means you will have the option to provide the selections for data extraction in SAP BW/4HANA.

DataSource	OLTP Source Version	Field Name	Properties of a DataSource Field	Relevance of a Field for Standard Extrac
ZRKGENDS1	A	ERDAT	P	Y
ZRKGENDS1	A	MATKL	P	Y
ZRKGENDS1	A	MATNR	P	Y
ZRKGENDS1	A	POSNR	P	Y
ZRKGENDS1	A	VBELN	X	Y
ZRKGENDS1	A	VKORG	P	Y

Figure 10.14 Table Fields Information

4. Next, check the table details at the transaction level. Open Transaction RSA2 and give the DataSource name in the **DataSource** field. In this case, enter "ZRKGENDS1". Click **Display** (see Figure 10.15).

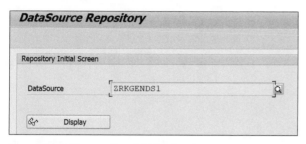

Figure 10.15 Transaction RSA2 Selection

5. You can now see the properties of the DataSource in three different tabs. The first tab, **General**, will have basic information about the DataSource, such as **Short Text** and **Created By**. The second tab, **Extraction**, is very important: it has essential metadata information about a DataSource, as shown in Figure 10.16.

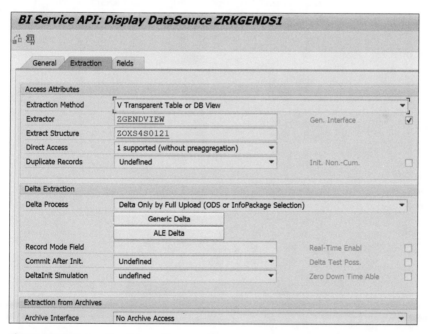

Figure 10.16 Extraction Properties

6. Choose the **Fields** tab to see a list of all the details of each field—for example, the properties for **Selection** or whether a specific field is set to **Transfer** (see Figure 10.17). Here, you can see that **VBELN** has **Selection** enabled.

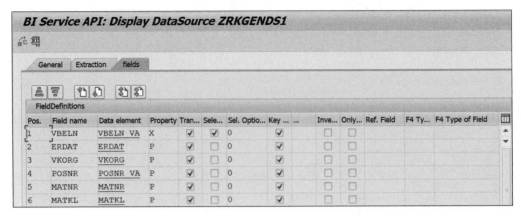

Figure 10.17 Fields of DataSource

Next, we'll walk through the steps to display DataSource data in SAP S/4HANA:

1. Open Transaction RSA3 and provide the DataSource name in the **DataSource** field. In this case, enter the name of the DataSource you created, "ZRKGENDS1". Click the **Execute** icon 🔄. You'll see that 3,402 records are selected. Click the **Display** icon ✅ see Figure 10.18).

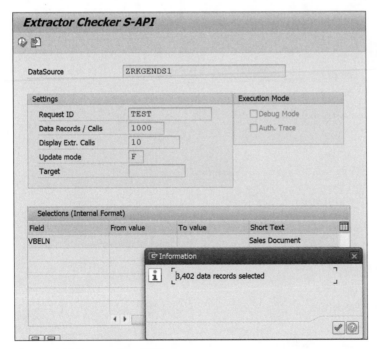

Figure 10.18 Transaction RSA3

2. Now choose the **ALV Grid** icon ⊞ to display the selected records as shown in Figure 10.19.

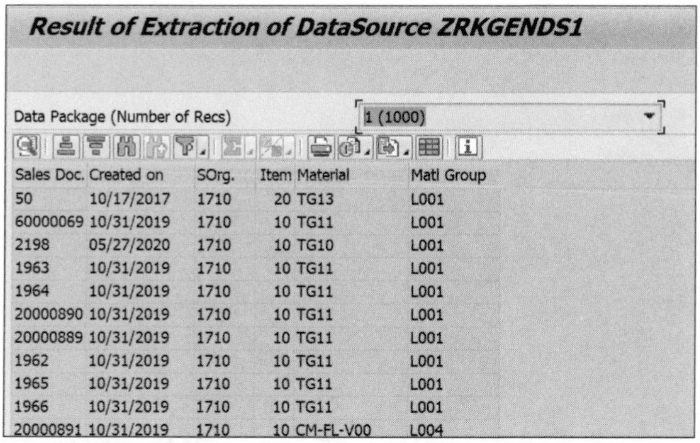

Result of Extraction of DataSource ZRKGENDS1

Data Package (Number of Recs) 1 (1000)

Sales Doc.	Created on	SOrg.	Item	Material	Matl Group
50	10/17/2017	1710	20	TG13	L001
60000069	10/31/2019	1710	10	TG11	L001
2198	05/27/2020	1710	10	TG10	L001
1963	10/31/2019	1710	10	TG11	L001
1964	10/31/2019	1710	10	TG11	L001
20000890	10/31/2019	1710	10	TG11	L001
20000889	10/31/2019	1710	10	TG11	L001
1962	10/31/2019	1710	10	TG11	L001
1965	10/31/2019	1710	10	TG11	L001
1966	10/31/2019	1710	10	TG11	L001
20000891	10/31/2019	1710	10	CM-FL-V00	L004

Figure 10.19 Display

3. There is a **Data Package (Number of Recs)** option here. If you select that drilldown option, as shown in Figure 10.20, there are four data package options. Each data package can hold 1,000 records. The first three data packages used 1,000 records each, and the last data package had the remaining records. If you choose to have more entries in the **Data Records/Call** setting, then this could have been reduced. You can test out a few trials of this in your system. For example, if **Data Records/Call** was set to 4,000 and **Display Extr Calls** was set to 10, then you will see all 3,402 records in the first data package. This is because the data package can hold up to 4,000 records with this setting. Setting **Data Records/Call** to 4,000 with up to 10 data packages means you can see 40,000 records in total. If you set **Data Records/Call** to 10,000 it would have the ability to hold 10,000 records per data package, so when you have more data in the base tables, then you should increase this value to see more records.

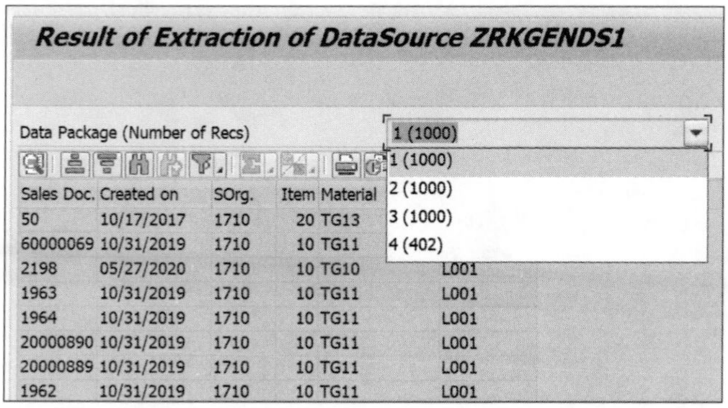

Figure 10.20 Total Packages

4. Because SAP BW/4HANA only supports DataSources that enabled for ODP, you should confirm that this DataSource is exposed to ODP. Table ROOSATTR can provide

this info. If the DataSource shows an **X** in the **Ind.** (indicator for expose external) column, as shown in Figure 10.21, then the DataSource is exposed to ODP.

Figure 10.21 Table ROOSATTR

10.2   Extract Data into SAP BW/4HANA Using Generic DataSources

In this section, we'll walk through extracting data from SAP S/4HANA using generic DataSources and transferring that data to SAP BW/4HANA.

10.2.1   Replicate the DataSource

Follow these steps to begin replication of the DataSource:

1. Replicate the DataSource based on the application component (see Figure 10.22). To do so, log onto the SAP BW/4HANA system, right-click the source system, and select **Replicate** to start the job for DataSource replication.

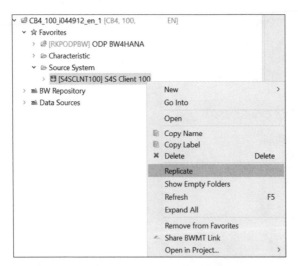

Figure 10.22 Replication

2. The screen will list all the DataSources that can be replicated, with the option to select and deselect DataSources. Choose the DataSource that you need to replicate, click **Select Displayed Datasources**, and then choose **Next**, as shown in Figure 10.23.

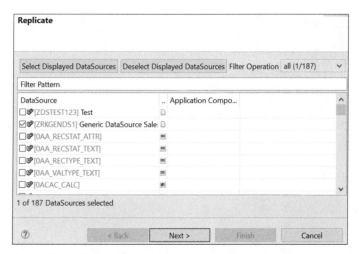

Figure 10.23 Choose Next and Finish

3. Before starting the replication process, first check the header table for the SAP BW DataSource, which is RSDS. Enter the name of the DataSource—for this example, "ZRKGENDS1"—in the **DataSource** field. You'll see that table RSDS doesn't have that specific field, as shown in Figure 10.24. Zero entries met the selection criteria.

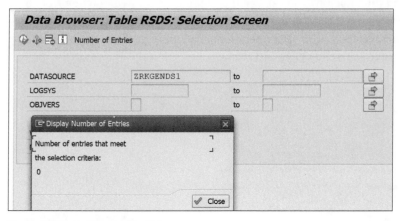

Figure 10.24 Before Replication

4. Meanwhile, the replication job should have finished. When the replication is successful with the activation and the DataSource is saved in SAP BW/4HANA (see Figure 10.25), you can open the DataSource and activate it using the ⬛ icon if it isn't active.

5. After the completion of the replication job, check table RSDS again. The DataSource is now available in in **M** and **A** versions, as shown in Figure 10.26.

Job Log Entries for RSDS_REPLICATION / 22464800

⊕ 🔲Long text 📋Previous Page 🔲Next page ⊞ 🔳

Job log overview for job: RSDS_REPLICATION / 22464800

Date	Time	Message text
28.02.2023	22:46:48	Job RSDS_REPLICATION 22464800 started
28.02.2023	22:46:48	Step 001 started (program RSDS_REPLICATION, variant &0000000000060,
28.02.2023	22:46:50	Saving DataSource ZRKGENDS1(S4SCLNT100)
28.02.2023	22:46:50	Job finished

Figure 10.25 Job Finished

Data Browser: Table RSDS Select Entries   2

🗋 ✏ ✂ 🔍 ⊕ Check Table...   🔳🔳 ≜ ☰ ☷ Σ ⓜ 🔳🔳🔳🔳 ⊞ ⊞ 🔳

DATASOURCE	LOGSYS	OBJVERS	OBJSTAT	ACTIVFL	TYPE	PRIMSEGID	OBJECTFD	APPLNM	BASOSOURCE
ZRKGENDS1	S4SCLNT100	A	ACT	X	D	0001			
ZRKGENDS1	S4SCLNT100	M	ACT	X	D	0001			

Figure 10.26 A and M Versions

6. To validate the DataSource replication, you need to search for the DataSource name in Eclipse and then open it. You can see that **Adapter** is set to **Extraction from SAP System by Operational Data Provisioning** and the **ODP Context** is based on **Data-Source/Extractors**. you can see the operational data provider with the name of the DataSource, **ZRKGENDS1** (see Figure 10.27).

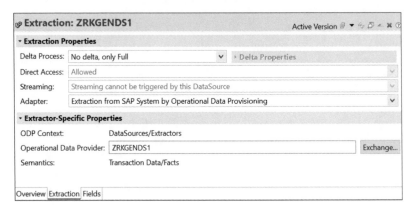

Figure 10.27 Eclipse DataSource

10.2.2   Data Modeling for Generic DataSources in SAP BW/4HANA

With the DataSource available, you can create the SAP BW data model using these steps:

1. Start with the creation of an aDSO with reference to the DataSource, as shown in Figure 10.28. In this example, to start, right-click the **RKPBGEN** InfoArea and choose to create an aDSO. You'll see the aDSO creation wizard as shown in Figure 10.28. Name the aDSO "ZADGEN" and provide the description. You can see that the aDSO is based on the DataSource, so choose **Browse** in the **DataSource** field and select **ZRKGENDS1** as the DataSource template. Once you choose the DataSource, the source system will be assigned by default. In this example, the source system is **S4SCLNT100**, which is the SAP S/4HANA system.

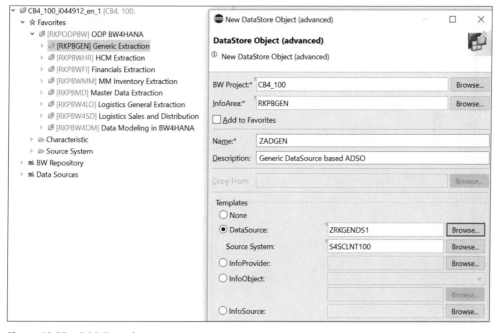

Figure 10.28 aDSO Template

Once the aDSO is created, activate it using the ⬛ icon. Create a transformation for the aDSO with the source as DataSource ZRKGENDS1 and activate it. Create the DTP for the aDSO from the transformation; you can see that the transformation is based on the same generic DataSource (ZRKGENDS1). Activate the transformation and DTP as shown in Figure 10.29.

The final dataflow that can be seen from the aDSO level is shown in Figure 10.30. The source system is S4SCLNT100, and it sends data to the ZRKGENDS1 DataSource. The ZADGEN aDSO fetches data using this DataSource. You can see the transformation and DTP in the dataflow between the DataSource and aDSO.

Figure 10.29 DTP for Generic Extraction

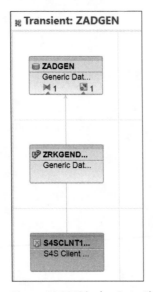

Figure 10.30 Display Data Flow

2. Now execute the DTP using ▶ ▾. You can see the request status in the web cockpit. Once you choose **Manage Request**, you can see the entries in the inbound table (see Figure 10.31), and they match the Transaction RSA3 results (shown earlier in Figure 10.18).

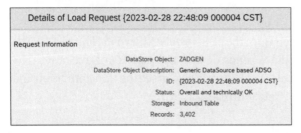

Figure 10.31 Inbound Table

3. From the **Manage Request** area, you can activate the aDSO request. To do so, select the **Activate** button. After the activation is completed, you can see the data in the active table, as shown in Figure 10.32.

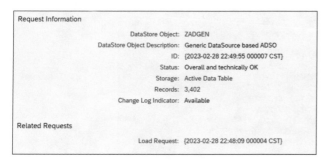

Request Information

DataStore Object:	ZADGEN
DataStore Object Description:	Generic DataSource based ADSO
ID:	{2023-02-28 22:49:55 000007 CST}
Status:	Overall and technically OK
Storage:	Active Data Table
Records:	3,402
Change Log Indicator:	Available

Related Requests

Load Request:	{2023-02-28 22:48:09 000004 CST}

Figure 10.32 Active Data Table Content

4. You can also check the active table for the aDSO based on the generic DataSource; as you know, the active table will end with 2. (See Figure 10.33.) In this example, the active table is /BIC/AZADGEN2 and it has 3,402 entries.

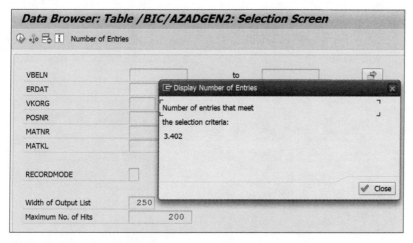

Data Browser: Table /BIC/AZADGEN2: Selection Screen

Number of Entries

VBELN		to	
ERDAT			

☞ Display Number of Entries

Number of entries that meet
the selection criteria:

3.402

✔ Close

VKORG	
POSNR	
MATNR	
MATKL	
RECORDMODE	
Width of Output List	250
Maximum No. of Hits	200

Figure 10.33 Active Table Contents

5. You can remove 200 from the **Maximum No. of Hits** field and click **Execute** or press F8 to see the total contents of the active table, as shown in Figure 10.34. The total number of records in the table (3,402) is shown in the upper-right corner.

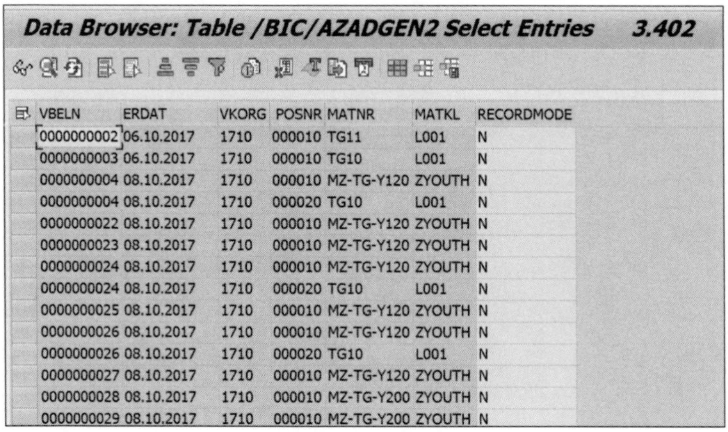

VBELN	ERDAT	VKORG	POSNR	MATNR	MATKL	RECORDMODE
0000000002	06.10.2017	1710	000010	TG11	L001	N
0000000003	06.10.2017	1710	000010	TG10	L001	N
0000000004	08.10.2017	1710	000010	MZ-TG-Y120	ZYOUTH	N
0000000004	08.10.2017	1710	000020	TG10	L001	N
0000000022	08.10.2017	1710	000010	MZ-TG-Y120	ZYOUTH	N
0000000023	08.10.2017	1710	000010	MZ-TG-Y120	ZYOUTH	N
0000000024	08.10.2017	1710	000010	MZ-TG-Y120	ZYOUTH	N
0000000024	08.10.2017	1710	000020	TG10	L001	N
0000000025	08.10.2017	1710	000010	MZ-TG-Y120	ZYOUTH	N
0000000026	08.10.2017	1710	000010	MZ-TG-Y120	ZYOUTH	N
0000000026	08.10.2017	1710	000020	TG10	L001	N
0000000027	08.10.2017	1710	000010	MZ-TG-Y120	ZYOUTH	N
0000000028	08.10.2017	1710	000010	MZ-TG-Y200	ZYOUTH	N
0000000029	08.10.2017	1710	000010	MZ-TG-Y200	ZYOUTH	N

Figure 10.34 Table Contents

10.2.3 Checking the ODQ

After the DTP is successful, you can see the status of the extraction job in the source system. Log onto SAP S/4HANA and execute Transaction ODQMON for the ODP-based delta queue. You'll see that the queue (**ZRKGENDS1**) for the generic DataSource is created in the queue view. If you need to see the queue name that was created, set **Request Select** to **All**: this will ensure that the full request is also selected and the respective queues are displayed (see Figure 10.35).

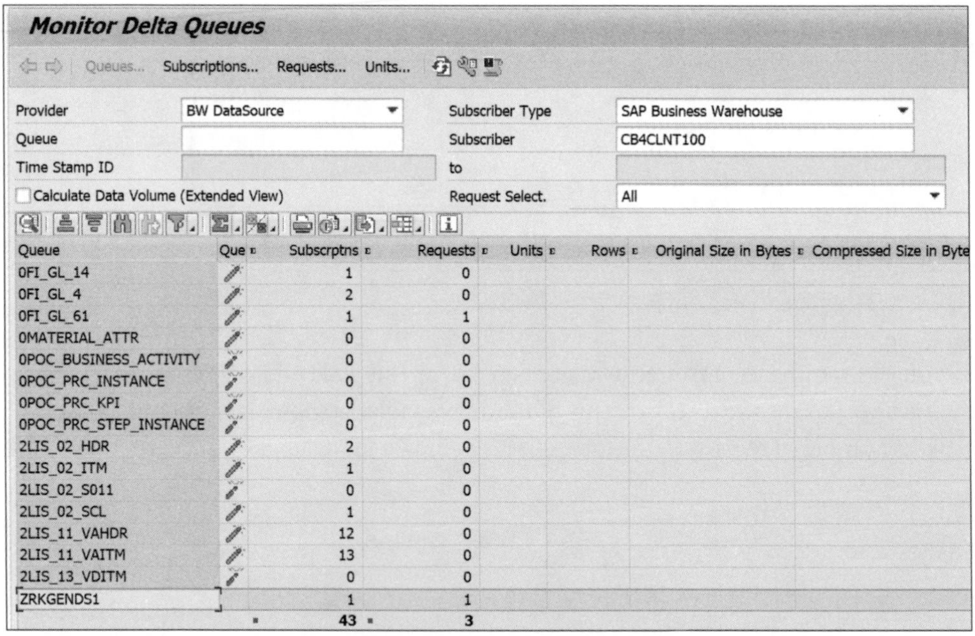

Queue	Que	Subscrptns	Requests	Units	Rows	Original Size in Bytes	Compressed Size in Byte
0FI_GL_14		1	0				
0FI_GL_4		2	0				
0FI_GL_61		1	1				
0MATERIAL_ATTR		0	0				
0POC_BUSINESS_ACTIVITY		0	0				
0POC_PRC_INSTANCE		0	0				
0POC_PRC_KPI		0	0				
0POC_PRC_STEP_INSTANCE		0	0				
2LIS_02_HDR		2	0				
2LIS_02_ITM		1	0				
2LIS_02_S011		0	0				
2LIS_02_SCL		1	0				
2LIS_11_VAHDR		12	0				
2LIS_11_VAITM		13	0				
2LIS_13_VDITM		0	0				
ZRKGENDS1		1	1				
		43	3				

Figure 10.35 Transaction ODQMON

From the queue view, you can get to the subscription view and then the request view. Finally, in the units view, you'll see the total number of rows is 3,402, matching the total number of records extracted using this DataSource. When you double-click that row, you can see the actual records that were sent to SAP BW/4HANA, and you'll see that **Storage** is now set to **ODQDATA_F** for a full upload (see Figure 10.36).

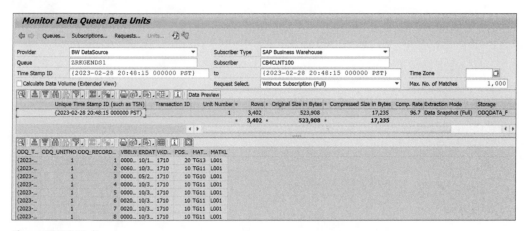

Figure 10.36 Units

The contents of table ODQDATA_F can be viewed as shown in Figure 10.37. You can see this table in Transaction SE16.

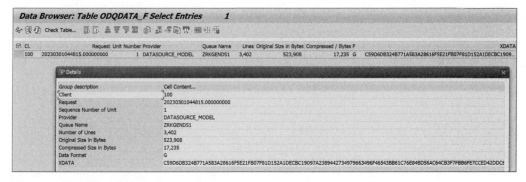

Figure 10.37 Table ODQDATA_F

10.3   Summary

With the completion of this chapter, you're ready to build a generic DataSource in SAP S/4HANA to extract data to SAP BW/4HANA. You've learned multiple options to create generic DataSources based on database views. You also learned how to consume generic DataSources in SAP BW/4HANA by creating custom objects. This entire process is considered an end-to-end extraction implementation as there are no standard-delivered contents available for the scenario. Implementing such a flow gives detailed insight into SAP BW/4HANA data modeling.

In the next chapter, we'll focus on extracting data from SAP BW 7.X systems to SAP BW/4HANA.

Chapter 11

Extracting SAP BW 7.x Data into SAP BW/4HANA

This chapter provides options to extract data from the SAP BW system to SAP BW/4HANA 2.0. When you migrate from SAP BW 7.x to an SAP BW/4HANA system using the shell conversion, where the data isn't migrated, you need to bring in the data from the old system and might need to load the data from old InfoProviders.

For customers with an SAP BW system landscape, there might be installations of SAP BW with different versions, and there might be a new migration to SAP BW/4HANA going on. If for any reason you need to extract the data from an SAP BW 7.x source to an SAP BW/4HANA target, then you need to follow a certain process to accomplish that. In the previous versions of SAP BW 7.x, there was an *export DataSource* that enabled the data from one SAP BW source system to be extracted to another SAP BW target system. But with SAP BW/4HANA, the export DataSource option can't be used anymore.

In Section 11.1, we'll explain the need for an SAP BW to SAP BW/4HANA data transfer, and in Section 11.2 you'll learn about the options to load data from a non–SAP HANA BW system to SAP BW/4HANA. In Section 1.3, we'll consume the 7.x objects in SAP BW/4HANA. Finally, we will validate the data with Transaction ODQMON in the sender SAP BW system.

11.1   SAP BW 7.x Extraction in SAP BW/4HANA

Consider the scenario shown in Figure 11.1. BW 7.x has InfoProviders such as classical DataStore Objects (DSO) and InfoCubes. If you need to extract data from these objects, then these InfoProviders must be accessed from another system. The first step in this process is to create a source system based on the sender SAP BW 7.5 or 7.x system under the **ODP_BW** folder. You'll have logical system names for the sender and target systems and create an RFC destination between the sender and receiver, then you'll connect both systems with the background user for the RFC. Once this is completed, create a source system with type **ODP Context** in the **ODP_BW** folder (see Chapter 3 for a refresher on these steps). Once you're done, you'll have a result like that shown in Figure 11.2, where the source system is created under the **ODP_BW** folder.

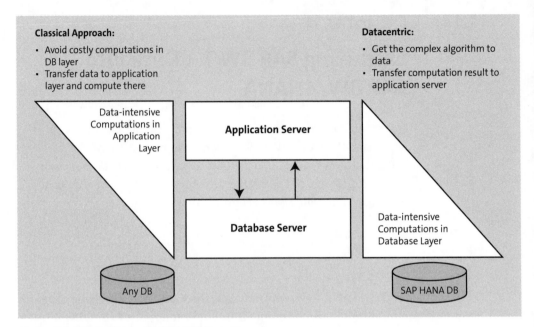

Figure 11.1 SAP BW 7.x to BW/4HANA Data Transfer

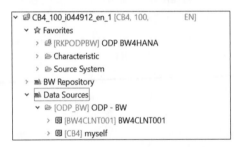

Figure 11.2 Source System BW4CLNT001 under ODP_BW

Log onto the SAP BW 7.5 sender system. From the SAP Easy Access screen, choose **System • Status** from the menu bar. You can see that the sender system is on **BW 7.5 SP19** (see Figure 11.3). You can see the details in the **Installed Product Versions** tab and the **Product** is **SAP NETWEAVER**. You'll extract the data from this system into SAP BW/4HANA.

So, the source system is connected to the target SAP BW/4HANA system as shown in Figure 11.4. Here you can see table RSBASIDOC, which has the information about the sender and target systems for the SAP BW source system connectivity. **SLOGSYS** is the sender logical system, which is **BW4CLNT001**, the SAP BW 7.5 system. **RLOGSYS** is the receiver logical system, which is **CB4CLNT100**, the target SAP BW/4HANA system. You can see that **OBJSTAT** is **ACT**, which means the source system connectivity is active.

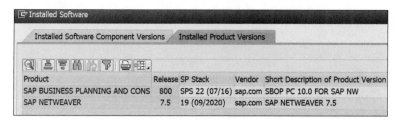

Figure 11.3 SAP BW Sender System Version

Data Browser: Table RSBASIDOC Select Entries   1

SLOGSYS	RLOGSYS	OBJSTAT	Details
BW4CLNT001	CB4CLNT100	ACT	

Group description	Cell Content
SLOGSYS	BW4CLNT001
RLOGSYS	CB4CLNT100
OBJSTAT	ACT
BIDOCTYP	
TSIDOC3X	000
TSPREFIX	9E
SRCTYPE	O

Figure 11.4 Source System Connectivity

As shown in Figure 11.4, the source system connectivity is working fine. In table RSBASI-DOC, the **OBJSTAT** field should have the value **ACT**, indicating it's active. If the source system connectivity is working fine and all the SAP BW background users in the sender system and receiver system have sufficient authorizations, then all prerequisites are completed.

11.2   SAP BW 7.x Objects for Data Loading

When you need to extract data from an SAP BW system, the source SAP BW system should have the data in InfoProviders. These InfoProviders will be used as the DataSources for the extraction. Say that you have an InfoCube called ZRKCUBS in a sender SAP BW 7.5 system, as shown in Figure 11.5.

The dataflow for the InfoCube is shown in Figure 11.6. As you can see, there is a flat file–based source system that sends data to the DataSource, and there is a classical DSO that gets data from the DataSource. There's also an InfoCube that fetches data from the classical DSO.

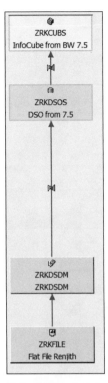

Figure 11.5 InfoCube Dataflow in SAP BW 7.5

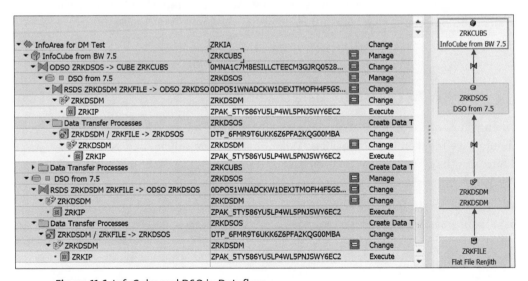

Figure 11.6 InfoCube and DSO in Dataflow

The InfoCube data for ZRKCUBS can be viewed as shown in Figure 11.7 by right-clicking the InfoCube and selecting **Display Data**.

"ZRKCUBS", List output

ZRKENUM	ZRKENAME	Employee City	ZRKEAGE	ZRKESAL
00001	EMP1	PHILADELPHIA	28	100.000,00
00002	EMP2	PHILADELPHIA	27	95.000,00
00003	EMP3	PHILADELPHIA	32	110.000,00
00004	EMP4	NEWYORK	35	120.000,00
00005	EMP5	NEWYORK	26	900.000,00
00006	EMP6	LAS VEGAS	24	850.000,00
00007	EMP7	HOUSTON	28	100.000,00
00008	EMP8	COLOMBUS	35	120.000,00
00009	EMP9	ILLINOIS	36	122.000,00
00010	EMP10	CHICAGO	29	98.000,00
00011	EMP11	BOSTON	30	100.000,00
00012	EMP12	LOS ANGELES	26	90.000,00
00013	EMP13	PHOENIX	38	130.000,00
00014	EMP14	SEATLE	40	135.000,00
00015	EMP15	WASHINGTON DC	32	110.000,00
00016	EMP16	DALLAS	27	95.000,00
00017	EMP17	SAN FRANSISCO	29	98.000,00
00018	EMP18	CALIFORNIA	30	100.000,00
00019	EMP19	CALIFORNIA	34	125.000,00
00020	EMP20	SAN JOSE	29	98.000,00

Figure 11.7 InfoCube Data

11.3   Consuming SAP BW 7.5 Objects in SAP BW/4HANA

There are two options to extract data from SAP BW systems: replication of SAP BW objects, and creating an SAP BW/4HANA DataSource using ODP. We'll walk through each option in the following sections.

11.3.1   Replicating SAP BW Objects

The first option is to do a replication in SAP BW/4HANA. Follow these steps:

1. As shown in Figure 11.8, right-click your SAP BW 7.x source system and select **Replicate**.

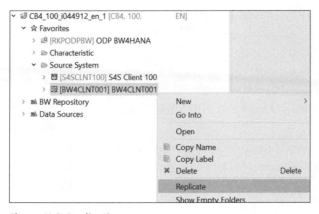

Figure 11.8 Replication

2. In the search bar, filter for the InfoCube name. Choose the DataSource that you need to replicate and activate it (see Figure 11.9). It has the InfoCube name, **ZRKCUBS**, plus **_F** at the end. Choose **Next** to proceed with the wizard.

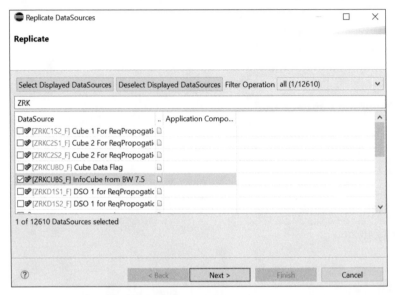

Figure 11.9 Replication of DataSource

3. You will see the message **DataSources will be created**, as shown in Figure 11.10. Choose the **Finish** option. This will trigger the background job (RSDS_REPLICATION).

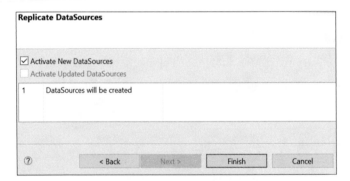

Figure 11.10 Activate DataSource Replication

4. You can see the status as shown in Figure 11.11. This job will create the DataSource in SAP BW/4HANA.

5. Now you can see the status of the DataSource in backend table RSDS. Check the table as shown in Figure 11.12. The newly created DataSource will be ZRKCUBS_F. If the Data-Source is activated, you can see the status as **A** in the table entry for the **ZRKCUBS_F** DataSource.

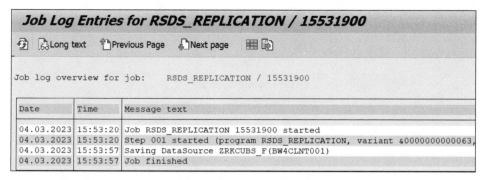

Figure 11.11 Job Log Entries Table

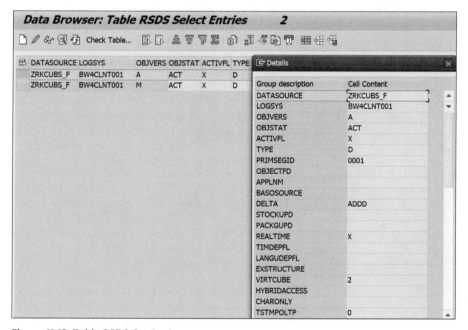

Figure 11.12 Table RSDS Content

6. You'll also see that the InfoArea will be replicated as shown in Figure 11.13. You can see the name of the InfoArea here, **ZRKIA**.

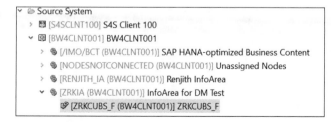

Figure 11.13 InfoArea

7. Double-click the DataSource that was created, as shown in Figure 11.14. It will have the **ODP Context** set to **SAP NetWeaver Business Warehouse** and **Operational Data Provider** set to **ZRKCUBS**.

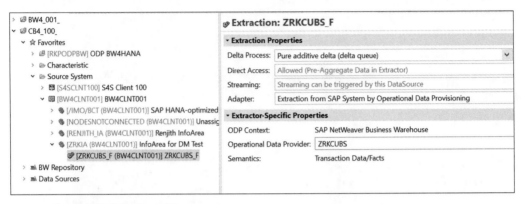

Figure 11.14 Adapter Settings

8. Create an aDSO based on this DataSource (see Figure 11.15). When you create the aDSO, you can use DataSource ZRKCUBS_F as the template to ensure that the aDSO will have all the required fields from the DataSource by default.

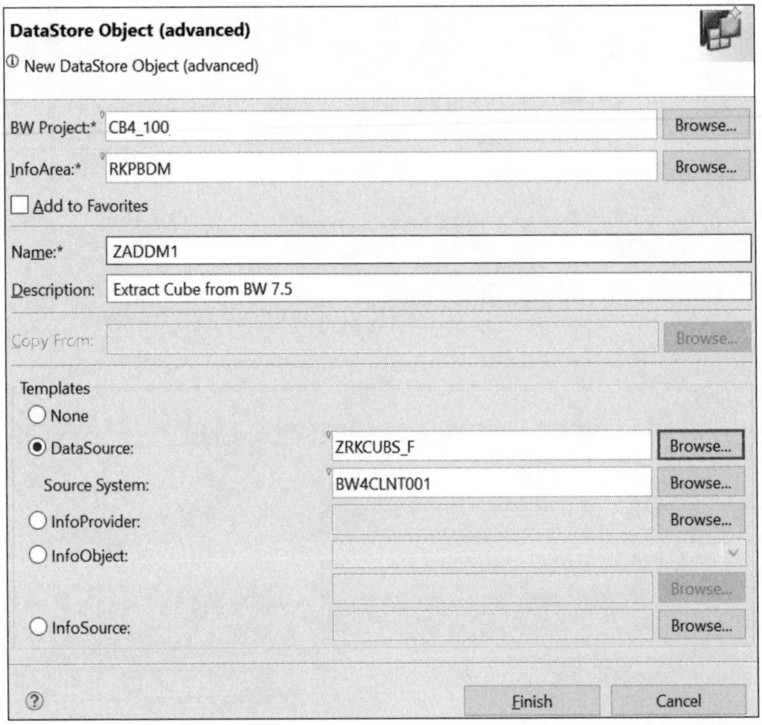

Figure 11.15 aDSO Creation

9. In the aDSO maintenance screen, choose the **Details** tab. Here you can choose the key fields for the aDSO in the **Manage Keys** section (see Figure 11.16). In this example, you'll see that **ZRKENUM** is the key field, and the icon for a primary key is shown.

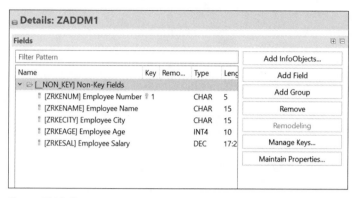

Figure 11.16 Keys

10. Once the aDSO is created, the next step is to create the transformation. You can see the mappings between the DataSource and the aDSO as shown in Figure 11.17. These transformation mappings will be created by default as you created the aDSO based on the DataSource.

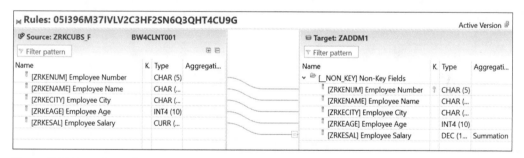

Figure 11.17 Transformation

11. The next step is to create the DTP as shown in Figure 11.18. You can create the DTP by right-clicking the transformation. The source of the DTP will be based on the transformation, which is the DataSource, and the target will be the ZADDM1 aDSO.

12. Execute the DTP using the ▶ ▼ icon and it will open the SAP BW web cockpit. The status of the activation can be seen here as shown in Figure 11.19. The data will be first loaded to the inbound table, where you can see there are 20 records that were extracted.

13. Once you execute the DTP, it will show the **Manage Request** screen. From here, you can view the contents of the inbound table (see Figure 11.20), which has 20 records.

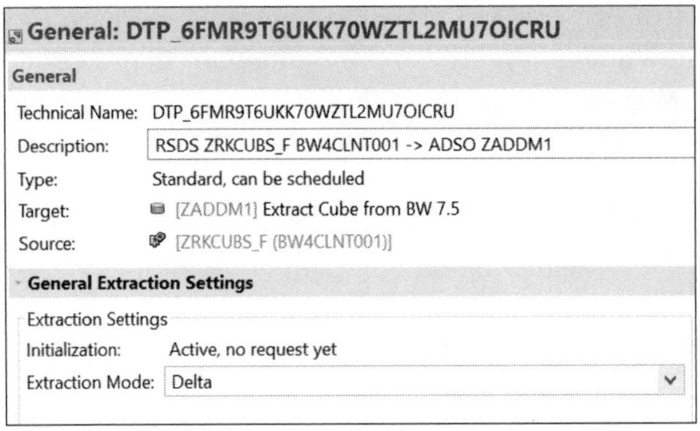

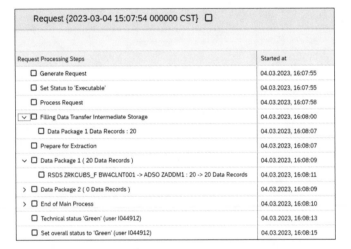

Figure 11.18 DTP Creation

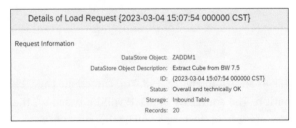

Figure 11.19 DTP Request Status

Figure 11.20 Inbound Table

14. If you click the **Inbound Table** link to the right of the word **Storage**, you'll see an option to display the table contents. Select it and the contents will be as shown in Figure 11.21. You'll see all 20 records that were extracted.

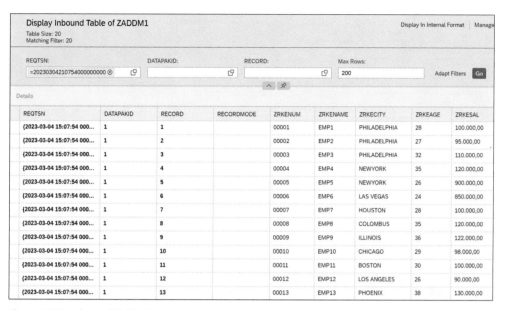

Figure 11.21 Inbound Table Contents

15. If you need to see the status of the aDSO request in a GUI, open Transaction RSMNG (Manage DataStore Object) to view the contents of the aDSO (see Figure 11.22). From Transaction RSMNG, once you see the **Load** column with a green indicator, you can activate the request as shown in Figure 11.22 by clicking the **Activate** button. The result is shown in Figure 11.23.

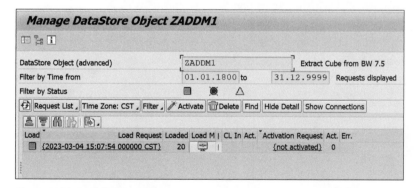

Figure 11.22 Before Activation

16. Now check Transaction RSMNG to view the status of the request, which is visible under **Activation Request** (see Figure 11.24).

Figure 11.23 After Activation

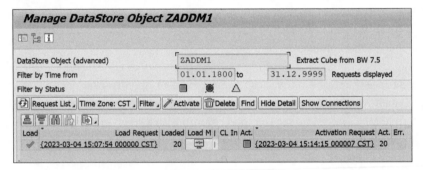

Figure 11.24 Transaction RSMNG: After Activation

17. Check the contents of the active table from Transaction RSMNG using menu path **Utilities • Display Active Data** (see Figure 11.25).

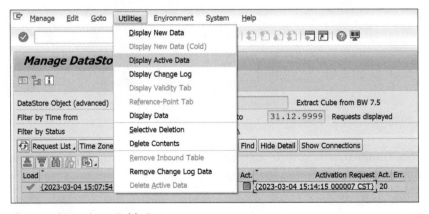

Figure 11.25 Activate Table Data

This opens the contents of the table, as shown in Figure 11.26.

Data Browser: Table /BIC/AZADDM12 Select Entries   20

ZRKENUM	RECORDMODE	ZRKENAME	ZRKECITY	ZRKEAGE	ZRKESAL
00001	N	EMP1	PHILADELPHIA	28	100.000,00
00002	N	EMP2	PHILADELPHIA	27	95.000,00
00003	N	EMP3	PHILADELPHIA	32	110.000,00
00004	N	EMP4	NEWYORK	35	120.000,00
00005	N	EMP5	NEWYORK	26	900.000,00
00006	N	EMP6	LAS VEGAS	24	850.000,00
00007	N	EMP7	HOUSTON	28	100.000,00
00008	N	EMP8	COLOMBUS	35	120.000,00
00009	N	EMP9	ILLINOIS	36	122.000,00
00010	N	EMP10	CHICAGO	29	98.000,00
00011	N	EMP11	BOSTON	30	100.000,00
00012	N	EMP12	LOS ANGELES	26	90.000,00
00013	N	EMP13	PHOENIX	38	130.000,00
00014	N	EMP14	SEATTLE	40	135.000,00
00015	N	EMP15	WASHINGTON DC	32	110.000,00
00016	N	EMP16	DALLAS	27	95.000,00
00017	N	EMP17	SAN FRANSISCO	29	98.000,00
00018	N	EMP18	CALIFORNIA	30	100.000,00
00019	N	EMP19	CALIFORNIA	34	125.000,00
00020	N	EMP20	SAN JOSE	29	98.000,00

Figure 11.26 aDSO Active Table

18. You've now loaded the data to the aDSO from the SAP BW system as a source. Figure 11.27 shows the dataflow that is created.

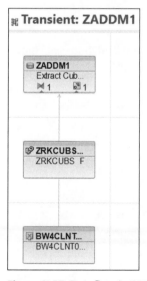

Figure 11.27 Dataflow in SAP BW/4HANA

19. Next, open Transaction ODQMON in the SAP BW system and go to the **Queues** tab (see Figure 11.28).

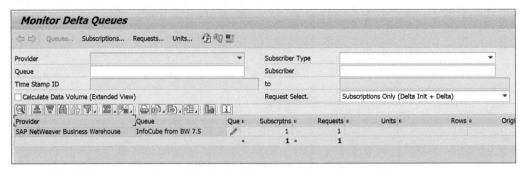

Figure 11.28 Transaction ODQMON

20. Once you double-click **SAP NetWeaver Business Warehouse**, it will take you to the screen shown in Figure 11.29, where you can review the subscriptions.

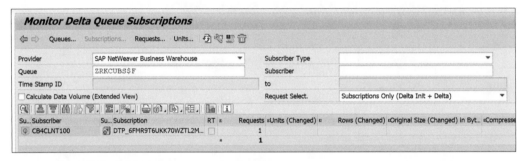

Figure 11.29 Subscriptions

21. You can navigate to the **Requests** tab (see Figure 11.30) or the **Units** tab (see Figure 11.31), where you can see the data loaded during the DTP execution.

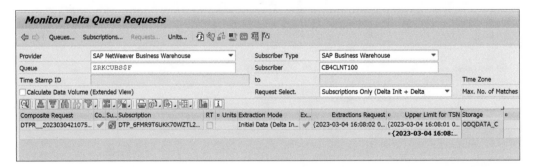

Figure 11.30 Requests Tab

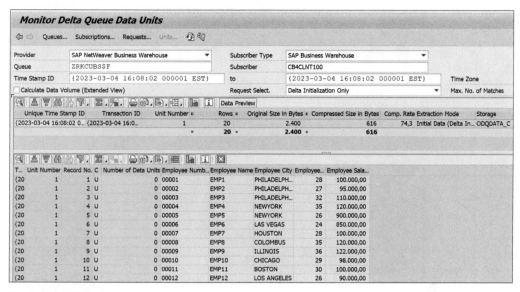

Figure 11.31 Units Tab

11.3.2   Creating an SAP BW/4HANA DataSource Using ODP

The second option to load the data from the SAP BW system is to create an SAP BW/4HANA DataSource using ODP. Follow these steps:

1. Open the SAP BW/4HANA system and navigate to the **Source** system folder, as shown in Figure 11.32. Right-click the logical system from which you need to create the DataSource. Select **New · DataSource**.

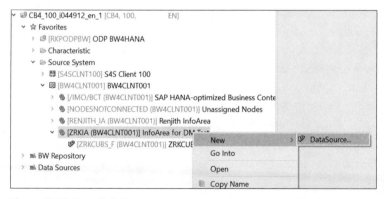

Figure 11.32 New DataSource

2. Create the DataSource as shown in Figure 11.33. Make sure that you see the right **Source System**. In this example, the source system is BW4 CLNT001, which is the SAP BW 7.5 system. Note that the **Source System Type** here is ODP.

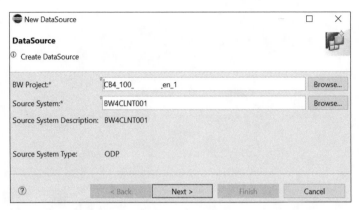

Figure 11.33 DataSource Creation

3. Choose **Next** in the wizard to reach the options shown in Figure 11.34. You can leave these options as-is.

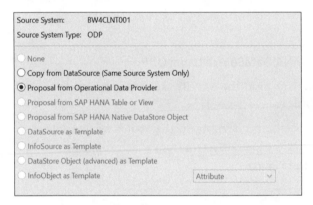

Figure 11.34 Proposal for ODP

4. Continue with the wizard and search for the pattern you require. For our example, we'll search for "ZRKD". You can see multiple search help options that appear as shown in Figure 11.35. Choose the correct DSO that you need to extract data from SAP BW 7.5 to SAP BW/4HANA and choose **Next**.

5. You'll see the confirmation shown in Figure 11.36. The **Name** of the DataSource is listed as **ZRKDSOS**, and you can see the **Description** for the DataSource and the **Data-Source Type** (**Transaction Data**). Choose **Finish** to complete the process.

6. Clicking **Finish** will complete the process and create the new DataSource (see Figure 11.37). You can see that the **ODP Context** is **SAP Netweaver Business Warehouse** and **Operational Data Provider** will show the name of the DSO—here, **ZRKDSOS**.

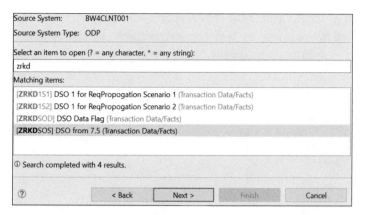

Figure 11.35 Selecting DataSource

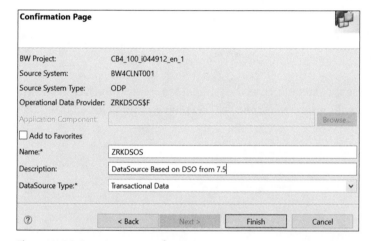

Figure 11.36 DataSource Confirmation

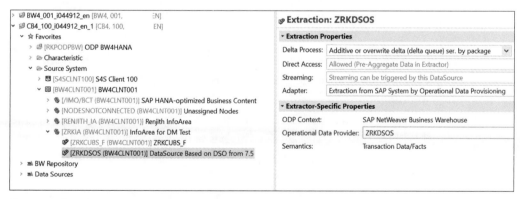

Figure 11.37 SAP BW–Based DataSource

You can see the fields of the DataSource as shown in Figure 11.38. You'll see all the fields that the DSO had in the sender system. For example, you can see the **ZRKE-NUM** field, which can be used as a primary key.

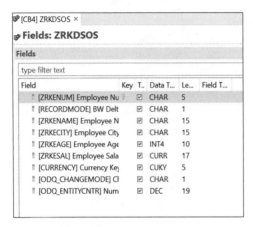

Figure 11.38 Fields

7. The next step is to use the DataSource as the template to create the aDSO, as shown in Figure 11.39. This will ensure that the aDSO will have same fields as the Data-Source.

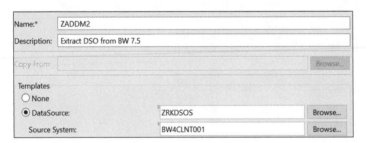

Figure 11.39 aDSO Creation

8. Finalize the key fields using the **Manage Keys** option as shown in Figure 11.40. Here, **Employee Number** will be the primary key, so that field (**ZRKENUM**) will be in the **Key Fields** folder.

9. Once this is completed, you can activate the aDSO using the 🔅 icon and see the contents of the source classical DSO. This has to be done from the source system, where you right-click the classical DSO (**ZRKDSOS**) and choose the **Display Data** option. You'll see the results shown in Figure 11.41.

10. Create the transformation between the DataSource and the aDSO, then create the DTP based on the transformation. Finally, active the request in the aDSO (see Figure 11.42).

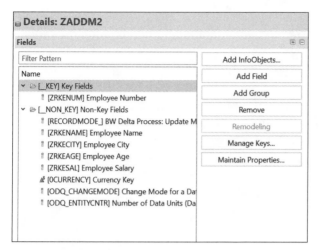

Figure 11.40 aDSO Keys

"ZRKDSOS", List output					
ZRKENUM	ZRKENAME	ZRKEAGE	Employee City	ZRKESAL	Currency
00001	EMP1	28	PHILADELPHIA	100.000,00	USD
00002	EMP2	27	PHILADELPHIA	95.000,00	USD
00003	EMP3	32	PHILADELPHIA	110.000,00	USD
00004	EMP4	35	NEWYORK	120.000,00	USD
00005	EMP5	26	NEWYORK	900.000,00	USD
00006	EMP6	24	LAS VEGAS	850.000,00	USD
00007	EMP7	28	HOUSTON	100.000,00	USD
00008	EMP8	35	COLOMBUS	120.000,00	USD
00009	EMP9	36	ILLINOIS	122.000,00	USD
00010	EMP10	29	CHICAGO	98.000,00	USD
00011	EMP11	30	BOSTON	100.000,00	USD
00012	EMP12	26	LOS ANGELES	90.000,00	USD
00013	EMP13	38	PHOENIX	130.000,00	USD
00014	EMP14	40	SEATLE	135.000,00	USD
00015	EMP15	32	WASHINGTON DC	110.000,00	USD
00016	EMP16	27	DALLAS	95.000,00	USD
00017	EMP17	29	SAN FRANSISCO	98.000,00	USD
00018	EMP18	30	CALIFORNIA	100.000,00	USD
00019	EMP19	34	CALIFORNIA	125.000,00	USD
00020	EMP20	29	SAN JOSE	98.000,00	USD

Figure 11.41 Data

Process	Action	Log	Last Timestamp	Name	Description	Type	Status
{2023-03-04 15:50:51 000021 CST}	☐ Removing	Log	04.03.2023, 16:50:51	ADSO_ZADDM2	Extract DSO from BW 7.5	Remove/Move Requests	Finished
Targets: Inbound Table							
{2023-03-04 15:50:47 000000 CST}	☐ Activating	Log	04.03.2023, 16:50:47	ZADDM2	Extract DSO from BW 7.5	Activate DSO Requests	Finished
Targets: Inbound Table, Active Data Table, Change Log Table							
{2023-03-04 15:50:14 000009 CST}	☐ Loading	Log	04.03.2023, 16:50:14	DTP_6FMR9T6UKK70...	RSDS ZRKDSOS BW4CLNT001 -> ADSO ZADDM2	DTP Load Data	Finished

Figure 11.42 Activate

11. This step will create the activation request as shown in Figure 11.43. This will popu-
    late the active table and change log table of the aDSO.

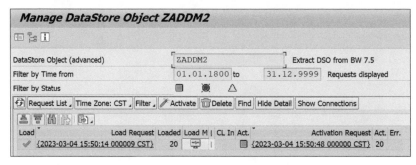

Figure 11.43 Activation Request

12. You can view the contents of the active table for the aDSO. The active table name
    ends with 2 (/BIC/AZADDM22; see Figure 11.44). The data is moved from the inbound
    table to the active table during the activation process.

Data Browser: Table /BIC/AZADDM22 Select Entries   20

ZRKENUM	RECORDMODE	RECORDMODE_	ZRKENAME	ZRKECITY	ZRKEAGE	ZRKESAL	CURRENCY	ODQ_CHANGEMODE	ODQ_ENTITYCNTR
00001	N		EMP1	PHILADELPHIA	28	100.000,00	USD	C	1
00002	N		EMP2	PHILADELPHIA	27	95.000,00	USD	C	1
00003	N		EMP3	PHILADELPHIA	32	110.000,00	USD	C	1
00004	N		EMP4	NEWYORK	35	120.000,00	USD	C	1
00005	N		EMP5	NEWYORK	26	900.000,00	USD	C	1
00006	N		EMP6	LAS VEGAS	24	850.000,00	USD	C	1
00007	N		EMP7	HOUSTON	28	100.000,00	USD	C	1
00008	N		EMP8	COLOMBUS	35	100.000,00	USD	C	1
00009	N		EMP9	ILLINOIS	36	122.000,00	USD	C	1
00010	N		EMP10	CHICAGO	29	98.000,00	USD	C	1
00011	N		EMP11	BOSTON	30	100.000,00	USD	C	1
00012	N		EMP12	LOS ANGELES	26	90.000,00	USD	C	1
00013	N		EMP13	PHOENIX	38	130.000,00	USD	C	1
00014	N		EMP14	SEATLE	40	135.000,00	USD	C	1
00015	N		EMP15	WASHINGTON DC	32	110.000,00	USD	C	1
00016	N		EMP16	DALLAS	27	95.000,00	USD	C	1
00017	N		EMP17	SAN FRANSISCO	29	98.000,00	USD	C	1
00018	N		EMP18	CALIFORNIA	30	100.000,00	USD	C	1
00019	N		EMP19	CALIFORNIA	34	125.000,00	USD	C	1
00020	N		EMP20	SAN JOSE	29	98.000,00	USD	C	1

Figure 11.44 Activate Table Contents

13. Once the request is available, you can check in Transaction ODQMON for the status
    of the data load (see Figure 11.45).

14. You can get into the units view to see the loaded records (see Figure 11.46). As you
    can see, there are 20 rows that were loaded. Clicking on that row will show the
    details of the 20 records.

15. In Transaction ODQMON, you'll now see two queues for SAP BW/4HANA, as shown
    in Figure 11.47.

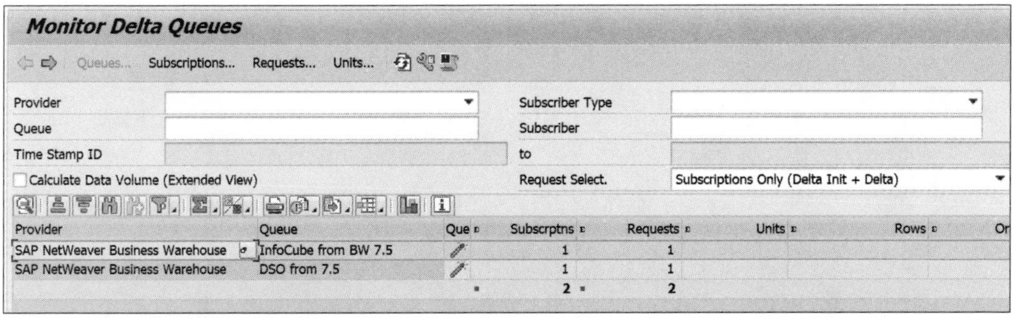

Figure 11.45 Transaction ODQMON

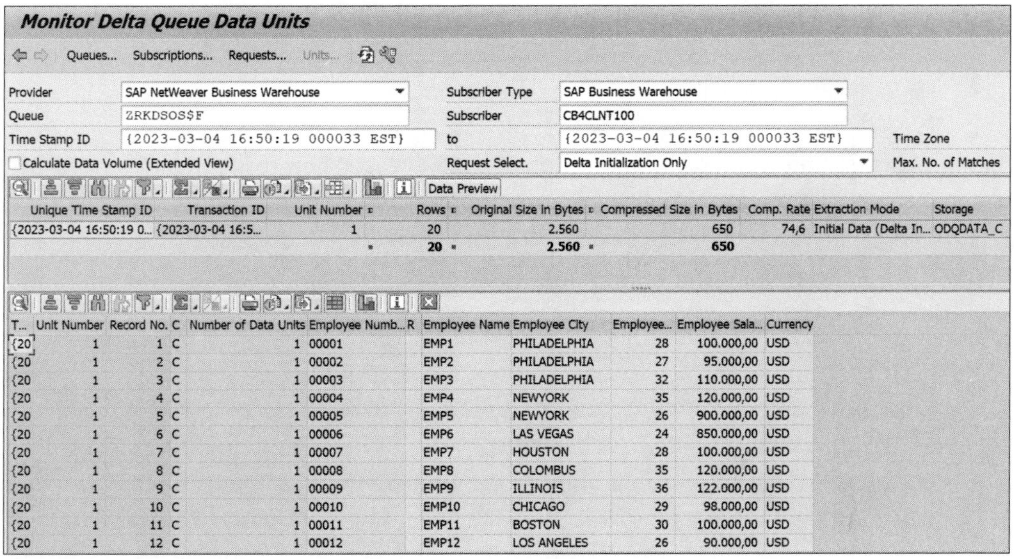

Figure 11.46 Units View

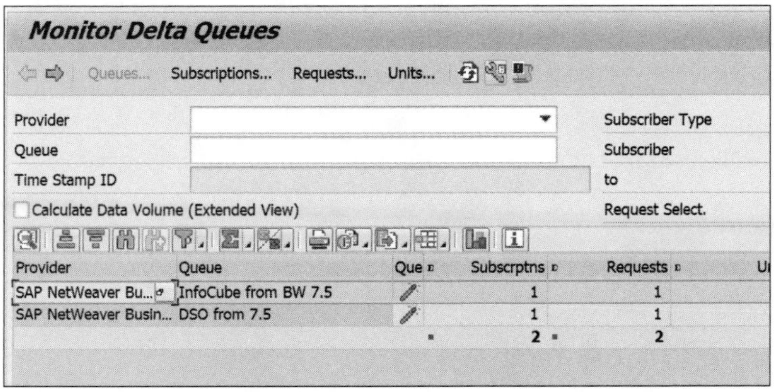

Figure 11.47 Two Queues

16. To see the technical names of the queues, you can use the wrench icon highlighted in Figure 11.48. Use the same icon to toggle between the technical names and descriptions.

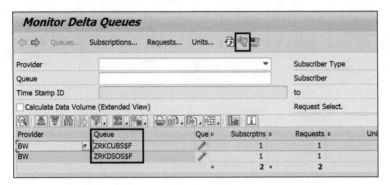

Figure 11.48 Technical Name

With the completion of this extraction flow, you've seen how to load data from SAP BW 7.x to SAP BW/4HANA. You'll need to use this process when you have to connect an SAP BW system to SAP BW/4HANA and fetch data from the SAP BW system.

11.4   Summary

With the completion of this dataflow, you're ready to build SAP BW/4HANA models by extracting data from classical SAP BW 7.x systems. Knowing about this process will be useful in SAP BW/4HANA migration projects, where there will be requirements to get data from InfoCubes and classical DSOs into SAP BW/4HANA aDSOs. You learned about multiple methods to bring in data from SAP BW 7.x systems. Knowing about a mix of classical and new extractors will help you design more efficient data models during SAP BW/4HANA implementation.

In the next chapter, we'll focus on extracting data from SAP S/4HANA systems with the help of core data services (CDS) views into SAP BW/4HANA.

Chapter 12

Extracting Data Using CDS Views

This chapter describes virtual data provisioning options from SAP HANA to SAP BW/4HANA. Effective data modeling can be achieved using the virtualization options for data extraction. These data provisioning methods will help you define and architect an analytics strategy for your complex landscape during SAP BW/4HANA implementation.

In this chapter, we'll start with an overview of the ABAP Dictionary in Section 12.1and then present an introduction to core data services (CDS) views in Section 12.2. We'll use multiple examples to create basic CDS views in Section 12.3, focusing on creating a view with joins and associations in Section 12.3.4. The most import part of the chapter explains how to consume the CDS views that have been created in SAP BW/4HANA. The consumption of CDS views is discussed in Section 12.4, where you'll learn about the end-to-end process of data provisioning from SAP S/4HANA to SAP BW/4HANA using CDS views. Section 1.5 will help you learn how to search for SAP-delivered CDS views for standard functional areas.

12.1   Understanding ABAP Dictionary

In the SAP system, data is distributed across multiple tables at the database level. When there's a reporting requirement for application-based data that resides in a database table, you need to create an ABAP report that executes in the frontend or on the application server. The selections are passed to the database layer, and the tables are joined using a join condition. Finally the results are sent to the application layer. In traditional programming styles, developers try to limit the number of hits to the database by transferring the maximum amount of data as much as possible to the application server. Operations then are done on those data using the internal tables to provide the desired results. The reason for this logic is that most traditional databases aren't capable of processing a large volume of data in real time, so fetching too much data from the database will be time-consuming. More time is spent on the data transfer and connectivity between the application server and the database server. This was a major challenge in traditional ABAP programming.

In any SAP system, Transaction SE11 is the ABAP Dictionary, which allows the creation of tables or database views. ABAP Dictionary views fetch the predefined data from the actual database. These dictionary views use SQL statements to get the data from the database for the application requirements. When you activate an ABAP Dictionary view, the SQL view is generated in the background. An ABAP report uses these ABAP Dictionary views to get the required data, which will use SQL in the database. You can think of these ABAP Dictionary views as intermediaries between ABAP and the database.

Let's look at the differences between the two ABAP program approaches, data-to-code and code-to-data:

- **Data-to-code**
  The traditional ABAP program approach involved bringing data from the database to the presentation server using the SQL generated by the view, and then doing data-intensive calculation and filtering, before presenting the filtered data to the user. This approach is called *data-to-code*. In ABAP programming, two kinds of SQL are used:
  - *Open SQL* permits you to access the database table which is declared among the ABAP Dictionary. It doesn't care what type of database underlies the system.
  - *Native SQL* will permit you to use database-specific SQL statements within an ABAP program, which implies that the statements will be dependent on the database and need to be supported by the database. In this method, you can use tables that aren't administered by the ABAP Dictionary. When you write an ABAP report, you write all native SQL statements with the EXEC and ENDEXEC SQL statements, which will be executed directly at the database level to optimize performance.

- **Code-to-data**
  SAP currently uses SAP HANA as its native database, which stores the data in columnar format. As you are aware, SAP HANA is more than a database, with additional benefits such as in-memory computing capabilities. The recommended approach is to push down the expensive or data-intensive mathematical calculations to the database layer. This in-memory capability helps to avoid unnecessary movement of huge volumes of data from the database to the presentation server, doing the data-intensive calculations within the database itself. Once the data-intensive calculation is completed in the SAP HANA database itself, the results are transferred to the ABAP program. This helps reports get more real-time data (see Figure 12.1).

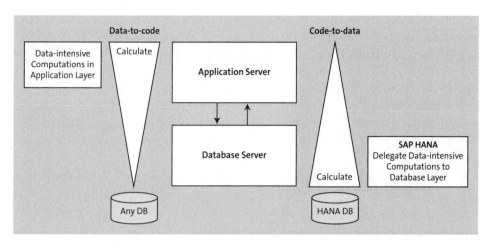

Figure 12.1 Code-to-Data and Data-to-Code

12.2 CDS Introduction

As you know, the code-to-data approach reduces system bottlenecks, and code push-down increases calculation speeds and drastically reduces the data movement from one layer to another. CDS views are more than Transaction SE11 views. CDS views are considered a collection of domain-specific languages (DSLs) and services for defining and consuming semantically rich data models. A CDS view is consumed in the ways shown in Figure 12.2. The data from the physical tables can be consumed by the CDS models, which will create a SQL view. You can use an ABAP report to consume the CDS views and create the reporting logic on top of it. CDS views can be used by OData services to be sent to the frontend and other applications, or they can be consumed by SAP S/4HANA. The SQL views generated by the CDS views can be consumed by SAP BW/4HANA as DataSources and further used by SAP Datasphere or SAP Analytics Cloud.

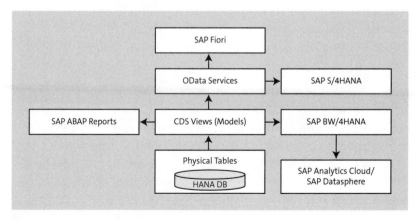

Figure 12.2 CDS Consumption

As you've seen, CDS views are defined as shown in Figure 12.3. The CDS is written in the application server in the ABAP perspective, and once it's activated, there's an equivalent database view in the SAP HANA database layer.

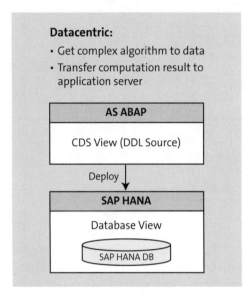

Figure 12.3 Deployment of CDS Views

The following list presents an overview of the basic details of CDS:

- CDS views have semantically rich data models that include DSLs such as data definition language (DDL), query language (QL), and data manipulation language (DML).
- CDS is completely based on SQL, which supports standard functionalities like joins, unions, and other built-in functions.
- CDS views create the database views in the SAP HANA layer.
- CDS has a common basis for domain-specific frameworks like business analytics, OData, and so on.
- CDS supports associations that capture relations between entities in data model path expression.
- ABAP CDS views can be extended.

When you see any CDS view, the first thing you'll notice is an *annotation*, which begins with @. CDS annotations are enablers that let you add SAP ABAP and component-specific data to the source code of any CDS entity. You already know that CDS views are created with Open SQL, and they're further enriched with these kinds of annotations. This helps to enrich the data model too. SAP CDS views are evaluated by SAP frameworks and can be either ABAP annotations or framework-specific annotations. When you create any CDS view, you'll see very important ABAP annotations in it such as @AbapCatalog, @AccessControl, and @EndUserText annotations.

The mandatory annotation for any CDS view is @AbapCatalog.sqlViewName. This will create a Transaction SE11 view for the corresponding CDS views, which helps in transporting the object. In the **Define View** section, you can provide the view name, such as the source of the data. The core annotations are checked by the ABAP Dictionary during activation and saved into the core metadata.

The next category is framework annotations, and these annotations are evaluated during runtime by specific frameworks such as analytics, enterprise search, UI, and so on. These annotations include the following:

- Analytics annotations
- Analytics details annotations
- Consumption annotation
- Default aggregation annotation
- Hierarchy annotations
- OData annotations
- Virtual data model (VDM) annotations

For SAP BW extraction scenarios, we'll use the analytics annotations that will be used by the analytics manager for multidimensional data consumption, performing data aggregation, and slicing and dicing data. SAP BusinessObjects BI frontends like SAP Design Studio and SAP Analysis for Microsoft Office can consume the data via the Analytics Manager. Let's discuss this more after a basic overview of the CDS views.

12.3   Create Basic CDS Views

To create a CDS view, you first need a package to contain all your views. We'll start with that before moving through the rest of the process. Before you begin, make sure that you are in the ABAP perspective in Eclipse.

12.3.1   Create Package

To create the package, log onto the relevant system and choose the ABAP Perspective option ![icon] from the SAP BW modeling tools. From the context menu of the system ID with the ABAP Project name, choose **New • ABAP Package**, as shown in Figure 12.4.

Provide the package name, such as "ZRKPCDS", and a description, and click **Next** to continue in the wizard as shown in Figure 12.5.

The wizard will prompt you for the component information. As shown in Figure 12.6, select **HOME** for **Software Component** using the **Browse** option and continue with the wizard.

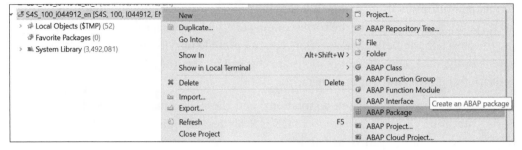

Figure 12.4 Create Package

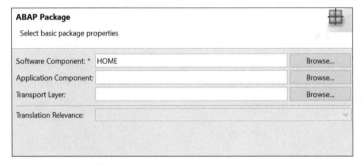

Figure 12.5 View Name

ABAP Package

Select basic package properties

Software Component: * HOME	Browse...
Application Component:	Browse...
Transport Layer:	Browse...
Translation Relevance:	

Figure 12.6 Component for View

You will see a prompt that will ask for the transport request number. Provide it and choose **Finish**. You'll see an option to activate the package, as shown in Figure 12.7.

Right-click the package (in this example, **ZRKPCDS**) and choose the **Activate** option. Once the package is activated, you can see the package name with the ⊞ icon. Next, you'll move this package to your favorites from the context menu of the CDS view. We will use this package to create the CDS views.

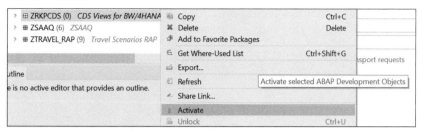

Figure 12.7 Activate View

12.3.2   Create CDS View with Data Definition

To create the CDS views, right-click the package you have created and choose **New · Other ABAP Repository Object**, as shown in Figure 12.8.

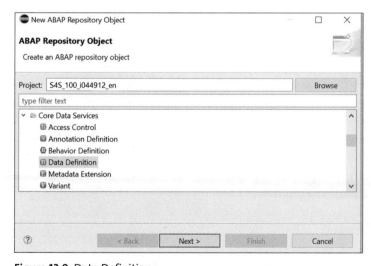

Figure 12.8 Other ABAP Repository Object Option

Once you select this, you can see the wizard. Choose the **Core Data Services** folder and select the **Data Definition** option, as shown in Figure 12.9.

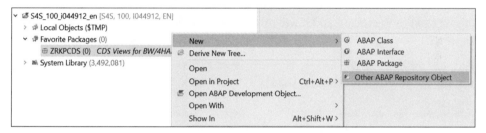

Figure 12.9 Data Definition

Continue in the wizard to see the screen shown in Figure 12.10. Provide the CDS view name—in this example, enter "ZRKCDS1".

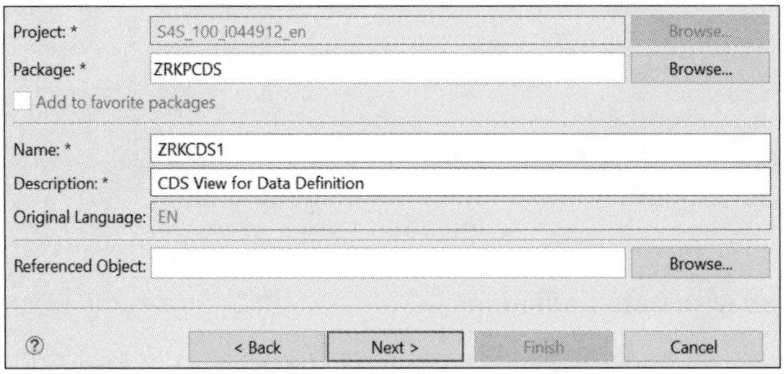

Figure 12.10 CDS View Name

Choose **Next** in the wizard and it will prompt you for a transport request, as shown in Figure 12.11.

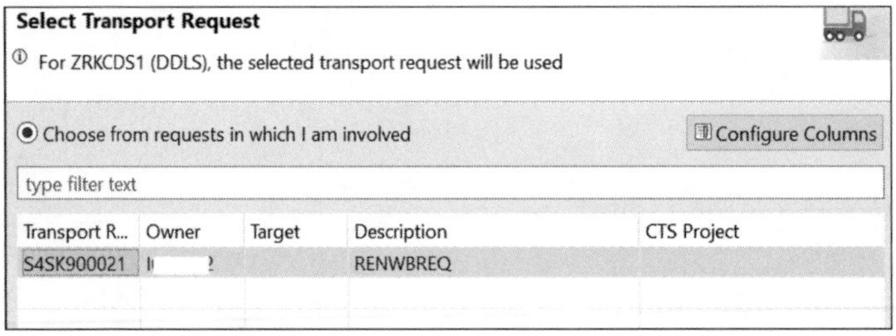

Figure 12.11 Transport Request

Choose **Finish** in the wizard and you'll see a screen with the CDS code, as shown in Figure 12.12.

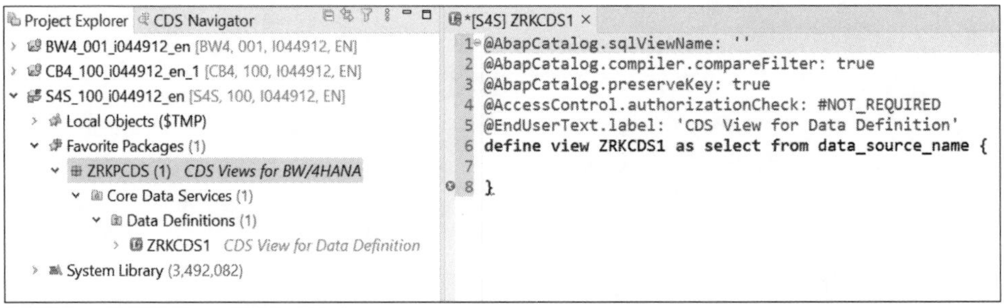

Figure 12.12 Initial View Screen

As you can see, the view is not completed, and it isn't yet active. Focus on this section in the CDS view editor:

```
@AbapCatalog.sqlViewName: ''
```

You'll see that this annotation has a blank value (' '). As a mandatory step, you have to provide the SQL view name within the quotes. This will be your SQL view name that you can see in Transaction SE11 once the view is activated. In the CDS view editor, you can see the following annotations available by default, which you can leave as is:

```
@AbapCatalog.compiler.compareFilter: true
@AbapCatalog.preserveKey: true
@AccessControl.authorizationCheck: #NOT_REQUIRED
@EndUserText.label: 'CDS View for Data Definition'
```

Now to write the logic of the CDS view, you need to write the code within the **Define View** section:

```
define view ZRKCDS1 as select from data_source_name {

}
```

This define view portion of the CDS view needs to be modified or added to in order to define a CDS view based on your requirements. We'll fetch a few fields from table VBAK here, as shown in Figure 12.13.

Dictionary: Display Table

Technical Settings   Append Structure...

Transparent Table	VBAK		Active			
Short Description	Sales Document: Header Data					

Attributes | Delivery and Maintenance | Fields | Input Help/Check | Currency/Quantity Fields | Indexes

Search   Built-In Type   1 / 228

Field	Key	Initi...	Data element	Data Type	Length	Decimal...	Coordinate	Short Description
MANDT	✓	✓	MANDT	CLNT	3	0	0	Client
VBELN	✓	✓	VBELN_VA	CHAR	10	0	0	Sales Document
ERDAT	☐	☐	ERDAT	DATS	8	0	0	Date on which the record was created
ERZET	☐	☐	ERZET	TIMS	6	0	0	Entry time
ERNAM	☐	☐	ERNAM	CHAR	12	0	0	Name of Person who Created the Object
ANGDT	☐	☐	ANGDT_V	DATS	8	0	0	Quotation/Inquiry is Valid From
BNDDT	☐	☐	BNDDT	DATS	8	0	0	Date Until Which Bid/Quotation is Binding (Valid-To Date)
AUDAT	☐	☐	AUDAT	DATS	8	0	0	Document Date (Date Received/Sent)
VBTYP	☐	☐	VBTYPL	CHAR	4	0	0	SD Document Category

Figure 12.13 Base Table for View

Now you'll create a CDS view that uses the VBELN, ERDAT, ERNAM, VBTYP, and NETWR fields. In the define view line, replace data_source_name with the table name that you will use to fetch the data . and modify the code with the view name as "ZRKCDS1". Enter the table name as "VBAK". This means we will fetch the data from the table VBAK. Then, after the first brace {, provide the table name and field name followed by a comma. Finally, leave the last table name and field name without a comma, then add the closing brace }. You can see this CDS code in Figure 12.14.

```
[S4S] ZRKCDS1 ×
 1⊖@AbapCatalog.sqlViewName: 'ZCDSVBAK'
 2 @AbapCatalog.compiler.compareFilter: true
 3 @AbapCatalog.preserveKey: true
 4 @AccessControl.authorizationCheck: #NOT_REQUIRED
 5 @EndUserText.label: 'CDS View for Data Definition'
 6
 7 define view ZRKCDS1 as select from vbak {
 8     vbak.vbeln,
 9     vbak.erdat,
10     vbak.ernam,
11     vbak.vbtyp,
12     vbak.netwr
13 }
14
```

Figure 12.14 Final CDS View Code

Examine the details shown in Figure 12.15:

❶ These are the standard annotations.

❷ This is the SQL view name. You must provide this for all CDS views that you create. This view will be created once the CDS view is activated. You can check the SQL view in Transaction SE11.

❸ This name, ZRKCDS1, is taken from the CDS name that you created.

❹ You need to provide the table name for the view source; in this example, use table VBAK.

❺ These are the view fields based on the table defined.

❻ Check and activate the view here.

❼ The final activated view is displayed here under your package.

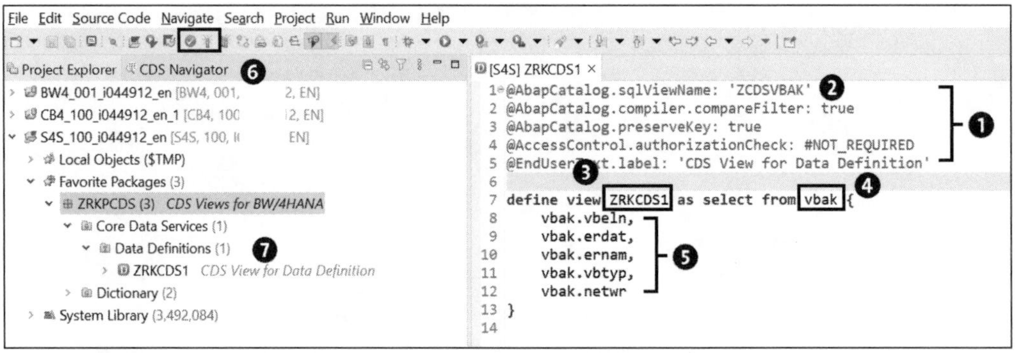

Figure 12.15 Interpretation of Basic CDS View

Once the view is activated, you can do a data preview as shown in Figure 12.16. The results are shown in Figure 12.17.

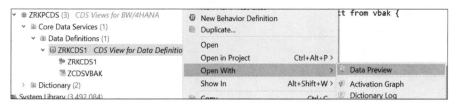

Figure 12.16 Data Preview

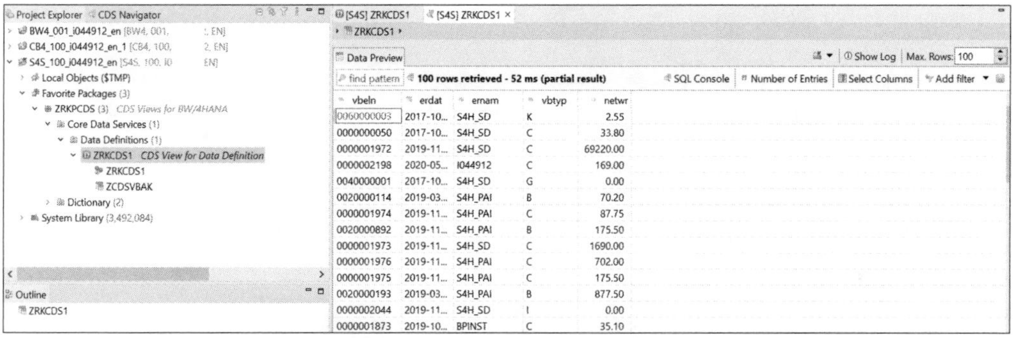

Figure 12.17 Data Preview Results

You can see that all the fields provided in the view are displayed, as shown in Figure 12.18. Note that **Max. Rows** is restricted to 100, which you can increase. There's also an option to filter when you have a large dataset like this.

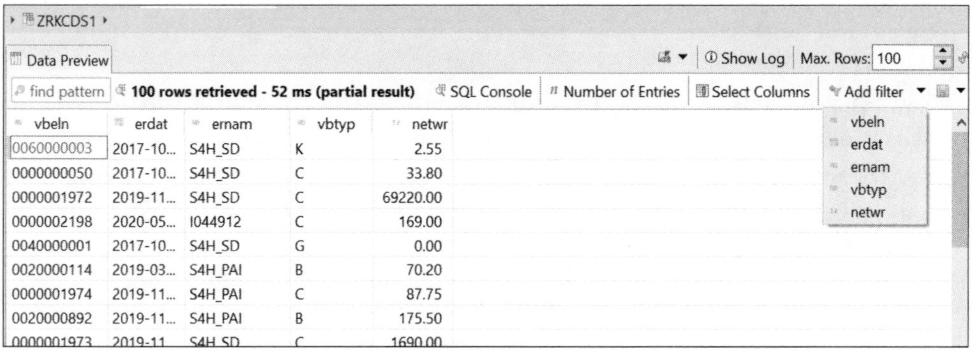

Figure 12.18 Add Filter on Dataset

When you click the **Number of Entries** button, you can see the results shown in Figure 12.19.

Open Transaction SE16 and select table VBAK. Select **Number of Entries** to get the total records of the table. You can see the table VBAK details, as shown in Figure 12.20.

479

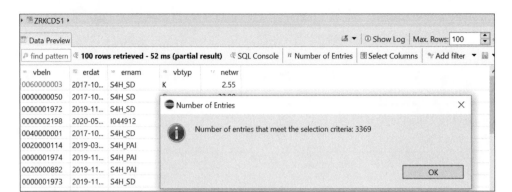

Figure 12.19 Total Count of Entries in Backend Table

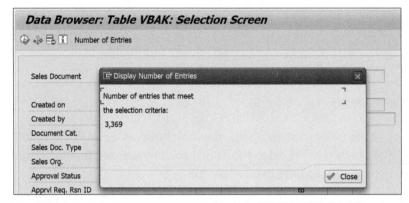

Figure 12.20 Total Count

You can also choose to display the results of only specific columns. To do that, choose **Select Columns** and to see the list of all fieds available. Uncheck the columns you don't want to see, for example **VBTYP** and **NETWR**, and you can see that the results will have only three fields (see Figure 12.21).

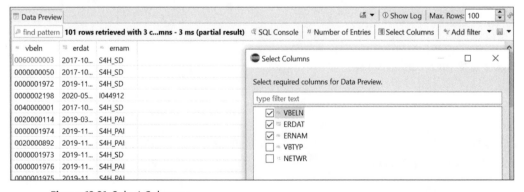

Figure 12.21 Select Columns

You have now created a view based on this statement, which has the sqlViewName as 'ZCDSVBAK':

```
@AbapCatalog.sqlViewName: 'ZCDSVBAK'
```

You can check for this view name in Transaction SE11, as shown in Figure 12.22. Choose the **View** radio button, enter "ZCDSVBAK" in the **View** field, and click **Display**.

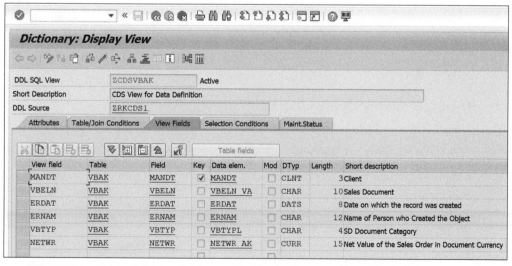

ABAP Dictionary: Initial Screen

- ○ Database table
- ⦿ View   ZCDSVBAK
- ○ Data type
- ○ Type Group
- ○ Domain
- ○ Search help
- ○ Lock object

Display   Change   Create

Figure 12.22 Display View

You'll see the generated view, as shown in Figure 12.23.

Dictionary: Display View

DDL SQL View	ZCDSVBAK	Active
Short Description	CDS View for Data Definition	
DDL Source	ZRKCDS1.	

Attributes | Table/Join Conditions | View Fields | Selection Conditions | Maint.Status

Table fields

View field	Table	Field	Key	Data elem.	Mod	DTyp	Length	Short description
MANDT	VBAK	MANDT	☑	MANDT	☐	CLNT	3	Client
VBELN	VBAK	VBELN	☐	VBELN_VA	☐	CHAR	10	Sales Document
ERDAT	VBAK	ERDAT	☐	ERDAT	☐	DATS	8	Date on which the record was created
ERNAM	VBAK	ERNAM	☐	ERNAM	☐	CHAR	12	Name of Person who Created the Object
VBTYP	VBAK	VBTYP	☐	VBTYPL	☐	CHAR	4	SD Document Category
NETWR	VBAK	NETWR	☐	NETWR_AK	☐	CURR	15	Net Value of the Sales Order in Document Currency

Figure 12.23 SQL View Definition

You can choose to display the contents of the view by selecting the display table contents using the ▦ icon. The results will be displayed as shown in Figure 12.24.

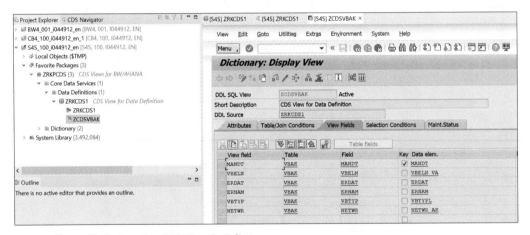

Figure 12.24 Contents Restricted to 200

In the ABAP development tools, from the CDS view data definition, if you choose the **Table** icon on the left ⊞, you can see the GUI screen shown in Figure 12.25 on the right side.

Figure 12.25 Opening SQL View in Eclipse

12.3.3   Using Joins in CDS Views

Like any standard SQL programming, you can use multiple join types in CDS views: inner joins, left outer joins, and right outer joins.

Let's join the sales header (VBAK) and sales item (VBAP) tables to get some fields. The join is carried out using the sales document number, VBELN. We'll use an inner join here so that only similar fields will be selected for the output, as shown in Figure 12.26. Create the view name, and the view will look as shown in Figure 12.27. You need to write the join conditions and fetch a few fields from table VBAP, such as VBELN, as shown in Figure 12.28.

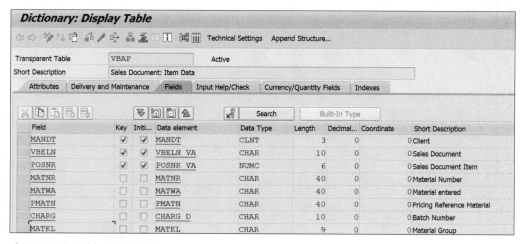

Figure 12.26 Table VBAP Fields

```
1 @AbapCatalog.sqlViewName: 'ZCDSJOIN1'
2 @AbapCatalog.compiler.compareFilter: true
3 @AbapCatalog.preserveKey: true
4 @AccessControl.authorizationCheck: #NOT_REQUIRED
5 @EndUserText.label: 'CDS View for Join'
6 define view ZRKCDS2 as select from data_source_name {
7
8 }
```

Figure 12.27 Base View

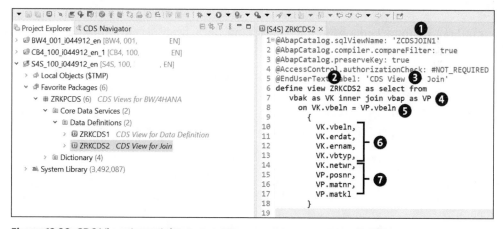

Figure 12.28 CDS View: Inner Join

In Figure 12.28, you can see the following:

❶ The SQL view name.

❷ The name of the CDS view that you created.

❸ The select statement.

❹ The select from table VBAP, referred to as VK, and the inner join table VBAP, referred to as VK.

❺ The condition for the select where VBAK-VBELN = VBAP-VBELN; replaced by aliases of both tables defined in an earlier statement.

❻ The first five fields are retrieved from table VBAK and hence you see VK in in front of the field names.

❼ The last three fields are retrieved from table VBAK and you refer to that with VP in in front of the field names.

When you do a data preview, you can see the result in Figure 12.29.

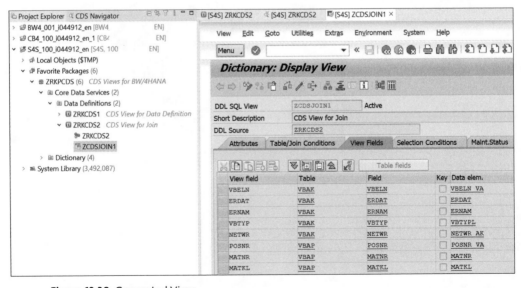

Figure 12.29 CDS Join: Data Preview

You can see the generated view in the backend. It will be displayed as **DDL SQL View**, as shown in Figure 12.30.

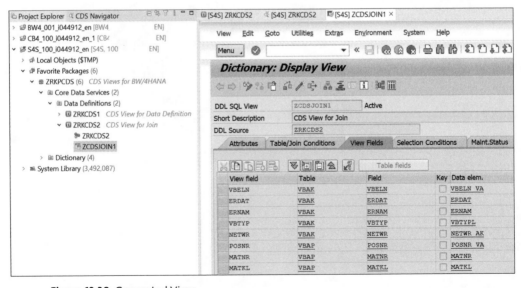

Figure 12.30 Generated View

You can create the left outer join just by changing the code as shown in Figure 12.31, replacing the inner join with the left outer join.

```
[S4S] ZRKCDS3 ×
 1 @AbapCatalog.sqlViewName: 'ZCDSJOIN3'
 2 @AbapCatalog.compiler.compareFilter: true
 3 @AbapCatalog.preserveKey: true
 4 @AccessControl.authorizationCheck: #NOT_REQUIRED
 5 @EndUserText.label: 'CDS View for Join'
 6 define view ZRKCDS3 as select from
 7    vbak left outer join vbap
 8      on vbak.vbeln = vbap.vbeln
 9        {
10            vbak.vbeln,
11            vbak.erdat,
12            vbak.ernam,
13            vbak.vbtyp,
14            vbak.netwr,
15            vbap.posnr,
16            vbap.matnr,
17            vbap.matkl
18        }
19
```

Figure 12.31 Left Outer Join

A data preview of the CDS view is shown in Figure 12.32.

vbeln	erdat	ernam	vbtyp	netwr	posnr	matnr	matkl
0060000003	2017-10-24	S4H_SD	K	2.55	000010	TG11	L001
0060000003	2017-10-24	S4H_SD	K	2.55	000020	TG11	L001
0000000050	2017-10-17	S4H_SD	C	33.80	000020	TG13	L001
0000000050	2017-10-17	S4H_SD	C	33.80	000010	TG13	L001
0000001972	2019-11-01	S4H_SD	C	69220.00	000010	F-10A	L004
0000001972	2019-11-01	S4H_SD	C	69220.00	000020	S-201	L003
0000002198	2020-05-27	I044912	C	169.00	000010	TG10	L001
0040000001	2017-10-16	S4H_SD	G	0.00	000010	TG12	L001
0020000114	2019-03-20	S4H_PAI	B	70.20	000010	TG11	L001
0000001974	2019-11-01	S4H_PAI	C	87.75	000010	TG12	L001
0020000892	2019-11-01	S4H_PAI	B	175.50	000010	TG12	L001

Figure 12.32 Left Outer Join Result

12.3.4   CDS Views with Associations

With association, you define a join on demand. This means the association will be executed only when the fields from the associated entity are referred to. You can consider CDS joins left outer joins. When you create a CDS view with a default template for the association, you can see this as shown in Figure 12.33. Write the code as shown in Figure 12.34.

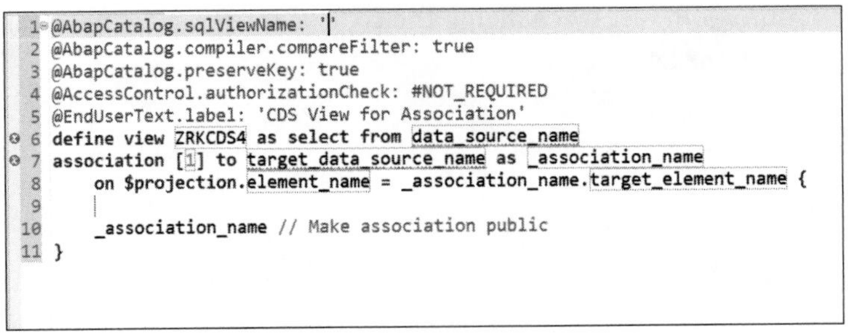

```
1° @AbapCatalog.sqlViewName: 'I'
2  @AbapCatalog.compiler.compareFilter: true
3  @AbapCatalog.preserveKey: true
4  @AccessControl.authorizationCheck: #NOT_REQUIRED
5  @EndUserText.label: 'CDS View for Association'
6  define view ZRKCDS4 as select from data_source_name
7  association [1] to target_data_source_name as _association_name
8      on $projection.element_name = _association_name.target_element_name {
9      |
10     _association_name // Make association public
11 }
```

Figure 12.33 Association Syntax

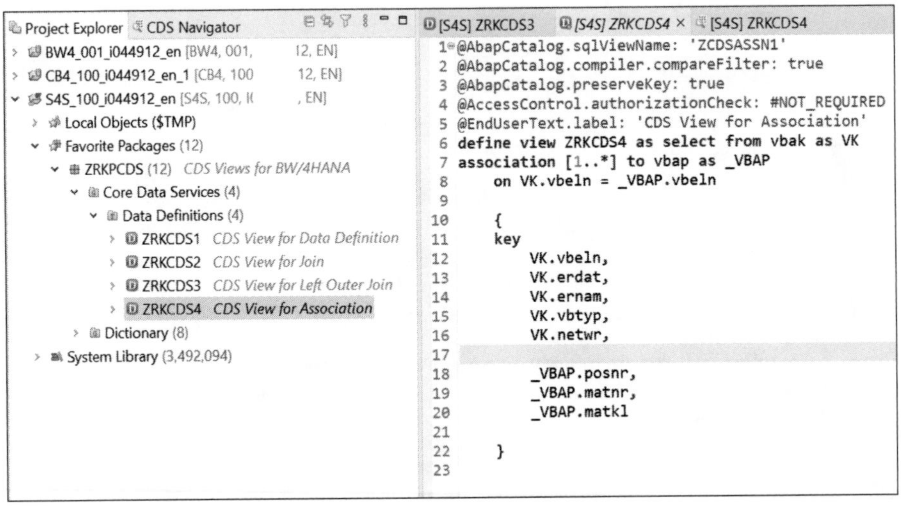

Figure 12.34 Association Code

The data preview of the CDS view is shown in Figure 12.35.

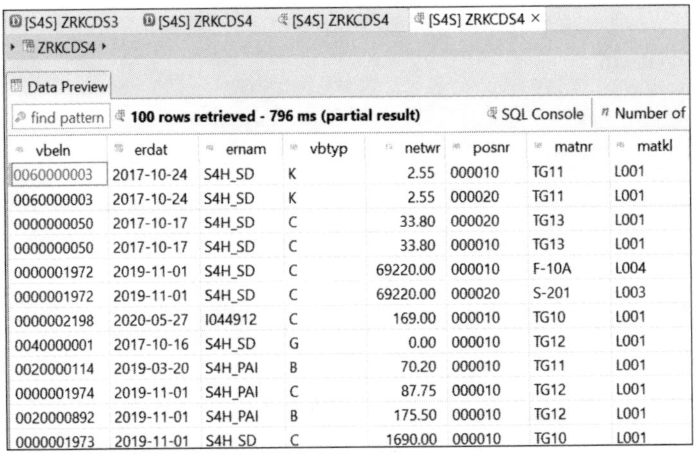

Figure 12.35 Data Preview for Association

12.4   Consume CDS Views in SAP BW/4HANA

In this chapter, you will learn how to consume the CDS views that were created earlier into SAP BW/4HANA. You will learn the CDS to BW extraction architecture and see how to create a DataSource based on CDS views. You will also learn to create CDS views with delta capability and test a CDS-based SAP BW/4HANA extraction for delta extraction.

With a solid understanding of creating CDS views established, it's time to show you how to consume CDS views in SAP BW in this section.

12.4.1   SAP BW CDS Extraction Architecture

The architecture of the SAP BW CDS extraction is shown in Figure 12.36. We have SAP S/4HANA as the source system and SAP BW/4HANA as the target system. There can be multiple tables in an SAP S/4HANA system, and we can create CDS views to consume the data from these tables using certain select statements or join conditions. The CDS view will create an internal SQL view in the database. The execution of a CDS view will trigger the internal view that will fetch the data from the table.

When you need to extract the data to SAP BW/4HANA, you'll add annotations related to the analytics in the CDS view. You need to make sure that there is a remote function call (RFC) connection and ODP_CDS source system connectivity in the SAP BW/4HANA system. The replication of CDS views will bring the view name provided in the @ABAP-Catalog.sqlviewname. It will be created as the DataSource in SAP BW/4HANA. You can create the aDSO based on this DataSource. When you execute the DTP for the ADSO, it will fetch the data from SAP S/4HANA using the code based on the CDS views. The data extraction can be seen in Transaction ODQMON, where the subscriber type is CDS. The extraction happens with the RFC, which is used to connect the sender and receiver.

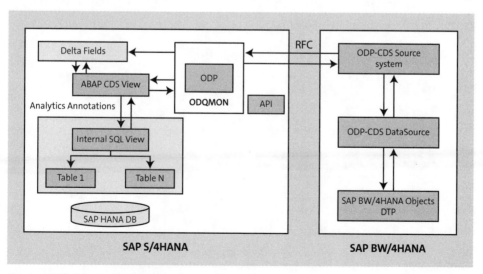

Figure 12.36 SAP BW CDS Extraction Flow

With this, you can create a CDS view in SAP S/4HANA and consume it in SAP BW/4HANA.

12.4.2 CDS Views Creation in SAP S/4HANA

Let's create a CDS view in SAP S/4HANA using the code shown in Figure 12.37.

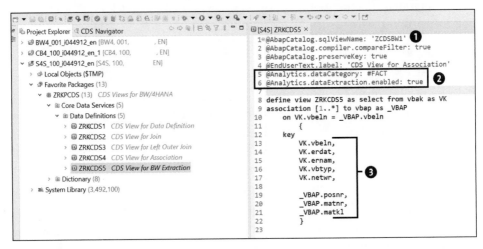

Figure 12.37 CDS Views

Here let's just modify the annotations in the old code from Figure 12.34, as shown in Figure 12.37. The key things to note here are as follows:

❶ Name of the SQL view

❷ The annotation for analytics (dataCategory #FACT means transaction data; data. Extraction.enabled: True will enable this CDS view for SAP BW extraction)

❸ The old code without any modification

You can see the data preview as shown in Figure 12.38.

vbeln	erdat	ernam	vbtyp	netwr	posnr	matnr	matkl
0060000003	2017-10-24	S4H_SD	K	2.55	000010	TG11	L001
0060000003	2017-10-24	S4H_SD	K	2.55	000020	TG11	L001
0000000050	2017-10-17	S4H_SD	C	33.80	000020	TG13	L001
0000000050	2017-10-17	S4H_SD	C	33.80	000010	TG13	L001
0000001972	2019-11-01	S4H_SD	C	69220.00	000010	F-10A	L004
0000001972	2019-11-01	S4H_SD	C	69220.00	000020	S-201	L003
0000002198	2020-05-27	I044912	C	169.00	000010	TG10	L001
0040000001	2017-10-16	S4H_SD	G	0.00	000010	TG12	L001
0020000114	2019-03-20	S4H_PAI	B	70.20	000010	TG11	L001
0000001974	2019-11-01	S4H_PAI	C	87.75	000010	TG12	L001
0020000892	2019-11-01	S4H_PAI	B	175.50	000010	TG12	L001

Figure 12.38 Data Preview

12.4.3 Creating CDS Views Based on DataSources in SAP BW/4HANA

The following sections will outline two options in SAP BW/4HANA to create CDS views: DataSource-based views and replicating CDS views into a DataSource.

Option 1: Create a DataSource Based on a CDS View

Sentence needed to lead into this list:

1. Create a CDS source system (see Figure 12.39), by right-clicking the source system folder in SAP BW/4HANA and choosing **New · Source system** (see Chapter 2, Section 2.2.5 for the details of creating an ODP_CDS source system).

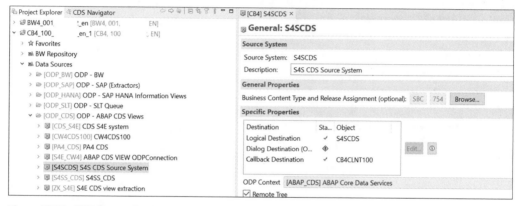

Figure 12.39 CDS Source System

2. Once the ODP_CDS source system is created, right-click the CDS source system and choose **New · DataSource**, as shown in Figure 12.40.

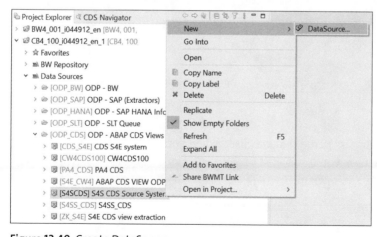

Figure 12.40 Create DataSource

3. Now choose the **Next** option in the wizard as shown in Figure 12.41. It will take you to the template selection.

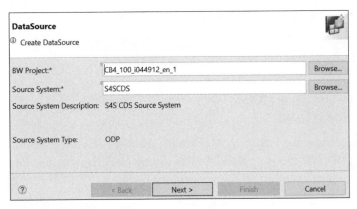

Figure 12.41 Choose Next

4. On the **Select Template or Source Object** screen, choose **Proposal from Operational Data Provider** as shown in Figure 12.42 and continue with **Next**.

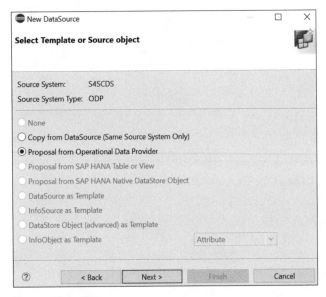

Figure 12.42 ODP

5. Search for the SQL view name that was used when you created the CDS view. Once you enter the pattern, you'll see a list of SQL view names. Enter "ZCDSBW1" for the search in this case, as shown in Figure 12.43.

> **Tip: CDS-Based DataSource Creation**
>
> If you search for the CDS name, you won't be able to see the correct result. Always use the SQL view name that you used in your CDS view to search when you're on the **Select Operational Data Provider** screen. That will be used for the DataSource creation.

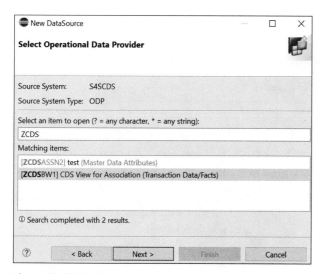

Figure 12.43 Name

6. On the **Confirmation** page, for the input field name, provide the name of the Data-Source that you created. For example, here we've entered "ZCDSBW1". Choose **Next** as shown in Figure 12.44.

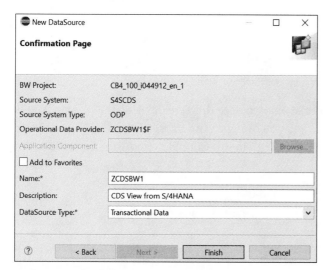

Figure 12.44 Name

You can see that the name of the DataSource and the description is provided. Select **Transactional Data** for the **DataSource Type**.

7. Once you choose **Finish**, you'll see the DataSource creation process, as shown in Figure 12.45.

491

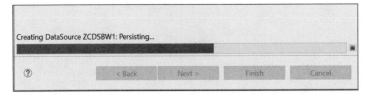

Figure 12.45 Creating DataSource

The DataSource will be inactive by default after creation, as shown in Figure 12.46. You can also see the ZCDSBW1 CDS view in Figure 12.46.

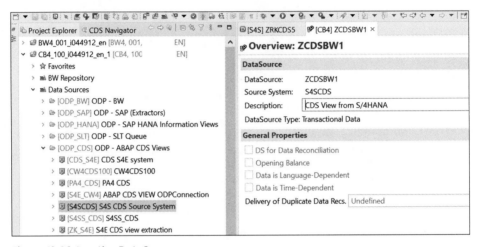

Figure 12.46 Inactive DataSource

You can activate the DataSource once you see this screen, using the ![icon] icon. You'll see the activated DataSource, and you can open the DataSource and navigate to the DataSource tabs as shown in Figure 12.47. In this example, choose the **Extraction** tab.

Extraction: ZCDSBW1

Active Version

Extraction Properties

Delta Process:	No delta, only Full
Direct Access:	Allowed (Pre-Aggregate Data in Extractor)
Streaming:	Streaming cannot be triggered by this DataSource
Adapter:	Extraction from SAP System by Operational Data Provisioning

Extractor-Specific Properties

ODP Context:	ABAP Core Data Services
Operational Data Provider:	ZCDSBW1 Exchange...
Semantics:	Transaction Data/Facts

Overview | Extraction | Fields

Figure 12.47 Extraction Fields

In the **Extraction** tab, you can see the **ODP Context** set as **ABAP Core Data Services** under **Extractor-Specific Properties**. You also can see that the **Operational Data Provider** is **ZCDSBW1**, which is your generated SQL view name that was provided in the CDS view.

8. If you navigate to the **Fields** tab, there will be a list of all the fields based on the CDS view that you created (see Figure 12.48).

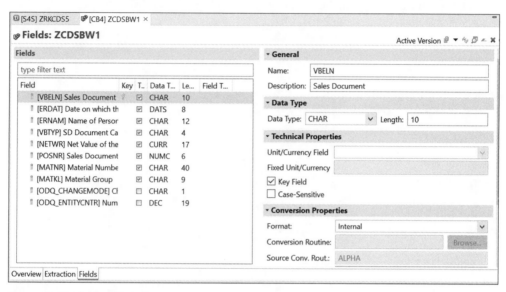

Figure 12.48 Fields of DataSource

Once the DataSource is activated, you can see it in table RSDS. **OBJVERS** will be set as **A**, which means the DataSource is active (see Figure 12.49).

Data Browser: Table RSDS Select Entries   2

DATASOURCE	LOGSYS	OBJVERS	OBJSTAT	ACTIVFL	TYPE	PRIMSEGID	TXTLG	OBJECTFD
ZCDSBW1	S4SCDS	A	ACT	X	D	0001	CDS View from S/4HANA	
ZCDSBW1	S4SCDS	M	ACT	X	D	0001	CDS View from S/4HANA	

Figure 12.49 Table RSDS

Option 2: Replicate a CDS View into a DataSource

If you don't want to use the preceding method, you can also use a replication-based method to replicate the CDS view from the source system. This will also create a DataSource. You can start the replication by opening the SAP BW/4HANA system and from the DataSource, choose the relevant CDS-based source system and choose **Replicate**. Follow the wizard as shown in Figure 12.50. You can search for the CDS-based SQL view name in the **Replicate** window; for example, here search for "ZCDS". You'll see a list of two DataSources available matching this pattern. Choose **ZCDSBW1** for the creation of the DataSource. From here, the steps are same as before: provide the name of the Data-Source like you did earlier as shown in Figure 12.43 through Figure 12.46, then activate the DataSource, which can be used in SAP BW/4HANA.

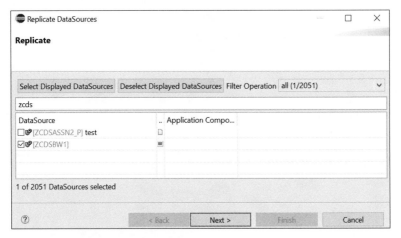

Figure 12.50 Replication-Based Method

With the options that we've discussed, you know two ways to create a DataSource in SAP BW/4HANA based on a CDS view. You can use these DataSources to create SAP BW data models.

12.4.4   Creating aDSOs Based on CDS View DataSources

Once a DataSource is created, you can follow the same steps to create an aDSO, as shown in Figure 12.51. Right-click the InfoArea and choose **New · DataStore Object (Advanced)**. In the wizard, provide the name of the aDSO and a description. Use the DataSource that was created based on the CDS view as the template. In this example, use the ZCDSBW1 DataSource, as shown in Figure 12.51.

The fields are shown in Figure 12.52. You can see that VBELN is part of the key fields and others are data fields.

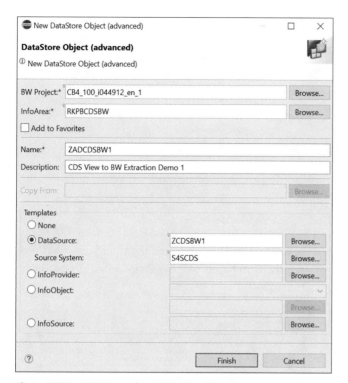

Figure 12.51 aDSO Based on CDS View DataSource

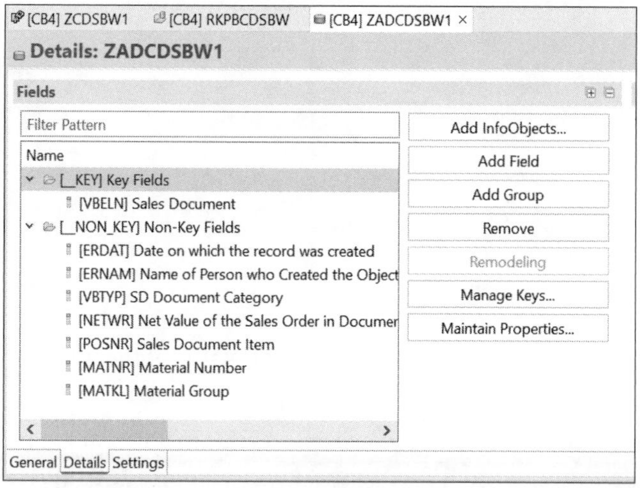

Figure 12.52 aDSO Fields

Once the aDSO is created, create a transformation based on the CDS view DataSource and a DTP, as shown in Figure 12.53.

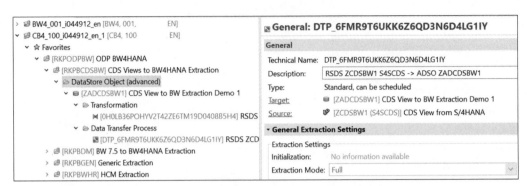

Figure 12.53 DTP and Transformation

Go to Transaction ODQMON in SAP S/4HANA (see Figure 12.54). Make sure **ABAP Core Data Services** is selected as the **Provider** and you have selected the right **Subscriber, SAP Business Warehouse**. You won't see the CDS-based SAP BW DataSource that you created because the DTP isn't yet executed.

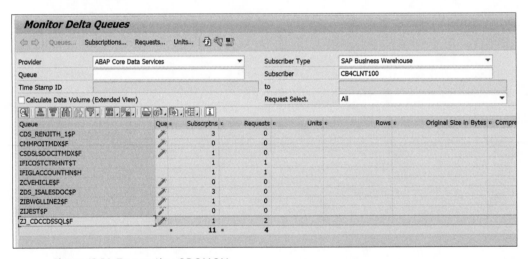

Figure 12.54 Transaction ODQMON

Now execute the DTP using the ⊙ ▼ icon and you can see the status of the inbound table, as shown in Figure 12.55. You can see that 3,470 records were extracted in the DTP.

In Transaction ODQMON, see if the queue has any subscriptions, as shown in Figure 12.56. Do a refresh using the 🔄 icon and you'll see that SAP BW DataSource **ZCDSBW1$F** is available in the **Queues** tab.

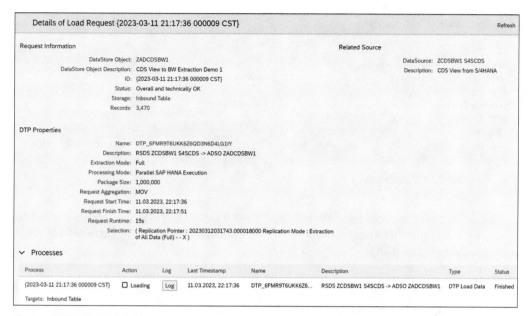

Figure 12.55 Inbound Table

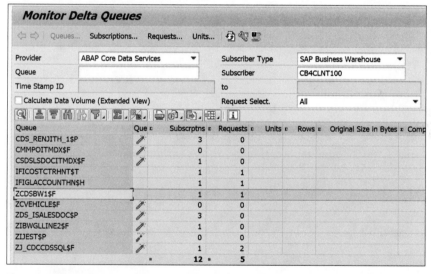

Figure 12.56 Transaction ODQMON: Queues

In the **Subscriptions** tab, you'll see that one request was generated in Transaction ODQMOM for the **ZCDSBW1$F** queue, as shown in Figure 12.57.

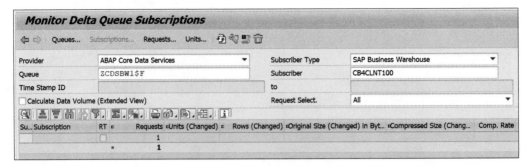

Figure 12.57 Subscriptions

Choose the next view tab, **Requests**, to see the requests (see Figure 12.58). Here you can see the **Composite Request** number and the extraction request. The **Extraction Mode** is **Snapshot Data (Full)**.

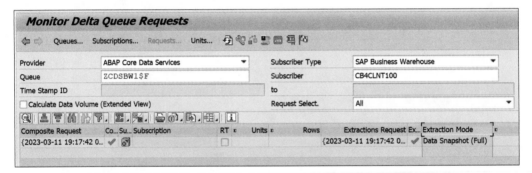

Figure 12.58 Requests

When you go to the **Units** view tab (see Figure 12.59), you'll see that the number of **Rows**, **3,470**, will match the inbound table contents you saw earlier in Figure 12.55.

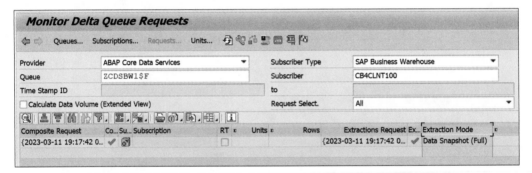

Figure 12.59 Units

Activate the aDSO using the ⬛ icon. During this process, the number of records might be reduced due to the overwrite functionality in SAP BW/4HANA (see Figure 12.60).

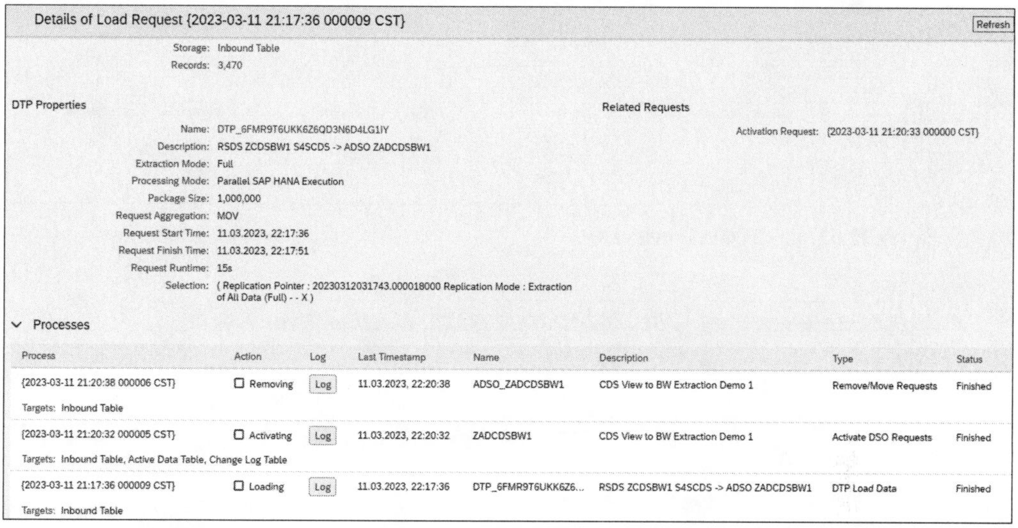

Figure 12.60 aDSO Activation

You can see the data preview of the aDSO using the ⬛ ▼ icon. Filter for a few fields you saw in Transaction ODQMON (see Figure 12.61).

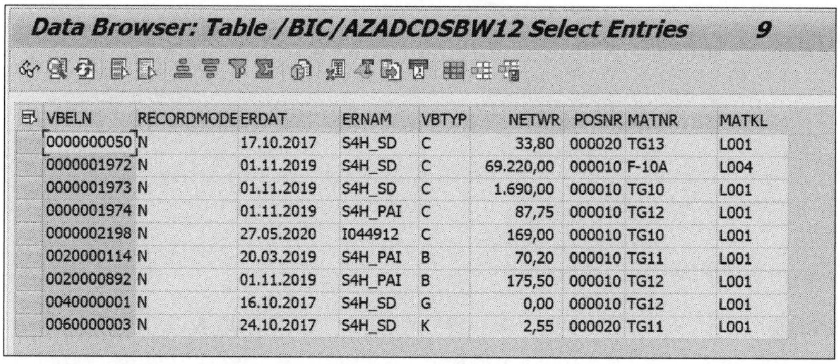

Figure 12.61 Filtered aDSO Active Table

You can see results of the data preview in Figure 12.62. If you open the aDSO active table that ends with 2 in Transaction SE16, you can see the total number of records, as shown in Figure 12.63. There are **3,369** records here.

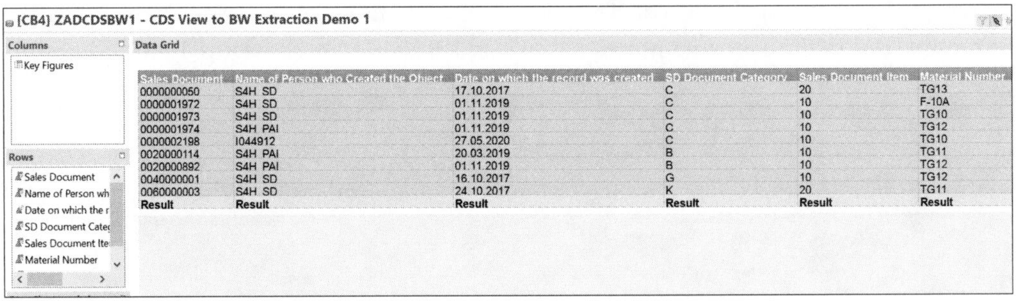

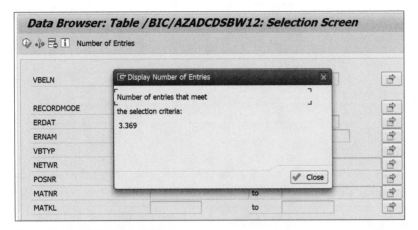

Figure 12.62 aDSO Data Preview

Figure 12.63 Total aDSO Records

The number of records was reduced from 3,470 due to the aDSO overwrite option.

Now you know how to consume CDS views from SAP S/4HANA in SAP BW.

12.4.5   CDS Views with Delta Extraction

The architecture of CDS delta extraction is shown in Figure 12.64. As you can see, there are base tables in the SAP HANA database and CDS views are created that will create the internal SQL views. These views will be consumed by SAP BW systems. When you add the annotations related to the analytics that trigger deltas, that will initialize the Data-Source in Transaction ODQMON. The further posting of new and delta records will be captured by the ODP framework, and the delta is fetched using the delta load.

To test the delta extraction, create a new CDS view data definition like the old CDS view and provide a different SQL view name; here we use "ZCDSBW2". The code is the same, as shown in Figure 12.65.

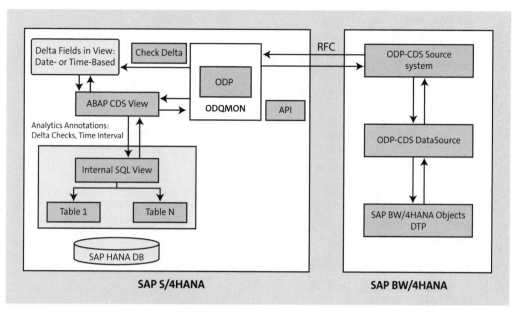

Figure 12.64 CDS View for Delta: Flow

```
  [S4S] ZRKCDS5    [S4S] ZRKCDS2    [S4S] ZRKCDS6 ×
 1 @AbapCatalog.sqlViewName: 'ZCDSBW2'
 2 @AbapCatalog.compiler.compareFilter: true
 3 @AbapCatalog.preserveKey: true
 4 @EndUserText.label: 'CDS View for Association'
 5 @Analytics.dataCategory: #FACT
 6 @Analytics.dataExtraction.enabled: true
 7
 8 define view ZRKCDS6 as select from vbak as VK
 9 association [1..*] to vbap as _VBAP
10    on VK.vbeln = _VBAP.vbeln
11       {
12    key
13       VK.vbeln,
14       VK.erdat,
15       VK.ernam,
16       VK.vbtyp,
17       VK.netwr,
18
19       _VBAP.posnr,
20       _VBAP.matnr,
21       _VBAP.matkl
22       }
23
```

Project Explorer / CDS Navigator
- BW4_001_i044912_en [BW4, 001, I044912, EN]
- CB4_100_i044912_en_1 [CB4, 100, I044912, EN]
- S4S_100_i044912_en [S4S, 100, I044912, EN]
  - Local Objects ($TMP) (52)
  - Favorite Packages (15)
    - ZRKPCDS (15) *CDS Views for BW/4HANA*
      - Core Data Services (6)
        - Data Definitions (6)
          - ZRKCDS1 *CDS View for Data Definition*
          - ZRKCDS2 *CDS View for Join*
          - ZRKCDS3 *CDS View for Left Outer Join*
          - ZRKCDS4 *CDS View for Association*
          - ZRKCDS5 *CDS View for BW Extraction*
          - ZRKCDS6 *CDS View for BW Extraction with Delta*
      - Dictionary (9)
- System Library (3,492,105)

Figure 12.65 CDS View Copy

Now you need to change the code by adding an annotation: @Analytics.dataEx-traction.enabled.: True. When you make this true, the delta changes for the field are captured. But before that, you need to know the field that's used to trigger the delta. You'll get the delta based on the change date, so check in table VBAK to confirm that, as shown in Figure 12.66.

501

Figure 12.66 AEDAT Field in Table VBAK

First, add the AEDAT field to the CDS output list. This will appear as as VK.aedat in the CDS code. This is the field for the change date. Now you need to add the analytics annotation (see Figure 12.67). You can see annotations such as @Analytics.dataextraction.enabled: true and @Analytics.dataCategory: #FACT.

```
1 @AbapCatalog.sqlViewName: 'ZCDSBW2'
2 @AbapCatalog.compiler.compareFilter: true
3 @AbapCatalog.preserveKey: true
4 @EndUserText.label: 'CDS View for Association'
5
6 @Analytics.dataExtraction.enabled: true
7 @Analytics.dataCategory: #FACT
8 |
9 define view ZRKCDS6 as select from vbak as VK
10 association [1..*] to vbap as _VBAP
11     on VK.vbeln = _VBAP.vbeln
12     {
13     key
14         VK.vbeln,
15         VK.erdat,
16         VK.ernam,
17         VK.vbtyp,
18         VK.netwr,
19         // Change Date
20         VK.aedat,
21
22         _VBAP.posnr,
23         _VBAP.matnr,
24         _VBAP.matkl
25     }
26
```

Figure 12.67 AEDAT Field

Add the delta annotations, as shown in Figure 12.68:

❶ These are standard analytics annotations.

❷ These two annotations are to capture change documents. 'LastChangedAt' needs to be associated with AEDAT in the list output. maxDelayInSeconds is 1800, which means it checks the change documents once every 30 minutes.

❸ Here you assign the AEDAT field to 'LastChangedAt' so that this is known as the field that is responsible for delta checks.

```
 1 @AbapCatalog.sqlViewName: 'ZCDSBW2'
 2 @AbapCatalog.compiler.compareFilter: true
 3 @AbapCatalog.preserveKey: true
 4 @EndUserText.label: 'CDS View for Association'
 5 @Analytics.dataExtraction.enabled: true                    ❶
 6 @Analytics.dataCategory: #FACT
 7 @Analytics.dataExtraction.delta.byElement.name: 'LastChangedAt'
 8 @Analytics.dataExtraction.delta.byElement.maxDelayInSeconds: 1800     ❷
 9
10 define view ZRKCDS6 as select from vbak as VK
11 association [1..*] to vbap as _VBAP
12     on VK.vbeln = _VBAP.vbeln
13     {
14     key
15         VK.vbeln,
16         VK.erdat,
17         VK.ernam,
18         VK.vbtyp,
19         VK.netwr,
20
21         @Semantics.systemDate.lastChangedAt: true
22         VK.aedat as LastChangedAt,   ❸
23
24         _VBAP.posnr,
25         _VBAP.matnr,
26         _VBAP.matkl
27     }
```

Figure 12.68 Annotations

12.4.6   Extract the Delta CDS in SAP BW

In an ERP system, there will be many new documents created each hour, and there will also be many changes to existing documents. You need to use the CDS view to extract these new and changed documents to SAP BW/HANA 2.0 Follow these steps to implement the delta extraction in CDS views:

1. In SAP BW/4HANA, replicate the CDS view and create a DataSource. Then create an aDSO (see Figure 12.69).

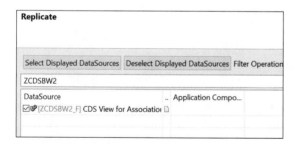

Figure 12.69 CDS Replication

2. Once this is done, the CDS-based DataSource will be created with the same name (**ZCDSBW2_F**). You can see that _F is added to the CDS-based SQL view name, and the **DELTA** field now shows **AIM**, as shown in Figure 12.70.

DATASOURCE	LOGSYS	OBJVERS	OBJSTAT	ACTIVFL	TYPE	PRIMSEGID	OBJECTFD	APPLNM	BASOSOURCE	DELTA
ZCDSBW2_F	S4SCDS	A	ACT	X	D	0001				AIM
ZCDSBW2_F	S4SCDS	M	ACT	X	D	0001				AIM

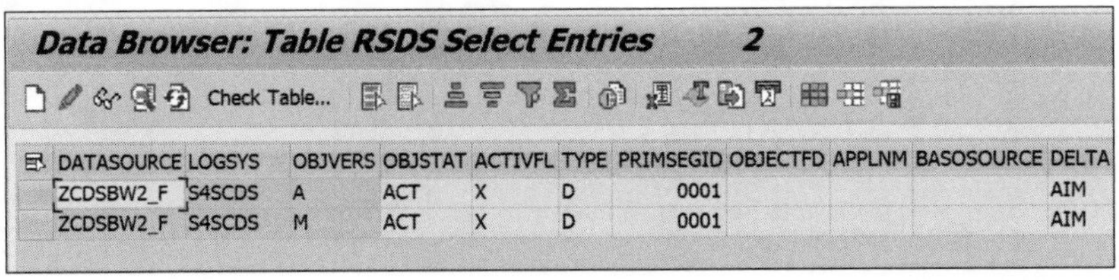

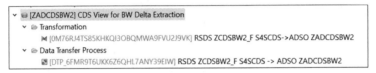

Figure 12.70 Delta Table

3. Create an aDSO based on this DataSource and create a transformation and DTP for the same. Execute the DTP; you can see the activated DTP status as shown in Figure 12.71.

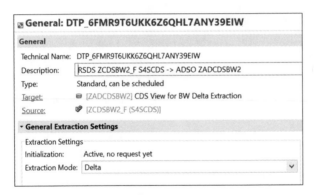

Figure 12.71 DTP and Transformation for CDS Delta

4. You can see that delta mode is now available in the DTP (see Figure 12.72).

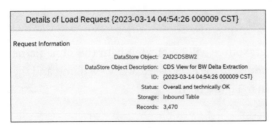

Figure 12.72 DTP Delta Mode

After the DTP execution using ▶ ▾, you can see the status of the inbound table (see Figure 12.73). It has 3,470 records.

Figure 12.73 DTP Inbound Table

5. In Transaction ODQMON, for the sender (see Figure 12.74), you can see the SAP BW DataSource **ZCDSBW2_F** in the queue name.

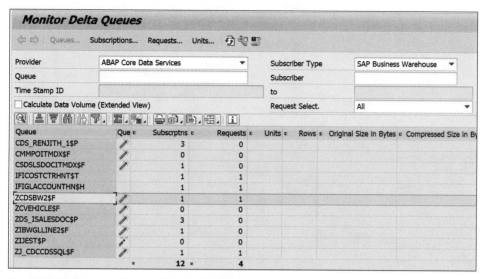

Figure 12.74 Queue in Transaction ODQMON

You can double-click the queue name to go to the subscriptions view. You can see that **Request Select.** is set to **Delta Initialization Only** (see Figure 12.75).

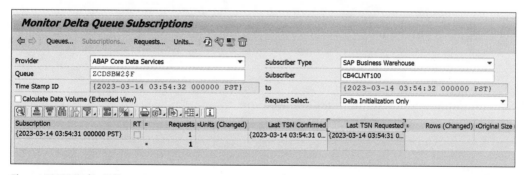

Figure 12.75 Delta Init

Now you can see the requests as shown in Figure 12.76. You'll see the composite request. The status is green, and it has **Extraction Mode** set to **Initial Data** and **Storage** set to **ODQDATA_C**.

If you double-click the request, you'll go to the units view, as shown in Figure 12.77.

6. Activate the aDSO using the ![icon] icon and you can see the records in the active table (see Figure 12.78).

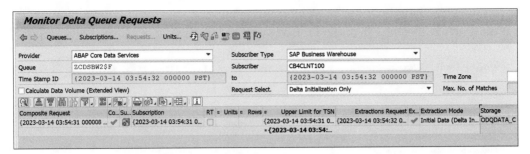

Figure 12.76 Requests

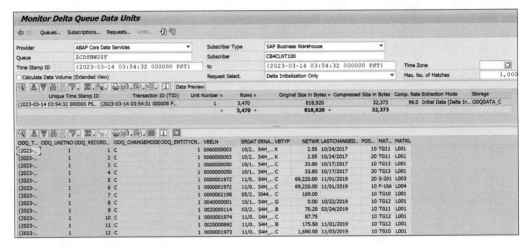

Figure 12.77 Units

Figure 12.78 aDSO Activation

7. Post the delta document in SAP ERP and you can see the new delta posted (see Figure 12.79).

Figure 12.79 New Sales Order

In the SAP S/4HANA system, check table VBAK table for the delta record, as shown in Figure 12.80.

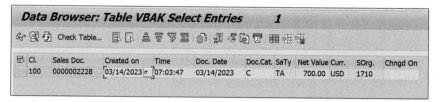

Figure 12.80 New Document after Delta Init

8. Execute the same DTP again using the ▶ ▼ icon and you can see that data package 1 has no data (see Figure 12.81).

Request Processing Steps	Started at	Total Runtime	Process Runtime	Details
☐ Generate Request	14.03.2023, 07:08:37	1s		Display Messages
☐ Set Status to 'Executable'	14.03.2023, 07:08:38	1s		Display Messages
☐ Process Request	14.03.2023, 07:08:39	2s		Display Messages
☐ Filling Data Transfer Intermediate Storage	14.03.2023, 07:08:41	4s		Display Messages
☐ Prepare for Extraction	14.03.2023, 07:08:45			Display Messages
☐ End of Main Process	14.03.2023, 07:08:45			
☐ Technical status 'Green' (user I044912)	14.03.2023, 07:08:46			Display Messages
☐ Data Package 1 (0 Data Records)	14.03.2023, 07:08:46			
☐ Set overall status to 'Green' (user I044912)	14.03.2023, 07:08:46			Display Messages

Request {2023-03-14 05:08:37 000013 CST}   ☐   Refresh   Job Overview

Figure 12.81 No Data

The reason for this is that you created a new document and the delta is based on that field only, so you need to change a document using VA02 to see data changes here. So, go ahead and change the order (see Figure 12.82 and Figure 12.83).

Figure 12.82 Changed Order

Data Browser: Table VBAK Select Entries   1

&⅌ ⅗ ⅍ Check Table...   ⊞ ⊟ ⥮ ⥯ ⥰ ⅀ ⊚ ⅊ ⅏ ⊞ ⊞ ⊞

Cl.	Sales Doc.	Created on	Time	Doc. Date	Doc.Cat.	SaTy	Net Value	Curr.	SOrg.	Chngd On
100	0000000050	10/17/2017	11:39:01	10/17/2017	C	TA	103.80	USD	1710	03/14/2023

Figure 12.83 AEDAT Updated

You can see the details as shown in Figure 12.84; new documents have been posted.

12

507

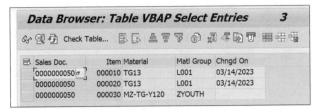

Figure 12.84 Table VBAP

Execute the same DTP using the ▶ ▼ icon again. You'll see that three line items are extracted (Figure 12.85). This can be seen in the inbound table with three records.

Figure 12.85 Inbound Table

View the contents of the inbound table by selecting **Display Contents**, as shown in Figure 12.86.

REQTSN	DATAPAKID	RECORD	RECORDMODE	VBELN	ERDAT	ERNAM	VBTYP	NETWR	LASTCHANGEDAT	POSNR	MATNR	MATKL
{2023-03-14 05:1...	1	1		0000000050	17.10.2017	S4H_SD	C	103,80	14.03.2023	10	TG13	L001
{2023-03-14 05:1...	1	2		0000000050	17.10.2017	S4H_SD	C	103,80	14.03.2023	20	TG13	L001
{2023-03-14 05:1...	1	3		0000000050	17.10.2017	S4H_SD	C	103,80	14.03.2023	30	MZ-TG-Y120	ZYOUTH

Display Inbound Table of ZADCDSBW2

Table Size: 3
Matching Filter: 3

REQTSN: =20230314111727000005000

DATAPAKID:

RECORD:

Max Rows: 200

Display In Internal Format   Manage

Adapt Filters   Go

Figure 12.86 Inbound Table: Last Changed At

Check Transaction ODQMON again or do a refresh using the 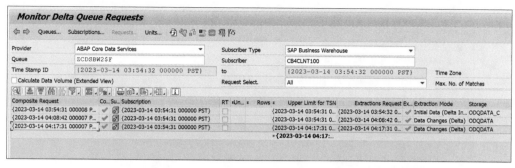 icon. You'll see that in the composite request status, as shown in Figure 12.87, the **Extraction Mode** is **Data Changes**.

Figure 12.87 Transaction ODQMON

12.5   Finding Standard CDS Views for SAP Applications

In this section, you'll learn how to search for CDS views that are delivered by SAP for the standard functional areas. This will be one of the requirements when you implement SAP BW/4HANA. If you know how to find the right CDS views for an application, then you can start the data modeling in SAP BW/4HANA based on that view.

12.5.1   Finding the CDS Views for Applications Using SAP Table

1. Log onto the SAP S/4HANA system and open table IXTRCTNENBLDVW using Transaction SE11, as shown in Figure 12.88.

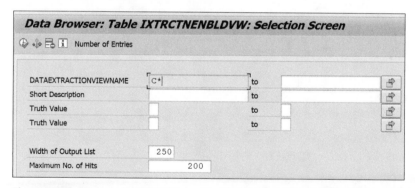

Figure 12.88 Table to Find CDS Views Enabled for Data Extraction

In table IXTRCTNENBLDVW, you can search with "C*" in **DATAEXTRACTIONVIEWNAME**, which will give you the standard CDS views that are delivered by SAP. The list shown in Figure 12.89 highlights a few views based on sales and purchasing applications.

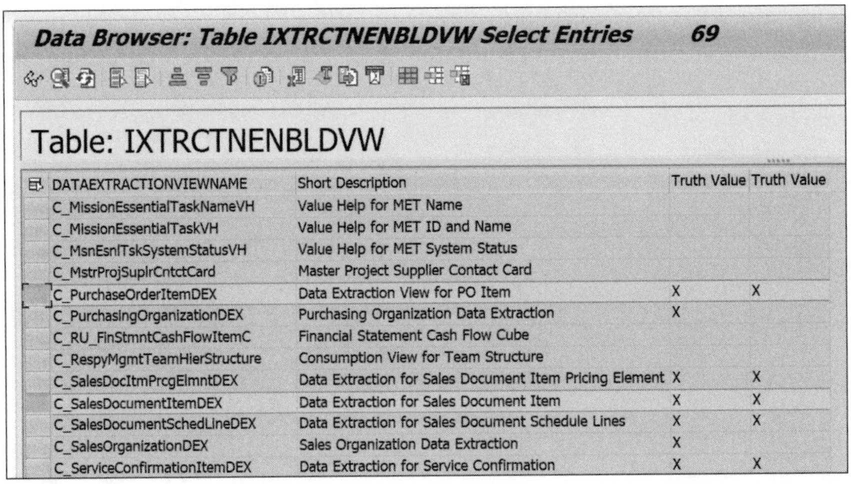

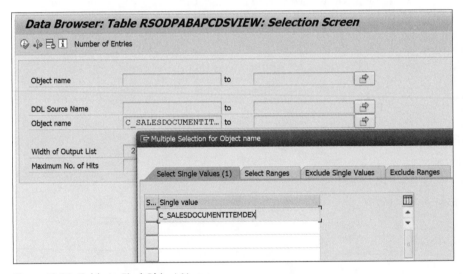

Figure 12.89 Available CDS Views

2. To find the data definition you can copy the **DATAEXTRACTIONVIEW** name; for example, here we'll copy **C_SalesDocumentIteaDEX**. Search the table by providing the same name in the **Object Name** field (see Figure 12.90).

Figure 12.90 Table to Find Object Name

Once you execute, you'll see the **Obj. Name** results as shown in Figure 12.91. This will be the SQL view name that you'll be using for DataSource creation.

If you need to find the details of the fields, you can copy the view name from table RSOD-PABAPCDSVIEW and find that in Transaction SE11, which will give the field name and the associated CDS view (see Figure 12.92).

Figure 12.91 Object Name of CDS View

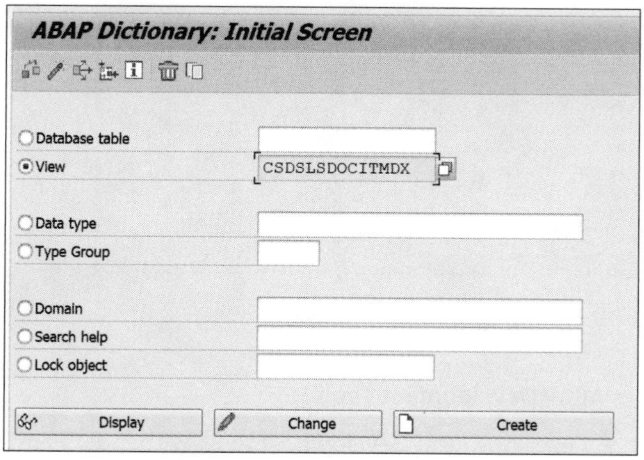

Figure 12.92 CDS SQL View Name

Once you choose the **Display** option, you'll see the screen shown in Figure 12.93.

Figure 12.93 Data Definition of CDS View

If you double-click the data definition, you can see the view definition, as shown in Figure 12.94.

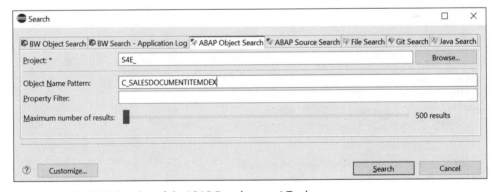

Display Data Definition

Data Definition   C_SALESDOCUMENTITEMDEX   Active

Properties   Source Code

ADT-Link: adt://S4E/sap/bc/adt/ddic/ddl/sources/c_salesdocumentitemdex

```
 1  @AbapCatalog.sqlViewName: 'CSDSLSDOCITMDX'
 2  @AbapCatalog.compiler.compareFilter: true
 3  @AbapCatalog.preserveKey: true
 4  @AccessControl:{
 5      authorizationCheck: #CHECK,
 6      personalData.blocking: #('TRANSACTIONAL_DATA')
 7  }
 8  @EndUserText.label: 'Data Extraction for Sales Document Item'
 9  @ClientHandling.algorithm: #SESSION_VARIABLE
10  @ObjectModel.usageType.dataClass: #TRANSACTIONAL
11  @ObjectModel.usageType.serviceQuality: #D
12  @ObjectModel.usageType.sizeCategory: #XL
13  @ObjectModel.representativeKey: 'SalesDocumentItem'
14  @VDM.viewType: #CONSUMPTION
15  @Metadata.ignorePropagatedAnnotations: true
16
17  @Analytics: {
18      dataCategory: #FACT,
19      dataExtraction: {
```

Figure 12.94 Data Definition

12.5.2   Finding CDS Views in ABAP Development Tools

You can also search for the CDS view in the ABAP development tools, with these steps:

1. Open the ABAP development tools perspective in Eclipse and open the search area, shown in Figure 12.95.

Search   □   ✕

BW Object Search | BW Search - Application Log | ABAP Object Search | ABAP Source Search | File Search | Git Search | Java Search

Project: *   S4E_   Browse...

Object Name Pattern: C_SALESDOCUMENTITEMDEX

Property Filter:

Maximum number of results: ▉   500 results

Customize...   Search   Cancel

Figure 12.95 CDS View Search in ABAP Development Tools

The search results are shown in Figure 12.96, which shows the details of the CDS views.

2. Open the view, and you can see the CDS view data definition, as shown in Figure 12.97.

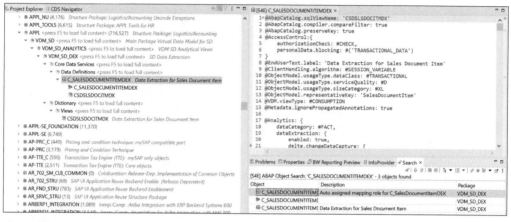

Figure 12.96 Search Results for CDS Views

Figure 12.97 CDS View in ABAP Development Tools

With this information, you can use this CDS view for data extraction in SAP BW/4HANA. These standard SAP-delivered CDS views will have the delta enabled with change data capture, which will help you to get the delta in real time from SAP S/4HANA. There is a separate annotation for enabling change data capture in the development of CDS views. Alternatively, you can also use the streaming process chain in SAP BW/4HANA, which will fetch the real-time data.

12.6 Summary

With the completion of the dataflow based on the CDS views, now you're ready to build the SAP BW/4HANA model to extract the data from SAP S/4HANA using the custom-developed or SAP-delivered standard CDS views. Having good know-how on this topic is essential as more companies are using CDS-based extraction on account of the impressive performance gains in the data load and support for the real-time extraction. The data modeling with CDS views will help you have more virtualization in your system design, which will be a key benefit of SAP BW/4HANA. Knowing about a mix of classical and new extractors will help you design more efficient data models during SAP BW/4HANA implementation.

In the next chapter, we'll focus on extracting the data from SAP S/4HANA using open ODS views to SAP BW/4HANA.

Chapter 13

Extraction Using Open ODS Views

This chapter describes the virtual data provisioning options from SAP HANA to SAP BW/4HANA. Effective data modeling can be achieved using the virtualization options for data extraction. These data provisioning methods will help you define and architect an analytics strategy for your complex landscape during SAP BW/4HANA implementations.

Open ODS views enable you to define data models for objects like database tables, database views, or DataSources (for direct access). These data models allow flexible integration without the need to create InfoObjects. This flexible type of data integration makes it possible to consume external data sources in SAP BW/4HANA without staging, combine data sources with SAP BW/4HANA models, and physically integrate (load) external data sources by creating DataSources.

The open ODS view is an SAP BW/4HANA metadata object that provides a structure description with attributes (fields) and data types. It represents a view of a source and adds analytic metadata to this source. Supported data sources are objects, which describe their data in a structure with attributes and data types (such as database tables), views, or SAP BW/4HANA DataSources. The open ODS view doesn't have separate storage for transaction data or master data. This means persistency and analytic modeling are decoupled for the open ODS view.

When you use open ODS views, there are many semantics that let you categorize the data you use. The source data can be categorized as facts, master data, or texts. The open ODS view can get data from multiple sources:

- SAP BW DataSources
- aDSOs
- Database tables or views
- Virtual tables using SAP HANA smart data access
- SAP BW transformations

In this chapter, we'll start with an introduction to open ODS views, followed by the detailed steps to create the same. We'll first look at open ODS views based on Data-Sources (Section 13.1.1), then create the CDS view and consume the view in an open ODS view in Section 13.1.2. Finally, we'll create a table in the SAP HANA database and consume the table using open ODS views in Section 13.1.3. Completing this chapter will give a solid foundation to data provisioning using open ODS views and help you create efficient SAP BW/4HANA data models with more virtualization options.

13.1   Creating Open ODS Views

Let's explore the creation of open ODS views based on a few source options: SAP BW DataSources, CDS views, and SAP HANA database tables.

13.1.1   Open ODS Views Based on SAP BW DataSources

To create open ODS views based on SAP BW DataSources, follow these steps:

1. Create a DataSource in SAP S/4HANA using Transaction RSO2 (see Chapter 10, Section 10.1.3 for how to create the generic DataSource). Here we'll use table EBAN to create the DataSource. The ZRKOOVDS DataSource is based on table EBAN, which holds information about the purchase requisition. BANFN is the field for the purchase request number. Make that the selection field, as shown in Figure 13.1.

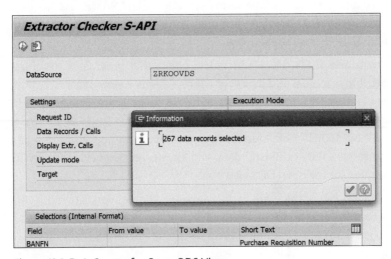

Figure 13.1 DataSource for Open ODS View

2. Once you press the green checkmark and then choose the ALV grid display, the records can be seen (see Figure 13.2).

3. Replicate this DataSource in SAP BW/4HANA from the **ODP_SAP** DataSource tree and activate the DataSource. Make sure the DataSource is shown as the A version in table RSDS, as shown in Figure 13.3. **ZRKOOVDS** shows **A** in the **OBJVERS** column, which means it's active.

Result of Extraction of DataSource ZRKOOVDS

Data Package (Number of Recs)   1 (100)

Purch.Req.	Item	Doc. Type	Cat	Ctl	D	S	C	Rel	Release	RS	PGr	Created by	Changed On	Requisitioner	Short Text
10000020	10	NB	B		B	R					001		10/16/2017		Requisition 1
10000010	10	NB	B		B	S					003		10/09/2017	S4H_MM	Office supply
10000011	10	NB	B		B	S					003		10/09/2017	S4H_MM	Office
10000021	10	NB	B		B	V					001		10/16/2017		Trad.Good 10,PD,Third Party
10000000	10	NB	B		B	V					001		10/16/2017		Trad.Good 10,PD,Third Party
10000022	10	NB	B		B	V					001		10/17/2017		Trad.Good 10,PD,Third Party
10000022	20	NB	B		B	V					001		10/17/2017		Trad.Good 10,PD,Third Party
10000023	10	NB	B		B	V					001		10/17/2017		Trad.Good 13,Reorder Point,Thrd Party
10000023	20	NB	B		B	V					001		10/17/2017		Trad.Good 13,Reorder Point,Thrd Party
10000535	10	NB	B		N	V	X				001		10/25/2018		Dummy Text
10000781	10	RV	B	R	K	R					001		10/15/2019		Trad.Good 10,PD,Third Party

Figure 13.2 Result of Check

Data Browser: Table RSDS Select Entries   2

Check Table...

DATASOURCE	LOGSYS	OBJVERS	OBJSTAT	ACTIVFL	TYPE	PRIMSEGID
ZRKOOVDS	S4SCLNT100	A	ACT	X	D	0001
ZRKOOVDS	S4SCLNT100	M	ACT	X	D	0001

Figure 13.3 DataSource in Table RSDS

4. Right-click on the InfoArea folder and select **New · Open ODS View**, as shown in Figure 13.4.

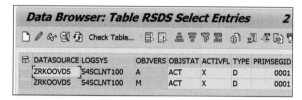

∨ 📖 [RKPODPBW] ODP BW4HANA		
› 📖 [RKPBOOV] Open ODS View Extraction	New >	🔳 Data Flow Object...
› 📖 [RKPBCDSBW] CDS Views to BW4HA		🔗 Process Chain...
› 📖 [RKPBDM] BW 7.5 to BW4HANA Extra	Open	📑 CompositeProvider...
› 📖 [RKPBGEN] Generic Extraction	📋 Copy Name	📑 Open ODS View...
› 📖 [RKPBWHR] HCM Extraction	📋 Copy Label	🌀 Aggregation Level...
› 📖 [RKPBWFI] Financials Extraction		

Figure 13.4 Open ODS View Creation

5. Provide the **Name** and **Description**, and under **Semantics**, choose **Facts**, as shown in Figure 13.5.

6. Choose the **DataSource (BW)** option for **Source Type** as shown in Figure 13.6, then choose **Next** in the wizard.

7. On the next screen, search for your DataSource name. Here we entered "ZRKOO". You'll see a similarly named DataSource in the **Matching Items** box. Choose the required DataSource and click **Next** in the wizard (Figure 13.7).

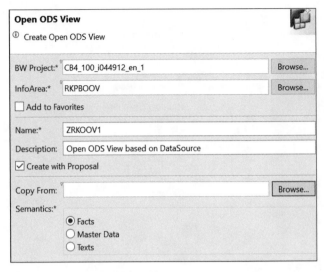

Figure 13.5 Open ODS View Name

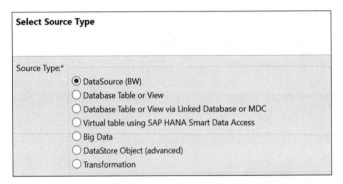

Figure 13.6 Source Type for Open ODS View

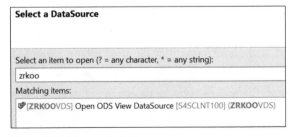

Figure 13.7 Choose DataSource

8. The wizard will take you to the **Confirmation Page**, where you can see the name of the open ODS view and the semantics used for this view, along with the source type and name, as shown in Figure 13.8.

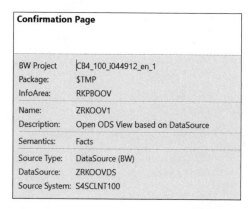

Figure 13.8 Confirmation Page for Open ODS View Creation

9. Once you select **Finish** from the wizard, the open ODS view will be created. Activate it and you can see its details, as shown in Figure 13.9.

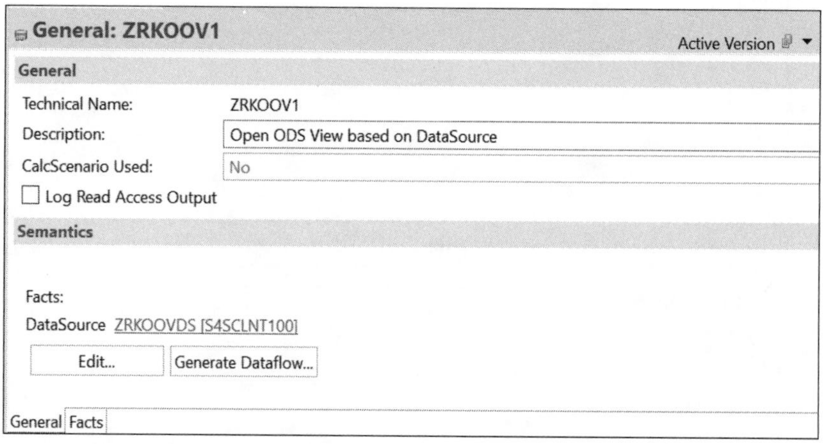

Figure 13.9 Open ODS View Screen

10. Now you've created the open ODS view. You can see that under **Semantics** it shows **Facts** and that it's based on the **ZRKOOVDS DataSource**, which is created from the source system **S4SCLNT100**. You can see the **Facts** tab now (Figure 13.10), which shows the details of the source fields and the open ODS view fields. **BANFN** is used as the key field, and it has used a system-wide unique name.

11. Create a query based on the open ODS view (see Figure 13.11).

12. Enter the name and you'll land on the screen shown in Figure 13.12. You can see the InfoProvider is ZRKOOV1, which is an open ODS view.

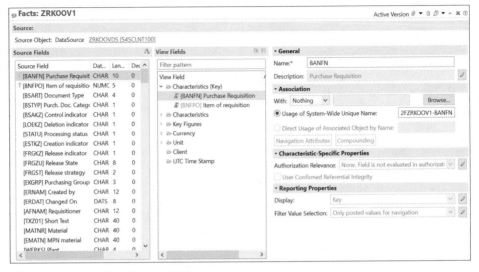

Figure 13.10 Facts Tab: Open ODS View

Figure 13.11 Query Creation

Figure 13.12 Query General View

13. Provide the sheet definition by choosing from the views (see Figure 13.13).

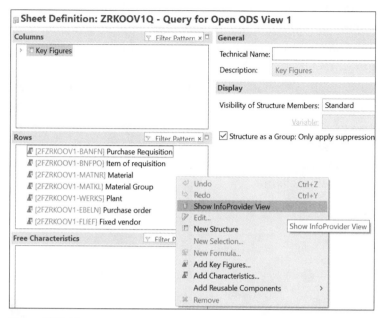

Figure 13.13 Views

14. Drag and drop from the right (see Figure 13.14).

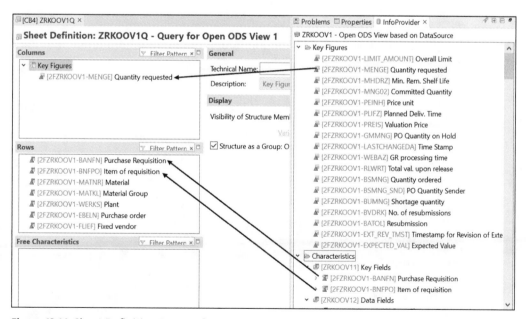

Figure 13.14 Sheet Definition Drag and Drop

15. You can see the final fields in Figure 13.15:

    ❶ In the **Sheet Definition** tab, define the rows for the reports and choose the key figures for the reporting view.

    ❷ Choose the rows from the InfoProvider view. These are the fields that will part of the rows in the report output.

    ❸ Choose the key figures from the InfoProvider view. These fields will be displayed in the report.

    ❹ If you want to suppress the results, you can make it **Never**. You need to do this for all fields in the row. But if you need to see the results, then you can choose the other options that are available, like **Always** or **Only of More than 1 Child**. For this example, choose **Never** for all rows.

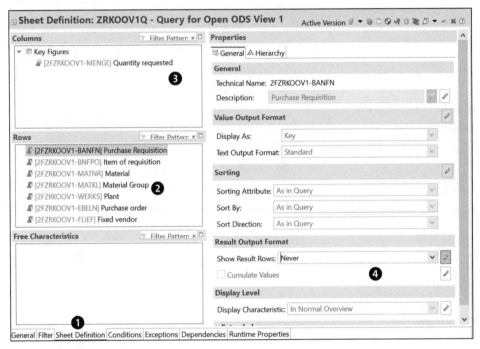

Figure 13.15 Sheet Definition Tab

16. Save the query and do a data preview, as shown in Figure 13.16:

    ❶ Generate the query.

    ❷ In the dropdown, select **Reporting Preview**.

Figure 13.16 Generate Data Preview

17. Alternatively, you can use the **Data Preview** option shown in Figure 13.17.

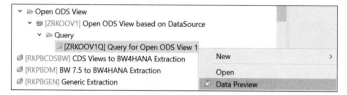

Figure 13.17 Data Preview

18. Either option will bring you to the results shown in Figure 13.18.

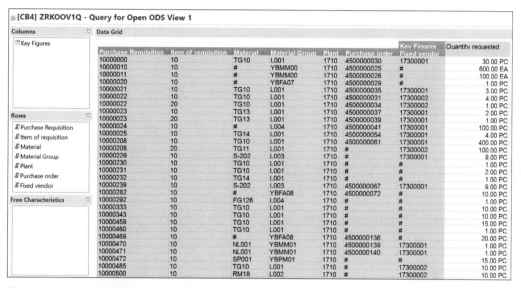

Figure 13.18 Reporting Preview

Note the following points:

- The query was executed based on the open ODS view, but it did not persist the data in SAP BW/4HANA.

- We did not create a transformation or DTP for the open ODS view.

- When the query is executed, it triggers the open ODS view, which in turn calls the DataSource in SAP S/4HANA, and the result is extracted from SAP S/4HANA.

- This is called *virtualization* in SAP BW/4HANA, where you do not stage the data and there is no persistence.

There's an option to generate a dataflow in the **General** tab of the open ODS view, as shown in Figure 13.19.

For open ODS views with a database table or virtual table source type using SAP HANA smart data access or an SAP BW DataSource, you can create a dataflow with an aDSO or a transformation (see Figure 13.20). This can be done using the **Generate Dataflow**

523

option in the **General** tab of the open ODS view. When the dataflow is created, the source of the open ODS view is automatically replaced with the created object.

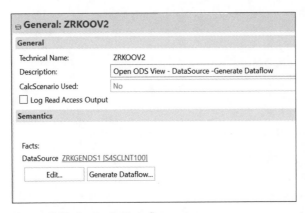

Figure 13.19 Generate Dataflow

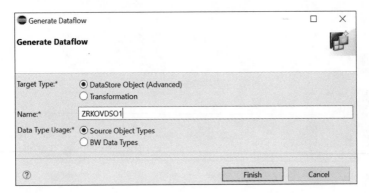

Figure 13.20 Name of aDSO

You can see that the source object will be now changed to the aDSO, as shown in Figure 13.21.

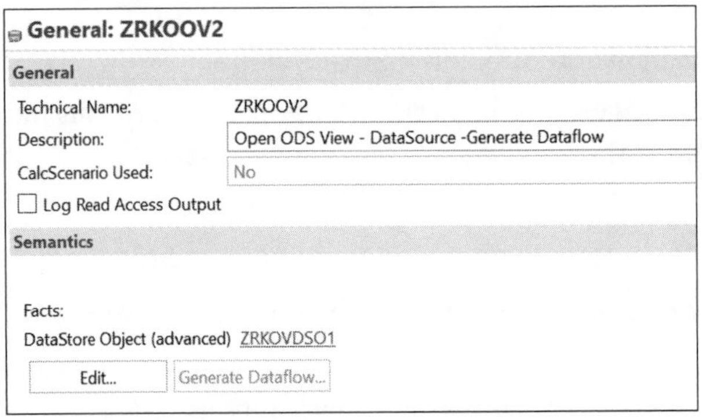

Figure 13.21 Generated aDSO

This will create the flow shown in Figure 13.22. You can see that the aDSO gets data from the DataSource.

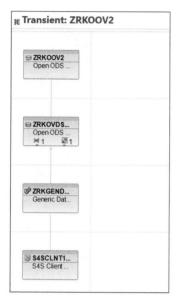

Figure 13.22 Generated Dataflow

You can create an aDSO with a dataflow as data persistency for the open ODS view. In this case, it's comparable with a persistent staging area (PSA) in which data can be further processed. For reporting purposes and for using the CompositeProvider, it's recommended to use the open ODS view directly.

13.1.2   Open ODS View Based on CDS

The most common use case is to use CDS views as the sources for open ODS views.

The CDS view shown in Listing 13.1 was created in SAP BW/4HANA based on table SFLIGHT. Use the ABAP perspective to create this CDS view.

```
@AbapCatalog.sqlViewName: 'ZRKBWCDS_1'
@AbapCatalog.compiler. compareFilter: true
@AbapCatalog.preserveKey: true
@AccessControl.authorizationCheck: #NOT_REQUIRED
@EndUserText.label: 'CDS View Demo 1'
@Analytics.dataCategory: #FACT
@Analytics.dataExtraction.enabled: true
define view ZRKBWCDS1 as select from sflight
  {
  key sflight.carrid,
  key sflight.connid,
```

```
  key sflight.fldate,
  sflight.planetype,
  sflight.price
}
```

Listing 13.1 CDS View for Table SFLIGHT

Once the CDS view is created, right-click the CDS view and select **Data Preview**. The results are shown in Figure 13.23.

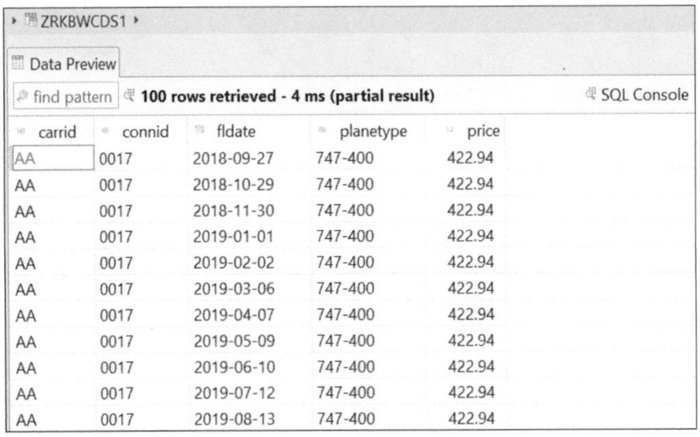

carrid	connid	fldate	planetype	price
AA	0017	2018-09-27	747-400	422.94
AA	0017	2018-10-29	747-400	422.94
AA	0017	2018-11-30	747-400	422.94
AA	0017	2019-01-01	747-400	422.94
AA	0017	2019-02-02	747-400	422.94
AA	0017	2019-03-06	747-400	422.94
AA	0017	2019-04-07	747-400	422.94
AA	0017	2019-05-09	747-400	422.94
AA	0017	2019-06-10	747-400	422.94
AA	0017	2019-07-12	747-400	422.94
AA	0017	2019-08-13	747-400	422.94

Figure 13.23 Data Preview

Once the CDS view is created and the data preview is tested, the next step is to consume the CDS view in SAP BW/4HANA. You need to first create the `ODP_CDS` source system in SAP BW/4HANA (see Chapter 3 for how to create an ODP-based source system; Section 3.2.5 deals specifically with `ODP_CDS`). Once the source system is created, in the CDS-based source system, you need to follow these steps:

1. Replicate the CDS view as a DataSource in SAP BW/4HANA. Once the replication is completed, the DataSource will be saved as shown in Figure 13.24. During the replication, the SQL view name will be used for the DataSource; in this case, the SQL view name is `ZRKBWCDS_1`. For the DataSource, _F is added, so the DataSource name is `ZRKBWCDS_1_F` (see Figure 13.24).

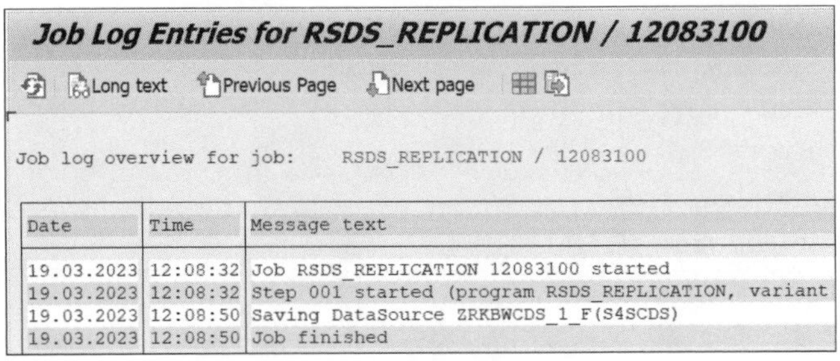

Date	Time	Message text
19.03.2023	12:08:32	Job RSDS_REPLICATION 12083100 started
19.03.2023	12:08:32	Step 001 started (program RSDS_REPLICATION, variant
19.03.2023	12:08:50	Saving DataSource ZRKBWCDS_1_F(S4SCDS)
19.03.2023	12:08:50	Job finished

Figure 13.24 Replication

After the replication, you can see the DataSource. Open it and you'll see that **ODP Context** is **ABAP Core Data Services** and **Operational Data Provider** is the CDS view, **ZRKBWCDS_1_F**, as shown in Figure 13.25. Make sure that you activate the Data-Source.

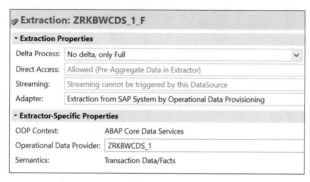

Figure 13.25 DataSource Based on ODP CDS

2. Create the open ODS view based on this CDS view. You can follow the same steps to create the open ODS views that you saw earlier in Figure 13.4, but choose the **Views** option (see Figure 13.6). Once you provide the CDS view name and confirm the creation process, you can see the open ODS view as shown in Figure 13.26. The open ODS view name will be ZRKOOV3 with the DataSource ZRKBWCDS_1_F, based on the CDS source system.

General: ZRKOOV3

General	
Technical Name:	ZRKOOV3
Description:	Open ODS View based on CDS View
CalcScenario Used:	No
☐ Log Read Access Output	

Semantics

Facts:

DataSource ZRKBWCDS_1_F [S4SCDS]

| Edit... | Generate Dataflow... |

Figure 13.26 Open ODS View Based on DataSource that Uses CDS Views

Once the open ODS view is created, do a data preview on this open ODS view. Right-click the open ODS view and choose **Data Preview**. You'll see the results as shown in Figure 13.27.

Now you've consumed the data from the SAP S/4HANA system using an open ODS view.

[CB4] ZRKOOV3 - Open ODS View based on CDS View

Columns	Data Grid

Key Figures

Airline Code	Flight Connection Number	Flight date	Aircraft Type	Key Figures · Airfare
AA	17	27.09.2018	747-400	422.94
AA	17	29.10.2018	747-400	422.94
AA	17	30.11.2018	747-400	422.94
AA	17	01.01.2019	747-400	422.94
AA	17	02.02.2019	747-400	422.94
AA	17	06.03.2019	747-400	422.94
AA	17	07.04.2019	747-400	422.94
AA	17	09.05.2019	747-400	422.94
AA	17	10.06.2019	747-400	422.94
AA	17	12.07.2019	747-400	422.94
AA	17	13.08.2019	747-400	422.94
AA	17	14.09.2019	747-400	422.94
AA	17	16.10.2019	747-400	422.94
AA	17	**Result**	**Result**	**5.498.22**
AA	64	29.09.2018	A340-600	422.94
AA	64	31.10.2018	A340-600	422.94

Rows

- Airline Code
- Flight Connection Number
- Flight date
- Aircraft Type

Figure 13.27 Data Preview from Open ODS View

13.1.3   Open ODS View Based on SAP HANA Database Table

Assume that you have a table in an SAP HANA database. Tables will be generally listed under the specific schema in a folder called **Tables**. This can be seen in the SAP HANA administration console perspective. For our demo, we'll start with creating the table in the SAP HANA database.

Create a Table in SAP HANA Database

In the SAP HANA admin perspective, follow the path **Schema · Tables · New Table** as shown in Figure 13.28.

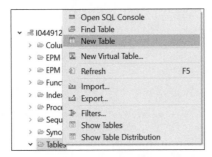

Figure 13.28 Create a Table under the Schema

Once you create the table, you need to give the fields that will be used in the table. Enter "PRODUCT" for the **Table Name**. You'll see the **Schema** name for the table, and the **Type** of the table will be **Column Store**. The next step is to add the names of fields like **Product_ID**, **Supplier_ID**, **Category**, and **Price** with their data types and dimensions, as shown in Figure 13.29.

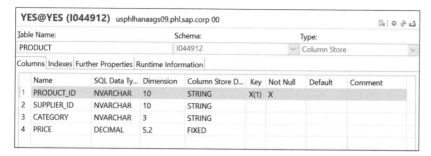

Figure 13.29 Table Fields and Data Types

You can see the path of the table under **SystemID · Catalog · <Schema Name> · Tables · <Table name>**, as shown in Figure 13.30:

❶ This is the **Catalog** folder in the SAP HANA admin console.

❷ Choose the schema that you are working on.

❸ The folder table is used to create and display the tables within the schema.

❹ Once you double-click on the table you can see the table name and the name of the fields.

❺ Here you can find the schema name.

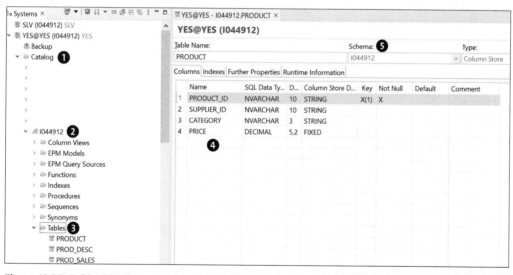

Figure 13.30 Table Details

Insert Data in SAP HANA Table

Once the table is created in the SAP HANA database, the next step is to insert the data into the table. To do that, right-click the table name and select **Generate · Insert Statement** (Figure 13.31).

Figure 13.31 Insert Data

You have an option to use SQL to insert the data into the SAP HANA table "Product". See Figure 13.32 for the syntax of the insert statement. It uses the `insert into` statement with the schema name and the table name. You need to add the details in the brackets.

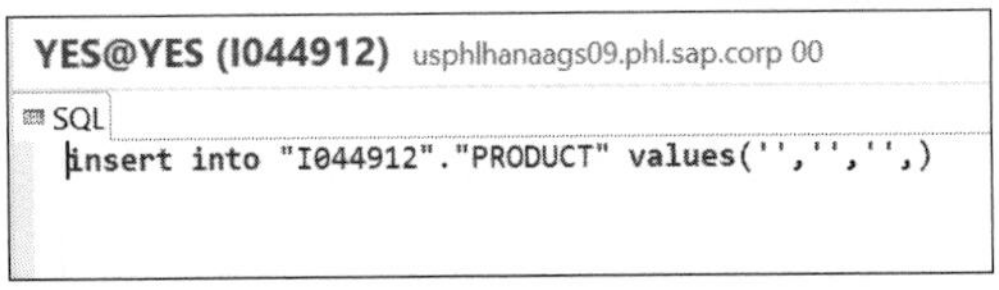

YES@YES (I044912) usphlhanaags09.phl.sap.corp 00

```
SQL
  insert into "I044912"."PRODUCT" values('','','',)
```

Figure 13.32 Insert Template

To add more rows to the table, you can use the SQL statement in Figure 13.32 with different values and execute. Once the statement is executed successfully, the table contents will be created (see Figure 13.33). You can see that five rows are inserted with the statement and it has multiple values within the parentheses.

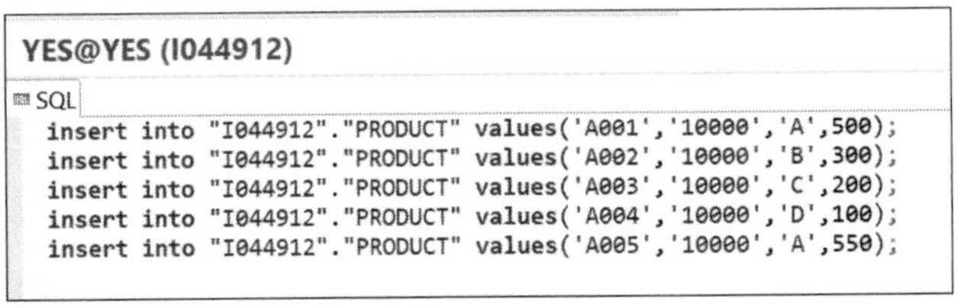

YES@YES (I044912)

```
SQL
  insert into "I044912"."PRODUCT" values('A001','10000','A',500);
  insert into "I044912"."PRODUCT" values('A002','10000','B',300);
  insert into "I044912"."PRODUCT" values('A003','10000','C',200);
  insert into "I044912"."PRODUCT" values('A004','10000','D',100);
  insert into "I044912"."PRODUCT" values('A005','10000','A',550);
```

Figure 13.33 Insert Statement Sample

Once the table content is created for the PRODUCT table, right-click the PRODUCT table and select **Open Content**, as shown in Figure 13.34.

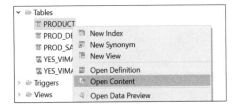

Figure 13.34 SAP HANA Database Table

The results are shown in Figure 13.35. You can see that five rows were retrieved and the fields are PRODUCT_ID, SUPPLIER_ID, CATEGORY, and PRICE.

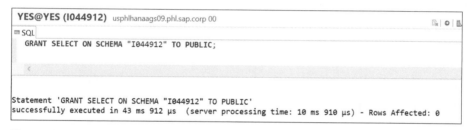

Figure 13.35 Table Data Preview

Before using this table in SAP BW/4HANA, users need grant access for this schema, which can be provided by the Basis or security team. For this example, let's grant access to all users. Execute the SQL shown in Figure 13.36 and make sure it's successful. In the real world, we won't provide grant access to the public; this access is controlled by the security team.

```
YES@YES (I044912)  usphlhanaags09.phl.sap.corp 00
SQL
  GRANT SELECT ON SCHEMA "I044912" TO PUBLIC;



Statement 'GRANT SELECT ON SCHEMA "I044912" TO PUBLIC'
successfully executed in 43 ms 912 µs  (server processing time: 10 ms 910 µs) - Rows Affected: 0
```

Figure 13.36 Grant Access

Consume SAP HANA Table with Open ODS View

The next step is to consume this SAP HANA table using an open ODS view from the SAP BW/4HANA system. Use the option shown in Figure 13.37. The creation of an open ODS view in SAP BW/4HANA will use a wizard to get details like the source type. You need to choose **Database Table or View** in this example, and in the second box you need to choose **Schema** as the source.

Once you choose the schema name and continue with the wizard, it will prompt you for the schema selection. You can search for the schema pattern and select the correct schema name from the list of **Matching Items** (Figure 13.38).

Select Source Type

Source Type:*
- ○ DataSource (BW)
- ◉ Database Table or View
- ○ Database Table or View via Linked Database or MDC
- ○ Virtual table using SAP HANA Smart Data Access
- ○ Big Data
- ○ DataStore Object (advanced)
- ○ Transformation

- ○ Existing BW Source System
- ◉ Owner / Schema

Figure 13.37 Database Table with Schema

Select a DB object schema

Select an item to open (? = any character, * = any string):

| I04 |

Matching items:

[I044912]

Figure 13.38 Choose Schema

Now choose the table name from the matching items. In this example, the table is **PRODUCT**, so choose that as shown in Figure 13.39.

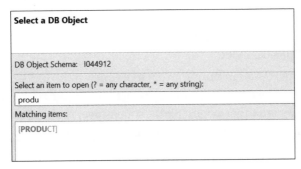

Select a DB Object

DB Object Schema: I044912

Select an item to open (? = any character, * = any string):

| produ |

Matching items:

[PRODUCT]

Figure 13.39 Choose Database Object

You can create the source system or use the existing source system. You need to choose a source system of type **SAP HANA Local Database Schema**. You've created this source system already, so choose source system **CB4_VIEW** as shown in Figure 13.40.

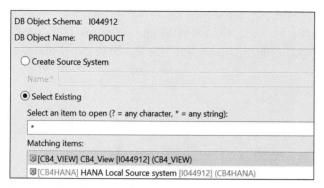

Figure 13.40 Choose Source System

If you check the DataSource in Eclipse, you can see that CB4_VIEW is a HANA_LOCAL source system, as shown in Figure 13.41.

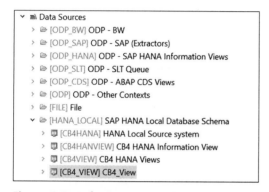

Figure 13.41 Reference HANA_LOCAL Source System

If you double-click the source system, you can see the **Connection Type** and the schema name, as shown in Figure 13.42.

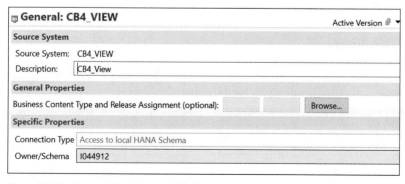

Figure 13.42 Connection Type and Schema

Back in the open ODS creation wizard, you can see the **Confirmation** page as shown in Figure 13.43. This page shows details such as the name of the open ODS view (**ZRKOOV4**) and the **Semantics** (**Facts**). The details of the **Source Type** will also be shown (**Database Table**).

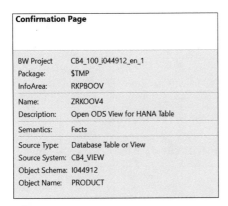

Figure 13.43 Confirmation

In the **General** tab you can find the source of the open ODS view under **Semantics**: **Database Table or View**, as shown in Figure 13.44.

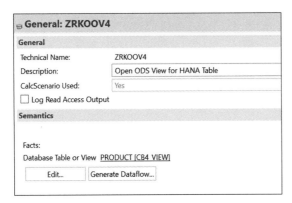

Figure 13.44 Open ODS View

Check the facts and you'll see that the fields from the CDS views are visible here (Figure 13.45). You can see fields such as [**PRODUC_ID**], [**SUPPLIER_ID**], [**CATEGORY**], and [**PRICE**]. If you double-click a field name, you can see the **Association With** information, showing the system-wide unique name.

Finally, you can do a data preview from the open ODS view (see Figure 13.46). You can see that without persisting in SAP BW/4HANA, you can read the data from the database table in SAP HANA. This is the major advantage of an open ODS view, which will help you implement data models with more virtualization.

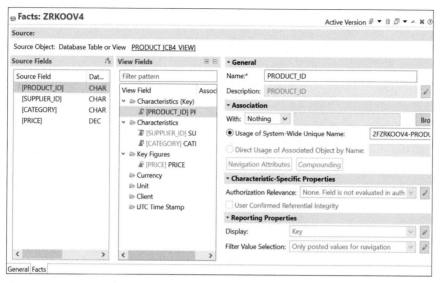

Figure 13.45 Facts in Open ODS

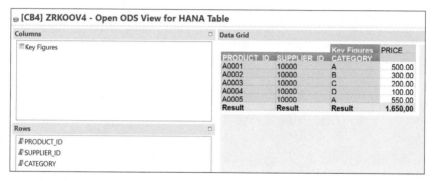

Figure 13.46 Data Preview in Open ODS

13.2   Summary

With the completion of the dataflow based on the open ODS views, now you're ready to build an SAP BW/4HANA model to extract data from SAP S/4HANA via a table or a CDS view. Having good know-how on this topic is essential as more companies are including more virtualization options in their data modeling for real-time extraction. Data modeling with open ODS views will help you have more virtualization in your system design, which will be a key benefit of SAP BW/4HANA. Knowing about a mix of classical and new extractors will help you design more efficient data models during SAP BW/4HANA implementation.

In the next chapter, we'll focus on extracting data from SAP S/4HANA using the SAP HANA calculation views to SAP BW/4HANA.

Chapter 14

Extracting Data Using SAP HANA Calculation Views

This chapter describes the virtual data provisioning options from SAP HANA to SAP BW/4HANA. Effective data modeling can be achieved using the virtualization options for data extraction. These data provisioning methods will help you define and architect an analytics strategy for your complex landscape during SAP BW/4HANA implementation.

The data in SAP S/4HANA can be consumed in real time using the native SAP HANA calculation views based on the tables. In this chapter, we'll start with a basic overview of the SAP HANA admin perspective in Section 14.1, then we'll create SAP HANA calculation views in Section 14.2. Consuming the SAP HANA calculation views in SAP BW/4HANA is discussed in Section 14.3. The options to consume SAP HANA calculation views with persistency and virtualization are discussed in Section 14.4. Finally, additional SAP HANA calculation views with input parameters are explained in Section 14.5. Upon completing this chapter, you'll know how to consume data from SAP S/4HANA using SAP HANA calculation views.

14.1 Understanding the SAP HANA Admin Perspective

In any SAP system based on the SAP HANA database, you'll have an SAP HANA administration perspective in which database administration takes place. If you need to work on SAP HANA calculation views, you must have an SAP HANA database user that has access with the relevant privileges.

First, open the SAP HANA admin perspective as shown in Figure 14.1:

❶ Choose the **Open Perspective** icon 🗗.

❷ Select **SAP HANA Administration Console** 🦺.

❸ Click the **Open** button.

You will then be in the admin console, and as shown in Figure 14.2, you need to add the equivalent SAP HANA database system for SAP BW/4HANA ❶ or SAP S/4HANA ❷. The first step is to know the database system IDs for SAP S/4HANA and SAP BW/4HANA. You can get that info by launching SAP GUI and selecting menu option **System • Status**.

The database system ID will be in the **Name** box and the type of database in the **Data-Base System** box.

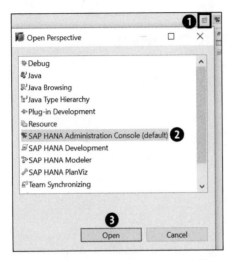

Figure 14.1 SAP HANA Admin Console Perspective

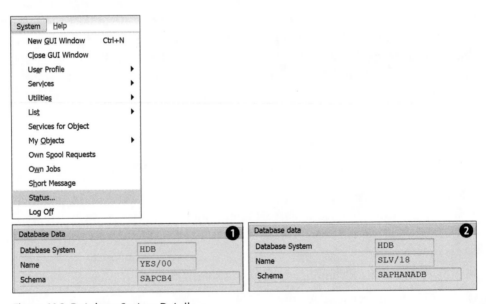

Figure 14.2 Database System Details

Once you have the user name and password for these database systems, you need to add them to SAP HANA Studio in the Admin Console. It will look as shown in Figure 14.3. To add a new SAP HANA database system, right-click in the **Systems** navigator space and select **Add System**. You'll see a wizard that will prompt you to provide the **Host Name**, **Instance Number**, and **Description**. Provide those details and click **Next**.

You'll be asked to provide the SAP HANA database **User Name** and **Password**. Enter that information and choose **Finish** to complete the process of adding the SAP HANA database system. You'll see the system ID once it's added under the **Systems** space.

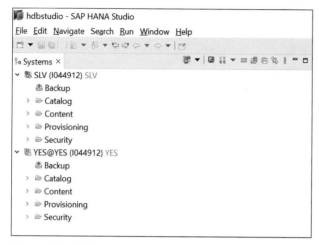

Figure 14.3 Adding SAP BW/4HANA and SAP S/4HANA Database Systems

You can see that two database systems have been added. **SLV** is the database system name for SAP S/4HANA and **YES** is the database system name for SAP BW/4HANA. You'll also see these folders:

- The **Catalog** folder represents the SAP HANA dictionary, which has all the system-defined or user-created schemas; for example, you'll see **_SYS_BI** and **_SYS_BIC** here (see Figure 14.4).

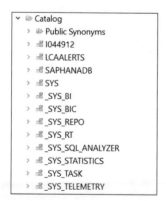

Figure 14.4 Catalog Folder

- The **Content** folder stores custom information models that a user creates. Here you can find the package for views (see Figure 14.5).

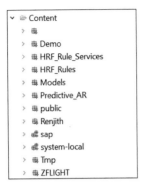

Figure 14.5 Content Folder Sample

You can see that a package has been created for this user. Note the **system-local** package, which is used to consume the objects that are exposed from SAP BW/4HANA (see Figure 14.6).

Figure 14.6 System Local

- The **Provisioning** folder is used to configure the remote sources that are used in SAP HANA smart data access (see Figure 14.7).

Figure 14.7 Provisioning

- The **Security** folder contains information about users and roles that are defined for a specific system (see Figure 14.8).

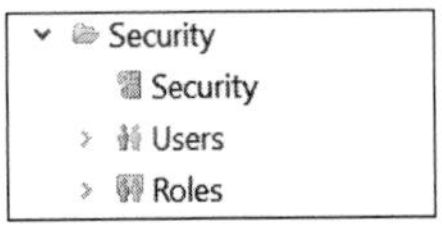

Figure 14.8 Security Folder

14.2   Creating SAP HANA Calculation Views

To create SAP HANA calculation views, you need to first log into SAP HANA Studio in Eclipse in the SAP HANA Admin Console perspective. We'll walk creating a package and calculation views in the following sections.

14.2.1   Creating a Package

Create a new package under the **Content** folder as shown in Figure 14.9.

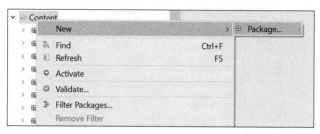

Figure 14.9 Package Creation

Provide the **Name** of the package and the **Description** (see Figure 14.10).

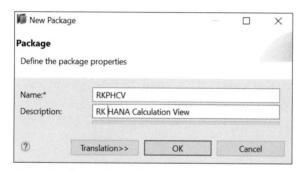

Figure 14.10 Package Details

Once you press **OK**, you'll see the screen shown in Figure 14.11.

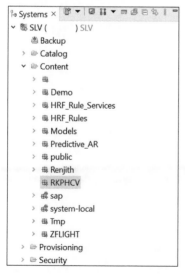

Figure 14.11 Package after Creation

14.2.2   SAP HANA Calculation Views

To create SAP HANA calculation views, follow these steps:

1. Right-click your package and select **New • Calculation View**, as shown in Figure 14.12.

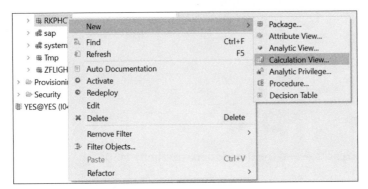

Figure 14.12 Create Calculation View

2. You'll see the screen shown in Figure 14.13. Provide the **Name** and a description in the **Label** field. The **View Type** is **Calculation View** by default and the **Type** is **Graphical**.

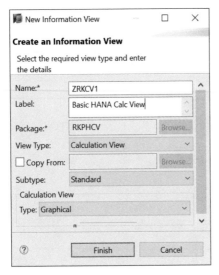

Figure 14.13 Name and Label

3. Once you choose **Finish**, you'll see the view editor, as shown in Figure 14.14:

   ❶ The package name is listed under the **Content** folder; you can create views under this package.

   ❷ The created SAP HANA calculation view name is listed here.

   ❸ The operations on SAP HANA calculation views can be carried out from these nodes.

❹ The SAP HANA calculation view can be created here. You can adjust the size of this frame by dragging the both sides of the frame.

❺ The details of the SAP HANA views can be seen under the multiple tabs listed here. You can see the properties, define parameters, and more.

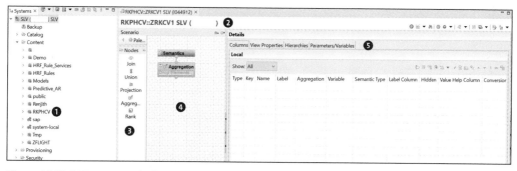

Figure 14.14 SAP HANA Calculation View Editor

Let's create a very simple SAP HANA calculation view that gets all data from table MARA, the material master header table. Follow these steps:

1. To view all data from a table, you can use the **Projection** option. Drag the **Projection** node from the left to the view editor, as shown in Figure 14.15.

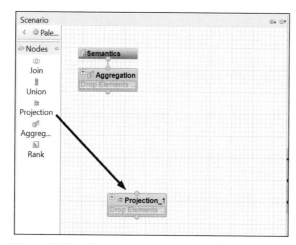

Figure 14.15 Projection

2. Insert the table name into the projection node by right-clicking the node and choosing **Add Objects** (see Figure 14.16).

3. Insert the table as shown in Figure 14.17. You first need to search for the table name in the **Find** window. You'll get multiple search help results. You can choose a table name from the search help—in this example, table MARA for general material data.

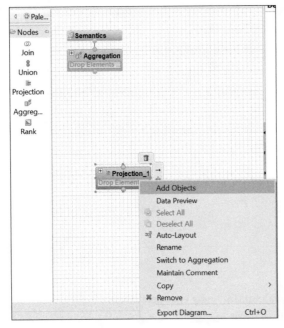

Figure 14.16 Add Objects

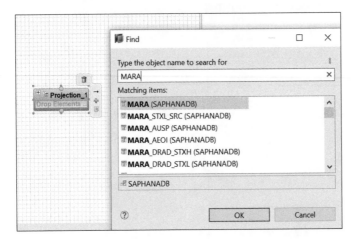

Figure 14.17 Insert Table

4. Once you choose **OK**, the editor will change and you'll see the options for the node; in this case, you can see that the **Projection** node now has the name of the table set as **MARA**. Under the **Details** section you can see all the fields from table MARA in grey. **SAPHAADB** before table MARA is the schema where the table is stored. In the last frame, you can see the output options for this node, such as **Columns**, **Calculated Columns**, **Input Parameters**, and **Filters**. Finally, you will see the properties for the node such as **View Name**, **Label**, **Changed By**, and **Package**. The base project screen will look as shown in Figure 14.18.

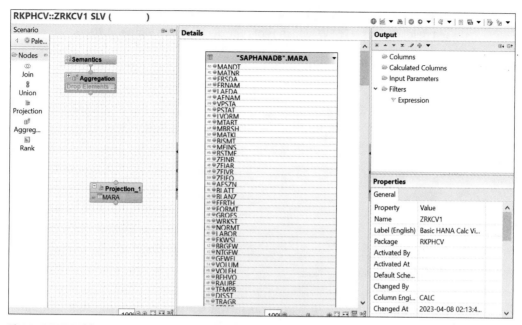

Figure 14.18 Table Projection

5. If you need to choose certain fields from the table, you need to click the field name in the center **Details** pane. The table along and its fields are shown here. You can choose five fields from this table; when you select the fields, the grey color will change to orange and the columns in the output will have those fields added. Start by selecting the **MATNR** field (see Figure 14.19).

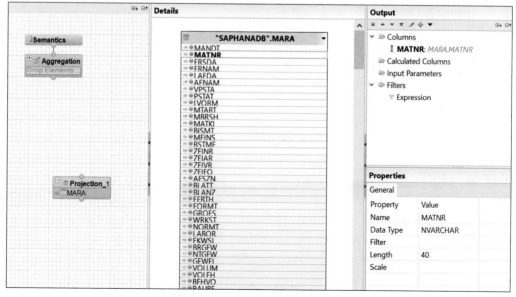

Figure 14.19 Choose Field for Selection

6. Choose other fields in the same way. Make sure you choose at least one numeric-based field, such as **NTGEW**, which is of type decimal (see Figure 14.20).

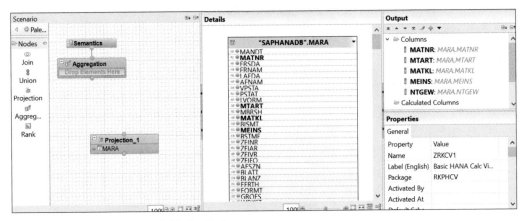

Figure 14.20 Output Fields for Node

7. If you need to rename the node, you can do that by right-clicking the node name and choosing **Rename**, but you can always leave it as it is with the same name as **Projection_1** (see Figure 14.21). We chose to rename our node here to **Projection_mara**.

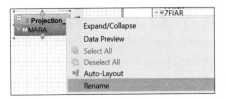

Figure 14.21 Option to Rename Node

8. Now use the **Create Connection** functionality to create a connection to the aggregation node. Choose the arrow icon from the node as shown in Figure 14.22. Drag the arrow to connect to the next node. In this case, point to the **Aggregation** node, as shown in Figure 14.23.

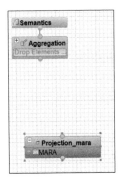

Figure 14.22 Create Connection

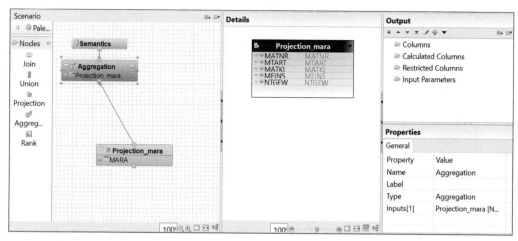

Figure 14.23 Aggregation Node

9. You can see that the **Aggregation** node now has the name of the **Projection_mara** node and the **Details** tab has only the fields that were selected for output in the previous node. But all four fields are grey, which means they're not selected for output in this node. You can see that the **Columns** folder in the **Output** area is blank as no fields are selected for the output. Choose all the fields in the **Details** frame and you will see the results shown in Figure 14.24. When you use the aggregation node, the common fields will be aggregated, so you need to test the behavior.

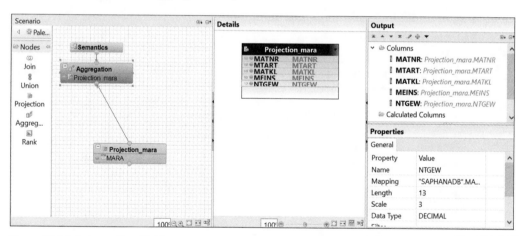

Figure 14.24 Aggregation Fields

10. If you right-click the **Graphical** pane, you can select **Auto Layout** as shown in Figure 14.25.

11. Earlier in Figure 14.25, the nodes were scattered, but with auto layout, you can see that the nodes are aligned properly in a vertical line in the graphical pane, as shown in Figure 14.26.

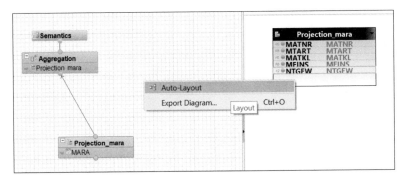

Figure 14.25 Auto Layout

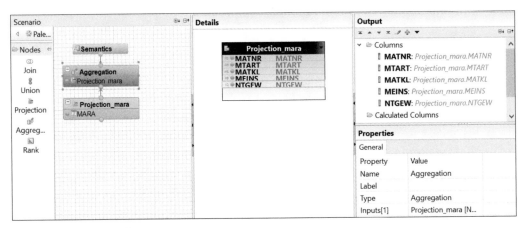

Figure 14.26 After Auto Layout

12. Click the **Semantics** node and you can see the view-based tabs, including the **Column** tab (see Figure 14.27).

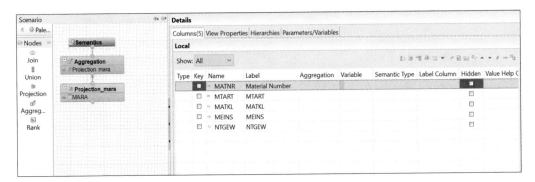

Figure 14.27 Semantics: Column Tab

13. Choose the **Properties** tab as shown in Figure 14.28.

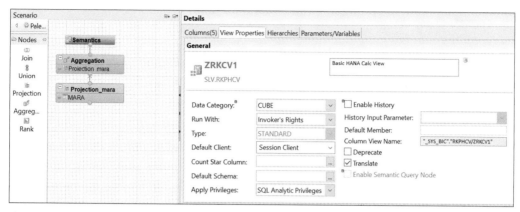

Figure 14.28 Properties Tab

14. You have the option to choose the **Default Client**, which should be **Cross-Client** (see Figure 14.29).

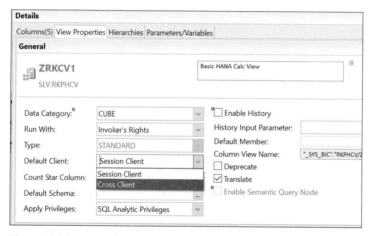

Figure 14.29 Cross-Client

15. Choose the **Classical Analytic Privileges** option from the dropdown in the **Apply Privileges** field (see Figure 14.30).

16. Changing both **Default Client** to **Cross-Client** and **Apply Privilege** to **Classical Analytic Privilege** will make the **View Properties** tab appear as shown in Figure 14.31.

17. Activate the view using the **Save and Activate** option (⊚ ▼ ; see Figure 14.32).

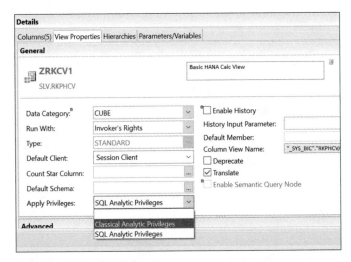

Figure 14.30 Apply Privileges

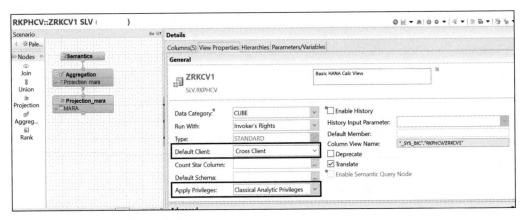

Figure 14.31 Properties Settings

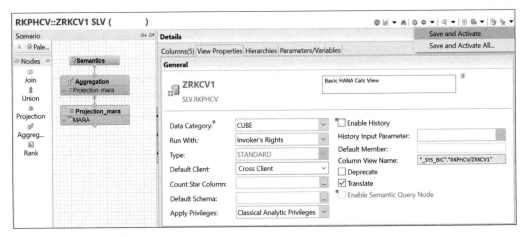

Figure 14.32 View Activation

18. You should see a message such as the one shown in Figure 14.33.

Figure 14.33 Job Status

19. Right-click the **Semantics** node and choose **Data Preview**, as shown in Figure 14.34.

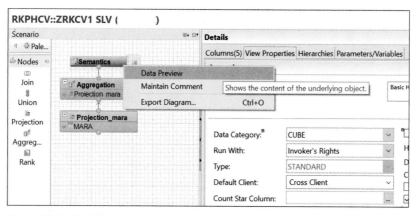

Figure 14.34 Data Preview

20. You can see the new tab, as shown in Figure 14.35. You'll see tabs such as **Analysis**, **Distinct Values**, and **Raw Data**.

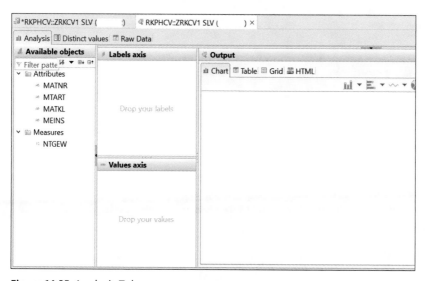

Figure 14.35 Analysis Tab

21. Choose **Raw Data** (see Figure 14.36).

MATNR	MTART	MATKL	MEINS	NTGEW
TG10	HAWA	L001	ST	180
RM1_CP	ROH	L002	ST	20
TG12	HAWA	L001	ST	18
TG13	HAWA	L001	ST	18
TG14	HAWA	L001	ST	180
TG20	HAWA	L001	ST	180
TG21	HAWA	L001	ST	18
RMME02	ROH	L002	EA	0.8
NS0002	NLAG	YBMM01	ST	0
SRV_CONT...	SERV	P001	LE	0
TG0001	MAT	L001	ST	0
TG0013	MAT	L001	ST	9
TG0012	MAT	L001	ST	1.8
000000000...	FERT		ST	0
NS0001	NLAG	YBMM01	ST	0
OM006	HALB	L003	KG	0

Analysis Distinct values Raw Data
Filter pattern 200 rows retrieved - 588 ms

Figure 14.36 Output

22. You can filter using the **Add Filter** option. You can also see the row count restricted to 200, as shown in Figure 14.37.

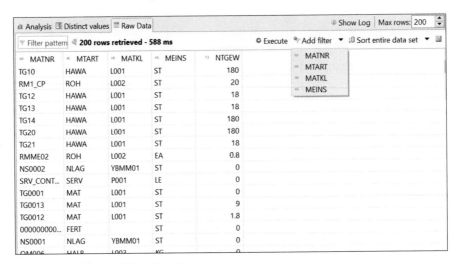

Figure 14.37 Filter and Row Count

23. The view and the results are shown in Figure 14.38, which shows the following information:

❶ The SAP HANA calculation view can be seen under your package.

❷ The data preview can show the results under the **Raw Data** tab.

❸ You can restrict the results by using the **Add Filter** option, which can help you view a specific record.

❹ You can increase the total rows displayed as raw data by increasing the value here. For example, if you set this to 500, then you can see 500 rows in the **Raw Data** tab.

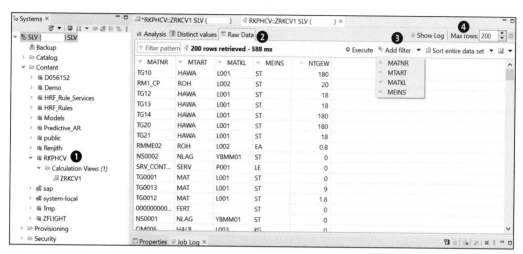

Figure 14.38 View and Results

With this, you've created an SAP HANA calculation view in the SAP S/4HANA system. Before you move to the next section, jot down the name of the view: ZRKCV1.

14.3   Prerequisites for Consuming SAP HANA Calculation Views

There are certain prerequisites before you consume an SAP HANA calculation view in SAP BW/4HANA:

1. The first step is to create an SAP HANA–based source system under the **DataSource** folder in SAP BW/4HANA. You'll use this source system to consume SAP HANA calculation views (see Figure 14.39).

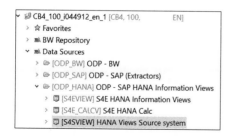

Figure 14.39 ODP_HANA Source System

The source system properties are shown in Figure 14.40.

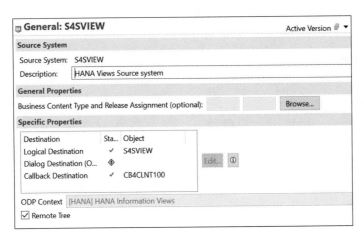

Figure 14.40 SAP HANA Properties

2. You need to make some configuration settings in SAP BW/4HANA. Use Transaction SPRO in SAP BW/4HANA and choose as **SAP Reference IMG** shown in Figure 14.41.

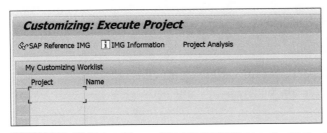

Figure 14.41 SPRO

3. You'll arrive at the screen shown in Figure 14.42. Select **Settings for Consumption of SAP HANA Views**.

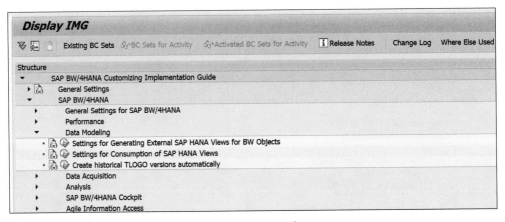

Figure 14.42 Settings for SAP HANA View Consumption

4. Choose the **Hybrid Mode** option shown in Figure 14.43.

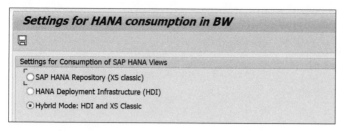

Figure 14.43 Settings

5. Save these settings.

14.4   Consuming SAP HANA Calculation Views

There are two major options to consume SAP HANA calculation views. You can replicate the SAP HANA views as DataSources in SAP BW/4HANA and create aDSOs on top of them to persist the data. Alternatively, you can consume the SAP HANA calculation views directly in the SAP HANA composite provider without persisting the data. We'll walk through each option in the following sections.

14.4.1   Consuming SAP HANA Calculation Views in SAP BW/4HANA as aDSOs

To consume SAP HANA calculation views, follow the navigation path shown in Figure 14.44 in SAP BW/4HANA: **Data Sources · ODP_HANA Folder · [Your source system] · New · DataSource**.

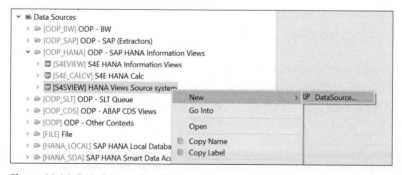

Figure 14.44 DataSource Creation

You'll see the wizard shown in Figure 14.45. Continue with the wizard by choosing **Next**.

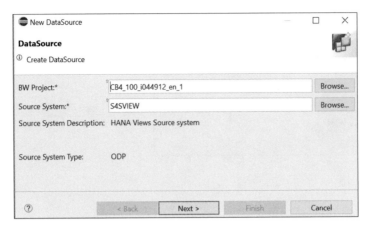

Figure 14.45 Wizard

On the screen shown in Figure 14.46, choose the **Proposal from Operational Data Provider** and continue with the **Next** button.

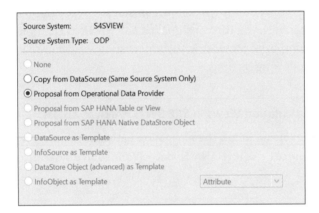

Figure 14.46 Proposal from Operational Data Provider

In the wizard, you can search for the providers as shown in Figure 14.47. You need to give the name of the calculation view that you created in the source system. Note that you always give the package name where you created the SAP HANA calculation view; it will list all the views that are created and you can select the SAP HANA calculation view. When you're done, choose **Finish**.

After you click **Finish**, you'll see the confirmation page shown in Figure 14.48. It will have the **Name** and **Description** of the DataSource that you're going to create. You'll need to choose the DataSource type; in this example, select **Transactional Data**.

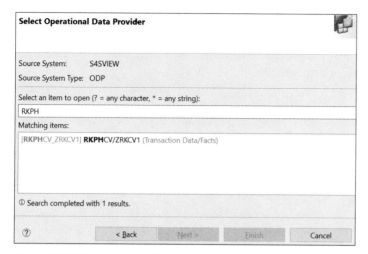

Figure 14.47 Choose a Provider

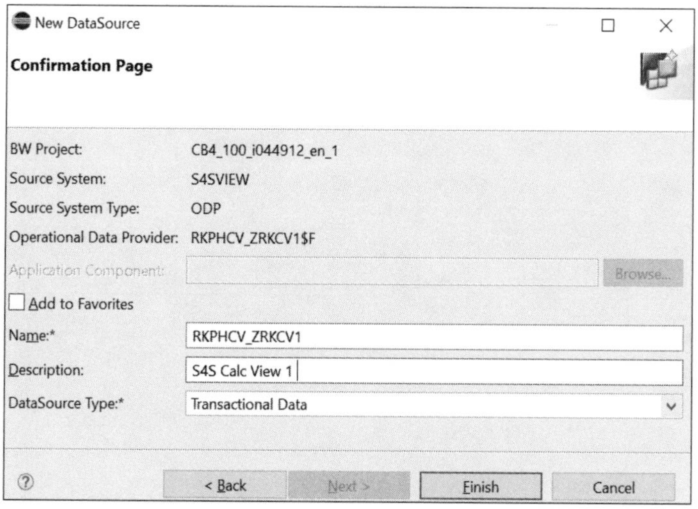

Figure 14.48 Confirmation

After the previous step, the system will create the new DataSource as shown in Figure 14.49. You can see that in the **Extraction** tab of the DataSource maintenance screen, the **ODP Context** is **HANA Information Views** and the **Operational Data Provider** is the SAP HANA calculation view that you created. Also note that **Semantics** is **Transaction Data**.

If you select the **Fields** tab of the DataSource maintenance screen, you can see the fields as shown in Figure 14.50. These fields are based on the SAP HANA calculation views that you created in the sender system. You can see that the DataSource has two additional fields: **ODQ_CHANGEMODE**, which can have values such as **C** for a new record, **U** for a changed record, and **D** for deleted record; and **ODQ_ENTITYCNTR**, which has values such as **(1, -1, 0)** for after image and before image. With the combination of these two field values, the **RECORDMODE** value is determined in SAP BW/4HANA to tell if a record is new image, after image, or before image.

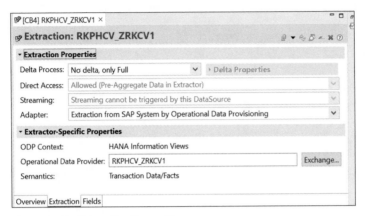

Figure 14.49 Extraction Properties

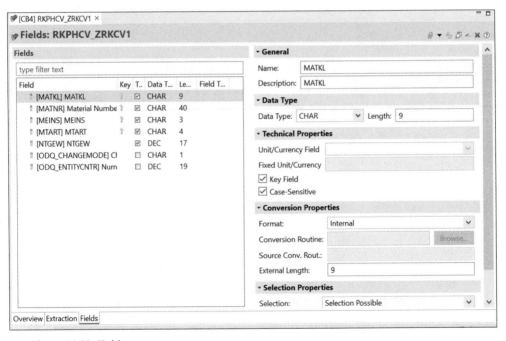

Figure 14.50 Fields

Once the DataSource based on the SAP HANA calculation view is created, the next step is to create the aDSO based on the DataSource (see Figure 14.51).

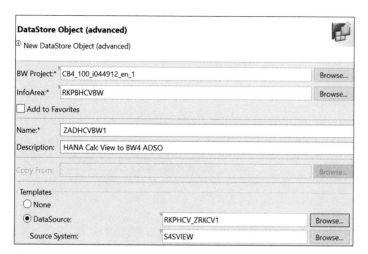

Figure 14.51 ADSO Based on SAP HANA Calculation View

The created aDSO will have fields based on the DataSource (see Figure 14.52). You can see that there are four key fields and one nonkey field in the aDSO. Activate the aDSO.

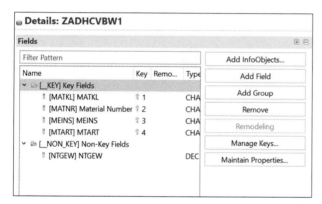

Figure 14.52 ADSO Fields

After the aDSO is activated, the next step is to create the transformation from the SAP HANA calculation view–based DataSource and then finally create the DTP, as shown in Figure 14.53.

To validate the data load in SAP BW/4HANA, log into SAP S/4HANA and check the total records in table MARA (see Figure 14.54). You can see that table MARA has 2,543 records, so the first execution of the DTP will bring in all these records.

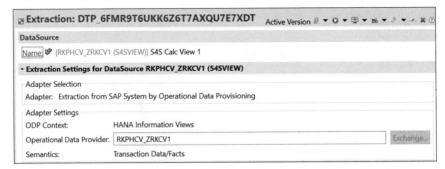

Figure 14.53 DTP Settings

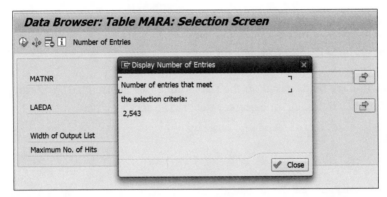

Figure 14.54 Total Records in Table MARA

In SAP S/4HANA, open the SAP HANA calculation view and do a data preview. You can see that the total records number in the SAP HANA calculation view is 2,543 which matches the table MARA entries (see Figure 14.55).

MATNR	MTART	MATKL	MEINS	NTGEW
TG10	HAWA	L001	ST	180
RM1_CP	ROH	L002	ST	20
TG12	HAWA	L001	ST	18
TG13	HAWA	L001	ST	18
TG14	HAWA	L001	ST	180
TG20	HAWA	L001	ST	180
TG21	HAWA	L001	ST	18
RMME02	ROH	L002	EA	0.8
NS0002	NLAG	YBMM01	ST	0

Figure 14.55 Total Records in SAP HANA Calculation View

Now log onto SAP BW/4HANA and execute the DTP that you created based on the SAP HANA calculation view DataSource–based aDSO. You can see the result of 2,543 records, as shown in Figure 14.56. The data will be first staged in the inbound table. But you can confirm that the same data was seen in table MARA and the SAP HANA calculation view in SAP S/4HANA, and the same records are extracted to SAP BW/4HANA.

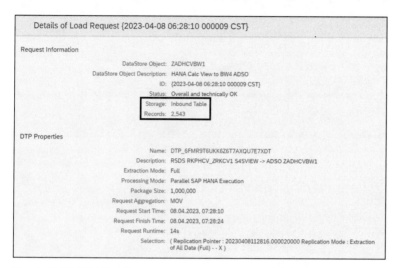

Figure 14.56 DTP Monitor

To see how the ODP is behaving when you use an SAP HANA calculation view, log onto SAP S/4HANA and check Transaction ODQMON. Choose **HANA Information Views** as the **Subscriber** (see Figure 14.57). You'll see a list of SAP HANA calculation views.

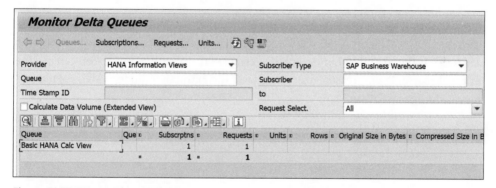

Figure 14.57 Transaction ODQMON

Select the SAP HANA calculation view that you created. Double-click it to go to the subscription view, where can now see other details, such as the target SAP BW system (see Figure 14.58).

If you double-click the subscriber, it will take you to the requests view, as shown in Figure 14.59. Here you can see the details of the composite request and the subscription with the DTP details. You can see that **Storage** is **ODQDATA_F**, which indicates that this is a full extraction.

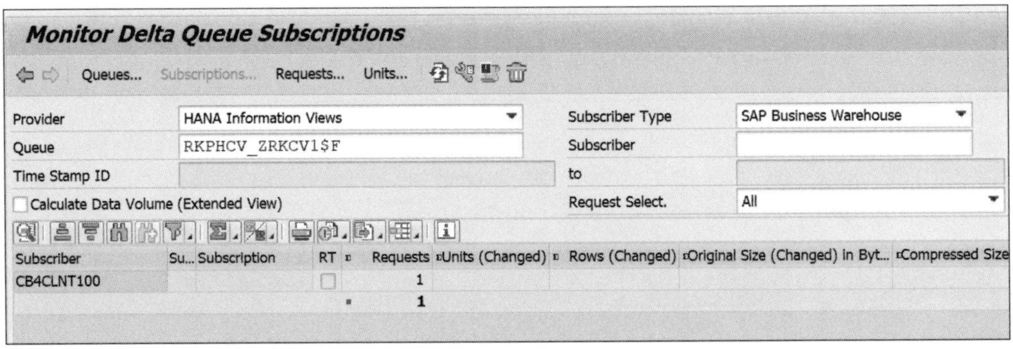

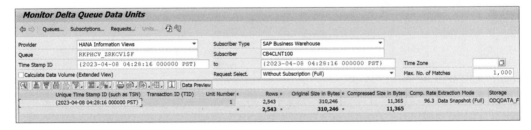

Figure 14.58 Queues

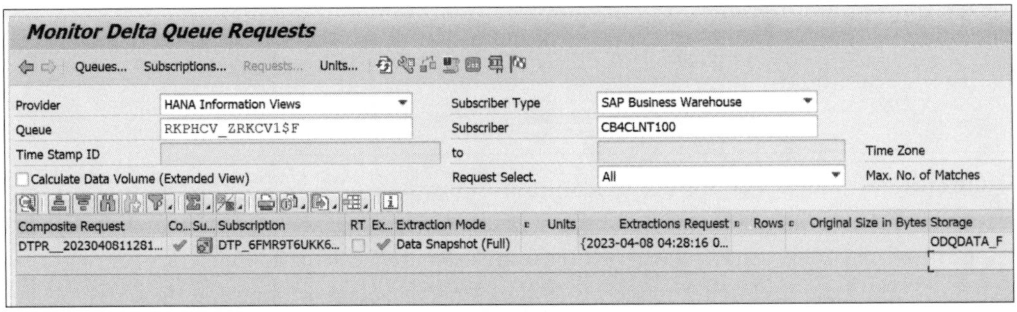

Figure 14.59 Requests

From the requests, if you double-click the composite request row, you'll go to the units view, as shown in Figure 14.60. This view will have the details such as **Rows with Value 2543**: this is the total number of records extracted to SAP BW/4HANA. You can see the original size and compressed size, along with the **Extraction Mode**, which is **Full**, and hence **Storage** is **ODQDATA_F**.

Figure 14.60 Units

You can see here that the aDSO persisted the data from the SAP HANA calculation view.

14.4.2 Consuming SAP BW/4HANA Calculation Views Using SAP HANA Composite Providers

When you want to consume SAP HANA calculation views in the same database, you need to create an SAP HANA calculation view in the database of the SAP BW/4HANA system. This is the base table that we will use for the calculation view creation (see Figure 14.61). The data for the calculation view will be fetched from this table.

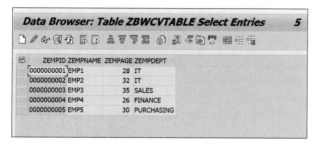

Figure 14.61 Base Table

Create a projection on this table (see Figure 14.62) and enable the fields required for the output in the **Details** tab. You can see that four fields are selected in the **Output** folder.

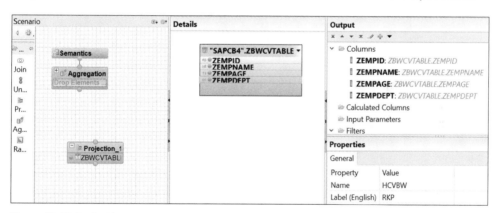

Figure 14.62 Projection

Once the **Projection** node is complete, drag the aggregation node and connect the projection node to the aggregation node. Choose the fields that you require for output in the aggregation node. Once the aggregation is over, check the data preview as shown in Figure 14.63.

Right-click the aggregation node and choose the **Data Preview** option. You'll see the results with the records listed as shown in Figure 14.64.

Once the SAP HANA view is tested and activated, the next step is to create an SAP HANA composite provider in SAP BW/4HANA (see Figure 14.65). After you've done so, right-click the graphical pane and you'll see an option to add the objects.

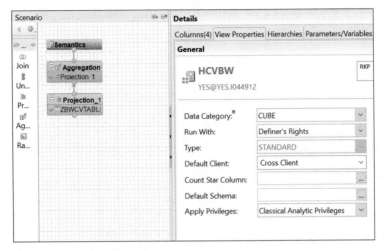

Figure 14.63 Calculation View

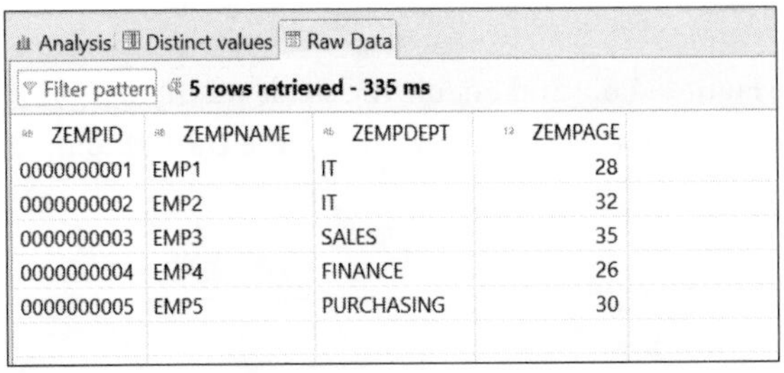

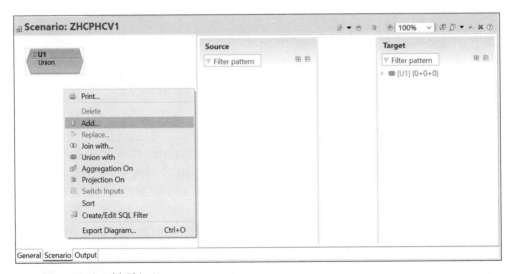

Figure 14.64 Data Preview

Figure 14.65 Add Objects

Once you see the **Add Provider** window, search for the SAP HANA calculation view object and choose it (see Figure 14.66).

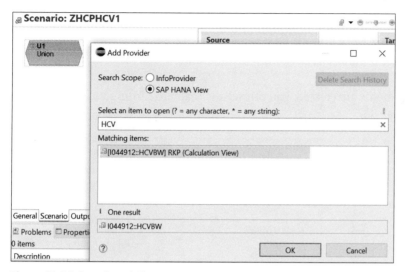

Figure 14.66 Search and Choose

Once you choose **OK**, you'll see the SAP HANA calculation view, as shown in Figure 14.67. The SAP HANA composite provider will bring in data from the listed SAP HANA calculation view. This will be a virtual model as the SAP HANA composite provider directly calls the SAP HANA calculation view for any reporting requirements. We won't stage the data in SAP BW in this scenario.

Figure 14.67 Source Tab

The next step is to right-click **Nongrouped Fields** and choose **Create Assignments** as shown in Figure 14.68. This will create the assignment from the source fields to the target fields in the SAP HANA composite provider.

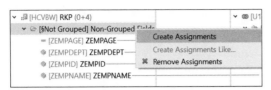

Figure 14.68 Create Assignments

Once the assignments are created, you can see the mappings from source to target as shown in Figure 14.69.

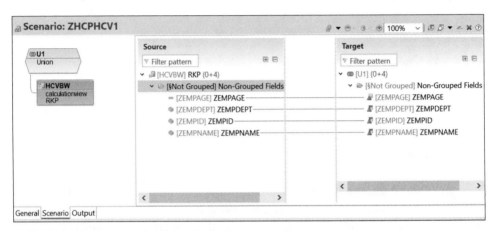

Figure 14.69 Scenario Tab after Assignment

Choose the **Output** tab as shown in Figure 14.70. This tab will have the details of the output fields of the SAP HANA composite provider.

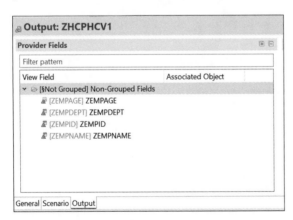

Figure 14.70 Output Tab

Once you've completed these steps for all tables of the SAP HANA composite provider, activate it (see Figure 14.71).

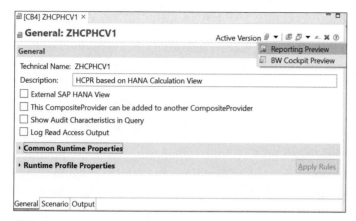

Figure 14.71 Activate and Reporting Preview

After the activation, you can right-click the SAP HANA composite provider and choose **Data Preview**. The output of the reporting is shown in Figure 14.72. These results are fetched from the SAP HANA calculation view execution.

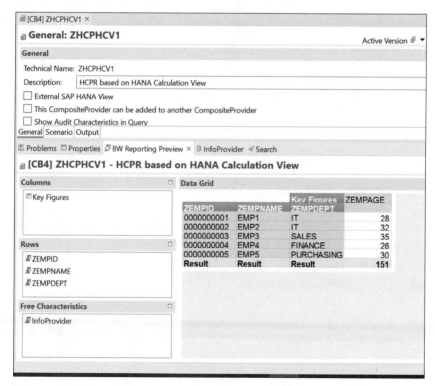

Figure 14.72 SAP HANA Composite Provider Reporting Preview

14.5   Creating Data Models Using SAP HANA Calculation Views

In this section, you'll see how to create SAP HANA calculation views with joins and how to use aggregation nodes on top of these joins. You'll also learn how to add an input parameter to restrict the results from the SAP HANA calculation views. Finally, you'll learn how to extract the created SAP HANA calculation view in SAP BW/4HANA.

14.5.1   Creating a New Calculation View

In this example, you need to join two tables and create an SAP HANA calculation view. Open SAP HANA Studio in the SAP HANA admin perspective and create a new SAP HANA calculation view. Follow these steps:

1. Create a new SAP HANA calculation view (see Figure 14.73), as we discussed in Section 14.2.2.

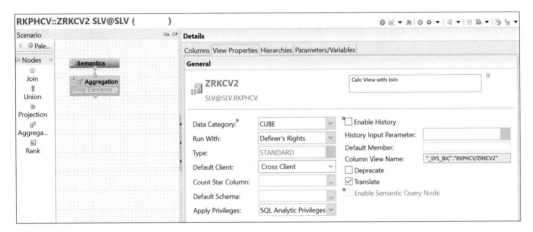

Figure 14.73 Calculation View Properties

You can see that **Default Client** is set to **Cross-Client**, and for **Apply Privileges** we've selected **SQL Analytic Privileges**.

2. Drag two more projection nodes in. The editor should look as shown in Figure 14.74, where you can see **Projection_1** and **Projection_2**.

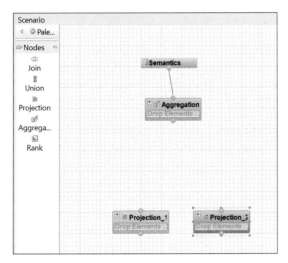

Figure 14.74 Projection Nodes

3. Click the ⊞ icon or right-click the projection node and select **Add Objects**. Choose the table name that you want to add (see Figure 14.75).

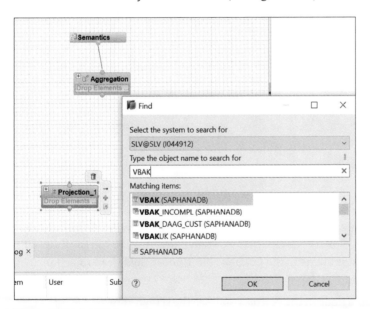

Figure 14.75 Add Elements

4. Add table VBAK in **Projection_1** and table VBAP in **Projection_2**. The final editor will look as shown in Figure 14.76.

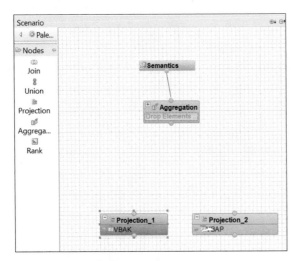

Figure 14.76 Projection

5. Choose **Projection_1** and select the fields that you need, as shown in Figure 14.77.

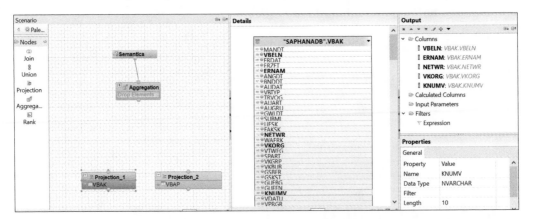

Figure 14.77 Projection_1 Fields

6. You can see that five fields are enabled in the **Details** pane, and you can see those five field names in the **Output** pane in the **Columns** tab. Choose fields for **Projection_2** in the same way (see Figure 14.78).

7. Drag and drop the **Join** node in the editor; you'll see the screen shown in Figure 14.79. The name will be **Join_1**.

8. Connect the link between **Projection_1** and **Projection_2** to **Join_1**, as shown in Figure 14.80.

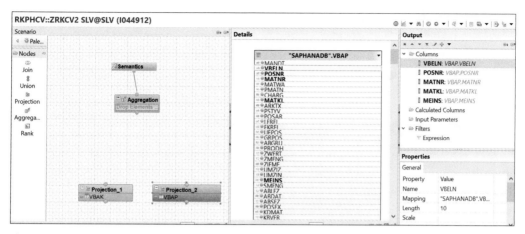

Figure 14.78 Projection_2 Fields

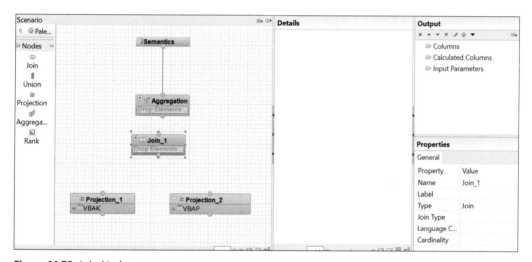

Figure 14.79 Join Node

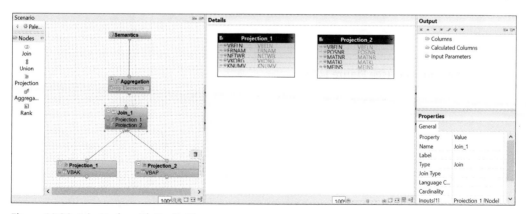

Figure 14.80 Join Node with Projections

9. In the **Details** pane, connect the join conditions from **Projection_1** and **Projection_2** as shown in Figure 14.81. You need to map and connect the fields from **Projection_1** to **Projection_2** manually, so make sure you connect the same fields; for example, **VBELN** in **Projection_1** should be connected to **VBELN** in **Projection_2**.

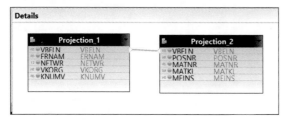

Figure 14.81 Join Conditions

10. If you double-click the **Join** line, you can see the type of join, as shown in Figure 14.82.

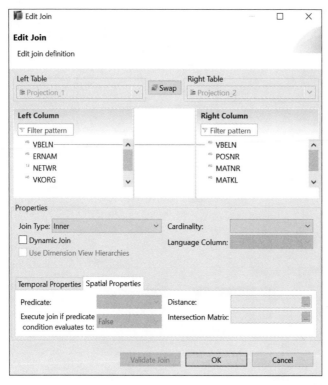

Figure 14.82 Inner Join

11. If you need to see the available joins, you can see that from the dropdown menu under **Join Type**. The list of available joins is shown in Figure 14.83. You can use joins such as inner join, left outer join, right outer join, text join, and full outer join.

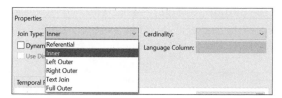

Figure 14.83 Join Type

12. For this example, stick with the **Inner Join**, which is the default. Chose the fields that you need from both projections (see Figure 14.84). In this example, fields **VBELN**, **ERNAM**, **NETWR**, **VKORG**, and **KNUMV** are selected from **Projection_1** and fields **POSNR**, **MATNR**, **MATKL**, and **MEINS** are selected from **Projection_2**. These fields are shown in the **Output** folder.

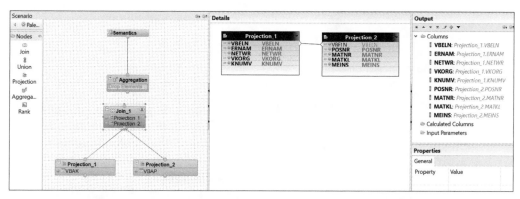

Figure 14.84 Output Field Selection

13. Connect the **Join_1** node to the **Aggregation** node (see Figure 14.85). This can be done just by dragging **Join_1** to **Aggregation**; you'll see the connection appear. You'll see that fields will be in gray initially in the aggregation node.

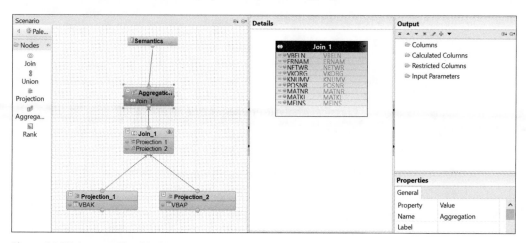

Figure 14.85 Aggregation Node

14. Now choose the fields required for the output (see Figure 14.86). You need to click each field name in the **Details** section of the aggregation node, and those fields will be shown in the **Output** folder.

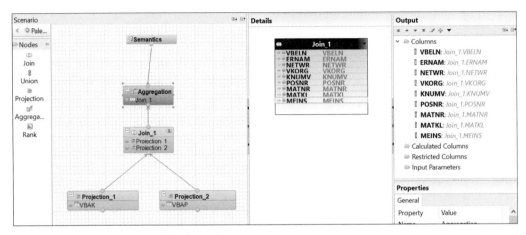

Figure 14.86 Aggregation Output

15. To make the graphical view more aligned, right-click in the graphical editor and choose **Auto Layout**. The view will be aligned properly, as shown in Figure 14.87.

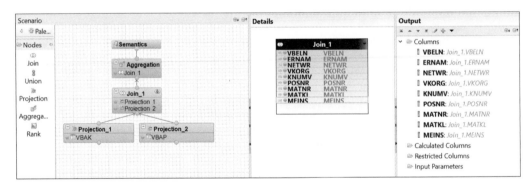

Figure 14.87 Auto Layout

16. In the semantics layer, make sure all the essential properties are set. There are two important properties here: make sure you set **Default Client** as **Cross-Client** and **Apply Privileges** as **Classical Analytic Privileges** (see Figure 14.88).

17. Now save and activate the view using the ⊙ ▼ icon. This will check for any errors and activate the view if there are none (see Figure 14.89).

18. You'll see the status of the activation, as shown in Figure 14.90.

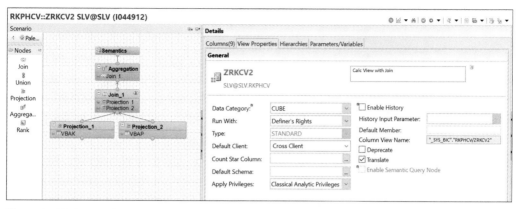

Figure 14.88 Semantics Layer

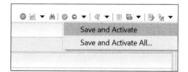

Figure 14.89 Save and Activate

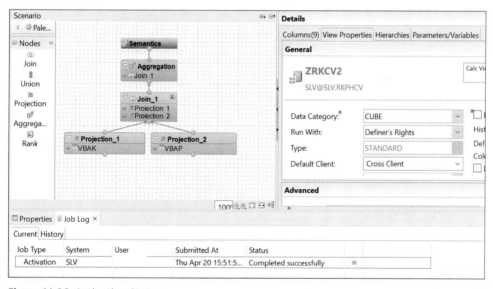

Figure 14.90 Activation Status

19. Once this is done, you can do a data preview of the SAP HANA calculation view as shown in Figure 14.91. Under the **Content** folder, in the folder for your package, right-click the SAP HANA calculation view name and select **Data Preview**.

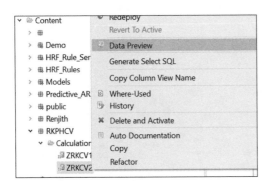

Figure 14.91 Data Preview

20. The result is shown in Figure 14.92. You need to choose the **Raw Data** tab to see the results.

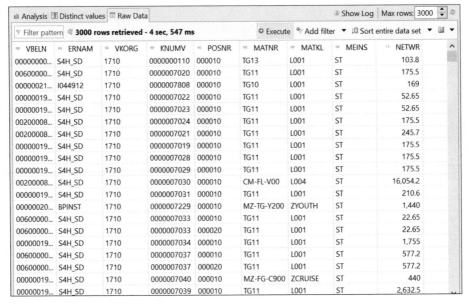

VBELN	ERNAM	VKORG	KNUMV	POSNR	MATNR	MATKL	MEINS	NETWR
00000000...	S4H_SD	1710	0000000110	000010	TG13	L001	ST	103.8
00600000...	S4H_SD	1710	0000007020	000010	TG11	L001	ST	175.5
00000021...	I044912	1710	0000007808	000010	TG10	L001	ST	169
00000019...	S4H_SD	1710	0000007022	000010	TG11	L001	ST	52.65
00000019...	S4H_SD	1710	0000007023	000010	TG11	L001	ST	52.65
00200008...	S4H_SD	1710	0000007024	000010	TG11	L001	ST	175.5
00200008...	S4H_SD	1710	0000007021	000010	TG11	L001	ST	245.7
00000019...	S4H_SD	1710	0000007019	000010	TG11	L001	ST	175.5
00000019...	S4H_SD	1710	0000007028	000010	TG11	L001	ST	175.5
00000019...	S4H_SD	1710	0000007029	000010	TG11	L001	ST	175.5
00200008...	S4H_SD	1710	0000007030	000010	CM-FL-V00	L004	ST	16,054.2
00000019...	S4H_SD	1710	0000007031	000010	TG11	L001	ST	210.6
00000020...	BPINST	1710	0000007229	000010	MZ-TG-Y200	ZYOUTH	ST	1,440
00600000...	S4H_SD	1710	0000007033	000010	TG11	L001	ST	22.65
00600000...	S4H_SD	1710	0000007033	000020	TG11	L001	ST	22.65
00000019...	S4H_SD	1710	0000007034	000010	TG11	L001	ST	1,755
00600000...	S4H_SD	1710	0000007037	000010	TG11	L001	ST	577.2
00600000...	S4H_SD	1710	0000007037	000020	TG11	L001	ST	577.2
00000019...	S4H_SD	1710	0000007040	000010	MZ-FG-C900	ZCRUISE	ST	440
00000019...	S4H_SD	1710	0000007039	000010	TG11	L001	ST	2,632.5

Figure 14.92 Data Preview

21. If you choose the **Show Log** button, you'll see the popup shown in Figure 14.93.

22. Choose **Generated SQL** to see the SQL code that's been generated, as shown in Figure 14.94.

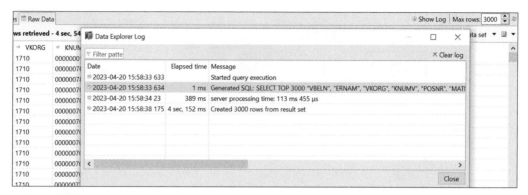

Figure 14.93 Show Log

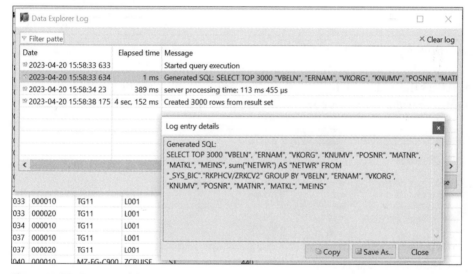

Figure 14.94 Generated SQL

14.5.2   Aggregation Behavior

If there is a key figure in the SAP HANA calculation view, then when you're using the aggregation node, you can decide how the key figure can be aggregated based on the primary key. In Figure 14.95, you can see that when the aggregation node is selected, you'll see a list of fields that are enabled for the output in the **Join_1** node. When you choose the **NETWR** key figure in the output list, the properties of that field are listed in the **Properties** window. For the **Aggregation Type** field, the default value is **SUM**. This means that when there is a key field, then based on the occurrence of the key field, it will sum up the key figure values. The final summation value will be displayed in all the rows where the primary key field is listed (see Figure 14.95).

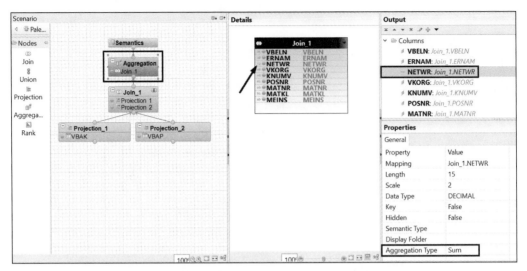

Figure 14.95 Aggregation for NETWR

Let's check the backend table for a specific sales order number. The results showing the summation value for **NETWR** are shown in Figure 14.96.

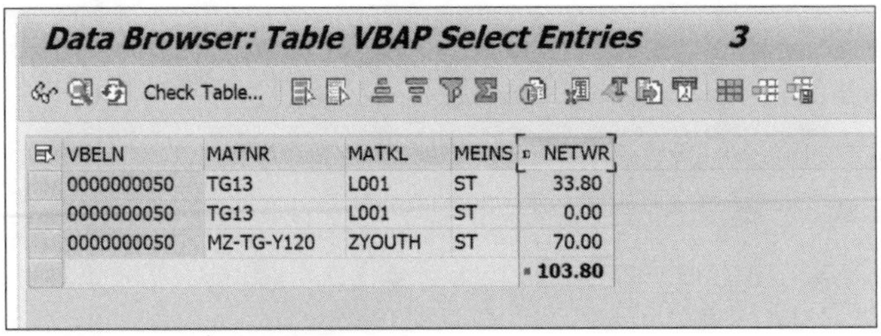

Data Browser: Table VBAP Select Entries   3

&r ⬚ ⬚ Check Table...   ⬚ ⬚   ⬚ ⬚ ⬚ ⬚ ⬚ ⬚ ⬚ ⬚ ⬚ ⬚ ⬚ ⬚

VBELN	MATNR	MATKL	MEINS	NETWR
0000000050	TG13	L001	ST	33.80
0000000050	TG13	L001	ST	0.00
0000000050	MZ-TG-Y120	ZYOUTH	ST	70.00
				▪ 103.80

Figure 14.96 Table VBAP Entry

If you filter the SAP HANA calculation view with the **VBELN** value, you'll see that the summed value of **NETWR** is shown in all the rows (see Figure 14.97).

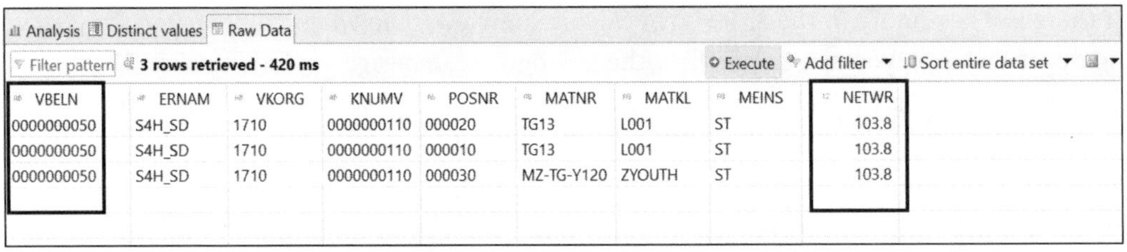

⬚ Analysis ⬚ Distinct values ⬚ Raw Data								
⬚ Filter pattern ⬚ 3 rows retrieved - 420 ms						⬚ Execute ⬚ Add filter ▼ ⬚ Sort entire data set ▼ ⬚ ▼		
VBELN	ERNAM	VKORG	KNUMV	POSNR	MATNR	MATKL	MEINS	NETWR
0000000050	S4H_SD	1710	0000000110	000020	TG13	L001	ST	103.8
0000000050	S4H_SD	1710	0000000110	000010	TG13	L001	ST	103.8
0000000050	S4H_SD	1710	0000000110	000030	MZ-TG-Y120	ZYOUTH	ST	103.8

Figure 14.97 Summation Behavior

There are many aggregation options, and you can see them from the dropdown in the **Aggregation Type** selection field, shown in Figure 14.98.

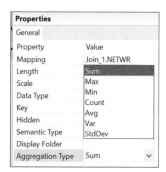

Figure 14.98 Aggregation Type

14.5.3   Using the Input Parameter

When you need to have an input parameter for selection in SAP HANA calculation views, you need to define the field in the semantics section. Let's copy the previous SAP HANA calculation view, using the instructions in Section 14.2.2. Select the **Copy From** checkbox (refer back to Figure 14.13), provide the name of the view that has to be copied, and choose **Finish**. Save and activate this new SAP HANA calculation view. The next step is to create a new parameter from the **Semantics** node, where you will see a **Parameter/ Variables** tab (see Figure 14.99).

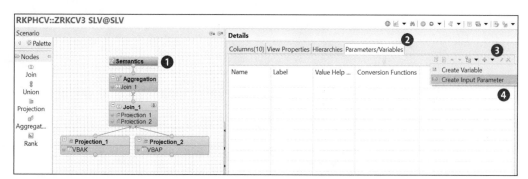

Figure 14.99 Input Parameter

As shown in Figure 14.99, here are the steps that you need follow:

❶ Choose the **Semantics** node in the SAP HANA calculation view.

❷ Select the **Parameters/Variables** tab.

❸ Choose the ➕ ▾ icon dropdown to see the **Create Variable** and **Create Input Parameter** options.

❹ Choose the **Create Input Parameter** option.

Once you choose **Create Input Parameter**, you'll see the popup shown in Figure 14.100. Provide the **Name** and **Label**, and in **Parameter Type** choose **Column**. That will help you choose the list from the column.

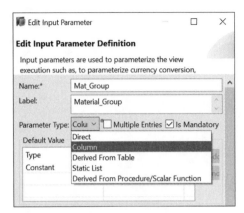

Figure 14.100 Input Parameter

You'll see the options in Figure 14.101. Choose **VBELN** for the value of the column.

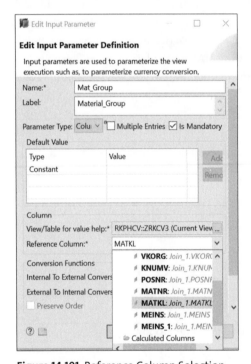

Figure 14.101 Reference Column Selection

Choose **MATKL** for the value and press **OK**. You'll see the values shown in Figure 14.102 in the **Parameter** tab.

Save and activate the SAP HANA calculation view. After the activation, you'll see the input parameter. You'll see how to use the input parameter later in this section, once you understand variables. Figure 14.103 shows how to create a new variable.

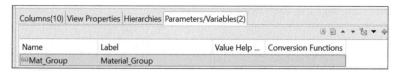

Figure 14.102 Parameter Tab

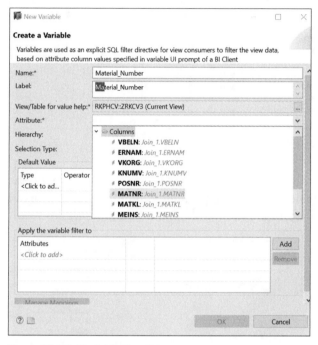

Figure 14.103 Variable Creation

Save and activate and do a data preview, as shown in Figure 14.104.

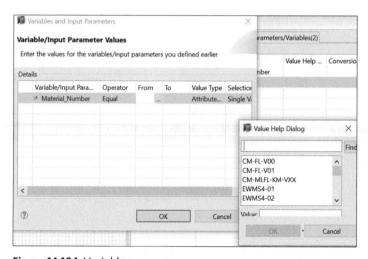

Figure 14.104 Variable

Choose the material number from the value help and you'll see only the desired results (see Figure 14.105).

VBELN	ERNAM	VKORG	KNUMV	POSNR	MATNR	MATKL	MEINS	MEINS_1	NETWR
0000001968	S4H_SD	1710	0000007032	000010	CM-FL-V00	L004	ST	ST	8,027.1
0060000015	S4H_SD_D...	1710	0000002250	000010	CM-FL-V00	L004	ST	ST	8,000
0000000728	S4H_SD	1710	0000002376	000020	CM-FL-V00	L004	ST	ST	0
0020000891	S4H_SD	1710	0000007030	000010	CM-FL-V00	L004	ST	ST	16,054.2
0000000729	S4H_SD	1710	0000002377	000010	CM-FL-V00	L004	ST	ST	0
0060000013	S4H_SD_D...	1710	0000002248	000010	CM-FL-V00	L004	ST	ST	8,000
0020000009	S4H_SD	1710	0000002374	000020	CM-FL-V00	L004	ST	ST	66,800
0000001951	S4H_PP	1710	0000006973	000010	CM-FL-V00	L004	ST	ST	8,000
0000001959	S4H_SD	1710	0000006994	000010	CM-FL-V00	L004	ST	ST	16,300
0000000162	S4H_SD	1710	0000000493	000010	CM-FL-V00	L004	ST	ST	8,000

Figure 14.105 Results

To define the input parameter, go to the projection node. The **Columns** folder on the right-hand side will have the folder for the input parameter and a filter where you can write the expression (see Figure 14.106).

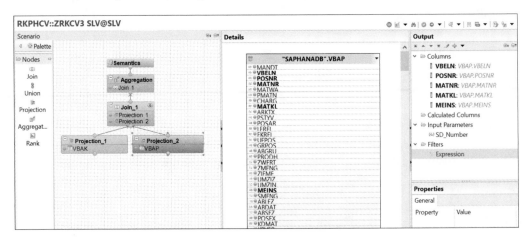

Figure 14.106 Expression

Create the filter expression in the expression editor, as shown in Figure 14.107. Save and activate, and when you do a data preview, you'll see the results shown in Figure 14.108.

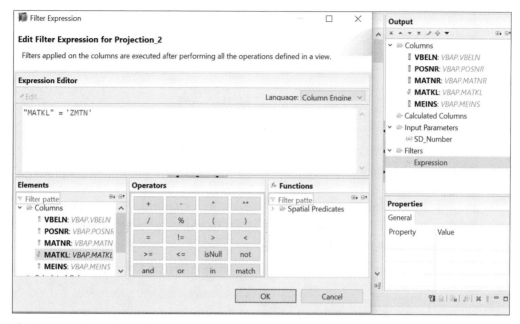

Figure 14.107 Expression Editor

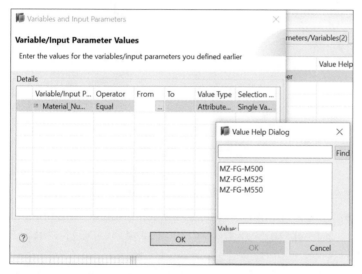

Figure 14.108 Reduced MATNR

Now if you choose any of the material numbers from the list shown in Figure 14.108, you'll see the output based on the material number, as shown in Figure 14.109.

⊞ VBELN	⊞ ERNAM	⊞ VKORG	⊞ KNUMV	⊞ POSNR	⊞ MATNR	⊞ MATKL	⊞ MEINS	⊞ MEINS_1	⊞ NETWR
0000000074	S4H_CO	1710	0000000144	000010	MZ-FG-M5...	ZMTN	ST	ST	2,667
0000000075	S4H_CO	1710	0000000145	000010	MZ-FG-M5...	ZMTN	ST	ST	2,667
0000000076	S4H_CO	1710	0000000146	000010	MZ-FG-M5...	ZMTN	ST	ST	13,335
0000000077	S4H_CO	1710	0000000147	000010	MZ-FG-M5...	ZMTN	ST	ST	16,002
0000000078	S4H_CO	1710	0000000148	000010	MZ-FG-M5...	ZMTN	ST	ST	9,779
0000000188	BPINST	1710	0000000579	000010	MZ-FG-M5...	ZMTN	ST	ST	889
0000000189	BPINST	1710	0000000580	000010	MZ-FG-M5...	ZMTN	ST	ST	1,778
0000000190	BPINST	1710	0000000581	000010	MZ-FG-M5...	ZMTN	ST	ST	8,001

Figure 14.109 Results

The SAP HANA calculation view will be the view with **Projection_2** with a **Filter** icon, as shown in Figure 14.110. You can also see that the **Input Parameters** and **Filters** are visible on the right side of the **Output** window.

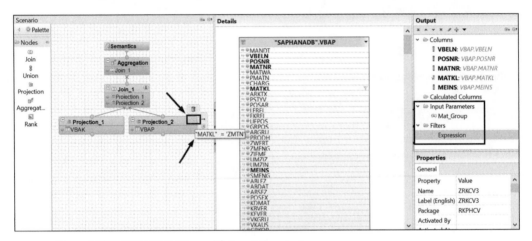

Figure 14.110 SAP HANA View with Input Parameter

14.5.4   Extracting the SAP HANA Calculation View in SAP BW/4HANA

To extract the data from the SAP HANA calculation view, follow these steps (refer to Section 14.4.1 for the essential steps to create the DataSource and the aDSO for the SAP HANA calculation view):

1. In the **ODP_HANA** (SAP HANA view source system) folder, create a DataSource based on the SAP HANA calculation view (refer back to Figure 14.44 through Figure 14.48). Once the DataSource is created, activate it (see Figure 14.111).

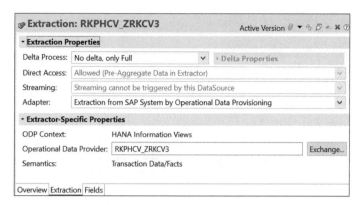

Figure 14.111 DataSource

2. Create an aDSO based on this DataSource (refer back to Figure 14.51) and create a transformation and DTP based on the same DataSource for the aDSO, and finally execute the DTP. Note that the DTP will be only in full update mode by default. The result of the extraction is shown in Figure 14.112.

Details of Load Request {2023-04-21 04:41:25 000000 CST}

Request Information

DataStore Object:	ZRKCV3
DataStore Object Description:	CV Test parameter
ID:	{2023-04-21 04:41:25 000000 CST}
Status:	Overall and technically OK
Storage:	Inbound Table
Records:	628

DTP Properties

Name:	DTP_6FMR9T6UKK6Z6UPW5HZK6BKXW
Description:	RSDS RKPHCV_ZRKCV3 S4SVIEW -> ADSO ZRKCV3
Extraction Mode:	Full
Processing Mode:	Parallel SAP HANA Execution
Package Size:	1,000,000
Request Aggregation:	MOV
Request Start Time:	21.04.2023, 15:11:25
Request Finish Time:	21.04.2023, 15:11:42
Request Runtime:	17s
Selection:	(Replication Pointer : 20230421094132.000016000 Replication Mode : Extraction of All Data (Full) - - X)

Figure 14.112 aDSO Content

3. Check the contents of the aDSO inbound table. Set the filter value of **MATKL** to **ZMTN**, because the view has a filter on that value, so this data will not be available in the inbound table due to the filter condition. In Figure 14.113, you can see that the aDSO has the data when only MATKL is equal to ZMTN ❶. When MATKL is not equal to ZMTN, there will be zero entries shown ❷. The reason for this behavior is that the SAP HANA calculation view has applied the filter on the lowest projection. The same data is extracted when the SAP BW/4HANA extraction is executed.

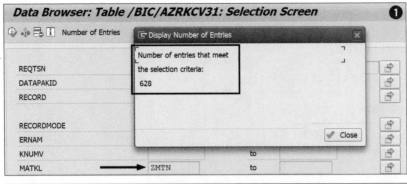

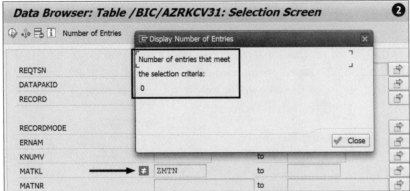

Figure 14.113 Inbound Table with Filter

14.6 Summary

With the completion of the dataflow based on the SAP HANA calculation views, you're ready to build the SAP BW/4HANA model to extract data from SAP S/4HANA system using custom-developed SAP HANA calculation views. These calculation views can be used along with CDS views. Having good know-how of these CDS and SAP HANA calculation views is essential as more companies are using SAP HANA calculation views or CDS-based extraction on account of the impressive performance gains during data load and support for the real-time extraction. Data modeling with SAP HANA calculation views will help you have more virtualization in your system design, which is a key benefit of SAP BW/4HANA. You can also create SAP HANA calculation views in the SAP S/4HANA system based on the generated views from the SAP BW/4HANA system. Knowing about a mix of classical and new extractors will help you design more efficient data models during the SAP BW/4HANA implementation.

In the next chapter, we'll focus on the multiple data provision options that can be used in SAP BW/4HANA. That will be the last chapter of this book.

Chapter 15

Implementing Mixed Modeling in SAP BW/4HANA

This chapter covers multiple data provisioning options from SAP HANA and non-SAP HANA systems to SAP BW/4HANA. These data provisioning methods will help you define and architect an analytics strategy for your complex landscape during SAP BW/4HANA implementation.

In this chapter, we'll first discuss SAP HANA smart data access in Section 15.1, which enables virtual access to remote sources, and then we'll discuss SAP HANA smart data integration in Section 15.1.2, which has replication and virtualization capabilities. We'll also discuss SAP Landscape Transformation Replication Server in Section 15.1.3. Finally in Section 15.2, we'll discuss the scenarios to implement mixed modeling, which will help you decide on an analytical strategy for a complex SAP BW system landscape.

15.1 Introduction to SAP HANA Smart Data Access

When you have an SAP HANA system, SAP HANA smart data access allows you to access the remote data as if the data was stored in the local tables of SAP HANA.

With the help of SAP HANA smart data access, SAP HANA can create a so-called virtual table, mapping to tables located in remote data sources, and then SAP HANA can access the data directly by accessing the virtual table. These tables can be manipulated by SAP HANA just like an ordinary table, which means operations such as select, update, insert, delete, and so on are all available for the virtual table.

The communication between SAP HANA and a remote data source is based on the ODBC protocol. To use the protocol, install the appropriate drivers for the databases you want to connect to using SAP HANA smart data access. All SAP HANA smart data access-supported remote sources require installation and configuration of the ODBC driver. If the corresponding ODBC driver isn't available, accessing that remote source can't be supported by SAP HANA smart data access even though it's listed. There are many sources supported for SAP HANA smart data access. To check the up-to-date list of sources, refer to SAP Note 2600176 (SAP HANA Smart Data Access Supported Remote Sources).

Figure 15.1 provides an overview of SAP HANA smart data access.

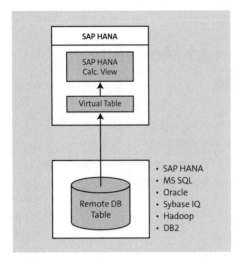

Figure 15.1 SAP HANA Smart Data Access Overview

In the following sections, you'll learn how to create remote sources for SAP HANA smart data access and get an introduction to SAP HANA smart data integration, followed by SAP Landscape Transformation Replication Server replication for SAP BW/4HANA.

15.1.1   Creating Remote Sources

If you need to connect an external source, you need to have SAP HANA smart data access and the equivalent adapter. Then you need to have database access to create the remote source

Follow these steps:

1. Log into the SAP HANA database system and go to the **Provisioning** folder.

2. Right-click the **Remote Sources** folder under the **Provisioning** folder and select **New Remote Source**, as shown in Figure 15.2.

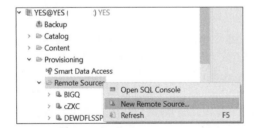

Figure 15.2 Create Remote Source

3. Enter the following information, as shown in Figure 15.3:

    ❶ Provide the **Source Name**.

    ❷ Choose the **Adapter Name**; in this case, it's **HANA (ODBC)**.

❸ Provide the application **Server** name.

❹ Provide the **Port** number.

❺ Provide the **User Name**.

❻ Provide the **Password**.

❼ Click **Execute** to finish the setup of the remote source.

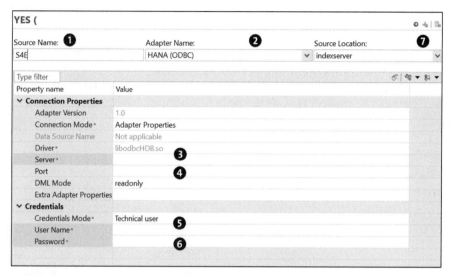

Figure 15.3 SAP HANA Smart Data Access Remote Source Setup

4. The remote source will be created as shown in Figure 15.4.

Figure 15.4 Remote Source

Once the remote source is created, make sure that you have access to all schemas. Execute the following SQL command for the SAP HANA database schema for your user to ensure the selection of the data from the database table that is available on your schema:

```
GRANT SELECT ON SCHEMA "Schema Name" TO <Username> WITH GRANT OPTION
```

This option can be discussed with Basis or security; they will have restricted access for the user in the database system in the operational environment.

5. Now you can see your schema and find the tables available in the system. Right-click the table that you want to access from the remote system and choose **Add as Virtual Table**, as shown in Figure 15.5.

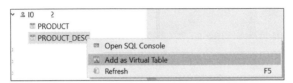

Figure 15.5 Enabling Virtual Table

6. You will see a prompt asking for the virtual **Table Name**. It will also show the details of the **Schema** to be created. Provide the table name and choose **Create**, as shown in Figure 15.6.

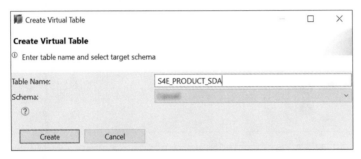

Figure 15.6 Virtual Table Name

7. You'll see a popup confirming that the virtual table is created, as shown in Figure 15.7.

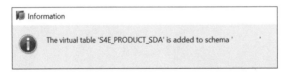

Figure 15.7 Confirmation

8. Once the table is created, check the **Catalog** folder and your schema in the SAP HANA database system. In the Admin Console perspective, follow path **Catalog · <Your schema name> · Tables · <Your table name>**, as shown in Figure 15.8.

9. The virtual table you've created using SAP HANA smart data access can be accessed in SAP BW/4HANA using an open ODS view extraction, which we discussed in Chapter 13. Refer to the architecture shown in Figure 15.9 to understand how the remote database table in SAP HANA is consumed in SAP BW/4HANA. There is an option to consume the remote table using an open ODS view, or you can create an SAP HANA calculation view on top of that table and consume that SAP HANA calculation view in

SAP BW/4HANA. Refer to Chapter 14 to learn how to create and consume SAP HANA calculation views in SAP HANA.

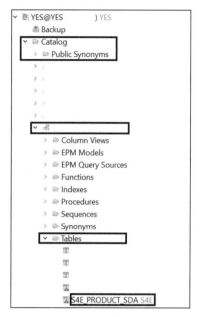

Figure 15.8 Virtual Table

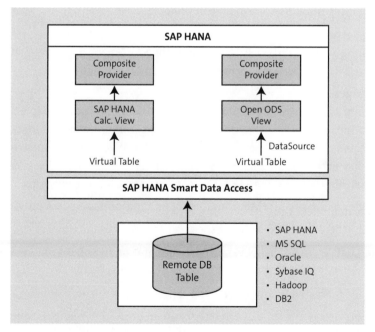

Figure 15.9 Consuming SAP HANA Smart Data Access-based Virtual Tables in SAP BW/4HANA

With SAP HANA smart data access, you can consume the virtual table using the remote data source.

15.1.2   SAP HANA Smart Data Integration

Now that you know about SAP HANA smart data access, next you should learn about SAP HANA smart data integration. SAP HANA smart data access can be seen as a subset of SAP HANA smart data integration, which comprises the functionality of common data manipulations and the data replication infrastructure. It represents a set of functions that you can use to retrieve data from external systems, transform it, and persist it in the SAP HANA database tables.

When you use SAP HANA smart data access, you'll see the index server, but with SAP HANA smart data integration, you'll have the data provisioning agent and server. With SAP HANA smart data access, you can have virtual access to the remote source, but SAP HANA smart data integration is an extract, transform, and load (ETL) tool that supports real-time replication and data virtualization. Here you can also have data persistence. The main features of SAP HANA smart data integration include the following:

- Physical replication in batch mode
- Physical replication in real-time mode
- Virtualization (like SAP HANA smart data access)

SAP HANA smart data integration has two main components:

- **Data Provisioning Server**
  The Data Provisioning Server is natively available in the SAP HANA database. You need to activate the Data Provisioning Server in the SAP HANA configuration.

- **Data Provisioning Agent**
  The Data Provisioning Agent manages all SAP HANA smart data integration adapters and connections to the SAP HANA database. It acts as the communication interface between SAP HANA and the adapter. The Data Provisioning Agent version must match the SAP HANA version. In this agent, different types of adapters are deployed that take care of the communication between the SAP HANA database and the source systems.

  You can see the architecture of SAP HANA smart data integration-based data provisioning in SAP BW/4HANA in Figure 15.10.

The steps to provision data from SAP HANA smart data integration to SAP BW/4HANA are as follows:

1. Once the virtual table is created in SAP HANA, you can create the calculation view.
2. When the calculation view is available, it can be consumed in SAP BW/4HANA using a composite provider. You learned how to create and consume SAP HANA calculation views based on tables in Chapter 14, and the same steps can be followed to consume these calculation views in SAP BW/4HANA.

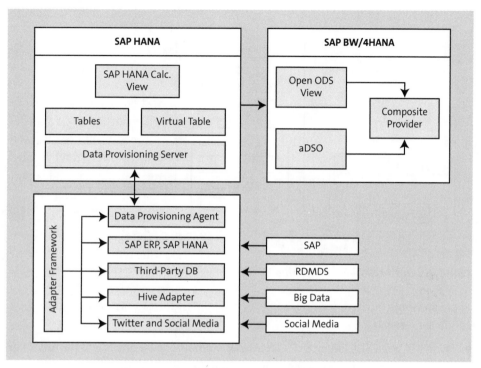

Figure 15.10 SAP HANA Smart Data Integration Overview

15.1.3   SAP Landscape Transformation Replication Server to SAP BW/4HANA

We'll start with an overview of the architecture for when you need to use the SAP Landscape Transformation Replication Server–based replication for SAP BW. The database triggers monitors for any events (insert, delete, modify, update, etc.) that take place in the application table. Database triggers will be created in the source system. If database triggers happen, then logging tables will store the triggered data, which is modified data, in the application table. Logging tables will be created in the source system. Then the read engine will be responsible for reading the data from the logging table and passing it to the SAP Landscape Transformation Replication Server. Finally, the mapping and transformation engine will be responsible for the structured transformation of the data as per the target SAP HANA database format. You can see the details of the SAP Landscape Transformation Replication Server architecture in Figure 15.11.

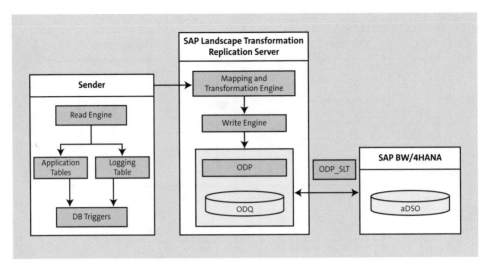

Figure 15.11 SAP Landscape Transformation Replication Server Architecture

There are some important things to note about SAP Landscape Transformation Replication Server to SAP BW replication:

- There will be an SAP ERP or SAP S/4HANA system where the document postings happen. This can be considered the source system for SAP BW/4HANA.

- SAP Landscape Transformation Replication Server is required for replicating the real-time data from the source.

- SAP BW/4HANA is used in to get the real-time data based on the SAP Landscape Transformation Replication Server replication from the application tables.

- You need to make the necessary configuration in the SAP Landscape Transformation Replication Server. Your source will be SAP S/4HANA and target will be SAP BW/4HANA.

- ODP will be used for the RFC connection with SAP BW/4HANA when you use SAP Landscape Transformation Replication Server–based replication.

- In SAP BW/4HANA, you'll have a DataSource with the ODP_SLT context, which should be active.

- Replicate the DataSource under the **ODP_SLT** folder and create the new DataSource.

- Once the SAP Landscape Transformation Replication Server–based DataSource is created and activated, the next step is to create an aDSO based on the same DataSource and start the data loading process using a transformation and DTP.

- You can use Transaction LTRC (SAP Landscape Transformation Replication Server Cockpit) to check the replication status, as shown in Figure 15.12.

- Once the replication is active, any changes in SAP S/4HANA will trigger the data in Transaction ODQMON. Select **SAP LT** for **Provider** and then check the rows in the units view.

Figure 15.12 SAP Landscape Transformation Replication Server Cockpit

- Once the DTP from SAP BW is triggered, it will fetch the data from Transaction ODQMON.

15.2 Sample Mixed Modeling Flow

Now that you know about the data modeling concepts discussed in the previous sections, you can implement SAP BW/4HANA by applying a mixed modeling approach. Here is a sample mixed modeling flow in SAP BW/4HANA 2.0:

1. The remote source is replicated as a virtual table in SAP HANA.

2. SAP HANA uses the calculation view to access the virtual table and the database tables.

3. The SAP HANA view is consumed by SAP BW/4HANA using an open ODS view.

4. The other SAP HANA calculation views created in SAP HANA are consumed by SAP BW/4HANA.

5. SAP BW/4HANA gets the data from the CDS view, which is replicated as the Data-Source, and the data is persisted in ADSO1.

6. SAP BW/4HANA accesses the data from the SAP HANA schema tables using the HANA_LOCAL connectivity, which is used by ADSO3.

7. You can send the data from the flat file for planning purposes using the flat file interface to SAP BW/4HANA. The data is persisted in ADSO3.

8. You can also expose the ADSO1 data as generated SAP HANA views in the SAP HANA database, which can be used by the native SAP HANA calculation views.

9. Finally, to implement mixed modeling you can join the open ODS view, SAP HANA calculation view, ADSO1, ADSO2, and ADSO3, in an SAP HANA composite provider.

10. You can build an SAP BW query on top of the composite provider and send the data to reporting tools like SAP BusinessObjects or SAP Analytics Cloud.

The mixed modeling architecture is shown in Figure 15.13.

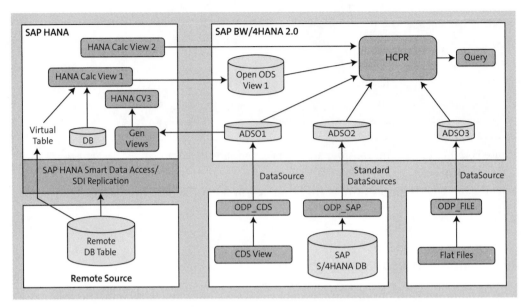

Figure 15.13 Mixed Modeling

The architecture summarizes all the data staging concepts that you've learned throughout this book. You learned about the extraction of flat files into SAP BW/4HANA in Chapter 1. In Chapter 2, we discussed data modeling in SAP BW/4HANA using flat file-based data staging as well as all major SAP BW modeling objects. In Chapter 3, you learned about creating ODP source systems of different contexts. Then you learned how to load data from multiple SAP application-based extractors using ODP_SAP in Chapters 4, 5, 6, 7, 8, 9, and 10. In Chapter 11, we discussed the extraction of data from an SAP BW 7.x system to SAP BW/4HANA 2.0. You learned about CDS view extraction in Chapter 12 and about open ODS view and SAP HANA calculation view extractions in Chapter 13 and 14. Finally, you learned about SAP HANA smart data access and SAP HANA smart data integration data provisioning in this chapter, Chapter 15. Completion of all these chapters will help you design a mixed modeling architecture in SAP BW/4HANA 2.0. Once you start to implement the dataflows in SAP BW/4HANA 2.0, you'll be on your way to building an efficient SAP BW/4HANA mixed modeling process in your implementation projects.

15.3   Summary

You've reached the end of the book! We hope you found this book useful and that it will be a valuable tool for you as you continue to learn, explore, and work with SAP BW/4HANA 2.0 and future versions. Happy learning!

The Author

Renjith Kumar Palaniswamy is an SAP BW/4HANA architect with over 15 years of extensive experience working with SAP BW/4HANA, SAP HANA, and SAP S/4HANA. Renjith currently serves as an SAP BW/4HANA services architect at SAP America, Inc., within the esteemed SAP Cloud Success Services Center of Expertise (SAP CoE). There, he specializes in extracting data from SAP S/4HANA for business intelligence analytical reporting. His expertise encompasses critical components such as SAP S/4HANA-based extraction and data staging, native SAP BW/4HANA data modeling, mixed SAP BW/4HANA modeling, native SAP S/4HANA modeling, and SAP BW/4HANA greenfield implementations and remote conversions.

Throughout his tenure at SAP America, Renjith has excelled as an SAP BW/4HANA architect and services consultant, collaborating with renowned Fortune 100 companies across North America. With a primary focus on SAP BW/4HANA data modeling utilizing mixed modeling techniques and data staging from SAP S/4HANA, Renjith has been pivotal in multiple SAP Business Warehouse (SAP BW) on SAP HANA migration projects and complex SAP BW/4HANA conversions across North America. Notably, he played a crucial role in overseeing the world's first and largest SAP BW migration powered by SAP HANA for a prominent retail company in North America. His expertise extends to native SAP HANA modeling and SAP BW/4HANA data staging implementations, as well as native and mixed SAP BW/4HANA modeling projects. Renjith has successfully led and played a crucial role in numerous large-scale SAP BW/4HANA implementation and conversion projects across multiple industry sectors, delivering valuable insights and solutions for organizational analytical strategy positioning.

Prior to joining SAP America, Inc., Renjith made significant contributions to SAP BW product support, serving as the global topic contact for the business content and extractors (BCT) component at SAP Labs India. His notable achievements include moderating the BCT space in SAP Community, authoring various SAP Notes, and publishing articles in international journals related to data warehousing. Renjith's expertise has guided and facilitated SAP BW-based initiatives for major companies worldwide, spanning across the Americas and Asia Pacific.

Index

T

Interested in reading more?

Please visit our website for all new book
and e-book releases from SAP PRESS.

www.sap-press.com